# Windows® 11

## ALL-IN-ONE

# Windows® 11

## ALL-IN-ONE

by Ciprian Adrian Rusen

A Wiley Brand

# Windows® 11 All-in-One For Dummies®

Published by: **John Wiley & Sons, Inc.**, 111 River Street, Hoboken, NJ 07030-5774, www.wiley.com

Copyright © 2022 by John Wiley & Sons, Inc., Hoboken, New Jersey

Published simultaneously in Canada

For general information on our other products and services, please contact our Customer Care Department within the U.S. at 877-762-2974, outside the U.S. at 317-572-3993, or fax 317-572-4002. For technical support, please visit https://hub.wiley.com/community/support/dummies.

Wiley publishes in a variety of print and electronic formats and by print-on-demand. Some material included with standard print versions of this book may not be included in e-books or in print-on-demand. If this book refers to media such as a CD or DVD that is not included in the version you purchased, you may download this material at http://booksupport.wiley.com. For more information about Wiley products, visit www.wiley.com.

Library of Congress Control Number: 2022930212

ISBN 978-1-119-85869-0 (pbk); ISBN 978-1-119-85870-6 (ebk); ISBN 978-1-119-85871-3 (ebk)

SKY10032643_020322

# Contents at a Glance

# Table of Contents

# Introduction

**W**elcome to *Windows 11 All-in-One For Dummies,* one of the most complete books you can find about the latest version of Windows. It's large and heavy because it has a lot to teach you.

This book is a great guide if you're upgrading to Windows 11 from Windows 10 or an older version such as Windows 7. And it's especially great if you're new to Windows. You'll learn everything you need to know about this operating system — and a bit more than most people. You won't become a tech support expert by the end of it, but you'll surely know enough to help others as well, especially when they're puzzled about the things Windows 11 can and can't do.

## About This Book

*Windows 11 All-in-One For Dummies* takes you through the Land of the Dummies — with introductory material and stuff your grandmother can (and should!) understand — and then continues the journey into more advanced areas, where you can truly put Windows to work every day.

I start with the basics about navigating Windows 11: turning it on and off, signing in, notifications, user accounts, and permissions. Then I dig into the desktop and the Start menu and take you through all the important pieces, one by one, in detail.

I don't dwell much on technical mumbo jumbo, and I keep the jargon to a minimum. At the same time, I tackle the problems you're likely to encounter, show you the major road signs, and give help where you need it the most.

Whether you want to get two or more email accounts set up to work simultaneously, personalize your Start menu, or learn the best way to protect your PC from viruses, this is your book. Or should I say ten books? I've broken out the topics into ten minibooks, so you'll find it easy to hop around to a topic — and a level of coverage — that feels comfortable. I didn't design this book to be read from front to back. It's a reference. Each chapter and each of its sections focus on solving a particular problem or describing a specific technique.

*Windows 11 All-in-One For Dummies* should be your reference of first resort, before you look for help online, on Google or Bing. You'll see that most topics of interest are already covered, and where there's more you can find online, I also give you references to articles and places that can help.

# Foolish Assumptions

I don't make many assumptions about you, dear reader, except to acknowledge that you're obviously intelligent, well-informed, discerning, and of impeccable taste. That's why you chose this book, right?

Okay, okay. The least I can do is butter you up a bit. Here's the straight scoop: If you've never used Windows, bribe your neighbor (or, better, your neighbor's kid) to teach you how to do four things:

>> Play a game with your fingers (if you have a touchscreen) or with a mouse (if you're finger-challenged). Any game that ships with Windows 11 or any free game in the Microsoft Store will do. If your neighbor's kid doesn't have a different recommendation, try the new Microsoft Solitaire Collection.

>> Start File Explorer.

>> Get on the web with Microsoft Edge, Chrome, or whatever you prefer.

>> Use the Start menu to turn Windows 11 off and then turn it back on.

That covers it. If you can play a game, you know how to turn on your computer, log in if necessary, click and drag (or tap and hold down). If you run File Explorer, you know how to click or tap a taskbar icon. After you're on the web, well, it's a great starting point for almost anything. And if you know that you need to use the Start menu, you're well on your way to achieving Windows 11 enlightenment. And that begins with Book 1, Chapter 1.

# Icons Used in This Book

Some of the points in *Windows 11 All-in-One For Dummies* merit your special attention. I set off these points with icons.

**TIP**

When I'm jumping up and down on one foot with an idea so cool that I can't stand it anymore, I stick a tip icon in the margin. You can browse any chapter and hit its highest points by jumping from tip to tip.

**REMEMBER**

You don't need to memorize the information marked with this icon, but you should try to remember that something special is lurking.

**WARNING**

Anywhere that you see a warning icon, you can be sure that it's important. Pay attention and don't do the opposite of what I recommend unless you want to get into trouble.

**TECHNICAL STUFF**

Okay, so I'm a geek. I admit it. Sure, I love to poke fun at geeks. But I'm a modern, New Age, sensitive guy, in touch with my inner geekiness. Sometimes, I just can't help but let it out, you know? That's where the technical stuff icon comes in. If you get all tied up in knots about techie-type stuff, skip these paragraphs. (For the record, I managed to write this entire book without telling you that an IPv4 address consists of a unique 32-bit combination of network ID and host ID, expressed as a set of four decimal numbers with each octet separated by periods. See? I can restrain myself sometimes.)

# Beyond the Book

When I wrote this book, I covered the initial release of Windows 11, dated October 5, 2021. Microsoft promises to keep Windows 11 updated each year. For details about significant updates or changes that occur between editions of this book, go to www. dummies.com, search for *Windows 11 All-in-One For Dummies*, and view this book's dedicated page.

In addition, the cheat sheet for this book has handy Windows shortcuts and tips on other cool features worth checking out. To get to the cheat sheet, go to www.dummies.com, and then type *Windows 11 All-in-One For Dummies Cheat Sheet* in the Search box.

# Where to Go from Here

That's about it. It's time for you to crack this book open and have at it. Read the first minibook for an overview of what you get and don't get in Windows 11. Then check the Table of Contents and decide where you want to go next.

**REMEMBER**

Don't forget to bookmark www.digitalcitizen.life. I lead this blog, which will keep you up to date on all the Windows 11 stuff you need to know — tutorials about the latest features and updates, fixes to annoying problems, and much more.

And if you want to contact me for advice about all things Windows, you'll find me at ciprianrusen@digitalcitizen.life. Sometimes, it's worth reading the Introduction, isn't it?

# 1

# Getting Started with Windows 11

# Contents at a Glance

IN THIS CHAPTER

» Understanding that hardware is hard — and software is hard, too

» Seeing Windows's place in the grand scheme of things

» Defining important technical terms

» Buying a Windows 11 computer

» Dealing with Windows 11 annoyances

# Chapter **1**

# Introducing Windows 11

We all started as newbies who did not know much about technology. If you've never used an earlier version of Windows, you're in luck because you won't have to force your fingers to forget so much of what you've learned! Windows 11 is a melding of Windows 10 and macOS, tossed into a blender, speed turned up to full, and poured out on your screen.

Although Windows 10 was a major improvement over Windows 8 and 8.1, some people still had problems understanding and using features such as tiles, Cortana, and the Settings app. Windows 11 makes the experience gentler for everyone. It also further optimizes the touchscreen approach so that it works well with a mouse, too. The user interface is more consistent, and it doesn't look like the old desktop and the new touchscreen approach forced to work together.

Some of you are reading this book because you chose to run Windows 11. Others are here because Windows 11 came preinstalled on a new computer or because your company forced you to upgrade to Windows 11. Whatever the reason, you've ended up with a good operating system, and — if you understand and respect its limitations — it should serve you well. However, you should know that other choices are available, and I present them in this chapter. Who knows, maybe you're considering returning your new Windows 11 PC already.

Before I get technical, I want you to take a quick look at Windows 11. Then, I explain some important technical terminology, and give an overview of what you need to keep in mind when buying your first Windows 11 PC, laptop, or tablet. Last but not least, I describe what you might not like about Windows 11. It's better to know all that sooner rather than later. Right?

# Taking Your First Look at Windows 11

First things first. Position yourself in front of your computer and press the power button to turn it on. This thing called Windows 11 will be staring at you, as shown in Figure 1-1. Microsoft calls this the lock screen, and it doesn't say *Windows*, much less *Windows 11*. The lock screen doesn't display much of anything except the current date and time, with a tiny icon or two to indicate whether your internet connection is working. You may also see the next meeting scheduled in your calendar, how many unopened emails await, or whether you should just take the day off because your holdings in AAPL stock soared again.

**FIGURE 1-1:**
The Windows 11 lock screen. Your picture may differ.

You may be tempted to sit and admire the gorgeous picture, whatever it may be, but if you swipe up from the bottom, click or tap anywhere on the picture, or press any key on your keyboard, you see the login screen, resembling the one in Figure 1-2. If more than one person is set up to use your computer, you'll see more than one name.

**FIGURE 1-2:**
The Windows 11
login screen.

The login screen doesn't say *Login* or *Welcome to Windows 11* or *Howdy.* It displays the names and pictures of the people who can use the computer. On the right, note the icons for things such as the language used for the keyboard, the network, accessibility, and power.

# Hardware and Software

At the most fundamental level, all computer stuff comes in one of two flavors: hardware or software. *Hardware* is anything you can touch — a computer screen, a mouse, a hard drive, a keyboard, a Blu-ray drive. *Software* is everything else: your Microsoft Edge browser, the movies you stream on Netflix, the digital pictures of your last vacation, and programs such as Microsoft Office. If you shoot a bunch of pictures, the pictures themselves are just bits — software. But they're probably sitting on some sort of memory card inside your smartphone or digital camera. That memory card is hardware. Get the difference?

Windows 11 is software. You can't touch it in a physical sense, even if you interact with it using the keyboard and a mouse, or a touchscreen. Your PC, on the other hand, is hardware. Kick the computer screen, and your toe hurts. Drop the big box on the floor, and it smashes into pieces. That's hardware.

Chances are good that one of the major PC manufacturers — such as Lenovo, HP, Dell, Acer, or ASUS — Microsoft, with its Surface line, or even Apple made your hardware. However, Microsoft, and Microsoft alone, makes Windows 11.

When you bought your computer, you paid for a license to use one copy of Windows on that PC. Its manufacturer paid Microsoft a royalty so it could sell you Windows along with the PC. (That royalty may have been close to zero dollars, but it's a royalty nonetheless.) You may think that you got Windows from, say, Dell — indeed, you may have to contact Dell for technical support on Windows questions — but Windows came from Microsoft.

If you upgraded from Windows 10 to Windows 11, you might have received a free upgrade license — but it's still a license, whether you paid for it or not. You can't give it away to someone else.

**REMEMBER**

These days, most software, including Windows 11, asks you to agree to an End User License Agreement (EULA). When you first set up your PC, Windows asks you to click or tap the Accept button to accept a licensing agreement that's long enough to reach the top of the Empire State Building. If you're curious about what agreement you accepted, take a look at the official EULA repository at www.microsoft.com/en-us/Useterms/Retail/Windows/11/UseTerms_Retail_Windows_11_English.htm.

# Must You Run Windows?

Are you wondering if you must run Windows? The short answer is that you don't have to run Windows on your PC.

The PC you have is a dumb box. (You needed me to tell you that, eh?) To get that box to do anything worthwhile, you need a computer program that takes control of the PC and makes it do things, such as show apps on the screen, respond to mouse clicks or taps, and print resumes. An *operating system* controls the dumb box and makes it do worthwhile things, in ways that people can understand.

Without an operating system, the computer can sit in a corner and display profound messages on the screen, such as *Non-system disk or disk error* or *Insert system disk and press any key when ready.* If you want your computer to do more than that, though, you need an operating system.

**REMEMBER**

Windows is not the only operating system in town. The other big contenders in the PC and PC-like operating system game are Chrome OS, macOS, and Linux:

>> **Chrome OS:** Created by Google, Chrome OS is the operating system used on Chromebooks. Affordable Chromebooks have long dominated the best-seller lists at many computer retailers — and for good reason. If you want to surf the web, work on email, compose simple documents, or do anything in a

browser — which covers a whole lot of ground these days — a Chromebook and Chrome OS are all you need. Chromebooks can't run Windows programs such as Office or Photoshop (although they *can* run web-based versions of them, such as Office Online or Photoshop Express Editor). Despite this limitation, they don't get infected and have few maintenance problems. You can't say the same about Windows: That's why you need a thousand-page book to keep it going. Yes, you do need a reliable internet connection to get the most out of Chrome OS. But some parts of Chrome OS and Google's apps, including Gmail, can work even if you don't have an active internet connection.

Chrome OS, which is built on Linux, looks and feels much like the Google Chrome web browser. There are a few minor differences, but in general, you feel like you're working in the Chrome browser.

» **macOS:** Apple has made great strides running on Intel processors even though they recently switched to making their own, including for the Mac. If you don't already know how to use Windows or own a Windows computer, it makes sense to consider buying an Apple computer or running macOS or both. Yes, you can build your custom computer and run macOS on it: Check out www.hackintosh.com. But, no, it isn't legal — the macOS End User License Agreement explicitly forbids installation on a non-Apple-branded computer. Also, installing it is certainly not for the faint of heart.

The performance of the latest MacBook Air and MacBook Pro, based on Apple's M1 chips, is breathtaking. However, they can natively run only macOS, not Windows. If you want Windows on the latest MacBooks, you must purchase Parallels Desktop 17 for Mac or newer, from www.parallels.com.

» **Linux:** The big up-and-coming operating system, which has been up-and-coming for a couple of decades now, is Linux (pronounced "LIN-uchs"). If you are not an IT professional and you plan to use your PC only to get on the internet — to surf the web and send emails — Linux can handle that, with few of the headaches that remain as the hallmark of Windows. By using free programs such as LibreOffice (www.libreoffice.org) and online services such as Google Workspace and Google Drive (www.drive.google.com), you can even cover the basics in word processing, spreadsheets, presentations, contact managers, calendars, and more. Even though Linux doesn't support the vast array of consumer hardware that Windows offers, it's popular with many software developers and power users.

In the tablet sphere, iPadOS and Android rule. Windows 11 doesn't compete with any of them, even though it works on Qualcomm chips designed for mobile devices, and is available on tablets and convertible devices such as the Surface line.

**WARNING**

Windows 10 in S mode and Windows 11 in S mode are a confusing development with an unclear future. Designed to compete with Chrome OS and iPads, *S mode* refers to a set of restrictions on "real" Windows. Supposedly in an attempt to improve battery life, reduce the chance of the PC getting infected, and simplify your life, the S mode in Windows 11 doesn't run most regular Windows programs. S mode limits users to only apps found in the Microsoft Store. You get Spotify and iTunes but not Google Chrome or Firefox. Fortunately, you can go to the Microsoft Store and upgrade a Windows 11 S mode system so that it's no longer in S mode.

What do other people choose? It's hard to measure the percentage of PCs running Windows versus Mac versus Linux. StatCounter (www.statcounter.com) specializes in analyzing the traffic of millions of sites globally and provides lots of useful statistics based on the data they collect. One stat tallies how many Windows computers hit those sites, compared to macOS and Linux. While their data may not be 100 percent representative of real-world market share, it does an excellent job of giving us an idea of operating system penetration. If you look at only desktop operating systems — Windows (on desktops, laptops, 2-in-1s) and macOS/OS X — the numbers in July 2021 (according to StatCounter) broke as shown in Figure 1-3. (Linux and Chrome OS barely have more than 1 percent market share, each).

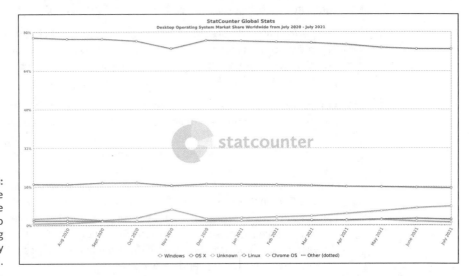

**FIGURE 1-3:** Worldwide market share of desktop operating systems from July 2020 to July 2021.

In July 2021, Windows had a market share of 73 percent of all desktop operating systems, and macOS had 15 percent. In Microsoft's world, Windows 10 is king with a 78 percent market share. Windows 7 is a distant second, with 16 percent, a value that is constantly declining because Microsoft declared its end of life on January 14, 2020. Users are no longer receiving support and updates for Windows 7, and they are highly encouraged to upgrade to Windows 10 or Windows 11. The graph doesn't include a market share for Windows 11 because it hadn't been launched. I expect it to reach levels similar to Windows 10 in just a couple of years.

**REMEMBER**

If you look at the bigger picture, including tablets and smartphones, the numbers change dramatically. As of July 2021, StatCounter says that 42 percent of all devices on the internet use Android, while 30 percent use Windows. Mobile operating systems are swallowing the world — and the trend has been in mobile's favor, not Windows. The number of smartphones sold every year exceed the number of PCs sold. According to Statista, in 2020, 54 percent of all internet traffic was made from mobile devices. And the data trends repeat the same story.

# Understanding Important Terminology

Some terms pop up so frequently that you'll find it worthwhile to memorize them or at least understand where they come from. That way, you won't be caught flat-footed when your first-grader comes home and asks to install TikTok on your computer.

**TIP**

If you want to drive your techie friends nuts the next time you have a problem with your Windows 11 computer, tell them that the hassles occur when you're "running Microsoft." They won't have any idea whether you mean Windows, Word, Outlook, OneNote, or any of a gazillion other programs. Also, they won't know if you're talking about a Microsoft program on Windows, the Mac, iPad, iPhone, Android, or even Linux.

Windows 11, the *operating system* (see the preceding section), is a sophisticated computer program. So are computer games, Microsoft Office, Microsoft Word (the word processor part of Office), Google Chrome (the web browser made by Google), those nasty viruses you've heard about, that screen saver with the oh-too-perfect fish bubbling and bumbling about, and more.

An *app* or a *program* or *a desktop app* is *software* (see the earlier "Hardware and Software" section in this chapter) that works on a computer. *App* is modern and cool; *program* is old and boring, *desktop app* or *application* manages to hit both gongs, but they all mean the same thing.

A *Windows app* is a program that, at least in theory, runs on any edition of Windows 11. By design, *apps* (which used to be called Universal Windows Platform, or UWP apps) should run on Windows 11 and Windows 10 on a desktop, a laptop, and a tablet— and even on an Xbox game console, a giant wall-mounted Surface Hub, a HoloLens augmented reality headset, and possibly Internet of Things tiny computers. They also run on Windows 11 in S mode (see the preceding section). Here's a neat trick that's available only in Windows 11: It can install and run *Android apps* too, but only through the Microsoft Store. I talk more about this topic in Book 5, Chapter 1.

**WARNING**

For most people, *Universal* Windows apps don't mean what they might think it means. Universal Windows apps *don't* work on Windows 8.1 or Windows 7 for example. They're universal only in the sense that they'll run on Windows 11 and Windows 10.

**REMEMBER**

A special kind of program called a *driver* makes specific pieces of hardware work with the operating system. The driver acts like a translator that enables Windows to ask your hardware to do what it wants. Imagine that you have a document that you want to print. You edit the document in Word, and then you click or tap the Print button and wait for the document to be printed. Word is an application that asks the operating system to print the document. The operating system takes the document and asks the printer driver to print the document. The driver takes the document and translates it into a language that the printer understands. Finally, the printer prints the document and delivers it to you. Everything inside your computer and all that is connected to it has a driver: The hard disk inside the PC has a driver, the printer has a driver, your mouse has a driver, and Tiger Woods has a driver (several, actually, and he makes a living with them). I wish that everyone was so talented.

Windows includes many drivers, some created by Microsoft and others created by third parties. The hardware manufacturer is responsible for making its hardware work with your Windows PC, and that includes building and fixing the drivers. However, if Microsoft makes your computer, Microsoft is responsible for the drivers, too. Sometimes you can get a driver from the manufacturer that works better than the one that ships with Windows.

When you stick an app or a program on your computer — and set it up so that you can use it — you *install* the app or program (or driver).

When you crank up a program — that is, get it going on your computer — you can say you *started* it, *launched* it, *ran* it, or *executed* it. They all mean the same thing.

If the program quits the way it's supposed to, you can say it *stopped, finished, ended, exited,* or *terminated.* Again, all these terms mean the same thing. If the app stops with some weird error message, you can say it *crashed, died, cratered, croaked, went belly up, jumped in the bit bucket,* or *GPFed* (techspeak for "generated a General Protection Fault" — don't ask), or employ any of a dozen colorful but unprintable epithets. If the program just sits there and you can't get it to do anything, no matter how you click your mouse or poke the screen, you can say that it *froze, hung, stopped responding,* or *went into a loop.*

A *bug* is something that doesn't work right. (A bug is not a virus! Viruses work as intended far too often.) US Navy Rear Admiral Grace Hopper — the intellectual guiding force behind the COBOL programming language and one of the pioneers in the history of computing — often repeated the story of a moth being found in a relay of an ancient Mark II computer. The moth was taped into the technician's logbook on September 9, 1947. (See Figure 1-4.)

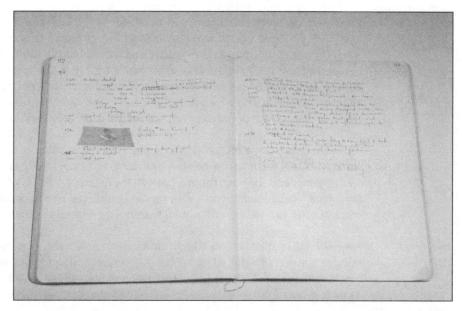

**FIGURE 1-4:** Admiral Grace Hopper's log of the first actual case of a bug being found.

Source: US Navy

The people who invented all this terminology think of the internet as being some great blob in the sky — it's *up,* as in "up in the sky." So, if you send something from your computer to the internet, you're *uploading.* If you take something off the internet and put it on your computer, you're *downloading.*

The *cloud* is just a marketing term for the internet. Saying that you put your data "in the cloud" sounds so much cooler than saying you copied it to storage on the internet. Programs can run in the cloud — which is to say that they run on the internet. Just about everything that has anything to do with computers can be done in the cloud. Just watch your pocketbook.

REMEMBER

If you use *cloud storage,* you're just sticking your data on some company's computers. Put a file in Microsoft OneDrive, and it goes onto one of Microsoft's computers. Put it in Google Drive, and it goes to Google's storage in the sky. Move it to Dropbox, and it's sitting on a Dropbox server.

When you connect computers and devices to each other, you *network* them. The network can be wired, using cables; wireless, often called *Wi-Fi*, the name for the main body of wireless networking standards; or a combination of wired and wireless. At the heart of a network sits a box, called a *router* or an *access point*, that computers connect to via cables or Wi-Fi. If the router has "rabbit ears" on top, for wireless connections, it's usually called a *Wi-Fi router*. Do keep in mind that some Wi-Fi routers have antennae hidden inside their box.

You can hook up to the internet in two basic ways: wired and wireless. *Wired* is easy: You plug one end of a network cable into a router or some other box that connects to the internet, and the other end into your computer. *Wireless* falls into two categories: Wi-Fi connections, as you'll find in many homes, coffee shops, airports, and all kinds of public places; and cellular (mobile phone–style) wireless connections. Cellular wireless internet connections are identified with one of the G levels: 2G, 3G, 4G, or maybe even 5G. Each G level is faster than its predecessor.

This part gets a little tricky. If your smartphone can connect to a 4G or 5G network, you can set it up to behave like a Wi-Fi router: Your laptop talks to the smartphone, and the smartphone talks to the internet over its 4G (or 5G) connection. That's called *tethering* — your laptop is tethered to your smartphone. Not all smartphones can tether, and not all manufacturers and mobile carriers allow it.

Special boxes called *mobile hotspot* units work much the same way: The mobile hotspot connects to the 3G or 4G (or 5G) connection, and your laptop gets tethered to the mobile hotspot box. Most smartphones these days can be configured as mobile hotspots.

If you plug your internet connection into the wall, you have *broadband*, which may run via *fiber* (a cable that uses light waves), *DSL* or *ADSL* (which use regular old phone lines), *cable* (as in cable TV), or *satellite*. The fiber, DSL, cable, or satellite box is called a *modem*, although it's really a *router*. Although fiber-optic lines are inherently much faster than DSL or cable, individual results can be all over the lot. Ask your neighbors what they're using and then pick the best. If you don't like your current service, vote with your wallet.

**TECHNICAL STUFF**

Turning to the dark side of the force, Luke, the distinctions among *viruses, worms,* and *trojans* grow blurrier every day. That's why most journalists and tech specialists use the generic term *malware* to describe anything that can harm a computer. In general, they're programs that replicate and can be harmful, and the worst ones blend different approaches. *Spyware* gathers information about you and then phones home with all the juicy details. *Adware* gets in your face with dodgy ads, all too frequently installing itself on your computer without your knowledge or consent. *Ransomware* scrambles (or threatens to scramble) your data and demands a payment to unscramble it.

If a bad guy manages to take over your computer without your knowledge, turning it into a zombie that spews spam by remote control, you're in a *botnet*. (And yes, the term *spam* comes from the immortal *Monty Python* routine that's set in a cafe serving Hormel's Spam luncheon meat, the chorus bellowing "lovely Spam, wonderful Spam.") Check out Book 9 for details about preventing malware and the like from messing with you.

The most successful botnets employ *rootkits* — programs that run underneath Windows, evading detection because regular antivirus programs can't see them. The number of Windows 10 and Windows 11 computers running rootkits is probably two or three or four orders of magnitude less than the number of zombified Windows XP computers. However, as long as Windows XP computers are out there, botnets will continue to be a major threat to everyone.

TIP

This section covers about 90 percent of the buzzwords you hear in common parlance. If you get stuck at a party where the bafflegab is flowing freely, do not hesitate to invent your own words. Nobody will ever know the difference.

# Buying a Windows 11 Computer

Here is how it usually goes: You decide that you need to buy a new PC, and then spend a couple weeks brushing up on the details — price, storage, size, processor, memory — and doing lots of comparison shopping. You end up at your local Computers Are Us shop, and the guy behind the counter convinces you that the best bargain you'll ever see is sitting right here, right now, and you better take it quick before somebody else nabs it.

Your eyes glaze over as you look at yet another spec sheet and try to figure out one last time whether a RAM is a ROM, whether a solid-state drive is worth the effort, and whether you need a SATA 6 Gbps, or NVMe, or USB 3 or C. In the end, you figure that the person behind the counter must know more than you, so you plunk down your credit card and hope that you got a good deal.

The next Sunday morning, you look at the ads on Newegg (www.newegg.com) or Best Buy (www.bestbuy.com) or Amazon (www.amazon.com) and discover that you could have bought the same PC for 20 percent less. The only thing you know for sure is that your PC is hopelessly becoming out of date, and the next time you'll be smarter about the entire process.

## YOU MAY NOT NEED TO PAY MORE TO GET A CLEAN PC

I hate it when the computer I want comes loaded with all that nice, "free" crapware. I would seriously consider paying more to get a clean computer. You do not need an anti-virus and internet security program preinstalled on your new PC. It's going to open and beg for money next month. Windows 11 comes with Windows Security (formerly known as Windows Defender), and it works great — for free.

Browser toolbars? Puh-lease.

You can choose your own internet service provider. AT&T? Verizon? Who needs you?

And trialware? Whether it's Quicken or any of a zillion other programs, if you must pay for a preinstalled app in three months or six months, you don't want it.

If you're looking for a new computer but can't find an option to buy a PC without all the extras, look elsewhere. The big PC companies are slowly getting a clue, but until they clean up their act, you may be better served buying from a smaller retailer who has not yet presold every bit that isn't nailed down. Or you can buy directly from Microsoft: Its Surface tablets and laptops are as clean as the driven snow. Pricey. But blissfully clean.

The online Microsoft Store sells new, clean computers from major manufacturers. Before you spend money on a computer, check to see whether it's available crapware free (usually at the same price). Go to www.microsoftstore.com and choose any PC. The ones on offer ship without any of the junk.

If you bought a new computer with all that gunk, you can get rid of it by performing a reset or reinstall. See Book 8, Chapter 2 for details.

If that describes your experiences, relax. It happens to everybody. Take solace in the fact that technology evolves at an incredible pace, and many people can't keep up with it. As always, I'm here to help and share everything you need to know about buying a Windows 11 PC:

>> **Decide if you're going to use a touchscreen.** Although a touch-sensitive screen is not a prerequisite for using apps on Windows 11, you'll probably find it easier to use apps with your fingers than with your mouse. Swiping with a finger is easy; swiping with a trackpad works well, depending on the trackpad; swiping with a mouse is a disaster. However, if you know that you won't be using Windows 11 apps or Android apps optimized for touch from the Microsoft Store, a touchscreen won't hurt but probably is not worth the

additional expense. Experienced, mouse-savvy Windows users often find that using a mouse and a touchscreen at the same time is an ergonomic pain in the arm. Unless you have fingertips the size of pinheads — or you always use a stylus — using classic Windows programs on a touchscreen is an excruciating experience. Best to leave the touching to apps that are demonstrably touch-friendly.

**TIP**

There is no substitute for physically trying the hardware on a touch-sensitive Windows 11 computer. Hands come in all shapes and sizes, and fingers, too. What works for size XXL hands with ten thumbs (present company included) may not cut the mustard for svelte hands and fingers experienced at taking cotton balls out of medicine bottles.

>> **Get a screen that's at least 1920 x 1080 pixels — the minimum resolution to play high-definition (1080p) movies.** You probably want to stream movies from Netflix and watch videos on YouTube. For a pleasant experience, don't get stingy when purchasing a monitor. Make sure that it's at least full HD – meaning that it has 1920 x 1080 pixels in resolution. Going higher makes for an even better experience. Therefore, if you have the cash, you won't be sorry if you buy a 1440p or a 4K display.

>> **If you're going to use the old-fashioned Windows 7–style desktop, get a high-quality monitor, a solid keyboard, and a mouse that feels comfortable.** If you are upgrading your computer and love your keyboard and mouse, you may want to keep them. Corollary: Don't buy a computer online unless you know that your fingers are going to like the keyboard, your wrist will tolerate the mouse, and your eyes will fall in love with the monitor.

>> **Go overboard with hard drives.** In the best of all worlds, get a computer with a solid-state drive (SSD) for the system drive (the C: drive) plus a large hard drive for storage. For the low-down on SSDs, hard drives, backups, and putting them all together, see the upcoming section "Managing disks and drives."

**TIP**

How much hard drive space do you need? How long is a string? Unless you have an enormous collection of videos, movies, or songs, 1TB (=1,024GB = 1,048,576MB) should suffice. That's big enough to handle about 1,000 broadcast-quality movies. Consider that the printed collection of the US Library of Congress runs about 10TB.

If you're getting a laptop or ultrabook with an SSD, consider buying an external 1TB or larger drive at the same time. You will use it. External hard drives are cheap and plug-in easy to use.

Or you can just stick all that extra data in the cloud, with OneDrive, Dropbox, Google Drive, or some competitor. For what it's worth, I used Dropbox in every phase of writing this book.

**REMEMBER**

If you want to spend more money, go for a faster internet connection and a better chair. You need both items much more than you need a marginally faster, or bigger, computer.

## Looking inside your PC

It's time to share some information about the inner workings of a desktop or laptop PC. The big box that your desktop computer lives in is sometimes called a *CPU*, or *central processing unit* (see Figure 1-5). Right off the bat, you're bound to get confused, unless somebody clues you in on one important detail: The main computer chip inside that big box is also called a CPU. I prefer to call the big box "the PC" because of the naming ambiguity, but you've probably thought of a few better names.

**FIGURE 1-5:**
The enduring, traditional desktop PC.

*Courtesy of Dell Inc.*

The big box contains many parts and pieces (and no small amount of dust and dirt), but the crucial, central element inside every PC is the motherboard. (You can see a picture of a motherboard here: www.asus.com/Motherboards-Components/Motherboards/PRIME/PRIME-Z590-V).

The following items are attached to the motherboard:

>> **The processor, or CPU:** This gizmo does the main computing. It's probably from Intel or AMD. Different manufacturers rate their processors in different ways, and it's impossible to compare performance by just looking at the part

number. Yes, Intel Core i7 CPUs usually run faster than Core i5s, and Core i3s are the slowest of the three, but there are many nuances. The same goes for AMD's Ryzen 7, Ryzen 5, and Ryzen 3 line-up of processors.

Unless you tackle intensive video games, create and edit audio or video files, or recalculate spreadsheets with the national debt, the processor doesn't count for much. You don't need a fancy processor if you're streaming audio and video (say, with YouTube or Netflix). If in doubt, check out the reviews at www.tomshardware.com and www.anandtech.com. Windows 11 requires an Intel Core processor from at least 2017, an AMD Ryzen processor from 2019 onward, or a processor from the Qualcomm Snapdragon 850 line-up.

» **Memory chips and places to put them:** Memory is measured in megabytes (1MB = 1,024KB = 1,048,576 characters), gigabytes (1GB = 1,024MB), and terabytes (1TB = 1,024GB). Microsoft recommends a minimum of 4GB of RAM. Unless you have an exciting cornfield that you want to watch grow while using Windows 11, aim for 8GB or more. Most desktop computers allow you to add more memory, while many laptops don't.

Boosting your computer's memory to 8GB from 4GB makes the machine snappier, especially if you run memory hogs such as Microsoft Office, Photoshop, or Google Chrome. If you leave Outlook open and work with it all day and run almost any other major program at the same time, 16GB is a wise choice. If you're going to do some video editing, gaming, or software development, you probably need more. But for most people, 8GB or 16GB will run everything well.

» **Video card:** Most motherboards include remarkably good built-in video. If you want more video oomph, you must buy a video card and put it in a card slot. Advanced motherboards have multiple PCI-Express card slots, to allow you to strap together two video cards and speed up video even more. If you want to run a VR or AR headset, such as an Oculus Rift, you'll need a much more capable video setup. Note that Windows 11 requires a DirectX 12–compatible video card, which means all video cards released in 2016 and beyond should be fine.

» **SSD:** Solid-state drives, or SSDs, are fast and cheap storage. You don't have to buy an expensive drive to benefit from tangible speed improvements. If you don't want to wait a lot for your programs to load, and you don't want Windows 11 to take minutes to boot, buying an SSD is a must. In comparison, hard disk drives (HDDs) are slow and dated. You should use an HDD for storing your personal files and backing up your data, not for running Windows 11, games, and apps. Remember, Windows 11 alone requires 64GB of storage, so don't be stingy with your SSD: Choose one with at least 256GB of storage space.

>> **Card slots (also known as expansion slots):** Laptops have limited (if any) expansion slots on the motherboard. Desktops contain several expansion slots. Modern slots come in two flavors: PCI and PCI-Express (also known as PCIe or PCI-E). Many expansion cards require PCIe slots: video cards, sound card, network cards, and so on. PCI cards don't fit in PCIe slots, and vice versa. To make things more confusing, PCIe slots comes in four sizes — literally, the size of the bracket and the number of bumps on the bottoms of the card is different. The PCIe 1x is smallest, the relatively uncommon PCIe 4x is considerably larger, and PCIe 8x is a bit bigger still. PCIe 16x is just a little bit bigger than an old-fashioned PCI slot. Most video cards these days require a PCIe 16x slot. Or two.

If you're buying a monitor separately from the rest of the system, make sure the monitor takes video input in a form that your PC can produce. See the upcoming section "Displays" for details.

>> **USB (Universal Serial Bus) connections:** The USB cable has a flat connector that plugs into your USB slots. Keep in mind that USB 3 is considerably faster than USB 2, and any kind of USB device can plug into a USB 3 slot, whether or not the device itself supports USB 3 level speeds.

USB Type-C (often called USB C) is a different kind of cable that requires a different kind of slot. It has two big advantages: The plug is reversible, making it impossible to plug it in upside down, and you can run a considerable amount of power through a USB-C, making it a good choice for power supplies. Many laptops these days get charged through a USB C connection.

Make sure you get plenty of USB slots — at least two and preferably four or more. Pay extra for a USB C slot or two. More details are in the section "Managing disks and drives," later in this chapter.

Here are a few upgrade dos and don'ts:

>> **Do not** let a salesperson talk you into eviscerating your PC and upgrading the CPU: Intel Core i7 isn't that much faster than Intel Core i5; a 3.0-GHz PC doesn't run a whole lot faster than a 2.8-GHz PC. The same is true for AMD's Ryzen 7 versus Ryzen 5.

>> **Do not** expect big performance improvements by adding more memory when you hit 16GB of RAM, unless you're running Google Chrome all day with 42 open tabs or editing videos.

>> **Do** consider upgrading to a faster video card or one with more memory if you have an older one installed. Windows 11 will take good advantage of an upgraded video card.

>> **Do** wait until you can afford a new PC, and then give away your old one, rather than nickel-and-dime yourself to death on little upgrades.

>> **Do** buy a new SSD if you can't afford to buy a new PC and you want more performance. Install Windows 11 and all your apps and games on the SSD. No other hardware component delivers bigger performance improvements than the switch from HDD to SSD.

TIP

If you decide to add memory, have the company that sells you the memory install it. The process is simple, quick, and easy — if you know what you're doing. Having the dealer install the memory also puts the monkey on the dealer's back if a memory chip doesn't work or a bracket snaps.

## Secure boot, TPM, and Windows 11

Windows 11 is a big deal when it comes to the security requirements it has for running on PCs and devices. Microsoft wants it to become the most secure Windows version ever and decided to enforce some stringent restrictions. As a result, for Windows 11 to work, your PC must have a processor with an embedded Trusted Platform Module (TPM) 2.0 and Secure Boot support. The TPM 2.0 chip has been a requirement for Windows devices since 2016, and Secure Boot has been around since the days of Windows 8. Because of that, you may think that these security features aren't be a big deal and that most computers should be able to handle Windows 11. However, many computers with a TPM 2.0 chip don't have it enabled by default, and you have to fiddle with your computer's BIOS to enable it — a task many users have no idea how to perform. To cope with this issue, motherboard manufacturers like ASUS have released new BIOS updates that enable this chip for you. Most probably others will follow their example. However, if your PC runs Windows 10 and you want to upgrade to Windows 11, you can't do that without enabling TPM and Secure Boot first.

TECHNICAL
STUFF

What is a TPM chip, you ask? It's a device used to generate and store secure and unique cryptographic keys. The cryptographic keys are encrypted and can be decrypted only by the TPM chip that created and encrypted them. Encryption software such as BitLocker in Windows 11 uses the TPM chip to protect the keys used to encrypt your files. Since the key stored in each TPM chip is unique to that device, encryption software can quickly verify that the system seeking access to the encrypted data is the expected system and not a different one.

Secure Boot, on the other hand, detects tampering attempts that may compromise your PC's boot process (which spans when you press the power button on your PC to when Windows starts) and key files of the operating system. When Secure Boot detects something fishy, it rejects the code and makes sure only good code is executed. Both security features are a big deal when it comes to protecting your data and your computer from all kinds of nasty cyberthreats.

These requirements significantly reduce the list of processors that work with Windows 11. To run this operating system, PCs and devices must have an Intel Core processor from at least 2017 or an AMD Ryzen processor from 2019 onward. They also need at least 4GB of RAM and 64GB of storage on their hard drives. It's ironic that Microsoft's own $3,499 Surface Studio 2 desktop, which was released at the end of 2018 and is still being sold, doesn't make the cut. New and expensive hardware like this isn't "good enough" for Windows 11. And I'm sure Microsoft's inflexible attitude on this subject will make many people frustrated.

TIP

Before upgrading a Windows 10 PC to Windows 11, it's a good idea to download and install the PC Health Check app from Microsoft (see Figure 1-6). Run it and click or tap Check Now. It tells you whether or not you can install Windows 11 and why. Download it here: `www.softpedia.com/get/System/System-Info/PC-Health-Check.shtml`

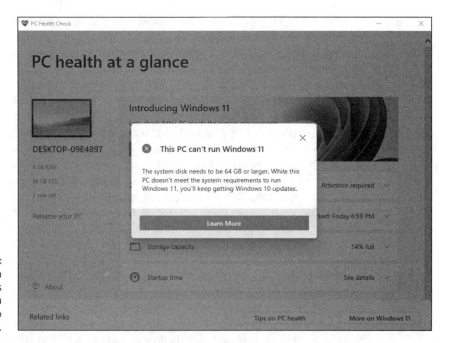

**FIGURE 1-6:**
The PC Health Check app tells you whether you can upgrade to Windows 11.

# Tablets

Although tablets have been on the market for more than a decade, they didn't really take off until Apple introduced the iPad in 2010. The old Windows 7 tablets required a *stylus* (a special kind of pen) and had truly little software that took advantage of touch input. Since the iPad took off, every Windows hardware manufacturer has been clamoring to join the game. Even Microsoft has entered the computer-manufacturing fray with its line of innovative tablets known as Surface.

The result is a real hodge-podge of Windows tablets, many kinds of 2-in-1s (which have a removable keyboard, as shown in Figure 1-7, and thus transform to a genuine tablet), and laptops and ultrabooks with all sorts of weird hinges, including some that flip around like an orangutan on a swing.

**FIGURE 1-7:** Microsoft Surface Pro tablets have tear-away keyboards.

*Courtesy of Microsoft*

The choice has never been broader. All major PC manufacturers offer traditional laptops as well as some variant on the 2-in-1, many still have desktops, and more than a few even make Chromebooks!

I did most of the touch-sensitive work in this book on an ASUS ZenBook Duo (see Figure 1-8). With a 10th-generation Intel Core i7-10510U processor, 16GB of RAM, and a 512GB solid-state drive, the ZenBook Duo is the fastest, most capable laptop I've ever used. It has a NVIDIA GeForce MX250 with 2GB of memory that works great for all kinds of professional tasks, including video editing and architectural drawing. I'm blown away by its dual-screen configuration and how it enhances my productivity.

The ZenBook Duo has two USB 3.1 ports, one USB C, an HDMI output for high-definition monitors (or TVs!), and a microSD card reader. Another cool feature is the webcam with facial-recognition support, which makes it easy to sign into Windows using your face instead of your password. Don't worry, your photo isn't sent to Microsoft; it is stored locally, on your PC.

Of course, this oomph comes at a price of around $2000. A couple thousand bucks for a desktop replacement is great, but if you just want a laptop, you can find respectable, traditional Windows 11 laptops (ultrabooks, whatever you want to call them), with or without touchscreens, for a few hundred dollars.

**FIGURE 1-8:**
The ASUS
ZenBook Duo
that I used for
writing parts of
the book.

*Courtesy of ASUS*

Microsoft's Surface Pro (refer to Figure 1-7) starts at $749 or so, without the keyboard. The Surface Laptop Go, including the keyboard, is $549 and up. The Surface Book, which is both a laptop and a tablet, starts at $1599.

If you're thinking about buying a Windows 11 tablet, keep these points in mind:

**REMEMBER**

>> **Focus on weight, heat, and battery life.** Touch-sensitive tablets are meant to be carried, not lugged around like a suitcase. The last thing you need is a box so hot that it burns a hole in your pants, or a fan so noisy you can't carry on a conversation during an online meeting.

>> **Make sure you get multi-touch.** Some manufacturers like to skimp and make tablets that respond only to one or two touch points. You need at least four just to run Windows 11, and ten wouldn't be overkill.

>> **The screen should run at 1920 x 1080 pixels or better.** Anything with a smaller resolution will have you squinting to look at the desktop.

>> **Get a solid-state drive.** In addition to making the machine much, much faster, a solid-state drive (SSD) also saves on weight, heat, and battery life. Don't be overly concerned about the amount of storage on a tablet. Many people with Windows 11 tablets end up putting all their data in the cloud using OneDrive, Google Drive, Dropbox, or Box. (For more info on cloud storage solutions, see Book 10, Chapter 6.)

>> **Try before you buy.** The screen must be sensitive to your big fingers and look good, too. Not an easy combination. You might have specific issues; for example, I dislike bouncy keyboards. Better to know the limitations before you fork over the cash.

>> **Make sure you can return it.** If you have experience with a "real" keyboard and mouse, you may find that you hate using a tablet to replicate the kinds of things you used to do with a laptop or desktop PC.

As the hardware market matures, you can expect to see many variations on the tablet theme.

## OLED VERSUS LED

OLED (organic light-emitting diode) screens are found on TVs, computer monitors, laptop screens, tablets, and even smartphones. Their prices are headed down fast. Can or should they supplant LED screens, which have led the computer charge since the turn of the century? That's' a tough question with no easy answer.

First, understand that an LED screen is an LCD (liquid crystal display) screen — an older technology — augmented by backlighting or edge lighting, typically from LEDs or fluorescent lamps. A wide variety of LED screens are available, but most of the screens you see nowadays incorporate IPS (in-plane switching) technology, which boosts color fidelity and viewing angles.

OLED is a horse of a different color. IPS LED pixels rely on the backlight or sidelight to push the color to your eyes. OLED (pronounced "oh-led") pixels make their own light. If you take an LED screen into a dark room and bring up a black screen, you can see variations in the screen brightness because the backlight intensity changes, if only a little bit. OLED blacks, by contrast, are uniform and thus deeper.

All sorts of new techniques are being thrown at LED, and LED screens are getting better and better. HDR (high dynamic range) improvements, for example, make LED pictures stand out in ways they never could before. Quantum dots improve lighting and color. Many people feel that OLEDs have blacker blacks, but the best LEDs produce better bright colors.

The huge difference is in price: OLED screens are still more expensive than LED, although the price of OLED is dropping rapidly. In addition, OLEDs don't last as long as LEDs — say, a decade with normal use. There is also some concern that OLEDs draw more power — and will burn through a laptop battery — faster than LCDs, but some contest that statement. Much depends on the particular LED and OLED you compare.

# Displays

The computer monitor or screen — and LED, LCD, OLED, and plasma TVs — use technology that's quite different from old-fashioned television circuitry from your parent's childhood. A traditional TV scans lines across the screen from left to right, with hundreds of lines stacked on top of each other. Colors on each individual line vary. The almost infinitely variable color on an old-fashioned TV combined with a comparatively small number of lines makes for pleasant but fuzzy pictures.

By contrast (pun intended, of course), computer monitors, touch-sensitive tablet screens, and plasma, LED, OLED, and LCD TVs work with dots of light called *pixels.* Each pixel can have a different color, created by tiny, colored gizmos sitting next to each other. As a result, the picture displayed on computer monitors (and plasma and LCD TVs) is much sharper than on conventional TV tubes.

REMEMBER

The more pixels you can cram on a screen — that is, the higher the screen resolution — the more information you can pack on the screen. That's important if you tend to have more than one word-processing document open at a time, for example. At a resolution of 1024 x 768, two open Word documents placed side by side look big and fuzzy, like caterpillars viewed through a dirty magnifying glass. At 1280 x 1024, those same two documents look sharp, but the text may be so small that you must squint to read it. If you move up to wide-screen territory — 1920 x 1080 (full HD), or even 2560 x 1440 (also called 1440p) — with a good monitor, two documents side-by-side look stunning. Run up to 4K technology, at 3840 x 2160 or better — the resolution available on many premium ultrabooks — and you need a magnifying glass to see the pixels.

A special-purpose computer called a *graphics processing unit (GPU),* stuck on your video card or integrated into the CPU, creates everything displayed on your computer's screen. The GPU has to juggle all the pixels and all the colors, so if you're a gaming fan, the speed of the video card (and, to a lesser extent, the speed of the monitor) can make the difference between a zapped alien and a lost energy shield. If you want to experience Windows 11 in all its glory, you need a fast GPU with at least 1GB (and preferably 4GB or more) of its own memory.

Computer monitors and tablets are sold by size, measured diagonally (glass only, not the bezel or frame), like TV sets. And just like with TV sets, the only way to pick a good computer screen over a run-of-the-mill one is to compare them side-by-side or to follow the recommendation of someone who has.

# Managing disks and drives

Your PC's memory chips hold information only temporarily: Turn off the electricity, and the contents of RAM go bye-bye. If you want to reuse your work, keeping it around after the plug has been pulled, you must save it, typically on a hard drive or possibly in the *cloud* (which means you copy it to a location on the internet).

The following list describes the most common types of disks and drives:

>> **Hard drive:** The technology's changing rapidly, with traditional hard disk drives (HDDs) now being replaced by *solid-state drives* (SSDs), which have no moving parts and, to a lesser extent, *hybrid drives,* which bolt together a rotating drive with an SSD. Each technology has benefits and drawbacks. Yes, you can run a regular HDD drive as your C: drive, and it will work fine. But tablets, laptops, or desktops with SSD drives run like lightning. The SSD wins as speed king. After you use an SSD as your main system (C:) drive, you'll never go back to a spinning platter, I guarantee.

SSDs feature low power consumption and give off less heat than HDDs. SSDs have no moving parts, so they don't wear out like hard drives. And, if you drop a hard drive and a solid-state drive off the Leaning Tower of Pisa, one of them may survive. Or maybe not.

SSDs are great for the main drive, but they may be too expensive for storing pictures, movies, and photos. Price and technical considerations (see the sidebar "Solid-state drives have problems, too") assure that hard drives will still be around.

Hybrid drives combine the benefits and problems of both HDDs and SSDs. Although HDDs have long had *caches* — chunks of memory that hold data before being written to the drive and after it's read from the drive — hybrid drives have a full SSD to act as a buffer.

**TECHNICAL STUFF**

If you can stretch the budget, start with an SSD for the system drive and a big hard drive (one that attaches with a USB cable) for storing photos, movies, and music, and then get another drive (which can be inside your PC, outside attached with a USB cable, or even on a different PC on your network) to run File History (see Book 8, Chapter 1).

If you want full on-the-fly protection against dying hard drives, get three hard drives — one SSD and two hard drives, either inside the box or outside attached with USB or eSATA cables — and run Storage Spaces (see Book 7, Chapter 4).

Many people opt for a fast SSD for files needed immediately coupled with cloud storage for the big stuff. Now that Google offers free unlimited photo storage — and with the rise of data streaming instead of purchased CDs — the need for giant hard drives has hit the skids.

For the enthusiast, a three-tier system, with SSDs storing data you need all the time, intermediate backup in the cloud, and multi-terabyte data repositories hanging off your PC is the way to go. Privacy concerns (and the, uh, intervention of various governments) have people worried about cloud storage. Rightfully so.

» **SD card memory:** Many smaller computers, and some tablets, have built-in SD card readers. (Apple and some Google tablets don't have SD — the companies would rather sell you more on-board memory at inflated prices!) You probably know Secure Digital (SD) cards best as the kind of memory used in digital cameras and smartphones (see Figure 1-9). A microSD card can be plugged into an SD card adapter to have it function like an SD card.

TIP

Many desktop computer cases have drive bays. Why not use one of them for a multifunction card reader? That way, you can slip a memory card out of your digital camera and transfer files at will. SD card, microSD card, CompactFlash, memory stick — whatever you have — a multifunction reader can read them all and costs a pittance.

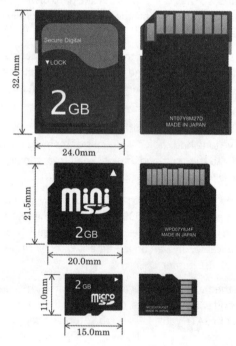

**FIGURE 1-9:**
Comparative sizes of an SD, a miniSD, and a microSD card.

*Source: Skcard.svg, Wikimedia*

» **CD, DVD, or Blu-ray drive:** Of course, these types of drives work with CDs, DVDs, and the Sony Blu-ray discs, respectively, which can be filled with data or contain music or movies. CDs hold about 700MB of data; DVDs hold 4GB, or six times as much as a CD. Dual-layer DVDs (which use two separate layers on top of the disc) hold about 8GB, and Blu-ray discs hold 50GB, or six times as much as a dual-layer DVD.

Fewer and fewer machines these days come with built-in DVD drives: If you want to schlep data from one place to another, a USB drive works fine — and going through the cloud is even easier. For most storage requirements, though, big, cheap USB drives are hard to beat.

» **USB drive or key drive:** It's half the size of a pack of gum and able to hold an entire PowerPoint presentation or two or six, plus a few full-length movies. Flash memory (also known as a jump drive, thumb drive, or memory stick) should be your first choice for external storage space or for copying files between computers. (See Figure 1-10.) You can even use USB drives on many DVD players and TV set-top boxes.

Pop one of these guys in a USB slot and suddenly Windows knows it has another drive — except that this one's fast, portable, and incredibly easy to use. It's okay to go for the cheapest flash drive you can find as long as it belongs to a recognized manufacturer.

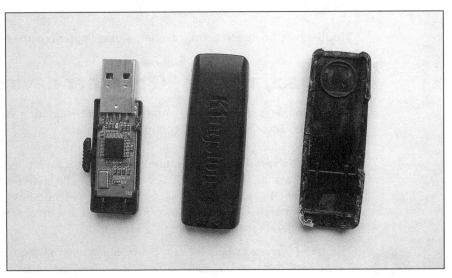

**FIGURE 1-10:**
The inside of a USB drive.

*Source: Wikipedia*

## SOLID-STATE DRIVES HAVE PROBLEMS, TOO

Although I love my SSD system drives and would never go back to rotating hard disk drives (HDDs), SSDs aren't perfect. First, they don't have any moving parts, and it looks like they're more reliable than HDDs. But when an HDD starts to go belly up, you can usually tell: whirring and gnashing, whining and groaning. Expiring SSDs don't give off advanced warning signals or sounds. When an HDD dies, you can frequently get the data back, although it can be expensive and time-consuming. When an SSD goes, you rarely get a second chance.

SSDs must take care of lots of internal bookkeeping, both for trimming unused space and for load balancing to guarantee uniform wear patterns. Trimming is the process in which the operating system tells the SSD which data blocks are no longer needed and can be deleted, or are marked as free for rewriting. SSDs slow down after you've used them for a few months or years. The speed decrease is usually associated with the bookkeeping programs kicking in over time.

**TIP**

What about USB 3? If you have a hard drive that sits outside your computer — an *external drive* — or a USB drive, it'll run faster if it's designed for USB 3 and attached to a USB 3 connector. Expect performance with USB 3 that's three to five times as fast as USB 2. For most other outside devices, USB 3 is overkill, and USB 2 works just as well.

This list is by no means definitive: New storage options come out every day.

## Connecting your PC to other devices

Your PC connects to the outside world by using a bewildering variety of cables and connectors. I describe the most common in this list:

>> **USB (Universal Serial Bus) cable:** This cable has a flat connector (known as *USB A*) that plugs into your PC, as shown in Figure 1-11. The other end is sometimes shaped like a D (called *USB B*), but smaller devices have tiny terminators (usually called *USB mini* and *USB micro,* each of which can have two different shapes).

**TECHNICAL STUFF**

USB 2 connectors work with any device, but hardware — such as a hard drive — that uses USB 3 will be much faster if you use a USB 3 cable and plug it into the back of your computer in a USB 3 port. USB 2 works with USB 3 devices, but you won't get the additional speed. Note that not all PCs have USB 3 ports, especially older PCs.

## USB Connection Type Reference Chart

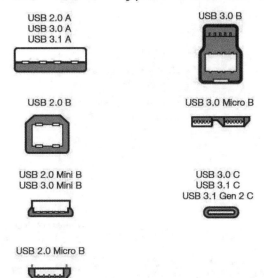

USB 2.0 A
USB 3.0 A
USB 3.1 A

USB 3.0 B

USB 2.0 B

USB 3.0 Micro B

USB 2.0 Mini B
USB 3.0 Mini B

USB 3.0 C
USB 3.1 C
USB 3.1 Gen 2 C

USB 2.0 Micro B

**FIGURE 1-11:**
The most common USB A, B, C, Mini, and Micro USB cables.

*Source: Wikimedia*

USB-C is a special kind of USB connection that supports amazingly fast data transmission and high levels of power. You know when you have USB-C because it's impossible to insert the plug upside down — both sides work equally well. It's becoming the go-to choice for connecting peripherals and, in some cases, power supplies.

**TECHNICAL STUFF**

USB is the connector of choice for just about any kind of hardware — printer, scanner, smartphone, digital camera, portable hard drive, and even the mouse. Apple's iPhones and iPads use a USB connector on one end — to plug in to your computers — but the other end is Lightning (common on Apple devices, not so common on Windows PCs) and doesn't look or act like any other connector.

If you run out of USB connections on the back of your PC, get a USB hub with a separate power supply and plug away.

**TECHNICAL STUFF**

» **LAN cable:** Also known as a CAT-5, CAT-6, or RJ-45 cable, it's the most common kind of network connector. It looks like an overweight telephone plug (see Figure 1-12). One end plugs in to your PC, typically into a *network interface card* (or *NIC*, pronounced "nick") or a network connector on the motherboard. The other end plugs in to your wireless router (see Figure 1-13) or switch or into a cable modem, DSL box, router, or other internet connection-sharing device.

**FIGURE 1-12:**
RJ-45 Ethernet
LAN connector.

*Source: David Monniaux, Wikimedia*

**FIGURE 1-13:**
The back of a
wireless router.

>> **Keyboard and mouse cable:** Most mice and keyboards (even cordless mice and keyboards) come with USB connectors.

>> **Bluetooth** is a short-distance wireless connection. Once upon a time, Bluetooth was finicky and hard to set up. In recent years, it has become quite useful and is now used to connect all kinds of accessories: speakers, headsets, mice, and keyboards.

>> **DisplayPort and HDMI connectors:** Modern computer monitors and smart TVs use small HDMI (see Figure 1-14), DisplayPort (see Figure 1-15) or mini DisplayPort connectors, which transmit both audio and video over one cable.

**FIGURE 1-14:**
HDMI replaces
the old VGA
and DVI-D video
adapters.

*Source: Amazon*

**FIGURE 1-15:**
DisplayPort
is a modern
alternative to
HDMI.

*Source: Wikimedia*

# Video, sound, and multimedia

Unless you're using a cheap laptop or a tablet, chances are good that you're running Windows 11 on a PC with at least a little oomph in the audio department. In the simplest case, you have to be concerned about four specific sound jacks (or groups of sound jacks) because each one does something different.

Here's how the four key jacks are usually marked, although sometimes you must root around in the documentation to find the details (see Figure 1-16):

>> **Line In:** This stereo input jack is usually blue. It feeds a stereo audio signal — generally from an amplified source — into the PC. Use this jack to receive audio output into your computer from your iPad, cable box, TV set, radio, CD player, electric guitar, or other audio-generating box.

» **Mic In:** This jack is usually pink. It's for unamplified sources, like most microphones or some electric guitars. If you use a cheap microphone for Skype or another VoIP service that lets you talk long distance for free, and the mic doesn't have a USB connector, plug in the microphone here. In a pinch, you can plug any of the Line In devices into the Mic In jack — but you may hear only mono sound, not stereo, and you may have to turn the volume way down to avoid some ugly distortion when the amplifier inside your PC increases the strength of an already amplified signal.

» **Line Out:** This stereo output jack is usually lime green. In many cases, it can be used for headphones or patched into powered speakers. If you don't have fancy output jacks (such as the Sony-Philips SPDIF), Line Out is the source for the highest-quality sound your computer can produce. If you go for a multi-speaker setup, Line Out is for the front speaker.

» **Rear Surround Out:** Usually black, this jack isn't used often. It's intended to be used if you have independent powered rear speakers. Most people with rear speakers use the Line Out connector and plug it into their home theater system, which then drives the rear speakers; or they use the HDMI cable (see the preceding section) to hook up to their TVs. If your computer can produce full surround sound output and you have the amplifier to handle it, you'll get much better results using the black audio jack.

**FIGURE 1-16:**
The audio jacks on the back of a desktop computer.

Many desktop computers have two more jacks: Orange is a direct feed for your subwoofer, and the gray (or brown) one is for your side speakers. Again, you must put an amplifier between the jacks and your speakers.

Laptops typically have just two jacks, pink for Mic In and lime for Line Out. If you have a headphone with a mic, that's the right combination. It's also common to plug powered external speakers into the lime jack.

Tablets and smartphones usually have headphone jack, which works just like a lime green Line Out jack.

High-end audio systems may support optical connections. Check both the computer end of the connection and the speaker/receiver end to make sure they'll line up.

**TIP**

PC manufacturers love to extol the virtues of their advanced sound systems, but the simple fact is that you can hook up a plain-vanilla PC to a home stereo and get good enough sound. Just connect the Line Out jack on the back of your PC to the Aux In jack on your home stereo or entertainment center. *Voilà!*

## Ultrabooks and convertibles

Netbooks, a popular concept in the days of Windows 7, were small laptops designed to provide the basics people needed from a laptop at an affordable price. Think of them as the precursor to today's Chromebooks.

Then along came the iPad, and at least 80 percent of the reason for using a netbook disappeared. Sales of netbooks have not fared well, and I don't see a comeback any time soon. Tablets blow the doors off netbooks, and 2-in-1s mopped up the remains.

Ultrabooks are a slightly different story. Intel coined (and trademarked) the term *Ultrabook* and set the specs. For a manufacturer to call its piece of iron an Ultrabook, it must be less than 21mm thick, run for five hours on a battery charge, and resume from hibernation in seven seconds or less. In other words, it must work a lot like an iPad.

Intel threw a $300 million marketing budget at Ultrabooks, but they fizzled. Now the specs seem positively ancient, and the term *Ultrabook* doesn't have the wow factor it once enjoyed.

If you're in the market for a new machine, drop by your favorite hardware store and look around. You might find something different that strikes your fancy. Or you may decide that you just want to stick with a boring desktop machine with a mechanical keyboard and a wide monitor the size of a football field. Guess what I work on, alongside the ZenBook Duo?

# What You Might Not Like about Windows 11

Windows 11 is not all greatness. There are frustrating bits, as in any operating system. Here are the negative aspects that I think every Windows 11 customer should know before using it:

>> **Forced updates:** Windows 11 users do not have any choice about updates. When Microsoft releases a patch, it gets applied. Considering the troublesome update history Windows 10 had, this is not a great policy on Microsoft's part. Unfortunately, all you can do is pause Windows 11 updates for up to five weeks. How annoying is that? Well, you'll soon find out.

>> **Inflexible hardware requirements:** As mentioned earlier in this chapter, you must have an Intel Core processor from at least 2017 or an AMD Ryzen processor from 2019 onward. As a result, only people with a new PC can run Windows 11, and they must also enable security features like the TPM chip and Secure Boot. I think these restrictions will lower the adoption rate for Windows 11 and drive many users mad. While Windows 11 is better than Windows 10, that doesn't justify the cost of replacing a not-so-old computer with a new one.

>> **Privacy concerns:** Microsoft is following the same path blazed by Google, Facebook, Apple (to a lesser extent), and many other tech companies. They're all scraping information about you, snooping on what you're doing, to sell you things. I don't think Microsoft is worse than the others, and Windows 11 has lots of privacy controls. In Book 2, Chapter 6, I talk about reducing the amount of data that Microsoft collects about you.

>> **Too many preinstalled apps:** Many people rely on apps to get their work done and to keep their lives sunny side up. The problem is that most Windows 11 PCs come with lots of crapware preinstalled: free apps and games that you don't need, which eventually ask you for money.

I've learned how to block Microsoft's forced updates and have come to peace with the fact that it's snooping on me. (Hey, I've used Google's Chrome browser for years, and it's been harvesting data the entire time.) Windows 11 may or may not give you more headaches than the alternatives, but it gives you more opportunities, too.

Welcome to Windows 11!

IN THIS CHAPTER

» **Rolling back to Windows 10**

» **Knowing how Windows 11 came about**

» **Understanding the types of apps available in Windows 11**

» **Checking what's new in Windows 11 for previous Windows users**

Chapter **2**

# Seeing What's New in Windows 11

Windows 11 is available as a free upgrade for Windows 10. You can get it from Windows Update, when Microsoft offers it to you, if your PC meets its steep system requirements, or upgrade manually using Windows 11 Installation Assistant at `www.microsoft.com/en-us/software-download/windows11`. You can also buy Windows 11 from Amazon and other shops and install it yourself, or get it preinstalled on a new laptop, tablet, PC, or hybrid device.

While it does have many cool features, new apps, and useful technologies (all covered in this chapter), Windows 11 initially proved to be relatively buggy. For example, soon after its launch, it was plagued by performance issues on systems with AMD Ryzen processors. If you have made the jump from Windows 10 to Windows 11 but find that it doesn't deliver suitable performance or stability, roll back to Windows 10 for a time, before making the jump again in a few months. I start this chapter by showing the steps required to get back to Windows 10.

Then I present the short story of Windows 11 and the principles Microsoft used in designing it. I also talk about the many different kinds of apps you can use in this operating system, including Android apps. Yes, you read that right!

Lastly, I describe all the new features and changes you might notice when you switch from a previous version of Windows to Windows 11.

# Rolling Back to Windows 10

Before digging into an examination of the new nooks and crannies in Windows 11, I'd like to pause for a second and let you know about an option you may have. If you upgraded from Windows 10 to Windows 11 in the past 10 days, and you don't like Windows 11, you can roll back to your old version. This works for only 10 days because a scheduled program comes in and wipes out the backup after 10 days.

If it's been 10 days or less since Windows 11 was installed and you want to roll back to Windows 10, the following steps show you how.

**WARNING**

Note that this technique is only for upgraders; it doesn't apply to new Windows 11 systems or computers on which you installed Windows 11 by wiping out the hard drive. For these systems, your only chance to go back to Windows 10 is to install it manually and erase Windows 11.

Settings

1. **Click or tap the Windows logo icon and then Settings. Alternatively, you can press Windows+I on your keyboard.**

   The Settings app opens.

2. **In the left column, choose System. On the right, click or tap Recovery.**

   You see the recovery options offered by Windows 11, as shown in Figure 2-1.

3. **Click or tap the Go Back button.**

   Microsoft asks you why you are going back, as shown in Figure 2-2.

4. **Choose a reason from the list and then click or tap Next.**

   Microsoft tells you that you should check for updates, because they might fix the problems you've been having. A funny but weak attempt to get you to stay with Windows 11, if you ask me.

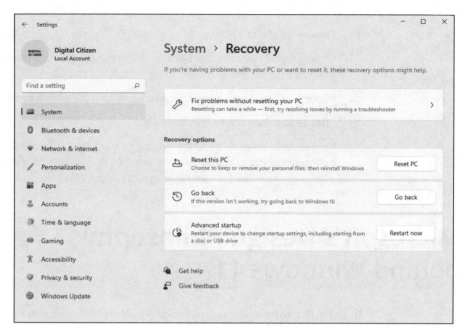

**FIGURE 2-1:**
The recovery options built into Windows 11.

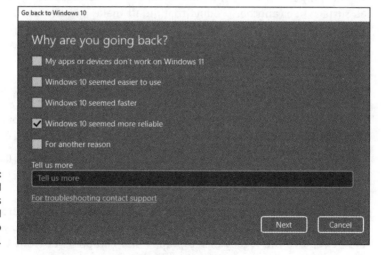

**FIGURE 2-2:**
When you roll back to Windows 10, you are asked why you want to go back.

5. **Click or tap No, Thanks.**

   Microsoft informs you that you won't be able to use your PC until the rollback is done. Also, after going back, you might have to reinstall some apps and might lose some settings.

6. **Click or tap No, Thanks.**

7. **Click or tap Next.**

   Microsoft gives you one last warning that you need to know the password of the user account that you used to sign into Windows 10.

8. **Make sure you remember this password and then click or tap Next.**

9. **Click or tap Go Back to Windows 10.**

   Your computer reboots and then restores Windows 10. This process takes quite a while and may involve some reboots. Arm yourself to be patient. If everything goes well, at some point you'll see the Windows 10 lock screen.

# Microsoft's Design Philosophy behind Windows 11

Initially, Microsoft planned to make Windows 10X (code-named Santorini), not Windows 11. Windows 10X was going to be a simplified version of Windows 10 that would compete with Chrome OS and be released on foldable mobile devices such as Surface Neo (another product that didn't make it to the market).

Windows 10X was expected to be released sometime in 2020, and it featured some significant changes compared to Windows 10:

>> A new taskbar with icons aligned to the center, rather than to the left

>> The removal of legacy components and legacy desktop apps from Windows 10 that were designed for PCs, not mobile devices with touchscreens

>> A redesigned Start menu without tiles and a friendlier user interface with an easier to use right-click menu

In May 2021, Microsoft announced that Windows 10X was cancelled but many of its features would be used in future products. In Windows 11, Microsoft didn't remove the legacy desktop apps and components from Windows 10, but it did adopt many of the user interface features that were developed for Windows 10X. The new operating system features a more pleasant-looking user interface, with lots of translucency effects, shadows, a new color palette, new icons, rounder corners for app windows, and sleek desktop backgrounds. Simply look at Figure 2-3 to see what I mean or give yourself a tour by opening the Start menu, File Explorer, Settings, and other Windows 11 apps.

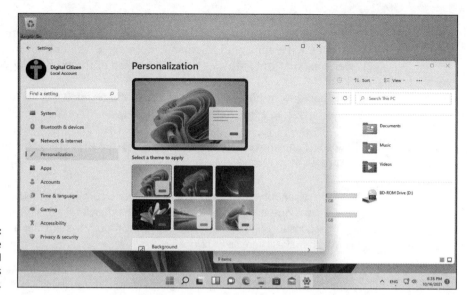

**FIGURE 2-3:**
Windows 11 is the
most beautiful
Windows
version yet.

Visually, Windows 11 is the most beautiful Windows ever. However, as you discover while reading this book and familiarizing yourself with Windows 11, it can also be one of the most frustrating Windows versions ever.

# Understanding the Types of Windows 11 Apps

Windows 11 can run several different kinds of programs. Computer programs (you can also call them applications or desktop apps if you want) work by interacting with an operating system. Since the dawn of Windows, programs have communicated with the operating system through a specific set of routines (application programming interfaces, or APIs) known colloquially and collectively as Win32. With rare exceptions, Windows desktop apps — the kind you use every day — take advantage of Win32 APIs to work with Windows.

In early June 2011, at the D: All Things Digital conference in California, Steven Sinofsky and Julie Larson-Green gave their first demo of Windows 8. As part of the demo, they showed off new Metro apps, which interacted with Windows in a different way. They used the newly minted API set known as Windows Runtime or, more commonly, the WinRT API. Microsoft started calling the WinRT based apps *immersive* and *full screen,* but most of the world settled on Microsoft's internal code name, Metro apps. Microsoft, however, has since changed the name to Modern

UI, then Windows 8 apps, Windows Store Apps, Modern apps, Universal Windows Platform (UWP) apps, and Microsoft Store apps. They all mean the same thing: newer apps that run with this new API instead of the traditional Win32 APIs.

In this book, to minimize confusion, I use the terms *Windows 11 app* and just *app* when referring to apps that use the new API.

Windows 11 apps have several characteristics that make them different from desktop apps:

>> They're sandboxed — stuck inside a software cocoon that isolates the apps from the operating system and from each other, so that it's hard to spread infections through them. These apps can't modify system files and settings, which makes them safer to use.

>> They can be easily interrupted, so their power consumption can be minimized. If a Windows 11 app hangs, it's almost impossible for it to freeze the machine.

>> They're designed to work both with touchscreens and a mouse and keyboard. In contrast, desktop apps were optimized for mouse and keyboard.

>> You can't run multiple instances of the same app in parallel like you do with many desktop apps or programs — or at least not yet.

>> They're distributed only through the Microsoft Store. In contrast, desktop apps can be downloaded from anywhere on the internet. One upside is that Windows 11 apps are updated automatically by the Microsoft Store app. Often, desktop apps need to be updated manually, or they have a separate updater that runs in the background.

>> When you buy an app from the Microsoft Store, Microsoft gets a commission. In contrast, you can buy a desktop app anywhere and Microsoft doesn't get a commission, unless you buy it from Microsoft or the app is made by Microsoft.

Android apps are another hot topic for Windows 11. According to Microsoft, in Windows 11, you'll be able to find Android apps in the Microsoft Store, which then hands you off to the Amazon Appstore. This feature wasn't available at launch, but the company says it soon will be. Basically, all the apps that work on Amazon's Kindle tablets that use Android should work on Windows 11 too. This move may increase the appeal for using Windows 11 on tablets and other touch devices, but many will be disappointed that this interconnectivity won't cover the Android apps from Google's Play Store.

Unlike Windows 10, the Microsoft Store for Windows 11 will host all types of apps: desktop apps, Windows 11 apps, and Android apps (again, not at launch, but they should show up soon after this book is published). To top things off, it also includes games, movies, and TV shows (see Figure 2-4).

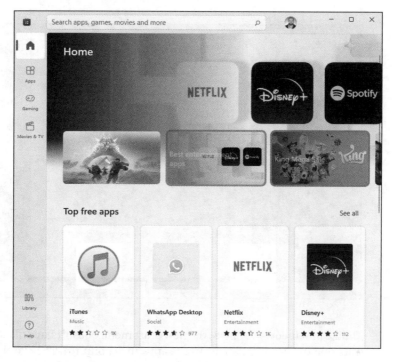

**FIGURE 2-4:**
The Microsoft Store includes apps, desktop apps, Android apps, games, movies, and TV shows.

Also, the Microsoft Store has more desktop apps, including Adobe Reader, VLC Media Player, Discord, and Zoom Cloud Meetings. After the appalling App Store for Windows 8 and the mediocre store for Windows 10, this seems a bit too good to be true, doesn't it?

Read Book 5, Chapter 1 to learn about the Microsoft Store and how to use it to find and install apps.

# Seeing What's New for the Windows Crowd

Depending on which version of Windows you're coming from, Windows 11 may be a bit different or a lot different. In the sections that follow, I present the most significant changes that you're likely to notice.

## A new Start menu and taskbar

Windows 11 has a new Start menu and taskbar. They're inspired by the world of macOS, so they're a lot more beautiful than previous incarnations but also less customizable. They're both centered on the screen, as shown in Figure 2-5.

**FIGURE 2-5:**
Windows 11 has a new taskbar and Start menu.

Unlike in Windows 10 and 8, the new Start menu doesn't have *tiles* (dynamic shortcuts that display live data from the apps they point to). The classic shortcuts from Windows 7 are back. (For details on personalizing the Start menu, see Book 3, Chapter 2.) Also, you can no longer resize the Start menu, and the way it is organized is fixed.

The taskbar looks good and works well with not only the mouse and keyboard but also touchscreen devices. However, you can't place it at the side of the screen, add toolbars to it, or change its size. (For more on working with the taskbar, read Book 3, Chapter 3.)

## Increased role for Settings

One of the things I love about Windows 11 is the new Settings app. First, it is better organized than it was in Windows 10 and a lot better than it was in Windows 8.

You can get where you need to faster because the categories in Settings appear in a column on the left, with the relevant settings alongside on the right, as shown in Figure 2-6. There's no intermediary step as there was in Windows 10. In addition, a Search box enables you to quickly find any setting.

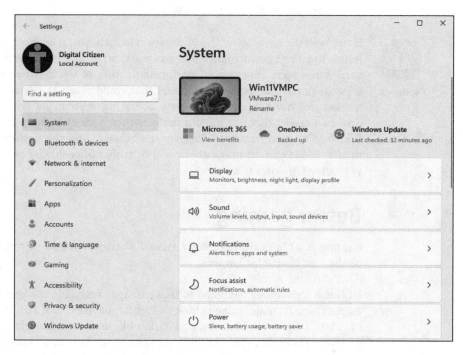

**FIGURE 2-6:**
The Settings app has received a major redesign in Windows 11.

Next, even more settings have migrated from the old Control Panel, making Settings even more useful than in Windows 10. However, I wish Microsoft would have finished this journey, so that I could stop having to use the dated Control Panel, which works well only with a mouse, not with touch.

## Improved performance

According to Microsoft, Windows 11 should offer more performance than Windows 10. Among all the improvements, one that caught my attention was that Windows 11 can prioritize apps in the foreground. Apps you're opening or using receive more hardware resources (including processor power) from the operating system than the ones in the background. That on its own should make apps feel faster in Windows 11.

Optimizations for laptop and tablet users mean the operating system uses less power than previous versions of Windows. For example, in Microsoft Edge, the Sleeping Tabs feature is on by default, putting open browser tabs in sleep mode after they haven't been used for a certain amount of time. According to Microsoft, this feature can lead to a huge decrease in processor and memory usage — about 30 percent less CPU time and RAM used.

If you read the news about the Windows 11 launch, you'll know that bugs and driver issues impaired performance. For example, on otherwise powerful AMD processors, some apps experienced performance hits of up to 5 percent, while some eSports games had performance hits that could reach 15 percent. The computer market has not supported this new operating system yet with fully optimized drivers. I expect that news about performance issues will be commonplace for the first 6 to 12 months after Windows 11's release. And the performance improvements that Microsoft brags about will be truly noticeable by everyone probably a year after Windows 11's launch.

## Better gaming

Gaming is a big deal in Windows 11, and Microsoft wants its operating system to be the best choice for gamers.

HDR is a technology designed to make images resemble the real world as closely as possible. To make images look authentic, devices with HDR use wider ranges of colors, brighter light areas, and darker blacks for shades. DirectX is a collection of application programming interfaces (APIs) for handling tasks related to games.

If you have a monitor with High Dynamic Range (HDR) support, you can take advantage of a cool aspect of Windows 11: The auto HDR feature (see Figure 2-7), which intelligently expands the color and brightness range up to HDR of DirectX 11 and DirectX 12 non-HDR games. This seamless feature will give you a new gaming experience that takes full advantage of your HDR monitor's capabilities.

There's also *dynamic refresh rate functionality*, which automatically helps you switch between different refresh rates. For example, Windows 11 might use 60 Hz when reading your email or a Word document on your laptop, which lowers battery consumption on your laptop, but it then switches to 120 Hz automatically when gaming to give you the most fluid gaming experience.

A more interesting technical feature of Windows 11 that will affect the gaming of tomorrow but not today's is *direct storage*. This feature allows your Windows 11 computer to bypass the processor when it needs to load data from an NVMe solid-state drive to the graphics card. NVMe, or Non-Volatile Memory Express, is a standard software interface that enables SSDs and other components to run directly through the PCI Express (PCIe) physical interface directly attached to a computer's processor.

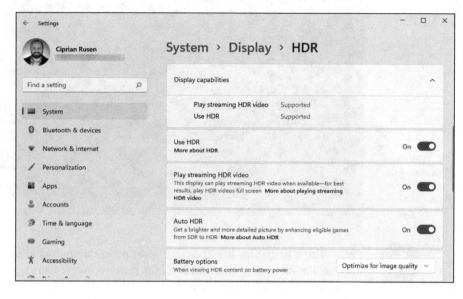

**FIGURE 2-7:**
Auto HDR makes non-HDR games more beautiful in Windows 11.

Direct storage decreases the amount of processor power required by games when loading textures (the graphics you see on the screen), which means that games should load faster too. However, games must implement specific support for direct storage and, when Windows 11 was launched, no games provided that support. I expect direct storage support in games to be the norm in a couple of years.

To cater to the needs of gamers, Windows 11, just like Windows 10, has a game mode that starts automatically when it detects that you're playing something. You can also start it manually. *Game mode* prioritizes the processor and graphics card resources to your game. It also stops Windows Update from installing driver updates or showing update notifications during your play. Another useful feature is that it stops all notifications from all apps so that they don't interfere with your game.

Another feature is the *Xbox game bar.* With it, you can take screen shots while you play and record videos of your gameplay. You can also use it to quickly adjust the audio and voice settings — useful when you play online with others and must coordinate with them. The Xbox game bar also shows you the performance of your computer (processor, RAM, and graphics card resource consumption) and allows you to chat and interact with your friends on Xbox, as shown in Figure 2-8.

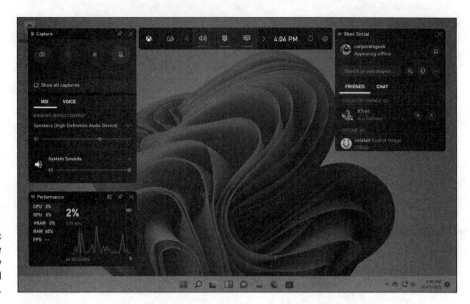

**FIGURE 2-8:**
The Xbox game
bar has many
features useful
to gamers.

**TIP**

Press Win+G to display the Xbox game bar at any time, including when you're not playing. Familiarize yourself with all the buttons and features, so that you can use it productively while you play games.

I discuss Windows 11 gaming more in Book 4, Chapter 9.

## Improved Microsoft Edge

Microsoft Edge has replaced Internet Explorer and is now based on the same Chromium open-source project found in Google Chrome and Opera.

The new Edge from Windows (shown in Figure 2-9) is a standards-compliant and screamingly fast browser, ready to take on just about any website anywhere. Microsoft Edge may see Microsoft taking back the mindshare it's been steadily losing on the browser front for the past decade or so. Recently, it managed the performance to overtake Mozilla Firefox in market share, which is quite something.

**REMEMBER**

Where Internet Explorer was frequently infected by wayward Flash programs and bad PDF files, Microsoft Edge is immune. And all the flotsam that came along with Internet Explorer — the ancient (and penetrable) COM extensions, custom toolbars, even Silverlight — are no longer used.

You learn about using Microsoft Edge in Book 3, Chapter 5.

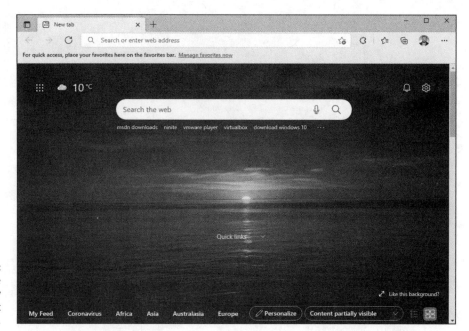

**FIGURE 2-9:**
Microsoft Edge
lets you finally
cut the Internet
Explorer cord.

## Less Cortana

Apple has Siri, Google has Google Assistant, and Amazon has Alexa. Microsoft has Cortana, the Redmond version of an AI-based personal assistant, shown in Figure 2-10. When Windows 10 was launched, Cortana was integrated into Windows Search, so it had the potential to know too much about what you do on your computer. Cortana never took off, and it was used a lot less than Siri or Google Assistant. Because of that, Microsoft decided to decouple it from the rest of Windows, and in Windows 11 it is a separate entity.

You can ignore it if you want, and you'll never know Cortana is part of Windows 11, or you can enable it, and have it sit in the background, listening for your commands. The choice is entirely yours, and the good news is that Cortana is no longer aggressively pushed by Microsoft.

I tell you much more about Cortana in Book 3, Chapter 6.

**FIGURE 2-10:**
Cortana is no
longer front
and center in
Windows 11, as it
was in
Windows 10.

## Improved security

Due to its strict security hardware requirements (supported processors, UEFI, Secure Boot, TPM), Windows 11 can be more easily secured by business organizations. Because of this hardline approach, you get the following benefits:

>> Encryption is turned on by default, which means that lost or stolen Windows 11 devices are harder to crack.

>> Chip-to-cloud protection (or virtualization-based security) is built-in, meaning that many cloud-based security solutions and services can be operated more securely, including in remote or hybrid work scenarios.

>> Container isolation for apps that are frequent targets for cyberattacks, such as Office or Microsoft Edge, means that a compromised app can't mess with the operating system, because it has no access to it, and can't cause even more damage.

>> Secure passwordless logins through biometric authentication, USB keys, or authentication apps provide for faster logins.

# Fine-tuned virtual desktops

Windows has had virtual (or multiple) desktops since Windows XP, but before Windows 10, you had to install a third-party app — or something like Sysinternals desktop from Microsoft — to get them to work. Windows 11 implements virtual desktops (see Figure 2-11) in a way that is useful and a bit less confusing than in Windows 10. For example, virtual desktops in Windows 11 no longer include the timeline from Windows 10.

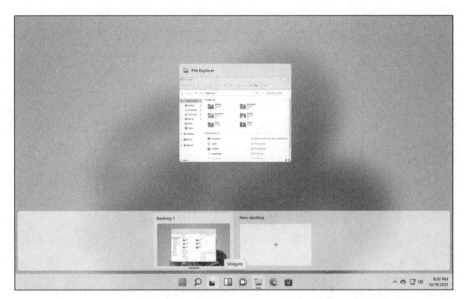

**FIGURE 2-11:**
Task view
displays all the
multiple desktops
you've set up.

You can name virtual desktops any way you want and change their desktop background, to help you keep track of which is which. It took Microsoft a long time to realize that this tiny improvement makes a world of difference.

Multiple desktops are handy if you tend to multitask. You can set up one desktop to handle your mail, calendar, and day-to-day stuff, and another desktop for your latest project or projects. Got a crunch project? Fire up a new desktop.

TIP

To start a new desktop, press Win+Ctrl+D. To see all available desktops, click or tap the task view icon on the taskbar (to the right of the search icon). App windows can be moved between desktops by right-clicking and choosing Move To. Alt+Tab still rotates among all running windows. Clicking or tapping an icon in the taskbar brings up the associated program, regardless of which desktop it's on.

You learn how to use virtual desktops in Book 3, Chapter 1.

# Improved window snapping and grouping

You use multiple windows and apps on your computer, and one of the easiest ways to organize them on the desktop is with the *snap feature.* It allows you to quickly position your windows on the screen by dragging them to the sides or corners. You can split the screen into two, three, or four areas. In Windows 11, snap is even better and easier to use: Hover your cursor on the square icon next to the close icon (X) in the top-right corner of any window, and you see a list of up to six snap layouts to choose from (Figure 2-12).

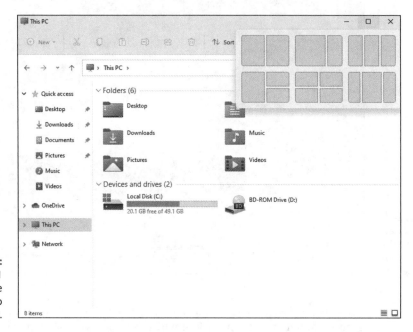

**FIGURE 2-12:**
Windows 11 has many more useful snap layouts.

**TECHNICAL STUFF**

The number of layouts depends on the resolution of your screen. Displays that are full HD or higher have six snap layouts. On older monitors or on resolutions lower than full HD (or 1080p), you get four snap layouts, as in Windows 10.

Open windows are also organized into snap groups that remember the positions of windows on the screen.

# Widgets are back

*Widgets* are a group of small graphical apps designed to provide at-a-glance information about news, weather, sports results, stocks, traffic, and the like, as shown in Figure 2-13. They are accessible straight from the taskbar and can be customized to show only the widgets you want. Widgets include a Bing search bar that opens results in Microsoft Edge.

**FIGURE 2-13:**
Widgets present
live news and
information.

The look and content delivery style of Windows 11's widgets are similar to the News and Interests widget in Windows 10 and the live tiles in the Windows 10 Start menu.

Read more about widgets in Book 4, Chapter 7.

## Other apps and improvements

Microsoft has given many built-in apps a much-needed makeover:

>> **Windows Terminal** is now built into Windows 11 instead of a separate app you download from the Microsoft Store. With it, you can use only one command-line shell for executing commands in PowerShell, Command Prompt, and Azure Cloud Shell.

>> **Paint** has a received a fresh look, with sleek menus and visuals and useful tools for basic image editing.

>> **Photos** has a better user interface, a new photo-viewing experience, and an updated photo-editing toolbar. Book 4, Chapter 3 shares what you need to know about using this app.

>> **Snipping Tool** combines the Snipping Tool and Snip & Sketch apps from Windows 10 into one screen shot–taking app. The new app from Windows 11 is better and simpler to use than its predecessors.

>> **Xbox** from Windows 11 is better than it was in Windows 10. If you have an Xbox Game Pass Ultimate subscription, the Xbox app lets you play through Xbox Cloud Gaming directly, with no browser required.

>> **Clock** now includes focus sessions, which help you improve productivity by implementing time-management methodologies such as the Pomodoro technique.

>> **Calculator** is even more advanced than in Windows 10 and can plot equations in graphing mode.

>> **Microsoft Store** looks better, works better, and includes a lot more useful apps than it did in Windows 10. Another cool aspect is that the search experience makes it easier to filter your results.

>> **Microsoft Teams** is now part of Windows 11 and added to the taskbar, to the right of the widgets icon. Read Book 6, Chapter 2, for more on Teams.

There are also some general improvements at a user interface level, which come in handy:

>> Quick settings are now separate from notifications and offer more things you can toggle on and off. Windows 11 apps can add their own quick settings (for example, Spotify), and they're easily accessible with a mouse and keyboard as well as touch. To see them in action, press Windows+A on your keyboard.

>> Microsoft has improved the touch experience, with more space between icons on the taskbar. Windows 11 also adds haptics to your digital pen, so you can hear and feel vibrations as you take notes or draw on the screen.

>> Windows 11 introduces voice typing and commands.

Chapter **3**

# Windows 11 Versions

B   ack in 2015, Microsoft told us that Windows 10 was the last version of Windows. Fast-forward to October 2021, and they changed their mind because we now have Windows 11. This won't be the last version of Windows, either, even if Windows 11 lives a long life, like Windows 10 still does. To make things even more confusing, Windows 11 has several editions, most of which you can ignore, and a Windows 11 Home in S mode edition that's quite troublesome if you run it when you don't know what it is. In this chapter, I explain how Windows 11 versions and editions are different and advise you on which one to buy.

Also, contrary to what you might expect, Windows 11 isn't free, even though you get it preinstalled on a new laptop, PC, Microsoft Surface, or All-In-One device or as a free upgrade to Windows 10.

**REMEMBER**

Here are some facts about purchasing Windows 11:

» You can upgrade from a genuine copy of Windows 10 to Windows 11 for free, if your PC meets the minimum system requirements that I detail in Chapter 1 of this minibook.

» If you're building a new PC, you must buy Windows 11. And if you buy a new PC with Windows 11 preinstalled, the PC manufacturer most probably paid for Windows 11 and passed along this cost in the price of the PC.

## EDITION VERSUS VERSION

Microsoft makes a distinction between *versions* and *editions* of Windows. *Windows versions* started with the venerable Windows 1.0, continued through Windows XP and Windows 7, and reached their lofty heights with Windows 10 and Windows 11. In the past, a version change was a big bump — from Windows 7, for example, to Windows 8, to Windows 10. With the launch of Windows 10 and Microsoft's Windows as a Service concept, the version bumps became tiny or almost imperceptible — but when you install a new version, you get a new copy of Windows.

Versions in Windows 10 often came with nonsensical names such as the Fall Creators update or May 2021 update. Many tech support engineers just give them numbers, which correspond roughly to when they were released: Windows 10 version 1507, 1709, 2009, 21H1, 21H2, and so on. When we got Windows 10, Microsoft released two versions of Windows per year. With Windows 11, Microsoft is going to release one version per year. A Windows 11 version represents a minor upgrade over the previous one, with just a few new features and improvements and several bug fixes.

*Windows editions,* on the other hand, refer to the capabilities of an individual copy of Windows. You probably know about Windows Home and Windows Pro. Once upon a time, we had a Windows Ultimate, but it died with Windows 7, which was the last to have some meaningful stuff added to it.

If you haven't yet bought a copy of Windows, you can save yourself some headaches and more than a few bucks by buying the right edition the first time. There are many versions and editions of Windows 11, and I explain them all in simple terms, so that you can understand which is best for you.

Finally, you may already have Windows 11 on your computer, but you don't know which edition and version you have. This information is helpful in understanding what you can and can't do with Windows 11, as well as when you need tech support. Read this chapter to its end for steps on finding the exact edition and version you're using.

# Windows 11 Editions

Windows 11 appears in seven different major editions. Fortunately, most people need to concern themselves with only two editions, and you can quickly narrow the list to one. Contemplating the 32-bit conundrum is no longer necessary, as it was with Windows 10 and Windows 7, because Windows 11 is available only in a 64-bit incarnation.

In a nutshell, the Windows 11 editions (and targeted customer bases) look like this:

**REMEMBER**

>> **Windows 11 Home** — the version you probably want — works great unless you need one of the features in Windows 11 Pro. A big bonus for many is that Windows 11 Home makes all the myriad Windows languages — 140 of them, from Afrikaans to Yoruba — available at no extra cost. Its biggest downside is that it doesn't include BitLocker encryption and Remote Desktop.

>> **Windows 11 Pro** includes everything in Windows 11 Home plus Encrypting File System and BitLocker (see the BitLocker sidebar later in this chapter) for protecting your hard drive's data; Hyper-V for running virtual machines; the software necessary for your computer to act as a Remote Desktop host — the "puppet" in remote desktop session; and the capability to attach the computer to a corporate domain network.

>> **Windows 11 Enterprise** is available only to companies that buy Microsoft's Volume License program. It offers a handful of additional features over those in Pro, but they don't matter unless you're going to buy a handful of licenses or more. There's also an Enterprise LTSC (Long-Term Servicing Channel) with new versions released once every two to three years and security updates for ten years after each version is released.

>> **Windows 11 Education** looks and works just like Windows 11 Enterprise but is available only to schools, through a program called Academic Volume Licensing. It also has a slightly smaller feature-set than the Enterprise edition.

>> **Windows 11 Pro Education** is a special edition of Windows 11 for the educational sector that's similar to Windows 11 Pro. It includes a Set Up School PCs app that allows provisioning settings using a USB flash drive. It does not have Cortana, Microsoft Store suggestions, or Windows Spotlight.

>> **Windows 11 Pro for Workstations** is designed for high-end hardware that costs a lot, intensive computing tasks, and the latest server processors and file systems. Unlike other editions of Windows 11, Pro for Workstations work on PCs with four processors (instead of a maximum two), and a maximum of 6TB of RAM (instead of a maximum 2TB). If you aren't a data scientist, CAD professional, researcher, or media producer, this edition isn't right for you.

>> **Windows 11 IoT** is designed for low-cost such as the Raspberry Pi and specialized machines, such as robots, ATMs, POS terminals, and barcode scanners. There are two editions of Windows 11 IoT: IoT Enterprise and IoT Core.

All editions except IoT run on only Intel and AMD processors. They're traditional Windows.

You'll hear about Windows 11 editions designed for ARM chips and Qualcomm processors — chips originally designed for smartphones. In theory, those editions work the same way as their Intel/AMD brethren but can run only emulated desktop apps.

To make your life a little bit more complicated, Windows 11 Home can run in S mode. Microsoft is peddling S mode as an alternative to Chromebooks — stripped down, fast starting, battery friendly, and offering better protection against infections with viruses and other forms of malware.

TECHNICAL
STUFF

Windows Vista and Windows 7 both had Ultimate editions, which included absolutely everything. Windows 11 doesn't work that way. If you want the whole enchilada, you must pay for volume licensing.

Windows Media Center — the Windows XP–era way to turn a PC into a set-top box — is not available in any version of Windows 11. Do yourself a favor and buy a Chromecast or use your cable company's DVR if you really have to record TV.

WARNING

Windows 11 Home running in S mode runs only apps. That bears repeating: **S mode doesn't run old-fashioned Windows programs.** It's restricted to running just Windows 11 apps from the Microsoft Store. Luckily, only Windows 11 Home can run in S mode. Other editions like Pro or Enterprise can't.

## Buying the right edition, the first time

What if you aim too low and buy Windows 11 Home and decide later that you really want Windows 11 Pro? Be of good cheer. Switching editions is not as tough as you think.

TIP

Microsoft chose the feature sets assigned to each Windows edition with one specific goal in mind: maximize Microsoft's profits. If you want to move from Windows 11 Home to Windows 11 Pro (the only upgrade available to individuals), you need to buy the Windows 11 Pro Pack. To buy an upgrade, click or tap the Start icon (shown in the margin), Settings, System, and then About. Then, inside the Related settings, find the Product key and activation information.

Similarly, moving from Windows 11 Home in S mode to plain Windows 11 Home requires only a trip to the Microsoft Store.

Upgrading is easy and cheap, but not as cheap as buying the correct version the first time.

# Narrowing the choices

If you're a regular home user, you can dismiss five Windows editions immediately:

>> **Windows 11 Enterprise** is an option only if you own a large business and want to go through Microsoft's Volume Licensing program or purchase a Windows 365 Enterprise or Microsoft 365 for Enterprise subscription.

>> **Windows 11 Education and Windows 11 Pro Education,** similarly, can be purchased only in large quantities. If you're a student, faculty member, or staff member at a licensed school, you must contact the IT department to get set up.

>> **Windows 11 Pro for Workstations** is useful only for professional users with expensive hardware and specific needs. Most people should ignore it.

>> **Windows 11 IoT** is a viable choice for enthusiasts and software developers who want to tinker with Raspberry Pi and program their own devices to perform specific tasks.

## BITLOCKER AND ENCRYPTING FILE SYSTEM

*BitLocker* was introduced in Windows Vista and has been improved since. BitLocker runs *underneath* Windows: It starts before the operating system starts. The Windows partition on a BitLocker-protected drive is completely encrypted, so bad guys who try to get to the file system can't find it.

*Encrypting File System (EFS)* is a method for encrypting individual files or groups of files on a hard drive. EFS starts after Windows boots: It runs as a program under Windows, which means it can leave traces of itself and the data that's being encrypted in temporary Windows places that may be sniffed by malicious programs. The Windows directory isn't encrypted by EFS, so bad people who can get access to the directory can hammer it with brute-force password attacks. Widely available tools can hack EFS if the cracker can reboot the computer that is attacking. Thus, for example, EFS can't protect the hard drive on a stolen laptop or notebook. Windows has supported EFS since Windows 2000.

EFS and BitLocker are complementary technologies: BitLocker provides coarse all-or-nothing protection for an entire drive. EFS lets you encrypt specific files or groups of files. Used together, they can be hard to crack.

There's also BitLocker To Go, which provides BitLocker-style protection to removable drives, including USB drives. You should use it when storing important data on your USB drives.

That leaves you with Windows 11 Home, unless you have the need to do one of the following:

>> **Connect to a corporate network.** If your company doesn't give you a copy of Windows 11 Enterprise, you need to spend the extra bucks and buy Windows 11 Pro.

>> **Play the role of the host in a Remote Desktop interaction.** If you're stuck with Remote Desktop, you must buy Windows 11 Pro.

Note that you can use Remote Assistance any time, on any Windows PC. (See Book 7, Chapter 3.) The Windows 11 Pro restriction is specifically for Remote Desktop, which is commonly used inside companies but not that much by other types of users.

TIP

Many business users find that TeamViewer, a free alternative to Remote Desktop, does everything they need and that Remote Desktop amounts to overkill. TeamViewer lets you access and control your home or office PC from any place that has an internet connection. Look at its website, www.teamviewer.com.

>> **Provide added security to protect your data from prying eyes or to keep your notebook's data safe even if the notebook is stolen.** Start by determining whether you need Encrypting File System (EFS), BitLocker, or both (see the BitLocker sidebar). Windows 11 Pro has EFS and BitLocker — with BitLocker To Go tossed in for even more protection.

>> **Run Hyper-V.** Some people can benefit from running virtual machines inside Windows 11. If you absolutely must get an old Windows 7 program to cooperate, for example, running Hyper-V with a licensed copy of Windows 7 may be the best choice. For most people, virtual machines are an interesting toy but not much more.

## 64-bit is the new normal

If you've settled on Windows 11 as your operating system of choice, there's no more stressing about whether you want the 32-bit flavor or the 64-bit flavor of the Home edition, as was the case with Windows 7 and Windows 10. That's because Windows 11 is the first consumer operating system from Microsoft to support only 64-bit processors. It doesn't work on older 32-bit processors, and it accepts only modern hardware that meets its strict security requirements.

Not being able to use Windows 11 on old hardware can be annoying, but there are important benefits to this enforcement on Microsoft's part:

>> **Performance:** The 32-bit flavor of Windows — the flavor that everyone was using more than a decade ago — has a limit on the amount of memory that it can use. Give or take a nip here and a tuck there, 32-bit machines can see, at most, 3.4 or 3.5 gigabytes (GB) of memory. You can stick 4GB of memory into your computer, but in the 32-bit world, anything beyond 3.5GB is simply out of reach. With many desktop apps acting like resource hogs, such as the Google Chrome browser, you want 4GB or more on any PC.

>> **Security:** Security is one more good reason for running a 64-bit flavor of Windows. Microsoft enforced strict security constraints on drivers that support hardware in 64-bit machines — constraints that just couldn't be enforced in the older, laxer 32-bit environment.

**WARNING**

There's only one problem with 64-bit Windows: drivers. Some people have older hardware that doesn't work in any 64-bit flavor of Windows. Their hardware isn't supported if the manufacturer decides that it isn't worth the money to build a solid 64-bit savvy driver so that the old hardware can work with the new operating system. You, as a customer, get the short end of the stick and are forced to buy new hardware.

Applications, however, are a different story. All 32-bit apps work on 64-bit Windows and shouldn't be an issue.

# Which Version of Windows Are You Running?

You may be curious to know which version of Windows you're running on your current machine. The easy way to tell is to first log in and press the Windows key on your keyboard. If your desktop is like

>> Figure 3-1, you're running some version of Windows 10. Note the Windows-logo wallpaper, the large Search box in the lower-left corner next to the Windows icon, and the large tiles on the right side of the Start menu.

>> Figure 3-2, you're running Windows 11. Note how the icons on the taskbar are centered, not left-aligned as they are in Windows 10. Also, the tiles from the Windows 10 Start menu are gone, replaced by traditional shortcut. And there's a new Recommended section that lists recent apps and recently opened files, for quick access.

**FIGURE 3-1:**
The desktop and
the Start menu in
Windows 10.

**FIGURE 3-2:**
The desktop and
the Start menu in
Windows 11.

If you have Windows 11, here's how to see your specific edition and version:

1. **Click or tap the search icon (magnifying glass) on the taskbar, and type** about.

   Search results appear. At the top of the stack you should see something like *About Your PC.*

**2.** **Press Enter or click or tap About Your PC.**

You see an About window with lots of technical details.

**3.** **On the right, scroll down until you get to Device Specifications, shown in Figure 3-3.**

To the right of System Type, you can see that you're using a 64-bit version of Windows 11.

**4.** **Scroll down a bit more until you see Windows Specifications.**

In this section, you see the edition of Windows 11, the version, the date it was installed, and the OS build number.

**TIP**

The OS build number is useful if you need to contact Microsoft's tech support service. It helps the support engineer figure out the exact build of Windows 11 and the appropriate patches or steps required to troubleshoot problems with your specific version.

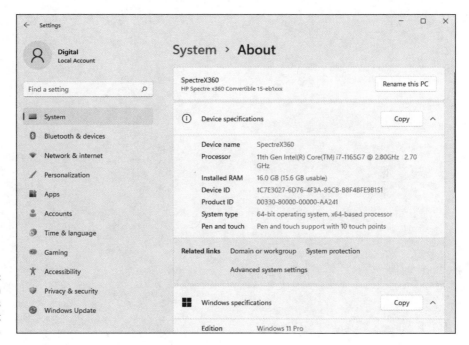

**FIGURE 3-3:** Full system information is in the About window.

# 2

# Personalizing Windows

# Contents at a Glance

# Chapter **1**

# Getting Around in Windows

Ready to get your feet wet, but not yet up to a full plunge?

Good. You're in the right place for a dip-your-toes-in kind of experience. Nothing tough in this chapter, just a bit of windows cruising. Lay of the land kind of stuff.

If you're an experienced Windows 7 user, you'll find parts of Windows 11 that look a bit familiar and parts that look like they were ripped from a Mac or an iPhone. If you're a Windows 10 user, you'll feel right at home, but will enjoy a more cohesive user experience.

Anyway, you surely know that to get around Windows you need to click or tap stuff, just like you do on your smartphone. Navigating the Windows 11 desktop is not difficult, but in this chapter I give you a quick tour. Also, I discuss how Microsoft approaches touchscreens in this version of Windows. It's a bit different and better than in Windows 10.

But what about turning Windows 11 on and off again? That question is a popular meme with people who do tech support for their friends and co-workers. Well, I show you how to do that, too, as well as how to take a screen shot when, for example, an error pops up on the screen.

Finally, I show you a few useful keyboard shortcuts, alongside the classic Ctrl+C and Ctrl+V that many know. Using shortcuts will make you more productive and help you find your way around Windows 11 more quickly.

# Navigating around the Desktop

Whether you use a mouse, a trackpad, or your finger, the desktop is the place where you're going to spend most of your time in Windows. Here's a guided tour of your PC, which you can perform with a mouse, a finger, or even a stylus, your choice:

1.  **Click or tap the Windows logo icon (Start), which is shown in the margin.**

    You see the Start menu (see Figure 1-1). Note the Search box at the top, the list of pinned apps, and the Recommended section populated with recent files and recently installed apps.

2.  **In the Pinned section, click or tap the Photos icon.**

    Microsoft's Photos app appears, as shown in Figure 1-2. Before you can use it, it may ask you to sign in.

3.  **Take a close look at the Photos app window.**

    Like other app windows, the Photos window can be resized by moving your mouse cursor over to an edge, and then clicking (or tapping) and dragging. You can move the entire window by clicking (or tapping) the title bar and dragging. You can minimize the window — make it shrink down to an icon on the taskbar — by clicking or tapping the horizontal line in the upper-right corner. And finally, you can close the app by clicking or tapping the X in the upper right.

4.  **At the bottom in the taskbar, next to the Start icon, click or tap the search icon (shown in the margin).**

    The Windows 11 search screen appears, where you can type the names of apps, files, folders, settings, or websites to find what you need.

**FIGURE 1-1:**
The Start menu is simpler and better than it was in Windows 10.

**FIGURE 1-2:**
The Photos app looks and works like many Windows 11 apps.

**5.** **In the search field (at the top), type the word** photos.

The first result is the Photos app, as shown in Figure 1-3. The results will also include settings, web results, and folders and files on your computer that contain the word *photos* in their name.

**FIGURE 1-3:**
Search is a useful feature of Windows 11.

**6.** **Click or tap the Task View icon (shown in the margin), which is to the right of the search icon.**

Windows 11 can have multiple virtual desktops, each running a separate set of apps. The first desktop is named Desktop 1, and you see it displayed at the bottom of the screen (see Figure 1-4).

**7.** **Click or tap the New Desktop button (above the taskbar).**

Desktop 2 is created and added to the list of virtual desktops. Any app that you open is then assigned to this virtual desktop.

8. **Move the mouse over Desktop 1, right-click (or tap and hold down on) the Photos app, and choose Move To ⇨ Desktop 2.**

   You've successfully moved the Photos app from Desktop 1 (the default) to Desktop 2, which you created in Step 7.

9. **Click or tap Desktop 2.**

   Note how the Photos app is now in Desktop 2 and no longer in Desktop 1.

10. **Inside the Photos app window, click or tap the X button in the top-right corner to close it.**

    Desktop 2 now has zero running apps.

11. **On the taskbar, click or tap the widgets icon (shown in the margin).**

    The Windows 11 widgets appear, as shown in Figure 1-5. They display useful information such as the weather forecast, the latest news, sports updates, stock market data, and traffic data.

12. **Click or tap somewhere on the desktop, outside the widgets.**

    You return to the Windows 11 desktop. Take a breather.

This was a quick tour of some of the highlights of the desktop. There's much, much more to discover — I only scratched a thin layer of the surface.

**Getting Around in Windows**

**FIGURE 1-5:**
The widgets
display useful
information.

# Using Windows 11 on Tablets and Touchscreens

Windows 10 had a special tablet mode optimized for touchscreens. While it wasn't perfect, it was easy to turn on and enabled you to use touch instead of the mouse and keyboard. Windows 11 has ditched tablet mode, but it does touch better than Windows 10 did. How is that possible?

Microsoft decided to stop offering two environments in parallel (one for the mouse and keyboard, and another for touch), and redesign the user interface so that it works equally well for both. As a result, when Windows 11 detects that you're using touch, it automatically increases the spacing between icons and other interface elements a bit, so that they're more touch-friendly. Most people can't tell the difference between Windows 11 on a desktop PC and on a laptop with touch. You must have a PC and a device with touch next to each other to notice the subtle differences.

To use Windows 11 on a touchscreen, you need to know a few basic gestures:

» **Tap** to select an item, such as a file or a shortcut. This gesture is the equivalent of a click.

» **Tap and hold down** to right-click an item.

>> **Double-tap** to open a file or an app. This gesture is the equivalent of a double-click.

>> **Tap and drag** to move an item across the screen.

Learning how to swipe with your fingers on the screen helps too:

>> **Swipe right to left** (in from the right side of your screen to the left) to open notifications and the calendar.

>> **Swipe left** (in from the left side) to view the widgets.

As you browse around Windows 11, notice how almost everything is a lot more touch-friendly than in Windows 10. I appreciate the new Settings app in Windows 11. It's simpler and better for both touch and mouse than Settings in Windows 10. Also, the highly improved File Explorer (see Figure 1-6) makes navigating files and folders much easier on a tablet.

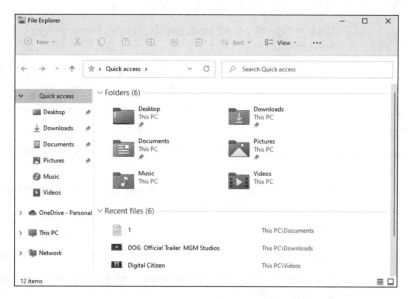

**FIGURE 1-6:** File Explorer in Windows 11 works much better on touchscreens.

# Shut Down, Sleep, Restart, Sign Out, Lock, Sleep

If you go away from your Windows 11 laptop, tablet, or computer for a long time, shut it down, meaning it is turned off completely and doesn't use energy. You restart it by simply pressing the Power button.

If you're taking a break for an hour or so, put your device to sleep. This mode turns off the display but keeps your computer awake and uses little energy. Also, your work is kept the way it was when you left, and your PC will start faster. To resume from sleep mode, move the mouse around, or press any key, or press the Power button.

Another option is to lock your Windows 11 computer so that others don't see your work and can't access your account.

If you have a family computer that you share with others, you should know how to sign out of your account, so that other people can sign in with theirs. Knowing how to restart your computer is helpful, too, especially after a Windows 11 update is installed or when you encounter problems.

Here's how to do all those tasks:

**1.** **Click or tap the Start icon.**

The Start menu is displayed. (Refer to Figure 1-1.)

**2.** **Click or tap the power icon, which is at the bottom-right corner of the Start menu.**

You see all the options from the Power menu, as shown in Figure 1-7. You can choose Sleep, Shut Down, or Restart.

WARNING

Clicking or tapping one of these options starts the specified action immediately.

**3.** **Click or tap your user account name in the bottom-left corner of the Start menu.**

A menu opens with options related to your user account, as shown in Figure 1-8, including Lock and Sign Out.

**4.** **Choose Sign Out.**

The Windows 11 lock screen is shown, where you see the time and date.

**5.** **Click or tap anywhere on the lock screen or press Enter. Enter your user password or PIN.**

You return to the Windows 11 desktop.

**FIGURE 1-7:**
Use the Power menu to sleep, shut down, or restart your device.

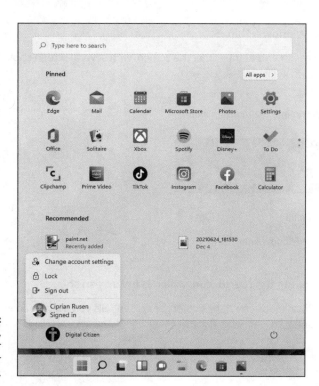

**FIGURE 1-8:**
From this menu, you can lock your computer or sign out.

Getting Around in
Windows

# Taking Screen Shots

One of these days, you'll be using an app on your Windows 11 PC and an error will occur. To find a solution, it's often helpful to take a screen shot of what you see on the screen and share it with others. In Windows 11, you can do so in many ways. You could press the Print Screen key on your keyboard, but that method stores your screen shot in the clipboard, and you must then paste the shot in an image-editing app such as Paint.

**REMEMBER**

A much better way to take a quick screen shot of the entire screen is to press Windows+Print Screen or Fn+Windows+Print Screen. Windows 11 saves the resulting image as a file in the Screen shots folder, which is inside your Pictures folder.

One cool aspect of Windows 11 is that Microsoft has decided to create a new and much improved Snipping Tool app. It's a mix of the old version in Windows 7 and the Snip & Sketch app in Windows 10, which many people ignored. With the snipping tool, you can capture a full-screen screen shot, a rectangular screen shot, a free-form screen shot (draw any shape you want on the screen), or the window of a specific app. The snipping tool calls those screen shots *snips.*

Here's how to use the snipping tool in Windows 11 to take a screen shot of the entire screen:

**1.** **Press Windows+Shift+S.**

You see a menu at the top of the screen, with several screen shot-taking icons, as shown in Figure 1-9.

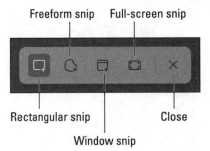

**FIGURE 1-9:**
The screen shot-taking options offered by the snipping tool.

**2.** **Click or tap the fourth icon, which is full-screen snip.**

A notification on the right side of the screen tells you that a snip was saved to the clipboard.

3. **Click or tap the Snipping Tool notification.**

   The Snipping Tool app opens (as shown in Figure 1-10), displaying the screen shot you just took. The app gives you access to plenty of image-editing tools, such as pens, highlighters, and erasers.

**FIGURE 1-10:**
Use the snipping tool to edit your screen shots.

4. **Click or tap the save icon (disk) at the top right of Snipping Tool.**

   The Save As dialog is shown, where you can choose the folder where the screen shot is saved. By default, screen shots are named using the date and time when they were taken. You can type a new name in the File Name field.

5. **Click or tap the Save button.**

   Your screen shot is saved in the Pictures folder.

6. **In the Snipping Tool window, click or tap X to close the app.**

# Keyboard Shortcuts

Windows 11 has hundreds of keyboard shortcuts. I don't use many of them because they're difficult to remember. However, some of them are easy to remember and will make your work with Windows 11 a lot easier.

Here are the keyboard shortcuts that everyone should know. They've been around for a long, long time:

>> **Ctrl+C** copies whatever you've selected and puts it on the clipboard. On a touchscreen, you can do the same thing in most applications by tapping and holding down, and then choosing Copy.

>> **Ctrl+X** cuts whatever you've selected and puts it on the clipboard. Again, you can tap and hold down, and Cut should appear on the menu.

>> **Ctrl+V** pastes whatever is in the clipboard to the current cursor location. Tap and hold down usually works.

>> **Ctrl+A** selects everything, although sometimes it's hard to tell what *everything* means — different applications handle Ctrl+A differently. Tap and hold down usually works here, too.

>> **Ctrl+Z** usually undoes whatever you just did. Few touch-enabled apps have a tap-and-hold-down alternative; you usually have to find Undo on a ribbon or menu.

>> When you're typing, **Ctrl+B, Ctrl+I,** and **Ctrl+U** usually change your text to bold, italic, or underline, respectively. Press the same key combination again, and the text returns to normal.

In addition to all the key combinations you may have encountered in previous Windows versions, there's a healthy crop of new combinations. These are the important ones:

>> The **Windows key** brings up the Start menu.

>> **Windows+A** opens Quick Actions.

>> **Windows+E** launches File Explorer.

>> **Windows+I** opens the Settings app.

>> **Windows+M** minimizes all open apps and windows on the current desktop.

>> **Windows+Tab** opens task view, with the virtual desktops listed at the bottom. In the middle is a preview of the open apps in each virtual desktop.

>> **Alt+Tab** cycles through all running apps on the current desktop, one by one. See Figure 1-11.

>> **Ctrl+Alt+Del** — the old Vulcan three-finger salute — brings up a screen that lets you choose to lock your PC, switch the user, sign out, or run Task Manager (see Book 8, Chapter 5).

**FIGURE 1-11:**
Alt+Tab cycles through all running apps.

You can also right-click (or press and hold down on) the Start icon or press Windows+X to display the Power User menu, which is shown in Figure 1-12.

**FIGURE 1-12:**
The Power User menu can get you into the innards of Windows 11.

And finally, the trick I know you'll use over and over: Whenever you want to type an emoji in a document, hold down the Windows key and press the period key. See Figure 1-13.

Who says Windows 11 isn't as cool as your smartphone?

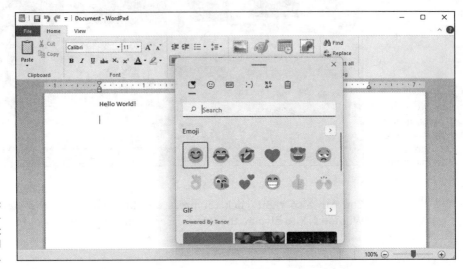

# Chapter **2**

# Logging into Windows 11

W indows 11 presents three hurdles for you to clear before you can get down to work (or play, or whatever):

» You have to get past the *lock screen*. This first-level hurdle is like the lock screen on a smartphone or an iPad and prevents your computer from being used by unauthorized people.

» If more than one person — more than one *account* — is set up on the computer, you must choose which person will log in. I go into detail about setting up user accounts in Book 2, Chapter 4.

» If a password is associated with the account, you must type it into the computer. Windows allows various kinds of passwords, which are particularly helpful if you're working on a touch-only tablet or a tiny screen. But the idea's the same: Unless you specifically set up an account without a password, you need to confirm your identity.

Only after clearing these three hurdles are you granted access to the desktop and, from there, to everything Windows 11 has to offer. In the sections that follow, you find out how to sign into Windows 11 and how to customize the lock screen and the login methods to suit yourself.

# Working with the Lock Screen

The very first time you start Windows 11, and anytime you shut it down, restart it, or let the machine go idle for long enough, you're greeted with the lock screen, as shown in Figure 2-1. The lock screen sports a beautiful image, with the date and time displayed in the middle, and small battery and network icons in the bottom-right corner. You don't see the battery icon in Figure 2-1 because I made the screen shot on a desktop PC, which doesn't have a battery. The icon is there on laptops and tablets — I promise.

**FIGURE 2-1:**
The Windows 11
lock screen.

You can get rid of the lock screen by doing any of the following:

>> Swipe up with your finger, if you have a touch-sensitive display.

>> Click with your mouse.

>> Press any key on the keyboard.

You aren't stuck with the lock screen Microsoft gives you. You can customize the picture and the little icons (or *badges*). The following sections explain how.

# Signing in

To sign in, make the lock screen go away by using any of the three methods just presented. You see the *sign-in screen,* with the name and picture for the last account that was used. Other accounts (if any) are listed on the bottom-left corner, as shown in Figure 2-2. The sign-in screen asks for your password, PIN, or biometric authentication (if it was set up). As soon as you comply, you are signed into Windows 11.

In the bottom-right corner of the sign-in screen are icons for your Ethernet or Wi-Fi connection, accessibility tools that can make your login easier, and the power button, so you can shut down, restart or put to sleep your machine.

TIP

If several languages or keyboard layouts are installed in Windows 11, you'll also see an icon for switching between keyboards in those languages.

# Changing the picture for the lock screen

Changing the picture for your lock screen is easy. (See the nearby sidebar "Individualized lock screens" for details about the difference between your lock screen and the system's lock screen.) Customizing the picture is a favorite trick at Windows 11 demos, so you know it must be easy, right? Here's how:

1. **Click or tap the start icon (shown in the margin), the Settings icon, and then Personalization.**

2. **On the right, choose Lock Screen.**

   The lock screen's preview window appears.

3. **In the Personalize Your Lock Screen drop-down list, try Windows Spotlight, if it's available (see Figure 2-3).**

   Windows Spotlight images come directly from Microsoft — more specifically, from Bing — and change frequently. Microsoft reserves the right to put advertising on Windows Spotlight screens to tell you about features in Windows 11 that you might not have used yet.

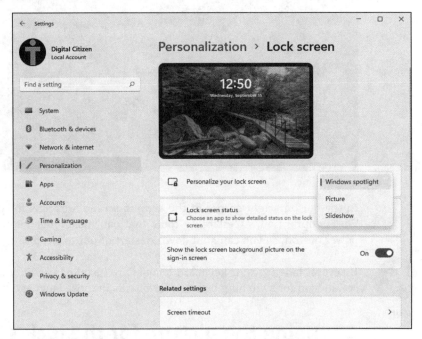

**FIGURE 2-3:**
Change your lock screen here.

4. **In the Personalize Your Lock Screen drop-down list, choose Picture and do the following:**

   a. *Choose a picture.* You have two options. If you like one of the pictures on offer, click or tap it. If you'd rather find your own picture, click or tap Browse Photos, and choose a picture of your own, as shown in Figure 2-4.

   b. *Decide whether you want your chosen picture to be overlaid with "fun facts, tips, tricks, and more on your lock screen."* Oh goodie.

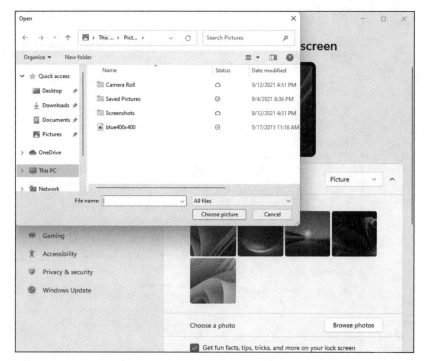

**5.** **If you would rather have a slideshow for the lock screen, choose Slideshow in the Personalize Your Lock Screen drop-down list and do the following:**

   *a. Click or tap Browse.*

   *b. Choose a folder containing pictures.* This option ties into the albums in the Windows 11 Photos app (see Book 4, Chapter 3). You can instead use your own folder of pictures.

   *c. Scroll down to the Advanced Slideshow Settings section and set the rules for your slideshow.* As shown in Figure 2-5, you can set whether the slideshow should be pulled from your camera roll, whether the chosen pictures have to be large enough to fit your screen, and more.

   You're finished. There's no Apply or OK button to click or tap.

Test to make sure that your personal lock screen has been updated. The easiest way is to go to the Start menu, click or tap your picture in the bottom-left corner, and choose Lock or Sign Out.

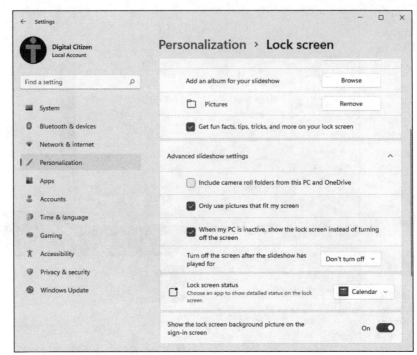

**FIGURE 2-5:**
Setting the
slideshow.

# INDIVIDUALIZED LOCK SCREENS

If you read the Microsoft help documentation, you may think that Windows 11 keeps one lock screen for all users, but it doesn't. Instead, it has a lock screen for each individual user and another lock screen for the system as a whole.

If you're using the system and you lock it — say, tap your picture on the Start menu and choose Lock — Windows 11 shows your personal lock screen, with the settings and data you've chosen. If you swipe up or click, you're asked to provide your PIN or password. There's no intervening step to ask which user should log in.

If, instead of locking the system when you leave it, you tap your picture and choose Sign Out, Windows 11 behaves differently. It shows the system's lock screen, with the system's settings. Your lock screen and data are nowhere to be seen. If you drag or swipe to go through the lock screen, you're asked to choose which user will log in.

Bottom line: If you change your lock screen using the techniques in this chapter, you change only *your* lock screen. Windows' idea of a lock screen stays the same.

# Adding and removing apps on the lock screen

*Badges* are the little icons that appear at the bottom of the lock screen. They exist to tell you something about your computer at a glance, without having to log in — how many email messages are unread, when your next meeting is, and so on. Some badges just appear on the lock screen, no matter what you do. For example, if you have an internet connection, a network badge appears on the lock screen. If you're using a tablet or laptop, the battery status appears; there's nothing you can do about it.

In addition to the badges that Windows 11 displays automatically, you can also choose to add a quick status badge that is important to you. The question I most often hear about badges is, "Why can't I just choose them all?" Good question. The apps that support these badges update their information periodically — every 15 minutes, in some cases. If you have a badge on your lock screen, the lock screen app that controls the badge must wake up every so often, so it can retrieve the data and put it on the lock screen. Putting everything on the lock screen drains your computer's battery and this may be an important reason why you can choose only one app to show a detailed status.

Here's how to pick and choose your quick status badge:

1.  **Click or tap the start icon and then the Settings icon.**

2.  **On the left, choose Personalization.**

3.  **On the right side of the Settings window, choose Lock Screen.**

4.  **Click or tap the Lock Screen Status drop-down list, and choose the app you want from the list (see Figure 2-6).**

    Choosing None means that no app can display a detailed status on the lock screen. Your changes are applied immediately.

**TIP**

Apps must be specially designed to display information on the lock screen. You're given a choice of all the apps that have registered with Windows 11 as being capable of displaying a quick status badge on the lock screen.

Go back out to the lock screen — click or tap the start icon, your picture, and then Lock — and see whether you like the changes. If you don't like what you see, start over.

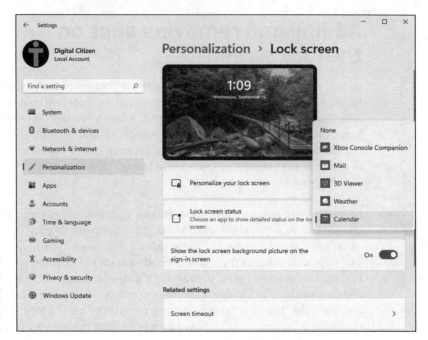

**FIGURE 2-6:**
Choose which
app displays
detailed
information on
the lock screen.

# Logging in without a Password

In this section, I step you through setting up a PIN and tell you how to show your face to Windows Hello.

## Creating a PIN

Everybody has PIN codes for ATM cards, telephones, just about everything.

**WARNING**

Reusing PIN codes on multiple devices (and credit cards) is dangerous — somebody looks over your shoulder, watches you type your Windows 11 PIN, and then lifts your wallet. Such nefarious folks can have a good time, unless the PINs are different. Word to the wise, eh?

PINs have lots of advantages over passwords and picture passwords. They're short and easy to remember. Fast. Technically, though, the best thing about a PIN is that it's stored on your computer — it's tied to that one computer, and you don't have to worry about it getting stored in some hacked database or stolen with your credit card numbers. In Windows 11, the PIN is part of Windows Hello, Microsoft's service for secure authentication options, which improves with each major update.

More on that in the next section of this chapter. For now, realize that creating a PIN is easy. Here's how to do it:

1. **Click or tap the start icon, the Settings icon, and then Accounts.**

2. **On the right, choose Sign-In Options.**

   The sign-in settings for your account appear, as shown in Figure 2-7.

3. **Click or tap PIN (Windows Hello) and then Set Up.**

   Windows 11 asks you to verify your user account password.

4. **Type your password and then click or tap OK.**

   Windows 11 gives you a chance to type your PIN, as shown in Figure 2-8, and then retype it to confirm it. *Note:* Most ATM PINs are four digits, but you can go longer, if you want — Windows 11 can handle any PIN you can throw at it.

5. **Type your PIN, confirm it, and click or tap OK.**

   You can include letters and symbols in your PIN, not just digits.

   The PIN is set and you can log in with it.

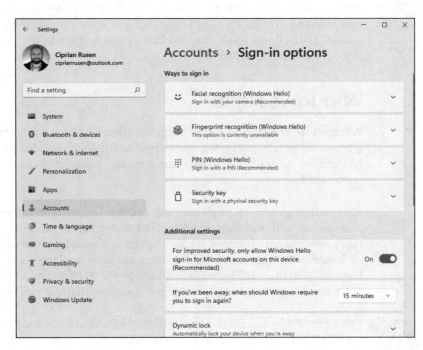

**FIGURE 2-7:**
The sign-in options available in Windows 11.

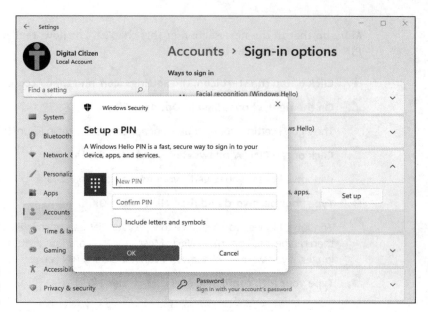

**FIGURE 2-8:**
Creating a
PIN is easy.

**TECHNICAL
STUFF**

Windows 10 offered picture passwords too. However, most people didn't use them, and they were also not that secure. Therefore, in Windows 11, Microsoft decided to hide them by default. They still exist, but you must jump through some hoops to enable them. I don't like them, and I think that logging in with a PIN or Windows Hello is a lot faster and safer.

## Windows Hello

Windows Hello offers biometric authentication — which is a lot faster than using a password or a PIN. The Windows Hello technology includes fingerprint or face recognition (or both) when you use a specially designed camera or fingerprint reader (or both).

Microsoft is gradually implementing fingerprint recognition with older finger scanners as well. But the hallmark Hello scan for your shining face is limited to fancy cameras with infrared sensors, which are included on an increasing number of Windows 11 laptops and tablets. There are some USB webcams too, such as the Logitech Brio Ultra HD webcam and Lenovo 500 FHD webcam, but they're harder to find and, with few exceptions, more expensive than normal webcams.

**WARNING**

I'm a fan of Windows Hello face recognition because it's fast, precise, and convenient. I can unlock my ASUS ZenBook Duo just by looking at it. However, there are some downsides too: Sometimes I sit in front of a PC and don't want to log in. If I put my face anywhere near the ZenBook when it's turned on, bang, I'm logged in. Also, if I want to log in to a different account, I have to manually log out first, which is annoying.

If your computer's webcam supports Hello face recognition, try it and see if you like it. Here's how:

1. **Click or tap the start icon, the Settings icon, and then Accounts.**

2. **On the right, choose Sign-In Options.**

   The sign in settings for your account appear (refer to Figure 2-7).

3. **Click or tap Facial Recognition (Windows Hello) and then Set Up.**

   The Welcome to Windows Hello window appears, as shown in Figure 2-9.

   If you see This Option Is Currently Unavailable, your Windows 11 computer doesn't support Windows Hello facial recognition.

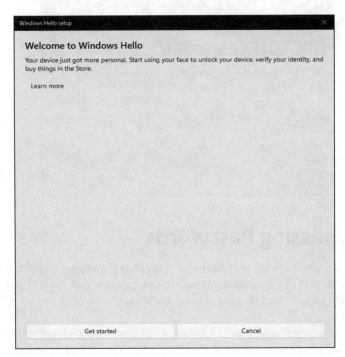

**FIGURE 2-9:**
Setting up facial recognition.

4. **Click or tap Get Started.**

   Windows 11 asks you to verify your user account password or PIN.

5. **Type your PIN or password, depending on what's asked of you.**

6. **When asked to look directly at your camera, as shown in Figure 2-10, do as instructed until you see a message that you're all set.**

7. **Click or tap Close.**

   Face recognition is set, and you can log in just by looking at your Windows 11 tablet or laptop.

**FIGURE 2-10:**
Look at your
camera as
instructed.

## Bypassing Passwords

So now you have three convenient ways to tell Windows 11 your password: You can type it, just like a normal password; you can pretend it's a smartphone and enter a PIN; or you can just look at your webcam.

But what if you don't want a password? What if your computer is secure enough — it's sitting in your house, it's in your safe deposit box — and you just don't want to be bothered with typing or tapping a password?

**TIP**

If you have a local account, you can just remove your password. Turn it into a blank. Follow the steps in Book 2, Chapter 4 to change your password but leave the New Password field blank.

Microsoft accounts can't have blank passwords, but local accounts can. If you have a blank password, when you click or tap your username on the login screen, Windows 11 ushers you to the desktop. If only one user is on the PC and that user has a blank password, just getting past the lock screen takes you to the desktop.

If you have a Microsoft account, you have to use your password (PIN, password, or Windows Hello) each time you reboot.

# Chapter **3**

# Handling Notifications and Quick Actions

I f you've ever used a moderately sentient smartphone or tablet, you already know about notifications and the notification center. Different devices do it differently, but the general idea is that the device monitors and gathers notifications — little warning messages or status reports — and then puts them in one place, where you can look at them and decide what to do from there.

In Windows 11, notifications are commonplace. The operating system sends you notifications, and so do many apps. Even websites can notify you when new articles are published. To make notifications manageable, Windows 11, like smartphones, gathers them into a dedicated center. Accessing and clearing notifications are easy. However, if you find notifications annoying or don't want to be bothered while you work, you can use the focus assist feature to make them go away automatically.

Windows 11 also has some useful icons for turning on and off different features, such as Bluetooth and Wi-Fi. These too work as they do on a smartphone and serve a similar purpose too. The only difference is that these icons are called quick actions in Windows 11 and accessing them involves a different approach. But I'm here to help you figure everything out, aren't I?

# What, Exactly, Is a Notification?

A *notification* is a message accompanied by a brief sound that you receive from Windows 11 or an app, informing you when something happens. The notification can be about anything: Windows telling you that you just plugged in a USB memory stick and asking you to choose what to do with it; a new email message in the Mail app; or Microsoft Store telling you that it has updated an app on your PC. Even websites can send you notifications when new content is posted if you allowed them to do so in your web browser.

Notifications are shown in the bottom-right corner of the screen (see Figure 3-1) and may contain the following elements:

>> A rectangular notice box, with the name and icon of the app or Windows feature sending the notification in the top-left corner.

>> The contents of the notification. If it's an email, you see who sent the email, the subject (if any), and a portion of the message.

>> Buttons for interacting with the notification. For example, an email has buttons so you can flag, archive, or dismiss the email. Some notifications, however, do not include buttons, such as a notification informing you that a Microsoft Store app was updated.

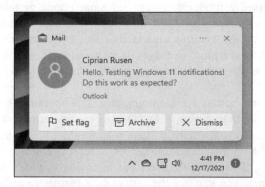

**FIGURE 3-1:**
A new email notification in Windows 11.

When you click or tap a notification, it takes you to the app or Windows feature that sent it to you. For example, if you click or tap an email notification, the Mail app opens the email you received so you can read and reply to it. Other notifications, like one you see when you plug in an external USB drive, might ask you to decide what to do next. Make your choice, and the notification is gone.

# Using the Notification Center

The place where notifications are stored is called the notification center. When it has notifications for you to see, a number is displayed in the bottom-right corner of the taskbar, next to the time and date. The number tells you how many unread notifications you have. If there are no new notifications for you to see, there is no number.

If you didn't click or tap a notification when it was displayed in the bottom-right corner, you can view it later, alongside all the other notifications you ignored, like this:

**1.** **In the bottom-right corner of the screen, click or tap the date and time.**

You see a calendar of the current month, with a list of notifications on top.

**2.** **Click or tap the downward-pointing arrow to the right of the current date.**

You now see only the notification center, as shown in Figure 3-2.

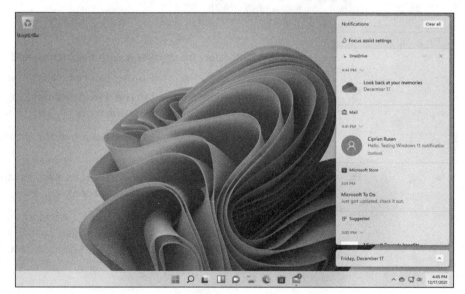

**FIGURE 3-2:**
The notification center in Windows 11.

**3.** **Hover the mouse cursor over a notification to see additional options for interacting with it.**

For example, in Figure 3-3, the three dots icon (Settings) and the X appear to the right of the notification.

**FIGURE 3-3:**
These options appear when you hover your cursor over a notification.

4. **To remove a notification, hover over it with the mouse, and click or tap the X to its right.**

5. **To expand a notification, click or tap the downward-pointing arrow below the name of the app displaying the notification.**

   Note the additional information (and buttons) displayed for the expanded notification, as shown in Figure 3-4.

6. **When you no longer want to see the notifications, click or tap the Clear All button in the top right of the notification center.**

   This action clears all notifications from Windows 11, and leaves room for new ones. Also, the notification center closes because it has nothing left to display. If you click the time and date instead of Clear All, the notifications are kept but the notification center closes.

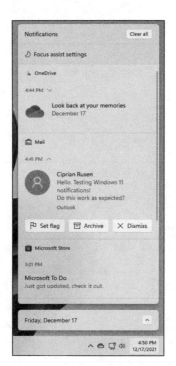

**FIGURE 3-4:**
An expanded
notification offers
more information
and interaction
options.

# Disabling Notifications

If a particular program is generating notifications that you don't want to see, you can stop it from doing so. And if you consider all notifications annoying, you can disable them all easily.

Here's how to disable notifications from a specific app or all notifications:

**1.** **Right-click (or press and hold down on) the time and date on the taskbar.**

The menu shown in Figure 3-5 appears.

**2.** **Choose Notifications Settings.**

The Notifications section of the Settings app appears, as shown in Figure 3-6.

**3.** **To silence just one app, scroll down, find the app, and move its switch to off. To turn off *all* notifications from all apps, including Windows 11, click or tap the Notifications switch on the top off.**

You're finished. You can close Settings or minimize it and do something else.

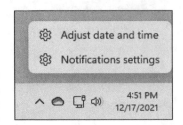

**FIGURE 3-5:**
Accessing the
Notifications
settings.

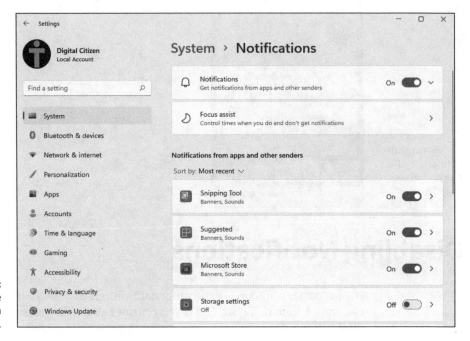

**FIGURE 3-6:**
Silence
notifications from
individual apps.

**TIP**

In Step 3, if you click or tap the name of an app instead of moving its switch, you get access to options for controlling how its notifications are displayed. For example, you can disable the sound played for each notification, change the number of notifications for that app visible in the notification center, set its priority, and more.

# Enabling Focus Assist

Focus assist is a Windows 11 feature that helps you remain focused by censoring the display of notifications based on rules you set. For example, you can enable focus assist automatically each time you duplicate your screen because you want to deliver a presentation, when you're playing a game, or when you're using an app in full-screen mode (such as PowerPoint). Last but not least, you can enable focus assist during a specific interval each day, such as when you are writing a book and don't want to be bothered by pesky notifications.

Here's how to configure focus assist in Windows 11:

**1.** **Right-click (or press and hold down on) the time and date on the taskbar and choose Notifications Settings.**

The Notifications section of the Settings app appears (refer to Figure 3-5).

**2.** **Click or tap Focus Assist.**

The Focus Assist settings appears, as shown in Figure 3-7.

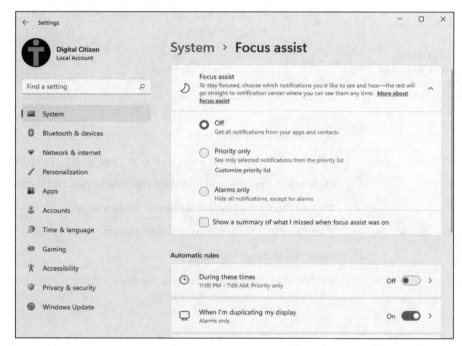

**FIGURE 3-7:**
Focus Assist
settings.

**3.** **In the Focus Assist section, choose Alarms Only.**

While focus assist is active, Windows 11 will hide all notifications and only display alarms (if any have been set).

**4.** **In the Automatic Rules section, click or tap During These Times. Then click or tap the switch to turn it on.**

Several settings are now displayed below the switch, as shown in Figure 3-8.

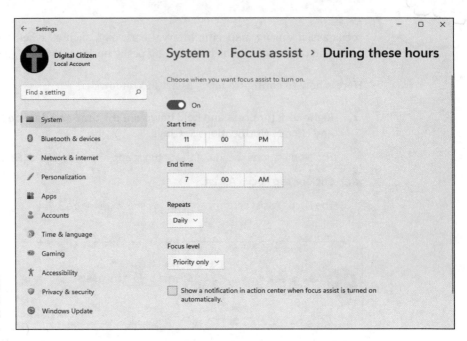

**FIGURE 3-8:**
Choose when you want Focus Assist to turn on.

5. **Set the start and end times.**

   It's a good idea to choose an interval when you tend to do most of your work.

6. **Click or tap Repeats and choose Daily, Weekends, or Weekdays.**

7. **Click or tap Focus Level and choose Alarms Only.**

   You will now see only alarms, not notifications.

8. **Close the Settings window.**

   Focus assist is now enabled during the days and times you chose, limiting your exposure to annoying notifications.

# Using Quick Actions

If you click or tap the volume, battery, or network icon in the bottom-right corner of the Windows 11 desktop, you'll see a readily accessible pane with quick actions, as shown in Figure 3-9. You can think of a quick action as a handy shortcut to a frequently adjusted setting, such as the screen's brightness, the sound volume, Bluetooth, or Wi-Fi. Quick actions mimic what you would find on a smartphone — airplane mode is an obvious example. In some cases, a quick action displays a Settings page or a pane with more options or toggles a specific setting.

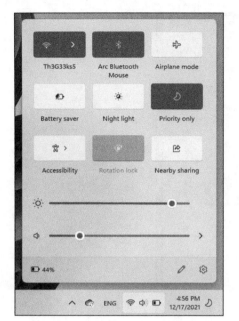

The quick actions available vary on whether you're using a desktop PC, laptop, tablet, or 2-in-1, the device's hardware configuration, and the apps installed. For example, if Spotify is installed, you may also see some controls for the music you play, allowing you to pause the current song or skip to the next one.

Unfortunately, you can't add your own quick actions, but you can control which quick actions are displayed. Here's how to exert as much influence as possible:

1. **Click or tap the network, volume, or battery icon.**

   Clicking any of them does the same thing, so it doesn't matter which one you choose. The quick actions appear on the right side of the screen.

2. **Click or tap the edit icon (pencil).**

   All quick actions become editable, as shown in Figure 3-10.

3. **To move an icon for a quick action, just click and drag it where you want (or tap and hold down on the icon while dragging).**

   You can't drag a quick action off the grid.

4. **To add quick action icons, click or tap the Add+ button, and make a selection from the list that appears.**

5. **To remove a quick action icon, click or tap its pin in the top right.**

6. **When you've set things the way you want them, click or tap Done.**

Table 3-1 explains what each configurable quick action icon does.

**FIGURE 3-10:**
Editing the list of quick actions.

**TABLE 3-1**     ## Quick Actions and What They Do

| Click or Tap This Icon | And This Happens |
|---|---|
| Accessibility | Turns on or off different accessibility tools such as Magnifier, Color Filters, Narrator, Mono Audio, and Sticky Keys. |
| Airplane mode | Turns all wireless communication on and off. See the Settings app's Network & Internet, Airplane Mode setting. |
| Battery saver | Cycles between two battery saver modes, dimming the display. It doesn't work if the laptop or tablet is plugged in. |
| Bluetooth | Turns Bluetooth on or off. |
| Brightness | Adjusts the screen brightness to the level you want. |
| Cast | Searches for wireless display and audio devices to project to — Miracast in particular. |
| Focus assist | Turns focus assist on or off. When turned on, all notifications are blocked. |
| Keyboard layout | Switches between multiple keyboard languages or layouts. |
| Project | Projects the image on your screen to an external display or a projector. |
| Rotation lock | Prevents the screen from rotating from portrait to landscape and vice versa. |
| Volume | Adjusts the screen's sound volume to the level you want. |

IN THIS CHAPTER

» Choosing an account type

» Weighing the pros and cons of Microsoft accounts

» Adding a user (local or Microsoft account)

» Adding a child account

» Modifying the settings of your accounts

» Switching between users

# Chapter **4**

# Managing User Accounts

M ost Windows PCs have just one user account. Although many PCs are each used by just one person, I think it's highly likely that people don't set up multiple user accounts on their PCs because they're intimidated. Not to worry. I take you through the ins and outs of this process.

Even if you're the only person who ever uses your PC, you may want to create a second account — another user, as it were — even if the second user is just you. Then again, you may not. And therein lies this chapter's story.

If you're running Windows 11 Enterprise or Windows 11 Pro and your PC is connected to a big corporate network (a *domain*), you have little or no control over who can log in to your computer and what logged-in users can do after they're on the machine. That's a Good Thing, at least in theory: Your company's network administrator gets to worry about all the security issues, relieving you of the hassles of figuring out whether the co-worker down the hall should be able to look at payroll records or the company Christmas card list. But it can also be a pain in the neck, especially if you have to install a program, like, right now, and you don't have a user account with sufficient capabilities. If your computer is attached to a domain, an administrator might install the program for you. This chapter applies only to PCs connected to small networks or to stand-alone PCs.

First, I present the types of Windows 11 accounts: standard accounts, administrator accounts, local account, and Microsoft accounts. You see know how they differ and how they mix with each other. I also show you how to add any account you want, including a special type called the child account, which is useful for families with children. Lastly, you see how to edit other user accounts from an administrator account and how to switch between accounts.

Here's hoping that this list of topics doesn't seem too long or intimidating.

# Understanding Why You Need Separate User Accounts

All sorts of problems crop up when several people share a PC. You may have set up your desktop just right, with all your shortcuts right where you can find them, and then your significant other comes along and changes the wallpaper, accidentally deletes some files you may need, and adds their own apps and shortcuts on the desktop. It's worse than sharing a TV remote.

Also, I'm sure you don't want others to open Microsoft Edge and take a peek into your Facebook account or see all the recent videos you've played on your computer. To get around this issue, it's a good idea to create a separate user account for each individual using your computer.

**WARNING**

If someone else can get their hands on your computer, it isn't your computer anymore. This can be a real problem if the cleaning staff uses your PC after hours or a snoop breaks into your study. Unless you use BitLocker (in Windows 11 Pro), anybody who can restart your PC can look at, modify, and delete your files or stick a virus on the PC. How? In many cases, a miscreant can bypass Windows 11 directly and start your PC with another operating system. With BitLocker out of the picture, compromising a PC doesn't take much work.

Windows 11 helps keep peace in the family — and in the office — by requiring people to log in. The process of *logging in* (also called *signing in*) lets the operating system keep track of each person's settings: You tell Windows 11 who you are, and it lets you play in your own sandbox.

# Choosing Account Types

When dealing with user accounts, you bump into one existential fact of Windows life repeatedly: The type of account you use puts limitations on what you can do.

Unless your PC is hooked up to a big corporate network, user accounts can generally be divided into two groups: the haves and the have-nots. (Users attached to corporate domains are assigned accounts that can exist anywhere on the have-to-have-not spectrum.) The have accounts are administrator accounts. The have-nots are standard accounts.

## What's a standard account?

If you're running with a *standard account*, you can do only standard tasks:

>> Run programs already installed on your computer, including programs on USB drives.

>> Use hardware already installed on your computer.

>> Create, view, save, modify, and use documents, pictures, and sounds in the Documents, Pictures, or Music folders as well as in the PC's Public folders.

>> Change your password or switch back and forth between requiring and not requiring a password for your account. You can also add a PIN. If your computer has the necessary hardware, you can use Windows Hello to set up a face scan, fingerprint, or retina scan — just like in the movies.

>> Switch between a local account and a Microsoft account. I talk about both in the next section of this chapter.

>> Change the picture that appears next to your name on the left side of the Start menu, change the desktop wallpaper, add items to the taskbar and Start menu, and make other small changes that don't affect other user accounts.

In most cases, standard users can change systemwide settings, install programs, and the like, but only if they can provide the username and password of an administrator account.

If you're running with a standard account, you can't even change the time on the clock. The account is quite limited.

On the upside, if you start Windows 11 with a standard account and accidentally run a virus, a worm, or some other piece of bad computer code, the damage is usually limited: The malware can delete or scramble files in your Documents folder and probably in the Public folders, but that's about the extent of the damage. Usually. Unless it's exceedingly clever, the virus can't install itself into the computer, so it can't run repeatedly, and it may not be able to replicate.

There's also a special limited version of the standard account called a child account. Child accounts can be controlled and monitored by those with standard and administrator accounts.

## What's an administrator account?

People using *administrator accounts* can change almost anything, anywhere, at any time. However, certain Windows folders remain off limits, even to administrator accounts, and you must jump through some difficult hoops to work around the restrictions. People using administrator accounts can even change other local accounts' passwords — a good thing to remember if you ever forget your password.

Someone with an administrator account can get into all the files owned by other users: If you thought that attaching a password to your account and putting a top-secret spreadsheet in your Documents folder would keep it away from prying eyes, you're in for a surprise. Anybody who can get into your machine with an administrator account can look at it. Standard users, on the other hand, are effectively limited to looking only at their own files.

## Choosing between standard and administrator accounts

REMEMBER

The first account on a new PC is always an administrator account. If you bought your PC with Windows 11 preinstalled, the account that you have — the one you probably set up shortly after you took the computer out of the box — is an administrator account. Or if you installed Windows 11 on a PC, the account you set up during installation is an administrator account.

When you create accounts, on the other hand, they always start out as standard accounts. That's as it should be.

Administrator accounts and standard accounts aren't set in concrete. In fact, Windows 11 helps you shift between the two as circumstances dictate:

>> If you're using a standard account and try to do something that requires an administrator account, Windows 11 prompts you to provide the administrator account's name and password or PIN, as shown in Figure 4-1.

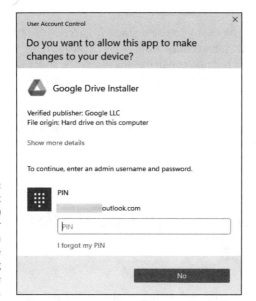

**FIGURE 4-1:**
User Account
Control (UAC)
asks for
permission
before
performing
administrative
actions.

**WARNING**

If the person using the standard account selects an administrator account without a password, simply clicking or tapping the Yes button allows the program to run. That's one more reason why you need passwords on all your administrator accounts, isn't it?

» Even if you're using an administrator account, Windows 11 normally runs as though you had a standard account, in some cases adding an extra hurdle (usually in the form of an additional confirmation dialog) when you try to run a program that can make substantial changes to your PC. You must clear the same kind of hurdle if you try to access folders that aren't explicitly shared (see Figure 4-2). That extra hurdle helps prevent destructive programs from sneaking into your computer and running with your administrator account, doing their damage without your knowledge or permission.

**FIGURE 4-2:**
Windows 11 lays
down a challenge
before you dive
into another
user's folder.

Managing User
Accounts

Some experts recommend that you use a standard account for daily activities and switch to an administrator account only when you need to install software or hardware or access files outside the usual shared areas. Most experts ignore their own advice: It's the old do-as-I-say-not-as-I-do syndrome.

TIP

Because you can add new users only if you're using an administrator account, I recommend that you save that one administrator account for a rainy day, and set up standard accounts for yourself and anyone else who uses the PC. Run with a standard account, and I bet you'll seldom notice the difference.

# Knowing What's Good and Bad about Microsoft Accounts

In addition to administrator and standard accounts (and child accounts, which are a subset of standard accounts), Microsoft has another pair of account types: Microsoft accounts, and local (also known as offline) accounts. You can have an administrator account that's a Microsoft account or a standard account that's a Microsoft account or an administrator account that's a local account, and so on.

The basic differentiation goes like this:

>> **Microsoft accounts** are registered with an email address. Most people use their @hotmail.com or @live.com or @outlook.com email addresses. Still, you can register any email address as a Microsoft account (details in the next chapter). Also, Microsoft accounts must have a password.

When you log in to Windows 11 with a Microsoft account, Windows goes out to Microsoft's servers in the cloud and verifies your password and then pulls down some of your Windows 11 settings and transfers them to the PC you just logged in to. You can control which settings get synced in the Settings app (click or tap the start icon, Settings, Accounts, and then Windows Backup), as shown in Figure 4-3.

If you change, say, your display language, the next time you log in to Windows 11 — from any machine, anywhere in the world — you see Windows in the new language. More than that, if the Microsoft account is set up to do so, you can get immediate access to all your email, OneDrive storage, and other Windows 11 features without logging in again.

>> **Local accounts** are regular, old-fashioned accounts that exist only on your PC. They don't save or retrieve your settings from Microsoft's computers. Such accounts may or may not have a password.

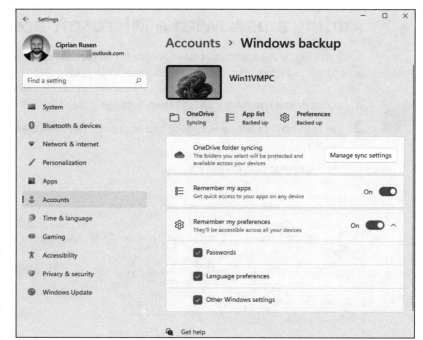

**FIGURE 4-3:**
Control which
Windows 11
settings are
synced across
your Microsoft
account.

**REMEMBER**

On a single PC, administrator accounts can add new users, delete existing users, or change the password of any local account on the computer. They can't change the password of any Microsoft accounts.

Microsoft accounts are undeniably more convenient than local (offline) accounts. Sign in to Windows 11 with your Microsoft account, and many of your apps will just realize who you are, pull in your email, sync your storage, and much more. On the other hand, using a Microsoft account means that Microsoft has a log of many of your interactions with your PC — when you signed in, how you used the Microsoft apps (including Edge), Bing search results, and so on. See Book 2, Chapter 5 for more about Microsoft accounts.

# Adding Accounts in Windows 11

In Windows 11, you can add three types of accounts: Microsoft accounts, local accounts, and child accounts. Let's discuss them one by one.

# Adding a user with a Microsoft account

After you log in to an administrator account, you can add more users easily. Here's how to add another user who has a Microsoft account:

1. **Click or tap the start icon and then Settings.**

2. **In the Settings window, click or tap Accounts, followed by Family & Other Users.**

   The screen shown in Figure 4-4 appears.

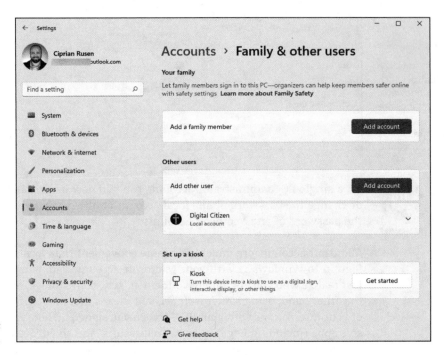

FIGURE 4-4:
Add other users.

3. **On the right, in the Other Users section, click or tap Add Account.**

   You see the challenging How Will This Person Sign In? dialog box, as shown in Figure 4-5.

4. **If the new user already has a Microsoft account (or a @hotmail.com or @ live.com or @outlook.com email address — which are automatically Microsoft accounts), type the email address in the box and then click or tap Next.**

5. **Click or tap Finish.**

   Windows 11 sets up your account and you see it in the list of users. You'll be asked to enter this account's password when you first sign in.

**FIGURE 4-5:**
Microsoft wants
you to set up
a Microsoft
account.

**TECHNICAL
STUFF**

If you have a Microsoft account, don't imagine that you can log in on any Windows 11 computer from anywhere. Before you can do that, a user who is an administrator needs to add your Microsoft account first, using the steps I just listed.

## Adding a local (offline) account

Don't get me wrong. There are good reasons for using a Microsoft account — such an account makes it much easier and faster to retrieve your mail and calendar entries, for example, or use the Microsoft Store or Microsoft Edge, bypassing individual account logins. It'll automatically connect you to your OneDrive too. Only you can decide if the added convenience is worth the decreased privacy. Book 2, Chapter 5 covers the details.

However, adding a local account is a good idea when you don't want Microsoft to know as much about what you do on your Windows 11 PC, or when you want to log in without a password. Here's how to add a local account in Windows 11:

1. **Click or tap the start icon and then Settings.**

2. **In the Settings window, click or tap Accounts, followed by Family & Other Users.**

   The Family & Other Users screen appears (refer to Figure 4-4).

3. **On the right, in the Other Users section, click or tap Add Account.**

4. **In the How Will This Person Sign In? dialog box, click or tap the link at the bottom that says I Don't Have This Person's Sign-in Information.**

   Windows 11 gives you yet another opportunity to set up a Microsoft account, as shown in Figure 4-6.

**FIGURE 4-6:**
Here's the second time Microsoft asks whether you want to set up a Microsoft account.

5. **Click or tap Add a User without a Microsoft Account.**

   Windows 11 (finally!) asks you to enter the local account name and password. See Figure 4-7.

6. **In the Who's Going to Use This PC? field, type a name for the new account.**

   You can give a new account just about any name you like: first name, last name, nickname, titles, abbreviations . . . no sweat, as long as you don't use the characters / \ [ ] " ; : | < > + = , ? or *.

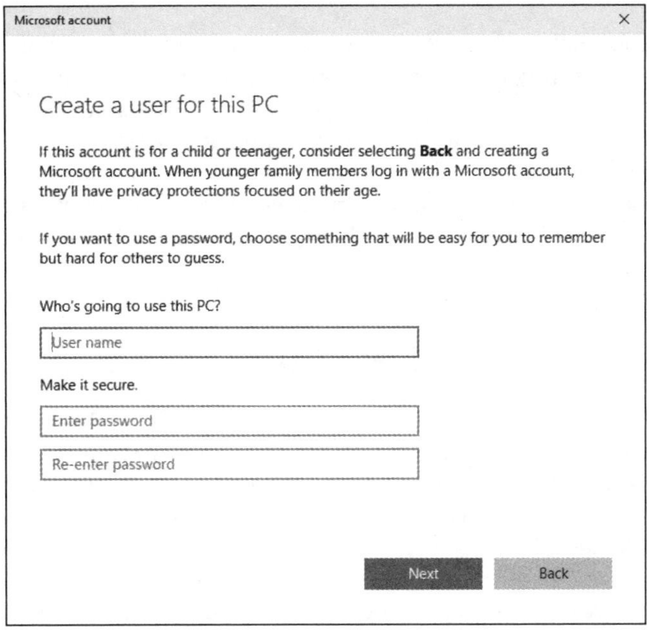

## Create a user for this PC

If this account is for a child or teenager, consider selecting **Back** and creating a Microsoft account. When younger family members log in with a Microsoft account, they'll have privacy protections focused on their age.

If you want to use a password, choose something that will be easy for you to remember but hard for others to guess.

Who's going to use this PC?

> User name

Make it secure.

> Enter password

> Re-enter password

> Next      Back

**FIGURE 4-7:**
Now you get to the "adding a new account" part.

**7.** **(Optional) Type a password twice and answer three security questions.**

If you leave the password fields blank, the user can log in directly by simply clicking or tapping the account name on the sign-in screen.

**8.** **Click or tap Next.**

You have a new standard local account, and its name now appears in the list of Other Users.

If you want to turn the new account into an administrator account, follow the steps in the section, "Changing Other Users' Settings," later in this chapter. To add an account picture for the sign-in screen and the Start menu, flip to Book 3, Chapter 2.

**TIP**

If you created a local account without a password, you can add a password later from Settings ⇨ Accounts ⇨ Sign-In Options ⇨ Password.

Managing User
Accounts

**TECHNICAL STUFF**

You aren't allowed to create a new account that's named Administrator. There's a good reason why Windows 11 prevents you from making a new account with that name: You already have one. Even though Windows 11 goes to great lengths to hide the account named Administrator, it's there, and you may encounter it by accident. For now, don't worry about the ambiguous name and the ghostly apparition. Just refrain from trying to create a new account named Administrator. You can create any account with any other name, with or without administrator permissions.

## Adding a Child Account

A child account is a standard Microsoft account that can be managed by parents. To manage a child account, you must have a Microsoft account on your Windows 11 PC that is set as administrator. From it, you can then add your child's Microsoft account, and set it as a member of your family, using Microsoft's Family Safety. For more details, visit: `www.microsoft.com/en-us/microsoft-365/family-safety`.

If you have created a Microsoft account for your child, and are logged in with your own Microsoft account, here's how to add your child's account to Windows 11:

1. **Click or tap the start icon and then Settings.**

2. **In the Settings window, click or tap Accounts, followed by Family & Other Users.**

   The Family & Other Users screen appears (refer to Figure 4-4).

3. **On the right, click or tap the Add Account button next to Add a Family Member.**

4. **Type the email address of your child's Microsoft account, and then click or tap Next.**

   You're asked about the role of this account, as shown in Figure 4-8.

5. **Choose Member and click or tap Invite.**

   Your child receives an email with an invitation to join your family. If your child accepts, you can set up Family Safety rules.

With Microsoft Family Safety, you can set screen time, app, and game limits; get access to reports about your child's activities; and have Microsoft Edge and Bing automatically filter inappropriate content online.

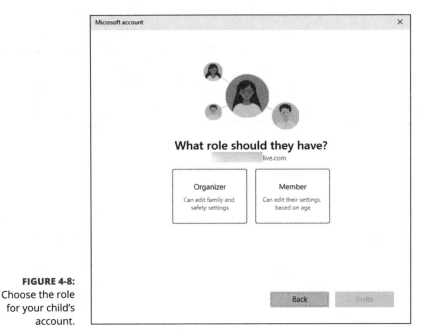

**FIGURE 4-8:**
Choose the role
for your child's
account.

# Changing Other Users' Settings

If you have an administrator account, you can reach in and change almost every detail of every single account on the computer. In this section, I cover the most important things you can do.

## Setting a standard account as administrator

To change another account from a standard account to an administrator account, do the following:

**1.** **Click or tap the start icon and then Settings.**

**2.** **In the Settings window, click or tap Accounts. On the right, choose Family & Other Users.**

A list of all the accounts on the computer appears.

**3.** **Click or tap on the account you want to change.**

For example, in Figure 4-9, I chose to change my local account called Digital Citizen.

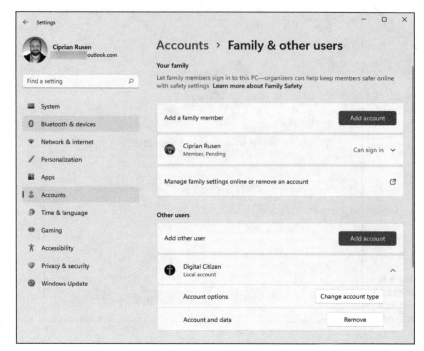

**FIGURE 4-9:**
Choose the
account you
want to change
from standard to
administrator, or
vice versa.

4. **Click or tap the Change Account Type button below the selected account.**

   Windows 11 responds with the option to change from a standard user account
   to an administrator account and back.

5. **Select the new account type and click or tap OK.**

   The account's type changes immediately.

## Modifying the settings of other accounts

For other kinds of account changes, you need to venture into the old-fashioned
Control Panel. Here's how to get to the options in the Control Panel:

1. **Click or tap the search icon on the taskbar and type** Control Panel.

2. **In the list of search results, choose Control Panel.**

   The Control Panel appears.

**3.** **Choose User Accounts, and then choose User Accounts again. Click or tap Manage Another Account.**

A list of all accounts on the computer appears.

**4.** **Click or tap the account you want to change.**

Windows 11 presents you with several options, as shown in Figure 4-10.

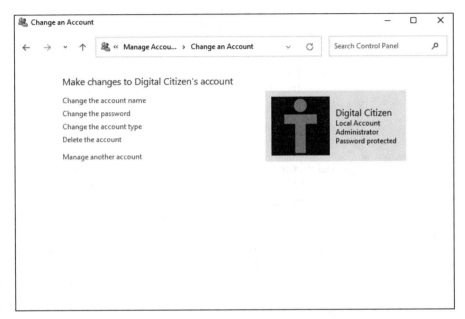

**FIGURE 4-10:** Maintain another user's account.

Here's what the available options entail:

>> **Change the Account Name:** This option appears only for local accounts. (It'd be problematic if Windows 11 let you change someone else's Microsoft account.) Selecting this option modifies the name displayed on the sign-in screen and the Start menu while leaving all other settings intact. Use this option if you want to change only the name on the account — for example, if Little Bill wants to be called Sir William.

>> **Create/Change a Password:** Again, this option appears only for local accounts. (*Create* appears if the account doesn't have a password; *Change* appears if the account already has a password.) If you create a password for the chosen user, Windows 11 requires a password to log in with that user account. You can't get past the sign-in screen (using that account) without it. This setting is weird because you can change it for other people. You can force Bill to use a password when none was required before, you can change Bill's password, or you can even make it blank.

**REMEMBER**

**WARNING**

Passwords are cAse SenSitive — you must enter the password, with upper-case and lowercase letters, precisely the way it was originally typed. If you can't get the computer to recognize your password, make sure that the Caps Lock setting is off. That's the number-one source of login frustration.

Much has been written about the importance of choosing a secure password, mixing uppercase and lowercase letters with punctuation marks, ensuring that you have a long password, and so on. I have only two admonitions: First, don't write your password on a yellow sticky note attached to your monitor. Second, don't use the easily guessed passwords that the Conficker worm employed to crack millions of systems, as listed in Table 4-1. Good advice from a friend: Create a simple sentence you can remember and swap out some letters for numbers (G00dGr1efTerry), or think of a sentence and use only the first letters! (toasaoutfl!) Of course, using a PIN, a Windows Hello mugshot, a fingerprint, or an iris scan makes even more sense.

>> **Change the Account Type:** You can use this option to change accounts from administrator to standard and back again.

>> **Delete the Account:** Get rid of the account, if you're that bold (or mad, in all senses of the term). If you're deleting a Windows 11 account, the account itself still lives — it just won't be permitted to log in to this computer. Windows offers to keep copies of the deleted account's Documents folder and desktop, but warns you quite sternly and correctly that if you snuff the account, you rip out all the email messages, user files, and other settings that belong to the user — definitely not a good way to make friends. Oh, and you can't delete your own account, of course, so this option won't appear if your PC has only one account.

>> **Manage Another Account:** Displays the list of accounts so you can choose another user and modify the user's account using the options just described.

**TABLE 4-1**    ## Most Frequently Used Passwords*

| Most Frequently Used Passwords | | | | | |
| --- | --- | --- | --- | --- | --- |
| 000 | 0000 | 00000 | 0000000 | 00000000 | 0987654321 |
| 111 | 1111 | 11111 | 111111 | 1111111 | 11111111 |
| 123 | 123123 | 12321 | 123321 | 1234 | 12345 |
| 123456 | 1234567 | 12345678 | 123456789 | 1234567890 | 1234abcd |
| 1234qwer | 123abc | 123asd | 123qwe | 1q2w3e | 222 |
| 2222 | 22222 | 222222 | 2222222 | 22222222 | 321 |

## Most Frequently Used Passwords

| | | | | | |
|---|---|---|---|---|---|
| 333 | 3333 | 33333 | 333333 | 3333333 | 33333333 |
| 4321 | 444 | 4444 | 44444 | 444444 | 4444444 |
| 44444444 | 54321 | 555 | 5555 | 55555 | 555555 |
| 5555555 | 55555555 | 654321 | 666 | 6666 | 66666 |
| 666666 | 6666666 | 66666666 | 7654321 | 777 | 7777 |
| 77777 | 777777 | 7777777 | 77777777 | 87654321 | 888 |
| 8888 | 88888 | 888888 | 8888888 | 88888888 | 987654321 |
| 999 | 9999 | 99999 | 999999 | 9999999 | 99999999 |
| a1b2c3 | aaa | aaaa | aaaaa | abc123 | academia |
| access | account | Admin | admin | admin1 | admin12 |
| admin123 | adminadmin | administrator | anything | asddsa | asdfgh |
| asdsa | asdzxc | backup | boss123 | business | campus |
| changeme | cluster | codename | codeword | coffee | computer |
| controller | cookie | customer | database | default | desktop |
| domain | example | exchange | explorer | file | files |
| foo | foobar | foofoo | forever | freedom | f**k |
| games | home | home123 | ihavenopass | Internet | internet |
| intranet | job | killer | letitbe | letmein | login |
| Login | lotus | love123 | manager | market | money |
| monitor | mypass | mypassword | mypc123 | nimda | nobody |
| nopass | nopassword | nothing | office | oracle | owner |
| pass | pass1 | pass12 | pass123 | passwd | password |
| Password | password1 | password12 | password123 | private | public |
| pw123 | q1w2e3 | qazwsx | qazwsxedc | qqq | qqqq |
| qqqqq | qwe123 | qweasd | qweasdzxc | qweewq | qwerty |
| qwewq | root | root123 | rootroot | sample | secret |
| secure | security | server | shadow | share | sql |
| student | super | superuser | supervisor | system | temp |

*(continued)*

**TABLE 4-1** *(continued)*

| Most Frequently Used Passwords | | | | | |
|---|---|---|---|---|---|
| temp123 | temporary | temptemp | test | test123 | testtest |
| unknown | web | windows | work | work123 | xxx |
| xxxx | xxxxx | zxccxz | zxcvb | zxcvbn | zxcxz |
| zzz | zzzz | Zzzzz | | | |

*From the Conficker worm, bowdlerized with an asterisk (*) as a fig leaf

# Switching Users

Windows 11 allows you to have more than one person logged in to a PC simultaneously. That's convenient if, say, you're working on the family PC and checking Billy's homework when you hear the cat making noise in the kitchen and your spouse wants to put digital pictures from the family vacation on OneDrive while you run off to check the microwave.

The capability to have more than one user logged in to a PC simultaneously is called *fast user switching*, and it has advantages and disadvantages:

>> **On the plus side:** Fast user switching lets you keep all your programs going while somebody else pops on to the machine for a quick jaunt on the keyboard. When that person is done and logs off, you can pick up precisely where you left off before you got bumped.

>> **On the minus side:** All idle programs left sitting around by the inactive (bumped) user can bog things down for the active user, although the effect isn't drastic. You can avoid the overhead by logging off before the new user logs in.

To switch users:

1. **Click or tap the start icon.**

2. **Click or tap your username or picture, in the bottom-left corner of the Start menu.**

   The menu shown in Figure 4-11 appears.

**FIGURE 4-11:**
The options
you have for
switching users.

## 3. Do one of the following:

- *Choose the name of the user you want to switch to (Digital Citizen in the figure). Authenticate using a PIN, a password, or Windows Hello.*

- *Choose Sign Out. On the sign-in screen, choose any user in the list and log in.*

TIP

If you're at work, it's a good idea to lock your computer each time you're not at your desk. To do that, at Step 3, choose Lock instead of Sign Out, or press Windows+L on your keyboard.

Managing User
Accounts

IN THIS CHAPTER

» Figuring out Microsoft accounts

» Deciding whether you even want a Microsoft account

» Getting a Microsoft account

» Cutting back on Windows 11 syncing through a Microsoft account

Chapter **5**

# Understanding Microsoft Accounts

Microsoft has been trying to get people to sign up for company-branded accounts for a long time.

In 1997, Microsoft bought Hotmail and took over the issuance of @hotmail.com email addresses. Even though Hotmail's gone through a bunch of name changes — MSN Hotmail, Windows Live Hotmail, and now Outlook.com, among others — the original @hotmail.com email addresses still work, and have worked, through thick and thin, except now it's called a *Microsoft account.* If you picked up an @msn.com ID, @live.com ID, Xbox ID, Skype ID, or @outlook.com ID along the way, it's now a Microsoft account as well.

In this chapter, I show you what's involved with a Microsoft account, and why it can be useful. Then, I explore the dark underbelly of Microsoft accounts and give you a trick for acquiring a Microsoft account that won't compromise much of anything. Finally, I show you how to limit the way Windows 11 syncs its settings through your Microsoft account.

# Realizing Which Accounts Are Microsoft Accounts

Microsoft has used many names and IDs for its accounts. However, in recent years, it has settled with the name Microsoft account. But what is that, you ask?

An email address that ends with @hotmail.com, @msn.com, @live.com, or @outlook.com is a Microsoft account. The same is true for Hotmail and Live and Outlook.com accounts in any country, such as @hotmail.co.uk. You don't have to use your Microsoft account. Ever. But you probably have one.

**REMEMBER**

Many people don't know that *any* email address can be a Microsoft account. It doesn't matter if that email address is from Gmail, Yahoo!, and so on. You need only register that email address with Microsoft; I show you how in the "Setting Up a Microsoft Account" section later in the chapter.

In the context of Windows 11, the Microsoft account takes on a new dimension. When you set up an account to log in to Windows, it can be either a Microsoft account or a *local account* (also called an *offline account*). The key differences follow:

>> **Microsoft accounts** are always email addresses and must be registered with Microsoft. As I explain in Book 2, Chapter 4, when you log in to Windows 11 with a Microsoft account, the operating system automatically syncs some settings — such as your passwords and language preferences — so if you change something on one machine and log in with the same Microsoft account on another, the changes go with you.

In addition, a Microsoft account gives you something of a one-stop login to internet-based Microsoft services. For example, if you have a OneDrive account, logging in to Windows 11 with a Microsoft account automatically hitches you up to your OneDrive files. Also, you can sign in with the same Microsoft account on your Windows 11 PC, Windows 10 computer, and your Xbox, or buy Xbox games from Windows 11 and have them available on your console right away.

>> **Local (offline) accounts** can be just about any name or combination of characters. If you sign in with a local account, Microsoft can't sync anything on different machines. Sign in with a local account, and you must sign into your OneDrive account separately. Windows 11 remembers your settings — your backgrounds, passwords, favorites, and the like — but they won't be moved to other PCs when you log in.

So, for example, phineasfarquahrt@hotmail.com is a Microsoft account. Because it's an @hotmail.com Hotmail email address, it's already registered with Microsoft. I can create a user on a Windows 11 machine with the name phineas farquahrt@hotmail.com, and Windows will recognize that as a Microsoft account.

On the other hand, I can set up an account on a Windows 11 PC that's called, oh, *Ciprian Rusen.* Because Microsoft accounts must be email addresses (you see why in the section "Setting Up a Microsoft Account"), the Ciprian Rusen account is an local (offline) account.

When you set up a brand-new Windows 11 PC, you must enter an account. If you're using Windows 11 Home, it must be a Microsoft account because Microsoft doesn't accept other types of accounts for this edition. If you're using Windows 11 Pro, you can also opt for local (offline) account. When you add a new account in Windows 11 Pro, Microsoft nudges you to use a Microsoft account, and makes it surprisingly difficult to create a local account. Still, it will begrudgingly let you (see Book 2, Chapter 4).

# Deciding Whether You Want a Microsoft Account

If Microsoft tracks a Microsoft account, you may ask, why in the world would I want to sign in to Windows 11 with a Microsoft account? Good question!

Signing in to Windows 11 with a Microsoft account brings a host of benefits. In particular:

>> **Some of your Windows 11 settings will travel with you.** Your user picture, desktop, Microsoft Edge favorites, and other similar settings will find you no matter which PC you log into. I find this helpful in some ways, and annoying in others. For example, suppose you have a Windows 11 desktop PC with a 4K monitor and a little Windows 11 tablet. If you put many shortcuts on the desktop, they look horrible on the tablet.

Your Windows 11 apps — the ones that came with Windows 11 or that you downloaded from the Microsoft Store — carry your settings and user content from one device to the next. For example, your open tabs in Microsoft Edge can be accessed from other PCs when you use the same Microsoft account. The settings for the Weather app travel from one device to the next. Even Windows 11 apps *that Microsoft doesn't make* may have their settings moved from machine to machine.

>> **Sign-in credentials for apps and websites travel with you.** If you rely on Microsoft Edge to keep sites' login credentials, those will find you if you switch machines.

>> **You will be automatically signed in to Windows 11 apps and services that use the Microsoft account.** Mail and Calendar, the Office apps from Microsoft 365, OneDrive, Teams, Skype, and the Microsoft website are all in this category.

In some sense, Microsoft dangles these carrots to convince you to sign up for, and use, a Microsoft account. But in another sense, the simple fact is that none of these features would be possible if it weren't for some sort of ID maintained by Microsoft.

**WARNING**

That's the carrot. Here's the stick. If you sign in with a Microsoft account, the company has a record of every time you've signed in to every PC you use with that account. More than that, when you start Microsoft Edge, you're logged in with your Microsoft account — which means that Microsoft keeps records about your browsing (except, presumably, InPrivate browsing). Bing gets to jot down your Microsoft account every time you search through it. Microsoft gets data on any app you access in the Microsoft Store. Even the weather you request ends up in Microsoft's giant database. And if you use Cortana, everything you ask it ends up in Microsoft's big database chock full of your history.

## WHAT IF MY HOTMAIL OR OUTLOOK.COM ACCOUNT IS HIJACKED?

So, you set up a Hotmail account or Outlook.com for logging in to your Windows PC, and all of a sudden, the account gets hijacked. Someone else gets into your account online and changes the password. The next time you try to log in to your Windows 11 PC, what happens?

Windows 11 doesn't let you log in, and gives you a link to reset your password and another for a Forgot Password? wizard. If you enabled two-factor authentication — where Microsoft sends you a text message on your smartphone or recovery email address (different from your Microsoft account email), you can proceed and change your password. But many people don't use two-factor authentication.

To get your account back, you need to contact the people at Microsoft and convince them that you're the rightful owner. Go to https://account.live.com/resetpassword. aspx, and complete as much information as possible. Depending on how you have set up your Microsoft account, and how correctly you answer all the questions, you may be able to recover your account relatively easily.

Perhaps it's true that you have no privacy and should get over it. Most people don't care about this subject. But if you do care, you should read the next chapter, where I talk about Windows 11's privacy settings.

# Setting Up a Microsoft Account

Just to make life a little more complicated, shortly before Microsoft released Windows 8, it decided to kill off the name Hotmail and replace it with Outlook.com. For the purposes of this chapter, Hotmail, Outlook.com, Live.com, Xbox LIVE, OneDrive, Skype, and MSN accounts are interchangeable: They're email addresses that have already been automatically signed up as Microsoft accounts.

If you don't have a Microsoft account, the way I see it, you have three choices for setting one up:

>> **You can use an existing email address.** But if you do that, Microsoft will be able to put that email address in its database. It can cross-reference the address to many things you do with Windows 11.

>> **You can use (or set up) a Hotmail, Xbox, OneDrive, Skype, or Outlook. com account.** If you already have one of these accounts, Microsoft tracks it already — Microsoft knows when you receive and send email, for example. But that's true of any online email program, including Gmail and Yahoo! Mail. Using an Outlook.com account to log in to Windows 11, though, means that Microsoft can track additional information and associate it with your Outlook. com account — the times you log in to Windows 11, your locations, and so on. You may be okay with that, or you may not want Microsoft to be able to track that kind of additional information.

>> **You can create an extra new Outlook.com account and use it only to log in to Windows 11.** The Outlook.com account is free and easy to create, and if you use it wisely, nobody will ever know the difference. The only downsides: If you use Outlook.com, you have to tell the Windows 11 Mail app to look in your other inbox; your existing Outlook.com contacts won't get carried over into the People app automatically; and Skype will want to work with your new ID.

# Creating an Outlook.com account

Here's how to set up a new Outlook.com account to use in Windows 11 and Microsoft's other products and services:

**1.** **Using your favorite web browser, go to www.outlook.com.**

The main screen lets you sign in or create a free account.

**2.** **Click or tap Create Free Account.**

You see the Create Account form, as shown in Figure 5-1.

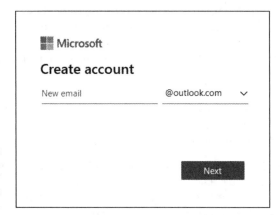

**FIGURE 5-1:**
Sign up for an
Outlook.com/
Microsoft
account.

**3.** **Type an account name and click or tap Next.**

If someone already has the email address you entered, type another and click or tap Next again.

**4.** **Type the password you want to use, deselect the box that tells Microsoft to send you information (another word for spam), and click or tap Next.**

**5.** **Fill out your first and last name, and then click or tap Next.**

**6.** **Give Microsoft your country (which they can find anyway by looking at your IP address) and fill out a birthdate. Click or tap Next.**

If your birthdate indicates that you're less than 18 years old, you may have problems using the account.

**7.** **Type the CAPTCHA code or solve the puzzle that Microsoft displays, to verify that you are human, and then click or tap Next.**

**8.** **If Microsoft asks if you want to stay signed in, click or tap Yes.**

Outlook.com loads your inbox and Microsoft's welcome message, as in Figure 5-2. That's it.

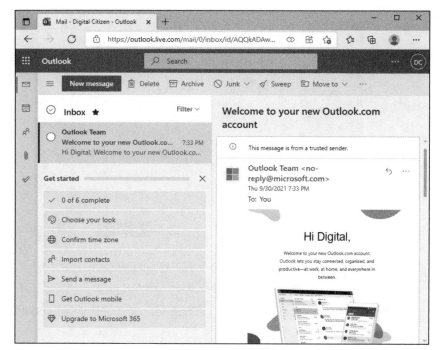

**FIGURE 5-2:**
Your new
Microsoft
account is live
and working.

You can now use your new Outlook.com account as a Windows 11 login ID. You can also use it for email, Skype, Xbox, OneNote, OneDrive, . . . just about anything from Microsoft. However, before you can log in to Windows 11 with this new Outlook.com account, you must add it as a user. Read Chapter 4 in this minibook to learn how.

## Making any email address a Microsoft account

You must follow a different procedure to turn any email address into a Microsoft account. The steps are simple, as long as you can retrieve the email sent to the address:

**1.** **Using your favorite web browser, go to** `https://signup.live.com`.

You see the Create Account message, as shown in Figure 5-3, where you can create a Microsoft account without a Microsoft email address.

**2.** **Type your email address from Gmail, Yahoo! Mail, or some other place. Then click or tap Next.**

Understanding
Microsoft Accounts

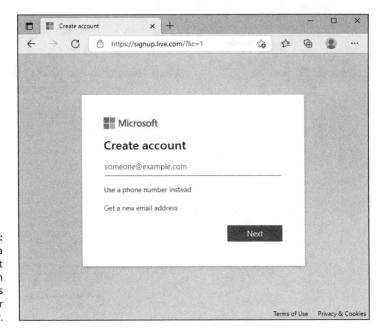

**FIGURE 5-3:**
Creating a
Microsoft
account with an
email address
from another
company.

3. **Enter the password you want to use and click or tap Next.**

**REMEMBER**

Note that the password you provide here is for your Microsoft account. It is *not* your email password. The password you enter here will be the password you need to use to log in to Windows 11 or any website that requires a Microsoft account. Most experts advise you not to reuse your email password as your Microsoft account password.

4. **Fill out a fanciful first and last name, and then click or tap Next.**

5. **Give Microsoft your country and fill out a birthdate. Click or tap Next.**

Microsoft sends a 4-digit verification code to your email address. If you do not see the email, check your Spam/Junk folder.

6. **Type the verification code, deselect the box that allows Microsoft to send you emails, and click or tap Next.**

7. **Type the CAPTCHA code or solve the puzzle that Microsoft displays, to verify that you are human, and then click or tap Next.**

8. **If Microsoft asks if you want to stay signed in, click or tap Yes.**

Your Microsoft account page is loaded, as in Figure 5-4.

# TWO-FACTOR AUTHENTICATION

Microsoft has a security feature called *two-factor authentication,* or *two-step verification,* and it's a great choice to enable and configure. Usually, when you log in with your Microsoft account using a machine that hasn't been explicitly identified (by you) as being an acceptable computer, Microsoft issues a challenge to verify that you are who you say you are. The authentication usually comes in the form of an SMS sent to your phone, a code displayed in a mobile app built for this purpose, or an email sent to another email address. The benefits are obvious: People may be able to steal your password, but it's rare that they get both your password and your computer (which bypasses two-factor authentication entirely), and almost impossible to get both your password and your smartphone — or access to your other email address.

Most people are leery about giving their phone numbers to Microsoft. However, Microsoft doesn't use your phone number for nefarious purposes. And smartphone-based two-factor authentication works great. You should try apps such as Microsoft Authenticator or Google Authenticator, which are available for Android and iPhone. I prefer the Microsoft app, but Google's is okay too.

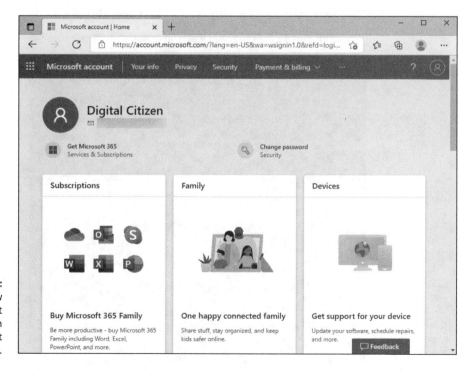

**FIGURE 5-4:**
Your new Microsoft account is alive, with an email that is not from Microsoft.

# Discontinuing Your Microsoft Account

So, you've read about the differences between a Microsoft account and local account, and you've decided that you just don't want to keep feeding Microsoft information. If you want to move to local account, do the following:

**1.** **Click or tap the start icon, Settings, and Accounts. On the right, choose Your Info.**

You see the account settings for your account.

**2.** **In the Account Settings section, click or tap the Sign In with a Local Account Instead link.**

**3.** **If you have a BitLocker-encrypted PC and see a warning that you should first back up a copy of your recovery key, close the warning, follow the instructions shown, and redo Steps 1 and 2. Then click or tap Skip This Step.**

**4.** **When asked whether you're sure you want to go ahead, click Next.**

Windows 11 asks you to enter your PIN or password.

**5.** **Type your current PIN/password and then click Next.**

Windows 11 presents you with the dialog shown in Figure 5-5.

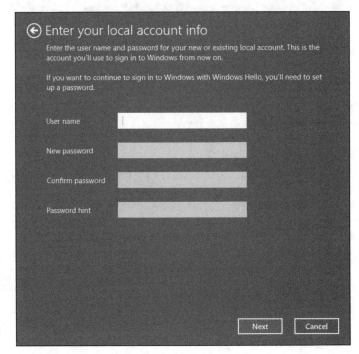

**FIGURE 5-5:**
Type the name of the local user account, its password, and the password hint.

6. **Enter the name of the local user account to use in place of your Microsoft account, the password you want, and a password hint. Then click Next.**

Windows 11 warns you to make sure you've saved your work — it's about to sign you out of your account.

7. **Click Sign Out and Finish.**

Windows 11 signs you out and displays the lock screen. Now you can sign in with your local account.

Note that your old Microsoft account is no longer valid for signing into this computer. Instead, you sign in only through the local account. If you want to switch back, follow Step 1 and at Step 2 click the Sign In with a Microsoft Account Instead link. Then, go through the hoops of adding the details of your Microsoft account.

# Taking Care of Your Microsoft Account

If you ever want to change the details in your Microsoft account, it's easy — if you know where to go.

For reasons understood only by Microsoft, to maintain your Microsoft account, go to `https://account.microsoft.com`. Sign in, and you see full account information (refer to Figure 5-4).

To change any of the information for your account, activate two-factor authentication, or change the password, tap or click the appropriate link for the item that interests you.

# Controlling Which Windows 11 Settings Get Synchronized

If you don't explicitly change anything, logging on to Windows 11 with a Microsoft account syncs some settings across all the PCs that you use. You can tell Microsoft that you don't want to sync specific items. Here's how:

1. **Click or tap the start icon, Settings, and Accounts.**

2. **On the right, click or tap Windows Backup.**

The screen shown in Figure 5-6 appears.

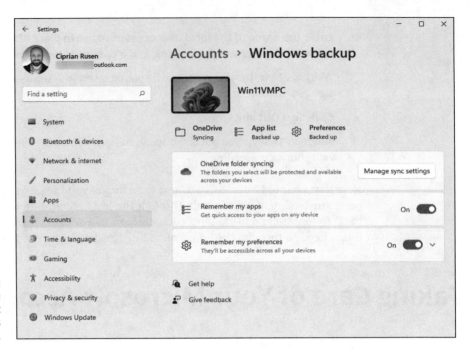

FIGURE 5-6:
Control the
way Microsoft
accounts
sync here.

3. **If you don't want Windows 11 to remember your apps and sync them across devices, turn off the switch for Remember My Apps.**

4. **If you don't want Windows 11 to sync your settings across devices, turn off the switch for Remember My Preferences.**

    No need to tap or click OK or Apply. The changes take effect with your next login.

Sync happens only when you log in with the same Microsoft account on two or more PCs.

REMEMBER

# Chapter **6**

# Protecting Your Privacy

"The best minds of my generation are thinking about how to make people click ads. That sucks."

— Jeff Hammerbacher, early Facebook employee

When you work with "free" services — search engines such as Google and Bing; social networks such as Facebook, Pinterest, and LinkedIn; online storage services such as OneDrive and Google Drive; email services such as Gmail, Outlook.com, and Yahoo! Mail — these services may not charge you anything, but they're hardly free. You pay for them with your privacy. Every time you go to one of these sites or use one of these products, with a few noteworthy exceptions, you leave a trail that companies are eager to exploit, primarily for advertising.

The exceptions? Google doesn't scan activity for any paid account or any educational account. Apple swears it doesn't wallow in the data-grabbing cesspool. Microsoft loves to say it doesn't scan the contents of Outlook.com messages. There are lots of if's, and's, but's, and nuances. But if it's free, you're the product, not the customer.

There's a reason why you buy something on, say, Alibaba, and then find ads for Alibaba appearing on all sorts of websites. One of the big advertising conglomerates has your data. Maybe just your IP address. Maybe a planted cookie. But they've connected enough dots to know that, whatever site you happen to be on at the moment, you once bought something on Alibaba.

Now, even when you log in to Windows 11 and use a Microsoft account, you leave another footprint in the sand. (I talk about Microsoft accounts in Book 2, Chapter 5.) This isn't horrible. It isn't illegal either — although laws in different countries differ widely, and lawsuits are reshaping the picture even as we speak.

In this chapter, I give you an overview of privacy settings — and some privacy shenanigans — inside Windows 11. You learn about the data collected by Microsoft when you use Windows 11, how to limit it, and also how to view it yourself. Then I talk about ads in Windows 11 and how to limit them too. Finally, I cover the very much disliked location tracking that we've grown accustomed to because of our smartphones.

# Realizing Why You Should Care about Privacy

People are becoming increasingly aware of how their privacy is being eroded by using the internet and social media. Some people aren't particularly concerned. Others get paranoid to the point of blocking anything that has a remote chance of tracking them. Chances are pretty good you're somewhere between the two extremes.

Windows 11 users need to understand that, similar to Windows 10, this operating system pulls in data from all over the web. Every time you connect to a service, you're connecting the dots for Microsoft's data-collection routines. And if you use a Microsoft account, Microsoft's dot connector is even more productive.

I'm not implying that Microsoft is trying to steal your data or somehow use your identity for illegal purposes. It isn't. At this point, Microsoft mostly wants to identify your buying patterns and your interests, so it can serve you ads that you will click for products that you will buy. Same as Google. That's where the money is.

Here's how the services stack up when it comes to privacy (or the lack thereof):

**TIP**

» **Google:** Without a doubt, this company has the largest collection of data. You leave tracks in the Google databases every time you use Google to search for a website. That's true of every search engine (except www.DuckDuckGo.com), not just Google, but Google has 90 percent or more of the search engine market worldwide. You also hand Google web-surfing information if you sign into your Google Chrome browser (so it can keep track of your bookmarks for you) or if you sign into Google itself (for example, to use Google Workspace or Google Drive). The native Android browser ties into Google, too, and using an Android smartphone or tablet also sends tons of data to Google.

Google also owns the former DoubleClick, now named Google Ad Manager. Any time you go to a site with a Google ad — most popular sites have them — a little log about your visit finds its way into Google's database.

» **Facebook:** Although Facebook may not have the largest collection of data, it's the most detailed. People who sign up for Facebook tend to give away lots of information, and the company knows their name, location, friends, relatives, specific interests, and everything they share on all its other services, such as Instagram, WhatsApp, and Messenger. Also, the company collects data even when you've left its websites and apps. Because many websites use Facebook's marketing tools, each time you visit them, Facebook gets some data too. That's why it's important to lock down your Facebook account (see Book 6, Chapter 1).

» **Microsoft:** Microsoft's internet access database may not be as big as Google's, or as detailed as Facebook's, but the company is trying to get there. One of the ways they're catching up is by encouraging you to use a Microsoft account. The other is to create all these connections to other data-collecting services inside Windows 11, such as Widgets and Cortana. Then there's Bing, which logs what you're looking for just like Google Search does.

Windows 11 is light-years ahead of earlier versions of Windows when it comes to harvesting your data. On the upside, it also provides more granular controls for protecting your privacy than Windows 10 did.

For an ongoing, authoritative discussion of privacy issues, look at the Electronic Frontier Foundation's Defending Your Rights in the Digital World page at www.eff.org/issues/privacy.

# Handling Your Privacy in Windows 11

Although Windows 11 can collect a large set of data about your activities compared to previous versions of Windows, it also offers the largest collection of controls for protecting your privacy. You can set detailed privacy permissions for more than 30 aspects of your daily computing activities, starting with general Windows 11 advertising and moving on to speech recognition, diagnostics and feedback, and which apps are allowed to take screen shots or download files automatically. Although most people will find the list of privacy controls intimidating, it's good to know where to find them:

1. **Click or tap the start icon and then the Settings icon.**

2. **On the left, click or tap Privacy & security.**

   The Privacy & security settings appear, as shown in Figure 6-1.

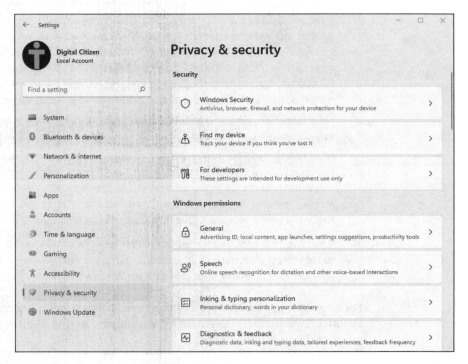

**FIGURE 6-1:** Windows 11's privacy and security settings.

3. **Scroll down the Windows Permissions section on the right and see the big categories of privacy settings available.**

   There aren't many, but they're all important, and you should look at how your permissions are set.

4. **Scroll further down to the App Permissions section.**

   This list is incredibly long. Simply scroll through it to understand just how many things you can set about your privacy in Windows 11.

# Limiting diagnostics and feedback data collection

Most of the snooping in Windows 11 is happening for its diagnostics and feedback collection, or the usual telemetry used for monitoring how software products work and improving them. Windows 11 collects data about the events that take place when you use it, the errors that show up, when users log in, online crashes, and the settings you change. Microsoft has a detailed description of its telemetry collection policy at `https://docs.microsoft.com/en-us/windows/privacy/configure-windows-diagnostic-data-in-your-organization`.

To limit the diagnostics and feedback data collection performed by Windows 11, you can set its telemetry to basic, like this:

1. **Click or tap the start icon and then the Settings icon.**

2. **On the left, click or tap Privacy & Security.**

   The Privacy & Security settings appear (refer to Figure 6-1).

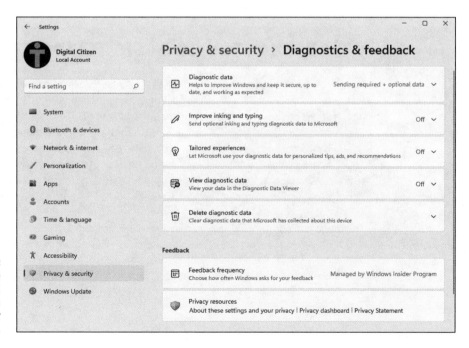

**FIGURE 6-2:** Configure the Windows 11 telemetry data collected by Microsoft.

3. **In the Windows Permissions section on the right, click or tap Diagnostics & Feedback.**

   The types of data collected appears in a list similar to Figure 6-2.

4. **Click or tap Diagnostic Data to display the section's contents, and set the Send Optional Diagnostic Data switch to off.**

   Microsoft will now collect only the basic telemetry data it needs about Windows 11.

5. **Click or tap Improve Inking and Typing to expand it and set its switch to off.**

   You've stopped Microsoft's data collection when you're using a pen or the touchscreen.

6. **Similarly, click or tap Tailored Experiences and set its switch to off.**

   Microsoft will no longer collect data for personalized ads and product recommendations.

7. **Close Settings when you're done.**

   Your settings are saved automatically.

**TIP**

If you want to delete all diagnostic data collected by Microsoft on your Windows 11 PC, in the Diagnostics & Feedback window, click or tap Delete Diagnostic Data and then the Delete button.

## WHAT, EXACTLY, IS BASIC TELEMETRY?

It probably won't surprise you to find out that Microsoft collects, as part of its Basic telemetry, roughly 2,000 data points per computer, updated every day. In April 2017, after a series of disclosures about privacy pursuits in the EU, Microsoft released a detailed list of its telemetry. You can see the list for basic-level telemetry in Windows on this web page: https://docs.microsoft.com/en-us/windows/privacy/basic-level-windows-diagnostic-events-and-fields-1903. A similar list for the full telemetry setting is at this page: https://docs.microsoft.com/en-us/windows/configuration/windows-diagnostic-data.

The lists are mind-numbing, as you might imagine, and exhaustive.

# Viewing the diagnostic data sent to Microsoft

Here's what I know:

» Microsoft collects telemetry — data about your use of Windows 11 — no matter what. You can minimize the amount of data collected (the basic setting, described in the nearby sidebar,) but you can't stop the flow unless you're connected to a corporate domain.

» The data being sent to Microsoft is encrypted. That means anyone who's snooping on your connection won't be able to pull out any useful information. Microsoft also offers the free Diagnostic Data Viewer app, which allows people to view the data sent to Microsoft from their Windows 11 PC.

To enable Diagnostic Data Viewer and use it to see the data sent to Microsoft, do the following:

1. **Click or tap the start icon, Settings, and then Privacy & Security. On the right, choose Diagnostics & Feedback.**

2. **Click or tap View Diagnostic Data to expand this section and then set the Turn On Diagnostic Data Viewer switch to on.**

3. **Click or tap the Open Diagnostic Data Viewer button.**

   Most probably the app is not installed on your Windows 11 PC, and you are taken to its Microsoft Store page.

4. **Click or tap Install.**

   Wait for the app to be installed on your PC.

5. **Click or tap Open, and then browse the data displayed by Diagnostic Data Viewer app, as shown in Figure 6-3.**

   As you can see, it's all very technical, and most people don't understand a thing of what's being collected.

**TIP**

If you need help understanding what Diagnostic Data Viewer is displaying, check out the following article on my blog: www.digitalcitizen.life/diagnostic-data-viewer-windows-10. Although the article was originally written for Windows 10, everything in it applies to Windows 11 too.

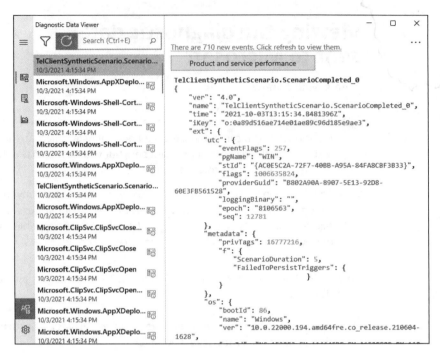

Diagnostic Data Viewer

≡ ▽ ↻ Search (Ctrl+E)

There are 710 new events. Click refresh to view them.

Product and service performance

TelClientSyntheticScenario.Scenario...
10/3/2021 4:15:34 PM

Microsoft.Windows.AppXDeplo...
10/3/2021 4:15:34 PM

Microsoft-Windows-Shell-Cort...
10/3/2021 4:15:34 PM

Microsoft-Windows-Shell-Cort...
10/3/2021 4:15:34 PM

Microsoft-Windows-Shell-Cort...
10/3/2021 4:15:34 PM

Microsoft.Windows.AppXDeplo...
10/3/2021 4:15:34 PM

TelClientSyntheticScenario.Scenario...
10/3/2021 4:15:34 PM

Microsoft.Windows.AppXDeplo...
10/3/2021 4:15:34 PM

Microsoft.ClipSvc.ClipSvcClose...
10/3/2021 4:15:34 PM

Microsoft.ClipSvc.ClipSvcClose
10/3/2021 4:15:34 PM

Microsoft.ClipSvc.ClipSvcOpen
10/3/2021 4:15:34 PM

Microsoft.ClipSvc.ClipSvcOpen...
10/3/2021 4:15:34 PM

Microsoft.Windows.AppXDeplo...
10/3/2021 4:15:34 PM

Microsoft.Windows.AppXDeplo...
10/3/2021 4:15:34 PM

TelClientSyntheticScenario.ScenarioCompleted_0
{
    "ver": "4.0",
    "name": "TelClientSyntheticScenario.ScenarioCompleted_0",
    "time": "2021-10-03T13:15:34.8481396Z",
    "iKey": "o:0a89d516ae714e01ae89c96d185e9ae3",
    "ext": {
        "utc": {
            "eventFlags": 257,
            "pgName": "WIN",
            "stId": "{AC0E5C2A-72F7-40BB-A95A-84FA8CBF3B33}",
            "flags": 1006635824,
            "providerGuid": "B802A90A-8907-5E13-92D8-
60E3FB561528",
            "loggingBinary": "",
            "epoch": "8106563",
            "seq": 12781
        },
        "metadata": {
            "privTags": 16777216,
            "f": {
                "ScenarioDuration": 5,
                "FailedToPersistTriggers": {
                }
            }
        },
        "os": {
            "bootId": 86,
            "name": "Windows",
            "ver": "10.0.22000.194.amd64fre.co_release.210604-
1628",

**FIGURE 6-3:**
Diagnostic Data
Viewer shows
you the telemetry
data collected by
Microsoft.

**WARNING**

If you want to minimize identifiable data harvested from you and don't feel comfortable with the fact that Microsoft collects data about you, it's best to switch to Linux. Then, avoid Google Chrome and use Firefox, use DuckDuckGo instead of Google Search, and always run a VPN (see Book 9, Chapter 4). Of course, you'd have to avoid using a smartphone and pay with cash or Bitcoin only. You'd also need to avoid walking in public, given the current state of facial recognition, and hope you never end up in a hospital!

# Knowing What Connections Windows Prefers

If you use Windows 11, parts of it are integrated well with services from other companies, while others are not. That's because Microsoft plays favorites with some online companies and shuns others as much as it possibly can:

>> **Microsoft owns part of Facebook.** You see Facebook here and there in Windows 11. There's a reason for that: Microsoft owns a 1.6-percent share of Facebook (at the time of this writing, anyway). But Facebook is ambivalent about Microsoft, at best.

>> **Microsoft doesn't play well with Google.** Windows 11 has some hooks into Google, but invariably they exist to pull your personal information out of Google (for example, Contacts) and put it in Microsoft's databases.

>> **Microsoft gives lip service to Apple.** There's no love lost between the companies. Microsoft makes software for Mac, iPhone, and iPad. (For example, Office for iPad is a treat, OneNote runs on any iPhone, and Office has been on the Mac for longer than it's been on Windows!) Apple makes little software for Windows. They're both fiercely guarding their turf. Don't expect to see any sharing of user information between the two companies.

>> **Microsoft once tried to buy Yahoo!, which owns Flickr.** Microsoft has hired a boatload of talented people from Yahoo!. Microsoft also still has contractual ties to Yahoo!.

And of course, you know that Microsoft also owns Skype, Hotmail/Outlook.com, Xbox, and OneDrive, right?

Your information — aggregated, personally identifiable, vaguely anonymous, or whatever — can be drawn from any of those sources and mashed up with the data that Microsoft has in its databases. No wonder data mining is a big topic on the Redmond campus.

# Seeing Fewer Ads in Windows 11

Ads are a major annoyance in Windows 10 and Windows 11. Microsoft has decided to plaster them all over the place, starting with your Start menu. For example, as soon as you install Windows 11 and open the Start menu, you see shortcuts to apps that are not installed, such as Photoshop Express and PicsArt. They're sponsored apps that Microsoft recommends to you. If you click or tap their shortcuts, these apps get installed automatically from the Microsoft Store.

Then, when you log in with a Microsoft account, the company creates an advertising ID for you that can be used to show you personalized ads. If you want to see fewer ads in Windows 11, or at least less personalized ones, here's what you have to do:

**1.** **Click or tap the start icon, Settings, and then Privacy & Security. On the right, choose General.**

The settings shown in Figure 6-4 appear.

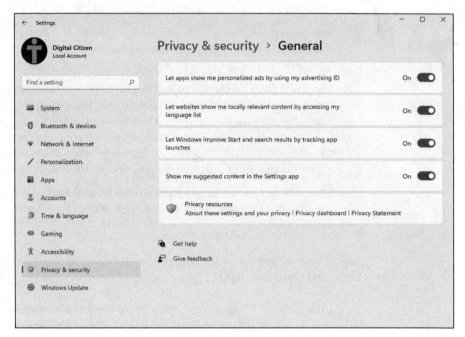

**FIGURE 6-4:**
You can disable some of the personalized ads in Windows 11.

2. **Set to off the switch for Let Apps Show Me Personalized Ads by Using My Advertising ID.**

3. **Set to off the switch for Let Websites Show Me Locally Relevant Content by Accessing My Language List.**

4. **In the column on the left, choose Personalization.**

   You see all the personalization options for Windows 11.

5. **On the right, scroll down to Device Usage and click or tap it.**

   You see several switches, as shown in Figure 6-5. They represent the types of activities you can perform on your Windows 11 PC and for which Microsoft can show personalized ads.

6. **Set to off all the switches, starting with Gaming and ending with Business.**

   Your settings are applied immediately, and you can close Settings when you're done.

TIP

To get rid of a pinned shortcut from the Start menu that's an ad for an app you don't want, simply right-click or press and hold down on it, and then choose Unpin from Start. That ad (pardon, app) is gone, and it won't come back.

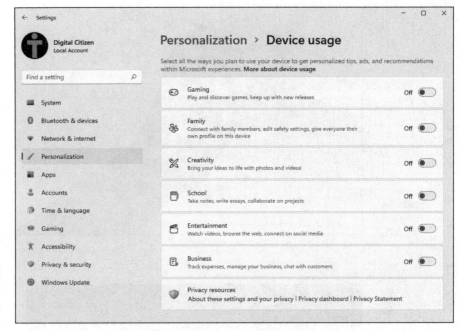

**FIGURE 6-5:**
Stop Windows 11 from showing you ads and tips about all kinds of apps and services.

# Controlling Location Tracking

Just like all the major operating systems out there, Windows 11 has *location tracking.* You must tell Windows 11 and specific applications that it's okay to track your location, but if you do, those apps — and Windows itself — know where you are. Like any technology, location tracking can be used for good or not-so-good purposes, and your opinion about what's good may differ from others'.

Also, location tracking isn't just one technology. It's several.

If your PC has a *GPS* (Global Positioning System) chip (see Figure 6-6) — they're common in tablets and laptops and rare in desktops — and the GPS is turned on, and you've authorized a Windows 11 app to see your location, the app can identify your PC's location within a few feet.

GPS is a satellite-based method for pinpointing your location. Commercial satellite clusters travel in specific orbits around the earth (see Figure 6-7); the orbits aren't geosynchronous, but they're good enough to cover every patch of land on earth. The GPS chip locates four or more satellites and calculates your location based on the distance to each.

**FIGURE 6-6:**
GPS chips
turn tiny.

*Source: OriginGPS Nano Hornet GPS chip*

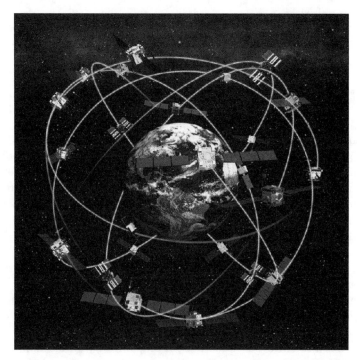

**FIGURE 6-7:**
Carefully crafted
orbits ensure
that a GPS chip
can almost
always find four
satellites.

*Source: Space.com*

# TRACKING YOUR SHOTS

Any time you put a GPS system and a camera together, you have the potential for lots of embarrassment. Why? Many GPS-enabled cameras — notably the ones in many smartphones and tablets — brand the photo with an exact location. If you snap a shot from your tablet and upload it to Facebook, Flickr, or any of a thousand photo-friendly sites, the photo may have your exact location embedded in the file.

Law enforcement has used this approach to find suspects. The US military warns active-duty personnel to turn off their GPSs to avoid disclosing locations. Even some anonymous celebrities have been outed by their cameras and smartphones. Be careful.

If your Windows 11 PC doesn't have a GPS chip or it isn't turned on, but you do allow apps to track your location, the best Windows 11 can do is to approximate where your internet connection is coming from, based on your IP address (a number that uniquely identifies your computer's connection to the internet). And in many cases, that can be miles away from where you're actually sitting.

When you start a Windows 11 app that wants to use your location, you may see a message asking for your permission to track it, as in the Weather app shown in Figure 6-8.

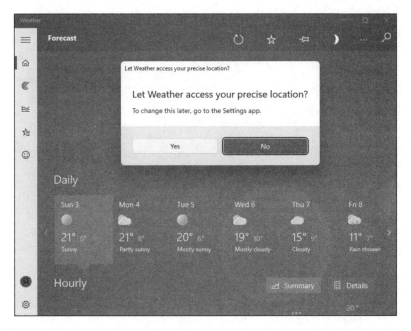

**FIGURE 6-8:** The Weather app wants you to reveal your precise location to show you the forecast.

If you've already turned on location services, each time you add another app that wants to use your location, you see a notification that says, "Let Windows 11 app access your precise location?" You can respond either Yes or No. The following sections explain how you can control location tracking in Windows 11.

## Blocking all location tracking in Windows 11

To keep Windows 11 from using your location in *any* app — even if you've already turned on location use in some apps — follow these steps:

1.  **Click or tap the start icon and then the Settings icon.**

2.  **On the left, click or tap Privacy & Security.**

3.  **On the right, scroll down to App Permissions, and click or tap Location.**

    The Location settings appear, as shown in Figure 6-9.

4.  **Set the Location Services switch to off.**

    That's all it takes to turn off location tracking — even if you've already given your permission to various apps to track your location.

As a bonus, click or tap the Clear button next to Location History, at the bottom of the screen. This deletes the recent location history stored by Windows 11.

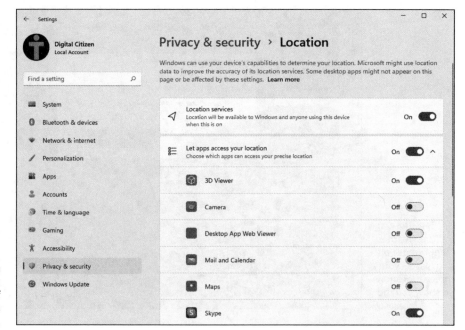

**FIGURE 6-9:**
This is where you turn on and off Windows 11's location tracking.

# Blocking location tracking in an app

You may not want to turn off location tracking for all apps in Windows 11, but only for some. To block location tracking for a specific app, do the following:

**1.** **Click or tap the start icon and then the Settings icon.**

**2.** **On the left, click or tap Privacy & Security.**

**3.** **On the right, scroll down to App Permissions, and click or tap Location.**

The Location settings appear (refer to Figure 6-9).

**4.** **Under Let Apps Access Your Location, scroll down until you find the app you want to cut off. If the list is not expanded, click or tap anywhere on Let Apps Access Your Location.**

You see the list of apps that can request access to your precise location, as shown in Figure 6-10.

**5.** **Find the app for which you want to block location tracking and click or tap its switch and set it to off.**

The app loses its permission to access your location.

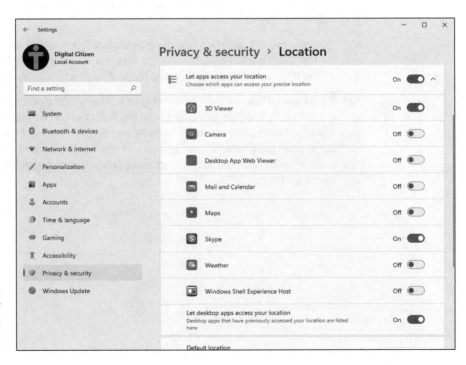

**FIGURE 6-10:** You can turn off location tracking for individual apps, as well.

# Minimizing Privacy Intrusion

Although it's true that using Windows 11 exposes you to some privacy concerns, you can reduce the amount of data kept about you by following a few simple rules:

>> **Set up an account solely for logging in to Windows 11.** If you want to log in to Windows 11 using a Microsoft account — and there are many good reasons for doing so — consider setting up a Microsoft account that you use only for logging in to Windows 11 (and possibly for OneDrive, Xbox, and Skype). See Book 2, Chapter 5, for details.

>> **Add a local account to Windows 11.** To increase your privacy in Windows 11, it's best to use a local account instead of a Microsoft account. This way, Microsoft has fewer logs about what you do, and its data collection is severely limited. Read Book 2, Chapter 4, for details.

>> **Use private browsing.** In Microsoft Edge, it's called *InPrivate;* Google Chrome calls it *Incognito;* Firefox says *Private Browsing.* Turning on private browsing mode keeps your browser from leaving cookies around, and it wipes out download lists, caches, browser history, forms, and passwords. Realize, though, that your browser still leaves crumbs wherever it goes: If you use Google to look up something, for example, Google still has a record of your IP address and what you typed.

Private browsing isn't the same thing as Do Not Track. In fact, as of this writing, Do Not Track is a largely futile request that you make to the websites you visit, asking them to refrain from keeping track of you and your information.

>> **If you use Office, turn off telemetry in it.** In any Office program, choose File ➪ Options ➪ Trust Center. Click or tap the Trust Center Settings button, and then on the left choose Privacy Options and then click or tap Privacy Settings. Deselect all the boxes you see and click or tap OK. The options displayed are ways in which Microsoft collects additional data about you and what you do in Microsoft Office.

# 3

# Working on the Desktop

# Contents at a Glance

Chapter **1**

# Running Your Desktop from Start to Finish

You'll spend most of your time in Windows 11 at the desktop, so you should personalize it and make it as visually pleasing as possible by changing the wallpaper and the theme. And if you're using dark mode on your mobile devices, you may want it on your Windows 11 PC too.

Next, adjust the display settings for blue-light filtering (to protect your eyes during the night), HDR, screen resolution and scaling, and refresh rate (especially important if you're a gamer). If you have issues that negatively affect your eyesight, you might also want to use Magnifier to make everything on the desktop bigger and more visible.

Interacting with the desktop and Windows in general involves using the mouse or the trackpad (on a laptop) or both. That's why it is a good idea to customize their sensitivity and buttons.

If you're a previous Windows 10 user, you may know about virtual desktops, and how you can use them to separate what you do in Windows. If not, it's time to familiarize yourself with this feature, which has been improved in Windows 11.

In this chapter, you learn about all this, as well as how to add shortcuts to the desktop, arrange them as you want, and work with the good old Recycle Bin. The chapter is long, but it's surely useful if you want Windows 11 to look and behave according to your preferences.

## Working with the Desktop

To begin, log into Windows 11. (Follow the instructions in Book 2, Chapter 2 if necessary.) Are you staring at a screen like the one in Figure 1-1? Good! Windows 11 shows you this screen, called the *desktop*, every time you log in.

**FIGURE 1-1:**
You start everything at the mighty Windows 11 desktop.

The desktop has a beautiful background, the Recycle Bin icon at the top left to hold all recently deleted files and folders, and the taskbar at the bottom. You can personalize many aspects of the desktop, to make it feel your own, and I cover them all in this section.

## Changing the background

You can start personalizing Windows 11 by changing the *wallpaper,* or the desktop background. If you bought a new computer with Windows 11 installed, your background might not be as beautiful as the one in Figure 1-1. Instead, it might promote a company such as HP, Dell, or Lenovo. Bah! Change your wallpaper by following these steps:

**1.** **Right-click or tap and hold down on an empty part of the desktop, and then choose Personalize.**

You see the Personalization section in Windows 11 Settings.

**2.** **Click or tap Background.**

The settings shown in Figure 1-2 appear, starting with recent images that were used as a desktop wallpaper.

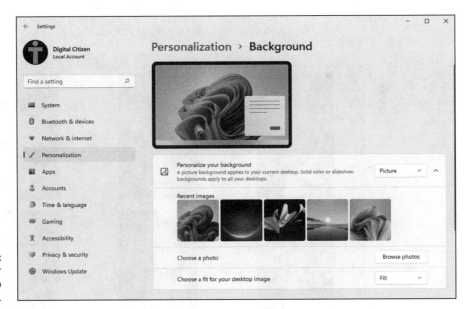

**FIGURE 1-2:** Choose your desktop background.

**3.** **Click or tap a background image you like.**

The image is applied immediately. You can choose one of the pictures that Windows 11 offers, a solid color, or a slideshow of the images in your Pictures folder.

**4.** **Now find a different background by clicking or tapping Browse Photos. When you find a picture you like, select it and click or tap Choose Picture.**

**5.** **If the picture looks like a smashed watermelon or is too small, click or tap the Choose a Fit for Your Desktop Image drop-down list, and make a selection:**

- Fill the screen. Windows 11 may stretch or crop the image to make this happen.

- Fit the image to the available space on the screen.

- Stretch the image so that it has the same dimensions as your screen.

- Tile the image. Windows 11 puts the image on the screen multiple times to fill up the space. See Figure 1-3.

- Center the image in the middle of the desktop.

- Span the image across multiple displays, if you have two or more.

**6.** **To close the Settings app, click or tap the close icon (X).**

Your new wallpaper settings take effect immediately.

**FIGURE 1-3:**
Tiling can be a
bit excessive.

# Switching Windows 11 themes

A *theme* is what Windows names the combination of a desktop background, a dominant color for the user interface, and a set of mouse cursors and system sounds. Windows 11 has six built-in themes, and you can switch among them easily. If you're bored by the default theme, here's how to change it:

1. **Right-click or tap and hold down on an empty part of the desktop, and choose Personalize.**

   You see the Personalization section in Windows 11 Settings.

2. **In the Settings app window, click or tap Themes.**

   The Windows 11 themes settings shown in Figure 1-4 appear.

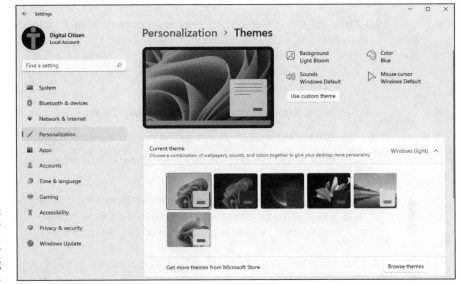

**FIGURE 1-4:** For more personalization, consider changing the theme.

3. **In the list below Current Theme, click or tap the available themes, one by one.**

   The desktop wallpaper, taskbar, Settings app, and Start menu change immediately.

4. **After you try all the available themes, click or tap the one you like.**

   I prefer the Captured Motion theme. It looks great and too few people know about it.

TIP

If you're not satisfied with the built-in themes, at Step 4, click or tap the Browse Themes button and navigate the Microsoft Store where you can find plenty of free themes for Windows. Click or tap the Get button for the theme you want to try, and then click or tap Open.

## Battling dark mode and light mode

Dark mode is a thing for smartphone users. I have many friends who want the screens of their mobile devices black at all times. Apparently, many believe that dark mode benefits their eyes and extends the battery of mobile devices. The battery improvements are measurable and provable, but I'm not so sure about the benefits for your eyes. Using a dark screen requires your pupils to dilate, which can make it harder to focus. I prefer light mode, which is the opposite of dark mode, using brighter and crisper colors.

While the world debates whether to go dark or light in Windows 11, let me show you how to quickly switch between the two:

1. **Right-click or press and hold down on an empty part of the desktop and choose Personalize.**

2. **In the Settings app window, click or tap Colors.**

   You see the settings shown in Figure 1-5.

3. **Click or tap the drop-down list for Choose Your Mode and select Light or Dark.**

   If you select Custom, you see additional options for choosing between dark mode and light mode for Windows and for apps separately. The colors used by Windows 11 change as soon as you've made a choice.

TIP

Changing between Dark Mode and Light Mode in the Colors settings window doesn't affect the wallpaper, sounds, and other elements. If you want the full dark mode or light mode experience, use the steps for changing the theme, shown in the preceding section, and choose between the Windows (Light) and Windows (Dark) themes.

REMEMBER

Switching from dark mode to light mode via themes does more than change the look of Windows 11. It changes the sounds as well. Sounds are soft and relaxing in dark mode but energetic and crisp in light mode. In this way, people with visual impairments have different experiences when using the two modes.

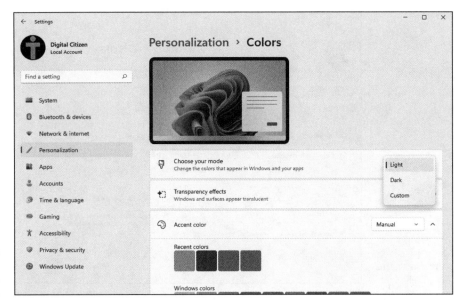

**FIGURE 1-5:**
Choose between
light mode and
dark mode.

# Setting Up Your Display

Technically, the desktop is only what you see after you log into Windows 11, although people think about the desktop as their screen or computer display too.

How text, icons and app windows are displayed on the desktop depends on your screen settings. In this section, you become familiar with the night light, HDR, screen resolution and scaling, refresh rate, magnification, and more. These topics will help you be more productive and protect your eyesight.

## Switching the night light on and off

If you use your laptop, tablet, or PC during the evening or at night, you might notice that it takes you longer to fall asleep. To help with this problem, Windows 11 includes a night light feature. When activated, it makes the screen display warmer colors, acting like a blue-light filter. The display is supposed to reduce eye fatigue at night and improve sleep cycles. Here's how to enable and configure the night light in Windows 11:

1. **Click or tap the start icon and then Settings.**

2. **On the left of the Settings window, make sure that System is selected. On the right, click or tap Display.**

   You see the Display settings shown in Figure 1-6.

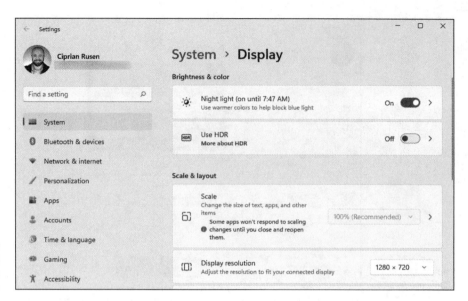

**FIGURE 1-6:**
It's a good idea
to enable the
night light.

**3.** **To turn on the night light immediately, click or tap its switch, setting it on.**

The colors on the screen should change immediately, to filter out the blue light.

**4.** **If you want to configure the night light:**

   a. *Click or tap its name, not its switch.* The strength slider and scheduling settings appear, as shown in Figure 1-7.

   b. *Configure the strength of the night light and its schedule.*

## Enabling HDR and auto HDR

HDR, or high dynamic range, is a display technology that offers a richer, more colorful viewing experience. With HDR turned on, you see more detail both in the shadows and highlights of a scene. You also get a brighter, more vibrant, and more detailed picture compared to a standard display. HDR is great for immersive video experiences, including movies and games. If you have a new laptop or PC with Windows 11 and its screen has support for HDR, you should turn it on.

If you're a gamer, you may also want to take advantage of the auto HDR feature built into Windows 11, which takes DirectX 11 or DirectX 12 non-HDR games and intelligently expands the color and brightness range up to HDR. This seamless feature gives you a new gaming experience that takes full advantage of your HDR monitor's capabilities. You enable this feature with a single switch.

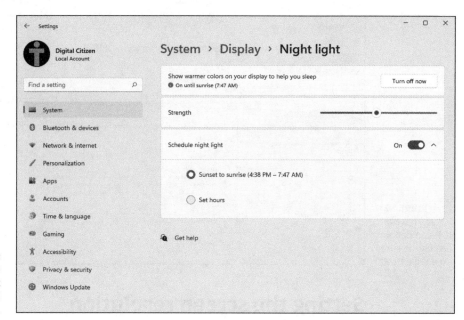

**FIGURE 1-7:**
Change the
night light
strength and
schedule.

If I've made you curious and you have a computer equipped with an HDR display, follow these steps to enable HDR and auto HDR:

1. **Click or tap the start icon and then Settings.**

2. **On the left of the Settings window, make sure that System is selected. On the right, click or tap Display.**

   The Display settings appear (refer to Figure 1-6).

3. **To turn on HDR immediately, click or tap the Use HDR switch to turn it on.**

   The colors on the screen change immediately to filter out the blue light.

4. **If you want to configure HDR:**

   *a. Click or tap the Use HDR text, not on its switch.*

   *b. Scroll down until you find the HDR settings shown in Figure 1-8.*

   *c. Turn on the switches for Use HDR, Play Streaming HDR Video, and Auto HDR.*

   HDR is now enabled for all types of activities, including watching video and playing games.

For more about the gaming features included in Windows 11, read Book 4, Chapter 9.

**TIP**

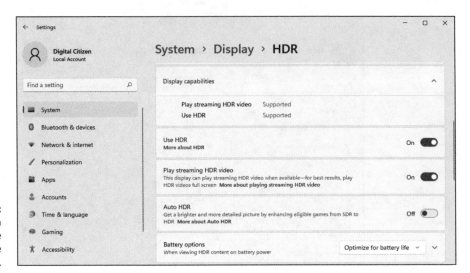

**FIGURE 1-8:**
If you have an
HDR-compatible
display, be sure
to enable HDR.

# Setting the screen resolution

If you have a 4K display and want to take full advantage of the screen space it has to offer, set its screen resolution to the maximum. However, when you do, the icons and text change size and might be so small that you can't read them, especially if you view the display from a distance.

In addition, video takes more time to render at higher resolutions, so video-intensive workloads such as games might be slower, especially if your video card can't meet the demands of the game. Other hardware components can negatively affect the experience too, but the video card plays a critical role. Because of these reasons, you may want to adjust the screen resolution to something that is more balanced. Here's how:

1. **Right-click or press and hold down on an empty space on the desktop.**

2. **In the menu that opens, choose Display Settings.**

   The Display settings appear (refer to Figure 1-6).

3. **Click or tap the Display Resolution drop-down list.**

   All available screen resolutions appear, as shown in Figure 1-9. The list depends on your display, its hardware specifications, the drivers installed, and the capabilities of your computer's graphics card.

4. **Click or tap the resolution you want in the list.**

   Windows 11 changes the resolution and asks you to confirm that you want to keep this setting.

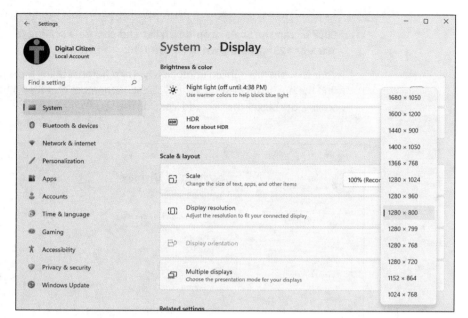

**FIGURE 1-9:**
Changing the
resolution can
improve or lower
the visibility of
items on the
screen.

5. **Do one of the following:**

   ● If you're happy with how everything looks, click or tap Keep Changes.

   ● If you're not happy with how everything looks, click or tap Revert or don't do anything for 15 seconds. The screen reverts to the previous resolution, and you can repeat from Step 3.

6. **When you're done, close the Settings app by clicking or tapping X in the top-right corner.**

## Changing the size of text, apps, and other items

When you increase the resolution, you get more space on the screen and can use more apps side by side. However, if you're using a 4K display, the icons and text may get ridiculously small and put a strain on your eyes. You can fix this problem by lowering the resolution (and losing some of the screen real estate) or by changing the scaling. I prefer the latter approach. Here's how to adjust the scaling to improve the size of text, apps, and other items:

1. **Right-click or press and hold down on an empty space on the desktop.**

2. **In the menu that opens, choose Display Settings.**

   The Display settings appear (refer to Figure 1-6).

3. **Click or tap the Scale drop-down list and choose a scaling factor (such as 100% or 125%), as shown in Figure 1-10.**

Your changes are applied immediately. Try different scaling factors until you find the one that's best for your eyesight. Remember that the higher the scaling, the bigger the text and icons on the screen.

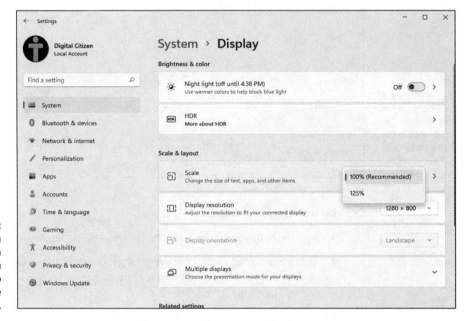

**FIGURE 1-10:** If you have a high-resolution display, it's a good idea to increase the scaling.

# Adjusting the refresh rate

The *refresh rate* tells you how many times per second the image displayed on the screen is updated. By default, Windows 11 sets a 60 Hz screen refresh rate on all computers, meaning that the image is updated sixty times per second. However, gaming laptops or desktop PCs have screens that can reach much higher refresh rates, such as 120 Hz, 144 Hz, or 165 Hz. The refresh setting is important in gaming because it affects motion handling. The higher the refresh rate, the more information reaches your eyes in the same amount of time, leading to smoother-looking motion.

If you have a computer with a display that's capable of high refresh rates, you can change the rate like this:

**1.** **Right-click or press and hold down on an empty space on the desktop.**

**2.** **In the menu that appears, choose Display Settings.**

You see the Display settings (refer to Figure 1-6).

**3.** **On the right, click or tap Advanced Display.**

Your see the display information from Figure 1-11.

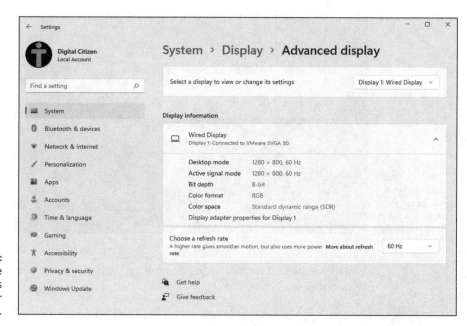

**FIGURE 1-11:**
Increasing the refresh rate is a good idea for gaming.

**4.** **Click or tap the drop-down list next to Choose a Refresh Rate, and choose the value you want.**

The screen refresh rates you see depend on your specific monitor.

Windows 11 changes the refresh rate and asks you to confirm that you want to keep these settings.

**5.** **Do one of the following:**

- If you're happy with how everything looks, click or tap Keep Changes.

- If you're not happy with the screen, click or tap Revert or don't do anything for 10 seconds. The screen reverts automatically to the previous refresh rate, and you can repeat from Step 4.

**6.** **Close the Settings app by clicking or tapping X in the top-right corner.**

## Using magnification

If you have eyesight problems and changing the resolution and the scaling doesn't help much, check out Magnifier by pressing the Windows and + keys simultaneously. By default, Magnifier zooms in to 200 percent, but you can increase the zoom in increments of 100 percent, up to 1600 percent. The app has simple controls for zooming in and out, as shown in Figure 1-12.

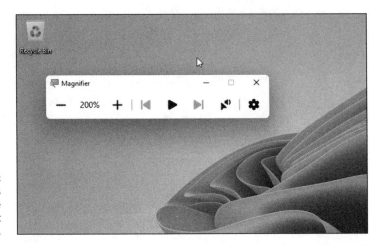

**FIGURE 1-12:**
Magnifier is useful for people with eyesight problems.

When you have finished using Magnifier, you can stop using it by pressing Windows+Esc.

If you would like to personalize how Magnifier works, open the Settings app, go to Accessibility, and then go to Magnifier. You can set the default zoom level, have Magnifier run before Windows boots, and more.

TIP

# Working with a Mouse and a Touchpad

For almost everyone, the computer's mouse (or the lowly touchpad) is the primary way of interacting with Windows 11. But you already knew that. You can click the left mouse button or the right mouse button, or you can roll the wheel in the middle (if you have one), and the mouse will do different things, depending on where you click or roll. But you already knew that, too.

Windows 11's Multi-Touch technology allows you to use all fingers simultaneously on your screen, making you look like Tom Cruise in *Minority Report*, if you have the bucks for expensive devices with Multi-Touch displays and the right application software. But for the rest of us, the mouse remains the input device of choice.

The best way to get the feel for a new mouse? Play one of the games that ships with Windows 11. Click the start icon, All Apps, and then Microsoft Solitaire Collection. Just realize that Microsoft will charge you for ad-free versions of their apps. In Figure 1-13, I'm playing a game of traditional Klondike, the type of game you think of when someone says "Solitaire."

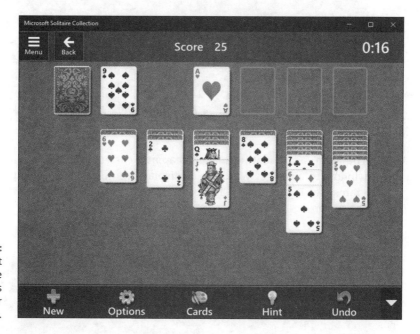

**FIGURE 1-13:** The Microsoft Solitaire Collection is great for mouse practice.

Try clicking in unlikely places, double-clicking, and right-clicking. I bet you'll discover several wrinkles, even if you're an old hand at the games.

## Snapping app windows

Windows 11 includes several gesture features that can save you lots of time. Foremost among them is a window docking capability called *snap*.

**REMEMBER**

If you click the title bar of a window and drag the window all the way to the left side of the screen, as soon as the mouse hits the edge of the screen, Windows 11 resizes the window so that it occupies the left half of the screen, docking it to the left edge. The same happens for the right side. Now it's two-drag easy to put a Word document and an Excel spreadsheet side by side or a list of files from File Explorer alongside your Solitaire game, as shown in Figure 1-14.

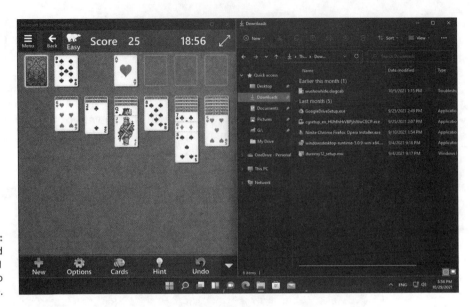

**FIGURE 1-14:**
Two drags and
Windows 11
arranges two
apps side by side.

The Snap Assist feature makes snapping easier than ever. If you snap one app window to an edge, Windows 11 displays thumbnails of all other running programs (see Figure 1-15). Click or tap a window, and it occupies the vacant part of the screen.

**FIGURE 1-15:**
Snap Assist
helps you put
two windows
side by side.

**TIP**

You can also drag to the corners of the screen and snap four app windows into the four corners. All these snapping features are controlled in the Settings app. Click or tap the start icon, Settings, System, and then Multitasking. You see all the settings for snapping app windows.

These aren't the only navigation tricks. If you drag a window to the top of the screen, it's *maximized*, so it occupies the entire screen. (Yeah, I know: You always did that by double-clicking the title bar.) And, if you click a window's title bar and shake it with the mouse (or your finger), all other windows on the screen move out of the way: They *minimize* themselves as icons on the taskbar.

**REMEMBER**

If you have rodent phobia, you can do the mouse tricks explained in this section by instead pressing the following key combinations:

>> **Snap left:** Windows key+left arrow

>> **Snap right:** Windows key+right arrow

>> **Maximize:** Windows key+up arrow

## Configuring the mouse

If you're left-handed, you can interchange the actions of the left and right mouse buttons — that is, you can tell Windows 11 that it should treat the left mouse button as though it were the right button and treat the right button as though it were the left. You can also reduce the mouse pointer speed (useful when you're older or not able to utilize your Windows computer normally), change how scrolling works, and so on.

To find all your mouse settings, do the following:

**1.** Click or tap the start icon and then Settings.

**2.** On the left of the Settings window, select Bluetooth & Devices.

**3.** On the right, click or tap Mouse.

The mouse settings appear, as shown in Figure 1-16.

**4.** Change the mouse settings that interest you, and then click or tap X to close Settings.

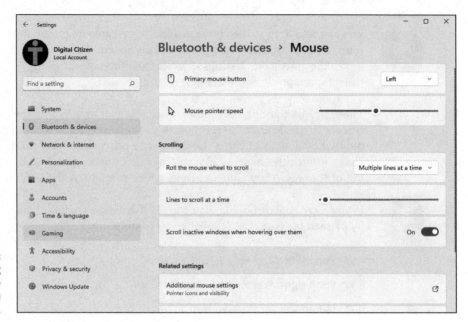

**FIGURE 1-16:**
Configuring
how your mouse
works makes you
more productive.

## Setting up the trackpad

Most laptops come with a trackpad. And premium ones come with precision touchpads that enable you to do all kinds of gestures, even with three of four fingers, that perform actions such as switching between apps and desktops. Whether or not you like using a touchpad, it's useful to know how to turn the touchpad on and off as well as where to find all touchpad-related settings:

1. **Click or tap the start icon and then Settings.**

2. **On the left of the Settings window, select Bluetooth & Devices.**

3. **On the right, click or tap Touchpad.**

   You see all touchpad settings, as shown in Figure 1-17. The settings you see depends on your laptop model and its touchpad's capabilities.

4. **To disable the touchpad, set its switch off.**

5. **If you keep the touchpad on, feel free to adjust the cursor speed and all the settings available for it.**

6. **To close Settings, click or tap X.**

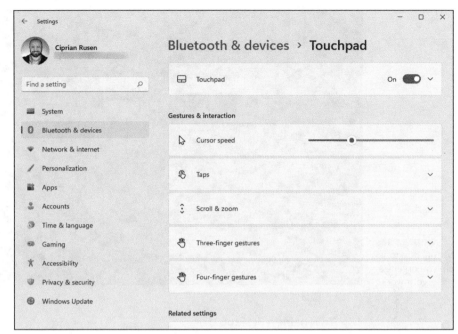

**FIGURE 1-17:**
Here you enable
or disable the
touchpad and
adjust its settings.

# Using Virtual Desktops

Just like Windows 10, Windows 11 can work with multiple desktops in parallel. One desktop can display your work, another your games, another your social media, and so on. Each desktop can have a specific name and desktop background, and you can switch between them with ease. Microsoft calls this useful feature *virtual desktops*.

To use virtual desktops, you first need to create ones, like this:

1.  **Click or tap the task view icon (shown in the margin) on the taskbar.**

    Task view displays the apps you have open and any desktops you've created, as shown in Figure 1-18. The current desktop is Desktop 1.

2.  **To create a virtual desktop, tap or click New Desktop +.**

    Desktop 2 is added to the list, at the bottom of task view.

3.  **Click or tap Desktop 2 to open it.**

    Note that the new virtual desktop is empty and has no running apps.

**FIGURE 1-18:**
Virtual desktops
help you organize
your work.

4. **To rename a desktop**

    a. *Click or tap the task view icon.*

    b. *Right-click (or tap and hold down on) the desktop you want and then choose Rename from the contextual menu.*

    c. *Type a name for the virtual desktop. Press Enter or click or tap outside the list of virtual desktops.*

**TIP**

In task view, if you right-click the name of a virtual desktop, you see the Choose Background option. You can then change the wallpaper for only that desktop, making it easier to tell them apart.

## Moving apps between virtual desktops

For virtual desktops to be useful, you need to be able to move apps between them. Here's how to do it:

1. **Create two virtual desktops, as shown in the preceding section.**

2. **Open Microsoft Edge by clicking or tapping its icon on the taskbar.**

3. **Click or tap the task view icon on the taskbar.**

    Task view is shown with the Microsoft Edge window in the middle.

4. **Right-click or tap and hold down on the Microsoft Edge app preview in task view.**

   The contextual menu shown in Figure 1-19 appears.

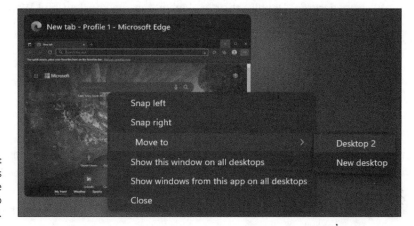

**FIGURE 1-19:**
Moving apps
from one
desktop to
another is easy.

5. **Choose Move To, and then click or tap the name of the desktop you want to move the window to.**

   The Microsoft Edge window is moved to the virtual desktop you chose.

6. **Click or tap the name of the desktop where you moved Microsoft Edge.**

   Note how the Microsoft Edge window moved to the virtual desktop you selected.

REMEMBER

This trick works with all apps and games, not just those made by Microsoft.

# Managing Icons and Shortcuts

When you first use Windows 11, you should see only one or two icons on the desktop: the Recycle Bin and perhaps Microsoft Edge. However, as you use Windows 11, you may want to add more shortcuts to your favorite apps, documents that you're working on, games, websites, and so on. In this section, I show you how to create shortcuts on the desktop and arrange them, and then tell you the basics about using the Recycle Bin.

# Creating shortcuts

Sometimes, life is easier with shortcuts. (As long as the shortcuts work, anyway.) So, too, in the world of Windows, where shortcuts point to things such as files, apps, or web pages. You can set up a shortcut to a Word document and put it on your desktop. Double-click or double-tap the shortcut and Word starts with the document loaded, as if you double-clicked or double-tapped the document in File Explorer.

You can set up shortcuts that point to the following items:

>> Windows programs and apps of any kind

>> Web addresses, such as www.dummies.com

>> Documents, spreadsheets, databases, PowerPoint presentations, and anything else that can be started in File Explorer by double-clicking or double-tapping

>> Folders (including the weird folders inside digital cameras and the Fonts folder)

>> Drives (hard drives, Blu-ray drives, and USB drives, for example)

>> Other computers on your network, and drives and folders on those computers, as long they're shared

>> Printers (including printers attached to other computers on your network), scanners, cameras, and other pieces of hardware

You have many different ways to create shortcuts. One way to create shortcuts to files and folders is from File Explorer, like this:

1. **Click or tap the File Explorer icon on the taskbar to open it.**

2. **Navigate to a file for which you want a shortcut, and right-click or tap and hold down on it.**

   You see a contextual menu with a few options.

3. **In the menu, choose Show More Options.**

   The old-school right-click menu from Windows 10 loads, as shown in Figure 1-20.

4. **Choose Send To and then Desktop (Create Shortcut).**

   A shortcut to your file is placed on the desktop.

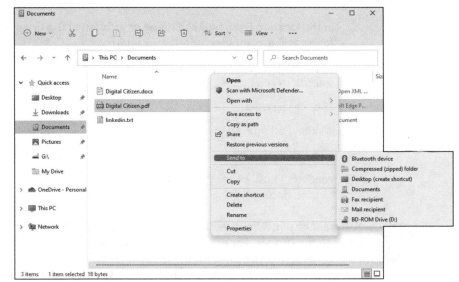

**FIGURE 1-20:**
The old right-click
menu is hidden
in Windows 11.

If you want to create shortcuts for other things, such as websites, shared folders, or computers on your network, use a more general-purpose method:

**1.** **Right-click or tap and hold down on a blank area on the desktop and choose New ⇨ Shortcut.**

The Create Shortcut wizard appears, as shown in Figure 1-21.

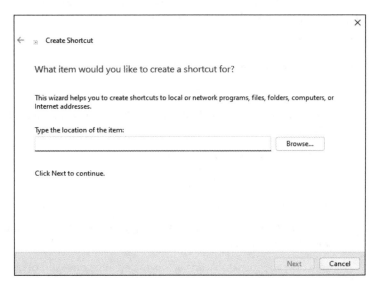

**FIGURE 1-21:**
Create shortcuts
the old-fashioned
manual way.

**2.** **In the location field, type the name or location of the program, file, folder, drive, computer, or internet address.**

You can also click or tap Browse, and then choose the item you want the shortcut to point to.

**3.** **Click or tap Next.**

Windows asks for a name for the shortcut.

**4.** **Give the shortcut a memorable name and click or tap Finish.**

Windows 11 places an icon for the program, file, folder, drive, computer, website, document — whatever — on the desktop.

**TECHNICAL STUFF**

Believe it or not, Windows thrives on shortcuts. They're everywhere, lurking just beneath the surface. For example, every entry on the Start menu is a (cleverly disguised) shortcut. The icons on the taskbar are all shortcuts. Most of File Explorer is based on shortcuts — although they're hidden where you can't reach them. Even the Windows 11 app icons work with shortcuts. So don't be afraid to experiment with shortcuts. In the worst-case scenario, you can always delete them. Doing so gets rid of the shortcut; it doesn't touch the original file that the shortcut pointed to.

## Arranging icons on the desktop

You can change the position of the icons on your desktop by dragging them with the mouse, your laptop's touchpad, or your finger (if you use a device with a touchscreen). Simply drag and drop any icon around the desktop and it will remain there.

However, if you're not happy with the icon's size or alignment, you can change it as follows:

**1.** **Right-click or tap and hold down on a blank area on the desktop and choose View.**

The options shown in Figure 1-22 appear.

**2.** **Choose an icon size (large, medium, or small).**

The change is applied immediately.

**3.** **To arrange the icons on your desktop a bit, repeat Step 1 and choose Auto Arrange Icons.**

Note how your desktop icons are arranged into some sort of order.

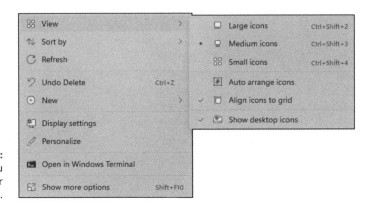

**FIGURE 1-22:**
Choose how you
want to view your
desktop icons.

# The Recycle Bin

The Recycle Bin is a special folder with a trash can icon that stores deleted files and folders. When you delete items from your computer or device, they're not removed permanently. Instead, they're moved to the Recycle Bin. Windows does this as a precaution in case you deleted something by mistake or later discover that you need a certain discarded file or folder.

Physically, deleted files continue to occupy the same space as before on your hard drive(s). However, once an item is deleted, you can't see it in the same location on your system and Windows displays it in the Recycle Bin. The Recycle Bin keeps the references to deleted files and folders, until they're permanently removed from your PC. Each hard drive in your computer has a Recycle Bin, but all the files you delete are displayed in this one folder on your desktop, represented by the trash can icon. If nothing has been deleted, the icon looks like an empty trash can. If at least one file or folder is deleted, the trash can becomes full, as shown in Figure 1-23.

**REMEMBER**

To completely remove all your deleted files, right-click or tap and hold down on the Recycle Bin icon on the desktop and then choose Empty Recycle Bin.

If you want to recover a deleted file, open the Recycle Bin, right-click (or tap and hold down on) the file, and choose Restore. You see the file in its initial location. This command can be used at any time, as long as you didn't empty the Recycle Bin. You can also drag a file from the Recycle Bin to another folder on your computer, rather than restoring it to its original location.

**FIGURE 1-23:**
Go to the
Recycle Bin to
find deleted files
and folders.

# Chapter **2**

# Personalizing the Start Menu

When it comes to the desktop, Windows 11 copied the approach used by Apple on the Mac. As a result, the Start menu and the taskbar are centered and the icons on the taskbar behave in a similar way as those on the Mac. I like this new approach, and I especially like the new Start menu, which is organized differently than it was in Windows 10, with new sections and items. Gone are the tiles from Windows 10, and back are the classic shortcuts from Windows 7. Hooray, right?

In this chapter, I give you a tour of the Windows 11 Start menu, explain how it's organized, and show you how to navigate it. You also find out how to personalize the different sections, add and remove folders, and align the Start menu to the left, like it was in older versions of Windows.

# Touring the Start Menu

The first thing you see when you click or tap the start icon is the Start menu shown in Figure 2-1. It is Microsoft's first centered Start menu in a Windows operating system, and it looks a lot different than the one in Windows 10.

**FIGURE 2-1:**
The normal mouse-and-keyboard version of the Start menu, in Windows 11.

Here's how the Start menu is organized:

» The top side of the Start menu contains a Search box that you can use to find anything from installed apps to settings to files or websites on the internet.

» Next is the Pinned section, which includes three rows of shortcuts to installed apps. These shortcuts are automatically set up by Windows 11, but you can personalize the list. Windows defaults to 18 shortcuts, but you can have more than the default (as I do in the figure). To navigate to the next screen of shortcuts, click or tap one of the dots to the right of the Pinned section.

» Just above the Pinned list, on the top right, you see the All Apps button. A click or tap on it opens a list of all the apps in Windows 11, as shown in Figure 2-2. Note the Back button, which, well, takes you back to the Start menu.

» Next is the Recommended section, which contains recently added apps, your most-used apps, and recently opened items. If you have more apps and items than can fit on the screen, you'll see a More button to the right of the section. Click or tap it to open a longer list filled with the same type of items.

>> The bottom of the Start menu has your username and picture on the left and the power icon on the right.

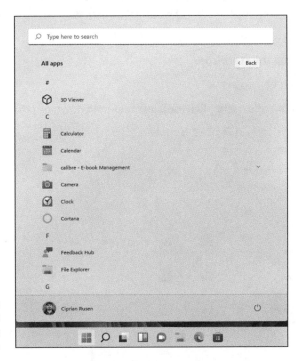

**FIGURE 2-2:**
The All Apps list
displayed by the
Start menu.

**REMEMBER**

An interesting but frustrating aspect about the Windows 11 Start menu is that it can't be resized like the one in Windows 10. You're stuck with its default size and sections.

The tiles you grew accustomed to in Windows 10 are gone from Windows 11 because most people didn't use them. I find the new Start menu a lot more useful and refreshing. Don't you?

# Modifying the Start Menu

You can customize many things about the Windows 11 Start menu. Let's take each option, one by one, and see how to personalize it to your liking.

# Adding, moving and removing pinned apps

The first thing you may want to do with the Start menu is remove the pinned app shortcuts you don't want, pin shortcuts to apps that you use regularly, and change the position of pinned shortcuts. The process involved is quite simple. Here's how it works:

**1.** **Click or tap the start icon.**

The Start menu opens.

**2.** **To unpin an app, right-click (or press and hold down on) the app shortcut.**

The menu shown in Figure 2-3 appears.

**FIGURE 2-3:**
Removing a
pinned app from
the Start menu.

**3.** **Click or tap Unpin from Start.**

The shortcut is no longer pinned, and another takes its place.

**4.** **Click or tap the All Apps button.**

You see a list with all the apps installed in Windows 11.

**5.** **To pin an app, scroll down the list of apps and right-click (or press and hold down on) the app.**

The menu shown in Figure 2-4 appears.

**6.** **Choose Pin to Start.**

The app is pinned to the Start menu.

**7.** **Click or tap the Back button to see the app in the Pinned list.**

**FIGURE 2-4:**
Pinning an app to
the Start menu.

**TIP**

If you don't see the app you just pinned in the Pinned section of the Start menu, it was added to the end of the list. Use the dots on the right side of the Pinned section to navigate to it. You will surely find the app.

**TIP**

To move a pinned app to the top of the list, drag it around with the mouse or your finger, if you have a touchscreen. You can also right-click (or press and hold down on) its shortcut in the Pinned section and choose Move to Top. The shortcut will now be the first in the Pinned section.

# Changing your picture

Another easy change to the Start menu is to swap out your picture in the bottom left.

Here's how to change your picture:

1. **Open the Start menu, tap or click your picture, and then select Change Account Settings.**

   Windows 11 takes you to the Settings app, where you can edit your information, as shown in Figure 2-5.

2. **If you already have a picture in mind, follow these steps:**

   a. *Next to Choose a File, click or tap Browse Files and navigate to the picture.*

   b. *Select the picture, and tap or click Choose Picture.* You return to the screen shown in Figure 2-5, with your new picture in place.

3. **If you'd rather take a picture with your computer's webcam:**

   a. *Comb your hair, pluck your eyebrows, and tap or click Open Camera (in that order).*

   b. *In the Camera app window, tap or click the Take Photo button, and confirm that you're happy with the picture by tapping or clicking Done.*

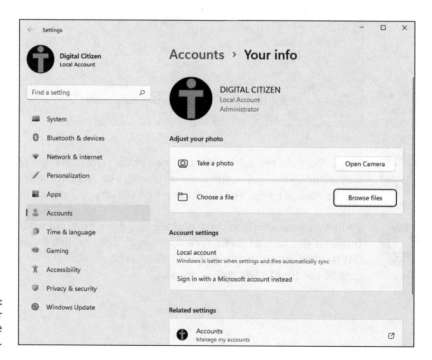

**FIGURE 2-5:** Change your picture in the Settings app.

Your new picture takes effect immediately — no need to click OK or anything of the sort.

**TIP**

Want a weird picture? Any picture you can find on the internet and download to your computer is fair game — as long as you're not violating any copyrights.

## Personalizing the Recommended section

By default, Windows 11 shows your recently added apps and opened items in the Recommended section of the Start menu. It can also show your most-used apps there too. Here's how to customize the Recommended section:

1. **Open the Start menu and click or tap Settings.**

2. **On the left side of the Settings app, choose Personalization.**

   You see a long list of settings on the right.

3. **Scroll down and click or tap Start.**

   The Start menu settings appear, as shown in Figure 2-6.

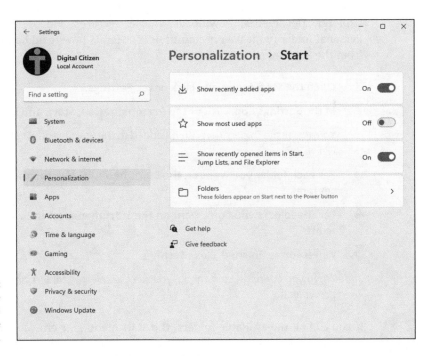

**FIGURE 2-6:**
Configuring the Recommended section of the Start menu.

4. **Depending on what you want, set the following switches on or off:**

- *Show Recently Added Apps:* Generally, it's useful to keep this setting enabled because you can quickly start recently added apps.

- *Show Most Used Apps:* Windows analyzes the apps that you frequently use and displays them in the Start menu.

- *Show Recently Opened Items in Start, Jump Lists, and File Explorer:* This setting affects all Windows 11 apps that can display recently opened items, not only the Start menu. For example, File Explorer is also affected by whether or not you enable this setting.

5. **When you're done, close Settings.**

   There's no Save button to press. The next time you open the Start menu, the *Recommended* section will display only the items you enabled.

## Adding and removing Start menu folders

By default, the bottom-right corner of the Windows 11 Start menu displays only the power icon. However, you can add several folders next to it to serve as quick shortcuts to places you visit frequently. You can add shortcuts to Settings, File Explorer, Documents, Downloads, Music, Pictures, Videos, Network, and the Personal folder (your user account folder). Here's how to add and remove folders from the Start menu:

1. **Open the Start menu and click or tap Settings.**

2. **In the Settings app, click or tap Personalization, Start, and then Folders.**

   You see all the folders that can be added to the Start menu, as shown in Figure 2-7.

3. **For each folder you want on the Start menu, click or tap the switch to set it on.**

4. **For the folders you don't want on the Start menu, set their switches to off.**

5. **When you're finished, close Settings.**

   When you open the Start menu, you see the selected folders next to the power icon.

**TIP**

If you add all the available folders, the Start menu gets crowded, making it difficult to tell each one apart. Therefore, it's best to enable only the folders you visit frequently, such as Documents, Downloads, Pictures, and Settings.

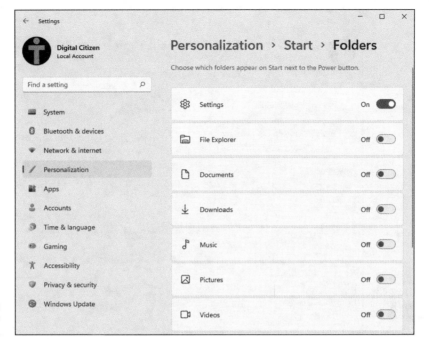

**FIGURE 2-7:**
Adding folders to
the Start menu.

# Moving the Start menu and taskbar to the left

In Windows 11, the taskbar and the Start menu are centered. This is different from Windows 10 and older versions of Windows, and you may want a more familiar setup, with everything aligned to the left side of the screen. Here's how to change the position of the taskbar and Start menu:

**1.** **Open the Start menu and click or tap Settings.**

**2.** **In the Settings app, click or tap Personalization and then Taskbar.**

The taskbar personalization options shown in Figure 2-8 appear.

**3.** **Scroll down to Taskbar Behaviors and click or tap this section.**

The section extends, as shown in Figure 2-9.

**4.** **Click or tap Taskbar Alignment and choose Left.**

Both the taskbar and the Start menu are now aligned to the left side of the screen.

**TIP**

I like the centered placement for the taskbar and the Start menu. I tried to go back to the classic, left-aligned placement, but gave up after a couple of minutes. If you want to return to the new layout too, choose Center in Step 4.

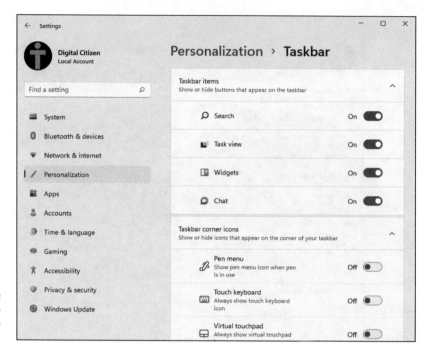

**FIGURE 2-8:**
Here is where
you personalize
the taskbar.

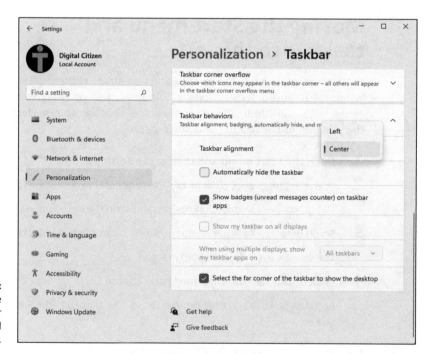

**FIGURE 2-9:**
Choosing the
alignment for
the taskbar and
the Start menu.

# Chapter **3**

# Exploring Search and the Taskbar

I n Chapters 1 and 2 of this minibook, you learn about the desktop and the Start menu: how they look, how they work, and how to personalize them. Now it's time to learn how to search for stuff in Windows 11, and how to use the operating system's search feature to quickly start apps. It's a pretty neat feature, and I use it regularly. Although Windows Search is fast, it doesn't search through everything on your computer. That can be changed, though, as you learn in this chapter.

Then you have the taskbar. It's sitting there on your desktop, and it helps you open the Start menu and your favorite apps. In Windows 11, the taskbar has undergone many changes, not all for the better. In this chapter, you discover the basics about how it works and some nifty tricks that will make you more productive. Lastly, you'll see how to pin the apps you want and remove the icons you don't want on your taskbar.

# Searching in Windows 11

Windows Search has been around for more than 15 years, starting with the ancient Windows Vista. It has evolved and matured over the years, and the latest iteration in Windows 11 is simpler, faster, and more efficient than previous versions. In this operating system, Windows Search can help you find apps, settings, documents, photos, emails, files, folders, and web results from several locations: your computer, the Bing search engine, OneDrive, OneNote, SharePoint, Outlook, and Mail.

To open Search in Windows 11, click or tap its icon, which is next to the Windows logo, or press Windows+S on the keyboard. You see the Windows Search window, as shown in Figure 3-1.

**FIGURE 3-1:**
Windows Search helps you find what you need.

The Windows 11 Search window has many useful links and settings. Starting from the top, the Type Here to Search field and the filters below it (All, Apps, Documents, Web, and More) can be used to restrict your searches. Next is Top Apps, a brief list of Windows 11 apps that you use the most. Finally, you have Recent, a list of your most recently accessed items. For users in the US, UK, and other countries, the Search window also displays the Quick Searches section next to Recent. These are powered by Microsoft's Bing search engine.

Here's the basics of how Search works in Windows 11:

1. **Click or tap the search icon on the taskbar.**

   Windows 11 displays the Search page (refer to Figure 3-1).

2. **Type** terminal **or another keyword for something you want to find on your computer or device.**

   The search results shown in Figure 3-2 appear. Note how the search results are split into several categories. First you see Best Match (the result that Windows 11 assumes is what you want), then Settings, Search the Web results, Photos, and so on.

**FIGURE 3-2:** Search results are presented in various categories.

3. **Look at the panel to the right of the Best Match result, and note the contextual options displayed. To extend the list, click or tap the downward-pointing arrow.**

   The list expands as shown in Figure 3-3, and includes even more options for what you can do with the Best Match result.

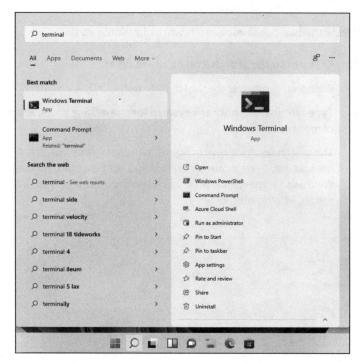

**FIGURE 3-3:**
Note how
many things you
can do with a
search result.

4. **To see more information about another search result, click or tap the right arrow next to it.**

   You see the contextual options for that result.

5. **Click or tap the Windows Terminal result (under Best Match) or the search result that interests you.**

   Search opens the result you've selected.

## Searching is the fastest way to start apps

If you pin apps to the Windows 11 taskbar, you can start them quickly, with a simple click or tap on their icon. However, pinning too many items on the taskbar makes it annoying to use. Luckily, you can use Windows Search to start any app you want in seconds. Here's how it works:

1. **Press the Windows key on your computer's keyboard.**

   The Start menu opens. This step may seem odd, but it will make sense in a moment.

2. **Type the name of the app you want to open. To follow along with the example, type** edge.

Windows Search displays Microsoft Edge as the Best Match, as shown in Figure 3-4. As you see, you don't have to type the full name of an app for Search to find it.

3. **Press Enter on your keyboard, and Microsoft Edge opens immediately.**

Repeat Steps 1 to 3 with other keywords for apps you want to start. This will train Windows Search to remember your searches and always provide the appropriate Best Match.

**FIGURE 3-4:**
After you press the Windows key, you can start searching for stuff in Windows 11.

**TIP**

Note how both the Start menu and the Windows 11 Search window have a Type Here to Search box at the top. You can use it to start searches from both places. Also, as you've seen, after you open the Start menu or the Search window you can also start a search by typing a keyword.

# Filtering search results to find what you need

You can do many things with search results in Windows 11, some more useful than others. For example, you might be looking for a setting that's buried inside the Windows 11 Settings app. To find what you want more quickly, you can use the filters in Windows Search. Here's how it works:

1. **Press the Windows key on your computer's keyboard or tap the search icon on the taskbar.**

2. **Type the word** mouse.

   Windows Search displays search results split by categories: Best Match, Settings, Search the Web, and so on.

3. **In the top-right corner of the Search window, click or tap More.**

   The search filters shown in Figure 3-5 appear.

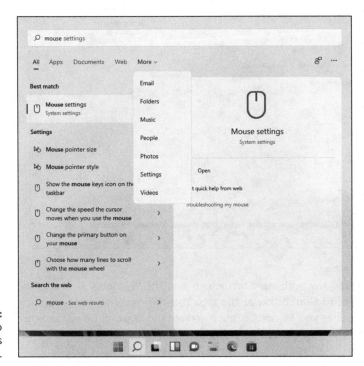

**FIGURE 3-5:**
Don't be afraid to use the Windows Search filters.

4. **In the filters list, select Settings.**

Note how Windows Search changes your search results to include all mouse-related settings, both from the Settings app and Control Panel.

5. **Click or tap the search result that interests you.**

The mouse setting you selected is shown on the screen.

REMEMBER

Using the filters in Windows Search helps you fine-tune the results you get, so that it's easier to find what you want. Don't hesitate to try them out.

## Starting apps as admin from a Windows search

By default, apps run in Windows 11 with standard permissions, meaning that they can't change operating system files and settings. Few people know that you can start apps with administrative permissions from Windows Search, not just the Start menu. This allows apps to make all the changes they want. Let's assume that you want to start PowerShell as an administrator. Here's what you must do:

1. **Press the Windows key on your computer's keyboard or tap the search icon on the taskbar.**

2. **Type the word** powershell.

Windows Search displays search results split by categories: Best Match, Apps, Settings, and Search the Web, as shown in Figure 3-6.

3. **To the right of the Windows PowerShell search result, click or tap Run as Administrator.**

Windows 11 asks if you want to allow this app to make changes to your device. These changes can be anything, from modifying system files to changing Windows settings.

4. **Click or tap Yes.**

Windows PowerShell opens with administrator permissions.

TECHNICAL STUFF

This procedure works for starting any desktop program with administrator permissions. You can't do this for Windows 11 apps designed for tablets and touchscreens, which can run only with standard permissions.

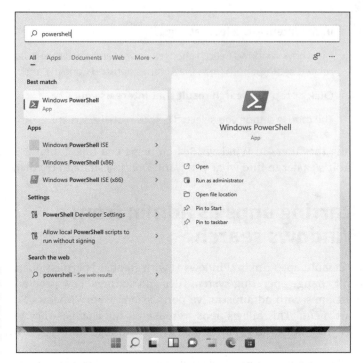

**FIGURE 3-6:**
For each search
result, you
have several
contextual
actions to
its right.

## Searching your entire PC

When it comes to searching for files and folders on your Windows 11 computer or device, Windows Search looks in only a few places, such as your user folders, the desktop, and the Start menu. If you have a computer with several partitions, it doesn't look on your other drives. However, you can set it to do so, like this:

1. **Click or tap the search icon on the taskbar.**

2. **In the Search window, click or tap the three dots in the top-right corner.**

   The menu shown in Figure 3-7 appears.

3. **In the menu, choose Indexing Options.**

   The Searching Windows page appears, as shown in Figure 3-8. At the top is Indexing Status, with how many files were indexed by Windows Search and how many are still pending.

4. **If you have a laptop or tablet, turn on the Respect Power Settings When Indexing switch by clicking or tapping it.**

   This action ensures that when your device is not plugged in, Windows Search is not busy indexing too many files and eating up your battery power.

**FIGURE 3-7:**
Accessing
indexing
options.

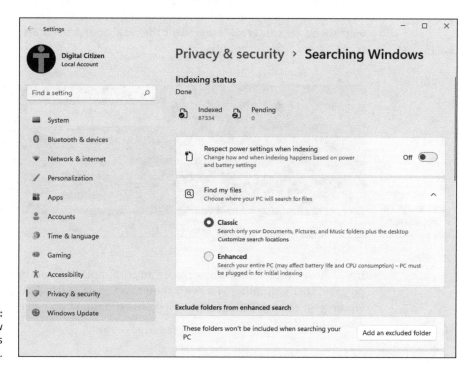

**FIGURE 3-8:**
Changing how
Windows
Search works.

5. **Under Find My Files, select Enhanced instead of Classic.**

    Windows Search will now index all the files on your PC, from all partitions, so that it can provide you with complete search results. See the progress of the indexing process in the Indexing Status section at the top of the window.

6. **Close Settings.**

    Indexing may take several hours, so don't expect to see any meaningful changes in your search results minutes after you've enabled this setting.

# Touring the Windows 11 Taskbar

Microsoft developers working on the old Windows 7 taskbar gave it a secret internal project name: the Superbar. Although one might debate how much of the *Super* in the taskbar is real, there's no doubt that the Windows 11 taskbar is a key tool for all users.

The Windows 11 taskbar is placed on the bottom of the screen, with several icons in the middle, as shown in Figure 3-9. One key difference is that it is no longer left aligned, as it was in Windows 10 and Windows 7. Microsoft has copied another page from Apple's workbook, and both the Windows 11 taskbar and the Start menu are centered. If you want the taskbar and the Start menu left aligned, read Chapter 2 in this minibook.

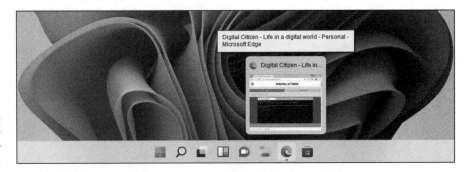

**FIGURE 3-9:**
The taskbar juggles many different tasks.

If you hover your mouse cursor over an icon, and the icon is associated with a program that's running, you see a thumbnail of what it's doing. For example, in Figure 3-9, Microsoft Edge is running, and the thumbnail gives you a preview of what's on offer.

**WARNING**

The Windows 11 taskbar is a lot less flexible than in Windows 10. For example, you can no longer change its size and location. It's stuck on the bottom of the screen no matter what. Also, the toolbars are gone, so you can't add any. I bet many people will dislike this a lot, and I hope Microsoft will soon change its course and bring back all the things we loved about the taskbar.

## Using the taskbar

The taskbar consists of two kinds of icons:

>> **Pinned icons:** Windows 11 ships with eight icons on the taskbar, one each for Start, Search, Task View, Widgets, Chat, File Explorer, Microsoft Edge, and the Microsoft Store. (Refer to the bottom of Figure 3-9.) When you install a program, you can tell the installer to put an icon for the program on the taskbar. You can also pin programs of your choice on the taskbar.

>> **Icons associated with running apps and programs:** Every time a program starts, an icon for it appears on the taskbar. If you run three copies of the program, only one icon shows up. When the program stops, the icon disappears.

To run a program from the taskbar, click or tap its icon. You can tell which icons represent running apps or programs because Windows 11 puts an almost imperceptible line under the icon for any running program. If a running app is minimized, the line below its taskbar icon gets smaller. If you have more than one copy of the program running, you see two transparent squares surrounding the taskbar icon. It's subtle. In Figure 3-9, Microsoft Edge has a line under its taskbar icon.

## Using jump lists and other taskbar tricks

If you right-click an icon on the taskbar or press and hold down on it, whether or not the icon is pinned, you see a bunch of links called a *jump list*, as shown in Figure 3-10.

The contents of the jump list vary depending on the program that's running, but the bottom pane of every jump list contains the name of the program and the entry Unpin from Taskbar (or conversely, Pin to Taskbar, if the program is running but hasn't been pinned).

Jump lists were new in Windows 7, and they haven't taken off universally. Implementation of jump lists ranges from downright obsessive (such as Microsoft Edge) to lackadaisical for many applications that aren't made by Microsoft.

**FIGURE 3-10:**
The jump list for
File Explorer.

Here are the jump list basics:

>> **Jump lists may show your frequent folders or files or the file history
of recently opened files.** For example, the File Explorer jump list shown in
Figure 3-10 displays the same Frequent list that appears inside the app. The
Paint jump list, which is shown in Figure 3-11, displays the Recent Files list
found in the app.

>> **It's generally easy to pin an item to the jump list.** When you pin an item,
it sticks to a program's jump list whether or not that item is open. To pin an
item, run your mouse cursor to the right of the item you want to pin and click
or tap the pushpin that appears. The item is now in a separate Pinned pane at
the top of the jump list.

>> **The jump list has one not-so-obvious use.** It lets you open a second copy
of the same app. Suppose you want to copy a handful of documents from the
Documents folder to a USB memory stick with the drive letter D:. Start by
clicking or tapping the File Explorer icon on the taskbar, and then clicking or
tapping Documents, on the left. You can select your documents, press Ctrl+C
to copy, use the list on the left of File Explorer to navigate to D:, and then
press Ctrl+V to paste. But if you're going to copy many documents, it's much
faster and easier to open a second copy of File Explorer and navigate to D: in
that second window. Then you can select and drag your documents from the
Documents folder to the D: drive.

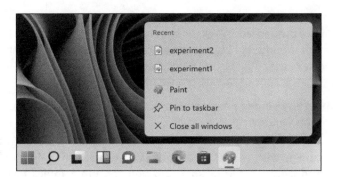

**FIGURE 3-11:**
Paint's jump list
shows recently
opened images.

TIP

To open a second copy of a running program without using the jump list, you can also

>> Hold down the Shift key and click or tap the program's icon on the taskbar.

>> Right-click the program's icon (or press and hold down on the icon, perhaps with a nudge upward), and choose the program's name.

In either case, Windows 11 starts a fresh copy of the program.

TIP

I've also discovered a few tricks with the taskbar that you may find worthwhile:

>> When you want to shut down all (or most) running programs, you can tell which are running by seeing whether their taskbar icon has an underline (refer to Figure 3-9). To close all instances of a particular program, right-click or press and hold down on its icon and choose Close Window or Close All Windows. Sometimes, if a program is frozen and won't shut itself down, forcing the matter through the taskbar is the easiest way to dislodge it.

>> Windows 11 minimizes all open windows when you move your mouse cursor to the lower-right corner and click or tap. Click or tap again, and Windows 11 brings back all minimized windows.

## Pinning apps to the taskbar

You can do several things to the taskbar:

>> **Pin a program on the taskbar:** Right-click or tap and hold down on the program and choose Pin to Taskbar. You can right-click the icon of a running program on the taskbar or its shortcut on the Start menu, the desktop, and other places.

Exploring Search and
the Taskbar

- » **Move a pinned icon:** Click (or tap) and drag the icon. Easy. You know, the way it's supposed to be. You can even drag an icon that isn't pinned into the middle of the pinned icons. When the program associated with the icon stops, the icon disappears, and all pinned icons move back into place.

- » **Unpin any pinned program:** Right-click or tap and hold down on the icon and choose Unpin from Taskbar.

Unfortunately, with a few exceptions, you can't turn individual documents or folders into icons on the taskbar. But you can pin a folder to the File Explorer jump list, and you can pin a document to the jump list for whichever application is associated with it. For example, you can pin a document to the jump list for Word.

Here's how to pin an app to the Windows 11 taskbar:

**1.** **Click or tap the start icon and then All Apps.**

You see a list with all the apps installed in Windows 11.

**2.** **Scroll down the All Apps list until you see the program you want to pin to the taskbar, and right-click or tap and hold down on it.**

A contextual menu appears, as shown in Figure 3-12.

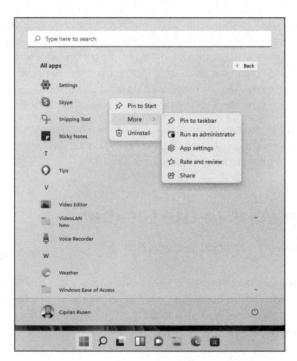

**FIGURE 3-12:**
Pinning apps to
the taskbar is a
no-brainer.

**3.** In the menu, choose More⇨Pin to Taskbar.

That's all it takes. The app's icon appears on the taskbar, and you can use it to quick launch the app.

# Adding and removing taskbar items

You can enable or disable some of the standard icons on the Windows 11 taskbar. And, if you have a tablet or a touchscreen, you might want to add icons for the pen menu, touch keyboard, or virtual touchpad. Here's how to add icons to and remove icons from the taskbar:

**1.** Right-click or press and hold down somewhere on the empty space on the taskbar and choose Taskbar Settings.

You see the settings for personalizing the taskbar, as shown in Figure 3-13.

**2.** Under Taskbar Items, turn off the switches of the icons you want to remove from the taskbar.

To change a switch from On to Off, click or tap it. If you don't use the Widgets or Chat, it's a good idea to disable their icons.

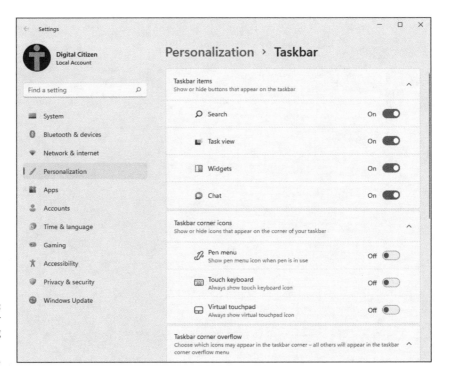

**FIGURE 3-13:**
Enabling or disabling Windows 11 taskbar icons.

3.  **If you have a tablet or a touchscreen, under Taskbar Corner Icons, enable the icons that you want to see in the right corner of the taskbar.**

    You can choose Pen Menu (useful only if you have a pen), Touch Keyboard (works well with all touchscreens), and Virtual Touchpad.

4.  **When you've finished, close Settings by clicking or tapping X in the top-right corner.**

    Your settings are applied immediately.

Chapter **4**

# Working with Files and Folders

ile Explorer and the right-click menu have received a major redesign in Windows 11. Compared to Windows 10, they look simpler and are easier to use. However, this does mean that you may feel lost for a time, until you get the hang of it.

To help you out, I give you a tour of all the basics you need to know about File Explorer: how to navigate it, view, open, and create files and folders, search for the stuff you need, sort and group files and folders as you like, and personalize the Quick Access section.

I also share some useful tricks on how to make File Explorer always display the extensions of your files, how to add check boxes that are useful for selecting stuff, and how to make File Explorer show hidden files.

Then, I cover the new ways of sharing items in Windows 11, and how to handle ZIP archives. Lastly, I cover the changes introduced by Microsoft to the right-click menu, and how to access the old one when you need to.

# Using File Explorer

The File Explorer app from Windows 11 includes many changes. The ribbon is gone, in favor of a more minimalist user interface, with icons for the most common actions shown on the top, as shown in Figure 4-1.

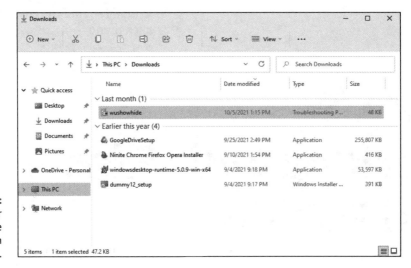

**FIGURE 4-1:**
The File Explorer user interface changed in Windows 11.

I prefer the new File Explorer to the old, and I think most people will like it too. However, there's a learning curve to get used to the latest version, so this section takes you through most of the significant changes to help you make sense of things.

## Navigating File Explorer

First, you should know how to start and navigate the File Explorer app in Windows 11. Here's a quick tour:

1.  **Click or tap the File Explorer icon on the taskbar, or open the Start menu and choose File Explorer.**

    The File Explorer app window appears, as shown in Figure 4-2. The app starts by displaying its Quick Access section, which includes shortcuts to useful places like the desktop, the Downloads folder, and your recent files.

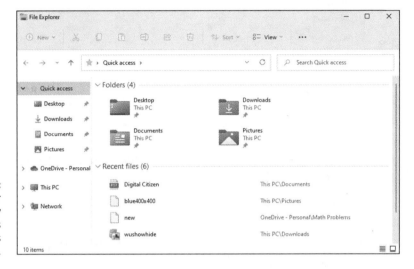

**FIGURE 4-2:**
File Explorer
starts by
displaying its
Quick Access
section.

2.  **On the left, in the column with shortcuts to places you can navigate on your computer, click or tap This PC.**

    You see your user folders (Desktop, Documents, Downloads, Music, Pictures, and Videos), and your devices and drives.

3.  **In the Devices and Drives section, double-click or double-tap the C: drive.**

    The files and folders on your C: drive are displayed.

4.  **To go back to the previous location, click or tap the back arrow in the top-left corner of File Explorer.**

5.  **To see the contents of the C: drive again, as in Step 3, click or tap the forward arrow (next to the back arrow).**

    Note how the address bar next to the back and forward arrows changes to display the current path, as shown in Figure 4-3. You can use the address bar in File Explorer to jump to a specific location.

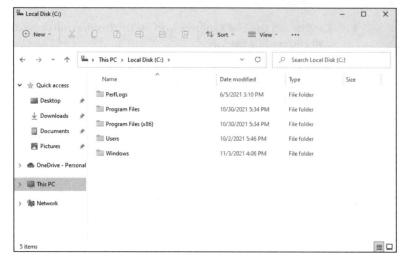

**FIGURE 4-3:**
Use the address
bar and the
arrows at the top
to quickly jump
between folders
and locations.

**6. To see how the address bar works, click or tap This PC in the address bar, not in the column on the left.**

You can do this with any folder or location displayed in File Explorer's address bar. This is a quick way to navigate your computer.

**7. To close File Explorer, click or tap the X in the top-right corner.**

You return to the desktop.

**TIP**

You can use the address bar in File Explorer to quickly run commands. For example, you can navigate to a folder you want, click or tap inside the address bar, type **cmd**, and press Enter on your keyboard. This runs Command Prompt using the current folder in File Explorer.

## Viewing and opening your file and folders

As you noticed in the preceding section, if you want to open one of the places shown on the left side of the File Explorer app window, you just click or tap its name. However, if you want to open a folder or a file shown on the right, you must double-click or double-tap. The double-click or double-tap applies to everything from folders to drives and partitions to files.

When you double-click (or double-tap) a file, it opens the file in the app set by Windows to open that file's type. For example, if you double-click a picture, it will open in the Photos app. If you double-click a PDF file, it will open in Microsoft Edge or Adobe Reader, depending on which app is set to open PDF files. Similarly, if you double-click a document, it will open in Microsoft Word, and so on.

By default, when you open a folder such as Downloads on your Windows 11 PC, File Explorer shows you the files and subfolders inside, as shown in Figure 4-4. For each file, you see its icon, name, date modified, type, and size. For each subfolder, you see its icon, name, and date modified.

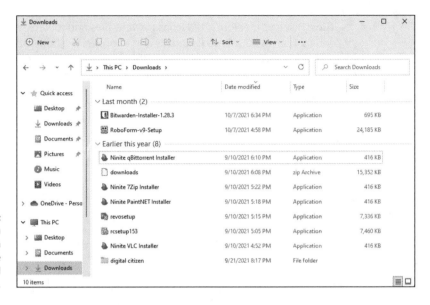

**FIGURE 4-4:** When you double-click a folder, you see its files and subfolders.

Depending on how the folders are set, they can show you more or less information about the files found inside. File Explorer applies different views to your folders, based on their content. For example, File Explorer applies the details view to your Downloads folder, but the large icons view to your Pictures folder. The menu in Figure 4-5 lists the views available in File Explorer:

>> **Extra Large Icons:** Offers the best previews of graphic and video files, and I recommend this view for pictures, media files, and PowerPoint presentations.

>> **Large Icons:** Useful when you want to see your photos without opening them. While its thumbnails are not as big as the ones you get with the extra-large icons view, they're larger compared to the other views.

>> **Medium Icons:** Displays thumbnails large enough to give you an idea about the content of media items but not big enough to distinguish among several similar graphics files. You're better off using the two previous views.

>> **Small Icons:** Displays items in columns with no thumbnails. The icons next to your files differ based on their type.

>> **List:** Displays just the filenames and the icons. Your files and folders are displayed as small icons, which makes it nearly indistinguishable from the small icons view.

>> **Details:** Provides detailed information about your files and folders, split by columns.

>> **Tiles:** Displays medium-sized icons for your files and folders, as well as basic details. Use it to display thumbnails and information about the type and size of your files. While not as detailed as the content and details views, the tiles layout is a useful mix between the medium icons and content views.

>> **Content:** Lists files and folders on separate rows. For each item you see details such as type, size, date modified, dimensions, and authors. This layout is a mix between the tiles and details views, although its thumbnails are slightly smaller than those used by the tiles view.

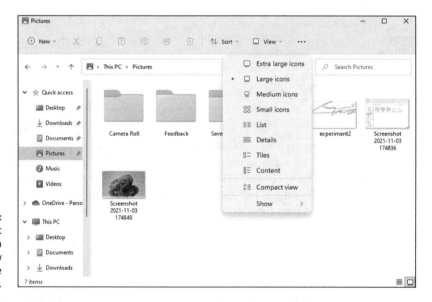

**FIGURE 4-5:**
The different ways in which you can view your files in File Explorer.

Here's how to switch between the views available in File Explorer:

1. **Click or tap the File Explorer icon on the taskbar, or click or tap the start icon and then File Explorer.**

2. **Click or tap your Pictures folder on the left.**

   You see all the subfolders in your Pictures folder, as well as all your pictures.

3. **At the top of the screen, click or tap View.**

   A menu appears with all available File Explorer views (refer to Figure 4-5). For your Pictures folder, the default view is large icons.

4. **Select Extra Large Icons in the View menu.**

   Note the change in the way your pictures are displayed. This view is useful for previewing the contents of multimedia files such as pictures and videos.

5. **Click or tap View and select List.**

   See how the list view differs from the extra-large icons view, displaying only the icon and name of each file and folder.

6. **Click or tap View and select Content.**

   Note how this view is different from the previous ones.

7. **Click or tap View and select Large Icons.**

   You return to the initial view of the contents of your Pictures folder.

TIP

You can switch between the different views using keyboard shortcuts too. Press Ctrl+ Shift+1 for extra-large icons, Ctrl+Shift+2 for large icons, up to Ctrl+Shift+8 for content view.

## Creating and managing files and folders

The toolbar at the top of File Explorer makes it easy to work with files and folders in Windows 11. The New icon opens a menu for creating new folders, shortcuts, and files, as shown in Figure 4-6.

To the right of the New icon, you have icons for cut, copy, paste, rename, share, and delete. If you don't select anything, these icons aren't active and appear dimmed. If you select a file or folder with a click or tap its name, these icons become usable. Here's how to use them:

1. **Start File Explorer and then click or tap your Pictures folder.**

2. **In the top-left corner of File Explorer, click or tap New.**

   You see the New menu (refer to Figure 4-6).

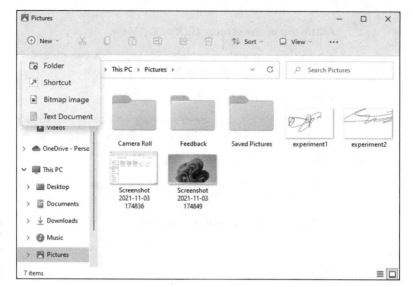

**FIGURE 4-6:**
Use the New
menu to create
folders, shortcuts,
and files.

3. **In the menu, choose Folder.**

   A new folder is created, waiting for you to edit its name, as shown in Figure 4-7.

4. **Type the name you want for the new folder and press Enter.**

5. **With that folder still selected, click or tap the rename icon at the top.**

   The rename icon is the fourth icon after the New icon. The folder's name becomes editable, and you can type a new name.

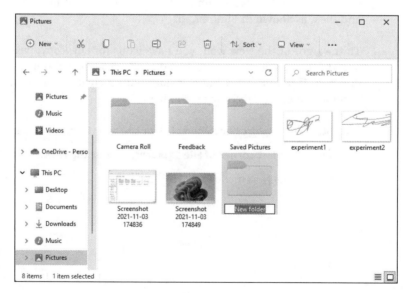

**FIGURE 4-7:**
Renaming folders
and files is easy.

6. **Type a new name and press Enter.**

7. **With that folder still selected, click or tap the delete icon (trash can) at the top.**

   The folder is deleted immediately, without any confirmation. You can find it in the Recycle Bin, on your desktop.

REMEMBER

You can always undo your previous action (delete, cut, paste, rename, and so on) by pressing Ctrl+Z.

TIP

You create files the same way you create folders. The only difference is that in Step 3, choose Bitmap Image or Text Document, depending on the type of file you want to create. When it's created, the file is empty and you can add content to it by opening it, editing it, and then saving it.

## Searching for files

One of the most useful features of File Explorer is search. If you want to find anything, use the Search box on the top right, like this:

1. **Start File Explorer and then open the partition (drive) or the folder where you want to find stuff.**

2. **In the top-right corner of File Explorer, click or tap in the Search box.**

3. **Type the name or partial name of the file or folder you want to find, and press Enter or click or tap the arrow.**

   After a few seconds, your search results are displayed, as shown in Figure 4-8.

4. **Double-click or double-tap the item you want to open.**

REMEMBER

The Search box in File Explorer searches only for items in the folder or location you're currently in. This approach narrows the search and returns your results faster. However, it's not helpful when you have no idea about the location of the item you're looking for. For example, if you search for a file in your Documents folder but the file is in your Downloads folder, you won't find it because you searched in the wrong place. If you don't have an idea about the location of a file, simply open the C: drive and make a search starting from there. Be warned that searching your entire C: drive will take much longer than using a specific folder.

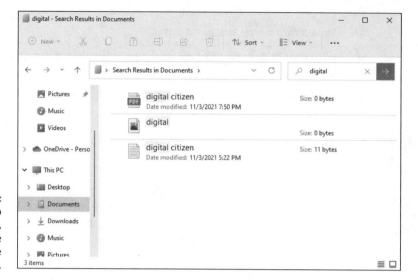

# Sorting and grouping files and folders

By default, File Explorer sorts your files and folders in ascending order by name (alphabetically), except for the items in the Downloads folder, which is sorted in descending order by date modified, with the newest downloads displayed at the top. Windows has approximately 300 sorting criteria to help you organize things, but most people need only the basics.

In addition to sorting files and folders, you can also group them. When using grouping, File Explorer organizes all the items in a folder, breaking them into separate sections, based on criteria you choose (name, size, date, and so on.) By default, items are not grouped in any way.

To familiarize yourself with how sorting and grouping work, do the following:

**1.** **Start File Explorer and then open a folder with lots of files.**

The Downloads folder might be an excellent choice.

**2.** **At the top of the screen, click or tap the Sort icon.**

The menu shown in Figure 4-9 appears. It includes the sorting and grouping options available in File Explorer.

**3.** **In the Sort menu, choose Type.**

Note how your files and folders are reorganized by type.

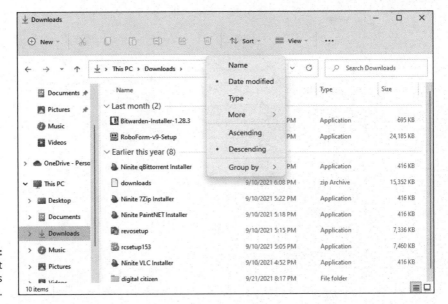

**FIGURE 4-9:**
The default
sorting options
in File Explorer.

4. **To change the order, click or tap Sort again, and choose Ascending or Descending.**

   Everything in the current folder is sorted again, based on the order you selected.

5. **To group items, click or tap Sort and then Group By.**

   The grouping options shown in Figure 4-10 appear.

6. **In the Group By menu, choose the grouping criteria you want.**

   For example, if you want to quickly identify the largest files, choose Size. The items inside your folder are grouped immediately. If you chose Size, you see the largest files in the current folder first.

## Displaying file extensions

A file, or filename extension, is a suffix at the end of a file on your computer. It comes after the period and is usually two to four characters long (for example, archive.7z, textfile.txt, picture.jpeg, or document.docx). Most files have extensions, and if you've opened a document or viewed a picture, you've probably noticed similar suffixes at the end of its name.

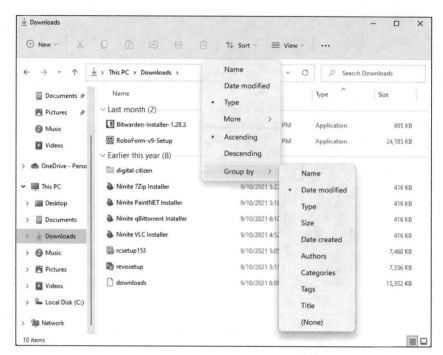

**FIGURE 4-10:**
Grouping items can be useful too.

Windows uses the file extension to identify the app associated with the file. It then uses that app to open the file. When you double-click or double-tap a file in Windows, the operating system looks for the app associated with its file extension, opens that app, and then loads the file in that app. For example, PNG or JPEG files are opened by the Photos app, .xlsx files are opened by Excel, PDF files are opened by Microsoft Edge or Adobe Reader, and so on.

By default, file Explorer doesn't display the extension of your files. For example, you don't see that Word documents have the file extension .doc or docx. Therefore, when you view a file named document.docx in File Explorer, you don't see the .docx part at the end. This is not necessarily a problem unless you're dealing with malware. Malicious files use this behavior of Windows to hide their real file extension. Therefore, you might end up with a file named document.docx.exe, but File Explorer displays only document.docx, without the .exe part at the end, which is the real file extension. When you double-click or double-tap the file, it's executed automatically, instead of opening in Word. If the virus is smart enough, the moment you run the file, your computer is infected.

To avoid such problems, you can set File Explorer to always display the file extension of all files:

**1.** **Click or tap the File Explorer icon on the taskbar, or click or tap the start icon and then File Explorer.**

**2.** **Click or tap the View icon.**

The View menu shown in Figure 4-11 appears.

**3.** **In the View menu, choose Show ⇨ File Name Extensions.**

File Explorer displays the file extension for all your files.

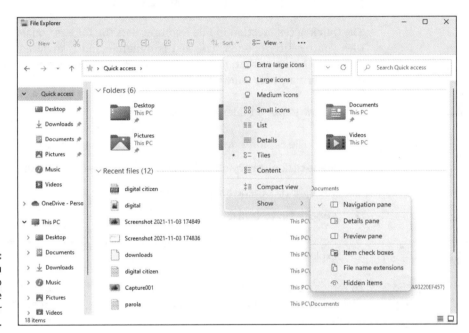

**FIGURE 4-11:**
The View menu enables you to display file extensions for all your files.

TIP

To learn more about securing Windows 11 against viruses, read Book 9, Chapter 2.

# Viewing hidden files

By default, File Explorer displays only files and folders that are not marked as hidden. The files you create as user are never marked as hidden and are always visible. The same happens with the files created by most apps. However, Windows itself, device drivers, and some apps may create files that are marked as hidden and cannot be seen when you browse your computer with File Explorer.

Luckily, you can set File Explorer to display all files and folders, including hidden ones, like this:

1. **Click or tap the File Explorer icon on the taskbar or click or tap the start icon and then File Explorer.**

2. **Click or tap the View icon, and then choose Show ⇨ Hidden Items.**

   File Explorer now displays hidden files too.

## Pinning items to and removing items from Quick Access

The Quick Access section in File Explorer lists the folders you use the most and the files you recently opened. This list is dynamic and is updated as different items are used. On top of that, you can also pin to Quick Access any folder you want, to have it permanently shown.

Here's how to pin a folder to Quick Access:

1. **Start File Explorer and then navigate to the folder you're interested in.**

2. **Right-click or tap and hold down on the name of the folder.**

   The right-click menu appears, as shown in Figure 4-12.

3. **Choose Pin to Quick Access.**

   Note how the folder is added immediately to the Quick Access section of File Explorer.

TIP

To remove a folder from Quick Access, navigate to the Quick Access section, right-click (or tap and hold down on) the folder's name, and choose Unpin from Quick Access.

## Enabling and disabling check boxes for files and folders

If you have a Windows 11 laptop or tablet with a touchscreen, you'll notice that all files and folder icons in File Explorer have a check box that becomes visible when you hover over them with the mouse cursor (or your finger) or when you click or tap them, as shown in Figure 4-13. This check box is useful when you want to select multiple items and then perform actions such as deleting them or copying them to another location.

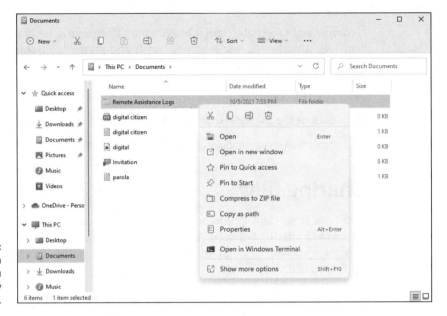

**FIGURE 4-12:**
Right-clicking a folder gives you access to many useful options.

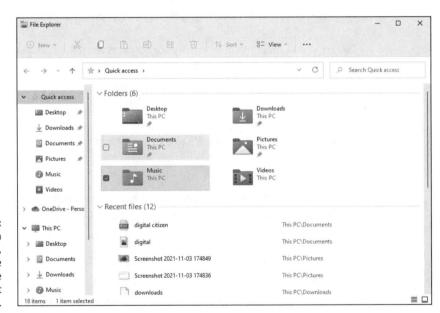

**FIGURE 4-13:**
On devices with touchscreens, items in File Explorer have a check box next to them.

You may want to enable check boxes on a PC without a touchscreen because you consider it useful. Or you may not like it and prefer to disable it. Both are done using the same procedure:

1. **Start File Explorer.**

2. **Click or tap the View icon and then choose Show ⇨ Item Check Boxes.**

   If this feature was initially enabled, it will be disabled and vice versa.

## Sharing files

Windows 11 no longer promotes the concept of home networks and the old way of network sharing between your computers. Instead, it focuses on the cloud and promotes sharing through other means: OneDrive, Mail, OneNote, and the other apps installed in Windows.

If you're navigating your OneDrive folders and files, sharing works as detailed in Book 4, Chapter 5. If you're browsing other parts of your computer that are not linked to OneDrive, the sharing options you get are limited to those in Figure 4-14:

» Email a Contact: You can email your contacts from the People app. Read Book 4, Chapter 2 for details.

» Share with App: You can share with your Windows apps, such as OneNote or Mail.

Here's how to share a file that's not in your OneDrive folder:

1. **Start File Explorer.**

2. **Navigate to the file you want to share, which is not stored in your OneDrive folder. Select the file by clicking or tapping its name.**

3. **Click or tap the share icon at the top of the File Explorer window.**

   The share icon is to the left of the trash can icon. You see the Share pop-up (refer to Figure 4-14).

4. **Choose the contact or the app you want to use for sharing.**

5. **If you selected to send the file by email, click or tap Send.**

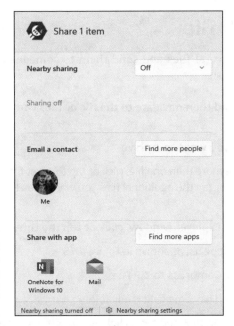

**FIGURE 4-14:**
Sharing in Windows 11 is quite different from Windows 7 or Windows 8.

# Working with ZIP Files

A ZIP file is an archive that contains one or more files and folders. The concept of archiving files by combining them into one file and compressing the space used in the process was born in the early years of the internet, when reducing the space used by a file was a big deal, resulting in many minutes saved in transferring files over slow dial-up internet connections. The ZIP file, and the high-performance compression that it enabled, received widespread support because its specifications were made public so that anyone could create apps to work with ZIP files.

Windows 11 can natively work with ZIP files, so you don't have to install a third-party app such as 7-Zip or WinRAR. However, Windows can't work with other types of file archives such as RAR or 7z, while specialized third-party apps can. For most people, this isn't a problem because they use only ZIP files to archive stuff.

# Creating a ZIP file

If you want to archive several files and send them to someone else in a ZIP file archive, follow these steps:

**1.** **Start File Explorer and then navigate to the file or files you're interested in archiving.**

**2.** **Click or tap the file you want to archive.**

If you need to archive more than one file, click or tap the first file, hold down the Ctrl key, and click or tap the additional files you want to include in your selection.

**3.** **At the top of the File Explorer window, click or tap the three dots icon.**

The See More menu appears, as shown in Figure 4-15.

**4.** **In the menu, choose Compress to ZIP File.**

A ZIP file is created, and its name field is editable.

**5.** **Type a name for the ZIP file, and then click or tap outside its name.**

You can then cut and paste the ZIP file where you want or use the sharing options described in the "Sharing files" section to send the ZIP file to someone.

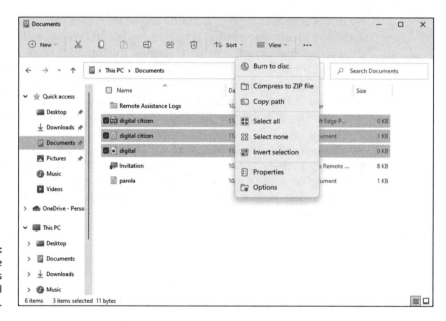

**FIGURE 4-15:** Clicking the three dots icon reveals an additional menu.

# Extracting a ZIP file

If you have received a ZIP file and want to see its contents, you can double-click or double-tap it, and it opens in File Explorer like a folder. If you want to extract its contents, do the following:.

**1.** **Start File Explorer and then double-click or double-tap the ZIP file to open it.**

You see the files inside the ZIP file, as shown in Figure 4-16.

**2.** **At the top of the window, click or tap the Extract All icon.**

The Extract Compressed (Zipped) Folders wizard appears, as shown in Figure 4-17.

**3.** **Choose the location where you want to extract the contents of the ZIP file and then click or tap Extract.**

The contents of the ZIP file are extracted and displayed in a separate File Explorer window.

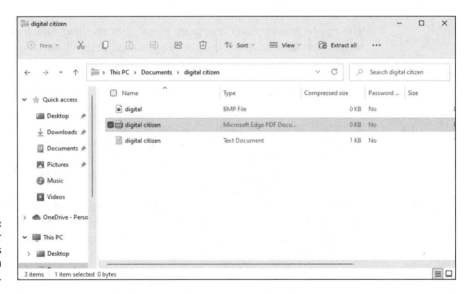

**FIGURE 4-16:** File Explorer can open ZIP files and show you what's inside.

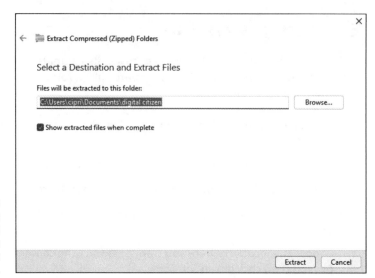

**FIGURE 4-17:**
The Extract
Compressed
(Zipped) Folders
wizard is quick
and simple.

# Right-Clicking in Windows 11

The right-click menu is a pop-up menu that provides shortcuts for actions you might want to take. You access it by pressing the right button on your mouse once or, if you're using a touchscreen, by pressing and holding down on the item for which you want the menu. Because the action list changes depending on the item that you right-click (or tap and hold down on), it's also called a contextual menu.

The problem with the right-click menu is that, over time, it has become increasingly difficult to navigate, especially on systems with lots of installed applications. This is because many apps add their respective action shortcuts to this menu. As a result, the most-used commands (cut, copy, paste, and so on) are far from the mouse pointer when you right-click, the menu is difficult to use, and the menu doesn't increase the speed at which you do things, as it was originally intended. Because of these issues, Microsoft decided to redesign the right-click menu in Windows 11. Look at Figure 4-18 to see how it looks when you right-click (or tap and hold down on) a file in File Explorer.

As you can see, the new right-click menu is less cluttered than in Windows 10 or Windows 8. It has a cool new ribbon with icons, close to the position of your mouse cursor (or finger). The ribbon contains the simplest and most common actions, such as cut, copy, rename, share, and delete.

Below the ribbon is a list of contextual actions, which vary based on the right-clicked item. This section is consistent and contiguous, as opposed to Windows 10, where the actions would sometimes be separated or split up.

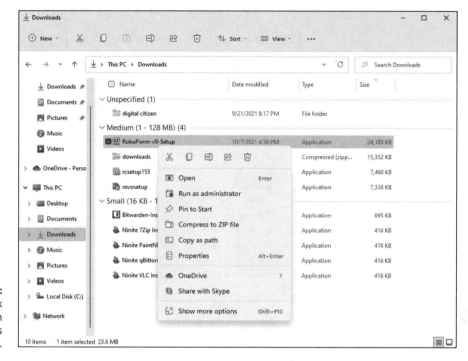

**FIGURE 4-18:**
The right-click menu in Windows 11 has been redesigned.

To keep the right-click menu simpler and more productive in Windows 11, Microsoft enforces stricter rules for the apps that want to add their own actions and sections. This, in theory, should make right-clicking (or tapping and holding down) more useful than it was in older versions of Windows.

The old right-click menu is not completely gone from Windows 11, just hidden. You need to perform an additional action to access it, like this:

**1.** **Start File Explorer and right-click or tap and hold down on a file.**

The right-click menu appears (refer to Figure 4-18).

**2.** **In the menu, choose Show More Options.**

The old right-click menu appears, as shown in Figure 4-19.

**3.** **Click or tap the option that you want to use from the old right-click menu.**

TIP

This trick works on the desktop too, not just in File Explorer. If you don't see the option you want in the new right-click menu, choose Show More Options.

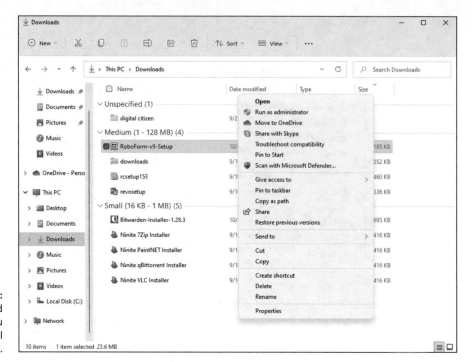

**FIGURE 4-19:**
The old
right-click menu
is one additional
click away.

Chapter **5**

# Connecting to the Internet and Browsing the Web

No PC or device in the world is truly useful if it's not connected to the internet. How else can you check someone else's Facebook profile or Twitter feed? Or, on a more serious note, how else can you find a new job or work remotely in these pandemic times?

As you see in this chapter, connecting to the internet is not rocket science. Plug a network cable into your PC and into your home router or connect to Wi-Fi on your Windows 11 laptop and — *bam!* — you're online.

Then you need a web browser. Microsoft wants you to use Edge, which isn't a bad browser even though Microsoft makes it. Other than the company that developed it, Edge has nothing in common with ill-famed Internet Explorer, which plagued the web for too many years. I like Edge more than Google Chrome, and you might enjoy using it too. In this chapter, I give you the basics about using Edge. By the end of the chapter, you might decide to stick with Microsoft Edge instead of trying another browser.

However, if you decide that you want to switch, the sad news is that Microsoft makes it hard to do so. This is one of the biggest annoyances in Windows 11, and for good reason. Don't fret, though. Read this chapter to its end, and you'll see how to switch from Edge to Chrome, Firefox, or Opera.

# Connecting to the Internet

To use the internet, you first must be connected to a network that is, in turn, connected to the internet. At home, a wireless router handles this task for you. At work, the network setup is a lot more complex, involving several routers, network switches, servers, and so on. However, to keep things simple, remember this: If you want internet access, you must connect to a network. If you use a desktop PC, you probably need to use a cable to connect it to a network. If you're using a laptop or a tablet, Wi-Fi is the way to go.

## Connecting a desktop PC to the network

If you have a desktop PC and want to browse the internet, you need to connect the PC to your home router or your company's network. Most desktop PCs don't have a wireless network card, but they do have an Ethernet port on the back that you can use to connect them to a network. Plug one end of the network cable into the Ethernet port on the back of your PC, and plug the other in one of the empty ports on the back of your home router (see Figure 5-1) or office network switch.

**FIGURE 5-1:**
Desktop PCs can be connected to the network using Ethernet cables.

After you connect your desktop PC to the network, note how the network icon appears next to the time and date, in the bottom-right corner of the desktop. Before connecting, the icon was a small globe with a disconnected sign on it. Now it's shaped like a PC with a network cable next to it. If you hover your mouse cursor over it, you see the text *Network Internet Access,* as shown in Figure 5-2.

**FIGURE 5-2:**
Your desktop PC is connected to the network and the internet.

Your PC is connected to the network and the internet. You can then fire up Microsoft Edge (see its section later in this chapter) and browse the web.

## Connecting your laptop or tablet to Wi-Fi

If you have a laptop or a tablet with Windows 11, you must connect it to Wi-Fi before you can go online. The process for doing this isn't rocket science, but it does take slightly longer than it did in Windows 10. Here's how it works:

**1.** **Click or tap the globe icon (internet or network) in the bottom-right corner of the desktop or press Windows+A on the keyboard.**

The Quick Settings panel appears, as shown in Figure 5-3.

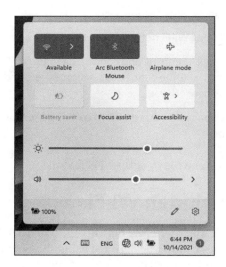

**FIGURE 5-3:**
First check whether the Wi-Fi icon appears dimmed.

2. **If the Wi-Fi icon in the Quick Settings panel is dimmed, click or tap it to activate the Wi-Fi chip on your laptop or tablet.**

3. **Click or tap the right arrow (>) next to the Wi-Fi icon.**

   Windows 11 displays the list of Wi-Fi networks available in your area.

4. **Locate the network you want to connect to and click or tap its name.**

   The options shown in Figure 5-4 appear.

**FIGURE 5-4:**
Choose your Wi-Fi
network and
connect to it.

5. **Select the box next to Connect Automatically and click or tap Connect.**

   You're asked to enter the network security key.

6. **Type the password of your Wi-Fi network and then click or tap Next.**

   Windows 11 tells you that it's verifying and connecting to the Wi-Fi network you chose. If everything works well, the connection is established, and *Connected* appears below the Wi-Fi network you chose.

7. **Click or tap an empty space on your desktop to close the Quick Settings panel, and you're done.**

   You're connected to Wi-Fi and can navigate the web.

## Connecting to hidden Wi-Fi

Some people choose to hide their wireless networks. Hidden Wi-Fi networks are not truly hidden because they can still be detected using the right tools, and hackers know how to find them with ease. However, a hidden Wi-Fi doesn't broadcast its name, and most people and devices don't see it and therefore won't try to connect to it.

**REMEMBER**

If you do have a hidden Wi-Fi you want to connect to, you must know the following details before trying to connect:

>> The exact name of the network, which is case sensitive

>> The Wi-Fi connection password

After you have these details, do the following to connect to a hidden Wi-Fi from Windows 11:

**1.** **Click or tap the globe icon in the bottom-right corner of the desktop or press Windows+A on your keyboard.**

The Quick Settings panel appears (refer to Figure 5-3).

**2.** **If the Wi-Fi icon in the Quick Settings panel appears dimmed, click or tap it to activate the Wi-Fi chip on your laptop or tablet.**

**3.** **Click or tap the right arrow (>) next to the Wi-Fi icon.**

Windows 11 displays a list with the Wi-Fi networks available in your area.

**4.** **Scroll to the end of the list, and choose Hidden Network, as shown in Figure 5-5.**

**FIGURE 5-5:**
Connecting to a hidden Wi-Fi network takes a bit more work.

5. **Select the box next to Connect Automatically and then click or tap Connect.**

   You are asked to enter the network name.

6. **Type the name of the hidden network and then click or tap Next.**

7. **Type the password for connecting to the hidden Wi-Fi and then click or tap Next.**

   If everything worked okay, the connection is established, and you see the word *Connected* below the network's name.

8. **Click or tap anywhere on an empty space on your desktop to close the Quick Settings panel.**

   You're now connected to the hidden Wi-Fi.

# Using Microsoft Edge

Windows 10 included both the old Internet Explorer and the new Microsoft Edge browser. In its initial versions, Edge was developed by Microsoft using a proprietary rendering engine that was different from Firefox and Chrome, with a unique set of features. Unfortunately, it didn't gain much market share, and Microsoft decided to change its strategy to: If you can't beat them, join them! As a result, since 2019, Microsoft has switched from its separate rendering engine to Chromium, the same open-source engine used by Google Chrome and Opera.

In Windows 11, only Microsoft Edge is installed, and the new Edge is a lot better than the previous incarnations in Windows 10. Not only that, but as the code for Chromium evolves and improves (partly due to Google, and Opera), Microsoft Edge improves too, and the other way around. If that won't make for a simpler web, I don't know what will. Also, Chrome extensions work in Microsoft Edge too, so you can expand this browser with any feature you want, just like with Google Chrome.

Microsoft Edge sits front and center on the taskbar on your Windows 11 desktop. To start Edge, just click or tap its shortcut, highlighted in Figure 5-6. The same shortcut can be found on the Windows 11 Start menu too.

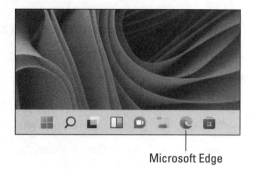

**FIGURE 5-6:**
The shortcut for
Microsoft Edge.

Microsoft Edge

## Familiarizing yourself with Microsoft Edge

Microsoft Edge works just like any other web browser, and its user interface should be familiar, especially if you've used Google Chrome. However, to make sure you feel right at home, let's go together through a tour of its user interface:

1. **Click or tap the Microsoft Edge icon on the taskbar or from the Start menu.**

   The browser loads its user interface. Look at the icons and buttons highlighted in Figure 5-7 to understand what they do.

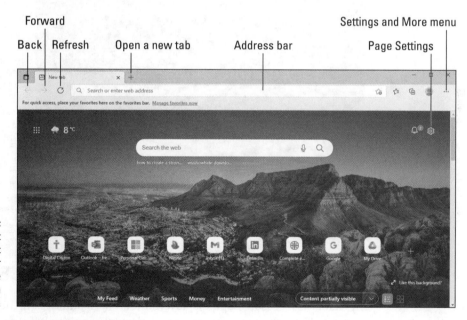

**FIGURE 5-7:**
The most
important
icons and user
interface
elements in
Microsoft Edge.

2. **In the address bar at the top, type** digitalcitizen.life **and press Enter.**

   The Digital Citizen website loads in Microsoft Edge.

3. **Click or tap + to the right of the current tab.**

   Microsoft Edge opens a new, empty tab.

4. **Click or tap the gear icon (page settings) near the top right.**

   A menu appears with several page layouts for the new tabs you open in Microsoft Edge.

5. **Switch between the available page layouts and choose the one you like.**

6. **In the address bar, type** dummies.com **and press Enter.**

7. **Click or tap the three dots icon in the top-right corner of Microsoft Edge.**

   The menu shown in Figure 5-8 appears. From this menu, you can access Edge's settings, favorites, and extensions.

8. **To close Microsoft Edge, click or tap X in the top-right corner.**

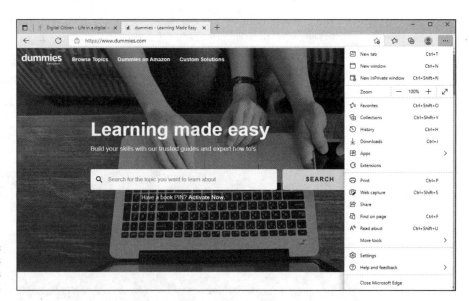

**FIGURE 5-8:** The Settings menu is quite long.

# Enabling vertical tabs in Microsoft Edge

By default, Microsoft Edge displays its tabs horizontally, on the top side of its window. However, you can also use vertical tabs, on the left side of the browser. To enable vertical tabs, do this:

1. **Click or tap the Microsoft Edge icon on the taskbar or from the Start menu.**

2. **Right-click or press and hold down on the new tab.**

   The contextual menu shown in Figure 5-9 appears.

3. **In the menu, choose Turn On Vertical Tabs.**

   Your tabs are immediately moved to the left side of Microsoft Edge.

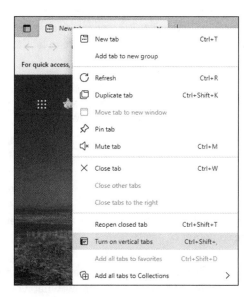

**FIGURE 5-9:**
Enabling vertical tabs in Microsoft Edge.

**TIP**

If you want the horizontal tabs back, repeat the same steps, but in Step 3, choose Turn Off Vertical Tabs. Alternatively, you can press Ctrl+Shift+, (comma) on your keyboard.

## InPrivate browsing with Microsoft Edge

InPrivate is the name given by Microsoft to Edge's private browsing mode. It provides a slightly more private way of browsing the web compared to normal web browsing. After you use InPrivate in Microsoft Edge to browse the web and close all private browsing tabs and windows, Edge does the following:

>> Deletes the cookies that were stored when using InPrivate browsing. If you log into Facebook, Gmail, YouTube, or some other website, and later close all private browsing tabs and windows, all the cookies generated by the sites you visited are deleted and you're automatically signed out. Suppose someone

else tries to visit the same websites in a new browsing window. In that case, they are not automatically logged in with your account(s). Cookies from normal browsing sessions remain as is.

>> Deletes its records of all the data you typed in forms, such as sign-up pages, login pages, and contact pages.

>> Deletes temporary files and the cache from your browsing session. When you visit a website, files such as images and styling files are downloaded to your computer or device. These files are stored on your computer for your private browsing session's duration to make browsing faster. When you close all private browsing tabs and windows, these files are deleted, so they can't be accessed and used by anyone else who knows where to look for them on the disk.

>> Deletes the browsing history from your browsing session. This way, other people with access to the same computer or device can't know what you have visited on the web just by looking at your web browser.

>> Does not store the search history from your browsing session. In all web browsers, you can search the web straight from the browser's address bar. You type some keywords, press Enter, and the keywords are sent automatically to the default search engine to return results. In regular browsing sessions, this data is stored for later reuse, to help you browse the web faster. In private browsing, this data isn't stored, so that others can't reuse it when accessing the same computer or device.

All these features enhance your privacy and confidentiality because other people who have access to the same computer don't know what you're doing online. However, private browsing doesn't mean that no one can track you. Your internet service provider still knows what you did online, as well as your network administrator, if you're at work. If you want to be private, you need to use a VPN with a strict no-logs policy. For more on that, read Book 9, Chapter 4.

If you want to browse privately with Microsoft Edge, do the following:

**1.** **Click or tap the Microsoft Edge icon on the taskbar or from the Start menu.**

**2.** **Click or tap the three dots icon in the top-right corner.**

The Settings and More menu appears.

**3.** **In the menu, choose New InPrivate window.**

You see a new InPrivate Browsing window opening, as shown in Figure 5-10.

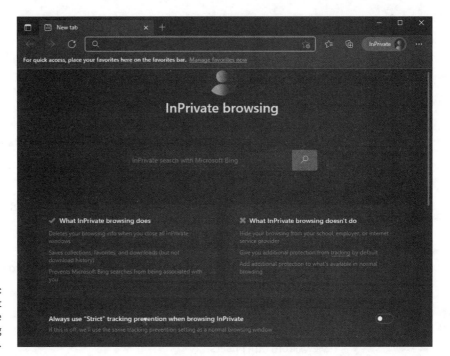

**FIGURE 5-10:**
Microsoft
Edge's InPrivate
Browsing
window.

TIP

If you want the most restrictive level of tracking prevention when using InPrivate browsing, click or tap the switch to on for Always Use "Strict" Tracking Prevention when Browsing InPrivate.

When browsing in Microsoft Edge's InPrivate window, any tab you open uses the same private browsing mode. The private browsing session ends only when you close the entire InPrivate browsing window and all its tabs.

TIP

You can open a new InPrivate browsing window by using the keyboard shortcut Ctrl+Shift+N.

REMEMBER

Few people know that you can use both normal and InPrivate browsing windows at the same time. They're separate and the cookies stored by one window don't affect the other.

## Adding extensions to Microsoft Edge

You can customize Microsoft Edge by adding the extensions or add-ons that interest you. They are a great way to modify your browsing experience and boost your overall productivity. For example, you can use Microsoft Edge extensions to add a password manager such as Bitwarden (read more in Book 9 Chapter 4), a Facebook video downloader, and an ad blocker.

Here's how to add extensions to Microsoft Edge:

1. **Start Microsoft Edge.**

2. **Click or tap the three dots icon in the top-right corner.**

   The Settings and More menu opens.

3. **In the menu, choose Extensions, and then click or tap Manage Extensions.**

   The Extensions tab opens, and you see all installed extensions, as shown in Figure 5-11.

   TIP

   If you want to install Google Chrome extensions in Microsoft Edge, click or tap the Allow Extensions from Other Stores switch.

4. **Click or tap the Get Extensions for Microsoft Edge button.**

   The Edge Add-Ons Store loads in a new tab. You can browse through the extension on the home page or search for a specific extension.

5. **Click or tap an extension you may want, such as AdBlock.**

   A page appears with screen shots and details about that extension, including reviews from other users.

6. **Click or tap the Get button, and then Add Extension.**

   The extension is installed in Microsoft Edge, and you can start using it.

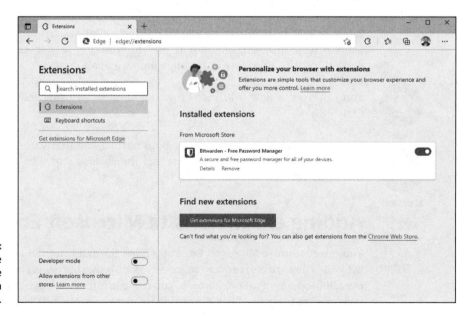

**FIGURE 5-11:**
This is where you manage extensions in Microsoft Edge.

# Using Other Web Browsers

Some people ask themselves, "Which browser is best?" Others simply don't care — and for good reason: All web browsers do the same things, with fewer differences than ever. You could stick with the Microsoft Edge browser and never miss a thing — especially because it now shares the same rendering engine as Google Chrome and Opera and can also use the same Chrome extensions.

However, here's how I view things:

» Microsoft Edge is a particularly good browser, with tons of cool features such as vertical tabs, strict private browsing, and shopping assistants. It evolves at a fast pace, and by the time this book is published, it will have some new features I haven't tested while writing it. I strongly recommend you try it before moving to another browser.

» Google Chrome is the king of web browsers mostly due to its integration with Google's services: Gmail, Google Docs, Google Drive, you name it. If you're an Android user, it makes sense to use Chrome on all your PCs and devices and have it synchronized through your Gmail account.

» Opera is another great browser I used to use before migrating to the new Microsoft Edge. It uses the same rendering engine as Edge and Chrome, and it has some cool integrations with WhatsApp, Facebook, Twitter, and other services. If you want to chat or interact on social media while doing your usual web browsing in a productive manner, Opera is a smart choice. It too can use Chrome extensions.

» Mozilla Firefox has been the most loved web browser for many years, but it recently faded from the headlines and users' attention. It is not backed by any big corporation, and it is not pushed by any major platform, except Linux. It also uses its own rendering engine, which may be problematic in the future, as fewer websites will support it. While Firefox is still a great browser, I expect it to become a niche product like Opera and continue to lose market share to Microsoft Edge and Google Chrome.

# Changing the Default Browser in Windows 11

One annoying thing in Windows 11 is that Microsoft aggressively pushes its Edge browser by making it difficult to change the default web browser. I like Edge and use it daily, but this approach is not cool.

If you want to switch your default browser from Microsoft Edge to Google Chrome (or some other browser that you've installed), here's what you must do:

**1.** **Click or tap the Start icon and then Settings, or press Windows+I on your keyboard.**

Windows 11 displays the Settings app.

**2.** **On the left side of the Settings app, choose Apps. On the right, click or tap Default Apps.**

This is where you set the defaults for applications in Windows 11.

**3.** **Scroll down the list of apps on the right until you find Google Chrome. Click or tap its name.**

You see a list of all the file types and link types that can be opened by Google Chrome. At this point, the default for most of them should be set to Microsoft Edge, as shown in Figure 5-12.

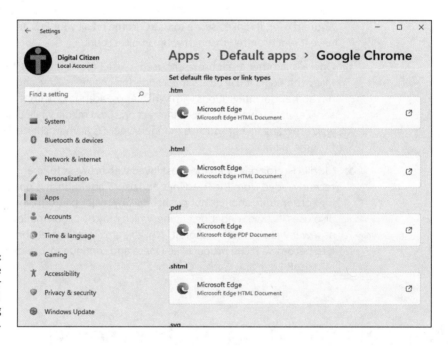

**FIGURE 5-12:**
Changing the default browser in Windows 11 is a frustrating experience.

4. **Under .htm, click or tap Microsoft Edge, Switch Anyway, Google Chrome, and then OK.**

That was annoying, wasn't it? Unfortunately, Microsoft chose to make it like this.

5. **Under .html, click or tap Microsoft Edge, Google Chrome, and then OK.**

6. **Repeat Step 5 for all entries where you see Microsoft Edge as the default instead of Google Chrome, including .pdf, .shtml, .sag, .xht, .xhtml, FTP, HTTP, and HTTPS.**

After you set Google Chrome as the default for all these entries, the browser will be your default. Your changes are applied immediately.

TIP

Follow the same procedure to set the default browser to Firefox or Opera. The only difference is that you select your browser instead of Google Chrome.

Chapter **6**

# Calling on Cortana

nitially launched on Windows Phone, back in 2014, Cortana is Microsoft's digital-assistant answer to Apple's Siri and Google's Assistant. In 2015, Cortana became available on Windows 10 and Android. Because Cortana is playing catch-up with the big guys, it hasn't helped with its adoption. Microsoft removed the Cortana app from many markets and it is now a stand-alone app for Windows. While the app still works well, Microsoft won't improve it as much as they tried in the past, and most people will continue to ignore it.

Although Cortana is not as advanced as the Google Assistant on your Android smartphone, it's worth getting to know the app. So in this chapter, I tell you all about Cortana: its backstory (it's quite cool), how to set it up, and how to use it as a virtual assistant. You also learn how to navigate its settings as well as some commands that you can use to interact with the app.

## The Cortana Backstory

Cortana is a fully developed artificial intelligence character from the video game series Halo. Cortana "lives" 500 years in the future. In the Halo series, Cortana morphs/melds into Master Chief Petty Officer John-117 and, in that position, tries to keep Halo installations from popping up all over the galaxy. Halo installations destroy all sentient life.

Cortana chose John-117, not the other way around. Cortana was supposed to be the resident AI on a ship, temporarily, but ended up the permanent AI apparently because of the deviousness of a Colonel Ackerson. It's not nice to fool Cortana, so it hacked into Ackerson's system and blackmailed him.

If that sounds a little bit like the kind of life you lead, well, you're ready for Cortana.

# Setting up Cortana

If you want to use Cortana, you need a webcam or a microphone on your Windows 11 computer or device. Make sure that it's plugged in and working. However, Cortana can be used only with a Microsoft account, a work account, or a school account. If you try to use Cortana on a local (non-Microsoft) account, it first asks you to sign in with a Microsoft account.

Here's how to set up Cortana when using a Microsoft account:

1. **Click or tap the Start icon, All Apps, and then Cortana.**

   Windows 11 displays the Cortana app, as shown in Figure 6-1.

**FIGURE 6-1:**
Time to sign in
with a Microsoft
account.

2. **Click or tap Sign In.**

3. **Choose your Microsoft account (if you're using one in Windows 11).**

4. **Click or tap Continue.**

   Cortana asks you to accept the fact that it needs to access some of your personal information to work.

5. **Click or tap Accept and Continue.**

   Cortana says "Hi" and lets you know what you need to do to use the app, as shown in Figure 6-2.

You can now use Cortana by typing text commands in its app window, or by clicking or tapping the microphone icon (in the lower right) and dictating what you want it to do. Try a first command like "What's Hello in Italian?"

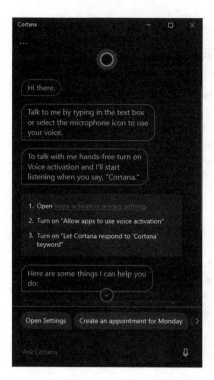

**FIGURE 6-2:**
Cortana is
ready to go.

# Turning on Voice Activation for Cortana

If you want Cortana to be as useful as it can be, you must enable voice activation in Windows 11. When you do, Cortana will listen in the background; when you say its name, it turns on and starts listening to your commands.

Here's how to set Cortana to reply when you say its name:

1. **Click or tap the Start icon and then Settings.**

   Windows 11 displays the Settings app.

2. **On the left, select Privacy & Security.**

   You see a long list of privacy and security-oriented features.

3. **On the right, scroll down to the App Permissions section, and click or tap Voice Activation.**

   Voice Activation settings appear, as shown in Figure 6-3.

4. **Click or tap the Cortana switch and set it to on.**

   Cortana is now allowed to respond to the "Cortana" keyword.

5. **Close Settings.**

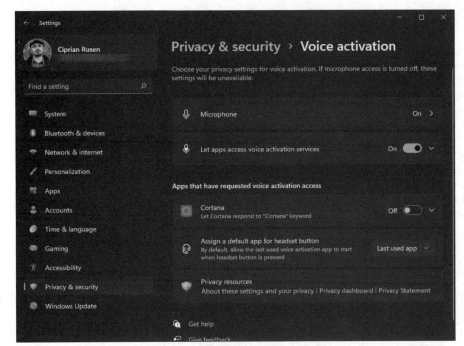

**FIGURE 6-3:**
Allowing Cortana
to reply when you
say its name.

If you want to start Cortana quickly without enabling voice activation, pin its shortcut to the taskbar. Open the Start menu, go to All Apps, right-click (or tap and hold down on) Cortana's shortcut, and choose More⇨Pin to Taskbar.

**TIP**

# Using Cortana

After you've set up Cortana, it's time to use the app. In this section, I show you how to start Cortana with the mouse and with voice commands, and how to interact with it through text and voice.

Before you proceed, make sure that you've enabled voice activation using the instructions in the preceding section. Now let's get started and use Cortana for a bit:

**1.** **Say, "Cortana."**

Cortana appears at the bottom of the screen, waiting for your command.

**2.** **Say, "Open Settings."**

Cortana launches the Settings app and replies, "I'll open Settings," as shown in Figure 6-4.

Calling on Cortana

FIGURE 6-4:
Cortana opens
Settings for you.

3. **Close Cortana by clicking or tapping the X in the top right.**

4. **Open Cortana again, this time with the mouse, by clicking or tapping the Start icon, All Apps, and then Cortana.**

   Cortana opens in a different looking window that includes the history of your previous interaction with it, as shown in Figure 6-5.

**REMEMBER**

Keep in mind that Cortana keeps a log of all your interactions with the app. Luckily, they're all displayed in the window, so there's no hidden stuff to worry about.

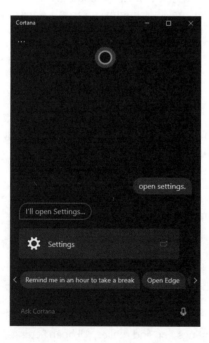

FIGURE 6-5:
Cortana keeps
your conversation
history.

5. **In the Ask Cortana field, type** Set a timer for 5 seconds **and press Enter.**

   Cortana sets and displays the timer. When it reaches 0, it starts playing an alarm sound.

6. **On the lower-right side of the screen, click or tap the Dismiss button for the timer set by Cortana.**

7. **In Cortana's app window, click or tap the microphone icon, and say, "What time is it in London?"**

   Listen to Cortana's reply.

8. **Practice asking all sorts of questions. When you're done, click or tap the X.**

   Cortana closes.

# Exploring Cortana's Settings

 To access Cortana's settings, click or tap the three dots in the top-left corner (and shown in the margin), and then click or tap Settings. You can set how you want to talk to Cortana (through typing, voice, or both) and change its permissions to access the microphone and speech (you want to give it these permissions if you want to talk to the app instead of typing).

The most interesting part is the Privacy section of Settings, shown in Figure 6-6, where you can revoke Cortana's permission to access your data (calendar, contacts, email, and so on) or clear your chat history with Cortana. You can also access the Microsoft Privacy dashboard, where Microsoft lists all the data about you stored in their cloud.

Keep in mind that turning off pieces of Cortana (say, its capability to keep track of your calendar details) deletes everything Cortana knows on this device but won't delete anything from Microsoft's servers. Give Microsoft an A for full disclosure but a D for how deep you must dig to find it.

The big Cortana off switch is in its settings: Go to the Privacy settings as just explained, and then click or tap the Revoke Permission and Sign Out button. Confirm your choice and Cortana is turned off.

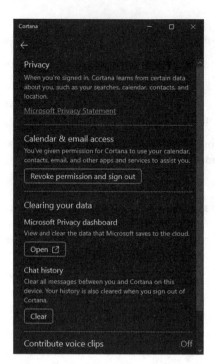

**FIGURE 6-6:**
Cortana's
settings lead
to interesting
places.

If you want to see the data that Microsoft has stored about you while using Windows 11 and Cortana, click or tap the Open button under Microsoft Privacy Dashboard in the same Privacy settings. Sign in with your Microsoft account again if you must. You get to the Privacy web page for your Microsoft account — in other words, the place Microsoft uses to store all sorts of nifty things about you, as shown in Figure 6-7.

You can see all the things that Microsoft has stored about you: your browsing history, search history, location activity, speech activity (from using Cortana), media activity, app and service activity, media activity, and more.

Spend some time looking through the types of information collected about you and click or tap Clear at will. Unfortunately, you can't see the details. But at least you can delete wide swaths of history from this web page.

**FIGURE 6-7:**
See what Microsoft knows about your activity.

# Useful or Fun Commands for Cortana

Cortana can be both useful and fun. Let's start with the fun part, and share some commands that have hilarious results:

>> Tell me a joke!

>> What's your favorite song?

>> Recite Shakespeare!

>> Can you talk like a pirate?

>> Tell me about Halo!

>> Make an impression!

>> What is the meaning of life?

>> Do you know Alexa?

>> What do you think about Google?

- » Testing!
- » Tell me an animal fact.
- » Can I borrow some money?

Leaving the jokes aside, Cortana can be a productive assistant too. Here's some of the stuff you can ask it to do:

- » **Check the weather.** "What's the weather in Tokyo?" "Is it going to rain tomorrow?"
- » **Ask questions.** "What's the tallest building in the world?" "What's the value of Apple stock?" "What's the Bitcoin exchange rate?"
- » **Check the news.** "Show me the latest news in Europe."
- » **Do math.** "What is 16 multiplied by 25?" "What is 100 by 25?"
- » **Make conversions.** "How many meters in a mile?" "How many liters in a gallon?"
- » **Define words.** "What's an epiphany?" "Define philosophy."
- » **Translate specific words.** "Translate something to Japanese."
- » **Start apps.** "Open OneNote." "Start Excel."

IN THIS CHAPTER

» **Formatting drives**

» **Freeing up storage space**

» **Checking the disk for errors**

» **Defragmenting drives**

» **Checking the system's health**

Chapter **7**

# Maintaining Your Drives

Windows 11, like all computer programs, will have problems. The trick lies in making sure that *you* don't have problems too. Windows is notorious for crashing and freezing, or garbling things so badly that you'd think the screen went through a garbage disposal. This situation is especially true when Microsoft launches a major update to Windows, which brings not only new features, apps, and improvements but also new bugs and problems. Microsoft has poured lots of time, effort, and money into teaching Windows 11 how to heal itself. You can take advantage of all that work — if you know where to find it.

While detailed troubleshooting tips are shared in Book 7, Chapter 3, this chapter is devoted to the topic of keeping the drives in your computer in tip-top shape. You learn how to free up storage space, defrag or check disks for errors, and quickly evaluate the health of your system.

If you've just bought a new PC with Windows 11, you may not need the tools presented in this chapter for a while. But when you do eventually encounter problems, you'll be glad that you've read this chapter.

# Using Maintenance Tools for Your Computer Drives

Hard drives die at the worst possible moments. A hard drive that's starting to act flaky can display all sorts of strange symptoms: everything from long pauses when you're trying to open a file to inexplicable crashes and other errors in Windows 11 itself. Windows 11 comes with a grab bag of utilities designed to help you keep your hard drives in top shape.

>> **Basic utilities:** Three simple utilities stand out as effective ways to care for your hard drives. You should get to know Check Disk, Storage Sense (an improved version of the old Disk Cleanup), and Defragment and Optimize Drives because they all come in handy in the right situation.

>> **Format utility:** When you format a data storage device (hard disk, solid-state drive, USB flash drive, and so on), you're preparing it for initial use. The process involves setting up a file system for the storage device and removing any data found on it.

>> **Storage Spaces:** This utility keeps a duplicate copy of every file in hot standby, in case a hard drive breaks down. But to use Storage Spaces effectively, you need at least three hard drives and twice as much hard drive space as you have data. Not everyone can afford that. Not everyone wants to dig into the nitty-gritty. See Book 7, Chapter 4 for more.

You must be a designated administrator (see the section on using account types in Book 2, Chapter 4) to get these utilities to work.

## Formatting drives

When you format a drive, you calibrate it: You mark it with guideposts that tell the PC where to store data and how to retrieve it. Every storage device (HDD, SSD, USB flash drive) must be formatted before it can be used. The manufacturer probably formatted your drive before you got it. That's comforting because every time a drive is reformatted, everything on the drive is tossed out, completely and (almost) irretrievably. Everything.

If you want to format a storage device such as a USB memory stick or an external hard disk you just bought, plug it into your computer, wait for Windows 11 to detect it, and do the following:

1. **Click or tap the File Explorer icon on the taskbar.**

2. **Click or tap This PC on the left.**

3. **Right-click (or press and hold down on) the drive that you want to format and a menu appears (see Figure 7-1). Choose Format.**

    The Format dialog appears, as shown in Figure 7-2.

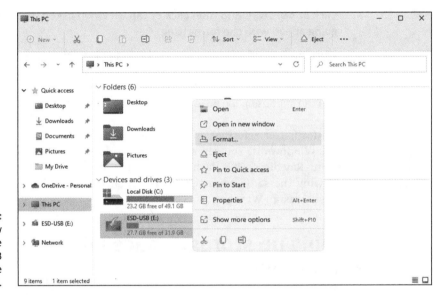

**FIGURE 7-1:**
Format a new storage device (HDD, SSD, USB drive) before using it.

**FIGURE 7-2:**
Choose how you want to format your drive.

4. **Click or tap the File System drop-down list and choose the file system you want.**

   For Windows 11, NTFS is the best choice.

5. **In the Volume Label field, type a name you want for your drive.**

6. **Select the Quick Format option, so that the process is finalized in seconds instead of minutes.**

7. **Click or tap Start, and then click or tap OK when asked if you're fine with going ahead with the formatting.**

   When the formatting is finalized, a confirmation message appears.

8. **Click or tap OK and then Close.**

   You can start using the drive you just formatted and store files on it.

**TIP**

You can format or reformat any hard drive or partition other than the one that contains Windows 11. You can also format — delete all the data on — rewritable DVDs, Blu-Ray discs, USB flash drives, and SD or other removable memory cards by following the same approach. To reformat the drive that contains Windows, you must reinstall Windows.

## Freeing up storage space with Storage Sense

Storage Sense is the Disk Cleanup replacement that Microsoft built for Windows 10 and Windows 11. It frees up storage space on your computer by removing things like the items in your Recycle Bin, temporary files, unused files in the Downloads folder, and unused Windows apps.

Here's how to use Storage Sense to clean up unused files from Windows 11:

1. **Click or tap the Start icon on the taskbar and then Settings.**

   Alternatively, you can press Windows+I on your keyboard.

2. **Make sure that System is selected on the left. On the right, click or tap Storage.**

   Storage Sense spends some time analyzing how your storage space is used, and then shows results similar to Figure 7-3.

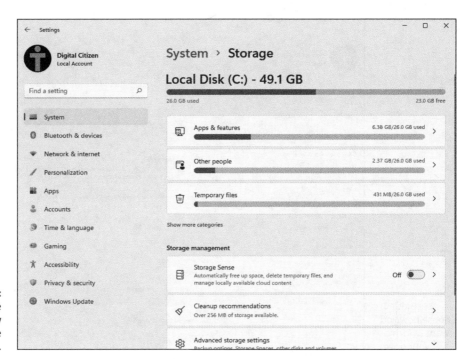

FIGURE 7-3:
Storage Sense
shows you how
your storage
space is used.

3. **Click or tap Cleanup Recommendations.**

   Storage Sense displays several recommendations for what you can delete, split into these categories: temporary files, large or unused files, files synced to the cloud, and unused apps. (See Figure 7-4.)

4. **Expand each category of recommendations one by one, select the items you want removed, click or tap Clean Up, and then click or tap Continue.**

   You return to Cleanup Recommendations, where you can repeat Step 4 as many times as you want.

5. **When you've finished cleaning up unused files, close Settings.**

## Running an error check on a drive

If a drive starts acting weird (for example, you see error messages when trying to open a file, or Windows 11 crashes in unpredictable ways, or a simple file copy takes hours instead of minutes), run the Windows error-checking routines.

TECHNICAL
STUFF

If you're an old hand at Windows (or an even older hand at DOS), you probably recognize the following steps as the venerable CHKDSK routine, in somewhat fancier clothing.

Maintaining Your
Drives

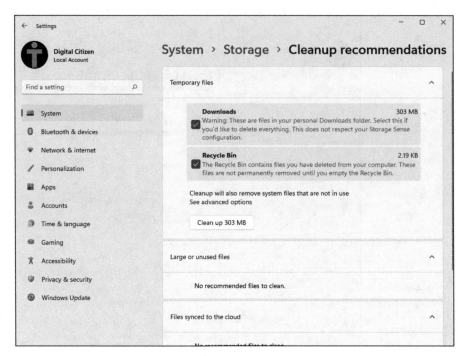

**FIGURE 7-4:**
Choose how you want to format your drive.

Follow these steps to run Check Disk:

**1. Bring up the drive you want to check in File Explorer:**

   *a. Click or tap the File Explorer icon.*

   *b. On the left, choose This PC.*

   *c. Right-click or tap and hold down on the drive that's giving you problems and choose Properties.*

   You see the Local Disk Properties dialog box.

**2. Go to the Tools tab, and click or tap the Check button, as shown in Figure 7-5.**

   Windows 11 may tell you that you don't need to scan the drive, because it hasn't found any errors on the drive. If you're skeptical, though, go right ahead and scan it.

**3. Click or tap Scan Drive.**

   Windows 11 tells you about any problems it encounters and asks for your permission to fix them.

**FIGURE 7-5:**
Run a check disk
in Windows 11.

# Defragmenting a drive

Once upon a time, defragmenting your hard drive rated as a Real Big Deal. Defragmentation is the process of instructing Windows to rearrange files on a hard drive so that the various parts of a file sit next to one another. Doing this increased the access speed to files by minimizing the time required to read and write files to and from the disk and by maximizing the transfer rate. Defragmentation helped on PCs that used traditional hard disks, with moving parts. However, Windows didn't automate the defrag process, so few people bothered. As a result, drives started to look like patchwork quilts with pieces of files stored all over the place. On the rare occasion that a Windows user ran the defragmenter, bringing all the pieces together could take hours — and the resulting system speed-up rarely raised any eyebrows.

Windows 7 changed that situation by quietly scheduling a disk defragmentation to run every week. Windows 11 continues that proud tradition. To defragment your drive, you don't need to touch a thing.

**TECHNICAL
STUFF**

Windows 11 doesn't run automatic defrags on SSDs because they're flash memory drives that don't have any moving parts. SSDs don't need defragmentation. In fact, defragmentation is actively bad for SSDs because it makes them wear out more quickly.

If you're curious about how your computer's doing in the defragmentation department, you can see the defragmenter report:

1. **Click or tap the search icon on the taskbar and type** *defrag*.

2. **Click or tap the Defragment and Optimize Drives search result.**

   The Optimize Drives dialog appears.

3. **Choose the drive you want to look at and click or tap Analyze.**

   You see how much of the drive is fragmented, or how many days have passed since the last retrim (for SSDs), as shown in Figure 7-6.

   A *retrim* is a rerun of the trim command, which I describe in the next section.

4. **If the fragmentation is more than 20 percent or a retrim hasn't been performed for more than a week, click or tap the Optimize button.**

   Windows 11 runs a defragmentation and optimization re-shuffling.

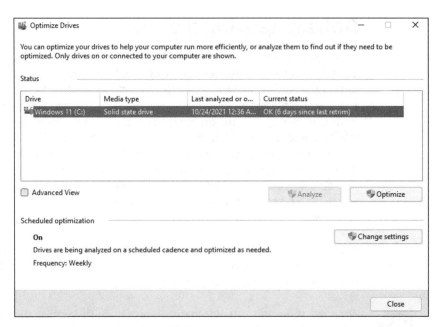

**FIGURE 7-6:**
Here's a full report of Windows 11's defragmenting activities.

## Maintaining solid-state drives

While the jury's still out on whether solid-state drives (SSDs) are much more reliable than hard disk drives (HDDs), just about everyone agrees that they're reliable. And there's no doubt that they're enormously faster. Change your C: drive over from a spinning platter to an SSD and strap on your seat belt.

However, SSDs are a completely different breed of cat. The only thing they need is for the defragmenter to run TRIM — a command that Windows uses to tell the SSD which data blocks are no longer needed and can be deleted or are marked as free for rewriting. In other words, TRIM helps the operating system know precisely where the data that you want to move or delete is stored.

Most SSDs these days are made using NAND flash memory, which is memory that doesn't lose its data when the power is turned off. Although an SSD may fit into a hard drive slot and behave much like a regular hard drive, the technology is different.

**WARNING**

SSDs have controllers that handle everything. Data isn't stored on SSDs in the same way it's stored on HDDs, and many purpose-built hard-drive tools don't work on SSDs. The controller must take on all the housekeeping that HDDs do automatically. For example, if you want to erase an HDD, you can format it or delete all the files on it. If you want to erase an SSD, you should use the manufacturer's utilities; otherwise, data can be left behind. For details, see the *Computerworld* article at `www.computerworld.com/article/2506511/solid-state-drives/can-data-stored-on-an-ssd-be-secured-.html`.

**TIP**

If you have an SSD or get an SSD, you should drop by the manufacturer's website and pick up any utilities it may have for the care and feeding of the furious little buggers. Windows 11 does a good job of looking after them, but the manufacturer may have a few tricks up its sleeve.

# Accessing the Health Report

The Windows Security app has a built-in device performance and health report that evaluates specific criteria including storage capacity, battery life, apps and software, and the Windows Time service (which updates the time and date on your PC). If you want to quickly check if everything is okay with your system, access this report and see what it says:

**1.** Click or tap the search icon on the taskbar and type *health*.

**2.** Click or tap the **Device Performance & Health** search result.

The Windows Security window appears, as shown in Figure 7-7.

**3.** If there's a problem with any of the things checked by this tool, click or tap the recommendation.

Follow the program's recommendation. Or if everything has a check mark in a green circle, there nothing to worry about.

**FIGURE 7-7:**
Windows
Security also
displays a device
performance &
health report.

# 4

# Using Windows Apps

# Contents at a Glance

Chapter **1**

# Using the Mail and Calendar Apps

The whole productivity app situation — Mail, Calendar, and People — has gone through enormous changes since the days of Windows 7. In the good old days, Mail, Calendar, and People were basically just one app — similar to the current situation in Office, where Outlook covers all the bases. That single app, confusingly, was called Windows Live Mail, even though it handled mail and contacts and calendar. It worked reasonably well, but it was old and clunky and didn't have many features.

In Windows 8, Microsoft created three separate apps: Mail, Calendar, and People. All three were connected, but each worked independently. Things improved with Windows 10, and a bit with Windows 11 too. We now have two apps: Mail and Calendar (which are just one app with two working modes), and People. In this chapter, I cover the Mail and Calendar side of things. The People app is covered in the next chapter of this minibook.

First, you learn about the various kinds of email services and apps available. Then you discover tips for choosing the right Mail/Calendar package and continue with the basics of using Mail and Calendar in Windows 11.

# THE MANY FACES OF MAIL

Like Gaul, all of email is divided into three parts.

- **Email programs,** commonly called *email clients, email readers,* or *mail user agents,* run on your computer. They reach out to your email, which is stored somewhere on a server (in the cloud, which is to say, on your email company's computer), bring it down to your machine, and help you work on it there. Messages get stored on your PC and, optionally, removed from the server when you retrieve them. When you write a message, it too gets stored on your machine, but it also gets sent out via your email company. Your email client interacts with your email company's server through strictly defined processes called *protocols*. The most common protocols are POP3 and IMAP. As is the case with most computer acronyms, the names don't really mean anything, although the protocols are quite different.

- **Online email,** most commonly, Gmail, Outlook.com, or Yahoo! Mail but there are many others, work directly through a web browser, or a program that operates much like a web browser but runs on your computer. You see mail on your computer, but it's stored on your email company's servers. To a first approximation anyway. You can log in to your mail service from any web browser, anywhere in the world, and pick back up right where you left off.

- **Hybrid systems** increasingly combine local mail storage on your machine with online email. Just as email clients are getting more online email characteristics, so too are online email systems adopting limited local storage. For example, Gmail — the prototypical online email program — can be set up to store mail on your machine, so you can work on email while away from an internet connection. The Windows 11 Mail app is a hybrid system, which can be set up to work with any email company's computers.

All the approaches are getting offshoots as email engulfs mobile devices. Microsoft now has Outlook variants on Windows 11 (with Office 2021 or Microsoft 365), iPad, Android, and directly through an internet browser on any kind of machine. The Android, iPad, and browser versions are free for personal use but require Microsoft 365 subscriptions for organizational use and to unlock certain features. With considerable effort from Microsoft, all these variants are starting to look and act like each other.

Google, similarly, has Gmail variants on Android, iPhone, and iPad, although Windows access to Gmail goes through a browser. Unlike Outlook, Gmail has consistently offered the same interface and the same behavior on all its different platforms. The free version of Gmail is identical to the organizational version, but organizations are required to sign up for (and pay for) Google Workspace.

Perhaps surprisingly, thanks to POP3 and IMAP, both Outlook and Gmail work well with just about any email account. You can use @gmail.com email addresses with Outlook and @outlook.com (and @hotmail.com, @msn.com, @live.com, and so on) addresses with Gmail. The people reading your messages will never know that you're consorting with the enemy.

That's just for email. When you enter the world of SMS (phone messages) and MMS (video/multimedia) instant messaging, life becomes more complex.

# Choosing Mail and Calendar Apps

The Windows 11 Mail app is shown in Figure 1-1. Your Mail may not look the same — the left column might be expanded and the preview pane on the right might not exist. There are differences between wide and narrow screens, and portrait and landscape mode.

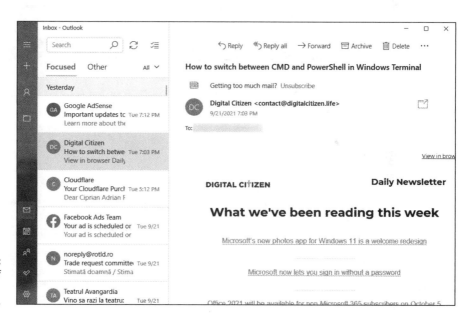

**FIGURE 1-1:**
A preview of the Windows 11 Mail app.

The Mail has improved a lot since its debut on July 29, 2015, back in Windows 10. Although it may never get the development attention lavished on the Outlook app from Microsoft 365 or Microsoft Office, Mail does see a steady trickle of improvements.

Before you jump into the productivity wallow, think about how you want to handle your mail and calendar.

## Comparing email apps

Windows 11 Mail has its benefits, but it may not best suit your needs. The most important question for you is whether the Mail app from Windows 11 is the right one for you. Life is full of difficult choices, and Microsoft sits behind many of them. For me, anyway.

Complicating the situation is that Mail isn't an either/or choice. For example, you can set up Outlook.com (see Figure 1-2) or Gmail accounts (see Figure 1-3), and then work with those accounts using either Mail or a web-based interface at www. outlook.com or www.gmail.com. In fact, you can jump back and forth between working online in your web browser of choice and working on your Windows 11 computer.

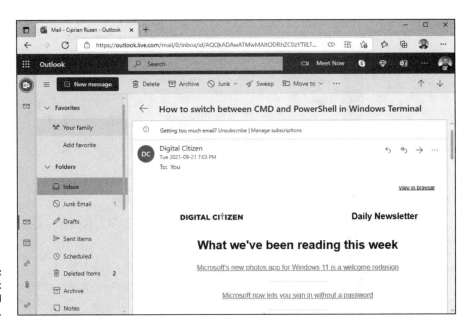

**FIGURE 1-2:**
I use Outlook for my personal email.

Windows 11's Mail functions as a gathering point: It pulls in mail from Outlook.com, for example, and sends out mail through Outlook.com. The same with Gmail, Yahoo!, and other email services. But when it's working right, the Mail app doesn't delete the mail: All your messages are still sitting there waiting for you in Outlook.com or Gmail. In most cases, you can use Mail in the morning, switch over to Gmail or Outlook.com when you get to the office, and go back to the Mail app when you get home — and never miss a thing.

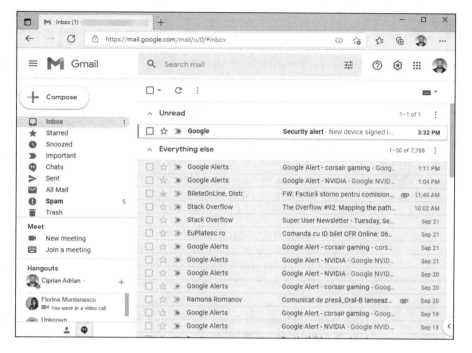

**FIGURE 1-3:**
I use Gmail as my
secondary email.

The current version of the Mail app can pull in mail from Outlook.com, Gmail, Exchange Server (a typical situation at a large office or if you use one of the Microsoft 365 business plans), Yahoo! Mail, and iCloud, as well as IMAP and POP3 (methods supported by most internet service providers).

That's the short story. Permit me to throw some complicating factors at you.

You can add your Outlook.com account to Gmail or add your Gmail account to Outlook.com. In fact, you can add just about any email account to either Outlook.com or Gmail. If you're thinking about moving to Windows 11 Mail just because it can pull in mail from multiple accounts, realize that Gmail (see Book 10, Chapter 4) and Outlook.com (see Book 10, Chapter 5) can do the same thing.

TIP

The main benefit to using Windows 11 Mail rather than Outlook.com or Gmail is that the Mail app stores some of your most recent messages on your computer. (Gmail running on the Google Chrome browser can do the same thing, but you must set it up.) If you can't get to the internet, you can't download new messages or send responses, but at least Mail enables you to look at your most recent messages.

Some people prefer the Mail app interface over Gmail or Outlook.com. I prefer Outlook.com's inbox, but you must decide for yourself. *De gustibus* and all that. Moreover, the interfaces change all the time, so if you haven't looked in the last year or so, it'd be worth the effort to fire up your web browser and have a look-see.

Outlook.com and Gmail are superior to the Mail app in these respects:

REMEMBER

>> Outlook.com and Gmail have all your mail, all the time — or at least the mail that you archive. If you look for something old, you may or may not find it with the Mail app — by default, Mail holds your mail from only the past few weeks, and it doesn't automatically reach out to Outlook.com or Gmail to run searches.

>> Gmail and Outlook.com display much more information on the screen. The Mail app has been tuned for touch, with big blocks set aside to make an all-thumbs approach feasible and lots of white space, while Outlook.com and Gmail are much more mouse friendly.

But wait! I've looked at only Windows 11 Mail, Outlook.com, and Gmail. Many, many more options exist in the mail game, to wit:

>> **Microsoft Outlook:** Bundled with Office since pterodactyls powered PCs, Outlook (see Figure 1-4) has an enormous number of options — many of them confusing, most of them never used. Or at least, that's what I keep telling myself. Outlook is the Rolls Royce of the email biz, with all the positive and negative connotations.

>> **Outlook.com (was known as Outlook Web App):** It isn't exactly Outlook — at least, not the kind that runs directly on your PC — but Microsoft marketing wants you to believe that it is. Big companies can run their own copies as part of Exchange Server. Most people just log in to www.outlook.com.

>> **Free, open-source alternatives:** These include Mozilla Thunderbird, SeaMonkey, and many more that have enthusiastic fan bases.

>> **Your Internet service provider (ISP):** Your ISP may well have its own email package. My experience with ISP-provided free email hasn't been positive, but the service generally doesn't hold a candle to Gmail, Outlook.com, Yahoo! Mail, or any of the dozens of competitive email providers. If you use ISP-based email, mail2web (www.mail2web.com) lets you get into just about any mailbox from just about anywhere — if you know the password.

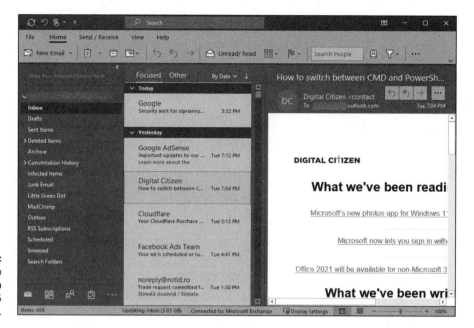

**FIGURE 1-4:**
The Outlook app included with a Microsoft 365 subscription.

## Comparing calendar apps

Calendars can also be handled by a bewildering array of packages and sites. Among the hundreds of competing calendar apps, each has a unique twist. The highlights:

>> **Google Calendar** (see Figure 1-5) is highly regarded for being powerful and easy to use. It's also reasonably well integrated with other Google apps, although you can use it — and share calendars with other people — without setting foot in another Google app. Put all your appointments in Google Calendar (https://calendar.google.com/), and you have instant access to your latest calendar from any computer, tablet, or smartphone that can get to the Internet.

>> **Outlook.com Calendar,** on the other hand, lives inside Outlook.com. It's reasonably powerful and integrated, and you can share the calendar with your contacts or other people (see Figure 1-6).

>> **Outlook** (the app from Microsoft 365) also does calendars, with so many options that you may feel intimidated.

**TIP**

If you want to schedule one conference room in an office with a hundred people, all of whom use Outlook, the Outlook Calendar is the way to go. If you want to keep track of your flight departure times, Aunt Martha's birthday, and the kids' football games, any of the calendar apps will work fine.

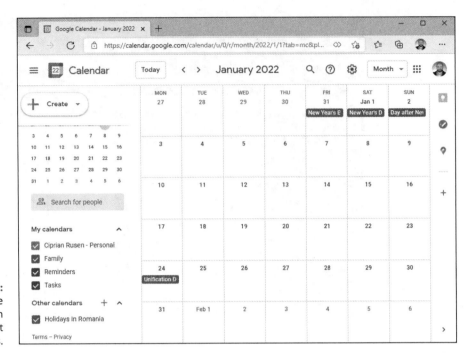

**FIGURE 1-5:**
I use Google
Calendar on
many different
devices.

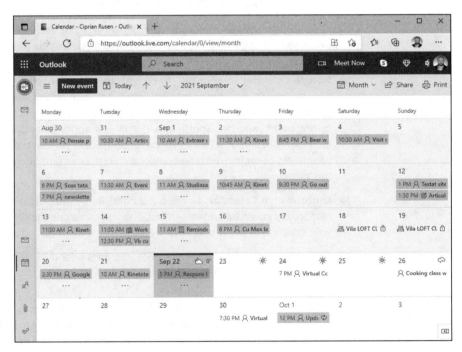

**FIGURE 1-6:**
The Outlook.com
Calendar has
lots and lots of
options.

I'm happy to say that the Windows 11 Mail and Calendar apps sync well with both Google Calendar and Outlook.com Calendar. Therefore, for your personal email and calendar, what Windows 11 has built in may be enough for your needs.

## Choosing the right package

So how do you choose mail and calendar programs? Tough question, but let me give you a few hints:

>> The Windows 11 productivity apps — Mail and Calendar — work well enough if your demands aren't great. If you also have an iPad, iPhone, or Android device, you may also want to use the Microsoft Outlook app for all mobile platforms. It offers a similar experience to the Mail and Calendar apps from Windows 11.

>> Online services — specifically Outlook.com and Gmail — have many more usable features than Windows 11 Mail. If you can rely on your internet connection, look at both before settling on a specific mail, contacts, and calendar program or programs.

>> Gmail and Outlook.com make it easy to use their programs to read ordinary email. I can set up my email account, `ciprianrusen@digitalcitizen.life`, to work through Gmail, for example, so mail sent to that email address ends up in Gmail. And if I respond to the message, it appears as if it's coming from `ciprianrusen@digitalcitizen.life`, not from Gmail.

TIP

A good compromise is to use either Gmail or Outlook.com most of the time but hook up Windows 11 Mail to the Gmail or Outlook.com account.

# Using the Mail App

The first time you click or tap the Mail shortcut from the Start menu, you're given the chance to add an account. If you signed into Windows 11 with a Microsoft account, you just click or tap a couple of times and end up at the Mail screen, which is shown in Figure 1-1 at the beginning of the chapter.

REMEMBER

If you signed in to Windows 11 with a local account — one that isn't known to Microsoft (see Book 2, Chapter 5) — or if you say that you want to add an email account, the Mail app presents you with the choices shown in Figure 1-7.

Table 1-1 explains the option you should choose, depending on your type of email provider.

**FIGURE 1-7:**
The Mail app
works with just
about any kind of
email account.

**TABLE 1-1**

## Mail Account Types

| Choose | For This Type of Email Account |
|---|---|
| Outlook.com | If you get your mail through Microsoft servers, which means you have an email address that looks like *something*@outlook.com, *something*@live.com, *something*@hotmail.com, or *something*@msn.com |
| Office 365 | If you get your mail through your company's Exchange mail server or you use Microsoft 365 (formerly known as Office 365) to handle your mail |
| Google | If you have a Google account, most commonly an email address that looks like *something*@gmail.com; or you use Google's servers for email, as you can with Google Workspace; or you've just registered your email address with Google and want to retrieve your mail through Google |
| Yahoo! | If you get your email from Yahoo!, in which case your email address looks like *somebody*@yahoo.com |
| iCloud | If you have an Apple account, that is, an @icloud.com, @me.com, or @mac.com address |
| Other | If you use any other kind of email address. When you type your email address, Microsoft looks for a bunch of associated information (such as the POP or IMAP server name) in its enormous database and can almost always set you up with a click (or tap) or two |
| Advanced setup | If you have an Exchange ActiveSync account or if Other fails to find your address, which is rare |

People trying to use work email on a computer may have to talk to their IT department for additional configuration options.

If you signed into Windows 11 with a local account and add a Microsoft account to the Mail app, you'll be asked if you want to change that local account into a Microsoft account everywhere, as shown in Figure 1-8.

**FIGURE 1-8:**
Unless you want to change your Windows 11 login to a Microsoft account, tell Windows to take a hike.

**WARNING**

Watch out! Do not click or tap Next. Instead, click or tap Microsoft Apps Only. Otherwise, Windows 11 takes that as permission to switch your local account over to a Microsoft account.

When you click or tap Microsoft Apps Only (you did heed the warning, didn't you?), you end up at the Mail main page, as shown in Figure 1-9. The Mail app pulls in about a month's worth of messages and shows them to you. (Details of the display vary depending on many things, including the width of the screen and whether the device is in tablet mode.)

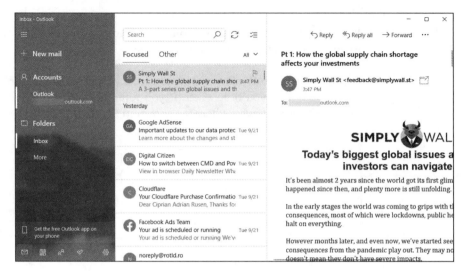

**FIGURE 1-9:**
The Mail app is displaying my Outlook.com emails.

Mail's standard layout has three columns:

» The left column holds a bunch of icons, which can be hard to decipher:

  ● The hamburger (three lines) icon, at the top, lets you look at all the options when the left column is minimized (see Figure 1-10).

  ● The plus icon starts a new message.

  ● The person icon lets you switch among accounts, if you have multiple email accounts.

  ● The folder icon lets you switch between your inbox, outbox, archive, and so on.

  ● The envelope icon doesn't do anything when viewing your email. If you're using one of the other Microsoft apps (such as Calendar or People), clicking or tapping the envelope icon takes you to Mail.

  ● The calendar icon launches the Calendar app.

  ● The two people icon opens the People app.

  ● The check mark takes you to Microsoft's To Do app (or to Microsoft Store so you can install the app).

  ● The gear icon brings up a Settings pane, which I discuss in the later section, "Mail Settings."

» The middle column lists all the messages in the selected folder. If you don't manually select a folder — by using the file folder icon and clicking or tapping to pin the specific folder — Mail selects the inbox for you.

» The right column shows you the selected message.

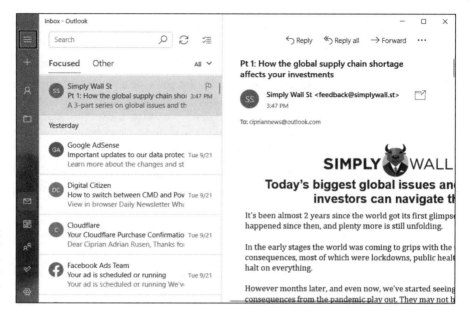

**FIGURE 1-10:**
Clicking or tapping the hamburger icon expands the left column.

## Creating an email message

When you reply to a message, Mail sets up a typical reply (or a reply to all) in a three-column screen, as shown in Figure 1-11. Similarly, if you click or tap the + icon in the upper left, Mail starts a new, blank message. Whether you reply or start a new message, your message is all set up and ready to go — just start typing.

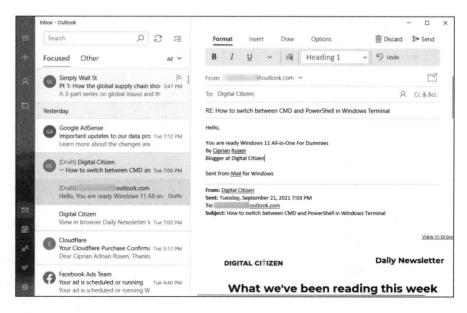

**FIGURE 1-11:**
When you reply to a message or compose a new message, Mail gives you these options.

Here's a quick tour of the features available to you as you create your email message:

>> **Format the text:** The new text you type appears in Calibri 11-point type, which is a good all-around, middle-of-the-road choice. Don't get me started on Comic Sans. If you want to format the text, just select it and click or tap the down arrow to the right of the underline icon; you see the formatting options in Figure 1-12.

Those who have a keyboard and know how to use it will be pleased to find out that many of the old formatting keyboard shortcuts still work. Here are the most-used shortcuts for formatting:

- *Ctrl+B* toggles bold on and off.

- *Ctrl+I* toggles italic on and off.

- *Ctrl+U* toggles underline on and off.

- *Ctrl+Z* undoes the last action.

- *Ctrl+Y* redoes the last undone action.

(In addition to the old stalwarts Ctrl+C for copy, Ctrl+X for cut, and Ctrl+V for paste, of course.)

You'll be happy to know that your old favorite emoticons work, too. Type :-) and you get a smiley face.

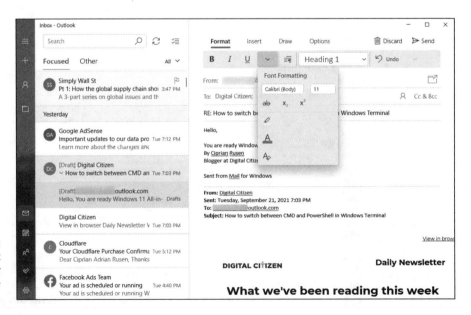

**FIGURE 1-12:**
Select the text and apply formatting in the usual way.

>> **Create bulleted or numbered lists or apply other paragraph formatting:**
Select the paragraph(s) you want to change, click or tap the paragraph
formatting icon and choose from the many paragraph formats, as shown in
Figure 1-13.

>> **Add an attachment:** At the top, click or tap Insert ⇨ Files. You see an Open
dialog box, where you can choose the file you want to attach. Click or tap the
file to select it and then click or tap Open.

>> **Add a message priority indicator:** At the top, choose the Options tab and set
the message to either High (exclamation point) or Low (down arrow) priority.

>> **Send the message:** Click or tap the Send icon in the upper-right corner, and
the message is queued in the outbox, ready to send the next time Mail syncs
for new messages.

>> **Delete or save the message:** If at any time you decide that you don't want to
send a message, click or tap the Discard icon in the upper-right corner. To
save a draft, you don't need to do anything: Windows 11 Mail automatically
saves everything, all the time.

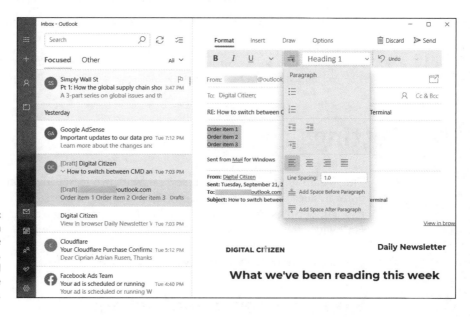

**FIGURE 1-13:**
To create a
bulleted list, type
the paragraphs,
select them, and
then select the
bullets style.

The Mail app's editing capabilities are impressive, with many of the features you
would expect in Microsoft Word. Styles, tables, fancy formatting, and easy manip-
ulation of inline pictures top the most-used list. The lack of customized folders
counts as a significant shortcoming for many.

## Searching for email in the Mail app

Searching for mail is easy if you remember two important details:

**REMEMBER**

>> **If you have multiple accounts, navigate to the account you want to search before you perform the search.** If you search while you're looking at the Gmail.com inbox, for example, you won't find anything in your Outlook. com account.

>> **Don't use Cortana.** It isn't up to the challenge. However, the Windows 11 Search might be useful in finding email messages.

To search for email messages:

1. **If you have more than one email account, move to the account you want to search.**

   The easiest way to do that is to click or tap the folder icon on the left and choose the account you want.

2. **At the top, above the second column, click or tap the magnifying glass.**

3. **Type your search term, and press Enter or tap the magnifying glass icon again.**

   Your results are shown in the middle column. Click or tap on a message, and it will appear on the right side of the Mail app.

# Mail Settings

The Windows 11 Mail app has several worthwhile settings. On the left, at the bottom, click or tap the gear icon (shown in the margin). If the window's wide enough, Settings appears on the right, as shown in Figure 1-14. (If the window isn't wide enough, Settings will tromp over to the left side.)

The next sections tell you what you can do.

## Adding a new email account

The Mail app has built-in smarts so you can connect to any Outlook.com, Gmail, Exchange Server (including Office 365), Yahoo!, iCloud, or IMAP or POP account. You can add any number of different types of those accounts — two different Gmail accounts and a few Outlook.com — no problem.

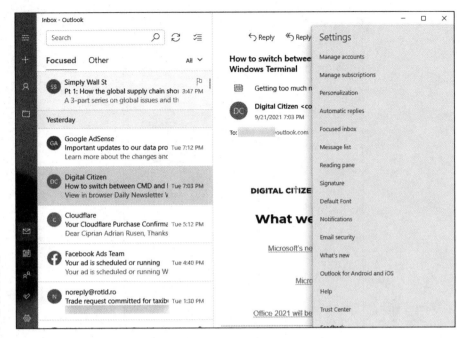

**FIGURE 1-14:**
If you want to add a new email address, click or tap Manage Accounts.

To add a new account:

**1.** **From the Mail app, click or tap the gear icon at the bottom left.**

The Settings menu appears (refer to Figure 1-14).

**2.** **Click or tap Manage Accounts ⇨ Add Account.**

The Add an Account list appears (refer to Figure 1-7).

**3.** **Click or tap the account type that you want to add.**

Refer to Table 1-1 for a list of account types. If you click or tap Outlook.com, you're telling Mail that you want to add a Microsoft account, so you see the dialog box shown in Figure 1-15.

**4.** **Enter your email ID and click or tap Next. Then enter your password and any ancillary information that may be required, and click or tap Sign In.**

Mail is probably smart enough to look up and find any other information it needs, but you may have to provide additional information (such as a POP3 mail server name) from your email provider.

**WARNING**

**5.** **If Mail presents you with an option to use this account everywhere on your device (refer to Figure 1-8), click or tap Microsoft Apps Only. (Don't click or tap Next.)**

When Mail comes back, your new account appears under the hamburger icon on the left.

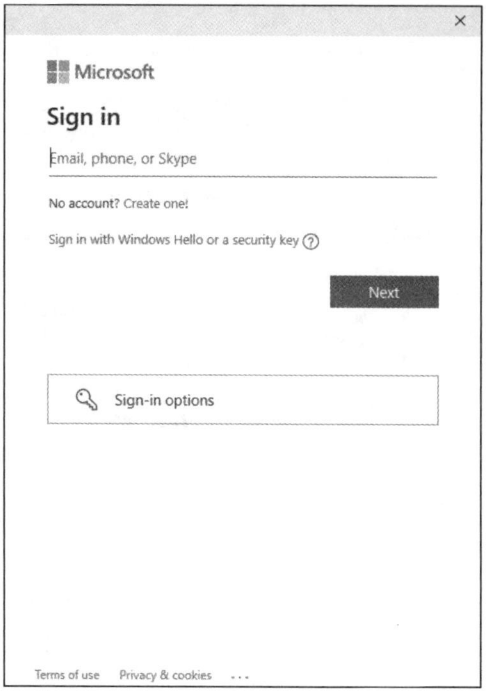

**FIGURE 1-15:**
Enter your
Microsoft email
account.

If you want to change the details about your account — in particular, if you don't want to see the name Hotmail, Outlook, or Gmail as an account name — click or tap the gear icon, click or tap Manage Accounts, and then click or tap the account you want to change. The Account Settings pane appears, as shown in Figure 1-16. In the top box, you can type a name that will appear in the first column of the Mail main page. If you also want to change the number of days' worth of email downloaded (the default is All Available Mail) or change the sync frequency, click or tap the link marked Change Mailbox Sync Settings.

## Setting extra options

In the Mail app, the Settings pane has several additional worthwhile options. To find them, click or tap the gear icon (Settings) at the bottom of the app. Then, you can do several things, including but not limited to the following:

>> **Personalization:** Change the picture that appears in the far-right pane when no mail has been selected or change the background for the entire app. You can also enable light or dark mode for the Mail app.

>> **Automatic Replies:** Have an account automatically send a response to any received message. (Spammers love this setting because it helps identify active accounts.)

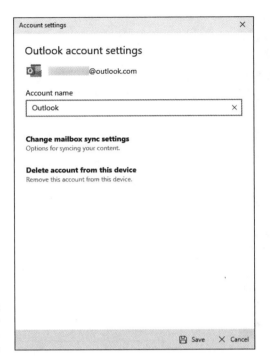

**FIGURE 1-16:**
Change the
details of an
account.

>> **Reading Pane:** Have Mail automatically open the next item when you're finished with the current message.

>> **Signature:** Put a signature (*Sent from Mail for Windows* is the default) on all new mail and all responses. Or disable the default signature if you don't want it.

>> **Default Font:** Change the default font, size, and formatting for one or all email accounts.

>> **Notifications:** Display notifications or play a sound when new mail arrives. Yes, "You've got mail" will work.

# Avoiding Calendar App Collisions

The Windows 11 Calendar is relatively straightforward, but the first time you bring up the Calendar app, you may think you're seeing double. Or triple. In Figure 1-17, you can see what I mean.

Don't panic.

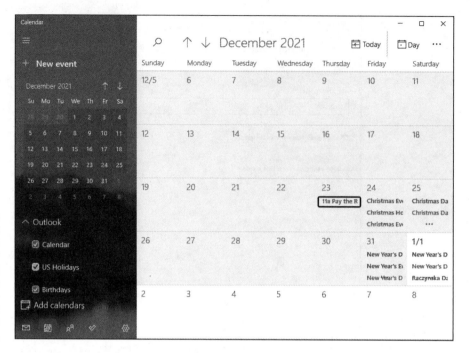

**FIGURE 1-17:**
Your first time
in Calendar app
may make your
head spin. Note
the duplicate
entries for Christ-
mas Day, from
two different
calendars.

The reason for the duplication? If you've added two or more accounts to Mail or Calendar, if one or more of the accounts has duplicated entries, the calendars associated with those accounts come along for the ride. Any appointment that appears in both calendars shows up as a duplicate on the consolidated calendar.

Fortunately, it's easy to see what's going on and to get rid of the duplicates. Or at least some of the duplicates. Maybe. Here's how to reorganize your calendar:

**1.** **Open the Start menu, and click or tap the Calendar shortcut p.**

You can also click or tap the calendar icon at the bottom of the Mail app.

If this is the first time you've looked at the Calendar app, it may appear like the one in Figure 1-17.

**2.** **Look at the selected boxes in the bottom left to see whether two or more of your calendars have a source that overlaps. If so, turn off one of the interfering calendars.**

For example, in Figure 1-17, I have both the Outlook calendar and a US Holidays calendar, but both have entries about holidays in the US. By simply turning off the US Holidays calendar, the main calendar goes back to looking somewhat normal, as shown in Figure 1-18.

**FIGURE 1-18:** Getting rid of the Holidays and Birthdays calendars cuts down the clutter.

3. **Go through the calendars, one by one, and set the color-coding for each calendar component to something your eyes can tolerate.**

4. **When you're finished, close the calendar.**

On the top, you can choose the detail of the calendar you want to see:

» **Day** brings up an hourly calendar, for two or more days (depending on the number of pixels across your screen).

» **Week** shows Sunday through Saturday.

» **Work Week** lists Monday through Friday of the current week only.

» **Month** displays one month at a time.

» **Year** shows a calendar for all the months of the current year.

**TIP**

In all cases, up and down arrows appear at the top of the screen to move one unit (day, week, month) earlier or later.

Click or tap the hamburger icon to get rid of the left column, and let the calendar take up the entire Calendar window.

## Adding calendar items

To add a new appointment or other calendar item, click or tap + New Event in the upper-left corner. Calendar shows you the Details pane, as shown in Figure 1-19.

**FIGURE 1-19:** Create a new appointment or calendar entry.

Most of the entries are self-explanatory, except these:

REMEMBER

>> **You must choose a calendar — actually, an email account — that will be synchronized with this appointment.** As soon as you enter the appointment, Calendar logs in to the indicated account and adds the appointment to the account's calendar.

>> **You may optionally specify email addresses in the People box.** If you put valid email address(es) in the People box, Calendar generates an email message and sends it to the recipient, asking the recipient to confirm the appointment.

When you're finished, click or tap Save or Send (in the upper-left corner), depending on whether you're setting the appointment or setting it and sending invitations.

TIP

If you click or tap the icon with two arrows chasing each other in a circle — the repeat icon — Calendar lets you choose how often to repeat and when to end the repetition.

## Struggling with the Calendar app's shortcomings

The Calendar app is a reasonable calendar program. It doesn't have any of the goodies you would expect from more advanced calendar apps, except for toaster-style slide-from-the-right notifications.

On the plus side, you can have calendar notifications placed on your lock screen. The notifications list individual appointments for the current day. See Book 2, Chapter 2 for details.

If you want to look at better calendars (which work from a browser, but not as an independent Windows 11 app), check out these:

>> **Google Calendar,** at calendar.google.com, is free and works well. It's especially useful if you have an Android smartphone.

>> **Outlook.com Calendar** is accessed from Outlook.com by clicking or tapping the calendar icon on the left. I use it alongside the Outlook mobile app for Android and iOS.

# Chapter **2**

# Keeping Track of People

O nce upon a time, contact lists were a big deal in the PC world. Being able to keep one single list of all your contacts — and keep their addresses, email addresses, and phone numbers all up to date — was one of the most important chores for a burgeoning PC.

Those days have long passed. Nowadays, contact lists get gummed up with outdated entries and useless information. Worse, the contact lists don't talk to each other: My contacts in Facebook, Skype, Gmail, my smartphones, Twitter, Pinterest, and Outlook just don't talk to each other. Which is all for the better, actually, because if they did start talking to each other, there'd be some really heated arguments and lots of name-calling.

Even if your contacts are better behaved than mine, changing a detail in one place — say, a new email address in Gmail — doesn't ripple to all the lists. Instead, it just means that one of the lists is out of sync with all the others.

I wish I could say that Microsoft has built a better contact list, but they haven't. The Windows 11 People app is a toy app, which may evolve into a superior central repository someday, but I'm not holding my breath. Until then, I will teach you how to use it. Unfortunately, starting it isn't intuitive, so I'll begin with that. Then you learn how to add accounts and contacts to the People app. I also briefly present some alternatives, for those who don't like the People app.

# Alternatives to the People App

Fortunately, while Microsoft's been playing at contacts with their People app, the rest of the world has zoomed right ahead. When you choose a contact app, your top consideration should be whether it runs on all your computers and devices: desktop, laptop, tablet, and smartphone. Windows 11 People doesn't even rate a meh on that scale.

If you're looking for a contact app and you aren't forced into People, try one of these free alternatives:

» **Contacts+:** Android, iOS, or online, syncs with Facebook, Twitter, and LinkedIn. It's very visual. Find it at www.contactspls.com.

» **Google Contacts:** It works like a champ and ties into Gmail, which I also use. Find it at https://contacts.google.com.

» **Sync.me:** Android, iOS, or online, works with Facebook, and LinkedIn contacts. Features are caller ID (a godsend if you get lots of spammy calls), social syncing, spam protection, a world phone book, and reminders. Find it at https://sync.me/.

A whole big world of contact apps is out there. You don't have to get stuck on one just because it ships with Windows 11. However, you may want to try the People app and see if I'm right. If that's the case for you, continue reading the remainder of this chapter.

# The Contact List in Windows 11

You may want to think of it as the Windows 11 People app (see Figure 2-1), but it's really just a basic contact list. Nothing pretentious about it. Unfortunately, the app doesn't have a separate shortcut in the Start menu, and it can be accessed only from Mail and Calendar. Therefore, when you're in Mail or Calendar, click or tap the people icon, which looks like two people sitting next to each other.

The People app keeps a list of contacts. If you hook things up right, it'll import contact lists from a variety of sources — the usual email contact lists (Office 365, Exchange, Outlook.com, Gmail.com, iCloud), plus a few contact list managers available in the Microsoft Store.

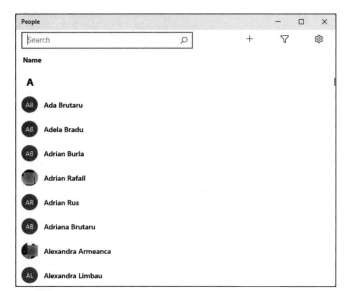

**FIGURE 2-1:**
The People app is a simple contact list.

# Adding Contacts in the People App

If you set up Mail with an Outlook.com, a Gmail, or an Exchange Server account, all the contacts belonging to that account have already been imported into People. If you set up more than one Outlook.com account, for example, all the contacts in both accounts have been merged and placed in People.

But you aren't even halfway done yet.

## Adding accounts to People

**REMEMBER**

Before you start pulling all your contacts from Outlook.com, Gmail, Exchange Server, and all the others, realize that doing so has side effects, not just in establishing Microsoft-controlled links with outside applications but even inside the core Windows 11 productivity apps (Mail, People, and Calendar).

Before you add an account to People, be aware of the effect it has in Mail and Calendar. Here's how connecting the following accounts with People affects other Windows 11 apps:

>> **Google account:** Connecting a Google account brings in your Gmail contacts. In addition, it adds your Gmail account to Windows 11 Mail and Calendar.

» **Outlook.com account:** Connecting an Outlook.com account brings in your Outlook.com contacts and hooks up the email account to the Mail and Calendar apps.

» **Other accounts:** Although you can add other accounts (POP3 and IMAP email accounts) to the Windows 11 People app, as best I can tell, doing so does not import anything to People. Rather, it simply adds the connected email account to the Mail app.

Now that you understand the implications, if you still want to add your contacts to the People app, do the following:

1. **Click or tap the Start icon and then Mail.**

   The Mail app opens. If you haven't added any email accounts, you may see a prompt to add an account. If so, click or tap Add an Account, and skip to Step 3.

2. **In the Mail app, click or tap the people icon (two people).**

3. **In the People app (refer to Figure 2-1), click or tap the gear icon at the top.**

   You see the Settings pane shown in Figure 2-2.

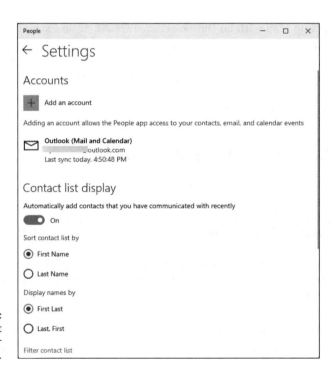

FIGURE 2-2:
Add an account
to your
People app.

## 4. If you have a contact list with entries that you want to see, pause and think about it a minute.

**TIP**

If you have old information in one or more of those accounts, you may want to think carefully about whether including all the contacts in your People list will be more of a pain than it's worth. Modifying existing contacts in People is time-consuming: You must click or tap each contact one by one, review the information about the contact, and modify it accordingly. Although the People app tries to identify duplicate entries — the same people coming from two different sources — and merge the data, it's not good at resolving differences.

## 5. If you want to proceed, click or tap Add an Account.

You see the Add an Account dialog box shown in Figure 2-3. Table 2-1 explains the option you should choose, depending on what kind of email provider you have.

## 6. Choose the type of account you have and follow the directions to add that account's contacts to People.

You're bound to find many duplicates and lots of mismatched data. Hang in there. There's another trick.

**FIGURE 2-3:**
The Add an Account dialog box looks just like the analogous dialog box in the Mail app.

**TIP**

If you added too many accounts to your People list, there's a way to prevent People from showing all the contacts from a specific source — without laboriously deleting individual entries.

**TABLE 2-1** **Mail Account Types when Adding an Account**

| Choose | For This Type of Account |
|--------|--------------------------|
| Outlook.com | If you get your email through Microsoft's servers and your address looks like *something@outlook.com*, *something@live.com*, *something@hotmail.com*, or *something@msn.com* |
| Office 365 | If you get your mail through a company's Exchange mail server or you use Office 365 to handle your mail |
| Google | If you have a Google account, most commonly an email address that looks like *something@gmail.com*; or you use Google's servers for email, as you can with Google Workspace; or you've just registered your email address with Google and want to retrieve your mail through Google |
| Yahoo! | If you have an @yahoo.com account. Yes, a few people still have @yahoo.com accounts |
| iCloud | If you have an Apple account, that is, an @icloud.com, @me.com, or @mac.com address |
| Advanced setup | If you have an Exchange ActiveSync account, or an IMAP or a POP3 email account |

Here's how:

1. **Bring up the People app from Mail or Calendar.**

   Click or tap the people icon on the left side of the app's window.

2. **In the People app (refer to Figure 2-1), click or tap the gear icon at the top.**

   The dialog box that was shown in Figure 2-2 appears.

3. **At the bottom, click or tap Filter Contact List.**

   The options shown in Figure 2-4 appear.

4. **In the Show Contacts From section, select and deselect the boxes, so you display only the contacts from the account you want to see.**

   It's easier to scale back duplicates this way — but harder to update older entries.

## SEARCHING FOR PEOPLE

Just to confuse things: Search in People looks only for the beginning of names. If you search for *umm*, you won't find *Dummy*, for example. That's usually not a big deal, unless you've imported names where both the first and last names have been mashed together and stuck in the First Name field.

**FIGURE 2-4:**
Disable all the contacts from a single source.

TIP

A little English translation: "Hide contacts without phone numbers — Off" means you want to see all your contacts, whether you have phone numbers for them or not.

## Editing a contact

If you want to change the information associated with a People contact, here's how to do it:

**1.** **Inside the People app, click or tap a contact's tile.**

The contact details appear, as shown in Figure 2-5. It's not at all obvious, but you can click or tap the email address and send a message or click or tap one of the Map links and see the Map app, pointing to the indicated address.

**2.** **Click or tap the edit icon.**

The Edit Outlook Contact pane appears.

**3.** **If you have multiple sources of contacts (say, multiple Outlook accounts, or accounts added in the Mail app), choose which contact you want to edit.**

Ultimately, you end up on the editing page, as shown in Figure 2-6.

**4.** **Change the information you want to change.**

See the next section for a list of the different data fields.

**5.** **Very important: Click or tap Save.**

WARNING

If you don't explicitly save your changes, they'll disappear, and you won't be warned.

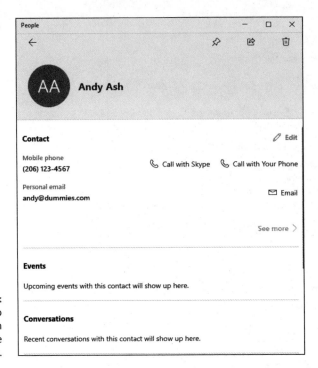

**FIGURE 2-5:**
The contact info for a person added to the People app.

**FIGURE 2-6:**
Change the contact's information here.

# Adding a contact

Adding a new contact in People isn't difficult, if you can keep in mind one oddity: You add *accounts* via the gear-shaped settings icon at the top, but to add a *contact*, you use the + (plus sign) icon.

**REMEMBER**

A contact in the People app doesn't have to be a person. Your local animal shelter is a person, too. Or at least a contact.

Here's how to add a new contact. Keep in mind that People alphabetizes by first name (unless you change the sort order in Settings) or by company name if there is no first or last name.

1. **Bring up the People app from Mail or Calendar.**

   To do so, click or tap the people icon on the left side of the app's window. That puts you on the main screen (refer to Figure 2-1).

2. **Click or tap + in the upper-right corner of the left pane.**

   The new contact dialog box shown in Figure 2-7 appears.

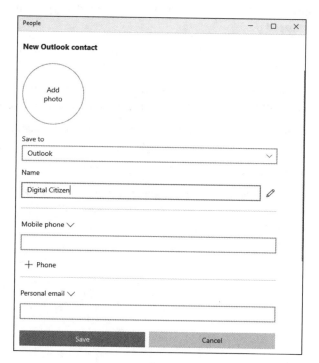

**FIGURE 2-7:**
Enter your new contact in the People app.

3. **In the Save To drop-down list, choose the account to which you want to sync this new contact, if you have two or more accounts in the People app.**

   You can choose from any account identified to the Mail app. When you add a contact to that account, People goes to the account and puts the person in your contact list for that account. Suppose that I add Peter Parker to my ciprian@outlook.com account. As soon as I'm finished, the People app will log in to my ciprian@outlook.com account and add poor Phineas to my contact list.

4. **Type a first and last name, keeping in mind that People alphabetizes by the first name, by default.**

   For additional name options — phonetic names, middle names, nicknames, title, or suffix — you can click or tap the pencil icon to the right of the Name field.

5. **If you have an email address for the contact, choose what kind of email address and then type the address in the box.**

   The types of email addresses are Personal, Work, and Other.

6. **Similarly, if you have a phone number, choose the type — and enter it in the indicated box.**

   The types of phone options are Mobile, Home, Work, Company, Pager, Work Fax, and Home Fax.

7. **If you want to add an address, scroll down below the Email entries, click or tap the Address button, and choose Home, Work, or Other Address.**

8. **As you feel inclined, fill in Other Info, such as Job Title, Significant Other, Website, and Notes.**

9. **Click or tap the Save button.**

   It takes a few seconds — People is going to your mail account and updating it — but you come back to the screen where you see the details of the newly added account.

# Chapter **3**

# Working with Photos

The Photos app in Windows 11 has been redesigned to match with the new visual design of the operating system, with rounded corners, updated typography styling, new theme specific color palettes, and more. It also has a few new features, but it isn't a whole lot different than its predecessor.

Overall, the Photos app is meant to give you a pleasing, straightforward way to look at your picture collection, coupled with some easy-to-use photo-editing capabilities. If your expectations go a bit beyond that, you'll be disappointed because only a few advanced options are available.

In this chapter, I introduce what Photos can do, starting with how to view pictures in the app and navigate around its user interface. Then, I explain how to add pictures from different sources, how to edit with the simple but surprisingly powerful Photos tools, and how to optimize some of its settings. Lastly, I show you how to organize pictures in your very own albums.

# Viewing Pictures with the Photos App

The Photos app from Windows 11 has a simple layout for viewing your photos. Here's what you get:

>> A central place to view photos from your Windows 11 computer and OneDrive

>> Help searching for a photo

>> A way to see your photos organized by date, by collections called *albums,* or by the source folder

To get you familiarized with the Photos app, let's start a mini-tour and see how you can view pictures from your computer:

1. **In the Start menu, click or tap the Photos shortcut. If you can't find it, go to All Apps and then Photos.**

   The first time you start the Photos app, it encourages you to keep your memories safe with Microsoft OneDrive and sign in with your Microsoft account, as shown in Figure 3-1.

**FIGURE 3-1:**
The Photos app actively promotes OneDrive.

**2.** **If you don't store your pictures in OneDrive, choose Not Now. Otherwise, choose Sign In and follow the onscreen instructions.**

The main screen of the Photos app appears, displaying the Pictures collection, as shown in Figure 3-2. The Photos app uses the dark mode implicitly for its user interface, ignoring the dark and light mode settings from Windows 11. Later in this chapter, you see how to change this behavior.

**TIP**

The collection is a simple reverse chronological view of all the pictures and videos in your computer's Pictures folder, combined with all your pictures and videos in the OneDrive Pictures folder. You can add additional folders, one by one, from the Settings pane (as described later in the chapter). Note that pictures outside your Pictures folder aren't included.

**FIGURE 3-2:**
Your pictures
are displayed
in reverse
chronological
order.

**3.** **To search for a specific photo, scroll using the slider on the right to find the date the photo was taken.**

You can also search for people, places, or things by using the Search box at the top.

**4.** **To view a picture from the Photos app, double-click or double-tap it.**

The picture opens in a different view, similar to Figure 3-3. You can use the thumbnails at the bottom to view the pictures that follow or precede the one you've opened.

Working with Photos

**FIGURE 3-3:**
The Photos app
in Windows 11
has a nicer way
of displaying
pictures than in
Windows 10.

5. **Navigate your pictures by clicking or tapping their thumbnail at the bottom.**

6. **To return to your Pictures collection, click or tap the back arrow at the top left.**

**TECHNICAL STUFF**

The Photos app can display an enormous variety of picture and video formats, including AVI, BMP, GIF (including animated GIFs), JPG, MOV, MP4, MPEG, MPG, PCX, PNG, many kinds of RAW (high-quality photos), TIF, WMF, and WMV files. That covers most picture and movie formats you're likely to encounter.

**REMEMBER**

The Photos app in Windows 11 uses dark mode for its user interface. For the remainder of this chapter, I use light mode so that the printed figures in the book will be clearer.

## Adding Photos

You can add pictures to your collection in the Photos app in three ways:

» **Add photos to OneDrive.** Putting photos into the OneDrive Photos folder is a simple drag and drop. File Explorer works great for this task.

>> **Import photos from a connected device.** You can import pictures from a camera or any removable device, including a USB drive, an SD card, or even a big honking external hard drive. See the next section, "Importing Pictures from a Camera or an External Drive," for details.

>> **Add pictures to your Pictures folder.** I call this the old-fashioned way, and it's how I add pictures to the Photos app (in addition to OneDrive). Simply flip over to the desktop and use File Explorer to stick photos and videos in your Pictures folder. Remember that videos in your Videos folder don't show up in the Photos app. You need to add the Videos folder to the Photos app folder watchlist, using the instructions in the "Adding folders to the Photos app" section, later in this chapter.

# Importing pictures from a camera or an external drive

It's easy to import pictures from a camera or any kind of external data source, including a USB–attached hard drive, an SD card, or a smartphone that's connected to your computer through USB. Just attach the camera, or plug in the data card or external drive, and wait for Windows 11 to recognize it. Then, do the following:

**1.** Click or tap the Start icon and then Photos.

**2.** At the top right of the Photos app, click or tap the Import button.

The action opens the menu shown in Figure 3-4.

**3.** Choose From a Connected Device.

You see a list of devices connected to your Windows 11 PC.

**4.** Click or tap on the name of the device you want to import from.

The Photos app takes some time to scan for pictures on the devices you selected.

**5.** Select the pictures you want to import, and then click or tap the Import button, which shows the number of pictures you've selected.

The Photos app copies all the pictures to your Pictures folder.

**6.** Click or tap OK and you're done.

You see the new pictures in your Photos collection.

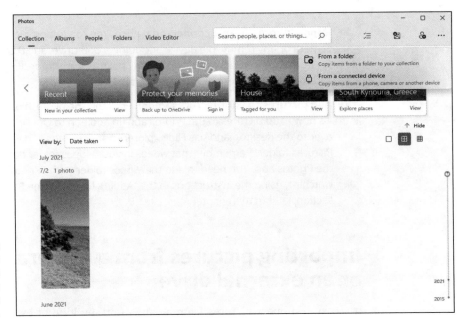

**FIGURE 3-4:**
It's easy to
import pictures
from anywhere
by using the
Photos app.

## Adding folders to the Photos app

By default, the Photos app from Windows 11 scans only your local Pictures folder
and the OneDrive Pictures folder (if you're using a Microsoft account). When you
open the app, you can't see pictures and videos from other folders. Even the video
files from your Videos folder are ignored. To fix that, and add other locations for
the Photos app to scan and manage, do the following:

**1.** **Start the Photos app and, on the top right, click or tap the three dots icon
(see more).**

**2.** **In the menu, choose Settings.**

The settings shown in Figure 3-5 appear.

**3.** **In the Sources section, click or tap Add a Folder.**

You see the Select Folder dialog.

**4.** **Browse your computer and select the folder you want to add. Then, click
or tap Add This Folder to Pictures.**

**5.** **If asked, confirm that you are okay to go ahead with this change.**

The selected folder is now listed in the Sources list that the Photos app is using.

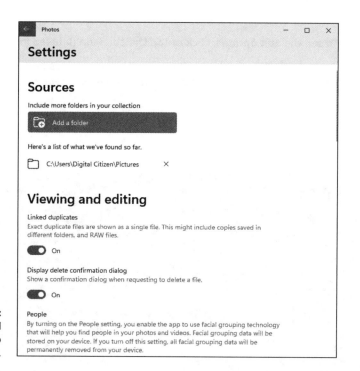

**FIGURE 3-5:**
Here you can add
more sources to
the Photos app.

# Editing Photos

The Photos app has underwhelming search capabilities, but editing a photo is easy. Although the tools at hand are rudimentary, they're also powerful. Here's how to edit a picture using the Photos app:

**1.** **Navigate to the photo in the Photos app, and click or tap it.**

An app bar appears at the top of the screen, as shown in Figure 3-6. You can (from the left): see all favorites, magnify it, zoom out, rotate it, edit it, draw on it, delete it, add it to your favorites, and see its file information. There's also an ellipsis that opens a menu with more options, including printing and resizing.

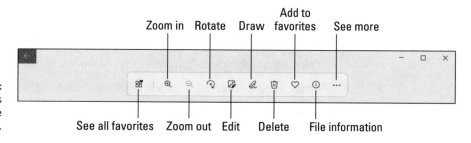

**FIGURE 3-6:**
Check the tools
available in the
Photos app.

Working with Photos

2. **To see the edit options, click or tap the edit icon (labeled in Figure 3-6).**

You have many options: add filters, create adjustments, straighten the photo, rotate it, flip it, and change its aspect ratio, as shown in Figure 3-7.

FIGURE 3-7:
The editing
options
offered by the
Photos app.

3. **To see the filter options, click or tap the filters icon (labeled in Figure 3-7).**

You have a wide variety of options for applying standard (and sometimes fanciful!) enhancement techniques to the picture.

4. **To see the adjustment options, click or tap the adjustments icon (labeled in Figure 3-7).**

The editing functions shown in Figure 3-8 appear:

- *Light:* Adjust a combination of contrast, exposure, highlights, and shadows.

- *Color:* Adjust saturation, from 0 for grayscale to 100 for ultra-saturated.

- *Clarity:* Increase the outline on automatically chosen edges.

- *Vignette:* Move the slider left to add white to the outer edges or right to add black.

- *Red eye:* Fix problems with red eyes when editing pictures of people.

- *Spot fix:* Click or tap on a spot or blemish to fix it.

**FIGURE 3-8:**
Many traditional
photo-adjusting
tools are a
swipe away.

5. **Try the red-eye function by clicking Red Eye and then clicking a specific eye or eyes with the blue dot that appears (see Figure 3-9).**

    The Photos app does a respectable job of automatically adjusting for red-eye.

6. **To blur part of the picture, click the Spot Fix button, and then click the part you want to blur a bit.**

7. **To save your changes, click Save a Copy. To quit without saving, click the X icon in the upper right.**

    You drop out of editing mode.

When you're ready to go back to your Pictures collection, click or tap the back arrow at the top left.

**FIGURE 3-9:**
Accurate red-eye
correction is just
a few clicks away.

# Switching to Light Mode in the Photos App

One aspect I don't like about the Photos app is that it insists on using dark mode for its user interface, ignoring the system settings made by the user. If you want to set it to use light mode or automatically respect the mode that you choose throughout Windows 11, do this:

1. **Start the Photos apps and, at the top right, click or tap the three dots icon.**

2. **In the menu that appears, choose Settings.**

   The settings shown previously in Figure 3-5 appear.

3. **Scroll down to the Appearance section.**

   You see the options shown in Figure 3-10.

4. **Choose Light or, better yet, choose Use System Setting, so that the Photos app changes according to your Windows 11 settings.**

   This change is applied the next time you start the Photos app.

TIP

If you want to know more about dark mode versus light mode in Windows 11, see Book 3, Chapter 1.

# Working with Albums

Once you have photos visible in the collection view at the top, the Photos app works hard at sorting your pictures into albums. It does this automatically if you use OneDrive to store your pictures. The sorting process can take hours for even a small photo collection, and as of this writing, there's nothing you can do to speed things up. Albums are created automatically, at a pace you can't control, based on the pictures you have and how many.

However, you can also create your own albums, like this:

**1.** **Start the Photos app and click or tap Albums, in the upper-left corner.**

**2.** **Click or tap New Album.**

The Create New Album wizard appears, as shown in Figure 3-11.

**3.** **Scroll down the list of pictures, and select the ones you want to add to the album.**

You can also use the Search box at the top to search for people, places, or things.

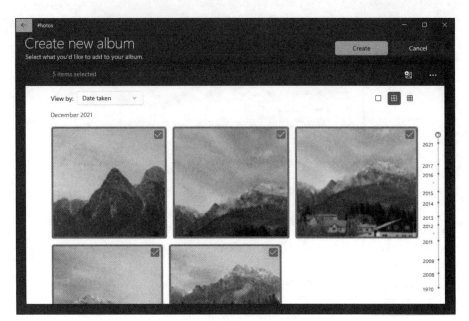

FIGURE 3-11:
Creating an
album.

4. **Click or tap Create, and then type a name for the album.**

5. **If you want the album saved on your OneDrive too, not just locally, click or tap Save in OneDrive.**

   The album is created, and you can go back to your list of albums to create another one.

**TIP**

If you want to stop the Photos app from generating albums automatically, click or tap the three dots icon at the top right, choose Settings, and set the Enable Automatically Generated Albums switch to off. (The switch is way down on the Settings screen.)

IN THIS CHAPTER

» **Getting started with OneNote**

» **Adding a notebook, sections, and pages**

» **Adding content to your notes**

» **Sending web pages to OneNote**

» **Tweaking OneNote's settings**

# Chapter **4**

# Note-Taking with OneNote

I f you haven't used OneNote, you've missed out on Microsoft's premier example of a cloud-first, mobile-first application. OneNote started as a small app in the Office suite. It's grown a lot during the years, and today it's part of Windows itself. It's arguably one of the most advanced Windows 11 apps, although Microsoft Edge fans may beg to differ.

**REMEMBER**

OneNote isn't Windows-only. Far from it. OneNote is available on the Mac, iPhones, iPads, Android smartphones and tablets, and other mobile devices. You can use OneNote to talk to yourself — pass all sorts of things around to your computers, your tablets, your smartphones. And the interface makes working with those things surprisingly easy. Your OneNote gets synchronized with the help of OneDrive and a Microsoft account.

If you install Microsoft Office or Microsoft 365, you'll get another OneNote app too. It's a desktop program like the others from the Office suite. In this chapter I don't cover the OneNote program. I show you the basics of using the OneNote app that comes with Windows 11. First, you learn how to start it and add an account to it, so that it can sync your notes. Then you see how to add content to OneNote and send stuff over from Microsoft Edge. Finally, you get to browse through OneNote's settings, so you can change the way it works.

# Getting Started in OneNote with or without a Pen

The nicest part about OneNote is that it's already installed with Windows 11. However, before you start using it, you need to set it up. Unfortunately, OneNote works only if you use a Microsoft, Work or School account. This is because OneNote syncs all your notes through the cloud, between all your devices, and it needs an account to tie them together. If you insist on using a local account, you can't use OneNote, and you need to switch to another account. For details about working with user accounts, read Book 2, Chapter 4.

Here's how to start OneNote and configure your account:

1. **Click or tap the Start icon and then All Apps.**

   You see all the apps from your Start menu.

2. **Scroll down the apps list to those that start with letter *O* and click or tap OneNote for Windows 11.**

   The OneNote app appears, asking you to pick an account to sign in, as shown in Figure 4-1.

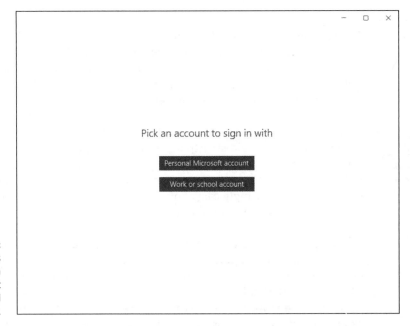

**FIGURE 4-1:**
OneNote asks you to use a Microsoft account or a Work/School account.

**3.** **Choose Personal Microsoft Account.**

A pop-up window appears with the Microsoft accounts that exist in Windows 11.

**4.** **Select your Microsoft account and click or tap Continue.**

A Windows Security prompt like the one in Figure 4-2 asks you to enter your PIN or password, depending on how your Microsoft account is set up.

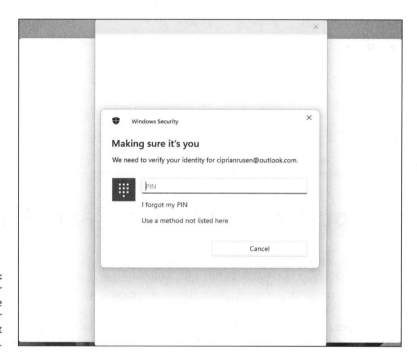

**FIGURE 4-2:**
Verify your identity before using your Microsoft account with OneNote.

**5.** **Enter your Microsoft account PIN or password.**

The OneNote app loads and displays the Untitled Page with an empty note, as shown in Figure 4-3.

**TIP**

Here's a tip for Surface Book and Surface Pro owners who have a sufficiently talented pen and have set up Windows 11 to start by using Hello face recognition (see Book 2, Chapter 2). After your machine is turned on, you may be able to crank up OneNote by simply clicking the top of the pen. That's a convenient shortcut because it's easy to start Windows 11 on a OneNote page, ready to take notes.

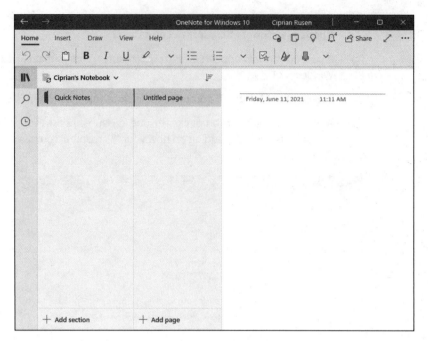

**FIGURE 4-3:**
OneNote is ready
for you to use.

# Adding Notebooks, Sections, and Pages

OneNote works with notebooks, just like Word works with documents, Excel with workbooks, and PowerPoint with presentations. Inside a notebook, there are sections. Within each section, there are pages. And on each page there can be many things: typed notes, screen shots, photos, voice recordings, marked-up web pages, tables, attached files, web links. Lots and lots of digital things. Only your imagination is the true limitation to what you can add to a OneNote page.

Here's how to get going with your very own notebook:

1. **Get OneNote fired up by clicking or tapping the Start icon, All Apps, and then OneNote for Windows 11. Or if you have a fancy pen, just click it.**

   If you've used OneNote before, you get a main screen that looks something like the one shown in Figure 4-3.

2. **Click or tap the downward-pointing arrow, to the right of the Notebook list.**

   You see the Notebook list shown in Figure 4-4.

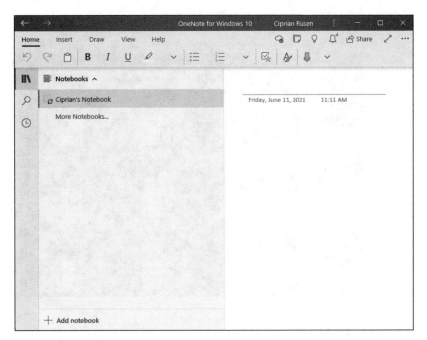

**FIGURE 4-4:**
OneNote's list of
notebooks.

3. **Click or tap the + Add Notebook link at the bottom of the list of available notebooks.**

   OneNote opens the New Notebook dialog, asking you to give your new notebook a name, as shown in Figure 4-5.

**FIGURE 4-5:**
Type the name of
the notebook.

4. **Type a name and press Enter or click or tap Create Notebook.**

   OneNote creates a new notebook and puts a link to it in your OneDrive's Documents folder. In Figure 4-6, the new notebook appears as Windows 11 For Dummies (the filename extension is .one, although you can't see it).

REMEMBER

   One weird aspect of OneNote is that your notebooks are saved not locally on your Windows 11 computer but in your OneDrive's Documents folder. Unless you set OneDrive to sync your local Documents folder with its Documents (see Book 4, Chapter 5), you won't see your OneNote notebooks in your File Explorer's Documents folder. But if you log in to OneDrive (www.onedrive.com), you'll see them.

Note-Taking with
OneNote

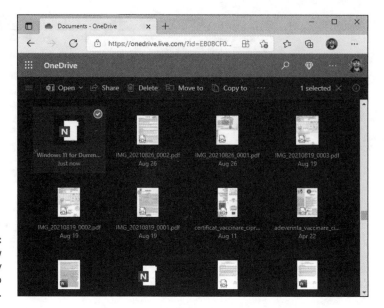

**FIGURE 4-6:**
The new
notebook really
does get saved to
your OneDrive.

Now that you have a new notebook, let's add a couple of sections. Like adding tabs in a web browser, adding new sections is flat-out simple:

1. **Return to the default notebook.**

   To do so, click or tap the arrow next to the new notebook and choose the default notebook, which should have your name.

2. **On the first tab (where it says Quick Notes in Figure 4-3), right-click or press and hold down, and then choose Rename Section.**

   You can also delete the section, change the section color, and do a lot more, as you can see in Figure 4-7.

3. **Type a new name, and press Enter.**

   The new name appears on the tab.

4. **To add another section, click or tap the + Add Section link at the bottom of the list of sections, type a name, and press Enter.**

   If you've ever worked with tabs in a browser, you already know all you need.

5. **To add pages to a section, click or tap + Add Page, at the bottom of the list of pages.**

   A new, empty, and untitled page appears, ready for you to fill it, as shown in Figure 4-8.

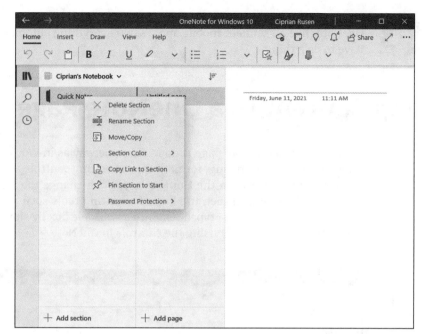

**FIGURE 4-7:**
Rename a tab —
a section — by
right-clicking.

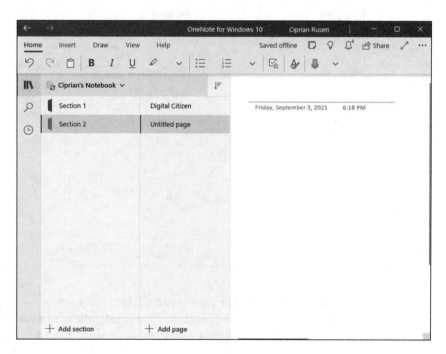

**FIGURE 4-8:**
Creating a page,
the OneNote way.

Note-Taking with
OneNote

**REMEMBER**

OneNote (like all sentient mobile apps) saves everything automatically. You don't have to do a thing.

# Adding Content to a OneNote Page

Writing inside a OneNote page is done the same way as in Word, Notepad, or any other text editor. The typing, formatting, and editing controls at the top work just like you would expect. On the Home tab, you can change the font used for your text notes, its size, and then use basic formatting tools such as bold, italic, and underline. In Figure 4-9, I typed text into a resizable box by simply typing on the keyboard and formatted it using the controls in OneNote.

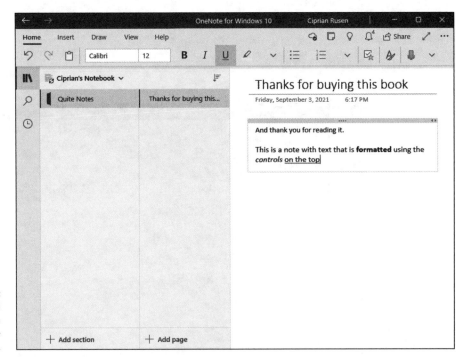

**FIGURE 4-9:**
Typing and formatting a OneNote page is easy.

You might think that you need a pen to draw in OneNote — and, believe me, a good pen helps! — but the fact is that you can doodle with your finger on a touch-sensitive computer, or with a mouse or trackpad if need be. It's just that some pens are sensitive to pressure, so lines and doodles you create with a pen look much more refined than they do with a mouse.

Here's how to draw on a OneNote page:

**1.** **Start with whatever OneNote page you want to doodle on. Then click or tap the Draw tab at the top.**

OneNote responds with the tools and palette shown in Figure 4-10.

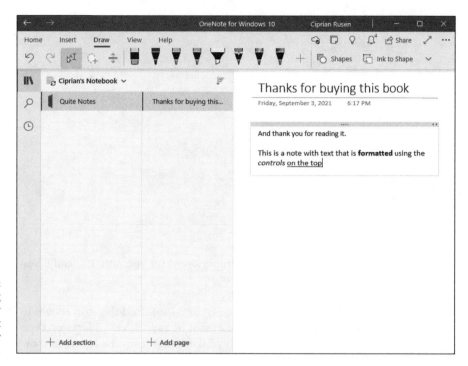

FIGURE 4-10:
Extensive drawing tools work better with a pen, but they'll do okay with a mouse.

**2.** **Prepare for drawing:**

a. *Select a pen — narrow, highlighter, multicolor.*

b. *Click or tap the down arrow at the bottom of the pen icon and choose a color.*

c. *Adjust the thickness of the pen by clicking or tapping the plus and minus signs or by choosing a bigger or smaller dot.*

The cursor turns into a circle.

**3.** **Draw away on the OneNote page on the right.**

See the quick drawing I made in Figure 4-11.

**4.** **If you don't like what you just drew, press Ctrl+Z.**

That deletes the drawing you just made on the notebook page and lets you start all over.

Note-Taking with OneNote

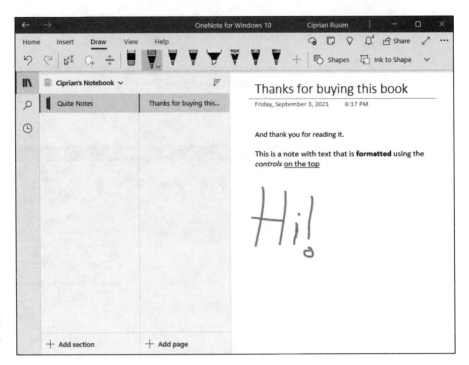

FIGURE 4-11:
Drawing — even
with a mouse —
is easy.

Remember that everything is saved for you automatically; you don't need to do a thing.

 On the Draw tab (refer to Figure 4-10), find the icon shown in the margin. If you hover your mouse cursor over it, it says Select Objects or Type Text. Use this icon to select text (say, to apply formatting from the Home tab) or to create a box into which you can type or insert a picture.

 The icon next to it, which looks like a dotted loop with a +, is lasso select. Use it to select items to move, copy, or delete as a group.

 The icon with two arrows pointing up and down and two lines in the middle lets you add or delete whitespace — kind of a move it down or up shortcut.

 The icon that looks like an eraser is an eraser (saints be praised!). If you're an experienced word-processing geek, it's a little difficult to think about the typed text as being just a picture, but you can erase it like a picture. Erase half a letter or right down the middle of a line. Go ahead. OneNote doesn't mind.

# Sending Sites from Microsoft Edge to OneNote

There is one surprising place where OneNote is reasonably well connected: Microsoft Edge. It's easy to take a snapshot of a web page from this browser and send it to OneNote. Here's how it works:

**1.** **Open Microsoft Edge and browse to a website you like.**

I chose my very own blog: `www.digitalcitizen.life`.

**2.** **Click or tap the three dots icon in the upper-right corner of Microsoft Edge and choose Share.**

OneNote shows you the Share Link pane, as shown in Figure 4-12.

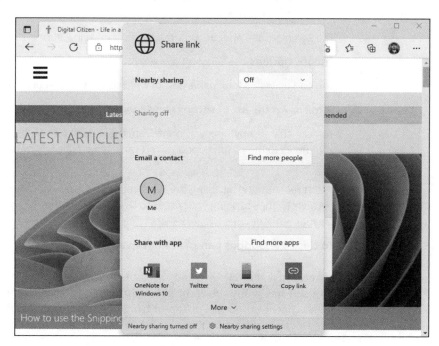

**FIGURE 4-12:**
Choose to share with OneNote.

**3.** **In the Share with App section, click or tap OneNote for Windows 11.**

You see the OneNote sharing window.

OneNote asks you to pick a default location for new notes.

4. **Choose the notebook you want from the drop-down list, enter a note, if you want, and click or tap Send.**

   The web page is sent to OneNote.

5. **Go to OneNote.**

   The page is sitting in the notebook you chose.

# Configuring OneNote's Settings

OneNote has a handful of settings you might want to try some day. Or maybe not. To see them, follow these steps:

1. **Inside OneNote, click or tap the three dots icon in the upper-right corner and choose Settings.**

   The Settings pane appears on the right, as shown in Figure 4-13.

2. **Choose Options.**

   You end up with a long pane, part of which is shown in Figure 4-14.

3. **Scroll down the list of settings and change what you want.**

   You can change anything you want, from the default font and size used for your notes to the pasting options. You can even enable legacy navigation panes.

   **WARNING**

   I don't recommend disabling the Sync Notebooks Automatically setting because it stops sending your notes to OneDrive, and they won't be accessible on your other devices.

4. **To close the Options pane, click or tap anywhere outside it.**

This chapter just scratched the surface of OneNote's capabilities. You'll find that the app itself has many different guises in many different locations — OneNote online (www.onenote.com) is different from OneNote for the iPad, which is different from OneNote for smartphones, and so on.

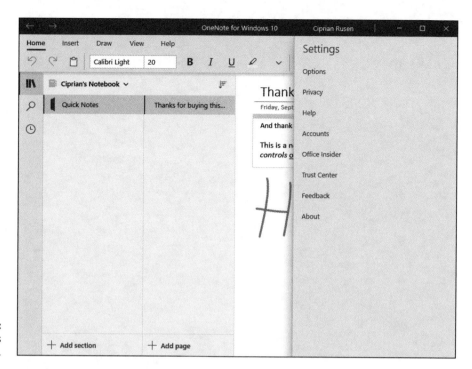

**FIGURE 4-13:**
OneNote's
Settings pane.

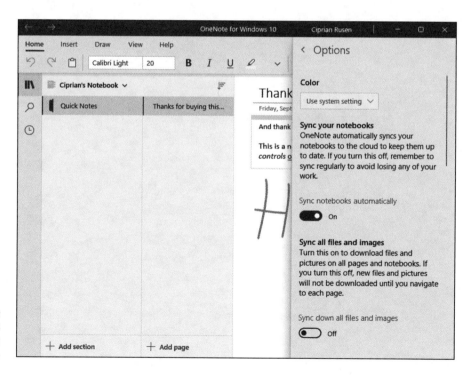

**FIGURE 4-14:**
A few settings
may prove
worthwhile.

Note-Taking with
OneNote

IN THIS CHAPTER

» **Introducing OneDrive**

» **Working with OneDrive through File Explorer**

» **Running OneDrive on the internet**

» **Files On-Demand**

» **Sharing files and folders on OneDrive**

# Chapter **5**

# Storing in OneDrive

L et's start with the basics: OneDrive is an online storage service, sold by Microsoft, which has some features woven into Windows to make it easier to work with your files stored on Microsoft's servers in the cloud. (*Cloud* is another word for the web or the internet.) "In the cloud" is just a euphemism for "stored on somebody else's computer."

If you have a Microsoft account (such as an Outlook.com ID, or Hotmail ID, or any of a dozen other kinds of Microsoft accounts — see Book 2, Chapter 5), you already have free OneDrive storage space, ready for you to use.

OneDrive has many competitors — Dropbox (which I used for this book), Google Drive (see Book 10, Chapter 4), Apple iCloud, SugarSync, Box, and many others. These competitors all have advantages and disadvantages — and the feature list changes constantly. However, OneDrive is here to stay, and it's embedded into Windows 11.

If you also use Microsoft Office or have a Microsoft 365 (formerly known as Office 365) subscription, you may want to use OneDrive, and use it productively. That's why, in this chapter, I show you just about everything you need to know to make OneDrive work for you: how to set it up, add files and folders, and share files and folders. You also learn about the states of OneDrive data.

# What Is OneDrive?

*OneDrive* is an internet-based storage platform with a chunk of space offered for free by Microsoft to anyone with a Microsoft account. Think of it as a hard drive in the cloud, which you can share, with a few extra benefits thrown in. One of the primary benefits: OneDrive hooks into Windows 11 and Windows 10. Microsoft, of course, wants you to buy more storage, but you're under no obligation to do so.

**REMEMBER**

As of this writing, OneDrive gives everyone with a Microsoft account 5GB of free storage (down from 15GB free in 2015), with the option to expand it to 200GB for $2/month. Many Microsoft 365 subscription levels have 1TB (1024GB) OneDrive storage, for as long as you're a subscriber. Back in 2015, the Office 365 subscriptions had unlimited storage, but Microsoft giveth and Microsoft taketh away.

Microsoft's offers change from time to time, but the general trend is that prices are going down.

The free storage is there even if you never use OneDrive. In fact, if you have a Microsoft account, you're all signed up for OneDrive, and you can access it straight from File Explorer. See Figure 5-1.

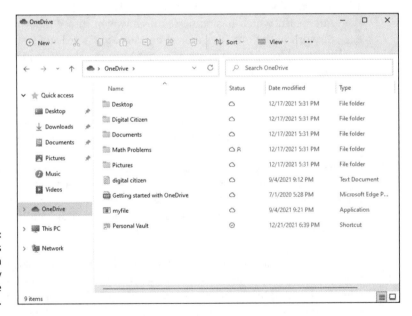

**FIGURE 5-1:** OneDrive files look and act a lot like everyday files, but they're different.

**REMEMBER**

Here are the keys to using OneDrive effectively:

>> OneDrive does what all the other cloud storage services do — it gives you a place to put your files on the internet. You need to log in to OneDrive with your Microsoft account (or Windows 11) to access your data.

>> OneDrive keeps a history of all changes you made to files over the past 30 days. That feature can be useful — and a lifesaver if you get hit by ransomware.

>> If you log in to a different device or computer (Windows, Mac, iPad, Android) using the same Microsoft account, you have access to all your OneDrive data.

>> You can share files or folders stored in OneDrive by sending or posting a link to the file or folder to whomever you want. So, for example, if you want Aunt Martha to be able to see the folder full of pictures of little Billy, OneDrive creates a link for you that you can email to Aunt Martha. You can also set a file or folder as Public, so anyone can see it.

>> To work with the OneDrive platform on a mobile device, you can download and install one of the OneDrive apps — OneDrive for Mac, iPhone, iPad, or Android. The mobile apps have many of the same features that you find in Windows 11.

>> In Windows 11, you don't need to download or install a special program for OneDrive — it's already baked into the operating system.

>> If you have the program installed, as soon as you connect to a network OneDrive syncs data among computers, smartphones, and tablets that are set up using the same Microsoft account. For example, if you change a OneDrive file on your iPad and save it, the modified file is put in your OneDrive storage area on the internet. From there, the new version of the file is available to all other computers with access to the file. Ditto for Android devices.

# Setting Up a OneDrive Account

If you sign in to Windows 11 with a Microsoft account, File Explorer gets primed automatically to tie into your OneDrive account, using the same Microsoft account ID and password you use to sign in.

But if you're using a local account (see Book 2, Chapter 4), life isn't so simple. You must either create a Microsoft account or sign into an existing Microsoft account (and thus an existing OneDrive account). Follow the advice in Book 2, Chapter 5 to get a Microsoft account set up. After you have a Microsoft account, here's how to set up OneDrive. Don't worry, you need to do this only once:

1. **On the taskbar, click or tap the File Explorer icon.**

   You see File Explorer.

2. **On the left, click or tap OneDrive.**

   You get a Set Up OneDrive splash screen, as shown in Figure 5-2.

**FIGURE 5-2:**
If you're using a local account, hook it into OneDrive with a Microsoft account.

3. **Type the email address of your Microsoft account, and then click or tap Sign In.**

4. **Enter the password and click or tap Sign In one more time.**

   OneDrive informs you that it respects your privacy and describes the type of data it gathers.

5. **Click or tap Next.**

   OneDrive asks about what kind of optional diagnostic and usage data you want it to collect.

6. **Choose Don't Send Optional Data and click or tap Accept.**

   OneDrive shares the location of the OneDrive folder. As you can see in Figure 5-3, it creates a OneDrive subfolder in your user folder.

**FIGURE 5-3:**
Choose where you want your OneDrive folder.

7. **If you're happy with the default location, click or tap Next. Otherwise, click or tap Change Location and select another folder on your Windows 11 PC.**

   OneDrive informs you that it's going to back up user folders such as Desktop, Documents, and Pictures.

8. **If you're happy with OneDrive backing up your user folders, leave them selected (I recommend that you do) and click or tap Continue. Otherwise, deselect them before clicking or tapping Continue.**

   OneDrive teaches you how to add items to the OneDrive folder, share files with others, and so on. Pay attention when you the screen about Files On-Demand, as shown in Figure 5-4. See the next section for details.

9. **Click or tap Next to navigate through all the screens.**

10. **When encouraged to Get the Mobile App, click or tap Later.**

    You're presented with an opportunity to open your OneDrive folder.

11. **Click or tap Open My OneDrive Folder.**

Now you're ready to set up synchronization between your PC and your OneDrive files in the cloud — which is to say, syncing between your PC and the copies of your files stored on Microsoft's computers.

**FIGURE 5-4:**
A short explainer
for Files
On-Demand.

# The Four States of OneDrive Data

On any given computer or device, all data in OneDrive exists in one of four states:

>> **Online-only:** Files you've stored in your OneDrive storage but not down-loaded locally. You can see a list of these files, even if you don't have an internet connection, but you can open them only if you have internet access.

>> **On this device:** Files from your OneDrive space that you have opened and File Explorer has downloaded and stored locally. These files can be reopened and used even when you don't have an internet connection. They are taking up space in your local storage. They get synchronized each time you're connected to the internet.

>> **Always available:** Files from your OneDrive that you've explicitly set to always be available offline. They are permanently taking up space on your local storage but are also always available for use, regardless of whether or not you have an internet connection. They get synchronized each time you're con-nected to the internet.

>> **In sync:** Files found in the middle of the synchronization process between your machine and Microsoft's computers.

That's the story behind the options shown in Figure 5-4.

**TIP**

Why wouldn't you choose to sync all your files and folders? Because the amount of data in your OneDrive cloud account could be enormous (5GB, just for starters). Syncing that data on your machine takes up not only disk space but also time and internet bandwidth because missing files will be downloaded and altered files will be uploaded, every time you're connected to the internet.

However, if you have lots of available disk space, and your internet connection is reasonably fast (and not hampered by ridiculous data caps), there's little reason to keep OneDrive files sitting stranded in the cloud and not copied to your machine.

**WARNING**

An important caveat: If you have OneDrive files or folders that you use all the time, you probably want to make them available on your machine. That way, if your internet connection is unavailable — say, you hop on a flight or a cruise with exorbitant Wi-Fi fees — you can continue to work on the files while the internet goes on without you. When you connect to the internet again, your files get synced with OneDrive in the cloud.

File Explorer tells you the status of every file and folder in your OneDrive by using tiny icons in the Status column, as shown in Figure 5-5:

» **Blue cloud icon:** The file or folder is available when online and is stored in the cloud, not on your machine.

» **White icon with a green check mark:** The item is available locally on your machine, not just on Microsoft's servers.

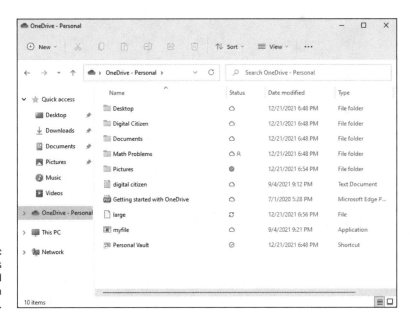

**FIGURE 5-5:**
The status icons for folders and files stored in OneDrive.

>> **Green icon with a white check mark:** The item is set to always be available on your device.

>> **Person icon:** The shared file or folders can be accessed by others. This icon is displayed alongside other status icons.

>> **Blue refresh icon:** The file is in the process of synchronizing with OneDrive.

To get OneDrive well and truly sorted, follow these instructions to step through the settings:

**1.** **Click or tap the OneDrive cloud icon on the right side of the taskbar, next to the time. Then click or tap the Help & Settings button.**

If you don't see the OneDrive cloud icon, click or tap the up arrow first.

The options shown in Figure 5-6 appear.

**2.** **Choose Settings, and then click or tap the Settings tab.**

The Microsoft OneDrive Settings pane appears, as shown in Figure 5-7.

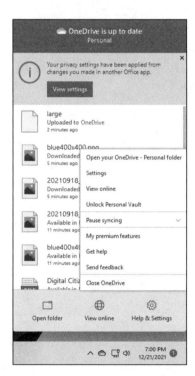

**FIGURE 5-6:**
Accessing OneDrive's settings.

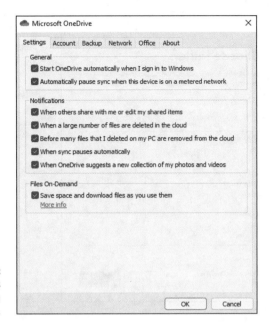

**FIGURE 5-7:**
Turn Files
On-Demand on
or off here.

**3.** **Make sure the box marked Save Space and Download Files as You Use Them is selected.**

As long as OneDrive is working properly (not an absolute given), you're better off with that box selected.

**4.** **Click or tap the Account tab, followed by Choose Folders.**

The Choose Folders pane appears, as shown in Figure 5-8.

**5.** **Do one of the following:**

- If you have a lot of room on your PC and have a reasonably good internet connection, select the Make All Files Available box. Click or tap OK.

- If you don't want to slavishly sync all OneDrive files onto this particular PC, deselect the Make All Files Available box, and select boxes next to the folders you want to sync. Click or tap OK.

**6.** **Click or tap the Backup tab and make your selections.**

The screen shown in Figure 5-9 appears. You can choose to back up to OneDrive your files in the Desktop, Documents, and Pictures folders, so that the files are protected even if your machine has problems. You also set whether you want to automatically save to OneDrive pictures and videos from the cameras, phones, and other devices you connect to your Windows 11 PC as well as screen shots you capture.

**FIGURE 5-8:**
Sync all OneDrive
data or choose
which folders
get the Files
On-Demand
treatment.

**FIGURE 5-9:**
Set what you
want OneDrive to
back up for you.

7. **If you want to automatically limit the effect OneDrive's synchronization can have on your internet connection, click or tap the Network tab and make your choices.**

   You can set throttles for both uploading (sending your data to OneDrive in the cloud) and downloading (pulling data from OneDrive onto your machine).

8. **If you want to disconnect sync for Office files — it's set up automatically, with Microsoft Office — choose the Office tab and go from there.**

9. **When you've finished setting OneDrive the way you want, click or tap OK.**

   It may take a while for OneDrive to sync, but when it's finished, all folders you've chosen to sync will appear in File Explorer with the appropriate status icons. Figure 5-10 shows the result of making the choices in Figure 5-8.

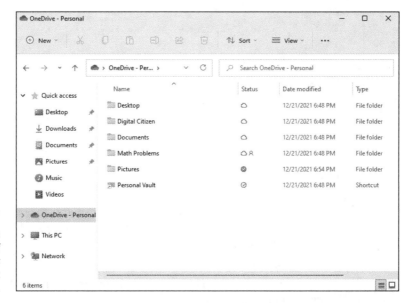

**FIGURE 5-10:** The result of applying your OneDrive sync settings.

# Adding Files and Folders to OneDrive

From the screen shown in Figure 5-10, you can add a file to any of the folders on OneDrive. After you've added files, you can delete them or you can download them to your computer by simply dragging and dropping, the way you usually move files.

Anything you can do to files anywhere, you can do inside the OneDrive folder — if you use File Explorer or one of the (many) apps, such as the Microsoft Office apps (see Figure 5-11), that behave themselves with OneDrive.

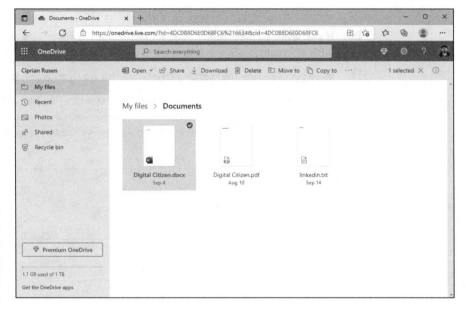

**FIGURE 5-11:**
If you open a
DOCX file from
onedrive.com,
Online Word
appears and
handles it.

For example, you can:

» Edit, rename, and copy files, as well as move vast numbers of them. The OneDrive folder in File Explorer is by far the easiest way to put data into and take data out of OneDrive.

» Add subfolders inside the OneDrive folder, rename them, delete them, move files around, and drag and drop files and folders in and out of the OneDrive folder to your heart's desire.

» Change file properties (by right-clicking or by pressing and holding down if you have a touchscreen).

» Print files from OneDrive just as you would any other file in File Explorer.

TIP

What makes the OneDrive folder in File Explorer unique is that when you drag files into it, the files are copied into the cloud. If you have other computers connected to OneDrive with the same Microsoft account, those other computers may or may not get copies of the files (depending on whether the Make All Files Available option in the PC's OneDrive is selected), but they can all access the files and folders through a web browser.

It may take a minute or two to upload the files, and then they appear everywhere, magically.

So, if you have other computers (or tablets or smartphones) that you want to sync with your computer, now would be a good time to go to those other computers and install whichever version of the OneDrive program is compatible with the device. Remember that a OneDrive app is available for Windows, Mac, iPad and iPhone. There's also a OneDrive app for Android smartphones and tablets. That's the one I use on my Samsung Galaxy smartphone, as shown in Figure 5-12.

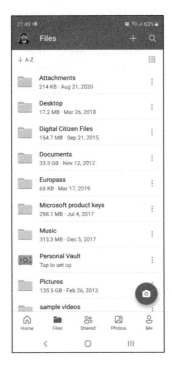

**FIGURE 5-12:**
The OneDrive app on an Android smartphone.

**WARNING**

Know that if you delete a folder or file marked Online-Only, you'll well and truly delete the file or folder — no extra copy is hanging around. However, OneDrive keeps deleted files for 30 days in a Recycle Bin folder, which you can access online at `https://onedrive.com/`. That's the only place where you have a chance of recovering them.

# Changing the States of OneDrive Data

It's remarkably easy to change among the four states of OneDrive data:

>> In the cloud only.

>> On your machine, synced.

>> On your machine, synced, and you've told OneDrive that you *always* want a copy of it on your machine.

>> On your machine but not yet synced (a sync may be in progress).

In general, all you have to do is right-click (or press and hold down on) a file or folder — even the entire OneDrive folder — and choose the correct option. For example, in Figure 5-13, I right-clicked the Math Problems folder, which is already synced.

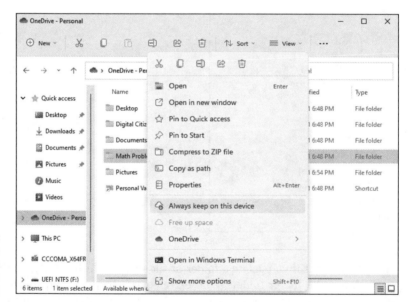

**FIGURE 5-13:**
Changing the
OneDrive state
of the Math
Problems folder.

From this point, I have two state-changing choices:

>> If I select Always Keep on This Device, OneDrive will change the state to Always Available and keep a copy on the PC.

>> If I select Free Up Space, OneDrive will delete the copy of data currently on the PC and set the state to Online-Only.

In general, after OneDrive has stopped syncing, you can change from one state to another by right-clicking (or pressing and holding down).

# Sharing OneDrive Files and Folders

Sharing files and folders with OneDrive couldn't be simpler. All it takes are just a few clicks (or taps). Here's how it is done:

**1.** **Open the OneDrive folder in File Explorer.**

**2.** **Navigate to the file or folder that you want to share, and right-click (or press and hold down on) it.**

The right-click menu opens, with several contextual options, as shown in Figure 5-14.

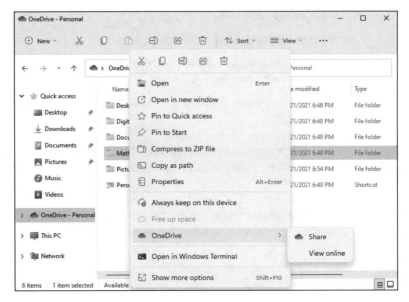

**FIGURE 5-14:**
Access OneDrive's
sharing options.

**3.** **Choose OneDrive and then Share.**

You can share the file or folder via email, copy a link to it that you can paste into a chat app or some other place, set the sharing permissions, and more, as shown in Figure 5-15.

**FIGURE 5-15:**
The OneDrive
Share dialog.

4. **Click or tap Copy Link.**

   You see the sharing link generated by OneDrive.

5. **Paste the sharing link from OneDrive anywhere you want (email, chat window, web browser, and so on).**

6. **When you're done, close the OneDrive Share window by tapping X in the upper right.**

TIP

If you click or tap Anyone with the Link Can Edit, you can also set an expiration date for the share. However, this option works only for premium (paid) versions of OneDrive.

OneDrive has many more capabilities. See the tutorials at `https://support. microsoft.com/en-us/onedrive` for an overview.

# Chapter 6

# Communicating with Skype

Everybody knows Skype, the instant-text-messaging, long-distance, telephone-killing video-chatting program. Not everybody knows that it started as something of a hacker's fantasy in 2003, in Estonia. Two of the key players in getting Skype to market, Janus Friis from Denmark and Niklas Zennstrom from Sweden, spent their earlier years getting Kazaa — the notorious file-sharing program that was used to distribute copyrighted content for free — off the ground.

Microsoft bought Skype in 2011, for a paltry $8.5 billion — yes, that's *billion* with a *b*. The management moved to Redmond, but most of the techies are still in Tallinn and Tartu, Estonia. As years went by, Skype has become a Microsoft product. One hundred percent. And this is not necessarily great.

Skype works, and it works well with iPhones, iPads, and Android smartphones and tablets, but it's had a difficult time with Windows. It took Microsoft a few years to get around to building a Skype app for Windows 8.1, and then the app was widely panned and shunned. The current Skype app for Windows 11 is better, but it's not actively promoted by Microsoft, as was the case in Windows 10. Microsoft prefers to promote Microsoft Teams instead.

Getting back to Skype, many folks swear by the browser-based version (you can find it at https://web.skype.com/). However, there's also a Skype app available for download. You find it at www.skype.com/en/get-skype/.

In this chapter, you look at the Skype app for Windows 11. I start by showing you how to set it up, and then cover how to add contacts, configure Skype, make and record calls.

## Signing Up with Skype

**WARNING**

If you're using a local account to sign in to Windows 11 — as opposed to a Microsoft account — and you crank up Skype, Skype prompts you immediately to use a Microsoft account. **If you want to use Skype, you must use it with a Microsoft account.**

With that warning out of the way, here's how to get started with Skype:

**1.** **Click or tap the Start icon, All Apps, and then Skype.**

Skype logs you in with your Microsoft account or nudges you to enter a Microsoft account.

**2.** **If you're starting Skype for the first time, click or tap Let's Go. Then, if you're not using a Microsoft account in Windows 11, click or tap Sign In or Create (see Figure 6-1)**

**3.** **Do one of the following:**

- *If you're logged into Windows 11 with a Microsoft account, you only need to select your account when shown.*

- *If you have a Microsoft account, and you logged into Windows 11 with a local account, enter the details of your Microsoft account and click or tap Next.*

- *If you don't have a Microsoft account, create one now and then click or tap Next.*

Skype may ask about updating your profile picture.

**4.** **If prompted to update your profile picture:**

- *To use the existing profile picture: Click or tap Continue.*

- *To update your picture: Click or tap Upload Photo, and choose another picture for Skype.*

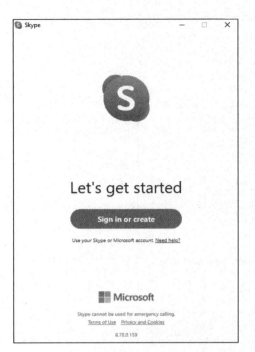

**FIGURE 6-1:**
It's time to sign
into Skype.

5. **When Skype asks you to test your audio (see Figure 6-2):**

   a. *Choose the microphone that you want to use, and start speaking.* You should see the volume dots picking up your voice.

   b. *Choose the device that you want to use for Speakers, and click or tap Continue.*

   c. *(Optional but recommended) Test the audio and make a free test call to see if your microphone and speaker settings work well.*

6. **When Skype asks you to test your video:**

   a. *Choose the webcam that you want to use and see if it works in the preview that appears.*

   b. *When everything works, click or tap Continue.*

7. **When Skype mentions finding contacts, click or tap OK.**

8. **When Skype asks about sharing optional and diagnostic data, choose Yes or No, depending on what you want.**

   Skype finally gets around to its main page, as shown in Figure 6-3.

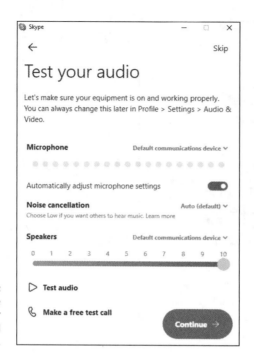

**FIGURE 6-2:**
Configure
and test your
microphone and
speakers.

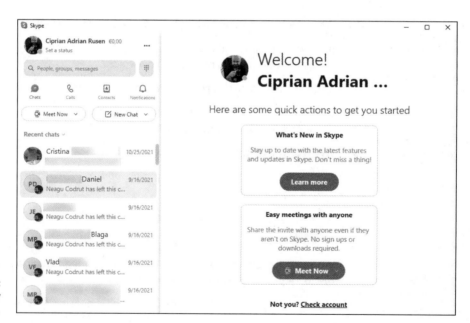

**FIGURE 6-3:**
Skype is ready
to use.

Note the following about the main Skype screen:

>> The you icon (a picture of you in the upper-left corner or an icon with the initials of your Skype name) displays details about your account. Skype may be smart enough to pull your picture from your Microsoft account. (You can change the photo directly, though.)

>> Click or tap the Contacts icon to display a list of your Skype contacts and bots, as shown in Figure 6-4. Note that Skype contacts are not the same as your People app contacts. They're unique to Skype. The bots, which look like regular contacts, are automated responders (chat algorithms) that provide some type of support service (for booking flights, troubleshooting technical problems, and so on).

>> Conversations appear in the left pane, under Recent Chats.

>> On the right side of the screen, you have room to keep track of your latest conversation with whichever contact you've chosen on the left.

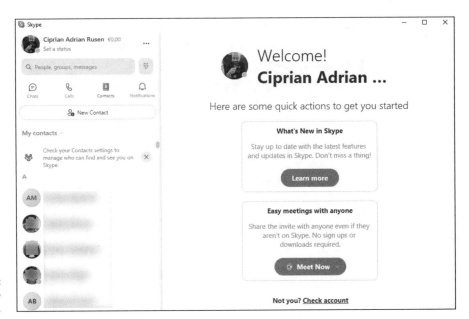

**FIGURE 6-4:**
Your Skype contacts.

# Adding a Contact

Before you can call someone, you must make the person an official contact — which means you have to ask for, and receive, permission to call.

**REMEMBER**

The methods for adding contacts vary depending on which version of Skype you're using. In most versions, you must go to the Contacts list before you can add a new contact. Here's how to add a contact in the Skype app from Windows 11:

1. **Open Skype and click or tap Contacts.**

   You get to the screen shown previously in Figure 6-4.

2. **Click or tap New Contact.**

   You see the Add a New Contact form, as shown in Figure 6-5. Yes, trying to search by name can be a hassle. Skype lets you search by name (such as Ciprian Rusen), Skype name (a name that predates the use of Microsoft accounts), or email (a Microsoft account).

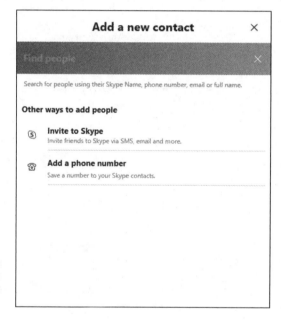

**FIGURE 6-5:**
From here you add new contacts on Skype.

3. **Type the name of the person you want to add. Then, right-click or tap and hold down on the name and click or tap View Profile.**

   Verify that the person you've selected is the one you want to converse with.

4. **Click or tap Add Contact, and then Send Message.**

Skype formulates and offers to send a message to that person. If you click or tap Say Hi, Skype sends the message and logs the fact on your call screen, as shown in Figure 6-6.

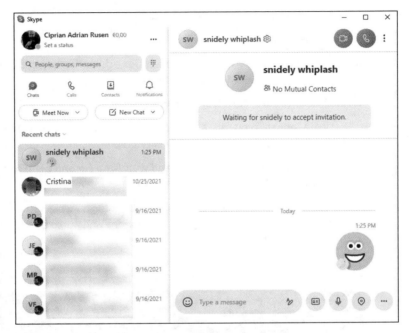

**FIGURE 6-6:**
Skype sends a message to the person you'd like to turn into a friend.

5. **Wait.**

If your contact-to-be clicks or taps the invitation, and either responds to it (as on the Android) or clicks or taps Accept, you'll suddenly find yourself able to communicate.

6. **Add a few more contacts, and you're ready to roll.**

If you close Skype (by clicking or tapping X), the app continues to run — it can notify you of any incoming calls — but it shows you as offline. A Skype icon is conveniently stuck on your taskbar, just to remind you that the program's alive and well.

# Testing Your Skype Settings

Each of the different versions of Skype — the Windows 11 app version, the desktop app version from the Skype website, the iPad or Android one, and so on — presents a slightly different way of working, but they all have the same basic core features. The location of features on the screen may vary, but the actions are all similar.

Before you get started with Skype, it's a good idea to make sure your microphone, speakers, and (optionally) camera are working. To do so, follow these steps:

**1.** **Open Skype and click or tap Contacts.**

You get to the screen shown in Figure 6-4.

**2.** **In the Search box at the top, search for** echo, **and then click or tap Echo/ Sound Test Service in the list of results.**

**3.** **Click or tap the Calls icon on the top right.**

Skype connects you with a test bot (Cortana should be jealous) that asks you to speak for a few seconds, as shown in Figure 6-7.

**4.** **Say something after the beep and wait for a second beep to be played. Don't close the call.**

After the second beep, the bot will play back to you what it heard. If you don't hear yourself, it means that your microphone and audio settings are configured incorrectly.

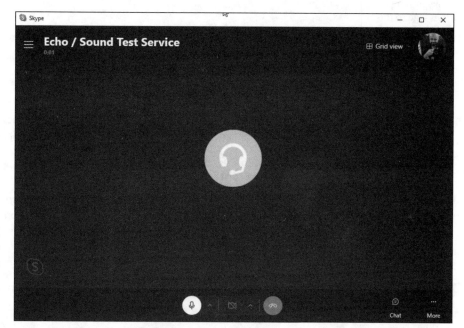

**FIGURE 6-7:**
Skype's Echo/
Sound Test
Service helps you
check whether
your microphone
is working.

# Improving Skype's Settings

If your earlier sound test failed or you just want to improve other aspects of Skype, here's how to access its settings:

**1.** **Open Skype and click or tap your picture (or the initials of your Skype name) in the upper left.**

A pane appears on the left side of Skype, as shown in Figure 6-8.

**2.** **Scroll down to the Manage section and click or tap Settings.**

Skype's Settings are shown in all their glory.

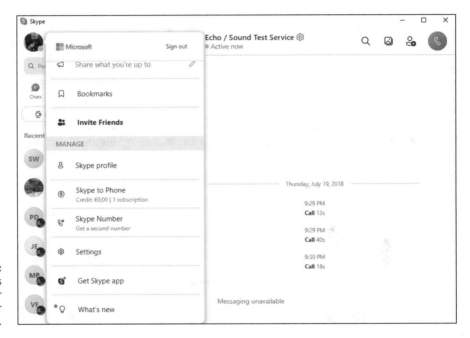

**FIGURE 6-8:** This pane gives you options for managing your Skype account.

**3.** **On the left, click or tap Audio & Video.**

The options shown in Figure 6-9 appear and you can set your webcam, microphone, and speakers. If you see yourself in the Camera section, you've chosen the correct webcam and it is working.

**4.** **When you've finished changing things, use the Make a Free Test Call option at the bottom, and try a similar test to the one described in the "Signing Up with Skype" section.**

CHAPTER 6 **Communicating with Skype** 353

FIGURE 6-9:
Settings for Skype
audio and video.

TIP

If you want to see fewer notifications from Skype, click or tap the Notifications section in Settings. The screen shown in Figure 6-10 appears, and you can change the way Skype notifies you and disable the notification sounds that may annoy you.

FIGURE 6-10:
Settings for
controlling Skype
notifications.

# Making Individual and Group Calls

The lockdown caused by the Covid-19 pandemic has forced many people to work from home and interact with their peers digitally. A useful feature of Skype is the option to easily make individual or group audio and video calls.

You can start a call in many ways. Here is the easiest method, from the Windows 11 Skype app:

1. **Open Skype and click or tap the Calls icon, near the top of the left pane.**

2. **Click or tap the New Call button.**

   Skype displays a list with your contacts.

3. **Select the person or the people you want to have a call with by clicking or tapping the circle next to each name to add a check mark (as shown in Figure 6-11), and then click or tap Call.**

   If you select one person, you start a one-to-one call. If you select two or more people, you start a group call. Your Skype voice call is initiated, and you can add a video feed to it even before the other participants answer by clicking or tapping the webcam icon at the bottom of the call screen.

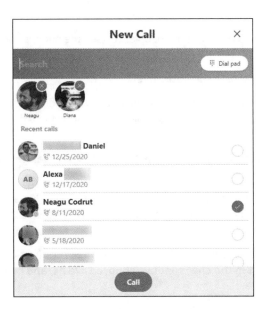

**FIGURE 6-11:**
Starting a group call in Skype for Windows 11.

REMEMBER

The procedure for starting a group call or a one-on-one call is the same in all versions of Skype, including Skype for Android, iPhone, or iPad. The only difference is that the buttons are placed in various locations.

WARNING

You can start calls in Skype for Web (https://web.skype.com/) too, but only if you load it in Google Chrome or Microsoft Edge. Microsoft doesn't provide this feature in other web browsers.

# Recording Calls

If you have an important Skype call and want to make sure you don't forget anything that was said, it's a good idea to record your call. The same is true if you're a teacher or a trainer who delivers a lesson or presentation to others.

You can record Skype calls with people using different platforms. Skype records everything during a call, including voice, everyone's combined video stream side-by-side, and screen sharing.

To record a Skype call, follow these steps:

1. **Start a Skype call.**

   The call can be with one or more people. You see the options shown in Figure 6-12.

2. **Click or tap Record, in the bottom left.**

   The recording starts. A banner at the top of the screen displays a reminder, as well as the elapsed time. People in your call are also notified that you're recording.

3. **To stop recording, click or tap Stop Recording in the banner at the top of the call screen or the Stop button at the bottom.**

   The recording is available in the conversation window for 30 days, to both you and the other participants. You can always access the conversation in the Recent Chats list.

4. **If you want to save the recording on your computer, right-click or tap and hold down on it in the chat window, choose Save As, and provide a name and location.**

TIP

Skype-to-Skype calls are free. But other options aren't. However, Skype options are usually much, much cheaper than normal long-distance phone charges. Skype has promotions all the time. You should see www.skype.com for starters.

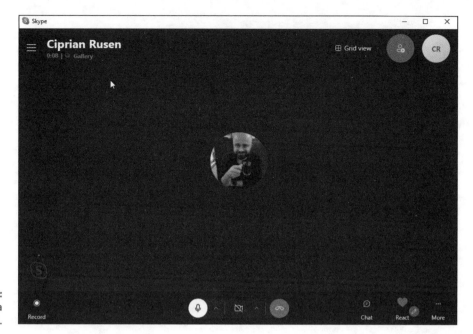

**FIGURE 6-12:**
Recording a
Skype call.

# Chapter **7**

# Using Widgets

L et's talk about a less-known feature of Windows 11: widgets. Microsoft has borrowed this concept from the smartphone world, but it's doing things differently, as always. First, widgets are tied to a Microsoft account. They don't seem to work at all with a local account. Second, although their purpose is to provide you with news that interests you or data that's useful to you, they also promote Microsoft's services, websites, and Edge browser. You may not like this, but it's how things are.

When you hear about Windows 11 widgets, you may also think of the desktop gadgets from the Windows 7 era. However, they're not similar in any way. In addition, the new Windows 11 widgets, unlike the old desktop gadgets, don't affect the performance of Windows. Widgets load only when you click or tap their shortcut, and they're just as fast no matter how many you add. The only things that might slow them down are your internet connection and how much time it takes to refresh their data.

To help you get the most of widgets, I explain what widgets are and how they work. You also learn how to customize Windows 11 widgets and change their order, how they look, and the data they display. Last but not least, you find out how to remove and add widgets.

# Working with Widgets

In Windows 11, a widget is a small app designed to display information that you might find useful, like the weather forecast, stock market data, traffic data, sports updates, and news. This feature is inspired from the News and Interests widget introduced in Windows 10 in May 2021. In Windows 10, News and Interests was more like a personalized news feed with stuff you might want to see. This concept was expanded in Windows 11 to allow other apps, such as Photos, Family Safety, Mail, Calendar, and Microsoft To Do, to install and display widgets.

 To open the widgets in Windows 11, click or tap the widgets icon on the taskbar, or press Windows+W on your keyboard. The widgets pane appears on the left side of the screen, occupying a large portion of it. Note how all the widgets are displayed as cards with different sizes, as shown in Figure 7-1.

**FIGURE 7-1:**
The Windows 11 widgets in all their glory.

On the top of the widgets pane, you see the current time, the icon of your Microsoft account, and a Search box powered by Bing. Below you see the cards with information, starting with the weather forecast for your current location.

If you scroll down the list of widgets, you get to the news section. For each news article, you see a picture, the title, the name of its publisher and reaction buttons such as those on Facebook. Microsoft learns what information to display based on how you use the reaction buttons.

Widgets contain clickable information. Unfortunately, most of them take you to a Microsoft site such as msn.com.

**WARNING**

Because Microsoft is fighting with Google for market share in the online space, the company has decided that Windows 11 widgets ignore your default browser setting, and load everything you click in Microsoft Edge. I find this annoying. Don't you?

# Customizing Widgets

Widgets can be dragged and dropped to any position you want, using both the mouse and touch. However, you can also change their size, customize the data they display, or remove them from your feed. Here's how to do all that:

1. **Click or tap the widgets icon on the taskbar.**

   Windows 11 displays the widgets pane on the left side of the screen.

2. **In the top-right corner of the Weather widget, click or tap the three dots icon.**

   The menu shown in Figure 7-2 appears.

3. **Choose Small or Large as the size of the Weather widget.**

   Note how the Weather widget gets smaller or larger, depending on what you chose.

4. **Click or tap the same three dots icon to the right of the Weather widget, and choose Customize Widget.**

   You see several options for how to customize the Weather widget, as shown in Figure 7-3.

5. **Enter the location for which you want to see the weather forecast.**

6. **Choose the units of measure (Fahrenheit or Celsius), and click or tap Save.**

   The Weather widget updates its forecast to the location you entered, using the units you selected.

7. **Click or tap the same three dots icon to the right of the Weather widget, and choose Remove Widget.**

   The weather forecast is gone from your feed, and the remaining widgets have shifted.

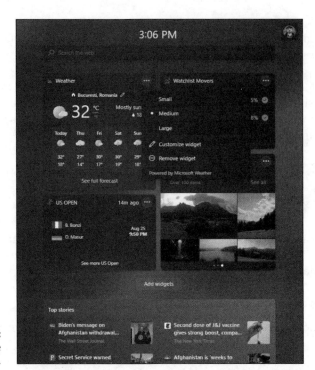

**FIGURE 7-2:**
Customizing the
Weather widget.

**FIGURE 7-3:**
Setting the
location and the
units of measure
for the Weather
widget.

**TIP**

Customizing other widgets works in a similar way. However, the customization options differ from widget to widget. Some widgets such as Photos don't offer a Customize Widget option. You can change only their size and position in the feed.

If you have changed your mind and want to use a widget that you've just removed, check out the next section.

# Adding Widgets

Microsoft is continuously expanding the list of widgets that you can add to your personalized feed. The process for adding a widget is not that difficult, even though you may not know where to start. But that's why I am here, to show you how:

**1.** **Click or tap the widgets icon on the taskbar or press Windows+W on your keyboard.**

Windows 11 displays the widgets pane.

**2.** **In the top-right corner of the widgets pane, click or tap your user icon.**

The Widget settings pop up, as shown in Figure 7-4.

**3.** **In the Add Widgets section, click or tap the + sign next to the Weather widget.**

The Weather widget is added back to your feed.

**4.** **Click or tap the + sign for each widget you want to add.**

**5.** **When done, click or tap the X button on the top-right corner of Widget Settings.**

Enjoy your newly added widgets. Don't hesitate to drag them around to the position you want.

Only a few widgets were available when I was writing this book, but by the time you read this, things will have changed. I'm curious as to whether apps other than ones developed by Microsoft will provide Windows 11 widgets, and turn this feature into a killer one, that many appreciate and use. I would like to see a Spotify widget, a Twitter widget, and more.

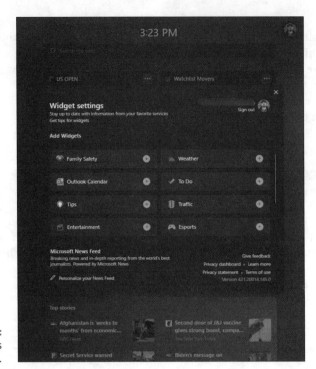

**FIGURE 7-4:**
Adding widgets
is not difficult.

# Chapter 8

# Handling Music, Movies, and Videos

I listen to music every day, especially when I write tutorials for Digital Citizen. I've listened to many songs while drafting this book. You may consider music a distraction, but for me it's how I get myself into a creative zone and start to become productive writing. Other times, music is also how I enhance my good mood and enjoy my day even more.

No matter if you're an audiophile or just your average computer user, you surely want to listen to music too. If you're on the old-school side of the music industry, you may still keep your music locally, on your PC or on audio CDs. If that's the case, you should give Groove Music and Windows Media Player a try. They're both included in Windows 11. If you're into online streaming, Spotify is the way to go, while it still has a free plan.

No matter which type of music listener you are, in this chapter, I show you how to work with all three music-related apps: Groove Music, Windows Media Player, and Spotify. I also take you into video territory and show you how to transform your vacation pictures into flashy homemade video creations. Lastly, I give you a quick tour of Windows 11's Movies & TV app, which unfortunately is quite underwhelming.

# Getting Your Groove Music On

Windows 11 includes the same Groove Music app from Windows 10. It's a stripped-down app compared to its initial vision as a Spotify competitor. The latest version can play only music stored locally on your computer and actively promotes Spotify as an alternative. A funny turn of events if you ask me.

By default, Groove Music looks for mp3s and other audio files in your Music folder. If it finds any, it can play them for you. If you're an old-school user that still has an ample collection of music on your computer, you can listen to it by following these steps:

1. **Make sure that your music collection is stored in your user's Music folder.**

2. **Click or tap the Start icon, All Apps, and then Groove Music.**

   If this is the first time you start the app, Groove Music, shown in Figure 8-1, spends some time setting things up and scanning your Music folder.

**FIGURE 8-1:**
Groove Music scans your Music folder and shows everything it finds.

### 3. Click or tap Songs.

You see a list with all the songs stored in your Music folder.

### 4. Find the song you want to play and double-click or double-tap it.

The song starts to play and, at the bottom of the screen, you see the music controls shown in Figure 8-2.

Now playing

Recent plays

My music

Search

**FIGURE 8-2:**
Groove Music's controls are like any other music player.

Settings

Create new playlists

Playlists

Handling Music, Movies, and Videos

5. **Play or pause the track, skip to the next track or the previous one in the list, and more.**

6. **If you want a more focused view, click or tap the now playing icon on the left, which looks like a sound equalizer.**

   The Now Playing view, shown in Figure 8-3, is much better for controlling the music you listen to.

**FIGURE 8-3:**
The Now Playing view is the way to go.

TIP

Groove Music can play the following music formats: .mp3, .flac, .aac, .m4a, .wav, .wma, .ac3, .3gp, .3g2, .amr, .mka, .ogg, and .opus. In File Explorer, if you double-click or double-tap a music file with one of these file extensions, the file opens in Groove Music by default and you can listen to it.

## Choosing where Groove Music looks for music

As mentioned, Groove Music actively monitors only the Music folder associated with your user account. If you want it to look for music in other folders, you must tell it to:

1. **Click or tap the Start icon, All Apps, and then Groove Music.**

   The Groove Music app opens (refer to Figure 8-1).

2. **On the left, click or tap the gear icon (settings).**

   The Groove Music Settings screen appears, as shown in Figure 8-4.

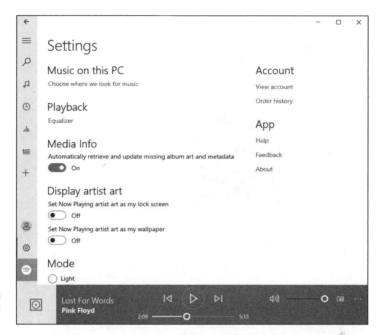

**FIGURE 8-4:**
Groove Music
settings.

3. **Under Music on This PC, click or tap the Choose Where We Look for Music link.**

   You see a list with the folders monitored by Groove Music.

4. **Click or tap +, select the folder you want to use, and then click or tap Add This Folder to Music.**

   The folder is added to the list.

5. **After you've finished adding folders to Groove Music, click or tap Done.**

6. **Click or tap the two musical notes icon (my music) on the left to see your updated collection.**

   If you have a large music collection, be patient while Groove Music scans everything.

# Creating playlists in Groove Music

As you've seen by now, the Groove Music app is basic and doesn't do a lot, except play the music stored on your Windows 11 computer. If you want to keep things well organized, you can use it also to create your own playlists, like this:

1. **Open the Groove Music app.**

2. **On the left, click or tap + (create new playlist).**

   The dialog shown in Figure 8-5 appears.

**FIGURE 8-5:** First, name your playlist.

3. **Type a name for your playlist and then click or tap Create Playlist.**

   The playlist is displayed but is empty. You need to add songs to it.

4. **Click or tap the Go To Albums link under Add Songs from My Collection.**

   You see all the albums found by Groove Music.

5. **Right-click or tap and hold down on the album you want to add.**

   The menu shown in Figure 8-6 appears.

6. **Select Add To, followed by the name of your playlist.**

   You see a notification at on the top right, indicating how many songs were just added to the playlist.

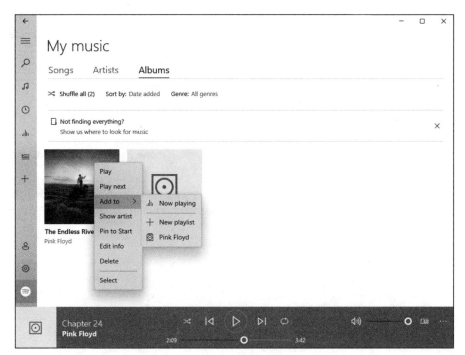

**FIGURE 8-6:**
Adding songs
to your playlist
involves a simple
right-click.

After Step 4, you can also navigate to Songs and Artists and repeat Steps 5 and 6 to add songs to the same playlist.

TIP

# Playing Videos and Music with Windows Media Player

While few people know about Windows Media Player, and even fewer use it, the program has survived in Windows 11. It hasn't been changed in many years, doing the same things it did in Windows 8 and Windows 10: It plays music, plays videos, and can be used as picture viewer. When you start Windows Media Player, it looks for content automatically in your local Pictures, Music, and Videos folders, as well as those found on your OneDrive. If it finds anything in the many formats it can play or view, you can interact with that content.

Here's how to use Windows Media Player to play music and videos:

1. **Click or tap the search icon on the taskbar and type** media player.

2. **Click or tap the Windows Media Player search result.**

   If this is the first time you start the program, you see a welcome message asking you to choose the initial settings.

3. **If you see the welcome page, choose Recommended Settings, and click or tap Finish.**

   You finally see the Windows Media Player program, as shown in Figure 8-7. The app spends some time scanning your Music, Videos, and Pictures folders, both locally and on your OneDrive.

**FIGURE 8-7:** Windows Media Player can play both music and videos.

4. **Click or tap Music, on the left, and then click or tap a song you want to play.**

   The song starts to play immediately, and you can use the controls at the bottom to pause, play, skip to the next song, and so on.

5. **Click or tap Videos, and then click or tap a video you want to view.**

   The video opens in a special window, with useful controls on the bottom, as shown in Figure 8-8.

6. **To close Windows Media Player, click or tap X.**

**FIGURE 8-8:**
Viewing a concert
recording with
Windows Media
Player.

**TIP**

Windows Media Player hasn't been updated in years, and it shows. If you want the best media player for movies that works with all formats, check out VLC Media Player. For more on why I recommend it, see Book 10, Chapter 6.

# Ripping Music from Your Old CDs

Do you have a large music collection stored on CDs? I do, and I love my Pink Floyd, Beatles, Rush, and Bob Dylan albums. The problem is that CDs wear over time, and they become unusable after several years. If you don't want to lose the songs stored on CDs, one solution is to rip them and store them on your PC. You might even want a cloud backup for your music on OneDrive or some other cloud-storage platform.

The process of *ripping* means copying the music from a CD to a computer, in a format such as mp3. Once you've ripped a CD, you can take the resulting mp3 files, move them anywhere you want, and listen to them without using the CD. This way, you can prolong the life of the CD by using it less frequently and playing the music you ripped from it instead.

To rip the music from a CD you own, plug it into the DVD/Blu-Ray drive of your desktop PC, and follow these steps:

1. **Click or tap the search icon on the taskbar and type** media player.

2. **Click or tap the Windows Media Player search result.**

**3.** **Wait a few seconds for Windows Media Player to read the disc, and then click or tap its name on the left, below Other Media.**

Windows Media Player displays the tracks and the album cover for your CD, as shown in Figure 8-9.

**FIGURE 8-9:**
Windows Media Player reads and plays your CDs with music too.

**4.** **To configure the ripping process, click or tap Rip Settings.**

The menu shown in Figure 8-10 appears.

**5.** **To set the format for your music files, choose Format, and then choose the format you want.**

I prefer MP3. Most probably you do too.

**6.** **In the same Rip Settings menu, choose Audio Quality, and then go for a high value such as 320 Kbps (Best Quality).**

You want your music to sound great, don't you?

**7.** **Click or tap Rip CD.**

Windows Media Player displays the ripping status for each track on your CD. In just a few minutes, all your songs should be ripped and stored on your PC.

**8.** **When the ripping process is over, click or tap X to close Windows Media Player, and then eject your CD.**

You'll find all your songs in the Music folder, in a folder named after the artist whose songs you've ripped.

**FIGURE 8-10:**
Configuring
the CD ripping
settings.

# Setting Up Spotify

Back when Windows 10 was launched, Microsoft launched Groove Music as a music-streaming service that competed with the likes of Spotify, Tidal, and Apple Music. Unfortunately, Groove Music has lost the battle and been turned into a basic app that plays music only locally. However, Microsoft has partnered with Spotify and actively promotes this music service, including on the Windows 11 Start menu.

If you want to stream music online for free, you can sign up to Spotify directly from Windows 11, like this:

**1.** **Click or tap the Start icon and then the Spotify shortcut.**

If you see a progress bar below the Spotify shortcut, Windows 11 is downloading the app from the Microsoft Store.

**2.** **When the Spotify app opens, click or tap Signup.**

The options shown in Figure 8-11 appear.

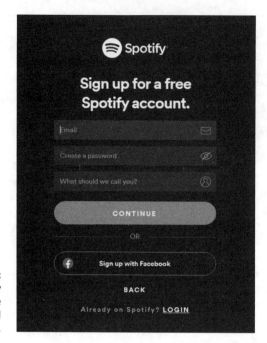

**FIGURE 8-11:**
To join Spotify
you must provide
some personal
details.

3. **Type your email (a real address please), a password, and your name. Then click or tap Continue.**

4. **Choose your date of birth and your gender, and click or tap Join Spotify.**

   You see the home screen for Spotify, as shown in Figure 8-12.

5. **Select one of the featured charts and click or tap the play icon.**

   Music starts playing, and you see the track controls at the bottom. They're similar to those from Groove Music and Windows Media Player, so you should feel right at home.

TIP

Spotify doesn't cost a thing to get started. You can listen to music for free for as long as you want. The two important downsides to the free plan are that you have to listen to ads every few songs and the quality of the music streaming is set to low. However, an individual plan ($9.99 per month) gets rid of ads and sets the audio quality to the maximum available. There are also plans for two people, families (of up to six people), and students (only $4.99/month).

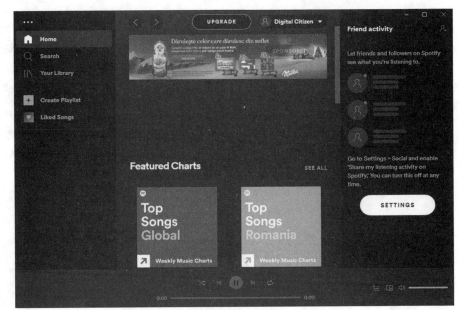

# Creating Your Own Videos

One of the coolest features of the Photos app (see Chapter 3 of this minibook) is that it also includes Video Editor. Video Editor is accessible as a separate tab in the Photos app but also has its own shortcut in the Start menu and other places.

With Video Editor, you can create your own movies from pictures you took. You can also add some videos you've recorded with your smartphone alongside your pictures, a soundtrack, and some cool effects. The result is a fun clip that you can share with others.

Video Editor is complex and includes many tools and options. Here's a basic tour of how to use it to create a video:

1. **Click or tap the search icon on the taskbar and type** video editor.

2. **Click or tap the Video Editor search result.**

   The Video Editor tab opens inside the Photos app, as shown in Figure 8-13.

3. **Choose New Video Project, enter a name for your project, and click or tap OK.**

   The Project Library shown in Figure 8-14 appears.

4. **Click or tap +Add and choose From This PC.**

   The Open dialog appears, where you can select pictures and videos on your PC.

**FIGURE 8-13:**
The Photos app has Video Editor built in.

**FIGURE 8-14:**
Add pictures and videos to the Project Library.

5. **Navigate to your PC, select the files you want to add to your video project, and then click or tap Open.**

The files you selected are shown in your Project Library.

6. **Drag your files to the storyboard at the bottom, where it says: "Drag Items from the Project Library Here."**

The items are shown on the storyboard in the order you've dragged them. You can move them around with the mouse (or your finger if you have a touchscreen).

7. **Click or tap Background Music at the top, choose the track you want to add to your video, and then click or tap Done.**

8. **Click or tap Finish Video, choose the quality you want, and then click or tap Export.**

9. **Select the folder where you want to save your video, type a name for it, and choose Export.**

Video Editor generates your video and then plays it back to you.

TIP

Use the tools above the timeline to add a title card, text, filters, and 3D effects that may make your movies even cooler.

# Using the Movies & TV App

The Movies & TV app behaves much like the initial Groove Music app from Windows 10, although it's considerably pushier about selling stuff. Click or tap the Start icon, All Apps, and then Movies & TV. The screen shown in Figure 8-15 appears.

Initially, Microsoft shows you only movies that they want you to buy. The Explore tab is all about discovering what movies and TV shows are on sale, and the company is aggressive about convincing you to buy. Luckily, you'll also find some free trailers to watch.

In the Purchased tab you see stuff you've already bought. Finally, on the Personal tab, you see the videos from your computer, and then only those stored in your Videos folder. If you have videos in other folders, the Movies & TV app won't display them, even though it may be able to play them.

Double-click or double-tap a video in the Movies & TV app or in File Explorer, and it plays in a letterboxed window, as shown in Figure 8-16. You have all the basic controls to play, pause, go back 10 seconds, move forward 30 seconds, change the volume, and display subtitles.

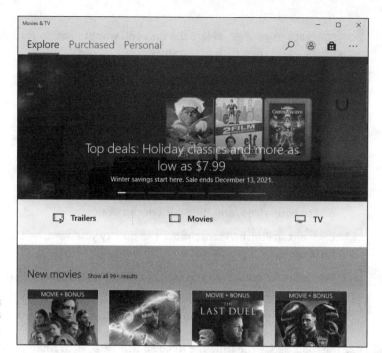

**FIGURE 8-15:**
Movies & TV tries hard to sell you stuff.

**FIGURE 8-16:**
Playing videos is easy.

The Movies & TV app isn't much more than a basic media player that works well with touchscreens too. If you want more features and a mature product that works with any movie format you can find on the internet, try VLC Media Player. It's available in the Microsoft Store.

IN THIS CHAPTER

» Searching for games in the Microsoft Store

» Playing with game mode

» Using the Xbox game bar

» Setting the default graphics card for your game(s)

» Finding old games, reborn

# Chapter **9**

# Playing Games

Microsoft has bragged a lot about Windows 11 and how it's the best operating system for gamers. The company did introduce some new features like direct storage and auto HDR, but for the most part, Windows 11 is identical to Windows 10 in this regard.

Direct storage is a technical feature that allows your PC to bypass the processor when it needs to load data from an NVMe solid-state drive to the graphics card. It decreases the amount of processor power required by games when loading textures, which means games should load faster. However, software developers need to implement direct storage in their games, and when Windows 11 was launched, no titles had this feature. Talk about a launch on paper, huh? I hope this situation will change in the next few years.

Auto HDR is a bit more interesting because it uses an algorithm to analyze the standard image from your game and convert it to HDR (high dynamic range). The algorithm pays particular attention to SDR (standard dynamic range) luminance data and upscales the image to a higher resolution, but with luminance data instead of resolution. If you have a monitor with HDR support, it's useful to enable it.

Other than these two features, Windows 11 comes with the same tools as Windows 10 did. It too has a game mode, an Xbox game bar, and so on. In this chapter I stick to what's visible to you, the user. I show you how to use the gaming features and tools from Windows 11. You learn how to enable game mode, access the Xbox game bar, and use the different widgets on it. Those with a gaming laptop can learn how to set the default graphics card for their favorite game.

Lastly, for casual gamers who miss classics like Solitaire and Minesweeper, I end the chapter by showing you how to get these games back.

# Searching the Microsoft Store for Games

Want to see what games will run on Windows 11? One way is to head to the Microsoft Store. Here's how:

1. **Click or tap the Microsoft Store shortcut on the taskbar or from the Start menu.**

    The Microsoft Store appears.

2. **On the left, click or tap Gaming.**

    An array of tiles for games appears, as shown in Figure 9-1. If you see a game that looks interesting, check it out.

**FIGURE 9-1:** Games offered at the Microsoft Store.

3. **Scroll down to Featured Free Games, and click or tap See All next to it.**

4. **Click or tap any game that interests you.**

   I chose Roblox, as shown in Figure 9-2. The Microsoft Store displays a complete description of the game and presents you with an opportunity to install the app. The description may include a notice that you can buy stuff when you're inside the game (Offers in-App Purchases). Scroll down farther and the description of the game includes some indication of what's available and how much it costs.

**FIGURE 9-2:**
If a game tickles your fancy, install it.

5. **To install the game, click or tap Get or Install (if the app is free) or the button with the price.**

6. **If there's a charge, verify your billing details and provide a password.**

   While it's downloading, you see a progress bar in the Microsoft Store.

   Games marked Game Pass are free as long as you have an Xbox Game Pass associated with your Microsoft/Xbox account.

REMEMBER

7. **To run the game, click or tap the play icon that appears after the game is downloaded and installed.**

   The game also appears in the Recommended list in the Start menu, just like any other newly installed Windows 11 app, as you can see in Figure 9-3. The game is also in the All Apps list.

**FIGURE 9-3:**
Games appear just like any other new app in the Recommended list.

Downloading and installing a game is one-click easy. Finding them and beating them are anything but.

**TIP**

Serious gamers should consider subscribing to Steam, the largest digital game distribution center on the internet. While the Microsoft Store is a decent distribution platform, it doesn't get close to Steam when it comes to how many titles are available. Steam works for PC, Mac, and Linux. It has built-in social networking, automated saved game backups, in-game achievement tracking, micropayments, and much more. See `https://store.steampowered.com/`.

# Enabling Game Mode

*Game mode*, which was introduced in Windows 10 and remains an active feature in Windows 11, is a set of tools, options, and settings that make gaming more pleasant. According to Microsoft, game mode helps games render more frames on the screen while you play them by focusing your PC's processing power on the game, not background tasks.

The basic idea is that you enable game mode when you play a game to avoid extreme slowdowns, drops in frame rates, interruptions caused by notifications, and other annoyances. In theory, Windows 11 detects when you're playing a game, and enables game mode automatically. But that doesn't work every time, especially when you're playing an older title.

To check to see if game mode is enabled — and to enable it if necessary — follow these steps:

**1.** **Click or tap the Start icon and then Settings.**

Windows 11 Settings opens.

**2.** **Click or tap Gaming. On the right, choose Game Mode.**

**3.** **Set the Game Mode switch to on, as shown in Figure 9-4.**

**4.** **Close Settings and start the game.**

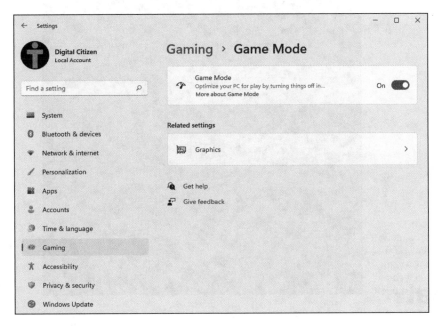

**FIGURE 9-4:**
Turning game mode on or off.

If you're playing an older game, and it doesn't look like Windows 11 is enabling game mode for it, do this:

**1.** **While the game is running, press Windows+G on your keyboard.**

The Xbox game bar appears, as shown in Figure 9-5.

**FIGURE 9-5:**
The Xbox game
bar appears at
the top of the
screen.

2. **Click or tap the gear icon (settings).**

   The Settings window appears, as shown in Figure 9-6.

3. **On the General tab, select the Remember This Is a Game option.**

   This tells Windows 11 that you're playing a game and it should enable game mode. If you don't see this option, the game is already in the list of officially supported titles, and everything is okay.

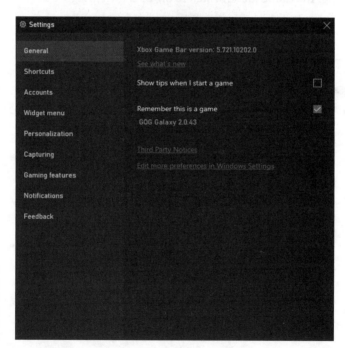

**FIGURE 9-6:**
Telling Windows
11 that you are
playing a game
and want game
mode.

# Using the Xbox Game Bar

Game mode in Windows 11 comes with a useful tool called the Xbox game bar. When you start a game, press Windows+G. The game bar appears over your game, with several widgets that offer useful settings and data, as shown in Figure 9-7.

Show previous widget     Performance     Enable click-through

Widget menu | Audio Capture |Show next widget| Settings

**FIGURE 9-7:**
Use the Xbox
game bar while
you play games in
Windows 11.

To become familiar with the game bar, follow these steps:

**1.** **Start a game that you want to play, and then press Windows+G.**

The game bar appears (refer to Figure 9-7).

**2.** **On the game bar, click or tap the widget menu icon (labeled in Figure 9-7).**

A menu with widgets that can be enabled and disabled is shown. A star to the right of a widget's name indicates that it's enabled. Click or tap their name to enable or disable them.

**3.** **Click or tap the audio icon to see how audio devices are set for your game. Change the settings, if necessary.**

**4.** **Click or tap the capture icon.**

The capture widget is displayed, with buttons for taking screen shots of your game, recording the last 30 seconds of gameplay, recording a video of your gameplay, and turning the microphone on and off.

5. **Click or tap the performance icon.**

   The performance widget is displayed, with real-time data about processor (CPU) usage, graphics card usage (GPU), RAM consumption, and the number of frames per second rendered on the screen (FPS). This data is useful to gamers who play demanding video games.

6. **Click or tap the Xbox Social icon.**

   If you don't see the icon, click or tap > until you do see it.

   The Xbox Social widget gives you tools to chat with friends, see who is online, invite them to a party, and so on.

7. **Click or tap the gear icon.**

   You get access to settings that you can use to personalize game mode and the game bar.

8. **To hide the game bar, click or tap anywhere outside it or press Windows+G.**

# Setting the Default Graphics Card

Many gaming laptops have two video cards: an integrated graphics chip that helps them provide basic video features at low power consumption and a dedicated video card for more demanding apps and games. By default, Windows 11 does a respectable job at using the correct video card, based on which apps and games you play. However, sometimes Windows might use the wrong card. Or you might want to force Windows 11 to use a specific graphics card for a specific game.

Here's how to set the default graphics card for a specific game that's installed on your PC:

1. **Click or tap the Start icon and then Settings.**

   Windows 11 Settings opens.

2. **Make sure that System is selected on the left, and then choose Display on the right.**

3. **Click or tap Graphics.**

   You see a list of apps and games, as shown in Figure 9-8.

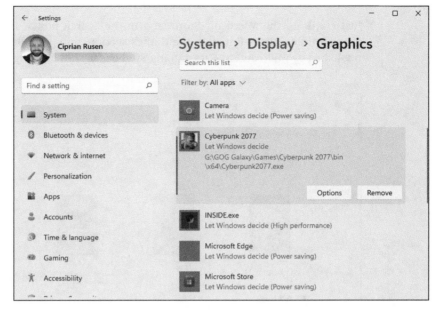

**FIGURE 9-8:**
The list of apps
and games for
which you can set
the default
graphics card.

4. **Click or tap the name of the game for which you want to set the default graphics card, and then click or tap Options.**

   If you don't see the game you want in the list, click or tap Browse, navigate to where the game is installed, and choose its default .exe file. Then continue with the next step.

TIP

5. **Choose between Power Saving (which uses the integrated graphics chip) and High Performance (which uses the dedicated video card), and then click or tap Save.**

   From now on, each time you play that game, Windows 11 uses the graphics card you chose, even if it may not be the optimal choice.

TIP

If you have a strong gaming PC and a monitor with HDR support, you 'll want to enable auto HDR for your games. To learn how to do that, read Book 3, Chapter 1, and look for the section about HDR in Windows 11.

# Bringing Back the Classics

Admit it. You want to play Solitaire on your new Windows 11 machine. And Minesweeper. Just like you did in Windows 7. Well, you're in luck — and they're easy to find if you know where to look.

Just crank up the Microsoft Store, and in the Search box at the top, type **Xbox Game Studios**. Press Enter. In the Games section, you get a list of all the games published by Microsoft and its gaming studios, as shown in Figure 9-9.

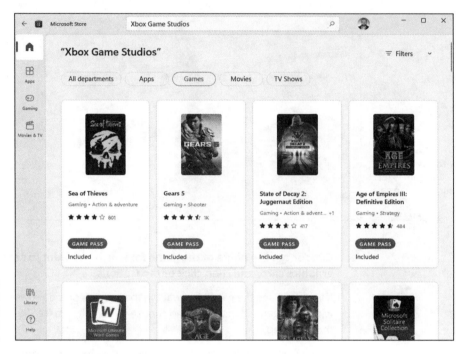

**FIGURE 9-9:**
These games
are published by
Microsoft's Xbox
Game Studios.

If you're an experienced Windows user, you might want to pick up some or all of these free games:

>> **Microsoft Solitaire Collection** includes Klondike (the game you no doubt remember as Solitaire, shown in Figure 9-10), Spider Solitaire, FreeCell, Pyramid, and TriPeaks. As mentioned in the "What is freemium?" sidebar, if you want your Solitaire Collection without ads, you must pay for the privilege.

   None of the old cheats work in Solitaire — you can't switch how many cards you flip in the middle of a hand or peek — but you can still play with hints, or choose between one-card and three-card draws.

>> **Microsoft Minesweeper,** the game that Bill Gates loved to hate, works very much like it has for many years, in many versions of Windows. See Figure 9-11.

>> **Microsoft Mahjong** brings the classic click-clack to the screen.

>> **Microsoft Sudoku** is another classic game that's easy to play, even on low-end PCs.

There are many more, but those Xbox Game Studios games should keep you going for hours. Or days.

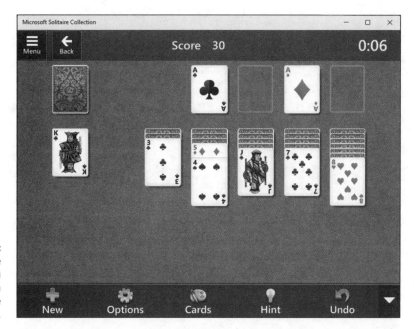

**FIGURE 9-10:** Klondike, the game you remember from when you were a kid.

**FIGURE 9-11:** Minesweeper works like the original but looks much better.

## WHAT IS FREEMIUM?

Microsoft has shifted to freemium games, to drive new income from its classic (and traditionally free) games. *Freemium* means that you can get the basic game for free, but you have to pay to get more features or — as is the case with Microsoft Solitaire Collection — to get rid of ads.

You can download and play Microsoft Solitaire forever, without having to pay for it. But if you want to get rid of the ads, you pay $14.99 a year for the Premium Edition. Is it worth the money? Good question. No easy answer.

# 5

# Managing Apps

# Contents at a Glance

Chapter **1**

# Navigating the Microsoft Store

I f you're familiar with buying apps in the Apple App Store or the Google Play Store, you already know about most of the features you'll find in the Microsoft Store. That said, the selection, breadth, and quality of apps are better in the App Store and the Play Store. The reason's simple: money. Large fortunes can be made with cool apps and games in the App Store and the Play Store because they have many more users.

Although the Microsoft Store used to include only Windows apps (designed to work just as well on touchscreens and with a mouse and keyboard), now the Microsoft Store carries all kinds of apps, including desktop programs and progressive web apps. You can also buy games, movies, and TV shows. Apps make or break any computer these days, and Microsoft knows it. That's why you find some popular apps in the Microsoft Store — it's good for you and good for Microsoft.

To make its Store more appealing, in July 2021, Microsoft announced that app developers can keep 100 percent of their revenue. However, game creators still need to pay a 30 percent share to Microsoft. While the 100 percent revenue share option doesn't apply to games, it's a significant policy shift. Now we just have to see if the new model is enticing enough to bring more developers to the Microsoft Store.

In Windows 11, the Microsoft Store looks better than it did in Windows 10 and is easier to navigate. In addition, at some point the Microsoft Store will offer Android apps that work in Microsoft's operating system.

It's time to show you the basics. In this chapter, you learn how to navigate the Microsoft Store, install the apps you want, and remove the apps you don't want.

# Understanding What a Windows 11 App Can Do

The longer the Microsoft Store is available, the more apps you'll find there. Each app must meet a set of requirements before Microsoft will offer it in the Microsoft Store. Here's a condensed version of what you can expect from any app you buy (or download) in the Microsoft Store:

>> **You can get both Windows 11 apps (which are supposed to run on any type of PC or device) and legacy-style apps (or computer programs) from the Microsoft Store.** If you want a new program for the desktop, you may be able to find it in the Microsoft Store, or you may be able to get it through all the old sources, such as its official website or monster download sites. But if you want a Windows 11 app, you must get it through the Microsoft Store — unless you have a big company. See the sidebar "Bypassing Microsoft Store restrictions." Also, check Book 1, Chapter 2 for a description of Windows 11 apps.

>> **Windows 11 apps can be updated only through the Microsoft Store.** When an update is available, the Microsoft Store automatically handles the upgrade process without any intervention from you. Read Chapter 4 in this minibook for details.

>> **Apps that use any internet-based services must request permission from the user before retrieving, or sending, personal data.**

>> **Each app must be licensed to run on up to ten computers at a time.** For example, if you buy the latest high-tech version of Angry Birds, you can run that same version of Angry Birds on up to ten Windows 11 devices — computers, tablets, laptops, Xbox One consoles, HoloLens augmented reality glasses, giant Surface Hubs — at no additional cost.

>> **Microsoft won't accept apps with a rating over ESRB *Mature,* which is to say adult content.**

>> **Apps must start in five seconds or less and resume in two seconds or less.** Microsoft wants apps to be speedy, not sluggish.

In addition to the basic requirements for any app, you're also likely to find that the following is true of most apps:

TIP

» **Microsoft's tools help developers create trial versions of their apps, so you can try before you buy.** The trial version can be limited in many ways — for example, it works only on a certain number of pictures, messages, or files, or only for a week or a month — before requiring payment. The developer must explain precisely what has been limited and what happens if you decide to purchase the app.

## BYPASSING MICROSOFT STORE RESTRICTIONS

Microsoft runs the Microsoft Store as a tightly held business and restricts what can be bought. The company can reject an application submitted to the Microsoft Store for a wide variety of reasons. Here's the key point you need to understand about the Microsoft Store: With two exceptions, the Microsoft Store is the *only place* where you can get Windows 11 apps.

The exceptions:

- Big companies can bypass the restriction and put their own apps on Windows machines using a technique called *sideloading*. At least in theory, sideloading can be accomplished only on machines locked into a corporate network.

- If you *jailbreak* your device, you may be able to put any Windows 11 app you like on it — Microsoft's censors no longer apply. On the other hand, jailbreaking your computer voids every warranty in existence and automatically disqualifies you from Microsoft support. Think: No security patches, lots of exposure. There's no incentive to jailbreak your computer.

*Unlocking* (which may or may not be accompanied by jailbreaking) allows you to switch carriers if you bought a Windows laptop or tablet with mobile connectivity from a carrier who's locked in its services. Some carriers in the United States, for example, may offer a discounted price for your Windows 11 tablet in exchange for a multiyear internet contract. If you unlock the device, you may (or may not) be able to hook it up to a different network. All sorts of penalties may apply. However, the case I am describing is not valid for most PCs because they are not bought from carriers. Most desktop PCs are not locked, so they don't need jailbreaking, especially those built by users or bought from traditional PC vendors such as Dell, HP, and ASUS.

>> **If an app breaks, you can complain to Microsoft, but the support responsibility lies 100 percent with the developer.** Although Microsoft acts as an agent in the distribution and sale of apps, Microsoft doesn't buy or sell or warrant anything at all.

>> **Many apps (and especially games) attempt to get you to buy more — more levels, more features, more content.** Microsoft has that covered, just like Apple and Google: Orders generated by the app must go through the Microsoft Store. Only Microsoft can fulfill the orders.

Don't confuse the Microsoft Store — which hooks directly into Windows 11 — with the Microsoft stores that existed in the real world for several years. Brick-and-mortar Microsoft stores were popping up all over the place until the Covid-19 pandemic. Then Microsoft decided to close them because they weren't exactly profitable.

Now we have the online version of the previous bricks-and-mortar Microsoft store at `www.microsoft.com/en-us/store/`. In the online store you can buy the new Microsoft Surface computers, applications that run on the desktop, as well as competitors' computers, Xboxes, headphones, mice, smartphones, Windows, Office — in short, everything that Microsoft has to offer to consumers.

# Browsing the Microsoft Store

When you're ready to venture into the Microsoft Store for Windows 11 apps and games, open the Start menu and click or tap the Microsoft Store shortcut. The screen shown in Figure 1-1 appears.

Moving around in the Microsoft Store isn't difficult. The navigation column on the left contains shortcuts to types of content like apps, games, and movies & TV. On the right, you see the content itself organized by categories and offers.

The following tips can help you move around and find what you're looking for:

>> **You no longer need a Microsoft account to get anywhere beyond basic searching and browsing, as you did in Windows 10.** Luckily, Microsoft has removed this limitation in Windows 11, and now both local and Microsoft accounts can have a similar experience, if they stick to free apps, games, and content. As soon as you try to buy something, the Microsoft account requirement splats you right in the face, as shown in Figure 1-2.

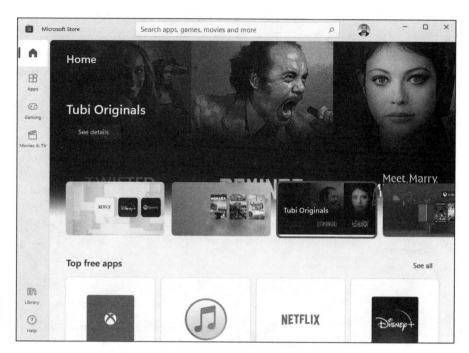

**FIGURE 1-1:**
Here's a peek
at the Microsoft
Store.

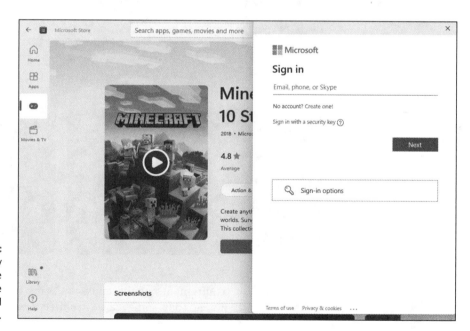

**FIGURE 1-2:**
You can't buy
stuff from the
Microsoft Store
with a local
account.

>> **To order an app or a game, click or tap its name**. The Microsoft Store takes you directly to the ordering screen for the app. For example, if you click or tap the Adobe Photoshop Elements app, you see the ordering page displayed in Figure 1-3. At the top is an overview of the app and its price. Scroll down, and you see screen shots, a description, ratings from other users, system requirements for using it, and additional information about its developer, release date, size, and so on.

>> **Use categories to find apps quickly.** If you scroll down the Apps section, you see all kinds of categories created by Microsoft: Top Free Apps, Essential Apps, Best Productivity Apps, and so on. For each category, click or tap the See All link to see everything inside that group. Check out Figure 1-4 to see what Microsoft considers Essential Apps. I don't know about you, but TikTok surely isn't essential to me.

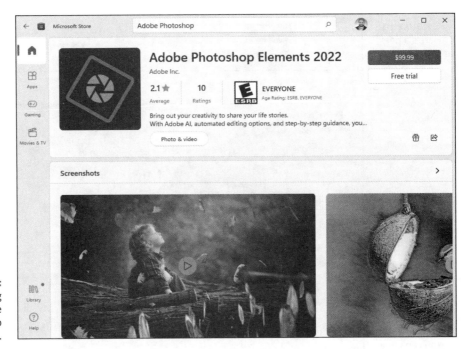

**FIGURE 1-3:**
The app-ordering page for the Adobe Photoshop Elements app.

If you read the system requirements of the apps you want to install from the Microsoft Store, you'll notice that some say "Architecture: neutral," others say "Architecture: x64," while others mention "Architecture: X86 X64 ARM." Those listed as "neutral" are Progressive web apps (see the "Progressive web apps" sidebar), those with x64 are classic desktop programs, and the others are Windows 11 apps.

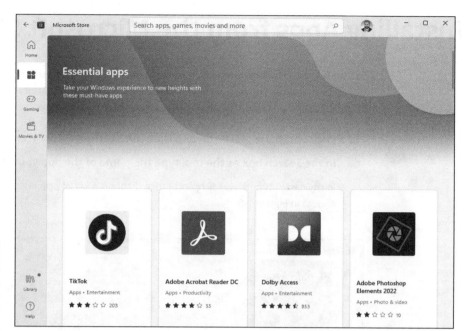

**FIGURE 1-4:**
Apps and
everything else
in the Store are
organized by
groups chosen by
Microsoft.

# PROGRESSIVE WEB APPS

A revolution is going on – from web apps running in a browser, to web apps running outside the browser, to hosted web apps, which are pulled down dynamically on execution, to progressive web apps, which blur the distinction between web-based apps and native apps.

Progressive web apps (PWAs) are a genuine attempt to make browser-based applications look and feel more like regular old apps. Chances are good that you've never seen a PWA in action, but they're here, including in the Microsoft Store. For example, Twitter and Facebook offer not native Windows 11 apps but PWAs. Any company that doesn't want to develop a specific app for Windows can easily make a PWA.

The theoretical benefits of PWAs are interesting. Just for starters, Windows 11 apps can run only in the stripped-down Windows 11 environment. PWAs, on the other hand, should be able to run on anything that supports a browser — particularly Chrome or Chrome OS. Yeah, that includes Chromebooks.

# Installing Apps from the Microsoft Store

If you want to find a specific app in the Microsoft Store, you can search for it using the Search box as the top, or you can browse the built-in categories. Here's how to install a free app, like the incredibly useful VLC Media Player:

1. **Click or tap the Start icon and then the Microsoft Store icon.**

2. **In the Search box as the top, type the name of the app you want to find.**

   In my case, I typed *vlc*. Microsoft Store displays a list of app suggestions, as shown in Figure 1-5.

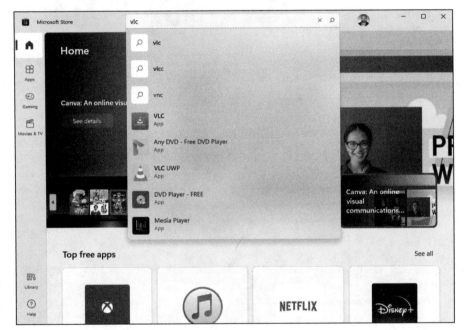

<br />

**FIGURE 1-5:** Searching for *vlc* in the Microsoft Store.

3. **Click or tap the name of the app you want.**

   In my case, I chose VLC, not VLC UWP (which is a different app). The Microsoft Store loads the app's page, with plenty of details, screen shots, user reviews, and system requirements, as shown in Figure 1-6.

4. **Click or tap the Get or Install button.**

   You see a bar that indicates the progress of the app's download and installation. You can minimize the Store and do something else while it handles everything for you. When the installation is complete, the app's shortcut appears in the Start menu's All Apps list or in the Recommended section.

<br />

<br />

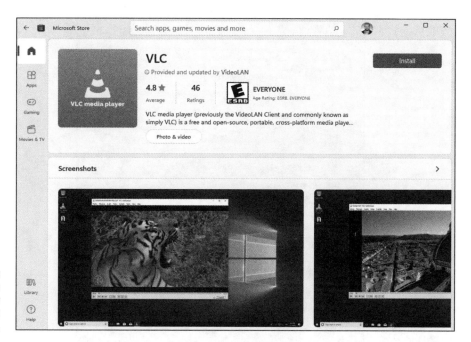

**FIGURE 1-6:**
The app's page
includes plenty
of details you
should look at.

**TIP**

If you're installing a desktop program from the Microsoft Store, at some point during the installation process you may see a User Account Control (UAC) prompt, asking you to allow the app to make system changes. If you don't click or tap Yes, the installation will fail. Read Book 9, Chapter 3 to learn more about UAC. This prompt is never shown for Windows 11 apps and PWAs.

# Uninstalling Windows 11 Apps

The process for uninstalling Windows 11 apps is different than the one for removing desktop apps. Also, it's much simpler and faster. All you have to do is this:

**1.** **Click or tap the Start icon and then All Apps.**

**2.** **Scroll down the list of apps until you find the one you want to remove.**

In this example, I am getting rid of Instagram.

**3.** **Right-click or tap and hold down on the app's name.**

A contextual menu appears, as shown in Figure 1-7.

**4.** **In the menu, choose Uninstall.**

**5.** **Confirm your choice by clicking or tapping Uninstall one more time.**

The Windows 11 app is removed immediately.

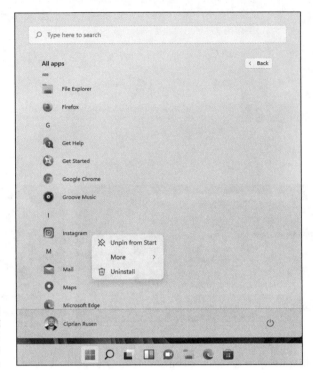

**FIGURE 1-7:**
Removing
Windows 11
apps takes only a
right-click.

**TIP**

You can follow the same steps for apps pinned to the Start menu or in the Recommended section. You don't have to go to the All Apps list. However, if you don't see a confirmation dialog after the first time you click or tap Uninstall, it means you've just removed a promoted app that wasn't installed on your machine. You had only a shortcut to it because Microsoft was paid to promote it.

IN THIS CHAPTER

» **Getting work done with focus sessions**

» **Writing with Notepad and WordPad for free**

» **Doing math on the Calculator**

» **Using the new Paint**

» **Creating sticky notes**

» **Keeping track of tasks**

» **Using the Maps app**

Chapter **2**

# Using Built-In Applications

W indows 11 comes with slightly fewer preinstalled apps than Windows 10. Initially, you may think otherwise because when you open the Start menu, you see shortcuts to several apps promoted by Microsoft. However, most are not preinstalled. They get installed only after you click or tap their shortcuts. If you remove their shortcuts, these apps will never get on your PC.

On the other hand, Windows 11 comes with several Microsoft apps built into the operating system itself. I cover a few of them elsewhere, such as the ones in Book 4. In this chapter, I cover the lesser-known ones.

I give you a tour of the following Windows 11 apps: Clock, Weather, Notepad, WordPad, Calculator, Paint, Sticky Notes, Microsoft To Do, and Maps. All were developed by Microsoft and are included with Windows 11. You learn where to find them and the basics about what they have to offer. Then it's your job to try them out, decide which ones you like best, and start using them regularly.

# Checking Out the New Clock App

The Clock app from Windows 11 is cool and a lot more useful than its Windows 10 counterpart. With it, you can do several things:

» Start focus sessions, which help you be productive for predefined periods of time (30, 45, or 60 minutes or more). When the time's up, the app encourages you to take a break before getting back to your computer for the next focus section. This is an easy way to implement the Pomodoro productivity technique. You can also connect the Clock app to Spotify, and have it recommend music to help you focus on your work. For more about setting up Spotify in Windows 11, read Book 4, Chapter 8.

» See your tasks from Microsoft To Do, check those you've finished, and add new ones.

» Set alarms to wake you up or remind you to stop working.

» Set and start a stopwatch to keep track of how much time it takes to do something you're interested in measuring.

» Use the world clock to keep track of different time zones. It's useful when you work with people from all over the world and don't want to bother them at the wrong time.

The time, alarm, and stopwatch features are easy to use and self-explanatory. In the following, you become familiarized with the focus sessions and see how they work:

**1. Click or tap the search icon and type the word** clock. **Then choose Clock in the list of search results.**

The Clock app appears. If this is your first time using it, it starts by welcoming you to focus sessions, as shown in Figure 2-1.

**2. Click or tap Get Started.**

You see the focus sessions options shown in Figure 2-2.

**3. Choose how long you want to focus and work without interruptions.**

The default is 30 minutes, but you can set the time as low as 15 minutes or as high as 240 minutes. If you choose a session above 30 minutes, the app automatically calculates how many 5-minute breaks you should take, so that you don't have an unhealthy work routine. For example, if you choose 75 minutes, the app will recommend that you take two breaks.

**4. Click or tap Start Focus Session and do your work.**

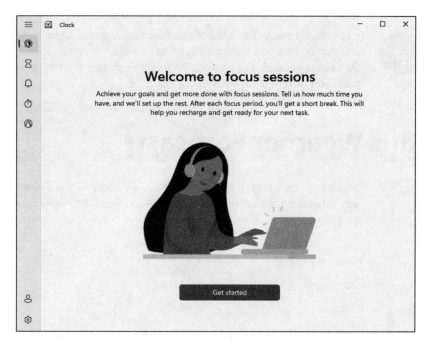

**FIGURE 2-1:**
The Clock app
welcomes you
to its new focus
sessions.

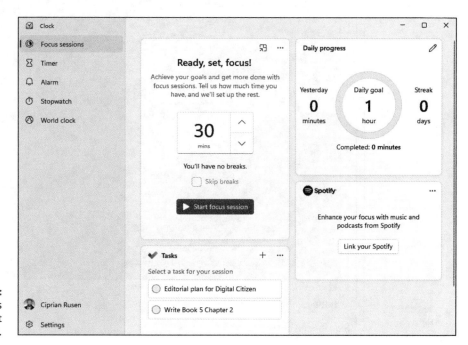

**FIGURE 2-2:**
Set up your focus
session and start
working.

Using Built-In
Applications

**TIP**

In the Daily Progress section of the Focus Sessions tab, you can set goals regarding how much time you want to spend daily doing focused work. Each time you finish a focus session, the app automatically updates your stats and shows you how much you have left towards you goal.

# Getting Weather Forecasts

Unlike the Clock app, the Weather app has remained the same in Windows 11. The only difference is that the weather forecast isn't displayed in a tile, because tiles are gone from Windows 11. You can see the Weather app in action in Figure 2-3.

Historical weather

Maps

Home

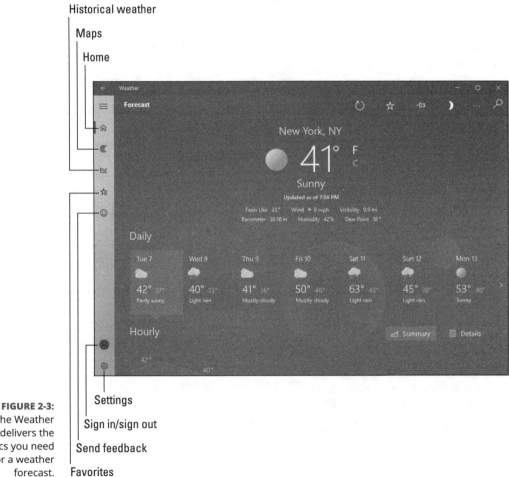

Settings

Sign in/sign out

Send feedback

Favorites

**FIGURE 2-3:**
The Weather app delivers the basics you need for a weather forecast.

You can have the app access your precise location and display its 10-day forecast, or you can check the forecast for any number of locations, from all over the world. On the left side of the app are several icons that give you access to the distinctive features of the app:

>> **Home icon:** Takes you to the app's home screen, displaying the default location you set for the weather forecast.

>> **Maps icon:** Displays different weather maps for any location you want. You can see how temperatures evolve over different regions, how the clouds move (viewed from satellites), precipitation maps, and so on. It's like the weather maps you see on TV.

>> **Historical weather icon:** Displays useful weather stats for your location with data about record highs and lows, average rainfall, snow days, and so on.

>> **Favorites icon:** Enables you to set several locations from all over the world as favorites and have them available for easy access.

>> **Send feedback icon:** Opens the feedback hub, which you can use to give feedback to Microsoft about the Weather app.

One thing I like about the Weather app is that it has a solid database that works well for most countries, not only the United States. If you're based in Europe, Asia, or some other continent, you won't be disappointed with its locations database.

# Editing Text Files with Notepad

Notepad was conceived, designed, and developed by programmers, for programmers — and it shows. Although Notepad has been improved over the years, many of the old limitations remain. Still, if you want a fast, no-nonsense text editor (certainly nobody would have the temerity to call Notepad a word processor), Notepad's a decent choice.

Notepad understands only plain, simple, unformatted text — basically the stuff you see on your keyboard. It doesn't understand formatting, such as bold text, or embedded pictures.

To top it off, Notepad is fast and reliable. Of all the Windows programs I come across, Notepad is the only one I can think of that has never crashed on me.

The following tidbits are all you'll likely ever need to successfully get in and around Notepad:

>> **To start Notepad, click or tap the Start icon and then All Apps. Then choose Notepad.** You can also double-click or double-tap any text (.txt) file in File Explorer. The screen shown in Figure 2-4 appears.

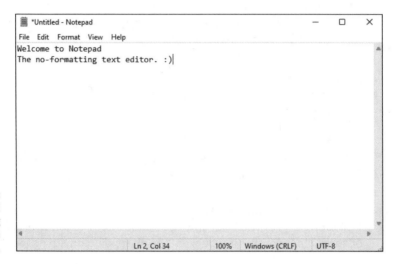

**FIGURE 2-4:**
Notepad is good
only for working
with plain
text files.

>> **Notepad can handle files of up to about 1GB.** If you try to open a file that's larger, a dialog box suggests that you open the file with a different editor.

>> **You can change the font, sort of.** When you first start Notepad, it displays a file's contents in 11-point Consolas font. Notepad's designers chose that font because it's easy to see on most computer monitors.

**REMEMBER**

Just because the text you see in Notepad is in a specific font, don't assume that the characters in the file itself are formatted. They aren't. The font you see on the screen is just the one Notepad uses to show the data. The stuff inside the file is plain, unformatted everyday text.

>> **To change the font displayed on your screen, choose Format and then Font and pick from the offered list.** You don't need to select any text before choosing the font because the font you choose is applied to all text onscreen. Also, your choice affects only the displayed text, not the contents of the file. The default Notepad font is *monospaced* — all the characters are the same width.

>> **You can wrap text.** Usually, text extends way off the right side of the screen. Notepad skips to a new line only when it encounters a line break — usually that means a carriage return character (or when someone presses Enter), which typically occurs at the end of every paragraph.

Notepad allows you to wrap text onscreen, so that you don't have to scroll all the way to the right to read every single paragraph. To have Notepad automatically break lines so that they wrap at the right edge of the window, choose Format and then Word Wrap.

TECHNICAL
STUFF

>> **Notepad has one little geeky time stamp trick.** You might find it amusing — and possibly worthwhile. If you type **.LOG** as the first line in a file, Notepad sticks a time stamp and date stamp at the end of the file each time it's opened.

TIP

Many alternatives to Notepad are available. Software developers need text editors, and many of them build their own. My favorite Notepad alternative is Notepad++ — and yes, I do type text quite a bit. Check out Notepad++ at `notepad-plus-plus.org/downloads/`. It's free and works well.

# Writing with WordPad

WordPad still exists in Windows 11, but you won't find its shortcut on the Start menu like you did in Windows 10. This app is even more hidden from view than it used to be. And for good reason: It's basic and hasn't been improved in many, many years. If you need to format a document and you can't get connected to Office Online (`www.office.com`) or you don't want to pay for Microsoft 365, WordPad will do, barely.

WordPad can work with DOCX format documents — the type of files that Word 2007 and later versions create by default. If you must edit a Word DOC or DOCX file with WordPad, follow these steps:

**1. Make a copy of the Word document and open the copy in WordPad.**

Do not edit original Word DOCX files with WordPad. Their formatting will become a mess as soon as you save them. Do not open Word docs in WordPad, thinking that you'll use the Save As command and save with a different name. You'll most probably forget.

**2. When you install Word, open the original document. On the Review ribbon, choose Compare, choose Combine, pick the WordPad version of the document, and then click or tap the Merge button.**

The resulting merged document is probably a mess, but it's a start.

Using Built-In
Applications

3. **Use the Review tab to march through your original document and apply the changes you made with WordPad.**

   This is the only reliable way to ensure that WordPad doesn't accidentally swallow any of your formatting.

WordPad works much the same as any other word processor. That said, WordPad isn't encumbered with many of the confusing features that make Word so difficult for the first-time e-typist, and it may be a decent way to start figuring out how simple word processors work.

To get WordPad going, click or tap the search icon, type **wordpad,** and then click or tap the search result with the same name. You then see the WordPad document editor in all its glory (see Figure 2-5).

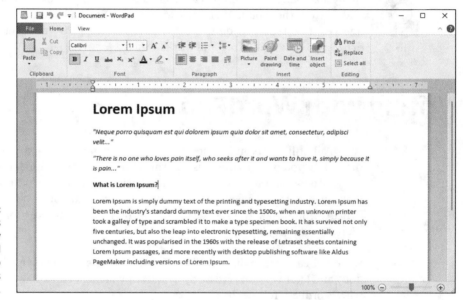

**FIGURE 2-5:**
WordPad includes rudimentary formatting and the capability to embed images for free.

WordPad lets you save documents in any of the following formats:

>> **Rich Text Format (RTF):** This ancient, circa-1987 format was developed by Microsoft and the legendary Charles Simonyi (yes, the space tourist) to make it easier to preserve some formatting when you change word processors. RTF documents can have some simple formatting but nothing nearly as complex as Word, for example. Many word-processing programs from many manufacturers can read and write RTF files, so RTF is a viable choice if you need to create a file that can be moved to many places.

>> **OOXML Text Document (DOCX):** This is the new Microsoft document standard file format, introduced in Word 2007 and used by default ever since. If you're going to use a document in Word, this is the format to choose.

**WARNING**

Note that WordPad can read and write DOCX files. Unfortunately, WordPad takes some liberties with the finer formatting features in Word. If you open a Word-generated DOCX file in WordPad, don't expect to see all the formatting. If you subsequently save that DOCX file from WordPad, expect it to clobber much of the original Word formatting.

>> **ODF Text Document (ODT):** This OpenDocument format is the native format for LibreOffice and OpenOffice.

>> **Text Document (TXT):** This format strips out all pictures and formatting and saves the document in a Notepad-style, regular old text format.

If you're just starting out with word processing, keep these facts in mind:

>> **To format text, select the text you want to format, and then choose the formatting you want in the Font part of the Home tab, on the ribbon.** For example, to change the font, click the down arrow next to the font name and choose the font you like.

>> **To format a paragraph, simply click once inside the paragraph and choose the formatting from the Paragraph group in the Home tab, on the ribbon.**

>> **General page layout is controlled by settings in the Page Setup dialog box.** General page layout includes things like margins and whether the page is printed vertically or horizontally. To open the dialog box, choose File⇨Page Setup.

>> **Tabs are complicated.** Every paragraph starts with tab stops set every half inch. You set additional tab stops by clicking in the middle of the ruler. (You can also set them by clicking the tiny side arrow to the right of the word *Paragraph* and then clicking the Tabs button.) The tab stops that you set up work only in individual paragraphs: Select one paragraph and set a tab stop, and it works only in the selected paragraph; select three paragraphs and set the stop, and it works in all three.

**TECHNICAL STUFF**

WordPad treats tabs like any other character: A tab can be copied, moved, and deleted, sometimes with unexpected results. Keep your eyes peeled when using tabs and tab stops. If something goes wrong, click the undo icon (to the right of the disk-like save icon) or press Ctrl+Z immediately and try again.

WordPad has a few features worthy of the term *feature:* bullets and numbered lists, paragraph justification, line spacing, superscript and subscript, and indentation. WordPad lacks many of the features that you may have come to expect from other word processors: You can't even insert a page break, much less a table. If you spend any time at all writing anything but the most straightforward documents, you'll outgrow WordPad quickly.

# Doing Math with Calculator

Windows 11 includes a capable Calculator app. Actually, Windows contains five capable calculators in this app, with several options for each one, plus a built-in units converter so you can translate furlongs per fortnight into inches per year. Before you run out and spend $20 on a scientific calculator, check out what the Calculator app can do.

To run the calculator, click or tap the Start icon and then Calculator. You probably see the standard calculator, as shown in Figure 2-6.

**FIGURE 2-6:**
The standard calculator, with a conventional keypad.

To use the calculator, click or tap its buttons or just type whatever you like on your keyboard, and press Enter when you want to carry out the calculation. For example, to calculate 123 times 456, you type or tap **123 \* 456** and press Enter.

The Calculator app comes in five modes: Standard, Scientific (which adds *sin* and *tan*, *x to the y*, and the like), Graphing, Programmer (hex, octal, Mod, Xor, Qword, Lsh), and Date calculation. You can flip among these modes by clicking or tapping the hamburger icon in the upper-left corner.

Calculator also has extensive unit conversion capabilities. After you click or tap the hamburger icon, look inside the Converter section and choose one of the unit converters: Currency, Volume, Length, Weight and Mass, Temperature, Energy, Area, Speed, Time, Power, Data, Pressure, or Angle. For example, if you choose Volume, you see the screen shown in Figure 2-7.

**FIGURE 2-7:**
The volume converter lets you choose from many different measures of volume.

The fun part of the converters is that they have little mind-jogging tips. For example, in Figure 2-7, you can see that 10 millimeters is about 2 teaspoons, but you can also see that it's about 0.68 tablespoons and 0.04 coffee cups. Play with it a bit, and you can see volumes in cubic yards and bathtubs, lengths in nautical miles, km and jumbo jet-lengths, weight in elephants, and much more.

**TIP**

You can also use Google or Bing for these options. You can type **32 C in F** in Google and get the answer back immediately. Google can calculate *1.2 euro per liter in dollars per gallon*, in one step — way beyond the Calculator app from Windows 11. Do a Google search for *mileage, lease payment,* or *amortization,* and you can find hundreds of sites with even more capable calculators.

A couple of Calculator tricks:

>> **Nope, an X on the keyboard doesn't translate into the times sign.** If you want times, you must click or tap the asterisk button on the Calculator, press the asterisk key (*), or use Shift+8.

>> **You can use the number pad, if your keyboard has one, but to make it work, you must turn on Num Lock.** Try typing a few numbers on your number pad. If Calculator sits there and doesn't realize you're typing, press the Num Lock key. The Calculator app should take the hint.

# Checking Out the New Paint App

Surprisingly, Microsoft has redesigned the Paint app for Windows 11. The new version is a modern spin on the classic app, with a new user interface with rounder corners but nothing worth mentioning in terms of new features.

If you want to fire it up and see how it looks, click or tap the Start icon, All Apps, and then Paint. You should see the new app in all its glory, as shown in Figure 2-8.

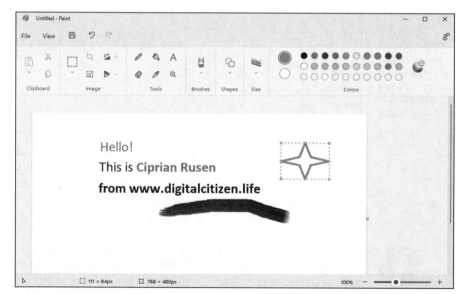

**FIGURE 2-8:**
Paint has received a fresh coat of paint.

As you can see, unlike in Windows 10, there's no longer a ribbon with several tabs. All the tools are at the top, logically organized, and easy to use on touchscreens as well as with the mouse. The File and View menus are easily accessible from the top-left corner. The toolbar is simplified, with new icons, a rounded color palette, and a new set of drop-down menus for tools such as brushes, stroke size, and flip and rotate controls.

Try it out and see the kinds of drawings and images you can create with the new Paint. I'm sure you're more talented than I am.

# Creating Sticky Notes

The Sticky Notes app in Windows 11 is the digital equivalent of real-life Post-It notes that stick anywhere, starting with your fridge and ending with your computer monitor. When you try to use them, Windows asks for a Microsoft account, even though regular local accounts can still create Sticky Notes. Microsoft does this because it has decided to take your notes to the cloud, back them up regularly, and synchronize them between PCs and devices.

To access the app, click or tap the Start icon, All Apps, and then Sticky Notes. The app is shown in Figure 2-9.

**FIGURE 2-9:**
The Sticky Notes app is easy to use.

To create a new note, click or tap + (plus) and start typing the note. You have some formatting options at the bottom of the note, and you can also add images. When you close a note, it's saved in the list shown in the middle of Sticky Notes.

While Sticky Notes is not as complex and feature-rich as OneNote, it's still a decent tool that many are going to appreciate, especially its simplicity. Its main purpose is to capture small pieces of information and keep them at hand. However, if you want a more advanced note-taking tool, with longer notes, and diverse content, read about OneNote in Book 4, Chapter 4.

# Keeping Track of Tasks with Microsoft To Do

Another app preinstalled in Windows 11 is Microsoft To Do. The app acts like a smart daily planner and is well integrated with the Mail app in Windows 11, Outlook in the Office suite and Microsoft 365, Cortana, the Clock app, and other Microsoft products and services.

You can use To Do individually or together with your family or with your co-workers, assigning tasks to each other. Microsoft To Do also has mobile apps for iOS and Android, so you can keep track of your tasks on all your PCs and devices. One neat little feature is that it automatically takes all your flagged messages from Mail or Outlook and shows them to you as tasks that you need to take care of.

To see it in action, click or tap the Start icon, All Apps, and then Microsoft To Do. The screen shown in Figure 2-10 appears.

Its user interface is simple to use and understand, split into logical categories. Its integration with many other Microsoft products and services is a big plus and, if you don't have a task planner, you should really try it out. It can help you become more productive and less forgetful, at both work and home.

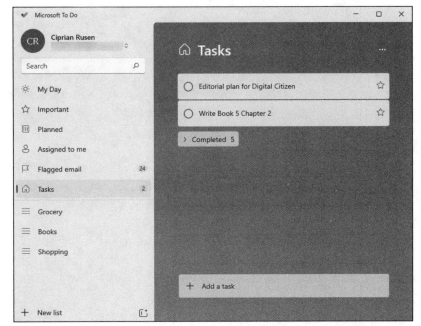

**FIGURE 2-10:**
Microsoft To Do
can enhance your
productivity.

# Navigating with Maps

The Maps app in Windows 11 is the same as the one in Windows 10. If you've ever used Google Maps (I do, every day) or the Apple Maps app, you already have a basic understanding of the Maps app in Windows 11.

To get the app started, click or tap the Start icon, All Apps, and then Maps. When you open the app, there are two basic views:

>> **Road** displays a traditional roadmap, at least to a first approximation. See Figure 2-11.

>> **Aerial** displays a satellite view of the terrain, augmented by superimposed roads. See Figure 2-12.

To switch between the two views, click or tap the down arrow at the top right and select the view you want.

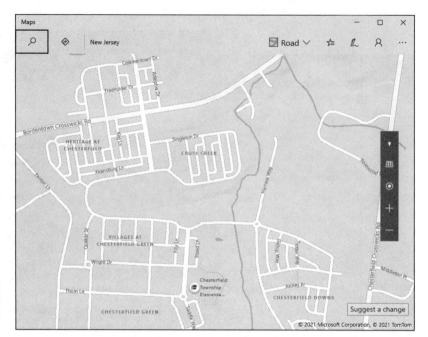

**FIGURE 2-11:**
The basic road view calls out the landmarks.

**FIGURE 2-12:**
Aerial view has a satellite shot with various notations.

**TIP**

At least in theory, both the road and aerial maps can be superimposed with traffic information, which appears color-coded on the roads. Again, click or tap the down arrow at the top right and turn the Traffic switch on or off. In my experience, traffic information is only occasionally useful. And in some cases, for reasons unknown, it doesn't appear at all. And if you don't have mobile data, traffic data isn't helpful.

If you want to see where you are, click or tap the the bull's-eye icon (show my location) on the right, above + and –. If you're mobile and have GPS turned on, the location is accurate. If you're working from a computer with a Wi-Fi connection, the best you're going to get is a rough approximation of the nearest phone company router.

There's a rotate-30-degrees-or-so tilt view, which you can enable or disable by clicking or tapping the grid icon above the bull's-eye. See Figure 2-13. The view isn't interesting — places that should have breathtaking elevation differences, such as the area surrounding Homer, Alaska, end up looking like Flatland.

**FIGURE 2-13:** Even places with lots of elevation differences look like a 12th-century depiction of a flat earth.

The map has the usual navigation controls: click (or tap) and drag to move the map, use the scroll wheel on the mouse (or pinch and unpinch) to zoom.

The Maps app is basic and doesn't hold a candle to the likes of Google Maps or Apple Maps. However, it's still useful for basic needs.

# Chapter **3**

# Getting Apps from the Web

U sing Windows alone is not enough to be productive or to have fun when using your computer. Yes, you can do plenty with the built-in apps and browse the web with Microsoft Edge, filling many hours of your day. However, you may need to work with all kinds of documents (such as PDF files) as well as cloud-storage apps not built into OneDrive, apps for viewing movies, desktop apps for unzipping file archives, and more.

Windows programs, or desktop apps, are downloaded by users from all over the internet, sometimes from illegal sources like torrents, using peer-to-peer file-sharing clients like eMule or Napster (are you also old enough to remember it?), and other times from legal and safe download sites like the Microsoft Download Center or Download.com.

The new and improved Microsoft Store has more apps than ever, but you still may not find there the programs you seek. And then comes the saga of searching for your favorite programs on the web, downloading them from a safe place, and confirming that they're safe.

In this chapter, I share recommendations on where to download your apps and how to check them before you use them. Finally, I show you how to remove (uninstall) a desktop app from Windows 11 when you no longer want to use it.

# Finding Safe Places to Download Desktop Apps

The first place to look for Windows 11 apps, including classic desktop programs, is the Microsoft Store, covered in Chapter 1 of this minibook. It's a safe place because all apps are reviewed by Microsoft, you can install only the app you want, without other bundled apps you don't need and ads. Not only that, but the Microsoft Store also keeps your desktop apps automatically updated, without any effort on your part.

Unfortunately, the Microsoft Store doesn't have that many desktop apps, and you may not find what you want. In this situation, doing an internet search for the name of the app you want to download is the way to go.

WARNING

Be wary when you download an app from someplace other than the Microsoft Store. The safest option is to download the app from its official site. Using third-party download sites such as softonic.com or filehippo.com can be a frustrating experience, filled with ads that promote downloading something other than what you want. Look at Figure 3-1, where I tried to download Google Chrome and got a large ad instead, recommending me to download Opera. Yes, Opera is a cool browser, but I wanted Google Chrome. Note how you barely see the link to refuse this offer and continue to download Google Chrome. If you don't pay attention, you'll fill your new Windows 11 computer with bloatware in no time. Unfortunately, the web is filled with download sites with similar practices.

TIP

To make things simpler and easier, here are my recommendations for locations for downloading desktop apps:

>> The Microsoft Store app from Windows 11

>> The official website of the app

>> Safe(r) download sites such as microsoft.com (for all everything made by Microsoft), softpedia.com, download.com, and github.com.

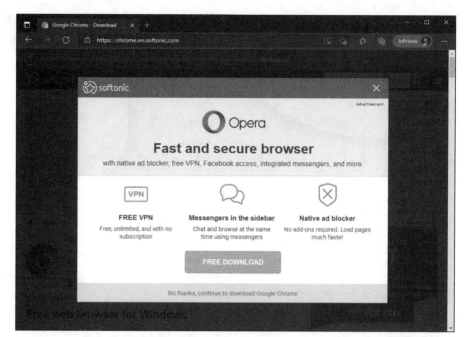

To navigate you through the process, let's download Adobe Reader, the official app from Adobe for opening and working with PDF files. We all need this app for work, right?

1. **Open Microsoft Edge and navigate to** `www.google.com`.

   Type *adobe reader* and press Enter. Google shows you a list of links, as shown in Figure 3-2.

2. **Scroll down the list of search results.**

   Note how the first result is from `https://get.adobe.com`, while others down are from play.google.com, apps.apple.com, softonic.com, and many other locations.

3. **Get back to the first result,** `https://get.adobe.com`, **and click or tap it.**

   Your browser should display something like Adobe Acrobat Reader DC Install for All Versions. Adobe also promotes all kinds of optional offers and additional apps from other vendors. Don't select any of them.

4. **Click or tap Download Acrobat Reader.**

When Adobe Reader finishes downloading, you can install it on your Windows 11 PC by double-clicking or double-tapping it. The setup file for the desktop app should have a name like readerdc_en_xa_crd_install.exe.

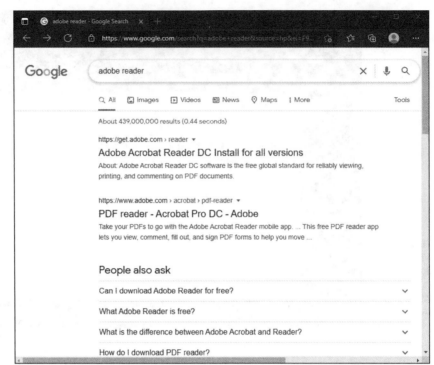

**FIGURE 3-2:**
Searching for
Adobe Reader on
Google reveals
many download
locations.

**WARNING**

When downloading desktop apps on Windows 11, pay attention to similar offers like the one from Adobe. Don't select any options other than the program you want. Otherwise, your computer will become filled with stuff you don't need and slow as molasses.

# Checking Apps for Malware

If you want to make sure that an app you just downloaded is safe to use, run an antivirus scan on it. To do so, navigate to www.virustotal.com and upload the file you want scanned. This site is particularly useful because it analyzes your file using all the major antivirus software on the market, from the likes of Symantec, Bitdefender, Avast, TrendMicro, and many others. For each file you analyze with VirusTotal, you see a summary like the one in Figure 3-3.

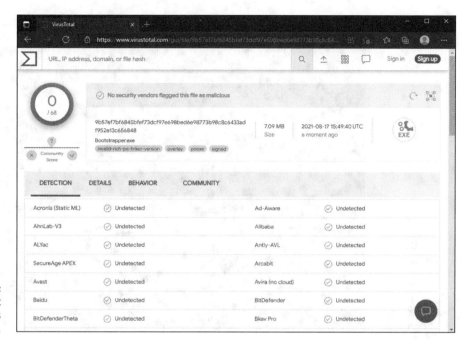

**FIGURE 3-3:**
VirusTotal is great at checking apps for viruses.

If you think that using VirusTotal is too cumbersome or time-consuming, Windows Security (which includes Microsoft Defender alongside other security tools) from Windows 11 is a good choice. Here's how to use it to check whether a file you just downloaded is secure:

1. **Open File Explorer and double-click or double-tap Downloads.**

2. **Right-click or press and hold down on the file you want to check and choose Show More Options.**

   If you downloaded Adobe Reader in the preceding section, you can right-click or press and hold down on the readerdc_en_xa_crd_install.exe file.

   The right-click menu extends to include more options, as shown in Figure 3-4.

3. **Choose Scan with Microsoft Defender.**

   The Windows Security app opens, where it displays the results of a scan, and whether it found any threats inside the file you scanned.

**WARNING**

If Windows Security tells you that threats were found inside the file you scanned, delete that file immediately. Never run it. It's highly likely that the file contains malware (such as a virus, trojan, or ransomware) that will harm your computer.

Getting Apps from the Web

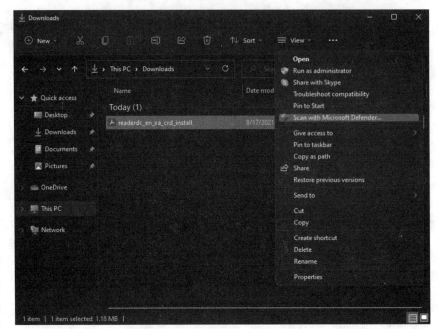

**FIGURE 3-4:**
The extended right-click menu includes the option to Scan with Microsoft Defender.

# Uninstalling Desktop Apps or Programs

If you no longer want to use a desktop app, you can remove it from Windows 11 to save space and optimize your system performance. Unfortunately, the process for removing desktop apps requires a few more steps than uninstalling Windows 11 apps. Here's one of the many ways to remove a desktop app in Windows 11:

**1.** **Click or tap the search icon on the taskbar and type** add remove.

Windows 11 displays a list of search results.

**2.** **Click or tap Add or Remove Programs.**

The Settings app opens to the Apps > Apps & Features section. You see a list of all installed apps, as shown in Figure 3-5.

**3.** **Find the app you want to remove and click or tap the three dots to the right of its name.**

You see a menu with two options: Modify and Uninstall.

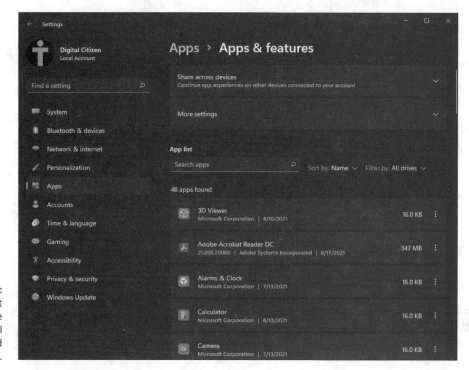
4. **Click or tap Uninstall, and then click or tap it again.**

5. **Follow the program's uninstall wizard.**

   This process usually means clicking or tapping buttons such as Next, Uninstall, Confirm, and Finish. The options you see differ from program to program.

As you can see, the process is not that difficult, and your Windows 11 computer or device now has more free space for you to use for other things.

# Chapter **4**

# Keeping Apps and Drivers Up to Date

I f you want to keep your PC as secure as possible and working in tip-top shape, it's not enough to keep only Windows 11 up to date with the latest patches and feature updates. You must also update your apps, desktop programs, and device drivers.

Apps and desktop programs get regularly updated by their developers to offer new features, to fix bugs and security glitches, and more. Drivers for hardware components like graphic cards or network cards receive similar updates. Driver updates are especially important if you are a gamer and want to play the latest titles with maximum performance and without lag. Often, new graphics drivers implement support for the newest games and offer specific optimizations that increase frame rates and overall performance. And new driver versions for your Wi-Fi network card can increase the speed or lower the latency you get when you play games online.

The task of keeping everything updated can be daunting, but the Microsoft Store can help you update Windows 11 apps and desktop programs. Also, Windows Update does a decent job updating drivers — but not updating all the hardware in your computer. For example, it's definitely not good enough for gamers who need the latest drivers for their NVIDIA, Intel, or AMD Radeon video card.

In this chapter, I cover the essentials of keeping Windows 11 apps, desktop programs, and device drivers updated on a regular basis.

# Updating Your Microsoft Store Apps

Microsoft updates all sorts of things through the Microsoft Store — not just apps you bought or downloaded from the Microsoft Store but also built-in Windows 11 apps.

Sometimes, the Microsoft Store doesn't update itself. From time to time, you should check that you have the latest updates for absolutely everything, including Microsoft Store. Here's how:

1. **Click or tap the Start icon and then Microsoft Store.**

   A Microsoft Store shortcut is probably also on your taskbar, not just on the Start menu.

2. **Click or tap Library, in the lower part of the left column.**

   You see all your Windows 11 apps, as well as which have updates available for installation, as shown in Figure 4-1.

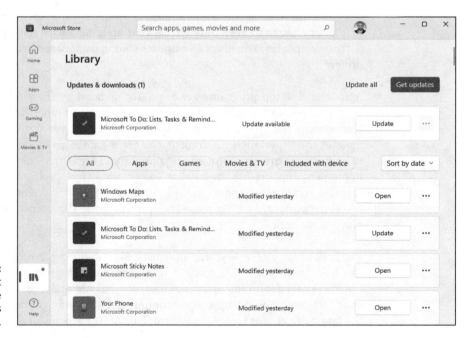

**FIGURE 4-1:**
Click or tap Get Updates to make sure everything is up to speed.

3. **Click or tap Get Updates.**

   Any waiting updates start installing, as shown in Figure 4-2.

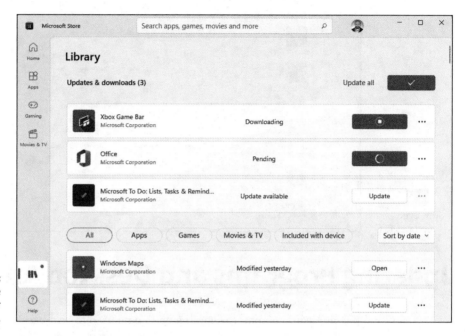

4. **If the Microsoft Store is updating your apps too slowly and seems to ignore your request to Get Updates, click or tap Update All in the top-right corner.**

   This action forces the Microsoft Store to focus on updating all your apps, right now.

In the normal course of events, you'll want to update all your apps, but if you know of a bad update (and they happen from time to time), you can choose which apps you want to bring up to date.

From time to time, you'll hit a problem with an update and an error will appear, as shown in Figure 4-3. To see more information, click or tap the app's name and then click or tap See Details. Check that your internet connection is working, and then try again by clicking or tapping the Retry button next to the app whose update has failed. If that doesn't work, do a web search for the error details or try contacting the app manufacturer. Good luck.

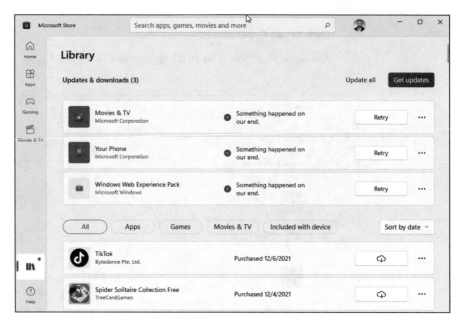

# Updating Programs and Desktop Apps

Keeping your computer programs up to date used to be a hassle, especially in the good old days of Windows 7. In recent years, the process has been easier for several reasons. One is that many desktop apps, especially web browsers, have their own update checker running from time to time in the background. For example, Opera (one of my favorite browsers), Firefox, and Microsoft Edge update automatically. When the browser upgrades to a new version, it loads a new tab to inform you that the browser is up to date and gives you a summary of what's new, as shown in Figure 4-4.

I like this approach because it ensures that I am always using the latest version of my web browser and am as secure as possible, with the latest bug fixes and security improvements.

Some Microsoft apps, such as Microsoft 365 and Office, can be updated through Windows Update. However, they don't do that by default; you need to enable the Receive Updates for Other Microsoft Products setting in Windows Update. For details, read Book 7, Chapter 2. Keeping Office up to date is important because its security bugs are often used for complex attacks, especially in business environments.

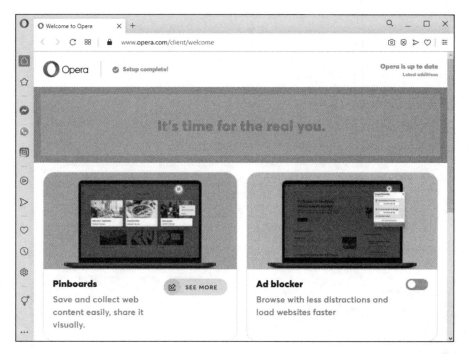

**FIGURE 4-4:** All major web browsers update themselves automatically.

Other programs use an approach similar to Paint.NET, which I present and recommend in Book 10, Chapter 6. When you start them, they check for updates. If they find any, they inform you and give you the option to update them now or later, as shown in Figure 4-5.

Still other apps and desktop programs are now distributed through the Microsoft Store, so Windows 11 updates them automatically, in the background. And, if the Microsoft Store hasn't updated them for some reason, you can do it yourself, using the steps in the preceding section. The automatic app-updating service is the main reason why I hope the Microsoft Store in Windows 11 will finally catch on with developers and users alike.

Lastly, you can use software updating programs. Some are decent but most of them are junk, filled with adware and other stuff you don't want. One of the best is Patch My PC Home Updater at `https://patchmypc.com/home-updater`. The program is free, has a database of over 300 desktop apps that it checks regularly for updates, and does an excellent job showing you which programs are outdated, as shown in Figure 4-6. A bonus is that it can update all your programs with just one click.

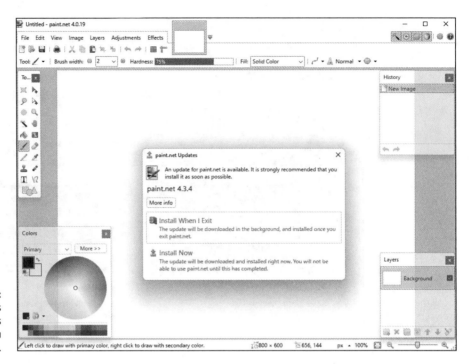

**FIGURE 4-5:**
Some programs
check for updates
each time you
start them.

**FIGURE 4-6:**
Patch My PC
Home Updater
can help you
keep your pro-
grams up to date.

# Updating Drivers

A *driver* is software that allows your operating system to start, use, and control a specific hardware device. In other words, drivers are the translators: When Windows (or any other operating system) wants a hardware device to do something, it uses its driver to make the request so that the hardware understands what it has to do.

Updating drivers is somewhat simpler than updating apps or programs because Windows 11 handles the process automatically through Windows Update. Windows does this for all kinds of devices, such as network cards, printers, video cards, and monitors. However, what you get from Windows are the latest drivers approved by Microsoft, not necessarily the latest drivers available from the manufacturer of the component. If you want the latest driver, check the official site of the company that manufactured the component.

Getting the latest driver for graphics cards is especially important for gaming. If you're a gamer, don't stick with what Windows 11 offers. Instead, manually download the latest driver for your graphics card. Here are the support sites for the most important manufacturers of video cards:

>> **AMD:** www.amd.com/en/support

>> **NVIDIA:** www.nvidia.com/Download/index.aspx

>> **Intel:** www.intel.com/content/www/us/en/download-center/home.html

**WARNING**

When downloading a driver it's vital to choose one made for your operating system (in this case Windows 11, not Windows 7 or Windows 8) and the exact model of the hardware component you're using. If you install a driver for the wrong component or the wrong operating system version, Windows 11 could crash. If that happens, boot Windows 11 in safe mode (read Book 8, Chapter 3) and uninstall the driver you just installed.

Let's assume that a hardware component in your computer isn't working well and you suspect that the driver is outdated. Use Windows 11 to search for updates, like this:

**1.** **Right-click or tap and hold down on the Start icon, or press Windows+X on your keyboard.**

The WinX menu opens.

## 2. Choose Device Manager.

The Device Manager program opens, as shown in Figure 4-7. You see all the hardware inside your computer and connected to it, organized by type. You can expand each hardware category with a double-click or double-tap.

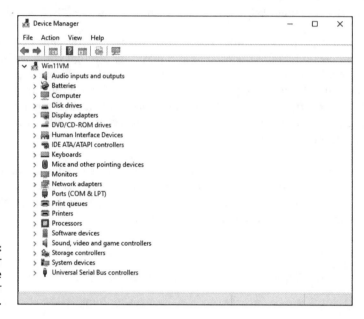

**FIGURE 4-7:**
Device Manager shows you all the hardware in your computer.

## 3. Expand the type of hardware for which you want to update the driver.

For example, to update the driver for a network card, expand Network Adapters.

## 4. Right-click or tap and hold down on the name of the hardware component that you want to update, and then choose Update Driver.

The options shown in Figure 4-8 appear.

## 5. Choose Search Automatically for Drivers.

Windows 11 checks for newer drivers. If it finds any, it informs you and installs them automatically.

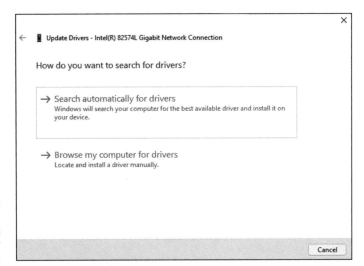

**FIGURE 4-8:**
Tell Windows 11
that you want
to search for
drivers.

6.  **If Windows 11 tells you that you have the best drivers already installed but you want it to keep looking, click or tap Search for Updated Drivers on Windows Update.**

    Windows 11 takes you to Windows Update, where you can click or tap Check for Updates, and see what updates are available.

# 6

# Sharing, Socializing, and Working Online

# Contents at a Glance

Chapter **1**

# Being Social on Facebook and Twitter

Everyone knows about Facebook and Twitter these days, and many people use them, all over the world. Facebook has been especially famous in the news, and not for positive reasons. If you haven't heard about it, look for The Facebook Papers on Google or Bing. It was quite an eye-opening investigation into Facebook's internal affairs.

In this chapter, I'm not going to debate about what's wrong with Facebook or Twitter. Instead, I'll show you the basics about using these social networks. My objective is to help you create a Facebook account, improve your privacy settings, and understand the basics about how it works. The same with Twitter.

Without further ado, let's get started. I'll cover Facebook first, and then Twitter.

## Getting Started with Facebook

If you don't yet have a Facebook account, more than 2.5 billion people are ahead of you. I have friends who figure Facebook is some sort of fad that's going away soon. They'd rather be offline for most of the day than put anything on Facebook. "You lose your privacy," they say. "I don't see any need for it." Even so, Facebook has become an important part of the daily routine of 1.8 billion people, and it claims that more than 2.5 billion registered users go online every month. It's been credited with starting revolutions. It's certainly a good source of news — almost as good as Twitter (described later in this chapter) — if you choose what and who you follow carefully.

REMEMBER

Facebook has fundamentally changed the way hundreds of millions of families interact, more so than any other invention since the telephone. It's altered the way people work. Businesses. Schools. Hospitals. Governments. Charities.

Facebook has even eaten into email and instant messaging, for heaven's sake. Email usage has gone down the past decade because Facebook's one-to-many nature reduces the need for email messages, and its embedded chat features are growing fast. To me, that's incredible. I'm tempted to stand up and bellow a chorus from Bob Dylan's "The Times They Are A-Changin'."

In this chapter, I only brush the surface of the capabilities available to Facebook users. You find a bit of depth about the Timeline, and I hit the privacy/security part because that's where you should concentrate your efforts when you're just starting out.

## Choosing the Facebook App or Facebook.com

Chances are that as soon as you log into Windows 11 for the first time and open the Start menu, you'll see the Facebook app shortcut in the middle of the Pinned section. It's right there, next to TikTok (one of its most important competitors) and Instagram, as shown in Figure 1-1.

When you click or tap the Facebook icon, Windows downloads the app from the Microsoft Store and then opens it for you. Unfortunately, this isn't a dedicated app for Windows but a progressive web app (PWA). This means that instead of having a Facebook app optimized for Windows like you do for Android and iOS, you have the Facebook website running inside a wrapper: something that appears to be an individual app but is actually Microsoft Edge running facebook.com in an app window named Facebook.

The Facebook company (now renamed Meta) ignored Windows for many years, so I don't find this approach surprising. The Facebook "app" for Windows works reasonably well, but many users don't appreciate it and prefer the mobile alternatives. I do too. And while I'm on Windows 11, I prefer to open facebook.com inside my favorite browser. It works better that way, and it's easier to deal with it inside a browser tab instead of as a separate app. To prove my point that the Facebook app for Windows is nothing but the facebook.com website in a wrapper, I've run them side by side, as shown in Figure 1-2. You can't tell them apart, right?

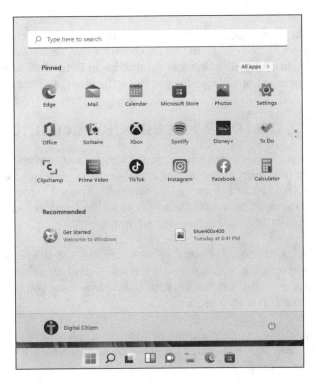

**FIGURE 1-1:**
Windows 11 often promotes the Facebook app.

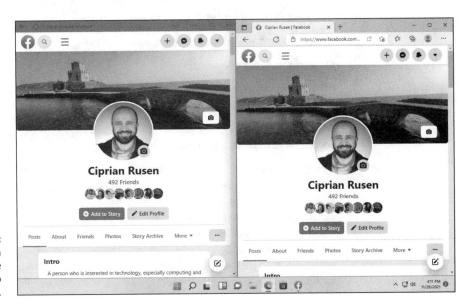

**FIGURE 1-2:**
Facebook.com on the right vs the Facebook app on the left.

And the funny thing is, if you log out from facebook.com inside Microsoft Edge, you'll also get logged out from the Facebook "app." Technically it makes sense, though, because all you're doing is using Edge in both situations, with the same cookies. Logging in one place logs you in on the other, and the other way around.

## Signing up for a Facebook account

If you don't yet have a Facebook account, I suggest you sign up. Don't worry — no one is going to steal your identity or mine your personal data. Facebook's free — and will be free to use forever, we're assured, although some features may cost something someday, and a few business-oriented features like promoting posts or other kinds of advertising do cost real money.

**WARNING**

There's one cardinal rule about Facebook, which I call the *prime directive:* Don't put anything on or in Facebook — *anything* — that you don't want to appear in tomorrow morning's news. Or your boss's inbox. Or your kid's school class. Privacy begins at home, doesn't it?

Now that you have the right attitude, all you need is a working email address, and if you state that you're at least 13 years old, you can have a Facebook account in minutes. Here's how:

**1. Use your favorite browser to go to www.facebook.com.**

The Log In or Sign Up page appears, as shown in Figure 1-3.

**2. Click or tap Create New Account.**

**3. Fill in your name and email address, give your new account a password, and make sure your birthday indicates that you're at least 13.**

The email address must be a valid one that you can get to because a confirmation email goes to that address.

This is *not* the way to set up an account for a celebrity, band, business, charitable organization, or knitting group. In all those cases, you need to set up an individual account first — follow the instructions here — and then after your individual account is ready, you add a *page* (sometimes known as a *business page*) to your individual account. I know it's complicated, but Facebook works that way. Even Coca-Cola's page is attached to an individual — presumably an employee from their Marketing department signed up and then created a page for Coca-Cola.

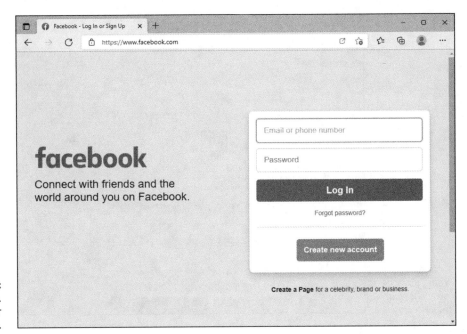

FIGURE 1-3:
The facebook.
com Log In or
Sign Up page.

**TIP**

There's no reason to give personally identifiable information in this sign-up sheet. Facebook may balk if you try to sign up as Mark Zuckerberg, but it (probably) won't have any problem with Marcus Zuckerbergus (although, now that I've mentioned it, the name may be added to Facebook's blacklist). Some people have had trouble using their stage names, even when their stage names are, legally, their real names. Facebook has a policy that you must use your real name, so if you don't want to provide yours, make sure whatever name you use looks real enough. (Apparently you can make up a silly middle name, though, and it's likely to be accepted.)

And if you figure your birthday is your business, the internet police aren't going to come knocking. The one item that must be valid, though, is the email address — which can come from a free site, such as Outlook.com or Gmail.

**4.** **Click or tap Sign Up.**

Facebook sends a confirmation email to the address you specified.

**5.** **Copy and paste the confirmation code. Click or tap Continue and then OK.**

If you live in Europe, Facebook asks about allowing it to use cookies.

**6.** **Click or tap Allow All Cookies if you see this prompt.**

You then see the facebook.com home page, which will look similar to Figure 1-4. At this point, your profile is empty: no picture, no friends, no content published on Facebook.

Next, you set up some basic settings and get your security locked down.

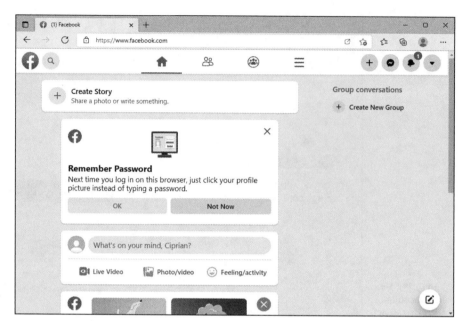

**FIGURE 1-4:**
Your Facebook profile is ready and also empty.

# WHAT, EXACTLY, IS A FRIEND?

Most people new to Facebook think that friends are, well, friends. Not so.

On Facebook, a *friend* is someone you're willing to interact with. If you're interested in interacting with someone who has a Facebook account — and want to let that person see what you've posted (typed in the What's on Your Mind box), look at your *Timeline* (a historic bulletin board), or look at the pictures you've posted on Facebook — you send a *friend request*. The person who receives the friend request decides to accept the request, decline it, or just sit on it.

Some of my Facebook friends are people I've never met. They are, however, people I trust enough to allow them to look at my vacation pictures, say, and people who are interesting enough that I want to look at what they post on their profiles. If the concept of a friend is a bit overwhelming at this point, don't worry about it. Find two or three people you know who have Facebook accounts, send friend requests to them, and watch what happens when they respond.

Get your feet wet with the concept before you start friending everything with two legs. Or four. You can always add new friends (or delete them — *unfriend* them — for that matter), but it's easier to start out slowly while you're getting the hang of it. Too many friends at first can be overwhelming.

## Improving basic Facebook privacy settings

Before you try to figure out what you're doing — a process that will take several days — go through setting up the rest of your Facebook account. One of the first things you should look at is your privacy settings. Here's how you can improve your privacy on Facebook:

1. **Log into Facebook and click or tap the down arrow, in the upper-right corner, and then choose Settings & Privacy, followed by Settings.**

   You see the General Account Settings page.

2. **On the left, choose Security and Login. Scroll down on the right until you see Use Two-Factor Authentication, and click or tap its Edit button.**

   The two-factor authorization (2FA) signup offer appears.

   **TIP**

   2FA is an important adjunct to any account — and I find text message 2FA is the easiest option. When you use the text message 2FA, the first time you log on to Facebook from a new device, Facebook automatically sends a text message to your smartphone with a confirmation code. You must enter the confirmation code before you can proceed.

3. **Click or tap Text Message (SMS). If you're asked to enter your Facebook password, do so.**

   The dialog box shown in Figure 1-5 appears.

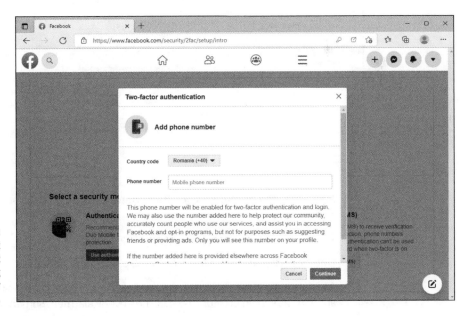

**FIGURE 1-5:**
The most important security setting is two-factor authentication.

**4.** **Type your phone number, and click or tap Continue. When the confirmation message appears on your phone, type the code in the confirmation box, and then click or tap Continue followed by Done.**

A pesky notification box asks you if it's okay to use your phone number to help you make connections and see ads that are more "relevant."

**5.** **Unless your friends are a whole lot friendlier than my friends, click or tap Not Now.**

You're informed that two-factor authentication is on.

**6.** **Click or tap the down arrow in the upper right, and then choose Settings & Privacy again, followed by Settings.**

You go back to the General Account Settings page.

**7.** **On the left, click or tap Privacy. Then, next to Who Can See Your Future Posts? choose Edit.**

The default sharing pane appears, as shown in Figure 1-6.

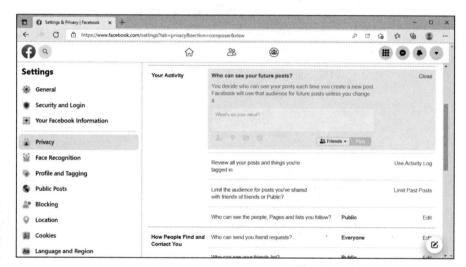

**FIGURE 1-6:**
The default is for all future posts to be visible only by friends.

**8.** **Make sure the drop-down box lists Friends and not Public, and then click or tap Close.**

You're back to the Privacy Settings and Tools page.

**9.** **One final check: On the left, click or tap Apps and Websites.**

A list of all apps that have permission to connect to your Facebook account appears, as shown in Figure 1-7. Don't be overly alarmed. Somehow, sometime, you gave those apps permission to hook into your Facebook account.

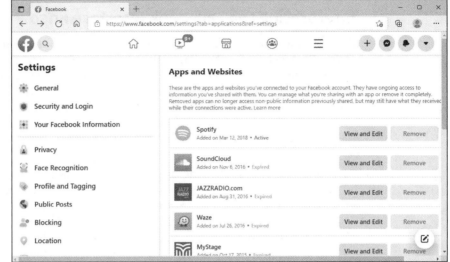

**FIGURE 1-7:**
Don't be too
surprised if
you see some
bizarre apps and
websites that
have access to
your Facebook
data.

**Being Social on Facebook and Twitter**

**10.** Delete any unwanted obtrusive app or website by clicking or tapping Remove next to its name, and confirming your choice.

**11.** Click or tap Home, up at the top, and go back to using Facebook.

# WHAT OTHER PEOPLE CAN SEE ABOUT YOU

Lots and lots of rumors circulate about what people can and can't see, so let me set the record straight.

If you look at someone's Timeline (or profile), the person you're looking up doesn't have any way to tell that you've looked. In fact, there's no way to tell how many times people have looked at a Timeline. There are lots of Facebook scams that offer to give you a list of who's visited your Timeline. They're just that — scams. It can't be done.

And if you confirm that only your friends can see your future posts, the amount of information that other people can see is small.

Although the ubiquitous Facebook Like button sits on millions of sites, Facebook doesn't give the people who run those sites any information at all about you. None. On the other hand, sites with the Like button allow Facebook to set third-party cookies on those sites. Facebook can trace your IP address as you go from site to site with the Like button. But the site itself doesn't get any information from Facebook.

## Interpreting the Facebook interface lingo

Now that you've taken the whirlwind tour, permit me to throw some terminology at you. Facebook used to be simple; it isn't anymore. To work with Facebook, you need to figure out the names of things and what the different pieces are supposed to do. The complicated part? Names have changed over the years, and you're bound to run into old names for new things — and vice versa.

Here's my handy translator:

>> **Home page (also called the News Feed)** is primarily about your friends. The important stuff is in the middle — navigation aids are on the left, and uninteresting things (including ads) are on the right. When you type something in the What's on Your Mind box, it's added to the top of the list, as well as at the top of your Timeline. When you add photos or videos, thumbnails of the photos go at the top of the list in the middle of the home page. Ditto for your friends' photos.

**REMEMBER**

When you click or tap Home at the top, you go to the home page or the News Feed. When you sign on to Facebook, you go to the home page.

Facebook has a secret algorithm that it uses to figure out which items appear on your News Feed and in what sequence. If you're mystified why something's on the top of the page but the important stuff is down farther, well, I'm frequently mystified, too.

At this moment, your home page also includes Top Stories and Facebook-generated Rooms just above the news feed. *Rooms* are a relatively new feature that allow up to 50 people to video chat at a time. There's no limit to how long you can talk.

>> **Timeline** is all about you. There's a big picture at the top, dubbed a cover, with your profile picture appearing to the left. Then there are all the settings you've made visible, followed by almost all the posts you've made over the years, in reverse-chronological order. I talk about the Timeline in the next section.

When you type something in the What's on Your Mind box, it's added to the top of the Timeline list, as well as at the top of your home page. Your friends can also post on your Timeline — in effect, leaving you a note.

**REMEMBER**

The Timeline appears when you click or tap your name at the top of the Facebook page. It also appears when someone clicks or taps your profile picture in something you posted.

# WHAT BUSINESSES CAN SEE ABOUT YOU

Many people starting out with Facebook are worried that businesses — particularly businesses that pay to advertise on Facebook — can see all their personal information.

Sorry. As much as I love a good conspiracy theory, it just isn't true.

Anybody who controls a business page can see the profiles of people who have clicked or tapped the Like button on the page and on the content they published on it. So, for example, if you go to the Ford page (which is a particularly good one, by the way), Ford will know that a person of a certain gender and age range visited the page. Ford will also get one more visitor tallied by city, country, and major language. If you arrived at the page by clicking or tapping a Facebook ad, that fact is also counted. But that's it.

When a business pays for an ad, it chooses the demographics (for example, "only show ads to males 18 to 24 living in Los Angeles") but there's no lingering information about who got served an ad, and no way to tie you, specifically, to a click or tap on an ad. Facebook has that information. The advertiser does not.

Facebook guards your information jealously. It doesn't sell your info to businesses or give it away, unless you specifically permit an app to pull the data from Facebook.

## Building a great Timeline

The Timeline — the place you go when you click or tap your name — is where people usually go when they want to learn about you. If somebody clicks or taps your picture in a post elsewhere in Facebook, that person is sent to an abbreviated version of your Timeline.

When you bring up your own Timeline, you get to see a great deal more than what the world sees, as in Figure 1-8.

**REMEMBER**

Keep in mind the prime directive: Don't put anything on or in Facebook — *anything* — that you don't want to appear in tomorrow morning's news. Fill in the details sparingly.

Follow these steps to personalize your Timeline:

**1.** **After you log in to Facebook, bring up your Timeline by clicking or tapping your name at the top right.**

Depending on how much you've done to your Timeline, it might look like the one in Figure 1-8.

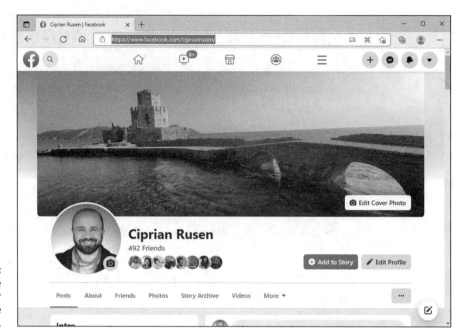

**FIGURE 1-8:**
Your Timeline
is your
resume in the
Facebook world.

2. **Click or tap the camera icon and follow the instructions that appear.**

   Facebook takes you through the steps of either uploading a new photo or choosing from one that you've already uploaded. The Facebook cover photo is 850 pixels wide x 315 pixels tall. Facebook will accept any picture as long as it's at least 720 pixels wide. When you drag the uploaded picture to fit it into the fixed-sized frame (in the next step), you're telling Facebook how to crop the picture to make it fit into the 850 x 315-pixel box. For best results, use a photo-manipulation program — or even Paint— to get the photo just right before you upload it.

**WARNING**

   If you don't have a suitable photo already, pre-fab Facebook cover photos are all over the internet. Just be careful when you go out looking: Any website that has you click (or tap) and log in to Facebook to deliver the photo may be gathering your Facebook login ID in the process. It's much safer to simply download the photo to your hard drive and then upload it yourself to Facebook.

3. **Drag the photo to the fixed-size frame. Then click or tap Save Changes.**

4. **To change your *profile picture* — the little picture on the left that also appears on anything that you post, click or tap it and choose Update Profile Picture.**

   Remember that your profile picture gets squeezed down most of the time, so a highly detailed photo usually doesn't work well.

**5.** **When you're finished editing your profile information, click or tap your name at the top of the screen to go back to the Timeline.**

Now it's time to change the contents of the Timeline itself.

**6.** **Scroll down the Timeline and find an item that you don't want other people to see. Then do the following:**

a. *Click or tap the ellipsis in the top-right corner of that item.* Facebook gives you the options shown in Figure 1-9.

b. *To remove that item from your Timeline, click or tap Move to Trash, and confirm your choice.* The item disappears immediately and is moved to Facebook's Trash. After 30 days, all items in Trash are automatically deleted for good.

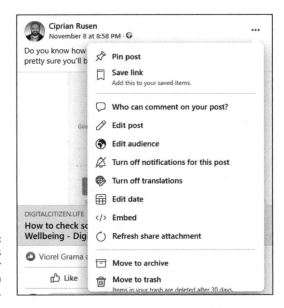

**FIGURE 1-9:**
The options available for every item in your Timeline.

**7.** **On the left, where it says Intro, consider clicking (or tapping) Edit Details, and providing data such as your school's name or current city, and clicking Save. Or click or tap Cancel and don't fill in anything.**

Either way, Facebook hits you with a barrage of questions that help flesh out your profile. Be careful to choose who can see all the information you add. By default, Facebook sets your school as public information, which is shared with everyone, not just your friends.

**8.** **Fill in the rest of your profile data. Or don't. Your choice.**

REMEMBER

As you get more adept at Facebook and figure out how to lock down your account, you may want to add more information to your profile. That's okay, as long as you understand the implications. For now, put in the minimum you feel comfortable about disclosing to the world at large. Remember, someday your boss or your son might read it.

Each line you can enter — from your schools and marital status to your religious views — has a choice to limit access to that information.

Access limitations are based on your lists. For example, if you identify Snidely Whiplash as a member of your family, Snidely can look at any items you've set to be visible to Family. Any friends who aren't on your Family list can't see the item.

For now, while you're still getting your feet wet, be very circumspect in what information you provide, *even if you limit access to the information to specific lists.* Give yourself awhile to get more friends. You can always update your profile.

If you've been using Facebook for a long time, your Timeline may go on and on and on. But I bet there's no chance you have your baby picture on it.

**9.** **To add something to your Timeline that goes way back (I'm talking years or decades, not centuries):**

a. *Click or tap the Life Event link in the What's on Your Mind box.* Facebook lets you identify the event, as shown in Figure 1-10.

b. *Choose a category for your life event.*

c. *Follow the instructions to give a date, choose or upload a picture, and provide more details about the event.*

d. *Click or tap Post.*

The item attaches itself to the appropriate place on your Timeline — even if it predates your joining Facebook.

It's your account. Take control of it.

TIP

As you get more adept at Facebook, you'll figure out how to tag photos; share things that have been posted to your home page or your Timeline; subscribe; set up groups; chat and make video calls; set up your own fan, business, group, or charity pages; post events; search; use GPS location-based features; set up your own lists — and much more. If Facebook intrigues you, I suggest you pick up a copy of *Facebook For Dummies,* by Carolyn Abram and Amy Karasavas. For a deeper look at the side of Facebook tailored for businesses, charities, and groups, look at *Social Media Marketing All-in-One For Dummies,* by Michelle Krasniak, Jan Zimmerman, and Deborah Ng.

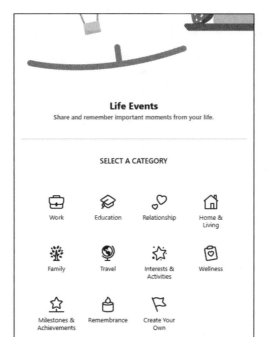

**FIGURE 1-10:** You can add items to the Timeline and mark them as a specific life event. Previous lives don't count.

# Downloading your Facebook data

Apps aren't allowed to download all your Facebook data. But you can. And doing that is a good idea, especially if you want to quit using Facebook or just want to see how much stuff they have about you. To do that, follow these steps:

1. **Log into Facebook. Click or tap the down arrow, in the upper right, and then choose Settings & Privacy, followed by Settings.**

   You see the General Account Settings page.

2. **On the left, choose Your Facebook Information.**

   You see all the options in Figure 1-11.

3. **Click or tap the View button next to Download Your Information.**

   The Download Your Information page appears, as shown in Figure 1-12.

4. **Select the Format, Media Quality and Date Range for the data you're interested in.**

5. **Choose all the types of information to download, and then click or tap Request a Download.**

   You receive an email from Facebook telling you that they'll send you another email when your data is ready for download. This process can take hours, so be patient.

**6.** **When that second email arrives, follow its instructions.**

The file with the information you requested will be in the same Download Your Information page, under Available Files.

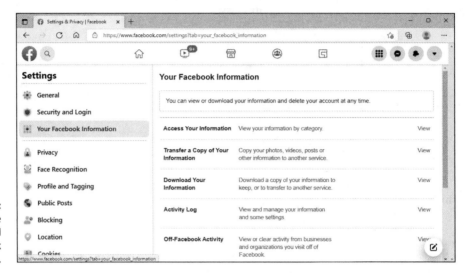

**FIGURE 1-11:**
This is where you access all Your Facebook Information.

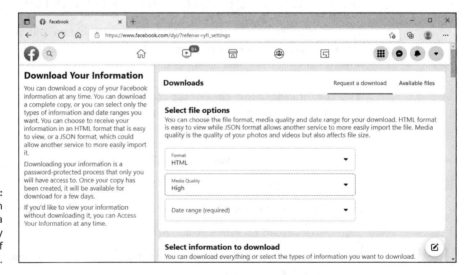

**FIGURE 1-12:**
You can download a surprisingly large amount of information.

# Using the other Facebook apps for Windows

I find it much easier to set up a Facebook account — and particularly keep on top of privacy settings — by using a web browser. For day-to-day use, though, most people rely on the Facebook mobile app. It's just simpler and faster to keep track of Facebook comings and goings with your smartphone or tablet. However, for chatting directly with people, you may want to try the Messenger app for Windows 11, available in the Microsoft Store. It's simple to use, and it works well. See it in action in Figure 1-13.

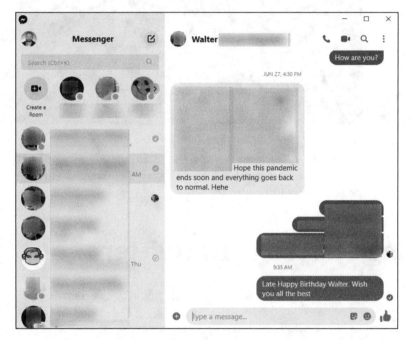

**FIGURE 1-13:** The Messenger app for Windows 11.

To chat with someone, select the person in the left pane or use the search field to search for the person. Type your message on the right, and press Enter or click or tap Send.

Another app that you might want to try is Facebook Watch for Windows 11 (see Figure 1-14), which is available in the Microsoft Store. Facebook Watch helps you discover videos from popular pages, friends, and other sources. Think of it as an inferior YouTube or TikTok competitor that's a great time waster. An upside of Facebook Watch is that you can use it without logging in with your Facebook account.

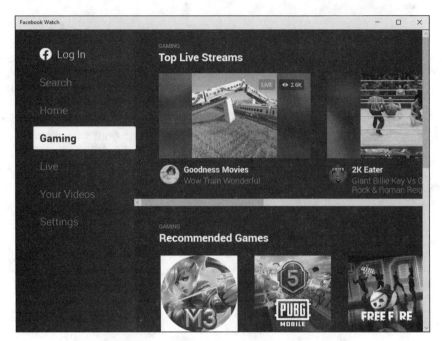

**FIGURE 1-14:**
The Facebook Watch app for Windows 11.

To watch a video, just click or tap it. To discover interesting videos, scroll through the available categories, or use the Search option and enter the subject, page, or person you're interested in.

# Getting Started with Twitter

The revolution will not be televised. It will be tweeted.

In March 2006, an amazing array of developers and entrepreneurs — originally intent on building a podcasting platform called Odeo — unleashed Twitter on an unsuspecting world. More than a decade and a half later, Twitter has been credited with helping to overthrow totalitarian governments, spread fear and mayhem, aid and abet leaks of embarrassing government documents, shed light on official dirty dealings, establish a rallying point for the Occupy disenfranchised, and let everyone know what Lady Gaga had for breakfast.

That's quite an accomplishment. In 2021, Twitter had more than 187 million daily active users, out of a total of 322 million users, with 19.4 percent of them based in the US. While Facebook dominates the social networking space in North America, Twitter takes the number 1 place in Japan, and it has an ever-increasing presence in Asia-Pacific and Europe. Those numbers are all industry estimates because Twitter doesn't divulge much, even though it's listed on the New York Stock Exchange.

I use Twitter regularly. I've used it to keep on top of important fast-breaking news, notify people around the world, talk with other writers in the computer business, keep tabs on political organizations important to me, track down details of obscure pieces of Windows 11, and point people to funny videos.

Just about every tech writer you can name is on Twitter. Every major news outlet is on Twitter — and breaking news spills out over Twitter much sooner than even the newspaper wire services. The Royal Society. The Wellcome Trust. Lots of people who are on the ground, relaying news as it happens, use Twitter. And did I mention Justin Bieber?

In short, Twitter's a mixed bag — but an interesting one.

Twitter's fast, easy, and free. It works with every web browser. It works with almost every smartphone and tablet. There's a Windows 11 app — an official one — that's not very inspiring, but it works. Tweets are short, concise, sometimes vapid, but frequently illuminating and witty. And every single piece of Twitter is limited to 280 characters.

In this section, I walk you through the basics of using Twitter: how to create a Twitter ID, how to communicate with others through Twitter, and what you need to know about hashtags. :)

## Understanding Twitter

When I explain Twitter to people who've never used it, I usually start by talking about mobile phone messaging — texting. A message on Twitter — a *tweet* (see Figure 1-15) — is much like a text message.

**FIGURE 1-15:**
A typical tweet from an atypical source.

Twitter is a simple one-to-many form of communication, kind of like texting all the people who have agreed, in advance, to receive your texts.

You usually send a text message to one person. If you have a business, you may send the same text message to many people all at once. Now imagine a world in which these are true:

>> You have an ID, not unlike a phone number, and you can send any messages *(tweets)* that you like, any time you want. The messages are limited to 280 characters (spaces included) — short and sweet.

>> You get to choose whose texts you want to see on Twitter. In Twitter parlance, you can *follow* anybody. If you get tired of reading their tweets, it's easy to *unfollow* them as well.

You have some leeway in what counts toward the 280-character limit. For example, when you

>> Reply to a tweet, @names don't count toward the 280-character limit

>> Add attachments, such as photos, GIFs, videos, polls, or quote tweets, that media isn't counted as characters in your tweet

Twitter has lots of bells and whistles — location tracking, if you turn it on, for example — but at its heart, Twitter is all about sending messages and wisely choosing whose messages you receive.

Spam texts and harassing phone calls may dog your days on the smartphone. On Twitter, while all is not happiness and light, such problems are less frequent and less severe.

If you follow someone who posts a tweet, you see the tweet when you log on to Twitter. If you keep Twitter running on your PC, smartphone, or tablet, the tweet appears in your Twitter window. When you tweet, the people who follow you can see it.

**WARNING**

In fact, *anybody* can see *every* tweet — a fact that's proved highly embarrassing to an amazingly substantial number of people. (Twitter has a Protected Tweets feature that lets you manually approve every person who's permitted to receive your tweets. But, in general, when you let it all hang out on Twitter, it's there for anyone to see.)

When you send a tweet, you can identify keywords in the tweet by using the # character in front of the keyword, creating a *hashtag*. See Figure 1-16.

Hashtag

**FIGURE 1-16:**
Tweet with a hashtag.

You can tell Twitter that, in addition to the tweets from people you follow, you also want to see all tweets that contain specific hashtags. For example, if you ask to see all the tweets with the hashtag #ForDummies, Twitter delivers to your web page or Twitter reader every tweet where the author of the tweet typed the characters #ForDummies.

Twitter (together with other sites, such as www.trendsmap.com) keeps track of all the hashtags in all the tweets. It posts lists of the most popular hashtags, so you can watch what's popular. Thus, hashtags not only make it easier for people to find your tweets but also publicize your cause — and many good causes have risen to the top of the hashtag heaps.

In fact, Twitter now keeps track of every phrase that's tweeted and compiles its trending lists from the raw tweets, with or without hashtags. You really don't need to use hashtags anymore. But you see them all the time in tweets, #knowwhatImean?

Google and Twitter have entered a partnership whereby Google scans tweets so that they show up in Google searches.

**TIP**

The power of Twitter — outside of gossip and teenage angst — lies in carefully choosing those you follow. If they, in turn, receive information from reliable sources and then retweet the results, you'll have a steady stream of useful information, each in 280-character capsules.

For example, during the Egyptian political crisis in January 2011, which saw the downfall of President Hosni Mubarak, Twitter played a pivotal (if controversial) role in aiding communication among protestors. One of the government's first acts was to shut down access to Twitter and Facebook. The protestors found ways around the government's shutdown.

There's a fascinating re-creation of the tweeting and retweeting that followed the January 25 start of demonstrations in Cairo. Data about tweets with the hashtag #jan25 was assembled by the University of Turin, the ISI Foundation, and a research institute at Indiana University, to come up with the graph you see in Figure 1-17.

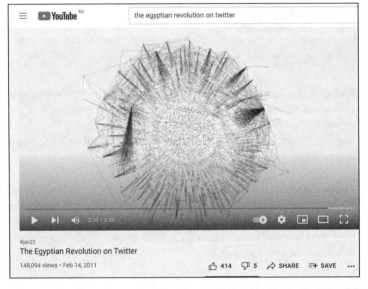

**FIGURE 1-17:**
The interconnections among Twitter users during the Egyptian uprising.

*Photo courtesy of* http://youtu.be/2guKJfvq4uI

In the graph, the points represent individuals, and the lines are tweets that go from one individual to another. It's downright explosive.

That's how a one-to-many social network like Twitter works. An important tweet (or even an unimportant but popular one) jumps from person to person.

My Twitter ID for tech articles and tutorials is @ciprianrusen, and you're welcome to follow me anytime you like.

## Setting up a Twitter account

Twitter has apps for all sorts of smartphones and tablets. You can use it on the iPhone, the iPad, and Android smartphones and tablets. There's also a Twitter app for Windows 11 in the Microsoft Store. I mention the Twitter app for Windows 11 only occasionally in this chapter because it's woefully underpowered, and just like the Facebook app, it's a progressive web app with limited functionality. If you want to get going with Twitter, it's much easier to start with a web browser, which is the primary emphasis here.

Starting a new account at Twitter couldn't be easier. Here's what you do:

1. **Fire up your favorite web browser, go to www.twitter.com, and click or tap Sign Up with Phone or Email.**

   You see the Create Your Account dialog, as shown in Figure 1-18.

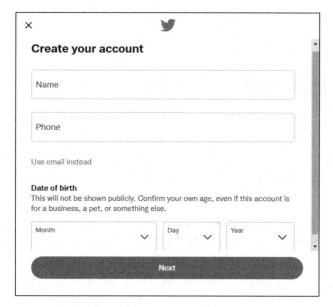

**FIGURE 1-18:** All you need to sign up for Twitter is a valid phone number or email address.

2. **Enter the name you want to use, your phone (or email), and your date of birth. Then click or tap Next.**

3. **Select how you want your Twitter experience to be (connect to others using your phone or email address, or see personalized ads), and click or tap Next.**

4. **Confirm that you want to create your account by clicking or tapping Sign Up.**

   Twitter sends a confirmation code to your phone or email address, depending on what you chose in Step 2.

5. **Type the confirmation code and then click or tap Next.**

   You're asked to set a password that has eight or more characters, as shown in Figure 1-19.

**FIGURE 1-19:**
Use a strong
password for
your Twitter
account.

6. **Type the password and click or tap Next.**

   You're asked to choose a profile picture for your Twitter account, as shown in Figure 1-20.

7. **Click or tap the profile icon, choose the picture you want, and click or tap Next. Or click or tap Skip for Now.**

   You're asked to describe yourself.

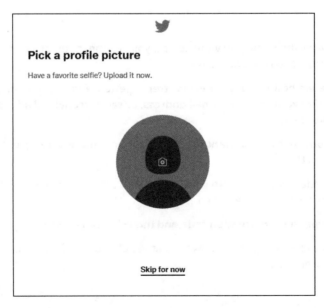

**FIGURE 1-20:**
Choose a picture
for your account.

8. **Type a short bio (up to 160 characters) and click or tap Next. Or click or tap Skip for Now.**

   You're asked to confirm your Twitter username.

**REMEMBER**

   Although you may be tempted to bypass typing your bio, give that choice some thought. If something about you is unique and you want the world to know — maybe you're an expert on 18th-century Tibetan bronzes — adding that to your bio may help someone else who shares the same interest find you. Your bio is accessible to anyone, so don't put anything in there that you don't want to be widely known.

9. **Type the username you want and click or tap Next. Or click or tap Skip to leave the one provided by Twitter.**

   You're asked if you want to turn on notifications.

10. **Choose Skip for Now, so that Twitter doesn't bother you with many notifications.**

   You're asked to choose your interests from a lengthy list that includes things such as sports, news, gaming, and music.

11. **Select the subjects that interest you and click or tap Next.**

   The things you choose are going to help Twitter recommend interesting accounts, as shown in Figure 1-21.

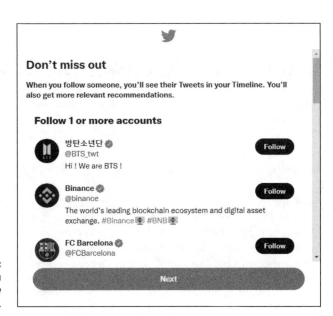

**FIGURE 1-21:**
Choose who you want to follow on Twitter.

**12.** **In the list of suggestions for you to follow, click or tap Follow for the accounts that interest you.**

If you don't know who to follow, consider the following:

- @ciprianrusen, @ForDummies, @AndyRathbone, who wrote the original *Windows For Dummies,* @windowsblog to keep up on the Microsoft party line, and some of the major news services — @BBCWorld perhaps and @BreakingNews.

- Try a few of the most-followed people on Twitter, @justinbieber at 114 million followers and @katyperry at 108 million and counting. You could even vote for @taylorswift13 by adding to her trove of 89 million followers.

You're finished and can finally use Twitter. :)

Celebrities and politicians don't have it so easy — many need to go through an independent confirmation step. But for normal dummies like you and me, the process is that easy.

At first, you probably just want to watch and see what others are tweeting to get a sense of how tweeting is done. Create a practice tweet or two and see how the whole thing hangs together.

On the Twitter home page, type your first tweet in the What's Happening field and then click or tap Tweet, as shown in Figure 1-22.

## TWO-FACTOR AUTHENTICATION (2FA)

Twitter supports two-factor authentication: Every time you start tweeting from a new device, it sends a confirmation text to your pre-established phone number, asking permission.

You can sign up for 2FA as part of the initial sign-up process. And if you have an account without 2FA, now's a good time to set it up.

To start using 2FA, log in to www.twitter.com, click or tap the ellipsis on the left, and choose Settings and Privacy. Go to Security and Account Access, followed by Security. Then choose Two-Factor Authentication, and decide how you want to verify your logins: through text messages, an authenticator app, or a security key.

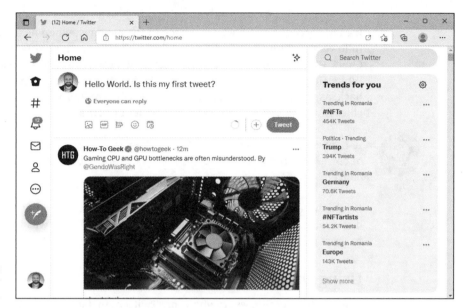

**FIGURE 1-22:**
Creating your
first tweet.

# Tweeting for beginners

On the surface, Twitter's easy and fun. Below the surface, Twitter's a remarkably adept application with lots of capabilities — and a few infuriating limitations.

## Beware of hacking

Before I dig into the more interesting parts of Twitter, permit me to give you just one warning.

**WARNING**

Unscrupulous people are on Twitter, just as they are anywhere else. If you get a tweet from someone with a gorgeous picture who's trying to convince you to sign up for something or hand over your password, ignore that account. If you get a tweet saying, "Somebody is writing bad things about you" or "Want to see a funny photo of you?" or "Find out who's been looking at your bio," ignore it.

Better yet, report the person as a spammer. Click or tap the spammer's name. That takes you to the spammer's profile page. In the upper right, click or tap the ellipsis icon and choose Block or Report. To complete a report, choose the reason from the list, and then click or tap Block.

If your Twitter account has been hacked — somebody talked you into clicking or tapping something that gets into your account or someone guessed your password — don't feel too bad about it. Fox News was hacked in July 2011. Mark Ruffalo (who plays The Hulk in *The Avengers*) got hacked in May 2012. Justin

Bieber's account was hacked — back in the old days, when he had only 20 million followers. Ashton Kutcher. Taylor Swift. *The Huffington Post. USA Today.* Senator Chuck Grassley. Brett Favre. Miley Cyrus. Reuters. Associated Press (bombs at the White House). *Newsweek.* Queensland Police Department. Chipotle (it also faked a hack, as a publicity stunt). Burger King. US Central Command. Even Twitter's own chief financial officer. And former President Obama.

TIP

It happens. If your account's been taken over, see the Twitter instructions at `https://help.twitter.com/en/safety-and-security/twitter-account-hacked`.

On the other hand, if you've posted some tweets that you want to categorically disavow, you can always *claim* that your Twitter account was hacked. You're sure to draw plenty of sympathy.

## Using the @ sign and Reply

You see the @ sign everywhere on Twitter. In fact, I used it when listing the people you may want to follow. The @ sign is a universal indication that what follows is an account name.

REMEMBER

In the not-so-great old days, sticking an @ and a username at the beginning of a tweet would limit the list of people who would automatically see the tweet. That's no longer the case. Anything you tweet goes out to all the people who follow you. Easy peasy.

The Twitter viewer on the internet has a Reply option to a tweet. On the Twitter website, hover your cursor over the speech bubble (see Figure 1-23) and you see Reply.

If you click or tap Reply, Twitter starts a new message with an @ sign followed by the sender's username. If you were to reply to the message in Figure 1-23, Twitter on the web creates a new tweet that starts: @ciprianrusen.

If you type a body to that message and click or tap Tweet, the message goes to people who are following you and an extra copy is sent to @ciprianrusen.

WARNING

A reply is *not* a private or hidden message. It's out in the open. Anybody who searches for your username or @ciprianrusen will see the message in its entirety.

FIGURE 1-23:
Reply to a tweet.

Reply    Retweet

## Retweeting for fun and profit

If you receive a tweet and want to send it to all the people who follow you, the polite way to do so is with a *retweet,* or *RT* for short. To give credit to the person who sent you the tweet, the retweet includes the person's username.

To retweet, click or tap the circling arrows icon (refer to Figure 1-23), and then choose a simple Retweet (Twitter builds a new tweet that copies the original tweet and adds the originator's username) or a Quote Tweet (you can add a comment to the original tweet), as shown in Figure 1-24. By retweeting a tweet precisely, you pass the information on to your followers yet preserve the attribution. If you want to add a comment to the original message, you can do so with ease, by choosing the Quote Tweet option.

## Direct Messaging

No discussion of the advanced part of Twitter would be complete without a mention of direct messaging (DM) — better known as *DM-ing.* Direct messages are private messages you send to another Twitter user. Unlike tweets, direct messages are not public and open. Think of DM as Twitter's internal chat feature.

Unfortunately, people screw up DMs all the time, and the results can be embarrassing. I suggest that you limit your use of DMs to situations where email may be a better approach, and that you studiously use the DM tools built into your Twitter account. You'll generally find DM hiding behind the Messages icon on the left (it looks like a sealed envelope).

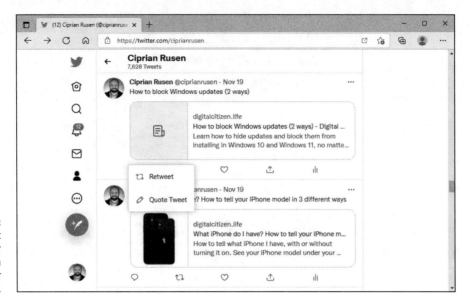

**FIGURE 1-24:**
Retweet a tweet to all your followers — with or without your own comment.

# Chapter **2**

# Mastering Tools for Remote Work

The COVID-19 pandemic, which is still a fact of life as I write this, has accelerated the remote work trend that was already gaining a lot of ground during the last decade. Because of the pandemic, we have to socialize with our colleagues on Teams and Zoom instead of enjoying face-to-face discussions during lunch breaks and business meetings at the office. We also have to spend way too many hours working from home, chatting with co-workers at crazy hours, and having "parties" online through Zoom to compensate for our lack of real-life socialization.

An unpleasant outcome of this trend is the so-called "Great Resignation." According to the U.S. Bureau of Labor Statistics, four million people quit their jobs in July 2021. Resignations peaked in April 2021 and remained abnormally high for several months, with a record-breaking 10.9 million open jobs at the end of July. And where do companies go looking for people to fill in those gaps? LinkedIn! Where do people go looking for new job opportunities? Again, LinkedIn! I must admit that Microsoft was smart in acquiring this social network. It will probably become a crucial platform for the future of work.

In this chapter, I begin by presenting the basics of LinkedIn. You discover how to create an account and get recommendations on using it effectively. I also talk a bit about the LinkedIn app situation.

Next, I take you through the basics of using Zoom. You discover how to download and install Zoom, create a free Zoom account, sign into Zoom, and schedule and then join Zoom meetings. Then, I cover the essentials of Microsoft Teams: setting up Teams integration, chatting with others, and starting a meeting.

Finally, I walk you through some tools for remote work: using Remote Desktop to connect remotely to another computer, connecting a second display to your laptop or PC, setting up a webcam, and keeping track of time zones.

# Getting Started with LinkedIn

In some ways, LinkedIn resembles Facebook — keeping up with people and expanding connections are grist for the mill. But in other ways, LinkedIn is different because it's focused on professional relationships, which LinkedIn calls *connections.*

You can use your LinkedIn connections to showcase products, look for a job, advertise a job, scout new business opportunities, find temporary help, stay up to date on companies that interest you — for any reason — or just replace the tattered box of business cards on your desk.

With more than 774 million subscribers (180+ million are in the US), LinkedIn has more than reached critical mass. Many businesspeople worldwide consider it a key part of their existence.

In December 2016, Microsoft completed its purchase of LinkedIn for $26.2 billion — the largest software purchase, anytime, anywhere. LinkedIn founder and Silicon Valley heavyweight Reid Hoffman joined Microsoft's board. Some feared that LinkedIn would let other platforms — iOS, Android, Mac — wither, but that hasn't been the case. Right now, it appears that Microsoft's main drive for LinkedIn is to integrate it with Microsoft 365 (formerly known as Office 365) and use it as a benefit for business customers, particularly enterprises.

## Signing up for LinkedIn

Don't have a LinkedIn account? Got a few minutes? Here's how to get started:

1. **Fire up your favorite browser, go to www.linkedin.com, and click or tap Join Now.**

   You see a sign-up page like the one in Figure 2-1.

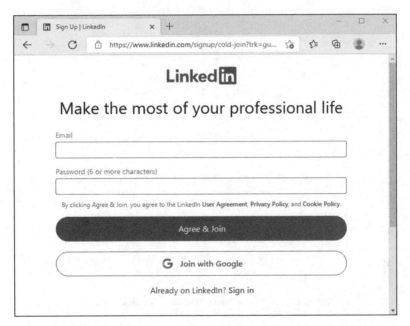

**FIGURE 2-1:**
Signing up for LinkedIn is easy.

2. **Fill in the blanks and click or tap Agree & Join.**

   Make sure you use a real email address: LinkedIn uses it to verify your account. You're better off *not* using an email address that's associated with your current employer. You want to be able to get into your LinkedIn account even if you get fired!

3. **Next, enter your first name and last name, and click or tap Continue.**

   You're asked to do a quick security check to verify that you're a real person.

4. **Click or tap Verify and follow the instructions on the screen to finish the security check.**

   The first profile page appears, as shown in Figure 2-2, asking you to enter your country and postal code or city/district.

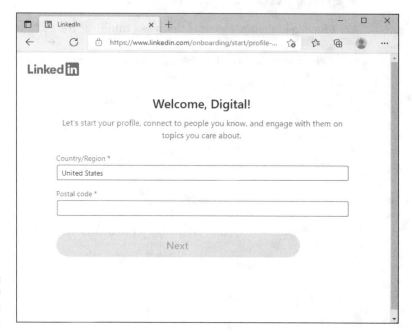

**FIGURE 2-2:**
You must provide
a lot of data for a
LinkedIn account.

5. **Enter your country, city, and postal code, and click or tap Next.**

   LinkedIn might ask for slightly different information based on your location. The screen shown in Figure 2-3 appears.

6. **Do one of the following and then click or tap Continue:**

   - Enter the information requested from you. Most probably you're asked to enter your most recent job title and some details about the job.

   - If you're a student, click or tap I'm a Student and then enter the required details.

   LinkedIn sends a verification code to your email address.

7. **Enter the verification code, and then click or tap Agree & Confirm.**

8. **When asked if you're looking for a job, answer as you see fit.**

**FIGURE 2-3:**
Give details about
whether you're
a student or an
employee.

9. **When LinkedIn asks to look inside your email account to find connections, click or tap Skip and confirm that you want to skip.**

   You can find your own contacts later.

10. **When asked if you want to connect with others, search for, and select specific people, or click or tap Skip.**

    You can add contacts later. The screen shown in Figure 2-4 appears.

11. **Click or tap Add Photo, choose a picture you like, and then save it.**

    LinkedIn says that you look great.

12. **Click or tap Continue.**

13. **When asked if you want to get the LinkedIn app, click or tap Skip.**

    You can install the app later, on your own terms, and log in.

14. **When LinkedIn recommends companies, people, or hashtags for you to follow, choose the companies or people you want, and then click or tap Finish.**

    LinkedIn takes you to your profile page, which looks more or less like Figure 2-5. Remember that just about anybody can see anything you post.

**TIP**

If you don't want to be bothered by the Messaging pane on the right, click or tap the inverted caret (downward-pointing arrow) in its upper-right corner.

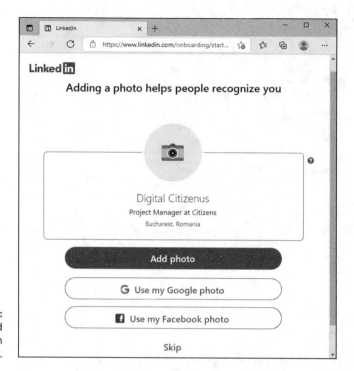

**FIGURE 2-4:**
It is time to add your LinkedIn picture.

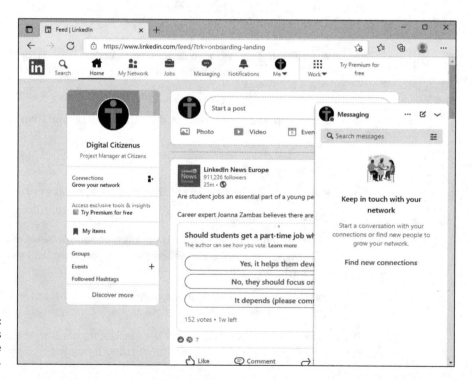

**FIGURE 2-5:**
LinkedIn takes you to the main page.

The social part of LinkedIn involves establishing connections — links with people you know or know of. To start filling in your connections list, click or tap the My Network button at the top of the home page, choose Connections, and add people based on their email addresses. You can also find people you know based on others' connections. Look for the little Connect buttons and links throughout the LinkedIn interface.

## Understanding LinkedIn basics

Using LinkedIn is both an art and a science. Here are a few tips I've acquired over the years:

>> **Use your current job title to your advantage.** LinkedIn seems to show your current job title almost everywhere. When people hover a mouse cursor over your picture, for example, they see your current job title and employer, and your location. Stock job titles (*CEO, Analyst, Nice Guy* — that's the one I use) don't have much sizzle. On the other hand, *M2M Executive with Expertise in the Rapid Implementation of CRM Solutions (M.S., Ph.D., O.B.E.)* certainly draws attention.

In some contexts, LinkedIn truncates your job title. Someone looking at your profile sees the entire title, but someone looking at search results, for example, sees only the first few words.

TIP

>> **Put a different, professional picture on your LinkedIn account.** Don't recycle your Facebook pic — you know, the one your friend took when you were plastered at the going-away party. Definitely a no-no in this arena. By all means, wear something professional if you feel more comfortable that way, but casual is okay, too. Just remember that the people you want to impress will look at your mug and make decisions based on it.

>> **If you graduated with honors, or there's something of note about your degree, include it in the Degree field.** Showing a college degree, such as B.A. Phi Beta Kappa or Summa Cum Laude or M.S.E.E. makes a greater impression than just listing your degree.

>> **Ask for recommendations, but don't use the stock request form.** Recommendations can make a difference in all sorts of situations, so don't be bashful about asking your friends to refer you. But when you do, take a few extra minutes and write a personal request message. Perhaps also tell the friend what you would like the recommendation to cover.

>> **Start slowly.** Take a few days to get a feel for LinkedIn before you invite everyone to become a connection. Look around and see how other people set up their profiles. Get a feel for what's acceptable and what's overly pushy. Only when you have your bearings are you ready to add all those old email contacts to your connections list. And when you start building your connections list, go slowly — just a handful of people a day.

Mastering Tools for Remote Work

After you have put together a few connections, you can view them by clicking or tapping My Network. You may find that you have a lot of people connected only two or three steps away; see Figure 2-6.

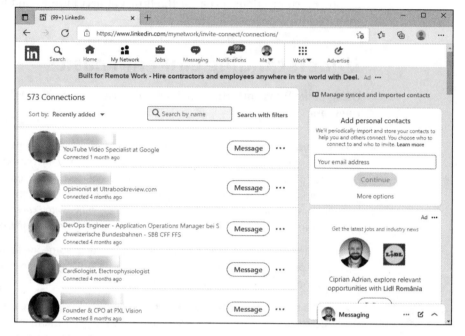

**FIGURE 2-6:**
Even if you're only moderately well connected, you can have hundreds of people three hops away.

Remember six degrees of separation?

LinkedIn allows you to follow industry leaders, groups, professional interests, and your local neighborhood firefly-collecting organization. The quality of the offered information varies widely, but it's king of the roost for business use.

**TIP**

Social networking works. Even if you don't use LinkedIn very much, having it available — just in case you're looking for a new job or for an expert in a particular field — is well worth the effort.

## Using LinkedIn apps for Windows and mobile devices

Although LinkedIn was purchased by Microsoft back in 2016, the company never fully integrated it into Windows. We have LinkedIn apps on Google Play and in the Apple App Store, but not in the Microsoft Store. Am I the only one who finds this weird?

All you can do in Windows is pin the LinkedIn.com website to the taskbar or the Start menu.

The only true integration developed by Microsoft is with Office. For example, in Word, you can use LinkedIn's Resume Assistant (see Figure 2-7). The tool shows you examples of how real people — in the fields you're interested in — describe their work experience and skills. It's useful when you want to find a new job. Resume Assistant is available to all Microsoft 365 subscribers.

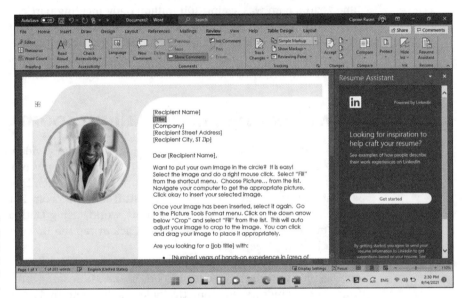

**FIGURE 2-7:** Resume Assistant is a useful integration of LinkedIn and Office.

By the time I write the next edition of this book, I hope Microsoft has developed a LinkedIn app for Windows 11 or some other form of useful integration between the two. Until then, head over to https://mobile.linkedin.com/ and install the mobile apps that you want.

# Video Conferencing with Zoom

As internet access expands and more online work tools emerge, an increasing number of people are working remotely from their homes instead of going into the office. Coupled with the pandemic and ever-shifting health regulations, a substantial percentage of the population has come to rely on online meetings and internet audio and video calls rather than face-to-face meetings with friends, family, co-workers, and business partners. This isn't a trend that makes me happy, and it probably doesn't make you happy either. However, we need tools to communicate online on a daily basis, whether for work or to stay connected with our families.

Alongside Microsoft and its Skype and Teams services, Zoom offers one of the best online meetings services on the market. And due to the pandemic, Zoom has become immensely popular, used by millions worldwide. For example, in June 2020, Zoom was seeing 300 million daily meeting participants. That's quite impressive, isn't it? Its popularity is deserved though, as Zoom has great apps for all platforms, including Windows PCs, Android devices, iPhones, and iPads. And, to make things even more interesting, Zoom is also available as a free plan, so anyone can try it, with reasonable limitations that don't annoy people.

## Downloading and installing Zoom

If you need to use Zoom for work, and join all kinds of video conferences, you can do that from many places. One way is to open your web browser and navigate to zoom.us/download. There, you'll find the Zoom Client for Meetings, which is what you need, but also other useful stuff like the Zoom Plugin for Microsoft Outlook (useful for those in the corporate world, using Outlook daily), and the Zoom mobile apps for Android and iOS. Click or tap the Download button for the Zoom Client for Meetings.

Another good place to download Zoom is the Microsoft Store. When you get it from there, Windows 11 automatically keeps Zoom up to date in the background, through its Microsoft Store updating infrastructure. I think the best place to get the Zoom app for Windows 11 is the Microsoft Store, not the official website.

1. **Click or tap the Start icon and then Microsoft Store.**

   You see the Microsoft Store home page.

2. **In the Search box at the top, type** zoom, **and press Enter on your keyboard.**

   You see a list of search results with Zoom in their name.

3. **Click or tap ZOOM Cloud Meetings.**

   The screen shown in Figure 2-8 appears.

4. **Click or tap the Install button.**

   Wait for the app to be downloaded and installed. This process may take a few minutes, depending on the speed of your internet connection.

**FIGURE 2-8:**
Zoom is available
in the Microsoft
Store too.

**TIP**

After you install it, the Zoom app shortcut should be visible in the Recommended section of the Start menu. For more about using and personalizing the Start menu, read Book 3, Chapter 2.

## Setting up a Zoom account

The Zoom client for Windows doesn't allow you to create an account. However, you can't use the app without one. If your company has a Business or Enterprise Zoom plan, the user account for Zoom is going to be provided by your company. However, you can also create a personal account for free, on the company's website, like this:

1. **Fire up your favorite browser, go to** `https://zoom.us/`, **and click or tap Sign Up, It's Free.**

   You see a sign-up page like the one in Figure 2-9, where you are first asked to enter your birth date.

2. **Enter your date of birth and click or tap Continue.**

3. **Next, enter your email address and click or tap Sign Up.**

   Make sure you're using a real email address: Zoom uses it to verify your account. Then, you're asked if you want to receive a newsletter from Zoom, with resources about using their service.

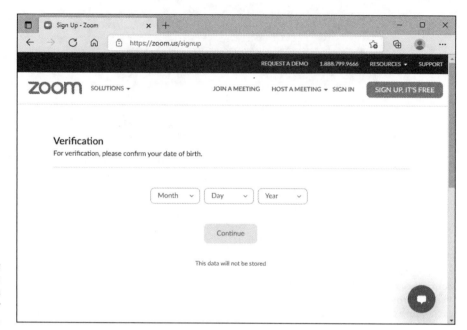

**FIGURE 2-9:**
Creating a Zoom account starts with checking for your birth date.

4. **Choose whether you want to receive the newsletter, and then click or tap Confirm.**

   You see a notification that the activation email was sent.

5. **Go to your inbox and click or tap the Activate Account button in the email you received from Zoom.**

   A web page opens where you are asked to enter information about your account, as shown in Figure 2-10.

6. **Enter your first name, last name, and the password that you want to use (twice). Then click or tap Continue.**

   You are asked whether you want to invite colleagues to Zoom, using their email addresses.

7. **Click or tap Skip This Step.**

8. **Do one of the following:**

   - *If you want to start a test meeting:* Click or tap Start Meeting Now. The Zoom client opens.

   - *If you don't want to start a test meeting:* Close the web page. You have finished creating your Zoom account.

Your Zoom account is now activated, and you can use it to schedule or join meetings at any time. All you need is a computer with a webcam installed. For more about using webcams in Windows 11, read "Installing a webcam," later in this chapter.

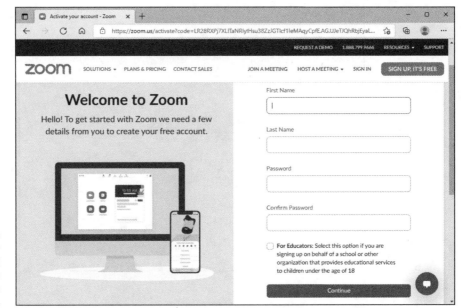

**FIGURE 2-10:**
Provide your
name and
password to
finalize the Zoom
account.

## Signing into Zoom cloud meetings

After you have installed Zoom on your Windows 11 PC and created an account, using the instructions shared earlier, it's time to sign into the Zoom client and start using it. To do that, follow these steps:

**1.** Click or tap the Start icon.

**2.** If you don't see the Zoom icon in the Recommended section, click or tap All Apps.

You see a lengthy list of all the apps installed on your Windows 11 PC.

**3.** Scroll down the list to the letter Z and click or tap Zoom.

The Zoom Cloud Meetings window appears, as shown in Figure 2-11.

**4.** Click or tap Sign In, and then enter the email and password for your Zoom account.

**5.** Select the box for Keep Me Signed In, and then click or tap Sign In.

The first time you're using Zoom, you should see a prompt about Zoom's terms and policies.

**6.** If you want to read Zoom's terms and policies, click or tap Terms of Service and Privacy Policy. Otherwise, click or tap Continue.

You see the Zoom Home screen, as shown in Figure 2-12. It includes options for joining meetings, scheduling new meetings, and more. You also see any upcoming Zoom meetings you've been invited to.

**FIGURE 2-11:**
Before using
Zoom, you need
to sign in.

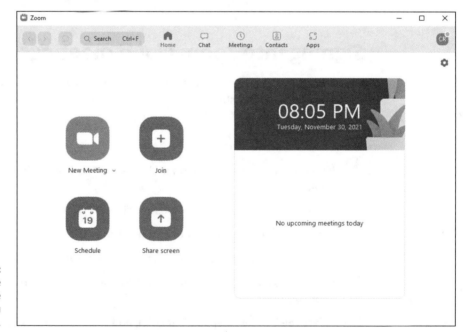

**FIGURE 2-12:**
The Zoom Home
screen is the
place where you
start everything.

## Scheduling a Zoom meeting

Anyone with a Zoom account can schedule a meeting, including those with a free
account. However, free accounts are limited to scheduling meetings that last a
maximum of 45 minutes. This is enough for most people, and one of the reasons
why Zoom is so popular nowadays.

If you want to schedule a Zoom meeting, follow these steps:

1. **Sign into Zoom, using the steps from the preceding section.**

2. **In the Zoom Home screen, click or tap Schedule.**

   You see the Schedule Meeting window, with the options shown in Figure 2-13.

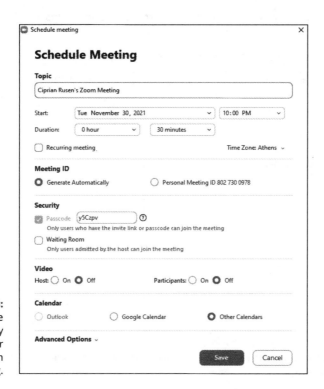

**FIGURE 2-13:**
Complete the necessary details for your scheduled Zoom meeting.

3. **Complete the topic of the meeting, and then choose the start date and time.**

4. **Choose a duration for your meeting.**

5. **In the Video section, choose whether you want the host and participants to join with their video on or off.**

6. **When you've finished setting things up, click or tap Save.**

   Zoom displays the details of your scheduled meeting.

7. **Click or tap Copy to Clipboard, and then paste the details into the email message you'll be sending to the people you want to invite.**

   The details generated by Zoom include the topic you've chosen, the scheduled time for the meeting, a meeting link, the meeting ID, and the passcode.

# Joining a Zoom meeting

Joining a Zoom meeting is not difficult. The simplest method is to click or tap the meeting link you've received via email (or some other method), and then allow your web browser to open Zoom for you. Another method is to use the meeting ID and password that you've received from the host, like this:

**1.** **Start Zoom and sign in using your account, and the instructions shared in previous sections of this chapter.**

**2.** **On the Zoom Home screen, click or tap Join.**

The Join Meeting dialog appears, as shown in Figure 2-14.

**FIGURE 2-14:**
Provide the meeting details to join.

**3.** **Type or copy and paste the meeting ID you've received and then enter your name.**

**4.** **Click or tap Join.**

**5.** **When asked, enter the meeting passcode, and click or tap Join Meeting.**

Depending on the meeting's settings, you may need to wait for the host to approve your join request. When you're in the call, you're asked if you want to join using computer audio.

**6.** **Click or tap Join with Computer Audio.**

You're inside the Zoom meeting. Feel free to start talking with others on the call.

**TIP**

If the microphone, doesn't work, click or tap the Mute button to unmute it. If you're not on mute, click or tap the upward-pointing arrow, next to the Mute button, and select the correct microphone. The same with Video: If the webcam is not turned on, click or tap Start Video. If it still doesn't show anything, click or tap the upward-pointing arrow next to it, and choose the right webcam.

# Contacting Others through Teams

Microsoft Teams is now embedded into Windows 11, and it has its own dedicated chat icon on the taskbar. The company has touted this integration as a big feature, but the truth is that it's underwhelming. And to my surprise, on some laptops, it crashed because of incompatibilities with certain drivers. I've reported this issue to Microsoft, and I hope it will be fixed, so that the experience is smooth and clean for everyone, on all Windows 11 laptops.

While my experience with this feature wasn't great, this new Teams integration is not useless. When it works, it does its job well, and it helps you start chat conversations and meetings faster. However, I wish Microsoft would have provided more capabilities, such as the option to schedule meetings.

Most probably, the Redmond giant will fine-tune the experience in future updates to Windows 11, and several years from now, this Teams integration may turn out to be better than Skype (read Book 4, Chapter 6), which is also available in Windows 11.

## Getting started with Microsoft Teams

Before you start using Microsoft Teams, you need either a Microsoft account (if you're a home user) or a business or school account. Then, to get started and use it, do the following:

1. **Click or tap the chat icon on the taskbar.**

   You see a brief description of the meet and chat features.

2. **Click or tap Get Started.**

   You see the name and picture of your Microsoft or work account, as well as the email address and phone number associated with it, as shown in Figure 2-15.

3. **If you want to sync Outlook.com and Skype contacts to find people you know on Teams, select this option, and then click or tap Let's Go.**

   The meet and chat features in Microsoft Teams are now ready for use, and you see a window like the one in Figure 2-16.

REMEMBER

The details shown in Figure 2-15 are what you should share with the people who want to find you on Teams.

From now on, each time you click or tap the chat icon on the taskbar, you see the options shown in Figure 2-16. Below the Meet and Chat buttons, you find your recent conversations, as well as the contacts synchronized through Outlook.com and Skype. The list is remarkably similar to what you see in the People app. Read Book 4, Chapter 2 for details about managing your contacts in Windows 11.

**FIGURE 2-15:** These are the details other people can use to contact you on Teams.

# Chatting from Windows 11

The chat icon on the taskbar aims to provide a quick way to start chats and meet-ings on Microsoft Teams. After you have set up Teams using the instructions in the preceding section, starting a chat conversation with someone takes a few clicks or taps, like this:

**1.** **Click or tap the chat icon on the taskbar.**

You see the options shown previously in Figure 2-16.

**2.** **Click or tap the Chat button.**

The New Chat window shows up. See Figure 2-17.

**3.** **In the To field on the top, type the name, email, or phone number of the person you want to find on Teams.**

As you type, Microsoft Teams searches for people, and it may provide you with suggestions.

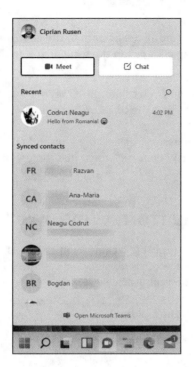

**FIGURE 2-16:**
The meet and chat features are now a click or tap away.

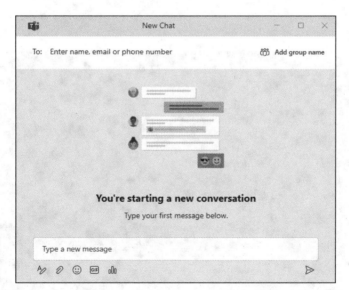

**FIGURE 2-17:**
Find the person(s) you want to chat with and send a message.

**4.** **Choose the person you want to chat with from the list.**

You can repeat Steps 3 and 4 and add more people to the chat, creating a group chat.

5. **In the Type a New Message field at the bottom of the chat window, type your message, and then click or tap the send arrow, in the lower-right corner.**

   The message is sent to the people you contacted. If they're using Windows 11, they should see a notification above the chat icon on their taskbar.

TIP

Don't hesitate to format your message, attach files, or add emoji and animated GIFs. All these options are displayed as icons just below the Type a New Message field.

## Starting a meeting from Windows 11

Besides chat conversations on Microsoft Teams, you can also start a meeting quickly. Before you do that, make sure you have a webcam installed and working on your laptop or desktop PC. Then follow these steps:

1. **Click or tap the chat icon on the taskbar.**

   The options shown previously in Figure 2-16 appear.

2. **Click or tap the Meet button.**

   The Meeting With window appears, as shown in Figure 2-18.

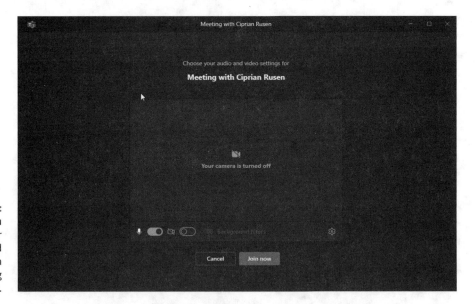

**FIGURE 2-18:**
Make sure you turn on your microphone and the webcam before starting the meeting.

3. **Make sure the switches for your microphone and video are turned on, so that others can hear you and see you.**

4. **When everything is set up the way you want, click or tap Join Now.**

   The meeting is started but there's only one participant: you! Microsoft Teams shows you several options to invite people to join you, as shown in Figure 2-19.

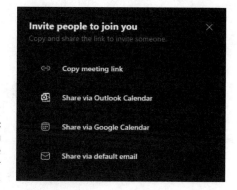

**FIGURE 2-19:**
Choose how you want to invite others to your meeting.

5. **Click or tap Copy Meeting Link, and then paste the link in an email message or chat window, where you invite others to join you.**

   This is the easiest way to invite someone.

6. **Click or tap the X button for the invitation options and wait for others to join the meeting.**

   The people that join your call are shown in the participants list on the right, and you can start talking with them as soon as they enter the meeting.

7. **When you want to exit the meeting, click or tap Leave in the top right.**

**TECHNICAL STUFF**

If the people you want in your meeting don't use Windows 11, and they want to join the call, they should install the Microsoft Teams app on their computer, as it may not be bundled automatically. They can download it from `www.microsoft.com/en-ww/microsoft-teams/download-app`.

## Accessing the full Microsoft Teams experience

The chat icon on the taskbar is just a quick way to introduce people to Microsoft Teams and its basic options. However, if you want to access the full Teams experience, click or tap the chat icon, and then the Open Microsoft Teams link at the bottom. This action opens the Microsoft Teams app, as shown in Figure 2-20.

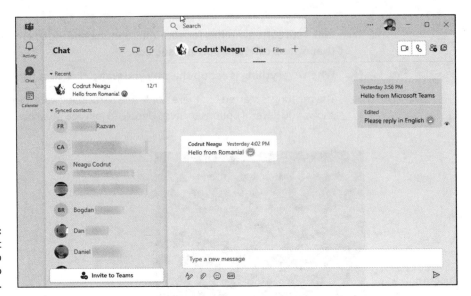

**FIGURE 2-20:**
The Microsoft
Teams app
is built into
Windows 11.

With it, you can chat with others, access your calendar, read a feed with your Microsoft Teams notifications, and so on. It works like the Teams app you may be familiar with on Windows 10 or other platforms. Don't hesitate to explore it and see what it has to offer.

# Working Remotely with Windows 11

The COVID-19 pandemic has changed the way we live and work. During the lock-down, millions of people had to work from home and required equipment that they may not have had in their homes: a webcam, a second display, a better keyboard, a computer desk, or even an office chair. They also had to familiarize themselves with apps and tools for working remotely.

In this section, I start with how to enable Remote Desktop and use it to connect remotely to another computer. This discussion ties in with Book 9, Chapter 4, where I discuss VPN. You may have to use VPN to connect to your company's network, and then use Remote Desktop to connect to a computer in your company's office. If that's the case, this section has you covered.

I also share how to connect a second display to your laptop or PC so that you can work productively on two monitors at once. In addition, I share some essential tips about what to look for in a webcam and how to set it up.

Finally, for readers who work with people from all over the world, I share some tips on how to keep track of time zones. You don't want to call someone on Skype or Teams late at night, do you?

## Enabling remote desktop connections

Remote Desktop connections allow Windows devices to connect to one another through the internet or your local network. When you connect remotely to another Windows PC, you see that computer's desktop. You can also access its apps, files, and folders as if you were sitting in front of its screen. This is useful for IT professionals and business users who must work remotely, especially during a lockdown.

If you want to use another PC to connect remotely to your own Windows 11 PC or you want to let others connect to it, you must enable Remote Desktop. Here's how:

WARNING

This procedure works on only Windows 11 Pro or Enterprise. If you run another edition, such as Windows 11 Home, you can't enable this feature. In Windows 11 Home, if you open the Remote Desktop section in the Settings app, you see a message stating that *Your Home edition of Windows 11 doesn't support Remote Desktop.*

**1.** **Click or tap the Start icon and then Settings.**

The Settings app opens.

**2.** **Choose the System category on the left, and then click or tap Remote Desktop on the right.**

On the right, you see the Remote Desktop settings, as shown in Figure 2-21.

**3.** **Click or tap the switch to enable Remote Desktop and then confirm your choice.**

You or others can now connect remotely to your PC, using any of the user accounts that have administrator permissions on it.

**4.** **Close Settings.**

REMEMBER

Don't forget that you turn on Remote Desktop to let other computers connect remotely to yours. You do not need to enable Remote Desktop if you want to connect from your computer to another. However, the computer to which you want to connect must have Remote Desktop enabled for the remote connection to work.

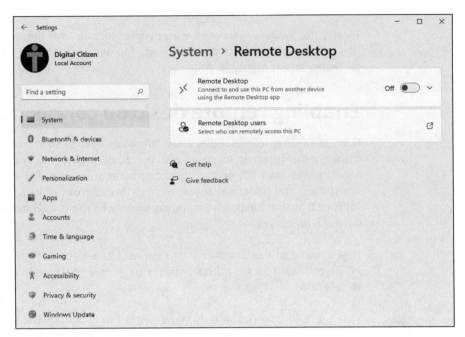

**FIGURE 2-21:**
Enabling Remote
Desktop in
Windows 11.

# Connecting with Remote Desktop Connection

If Remote Desktop is enabled on the PC that you want to connect to and you know the IP address and the credentials for a user account that exists on that computer, you can connect to it from your Windows 11 PC by using the built-in Remote Desktop Connection app. Here's how to establish a remote desktop connection from Windows 11:

1.  **Click or tap the search icon on the taskbar, type** remote, **and click or tap the Remote Desktop Connection result.**

    The Remote Desktop Connection app opens, asking you to enter the address of the computer that you want to connect to, as shown in Figure 2-22.

2.  **Enter the IP address of the computer you want to connect to, and click or tap Connect.**

    Remote Desktop Connection may take some time to establish the connection, after which it asks for the username and password to use to connect to that PC.

3.  **Enter the details of the user account to use to connect to the remote PC, and then click or tap OK.**

    If you plan to connect frequently to the remote PC, you may want to select the box for Remember Me, so that your connection details are saved and automatically used each time you log in.

**FIGURE 2-22:**
The Remote
Desktop
Connection app
allows you to
connect to other
computers.

4. **If you see a warning message that problems exist with the security certificate of the PC you want to connect to, click or tap Yes to continue.**

   When the connection is established, you'll see the desktop of the remote PC as if it were your own. A toolbar at the top displays connection information, as shown in Figure 2-23.

5. **When you've finished working on the remote PC, click or tap the X button in the toolbar at the top of the screen.**

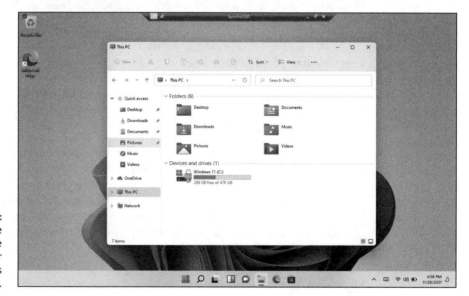

**FIGURE 2-23:**
You see the
desktop of the
remote computer
and can use it as
your own.

**TIP**

If you want to control how the Remote Desktop connection works, click or tap Show Options (refer to Figure 2-22), and configure the available settings. You can also save the username so that you don't have to enter it manually every time. Also, connect only to trusted computers.

# Connecting a second monitor

Working on two screens at the same time can increase productivity when you have to work from home. To connect a second display to your Windows 11 laptop or PC, first check out the ports on the display and on your Windows device. Figure 2-24 shows you how all the video ports look.

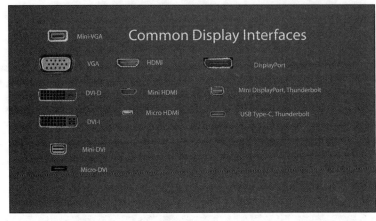

**FIGURE 2-24:** All the ports used by monitors, new and old.

*Wikipedia*

There are two possible situations:

>> **Your monitor and your laptop or PC share the same video port.** Buy a cable that has the same video port on both ends (HDMI, DisplayPort, USB Type-C, and so on).

>> **Your monitor and your laptop or PC do not share a common video port.** Buy an adapter to convert the video signal from your laptop or PC to the external monitor. Depending on what video ports you have on your laptop or PC and monitor, you might need a DisplayPort-to-VGA, HDMI-to-DisplayPort, USB-C-to-HDMI, DVI-to-HDMI, or Mini DisplayPort-to-DisplayPort adapter. You can find inexpensive adapters in electronics shops for almost any type of video connection.

After you have the necessary cable, do the following to connect the second monitor:

1. Using the appropriate cable, connect the monitor to your Windows 11 laptop or PC.

2. **Turn on the second monitor by plugging it into a power outlet and pressing its power button.**

   Windows 11 takes a few seconds to detect the external monitor. Note that the external monitor may not display anything after it's detected.

3. **Press Windows+P on your keyboard to display the Project options (see Figure 2-25).**

   You can view the desktop only on your PC screen (the main display) or only on your second screen, view the same desktop on both screens, or extend the desktop and have two different desktops side by side.

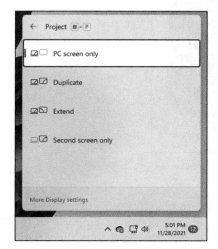

**FIGURE 2-25:**
The Project
options in
Windows 11.

4. **Press Windows+P to cycle through the Project options and view the results.**

   You can also click or tap to select an option. The image changes with each selection.

# Installing a webcam

During the COVID-19 lockdown, webcams became a hot item. Millions of people began working from home and had to rely on webcams to join countless conference calls. If you are in the market for a webcam, realize that most people don't need a high-end model with 4K video recording. A simple webcam with 720p or Full-HD video recording should suffice.

Installing a webcam is as simple as plugging it into a USB port on your computer and waiting for Windows 11 to detect it and install its drivers. One of my favorite webcams is Microsoft LifeCam HD-3000 (shown in Figure 2-26). It covers the basics, is affordable (it costs a bit less than $30) and is plug-and-play.

**FIGURE 2-26:**
Microsoft
LifeCam HD-3000.

Some webcams include software to activate features that may be useful to you. That's why it's a good idea to do a Google or Bing search for the Support page of the webcam's manufacturer and download from there the latest software and drivers for your webcam model. Install the webcam's software, and you should have no problems using it for Skype, Zoom, Teams, and Google Meet video calls.

I prefer webcams from proven manufacturers, such as Microsoft, Logitech, Asus, or Razer. Their webcams have many options at diverse price points.

TIP

## Adding clocks to the taskbar

If you work with a team from a multinational corporation, it's a good idea to set Windows 11 to display a clock from that corporation's time zone. That way, you can quickly check the time in the country of your team members. Here's how it works:

**1.** **Right-click or tap and hold down on the clock in the bottom-right corner of the screen.**

A contextual menu appears with a few options.

2. **Choose Adjust Date and Time.**

   The Settings app opens, displaying options about adjusting the date and time.

3. **On the right, scroll down to Related Links, and click or tap Additional Clocks.**

   The Date and Time dialog box appears, as shown in Figure 2-27.

**FIGURE 2-27:**
The Date and Time dialog box where you add clocks to the taskbar.

4. **Select the first Show This Clock box, choose a time zone from the list, and enter the name of the city or country that interests you.**

5. **Select the second Show This Clock box, choose another time zone from the list, and enter the name of the city or country that interests you.**

6. **Click or tap OK.**

To see the additional clocks, click or tap the clock on the taskbar. They are placed just above the calendar, as shown in Figure 2-28. If the calendar is minimized, you see only the additional clocks. Click or tap the upward-facing arrow to extend the calendar.

**FIGURE 2-28:**
The clocks you
added appear
just above the
calendar.

# 7

# Controlling Your System

# Contents at a Glance

**IN THIS CHAPTER**

» Checking out the Settings app

» Finding what's left in the Control Panel

» Putting shortcuts to settings on your desktop

» Using search to quickly find settings

» Adding new languages to Windows 11

# Chapter 1

# Navigating Windows Settings and Languages

Windows 11 has more settings than previous consumer operating systems from Microsoft, and that's to be expected since it has even more features than its predecessors. Most settings are found in the new Settings app, which is well organized and surprisingly easy to navigate.

**REMEMBER**

However, the old Control Panel, the bastion of Windows settings, still controls many aspects of how a Windows 11 PC works. While the Settings app controls several hundred settings, the Control Panel has a smaller yet still large enough number of Windows settings. And there's overlap between the two, but some settings can be changed only in the Settings app, and other settings can be changed only in the old-fashioned Control Panel. However, with each new major update to Windows 11, more settings get migrated from the old Control Panel to the new Settings app.

This chapter straddles both sides of the fence, both the new Settings app and the old Control Panel. The Settings app is sufficient, for the most part, but if you want to take greater control of your machine, you must learn how to live in both worlds.

For convenience, you may want to create shortcuts on your desktop to frequently used settings. In this chapter, I have some tips on how to do just that, quickly. There's also the world-famous God mode, which still works, and I haven't forgotten about it. You may want to try that too.

Lastly, some users need to use Windows in two or more languages. To help them out, I share how to install new languages in Windows 11 and how to switch between them.

# Understanding the Settings App

As mentioned, you can still use the old Control Panel to manage many settings. But the Windows 11 Settings app, shown in Figure 1-1, has a remarkable collection of settings arranged in a way that's infinitely more accessible than the old-fashioned desktop Control Panel.

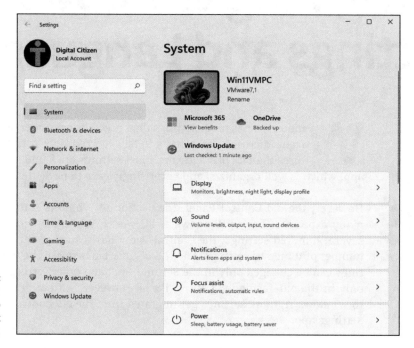

**FIGURE 1-1:**
The Windows 11 Settings app looks a lot more inviting.

Click or tap the Start icon and then the gear icon, and you see all Windows 11 settings organized by categories as follows:

>> **System:** This category includes settings for changing the display and sound settings, controlling notifications, controlling window snapping and multiple desktops, kicking in the battery saver, controlling how long the screen stays active when not in use, analyzing how much storage space is being used, configuring nearby sharing, and many other things. In the Storage pane of System (shown in Figure 1-2), you can tell Windows 11 where to store certain kinds of files.

>> **Bluetooth & Devices:** From here, you can control printers, scanners, cameras, and other connected devices; turn Bluetooth on and off; change mouse settings; manipulate the pen; and specify what AutoPlay program should kick in when you insert a USB drive or memory card. You can also link your Android smartphone or iPhone to your Windows 11 account.

>> **Network & Internet:** This category lets you turn Wi-Fi off and on, change your connection, and manage Ethernet (wired) network connections. You can also go into airplane mode, thus turning off both Wi-Fi and Bluetooth connections; set up a VPN; work with a dial-up connection; and manually set a proxy. You can also transform your Windows 11 laptop or tablet into a mobile hotspot.

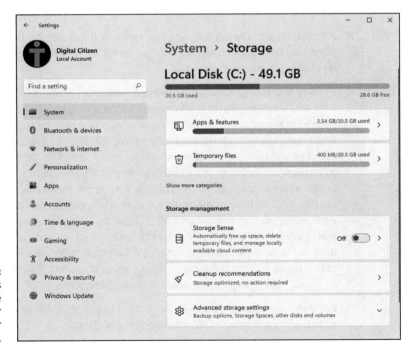

**FIGURE 1-2:**
System's Storage pane helps you better manage your storage space.

>> **Personalization:** This catchall category includes setting your wallpaper (background), adding a theme, choosing accent colors, putting a picture on your lock screen, and controlling the Start menu, the taskbar, the touch keyboard, and installed fonts.

>> **Apps:** Want to remove an app? Here's where you do it. You can also set default apps (for opening pictures and videos, for example), download offline maps, add optional features to Windows 11, and set the websites that can open in an app instead of a browser (like on Android). Finally, you also get access to settings involving video playback and which apps run at Windows startup.

>> **Accounts:** Disconnect a Microsoft account, set your account picture, and change information about your account with Microsoft's account database. Options enable you to add a new standard user, change your password, switch to a picture or PIN password, and switch between a Microsoft account and a local account. You can also set your Windows backup and sync settings through OneDrive and your Microsoft account (see Figure 1-3). There are also options for adding other accounts (children, work, or school accounts, and so on).

>> **Time & Language:** Set your time zone, manually change the date and time, set date and time formats, add keyboards in different languages, add new display languages, control how Windows 11 uses speech and spoken languages, and set up your microphone for speech recognition.

>> **Gaming:** Work with game mode, the Xbox game bar, and other gaming-related features. The Gaming category is your link to the Xbox-friendly part of your Windows 11 PC.

>> **Accessibility:** Microsoft has long had commendable aids for people who need help seeing, hearing, or working with Windows. All the settings are here, and there are surprisingly many.

>> **Privacy & security:** This section is huge, with an overwhelming list of options. First, this is where you access Windows Security. You can also set the Find My Devices feature (useful for laptops and tablets that may be stolen or lost) and access settings for web developers creating Windows 11 apps. Then there's the Windows permissions part, where you can turn off broadcasting of your advertising ID, maintained by Microsoft to identify you. Search settings are buried in here too. You can control how Search works, whether web results are filtered, and how indexing works, so that you get the search results you want. Next, you can turn on and off location tracking, and keep your webcam and microphone locked up. You can also control what apps get access to different features and personal data, including giving Windows 11 permission to send your full computer diagnostics data to Microsoft. Privacy is a huge deal, and I discuss it in more detail in Book 2, Chapter 6.

>> **Windows Update:** Control how Windows 11 updates itself, when it installs updates, when it reboots to install updates, and more.

All in all, the Settings pane is a well-thought-out subset of the settings that you may want to use.

**FIGURE 1-3:** Control what gets synced among computers using your Microsoft account.

# Exploring the Control Panel

The inner workings of Windows 11 also reveal themselves in the Control Panel. You may be propelled to the Control Panel via a link in the Settings app. But if you want to get in directly, of your own volition, click or tap the search icon on the taskbar and type **Control**. Choose Control Panel in the list of results. Figure 1-4 shows the Control Panel window.

Here's an overview of the main categories of the Control Panel:

>> **System and Security:** This category includes an array of tools for trouble-shooting and adjusting your PC. Check out Windows Defender Firewall and its settings, change power options, retrieve files with File History, manage Storage Spaces, and rifle through miscellaneous administrative tools. Use this part of the Control Panel with discretion and respect.

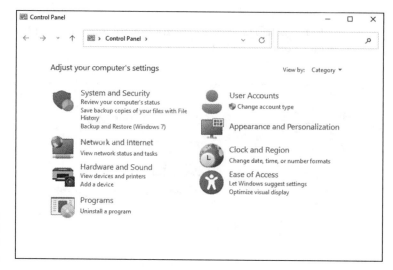

**FIGURE 1-4:**
You may still need to browse the Control Panel.

>> **Network and Internet:** Configure network sharing settings. Set up internet connections, particularly if you're sharing an internet connection across a network or if you have a cable modem or digital subscriber line (DSL) service.

>> **Hardware and Sound:** Add or remove printers and connect to other printers on your network. Troubleshoot printers, configure sound devices, and adjust the power settings for your laptop or tablet.

>> **Programs:** Add and remove specific Windows features and uninstall programs (desktop apps). Change the association between filename extensions and the programs that run them. Most of the functionality here is available in the Settings app, but a few laggards are still in the old Control Panel.

>> **User Accounts:** This group is a limited selection of actions that Microsoft hasn't yet moved to the Settings app. For example, you must go here to remove an account or manage credentials associated with an account.

>> **Appearance and Personalization:** Font management is in this section even though it exists in the Settings app too. You also get access to the Ease of Access Center and to File Explorer options.

>> **Clock and Region (and Language):** Set the time and date, or tell Windows to synchronize the clock automatically. You can also add support for complex languages (such as Thai) and right-to-left languages, and change how dates, times, currency, and numbers appear.

>> **Ease of Access:** Change accessibility settings to help you see the screen and better use the keyboard or mouse. You also set up speech recognition here.

If you want to change a Windows 11 setting, try the Control Panel, but don't be discouraged if you can't find what you're looking for. The Settings app is growing into a better alternative each year.

# Putting Shortcuts to Settings on Your Desktop

Want to see the Windows Update settings by simply clicking or tapping a shortcut on the desktop? Enable or disable your microphone with two clicks? Turn off your webcam? Manage your Wi-Fi settings? It's easy! Here's how:

**1.** **Right-click (or press and hold down on) any blank place on the desktop. Choose New ⇨ Shortcut.**

You see the New Shortcut Wizard shown in Figure 1-5.

**2.** **Choose one of the ms-settings apps listed in Table 1-1, and type it in the input box.**

For example, as shown in Figure 1-5, to go to the Data Usage app, type **ms-settings:windowsupdate** in the box marked Type the Location of the Item.

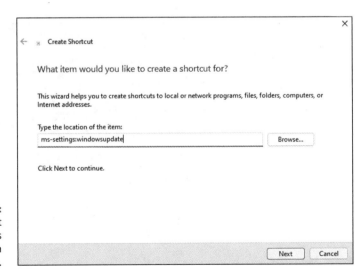

← ◫ Create Shortcut

What item would you like to create a shortcut for?

This wizard helps you to create shortcuts to local or network programs, files, folders, computers, or Internet addresses.

Type the location of the item:

ms-settings:windowsupdate     [ Browse... ]

Click Next to continue.

[ Next ]  [ Cancel ]

**FIGURE 1-5:**
Create a shortcut to the Windows Update pane in the Settings app.

**TABLE 1-1**     **Shortcuts to Settings App Panels**

| Settings App Page | Command |
|---|---|
| Access Work or School | ms-settings:workplace |
| Account Info | ms-settings:privacy-accountinfo |
| Airplane Mode | ms-settings:network-airplanemode |
| Backgrounds | ms-settings:personalization-background |
| Calendar (Privacy & Security) | ms-settings:privacy-calendar |
| Camera (Privacy & Security) | ms-settings:privacy-webcam |
| Captions (Accessibility) | ms-settings:easeofaccess-closedcaptioning |
| Colors | ms-settings:colors |
| Colors | ms-settings:personalization-colors |
| Contacts (Privacy & Security) | ms-settings:privacy-contacts |
| Contrast Themes | ms-settings:easeofaccess-highcontrast |
| Date and Time | ms-settings:dateandtime |
| Devices | ms-settings:connecteddevices |
| Devices (Bluetooth & Devices) | ms-settings:bluetooth |
| Diagnostics & Feedback | ms-settings:privacy-feedback |
| Dial-up | ms-settings:network-dialup |
| Display | ms-settings:display |
| Ethernet | ms-settings:network-ethernet |
| Family & Other Users | ms-settings:otherusers |
| For Developers | ms-settings:developers |
| Inking & Typing Personalization | ms-settings:privacy-speechtyping |
| Keyboard (Accessibility) | ms-settings:easeofaccess-keyboard |
| Language & Region | ms-settings:regionlanguage |
| Location (Privacy & Security) | ms-settings:privacy-location |
| Lock screen | ms-settings:lockscreen |

| Settings App Page | Command |
|---|---|
| Magnifier | ms-settings:easeofaccess-magnifier |
| Manage Known Wi-Fi Networks | ms-settings:network-wifisettings |
| Microphone (Privacy & Security) | ms-settings:privacy-microphone |
| Mobile Hotspot | ms-settings:network-mobilehotspot |
| Mouse | ms-settings:mousetouchpad |
| Mouse (Accessibility) | ms-settings:easeofaccess-mouse |
| Narrator | ms-settings:easeofaccess-narrator |
| Notifications | ms-settings:notifications |
| Offline Maps | ms-settings:maps |
| Optional Features | ms-settings:optionalfeatures |
| Personalization | ms-settings:personalization |
| Power & Battery | ms-settings:batterysaver |
| Privacy & Security | ms-settings:privacy |
| Proxy | ms-settings:network-proxy |
| Sign-in Options | ms-settings:signinoptions |
| Speech | ms-settings:speech |
| Start | ms-settings:personalization-start |
| Storage | ms-settings:storagesense |
| Themes | ms-settings:themes |
| Typing | ms-settings:typing |
| VPN | ms-settings:network-vpn |
| Wi-Fi | ms-settings:network-wifi |
| Windows Update | ms-settings:windowsupdate |

3. **Click or tap Next, give the shortcut a name, and then click or tap Finish.**

   A new shortcut appears on your desktop. Double-click or double-tap it, and the Settings app appears, as shown in Figure 1-6.

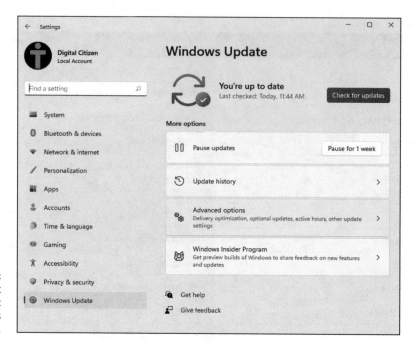

**FIGURE 1-6:**
The new shortcut
takes you straight
to the Windows
Update pane.

# God Mode (Still) Works in Windows 11

The Windows Vista–era parlor trick commonly called *God mode* is alive and well in Windows 11 too, as shown in Figure 1-7. I, for one, was quite surprised to see that God mode made the transition to Windows 11 because it's based on hooks into the Control Panel — and the Control Panel is being slowly retired.

The parts of God mode that appear in Windows 11 are slightly different from the elements in Windows 10 (which, in turn, is slightly different from Windows 8.1 and Windows 7). But the overall effect is the same.

Follow these steps to access God mode on your Windows 11 desktop:

1. **Right-click (or press and hold down on) any empty spot on the desktop. Choose New ⇨ Folder.**

   A new folder appears on your desktop, ready for you to type a name.

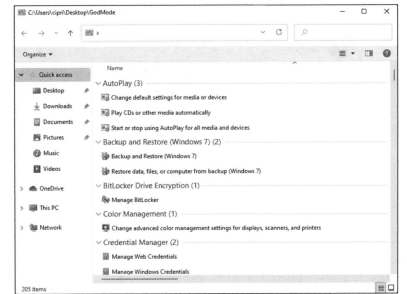

**FIGURE 1-7:**
God mode is a massive collection of more than 200 shortcuts to all sorts of Windows settings, many of which are obscure.

2. **Give the folder the following name, and then press Enter:**

   **GodMode.{ED7BA470-8E54-465E-825C-99712043E01C}**

   The name you just entered is going to disappear.

TIP

   The God Mode folder can be renamed to anything you want, after you first create it.

3. **Double-click or double-tap the folder to display the list you see in Figure 1-8.**

   It's a massive list of direct links to all sorts of settings. Most of them work.

Some of these links may be useful. For example, the AutoPlay option, when accessed through God mode, brings up the old Windows 7/8 AutoPlay dialog box, which is more advanced than the Windows 11 Settings version of AutoPlay (click or tap the Start icon, Settings, Devices, and then AutoPlay).

Navigating Windows
Settings and Languages

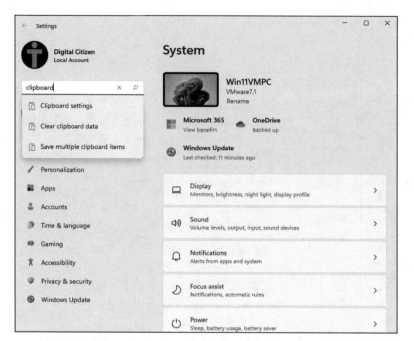

**FIGURE 1-8:**
Create a shortcut to the Windows Update pane in the Settings app.

# Using Search to Quickly Find Settings

Even though the Settings app is well organized, no one can know where every setting is located, unless they were on the development team that created Windows 11. To help you find the settings you're interested in, the Settings app has a search feature of its own. Here's how it works:

**1. Click or tap the Start icon and then Settings. Or press Windows+I on your keyboard.**

The Settings app opens to the System category.

**2. In the Find a Setting Search box, in the top-left of Settings, type** clipboard.

Note how the Settings app displays several search results with links to clipboard-related settings, as shown in Figure 1-8.

**3. Click or tap the Clipboard Settings search result.**

The Settings app takes you directly to its clipboard settings.

REMEMBER

Use the same process to find any setting that interests you, from Bluetooth to Active Hours to Family Options.

**TIP**

Control Panel has a similar Search box in the top-right corner of its window, and it works in a similar fashion.

# Installing New Languages in Windows 11

Many Windows 11 users use more than one language. You may know English but also Spanish, French, German, or Hindu. If you want to install a new display language, Windows 11 makes the process easy. Here is how it works:

**1.** **Click or tap the Start icon and then Settings.**

You see the Settings app.

**2.** **On the left, click or tap Time & Language.**

**3.** **On the right, click or tap Language & Region.**

You see the languages installed on Windows 11, as shown in Figure 1-9.

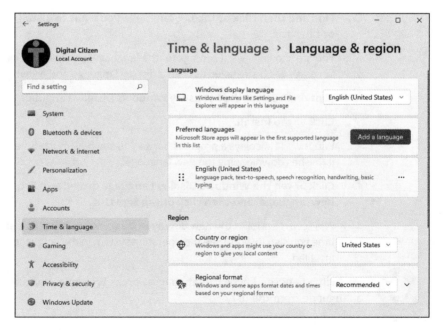

**FIGURE 1-9:**
Set your language and region.

**4.** **Click or tap the Add a Language button next to Preferred Languages.**

A surprisingly long list with all the available languages is displayed, as shown in Figure 1-10. Scrolling the list takes a long time, so you may want to use the Search box at the top of the language list.

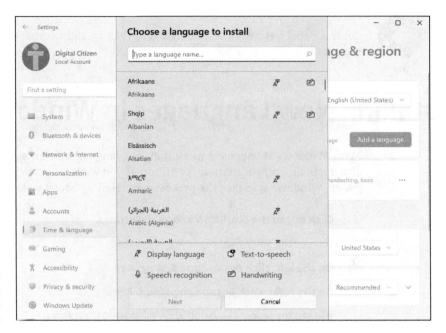

FIGURE 1-10:
Choose a
new language
to install.

5. **Find and then click or tap the language you want to install, and then click or tap Next.**

You are shown several settings for the language, as shown in Figure 1-11. The language will be installed as both a display language and a keyboard language.

6. **(Optional) Select the Set as My Windows Display Language option.**

7. **Click or tap Install.**

Windows 11 displays a progress bar so you see how much time remains before it finishes downloading the new language.

8. **Click or tap the Windows Display Language drop-down list, choose the new language, and then click or tap Sign Out.**

Windows 11 applies the new display language to your account, and the next time you sign in, you'll see the operating system in the language you just installed.

TIP

To switch between keyboard languages, press Windows+spacebar and then select a language from the list.

REMEMBER

Languages are applied per user account. Therefore, two user accounts can use different display and keyboard languages.

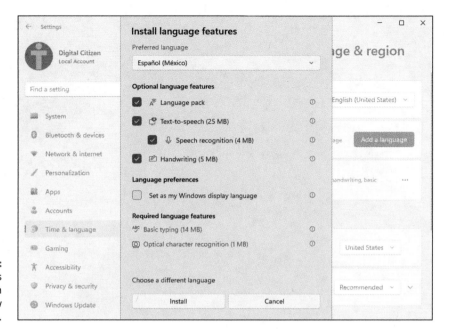

**FIGURE 1-11:**
The settings available when installing a new language.

# Chapter **2**

# Managing Windows Updates

M any users complain about Windows 11's forced patches and upgrades. Rightfully so. From the days of Windows 10, Microsoft has proved over and over that it can't be trusted to deliver reliable software fixes. No matter how much Microsoft fails and users complain, the company is not willing to improve its approach to Windows updates.

Windows 11 updates itself automatically, in the background, using criteria known only by Microsoft. If you don't go into Windows 11 and change things, it automatically assumes that you want to install Microsoft's changes the moment they appear. In the past, that's led to all sorts of problems, and I doubt that it'll change in the future. If you want a better computing experience, take control and use the Pause Updates feature, especially just before Microsoft releases a new feature update.

While Windows updates can be troublesome, updating from time to time is necessary. The same goes for Office. Few people know that Windows Update can be set to download and install Office updates too.

In this chapter I cover all the basics about updating Windows 11 and Office. I show you how to install updates, find information about them, remove those you don't need, and pause and block updates.

# Understanding the Terminology

Microsoft's terminology doesn't help users much. The official naming for Windows updates has changed several times. As of this writing, these are the patching terms you need to know:

» **Cumulative updates:** Microsoft calls them *quality updates.* These updates include a combination of security patches, bug fixes, and small changes to the operating system.

In theory, cumulative updates arrive once a month, on the second Tuesday of the month — so-called Patch Tuesday. Reality can be messier, though, with some cumulative updates pulled because of the issues they generate, then re-released a couple of days later, and so on.

» **Version changes:** Microsoft calls them *feature updates,* but they're really upgrades. These move you from one version of Windows 11 to the next. New versions of Windows 11 are supposed to appear once a year, usually in the fall.

» **Changes to the updating software itself:** *Servicing Stack updates* can appear unexpectedly just about any time. They're intended to make it easier to install patches.

» **Definition updates for Microsoft Defender Antivirus and the Windows Malicious Software Removal Tool (MSRT):** These updates happen all the time, and they're harmless. Don't worry about installing them. Read Book 9, Chapter 3 for more about the security tools built into Windows 11.

» **Drivers:** Microsoft's drivers are famous for creating mayhem where none was needed, even though most driver updates are harmless. Windows 11 regularly pushes out drivers for certain big-name hardware manufacturers through Windows Update. It's your decision whether to install them or not.

**WARNING**

If you're having problems with a driver pushed by Microsoft, uninstall it (I provide instructions later in the chapter), go to your hardware manufacturer's website, and get the latest driver from them.

» **Firmware changes (Microsoft Surface computers):** One of the joys of owning a Surface device is that Microsoft pushes system software updates — both firmware changes and driver changes — via Windows Update.

>> **Miscellaneous updates:** Microsoft occasionally pushes out patches specifically for Microsoft Edge, the .NET Framework used by software developers to create computer programs for Windows, and all sorts of additional pieces of Windows 11. In general, these patches are supposed to be rolled into cumulative updates. In practice, they are also delivered independently.

**TIP**

Confusingly, some miscellaneous patches get released as quality updates — and are thus subject to automatic update rules. Others float around until they're picked up by the next month's cumulative update. The definition of *quality* is tenuous at best.

Microsoft delivers its updates to Windows users through what it calls *servicing channels*. Each channel contains a set of devices that Microsoft deems suitable to receive a certain feature update. While I was writing this book, Microsoft used these servicing channels:

>> **General Availability Channel** means that the latest "stable" version of Windows 11 found in this channel is good enough to be sent out the door, usually to consumers. In this channel, feature updates are available annually, but unlike home users, businesses can delay them for as long as they want, to make sure that they won't cause havoc on their work computers.

>> **Long-Term Servicing Channel** (LTSC) applies to only Enterprise versions of Windows 11. In theory, it's a more stable version of Windows, suitable for environments that need to avoid update bugs. In practice, it's almost impossible to get real work done on an LTSC machine. Microsoft states that LTSC is not intended for machines that run, say, Microsoft Office, and it should be used for special-purpose devices only, like ATMs, medical equipment, and point-of-sale systems.

>> **The Windows Insider Program** includes people and organizations that want to test early builds for Windows 11 feature updates and provide feedback on what features will be shipped next. This channel delivers frequent updates, many of which are barely tested, and it is not intended for the faint of heart. However, anyone can join it with a Microsoft or work account.

That's the general framework of the Windows 11 patching phenomenon. Your job, should you choose to accept it, is to make the rules work for you — not blindside you.

# Installing Updates for Windows 11

Windows 11 automatically checks for updates when you use it, and you don't have to do anything to get them installed on your computer. The only thing that's necessary is a working internet connection.

However, you can manually check for updates, see what's available, and install them yourself, like this:

**1. Click or tap the Start icon and then Settings.**

The Windows 11 Settings are shown.

**2. On the left, choose Windows Update.**

You see the Windows Update options. By default, if an update is already available, you should see it at the top, as shown in Figure 2-1. For each update, you see its name and release date, without any meaningful details about what it does.

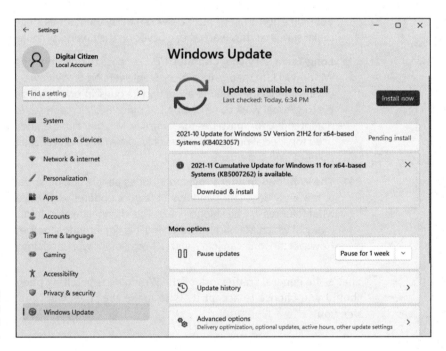

**FIGURE 2-1:**
This is where you update Windows 11.

**3. To install the latest update, click or tap Install Now.**

The progress is shown for each update. It first gets downloaded from Microsoft's servers, and then installed on your computer or device.

4. **If you want to finalize the installation of your available updates, first close all apps and files (so you don't lose any work), and then click or tap the Restart Now button when shown.**

   This last step is not required by all updates. Only those that change important system files require you to reboot before their installation is finalized.

# Postponing Windows 11 Updates

I think it's a good idea *not* to install feature updates for Windows 11 as soon as they're available. Postpone them for the maximum of 5 weeks instead. This ensures that you're not a beta tester. If there are any problems with a feature update, other people discover them (many times unwillingly), and Microsoft gets a chance to fix them before you get the update on your machine.

To pause Windows 11 updates, do the following:

1. **Click or tap the Start icon and then Settings. On the left, choose Windows Update.**

   The options shown previously in Figure 2-1 appear.

2. **Click or tap the drop-down list next to Pause Updates.**

   You see the options shown in Figure 2-2.

3. **Choose Pause for 5 Weeks.**

   On the top side of the Windows Update window, you see the date until updates are paused. Because cumulative updates normally arrive the second Tuesday of the month (Patch Tuesday), setting this pause to the last available date ensures that the update will be installed right before the next cumulative update is available.

4. **If you want to resume updating Windows 11 prior to the pause date, click or tap Resume Updates.**

**WARNING**

Pause updates takes precedence over all other settings. If you have Pause turned on, Windows 11 stops all updates but Microsoft Defender Antivirus updates. Microsoft is careful to mention that you can't reset the Pause Updates setting. If you try to turn it off and turn it back on again, "this device will need to get new updates before you can pause again." However, you can resume updates anytime you want before the pause period ends.

All sorts of things they don't teach you in Windows 11 school, eh?

# Getting Updates for Office

If you use many services and products from Microsoft, it may be a good idea to enable Windows Update to handle updates for them too. This approach is especially useful for Office, but it works for other Microsoft products too. Here's how to set Windows 11 to automatically install updates for Office and the like:

**1.** **Click or tap the Start icon and then Settings. On the left, choose Windows Update.**

**2.** **Click or tap Advanced Options.**

You see the options shown in Figure 2-3 and more.

**3.** **Click or tap the switch for Receive Update for Other Microsoft Products and set it on.**

The next time you click or tap the Check for Updates button, Windows Update will check for updates for Office and other Microsoft products.

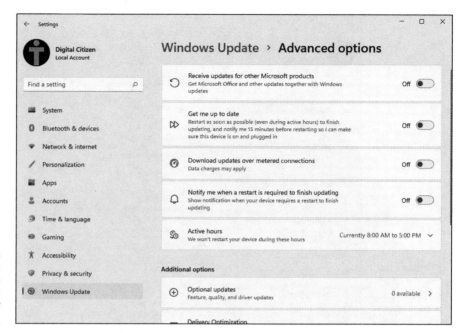

**FIGURE 2-3:**
This is where you control the more advanced features of Windows Update.

# Stopping Updates from Rebooting Your PC

Another annoying part of Windows 11 updates is that some require a reboot to get applied. Because of that, you may end up with your PC restarting while you're working, delivering a presentation at an event, or playing a game. To stop that from happening, Windows Update has a feature called Active Hours. You can set the interval during which you tend to use your PC, named Active Hours, and Windows 11 won't restart for updates during that time. Here's how to set it up:

**1.** Click or tap the Start icon and then Settings. On the left, choose Windows Update.

**2.** Choose Advanced Options.

**3.** Click or tap Active Hours to see more options.

**4.** Click or tap the drop-down list next to Adjust Active Hours and select Manually.

You can then change the interval for Active Hours, using the options from Figure 2-4.

**5.** Set the Start Time and End Time.

Windows needs an interval when it is allowed to install updates, but you are allowed to have a maximum of 18 hours between the start and end times. Your settings are applied immediately.

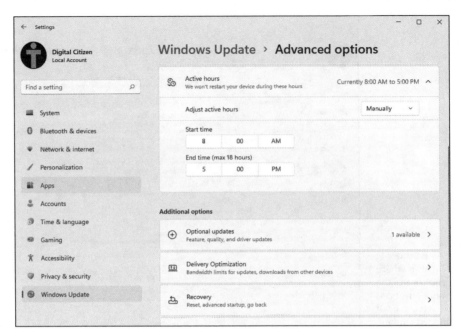

FIGURE 2-4:
Setting the hours
when Windows 11
doesn't restart
for updates.

You can also let Windows 11 automatically adjust your Active Hours. It does that by monitoring how you use your PC.

TIP

# Getting Information about and Removing Updates

Unfortunately, Microsoft doesn't make it easy for you to learn what an update does before it gets installed. However, it does provide plenty of useful information after the fact. If you recently installed an update and Windows 11 is misbehaving, you can learn more information about that update in particular and then remove it, like this:

**1.** **Click or tap the Start icon and then Settings. On the left, choose Windows Update.**

**2.** **Click or tap Update History.**

Windows displays all the updates installed on your machine, split by type, as shown in Figure 2-5.

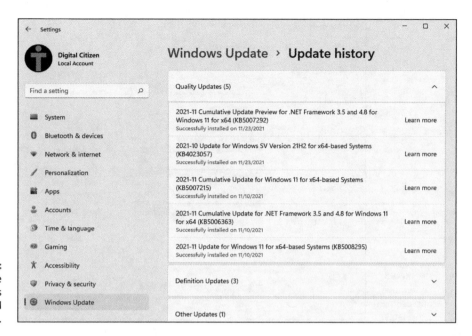

**FIGURE 2-5:**
Your Update History reveals plenty of useful information.

3. **Expand each category of updates with a click or tap on the arrow to the right of its name.**

    For each update, you see its name, when it was installed, and a Learn More link.

4. **To find out more about a specific update, click or tap the Learn More link to its right.**

    A web page is loaded in Microsoft Edge, sharing detailed information.

5. **To remove an update, get back to the Update History screen by clicking or tapping the Settings icon on the taskbar. Then, under Related Settings, click or tap Uninstall Updates.**

    The Installed Updates window appears, as shown in Figure 2-6. As you can see, this is in the Control Panel rather than Settings, and you now have both the Control Panel and Settings open.

6. **Click or tap the name of the update you want removed, and then Uninstall.**

7. **Confirm that you want the update removed by clicking or tapping Yes.**

    A progress bar appears during the uninstallation process. When done, the screen returns to the Installed Updates window.

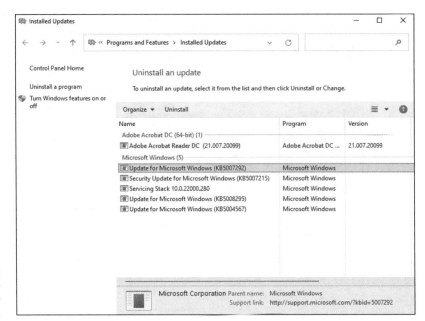

FIGURE 2-6:
Remove
troublesome
updates.

**TIP**

The problem with removing updates from Windows 11 is that Windows Update will install them back at some point. If you have problems with a specific update, you can block it from installing on your machine again by using Windows Update Manager — a free tool developed by a passionate developer — at `https://github.com/DavidXanatos/wumgr/releases`.

# The Case against Windows Automatic Update

Unfortunately, Microsoft still hasn't figured out how to deliver reliable Windows 11 patches. Patch Tuesdays have turned into beta-testing grounds where bugs crawl out of the woodwork in unpredictable ways. With a few notable exceptions, I don't blame Microsoft for the mayhem — patching the mess we know as Windows, in all its varied glory, is a difficult problem to tackle. Also, if everybody skipped automatic updates, we'd be in an unholy mess.

A few bad patches are particularly debilitating for most people and a nuisance for some. More to the point, the problems are avoidable if you just wait a few weeks for problem reports to die down and for Microsoft to get its patches patched. That's why pausing updates is a good practice, especially just before Microsoft announces the next feature update for Windows 11.

Even if Microsoft isn't at fault — and it frequently isn't — that's small consolation to folks who have their days disrupted by a weird conflict or their products clobbered.

Certainly, the wait-and-watch approach has downsides. Foremost among them is that if Microsoft patches a vulnerability in Windows 11 or Office and malware appears quickly to take advantage of a previously unknown security hole, those who are deferring updates might be caught flat-footed.

That scenario, however, has become uncommon. Sure, there are patches for *zero days* — Windows Update patches for security holes with known exploits — but this is a horse of a different color. Microsoft did a respectable job obfuscating its descriptions and preventing its patched code from fast reverse engineering. Could a massive reverse-engineered wave of malware roll out on some future Wednesday? Yes, and if it does, automatic updates will save the day.

**WARNING**

As with everything associated with patching Windows, there are pros and cons. You must weigh the possibility of a giant, quick reverse-engineered attack against the certainty of buggy patches. History shows that the risk of letting a Windows update install on day one exceeds the risk of delaying for a couple of weeks.

## Blocking Windows 11 updates

The trick to blocking updates on Windows 11 Home or Pro machines lies in a little-known setting called metered connection. As originally conceived, Microsoft put the metered connection setting in Windows 11 to let you tell Windows that you're paying for your internet access by the bit; which means you don't want Windows 11 to download anything unless it absolutely has to. From that fortunate beginning arises the best option for Windows 11 users to block updates.

**REMEMBER**

What goes through a metered connection? Hard to say, specifically, and Microsoft has made no commitments. But experience has taught us that the metered connection setting guards against any patches, except Microsoft Defender Antivirus updates — exactly what you would hope. No guarantees, of course, but metered connection looks like a decent, if kludgy, approach to blocking updates.

If you want to (temporarily!) block updates and Windows 11 version upgrades, follow these steps:

**1.** **Click or tap the Start icon and then Settings. On the left, choose Network & Internet.**

## 2. Do one of the following:

- *If you have a wired (Ethernet) connection, click or tap Ethernet.* You see the Ethernet configuration options shown in Figure 2-7.

- *If you have a wireless connection, click or tap Wi-Fi and then the name of your network connection.* You see the properties of your Wi-Fi connection, similar to Figure 2-8.

## 3. Set the Metered Connection switch on by clicking or tapping it.

Your internet connection is now set as metered and — unless Microsoft changes the rules — you're protected from both cumulative updates and version upgrades.

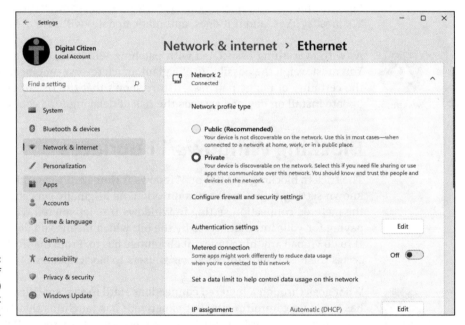

**FIGURE 2-7:**
The properties of a wired (Ethernet) connection look like this.

WARNING

*You must install updates eventually.* To resume them, follow the same steps, and set the Metered Connection switch to off. Then, read the next section for advice on choosing the right time to drop the big one.

# When is it a good time to unblock updates?

If you block updates, you're on the hook to unblock them, sooner or later. Generally, it takes several days for the worst cumulative update bugs to shake out, and weeks for the more subtle problems to appear, get diagnosed, and in some cases, fixed.

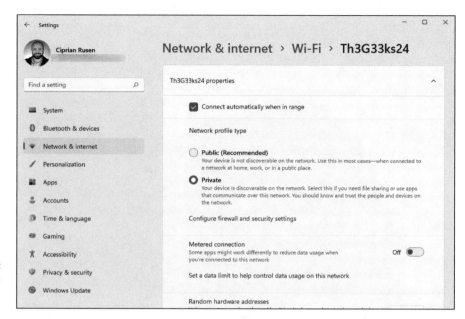

**FIGURE 2-8:**
If you have a
Wi-Fi connection,
it'll look like this.

Version upgrades, on the other hand, seem to follow Microsoft's original schedule. It really *does* take three or four months with the cannon fodder subjected to a new version to make sure it's stable enough to entrust your machine to the new order.

The deadline we're all fighting is the one imposed by the bad guys. If you delay patching long enough, something bad is going to hit, and it may hit quickly. We had a good example in February 2017, when Microsoft's patches, about six weeks after they were released, became crucial to block the WannaCry and NotPetya vulnerabilities. If you waited too long to patch in early 2017, your machine was wide open to some truly awful stuff.

**WARNING**

Conversely, if you install all patches soon after they're released, you expose yourself to the kind of problems we saw in January 2018. Back then, Microsoft released a bevy of Meltdown and Spectre patches that bricked large groups of PCs. It took Microsoft five days to identify the problem and pull the patch. Microsoft spent weeks patching, pulling patches, re-patching, and re-re-patching — and it had to counter bugs in Intel's patches at the same time. The result was an abominable mess that left many Windows users bewildered and more than a few staring at useless blue screens on bricked machines. The upshot? Every month is different. If you block updates and upgrades, you must stay on top of the latest developments and judge for yourself when it's safe to patch.

IN THIS CHAPTER

» **Using the Windows troubleshooting tools**

» **Fixing installation and update problems**

» **Running troubleshooting tools with Windows Terminal**

» **Taking screen shots of your problems**

» **Using Windows Sandbox**

» **Getting help from Microsoft**

» **Receiving remote assistance**

» **Getting help on the web**

Chapter **3**

# Troubleshooting and Getting Help

Your PC ran into a problem that it couldn't handle, and now it needs to restart. You can search for the error online, but the *error message goes by so fast that you can't possibly read it.*

Wish I had a nickel for every time I've seen that "blue screen" message. People write to me all the time and ask what caused the message, or one like. My answer? It could be anything. Hey, don't feel too bad: Windows couldn't figure it out either, and Microsoft spent hundreds of millions of dollars trying to avoid it.

Windows 11 arrives with automated tools to help you pull yourself out of the sticky parts. The troubleshooters really do shoot trouble, frequently, if you find the right one. Error logs and event trackers can keep you reading for many hours and provide some useful information too. However, if the tools built into Windows 11 don't help, you can try some of the advice shared in this chapter. I cover Windows 11 installation problems, and some of the headaches caused by faulty updates.

But if my advice doesn't help, I also share how to help yourself get some help: where to look for help online and how to take screen shots or record your problems, so that you can send the details to Microsoft Support or some tech geek you know.

Lastly, I also share detailed, simple, step-by-step instructions for inviting a friend to take over your computer, via the internet, to see what's going on and lend you a hand while you watch.

This chapter is long and technical but worth reading. So arm yourself with some patience, and let's get started.

# Troubleshooting the Easy Way

If something goes wrong, your first stop should be the troubleshooters built into Windows 11. *Troubleshooters,* as the name implies, take you by the hand and help you figure out what's causing problems — and, just maybe, solve them.

If you run into a problem and you're stumped, see whether Microsoft has released a pertinent troubleshooter by following these straightforward steps:

1. **Click or tap the search icon (magnifying glass) and type** troubleshoot.

2. **Click or tap Troubleshoot Settings.**

   The Troubleshooting section from the Settings app is loaded. Windows 11 might recommend some troubleshooters.

3. **To see all the troubleshooters available, click or tap Other Troubleshooters.**

   The list shown in Figure 3-1 appears. Scroll down and you'll see that it's a long list.

4. **Click or tap Run next to the troubleshooter that you think may help with your problem.**

   Windows 11 troubleshooters start by trying to detect your problem and what's causing it. The basic idea is to answer any questions the troubleshooter may ask, and follow its instructions.

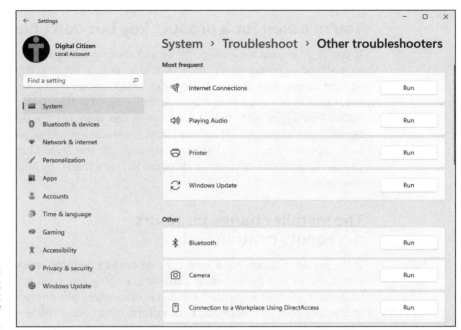

**FIGURE 3-1:**
Troubleshooting wizards can cut to the heart of a problem.

**TECHNICAL STUFF**

If you can't find a worthy troubleshooter, you may be able to unearth worthwhile content from your system's log using Event Viewer, a topic that I tackle in Book 8, Chapter 4.

# Troubleshooting the Hard Way

No troubleshooter available to whisk you out of harm's way?

That's a tough spot to be in. To help you out, I've come up with two lists of solutions that you may find enlightening or at least helpful. One deals with installing Windows 11, and the other deals with updating Windows 11.

## Tackling installation problems

This section is for folks who are using Windows 10 and trying to upgrade to Windows 11 but can't, and for those who are trying to move from one version of Windows 11 to the next. I have categorized some installation problems, including initial setup problems, and offer a bit of advice and some pointers, should you find yourself stuck.

## You're asked for a product key but don't have one

If you're prompted for a product key and are upgrading from a genuine Windows 10 machine or switching versions of Windows 11, click or tap Skip, Do This Later, or Next (depending on the dialog box). Don't bother trying to find a Windows 11 key. Chances are good that Windows will recognize the error of its ways and not bother you again, although it may take a few days for the activation routine to figure it out. If you get repeated prompts, see the upcoming section on activation problems. Another thing that may help is to use the same Microsoft account that you use in Windows 10. Usually, product keys are linked by Microsoft to Microsoft accounts.

## The installer hangs for hours or reboots continuously

If the installer hangs for a long time or keeps rebooting, make sure that you've disconnected any nonessential hardware: Unplug any hard drives other than the C: drive. Yank that external hard drive, disconnect peripherals that aren't absolutely necessary, including extra monitors, smart-card readers, weird keyboards, whatever. If possible, consider turning off Wi-Fi and plugging into a router with a LAN cable (that worked for me).

**TECHNICAL STUFF**

Second, make sure you have the right upgrade: Don't upgrade from 32-bit Windows 10 to 64-bit Windows 11. That won't work. This situation requires a clean installation of Windows 11, not an upgrade.

Also, if you started with Windows 10 Home, you should install Windows 11 Home. If you started with Windows 10 Pro, you should install Windows 11 Pro. If you're working with any Enterprise version of Windows 10, the upgrade isn't free; it's dependent on your company's license terms.

Then try running the upgrade again.

If you continue to have the same problem, Microsoft's best advice is to use the Windows 11 media creation tool to create a USB drive (or DVD). See the Download Windows 11 page at www.microsoft.com/en-us/software-download/windows11 for details, but be aware that your genuine license depends on running the upgrade sequence correctly. Specifically, you must first upgrade the PC instead of performing a clean install, to make sure your old Windows 10 license is recognized as a valid license for the free Windows 11 upgrade. If you start with a valid Windows 10 machine and use the media creation tool to move to the next version, you shouldn't have licensing problems.

For full instructions on installing Windows 11, go to www.digitalcitizen.life/install-windows-11. Make sure that you follow the steps in order.

# Problems with installing updates

Windows 11's forced updates drive everybody nuts. If you're having problems, you aren't alone.

Each new cumulative update is different and each situation is unique, but a handful of tricks seem to work in specific situations — and a handful of tricks may jolt your system back into consciousness no matter how hard the cumulative update fails.

Here are my recommendations for fixing an intransigent cumulative update. This isn't an exhaustive list of problems and solutions. Quite the contrary. It's a short (and I hope understandable) list of the most common problems and most common solutions.

## Before you do anything else

The very first thing to do is to make sure your antivirus software is turned off while you're troubleshooting. If you're using Microsoft Defender Antivirus (built into Windows Security), you're fine. But if you got suckered into installing something different, turn it off.

## Check for mundane hardware problems

Just because your PC has problems right after you installed the latest cumulative update, it doesn't mean the update caused the problem. Consider the possibility that your problem has nothing to do with the cumulative update. At the very least, someone with a cumulative update problem should right-click or tap and hold down on the Start icon, choose Windows Terminal (Admin), type the following in the box:

    chkdsk /f

and press Enter. This command will scan your main drive and fix any errors.

If you're having problems with a mouse, keyboard, monitor, or speaker, try plugging them into another computer to see if they're dead. This low-tech approach can save you from wasting time on a dead device.

## Recover from a bricked PC

For most people, a bricked PC is the scariest situation. The cumulative update installs itself (possibly overnight, while you aren't looking), you come back to your machine, and nothing happens. It's dead, Jim.

At least half the time, you can get back to a working machine by booting into safe mode, uninstalling the cumulative update, blocking it, and then rebooting normally. For the rundown on booting into safe mode, check out Book 8, Chapter 3.

## Make sure your problem isn't the latest Windows update

Try to uninstall the latest Windows 11 update and see if the problem goes away. To learn how to remove updates, read Book 7, Chapter 2.

After the update is removed and you restart, you should be on the previous (presumably functional) version of Windows 11. Immediately test to see if your problem went away. If it did, use the wushowhide tool (instructions in the next section) to hide the bad patch from installing again. If your problem persists, chances are good your problem isn't with this particular update.

## Break out of the endless update loop

Sometimes a Windows 11 update fails. You see a message saying "Installation failed" or some such followed by "Undoing changes." When your system comes back to life an hour or two later, it goes right back to trying to install the same problematic update. You get the same error. Wash, rinse, repeat. You might want to let your system go through the full self-mutilation cycle twice, just to see if you get lucky, but after that it's just too painful. You need to put Windows 11 out of its misery.

Fortunately, Microsoft has a tool that tells Windows Update to stop looking for the specific update that's causing problems. Here's how to use it:

1.  **Download Microsoft's Wushowhide tool at** https://download. microsoft.com/download/f/2/2/f22d5fdb-59cd-4275-8c95- 1be17bf70b21/wushowhide.diagcab.

2.  **Run the wushowhide.diagcab file you just downloaded.**

3.  **This part's important and easy to miss: Click or tap the Advanced link. Deselect the Apply Repairs Automatically option (see Figure 3-2). Click or tap Next.**

4.  **Wait for the tool to look for all pending updates on your system. When it's done, click or tap Hide Updates.**

    There should be one or more updates with a check box near them.

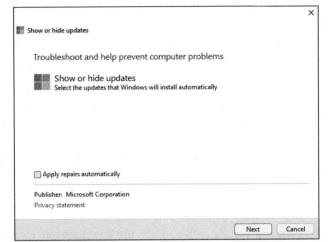

**FIGURE 3-2:**
To get
wushowhide to
hide updates, go
to the Advanced
options and turn
off Apply Repairs
Automatically.

5. **Select the check box next to the latest update you just uninstalled, click or tap Next twice, and close out of wushowhide.**

   Windows 11 hides the update for you. The Windows Update program won't even see the update unless you specifically unhide it.

If you've found a solution to your problem and want to reinstall the update, try this:

1. **Double-click or double-tap wushowhide.diagcab to run it.**

2. **Click or tap Advanced, and deselect the Apply Repairs Automatically option (refer to Figure 3-2). Click or tap Next.**

   Wait for wushowhide to look for all pending updates on your system.

3. **Click or tap Show Hidden Updates.**

4. **Select the box next to the update you want back, and then click or tap Next twice.**

5. **Click or tap Close.**

   That should unhide the update you previously hid and make it available for installation through Windows Update.

## Run SFC and DISM

Running SFC (System File Checker) and DISM (Deployment Image Servicing and Management) seems to be everyone's go-to suggestion for cumulative update installation problems. In my experience, it works only a small fraction of the time, but when it does, you come back from the brink of disaster with few scars to show for it.

System File Checker, better known as SFC, is a Windows 11 program that scans system files, looking to see if any of them are corrupt. There are ways to run SFC with switches to tell it to replace bad versions of system files.

If SFC can't fix the problem, a second utility called Deployment Image Servicing and Management (DISM) digs even deeper. Microsoft recommends that you run both, in order, regardless of the dirt dug up (or missed) by SFC.

Be painfully aware that SFC has flagged files as broken when in fact they weren't. You're looking for the automatic repair from SFC, not its diagnosis.

Here's how to run SFC:

1. **Right-click** or press and hold down on **the Start icon and choose Windows Terminal (Admin).**

2. **When the UAC prompt appears, choose Yes.**

3. **In Windows Terminal, type** sfc /scannow **and press Enter.**

   Yes, there's a space between *sfc* and */scannow*. It can take a couple of minutes or half an hour, depending on the speed of your storage drive. See Figure 3-3.

   If SFC reports "Windows Resource Protection did not find any integrity violations," you're out of luck. Whatever problems you have weren't caused by scrambled Windows system files. If SFC reports "Windows Resource Protection found corrupt files and repaired them," you may be in luck because the problem may have been fixed. If SFC reports "Windows Resource Protection found corrupt files but was unable to fix some of them," you're back in the doghouse.

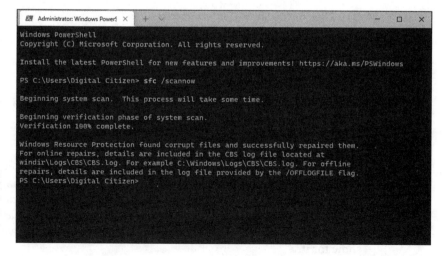

**FIGURE 3-3:**
The sfc /scannow command scans all your system files.

4. **Keep the same Windows Terminal (Admin) app open, type** DISM /Online /
Cleanup-Image /RestoreHealth **and press Enter.**

Again, spaces before all the slashes, and note that's a hyphen between *Cleanup*
and *Image*. Let it run: half an hour, an hour, whatever. If DISM finds any corrupt
system files, it fixes them.

5. **Reboot and see if your system has been fixed.**

The result of the scans is placed in the C:\Windows\Logs\CBS\CBS.log file. (*CBS*
stands for *Component Based Servicing*.) You may want to make a ZIP of that file, in
case one of Microsoft's helpers needs to take a look.

## Check the system event log

Everything, but everything (almost everything, anyway) gets posted to the system
event log. The biggest problem with the log? People get freaked out when they see
all the errors. That's why you rarely see a recommendation to check the log. It's
hard to believe that an error in a system event log is a natural occurrence.

Fair warning: Telephone scammers frequently have customers look at their system event logs to convince them that their computer needs repair.

To bring up the system event log and interpret its results, look at Book 8, Chapter 4.

## Refresh built-in Windows 11 apps

After the sfc /scannow run, refreshing the built-in apps is another common general recommendation for fixing a bad Windows 11 update. The command I recommend in the following reaches into your computer, looks at each app installed in
your user profile, and reinstalls a fresh, supposedly glitch-free copy:

1. **Right-click or press and hold down on the Start icon and choose Windows
Terminal (Admin).**

2. **Click or tap Yes when UAC asks for your confirmation.**

3. **In the Windows Terminal window, type the following (all on one line) and
press Enter:**

```
Get-AppXPackage -AllUsers | Foreach {Add-AppxPackage
    -DisableDevelopmentMode -Register "$($_.InstallLocation)\
    AppXManifest.xml"}
```

You see a bunch of red error messages (see Figure 3-4). Don't panic! Ignore
them. Yes, even the ones that say "Deployment failed with HRESULT," "The
package could not be installed because resources it modifies are currently in
use," and "Unable to install because the following apps need to be closed."

When the Get-AppXPackage loop finishes — even with all those red warnings — you'll be returned to the Windows Terminal prompt.

4. **Close Windows Terminal, reboot, and see if the demons have been driven away.**

   Although it sounds like this process will fix only errant built-in Windows 11 apps, people have reported that it fixes all manner of problems with Windows 11, including icons that have stopped responding, and Start menu and Cortana problems.

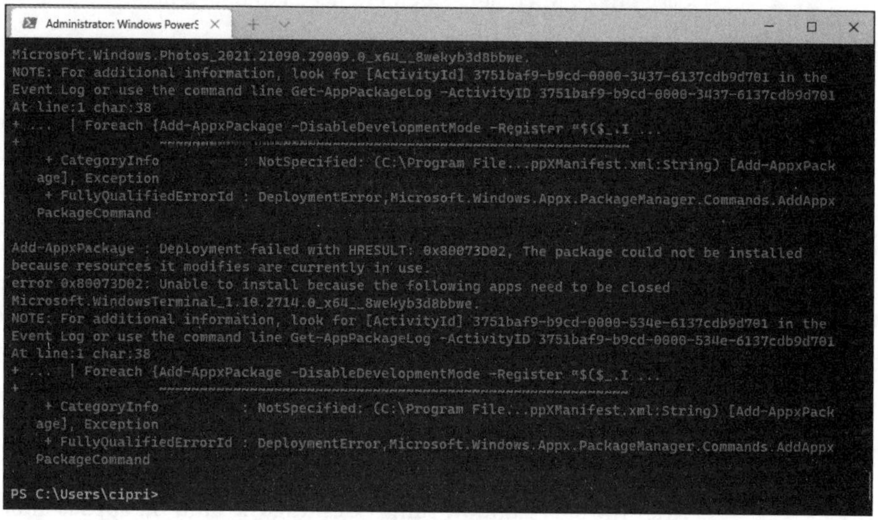

**FIGURE 3-4:**
Don't be scared of all the red error messages you see.

Even if an app refresh doesn't fix your machine, you've now undertaken the second standard approach (after sfc /scannow) that you'll find offered just about everywhere.

## Check Device Manager

Many problems can be traced back to non–Microsoft peripherals with drivers that don't work correctly. The first stop for bad devices is Device Manager:

1. **Right-click or tap and hold down on the Start icon and choose Device Manager.**

2. **Look for yellow icons in the list of devices.**

3. **If you find any:**

   a. *Double-click or double-tap the device that's causing problems.*

   b. *Click or tap the Driver tab.*

> c. *See if you can find a newer driver by clicking or tapping Update Driver and asking Windows 11 to find them through Windows Update, or by browsing for a driver you've downloaded locally.*

**TIP**

Download and install only Windows 11 drivers for your PC. If you can't find any, try Windows 10 64-bit drivers too. Don't go for Windows 8 or Windows 7 drivers because they will cause more problems than you already have.

## Just walk away and forget it

It's good to keep a bit of perspective. If the latest Windows 11 cumulative update won't install (or if it breaks something) and you can get your machine back to a normal state — using, perhaps, the uninstall/wushowhide sequence described at the beginning of this section — seriously consider doing nothing.

I know it's heresy, but the most recent cumulative update doesn't necessarily fix anything you need (or want!) to have fixed immediately.

Yes, security patches are tossed into the giant cumulative update, but Microsoft doesn't bother to split those out so you can install them separately. So you're stuck with an undifferentiated massive mess of fixes and security patches that may or may not be important to you.

There's no penalty for sitting out this particular cumulative update. The next one will come along, usually within a month, likely on Patch Tuesday (the anointed second Tuesday of the month) and it may well treat you and your machine better.

# Using Windows Terminal

In a previous section of this chapter, I mentioned Windows Terminal. This app is new to Windows 11 and comes as part of the operating system. Windows 10 users can have it too, but they have to download it separately from the Microsoft Store.

But what's Windows Terminal, you ask?

In geek talk, Terminal is a multi-tabbed command-line user interface designed to open and run any command-line application. In other words, Windows Terminal is itself an app that can load other command-line apps or shells such as Command Prompt (CMD) or PowerShell. By default, when you open Windows Terminal, it loads PowerShell behind the scenes, and you can enter commands optimized for this shell. However, you can open a new tab and run Command Prompt commands too, like this:

1. **Right-click** or tap and hold down on **the Start icon and choose Windows Terminal (Admin).**

2. **Choose Yes when UAC asks for your confirmation.**

3. **Click or tap the down arrow to the right of the + icon.**

   The menu shown in Figure 3-5 appears.

4. **Choose Command Prompt.**

   A new tab opens in the Windows Terminal window, that can take commands designed for the old Command Prompt.

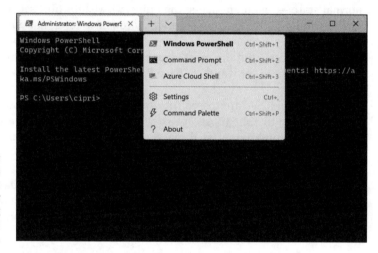

**FIGURE 3-5:**
Windows Terminal can work with many shells, including CMD and PowerShell.

**TIP**

You can also use keyboard shortcuts to open a Command Prompt tab in Windows Terminal: press Ctrl+Shift+2 for a new Command Prompt tab. Press Ctrl+Shift+1 for a PowerShell tab.

With Windows Terminal, Microsoft created something that is filled with useful tools and also compatible with any command–line app and shell. So, Windows Terminal not only enables you to run troubleshooting commands like those shared in this chapter, but also features the following:

» Split panes support enhancing the multi-tabbed Terminal environment enables you to see multiple command-line apps in a single tab, similar to how you can split your screen in Windows 11.

» Built-in zooming lets you make text larger or smaller without automatically changing the window's size as in regular Command Prompt or PowerShell windows.

>> Transparency support allows you to easily and quickly adjust the opacity of the Terminal window to get a nice futuristic effect.

>> Azure Cloud Shell connection gives you access to a tool that's particularly useful for IT admins and professionals working with Microsoft's Azure cloud services.

# Experimenting with Windows Sandbox

If you run Windows 11 Pro, Education, or Enterprise, you get access to Windows Sandbox. This useful app helps you run anything you want in an isolated environment. Sandbox is a virtual machine that simulates your Windows 11 PC while being separated from the real Windows 11 environment you're using.

While Sandbox is open, what you do in Sandbox remains there. Also, when you close it, everything you've done is deleted. Suppose you receive a weird link via email, download a file from an untrusted source, or download an app with an odd name. Start Windows Sandbox, run the link or file there, and see what it does. If it's malware, it will be gone the moment you close Windows Sandbox and your machine will not be affected. Isn't that better than having your PC locked down by ransomware or fighting off the Blue Screen of Death?

Windows Sandbox is not installed by default in Windows 11. Here's how to add it:

1. **Click or tap the search icon and type** features. **Click or tap Turn Windows Features On or Off.**

   The Windows Features window appears, as shown in Figure 3-6.

2. **Scroll down to Windows Sandbox and select its check box. Then click or tap OK.**

3. **When Windows 11 completes the requested changes, click or tap Restart Now.**

   After Windows 11 restarts and you log in, you can use Windows Sandbox.

To start Windows Sandbox, click or tap the search icon, type **sandbox** and click or tap the app's name. You then see another copy of Windows 11 loaded as if it were an app.

**FIGURE 3-6:**
Adding Windows
Sandbox to
Windows 11.

# Tricks to Using Microsoft Support

To go straight to the source of Windows help, fire up your favorite web browser and go to the `https://support.microsoft.com` website, as shown in Figure 3-7. This is Microsoft's official support site for all its products, including Windows and Office.

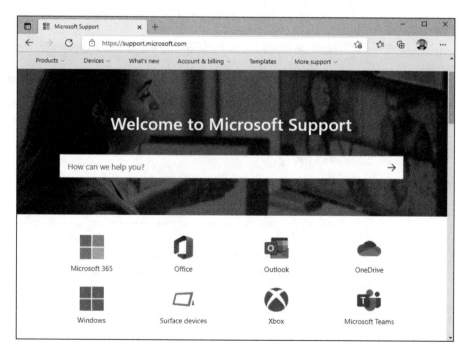

**FIGURE 3-7:**
I'm from the
Internet and I'm
here to help!

If you click or tap the Windows category, you get to the Windows Help & Learning center, which includes how-to articles, links to Microsoft's support community, and support service.

# The problems with Windows Help & Learning

Windows Help & Learning offers only the Microsoft party line. If a big problem crops up with Windows 11, you find only a brief report. If a product from a different manufacturer offers a better way to solve a problem, you won't find that information in Windows Help & Learning. Want searing insight or unbiased evaluations? That's why you have this book, right?

Windows Help & Learning exists primarily to reduce Microsoft support costs. Microsoft has tried hard to enable you to solve your own problems and to help you connect with other people who may be willing to volunteer. That's good. The new Answer Desk — where you get answers by chatting — is a great idea, but it doesn't always work well.

# Managing your expectations of Windows Help & Learning

Windows Help & Learning has been set up for you to jump in, find an answer to your problem, resolve the problem, and get back to work. Unfortunately, life is rarely so simple. You probably won't dive into Windows Help & Learning until you're feeling lost. Most of the content you find there falls into the following categories:

>> **Overviews, articles, and tutorials:** These explanatory pieces are aimed at giving you an idea of what's going on, as opposed to solving a specific problem.

>> **Tasks:** The step-by-step procedures are intended to solve a single problem or change a single setting.

>> **Walkthroughs and guided tours:** These multimedia demonstrations of capabilities tend to be light on details and heavy on splash.

>> **Troubleshooters:** These walk you through a series of (frequently complex) steps to help you identify and resolve problems. I talk about troubleshooters earlier in this chapter.

In my experience, Windows Help & Learning works best in the following situations:

>> You want to understand what functions the big pieces of Windows 11 perform (for example, Windows 11 widgets) and aren't overly concerned about solving a specific problem.

>> You have a problem that's easy to define (for example, *my printer doesn't print*).

>> You have a good idea of what you want to do (for example, use touch gestures), but you need a little prodding on the mechanics to get the job done.

This portal doesn't do much if you have only a vague idea of what's ailing your machine, if you want to understand enough details to think your way through a problem, or if you're trying to decide which hardware or software to buy for your Windows 11 computer.

For example, if you type **how much memory do I need?**, the answers you see talk about all sorts of things, but they don't tell you how much memory you need, as shown in Figure 3-8. For all that, and much more, you need an independent source of information — this book, for example.

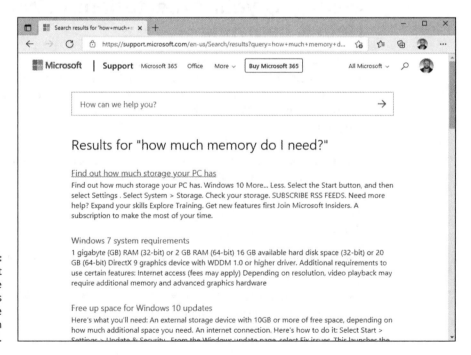

**FIGURE 3-8:** The Microsoft Support site doesn't always answer the question you asked.

## BEWARE OF "MICROSOFT" TECH SUPPORT SCAMS!

Somebody calls you, claims to be from Microsoft, and points you to a fancy website that says the caller's a Microsoft Registered Partner. The caller may even know your name or your phone number, or what version of Windows or what computer you're using. The scammer offers to check whether your system is still under warranty. Invariably, it just went out of warranty, and oh golly, you have to pay $35 or $75 or $150 to get all your problems solved.

These folks are clever. Many don't live in your home country, although they may sound like it. They may scrape your name from a tech support site and look up your phone number, or they may just make cold calls and figure there's likely to be a warm reception for anyone who claims to be from Microsoft and wants to help.

The websites with Microsoft Registered Partner qualifications may look impressive, but anybody — even you — can become a Microsoft Partner. The process takes a few minutes, and all you need is a free Hotmail or Outlook.com account or other Microsoft account. Drop by https://partner.microsoft.com/en-US/, and sign up!

I have a general explanation of the scam in Book 9, Chapter 1.

**REMEMBER**

Microsoft offers support by phone — you know, an old-fashioned voice call — but some pundits (including yours truly) have observed that you'll probably have more luck with a psychic hotline. Be that as it may, the telephone number for tech support in the United States is 800-642-7676, and you may have to press 0 three or more times to get a live person. In Canada, it's 905-568-4494. Have your computer handy.

# Snapping Your Problems

Since the dawn of Windows, you could take a snapshot of your desktop and put it on the clipboard by simply pressing the PrtScr or Print Screen key on your keyboard. Similarly, you could hold down the Alt key and press PrtScr, and Windows 11 would put a screen shot of the currently active window on the clipboard. From there, you could open Paint (or any other picture-savvy program, including Word), paste, and do what you will with the shot. That approach still works in Windows 11 — even in the Windows 11 apps — and in some circumstances, it's the right tool for the job.

However, Windows 11 has a new snipping tool, which is a more advanced tune on the same theme. With the snipping tool, shown in Figure 3-9, you click or tap New, and then drag and draw a rectangle around the area you want to capture. You can also capture a freeform area anywhere on the screen or automatically capture the current window or the full screen by choosing the type of screen shot you want to make before clicking or tapping New.

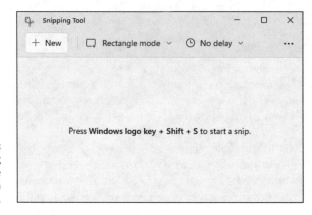

**FIGURE 3-9:**
The snipping tool can take screen shots in a few steps.

The snipping tool has tools for drawing on the captured screen, and the result can be copied to the clipboard, saved as a PNG, GIF, JPG, or HTML file, or automatically attached to a newly generated email message.

To bring up the snipping tool, click or tap the Start icon, All Apps, and Snipping Tool. The snipping tool appears, and if you click New, you can click (or tap) and drag whatever you want to snip. For more about taking screen shots with the snipping tool, read Book 2, Chapter 1.

REMEMBER

Windows has a third screen capture option, and in many circumstances, it's much handier. If you hold down the Windows key and press PrtScr or Print Screen on your keyboard, Windows takes a screen shot of the entire screen, converts it to a PNG file, and stores it in your Pictures\Screenshots folder. The file is given the name Screenshot (*x*).png, where *x* starts at 1 and increases by 1 with each shot.

# Recording a Video of Your Problems

If a screen shot's worth a thousand words, a video of the screen in action must be worth a thousand and one at least, right?

Windows 11 includes the magical *Steps Recorder (SR),* which lets you take a movie of your screen. To a first approximation, anyway, it's a series of snapshots, more like an annotated slideshow. You end up with a file that you can email to a friend, a beleaguered spouse, or an innocent bystander, who can then see which steps you've taken and try to sort things out. To read the file, your guru must run Microsoft Edge.

Here's how to record your problems:

**1.** **Make sure you remember which steps you have to take to make the problem appear.**

Practice, if need be, until you figure out how to get to the sorry state that you want to show to your guru friend.

**2.** **Click or tap the search icon and type** steps. **Or click or tap Steps Recorder.**

Steps Recorder, which resembles a full-screen camcorder, springs to life (see Figure 3-10). It isn't recording yet.

FIGURE 3-10:
The unassuming
Steps Recorder.

**3.** **Click or tap Start Record.**

The recorder starts. You know it's going because the title flashes *Steps Recorder — Recording Now.*

Note that the recorded slideshow will include the Steps Recorder window, so you may have to move it out of the way to display what you want to show your guru.

**4.** **(Optional) If you want to type a description of what you're doing or why or anything else you want your guru friend to see while they're looking at your home movie:**

a. *Click or tap the Add Comment button.* The recording pauses, and the screen dims. A Highlight Problem and Comment box appears at the bottom of the screen.

b. *Click or tap the screen wherever your problem may be occurring and drag the mouse cursor to highlight the problematic location.*

c. *Type your edifying text in the box, and click or tap OK.* Recording continues.

**5.** **When you're finished with the demo, click or tap Stop Record.**

Steps Recorder responds with the Recorded Steps dialog box, as shown in Figure 3-11. Take a good look at the file because what you see in the Save As box is precisely what gets saved — each of the screen shots, in a slideshow, precisely as presented. Remember, this isn't a video. It's an annotated slideshow.

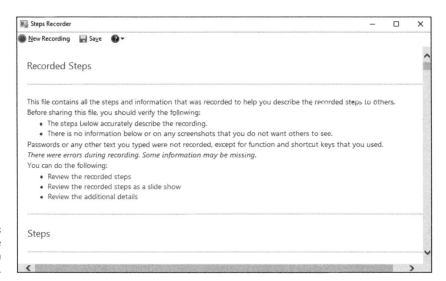

**FIGURE 3-11:**
Save the
recording as soon
as you finish it.

**6.** **Click or tap Save, type a name for the file (it's a regular ZIP file), and click or tap Save again.**

The ZIP file contains an MHT file, which can be reliably read only by Microsoft Edge — although you may have some luck reading the file in Firefox.

**7.** **When you're finished, click or tap X to close Steps Recorder.**

**8.** **Send the file to your guru friend through email, chat, or physically, on a USB drive.**

*Sneakernet* — the old-fashioned way of sticking the file on a USB drive and hand-delivering it — works.

**9.** **Tell your friend to open the ZIP file and then double-click or double-tap the MHT file inside.**

Microsoft Edge appears and displays the MHT file. The guru has several options; my favorite is to display the file as a slideshow (see Figure 3-12).

Realize that anything appearing on the screen is recorded by Steps Recorder. So don't record and send your salary information, okay?

REMEMBER

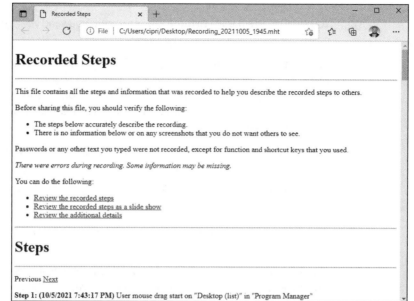

**FIGURE 3-12:**
The recording appears as a series of snapshots, with detailed accounts of what has been clicked (or tapped) and where.

# Connecting to Remote Assistance

Windows has long boasted the Remote Assistance feature, which lets a person on one computer control a second computer, long distance, while both watch what's on the screen. It's a great puppet/puppet master capability that allows someone to solve your problems remotely while you watch.

**WARNING**

If you're looking at these instructions because someone you don't know wants to get into your computer, stop. Right now. *Seriously. Stop.* Ask yourself how much you know about the person who's trying to look at your PC. Do you trust that person to take control of your PC — is it possible they'll trick you, even drop an infected file? If you have any qualms at all, DON'T DO IT. Scammers love to talk people into using Remote Assistance because they get full control over the PC, and if they work fast enough (or talk fast enough to convince you that what they're doing is legitimate), they can easily plant anything they want on your computer.

## Understanding the interaction

In a Remote Assistance session, the basic interaction goes something like this:

1. You create an invitation file for your guru friend, asking that person to look at your computer. Windows 11 creates a password for the invitation and shows it on your screen.

2. You send or give the file to the guru. Separately, you send your guru the password.

   Attach the file to an email message, send it via an instant messaging program that allows you to transfer files, put it on a network shared drive, post it on your company's intranet, copy it to a shared folder on OneDrive, copy it to a USB key drive, burn it onto a CD, or strap it to a carrier pigeon. It's just a text file. Nothing fancy.

3. Your guru friend receives the message or file and responds by clicking or tapping it and then typing the password.

4. Your PC displays a message saying that your guru friend wants to look at your computer.

5. If you give the go-ahead, your guru friend can see what you're doing — look, but not touch.

6. Your guru friend may ask to take over your computer. If you give your permission, your guru friend takes complete control of your machine, with the ability to start any program on your computer, go into Settings, and so on.

   You watch as your friend types and clicks (or taps), just as *you* would if you knew what you were doing. Your friend solves the problem as you watch.

7. Either of you can break the connection at any time.

The thought of handing your machine over to somebody on an internet connection probably gives you the willies. I'm not real keen on it either, but Microsoft has built some industrial-strength controls into Remote Assistance. Your guru friend must supply the password that you specify before connecting to your computer. Your guru friend may take control of your computer only if your friend requests it and you specifically allow it. And you can put a time limit on the invitation: If your friend doesn't respond within an hour, say, the invitation is canceled.

## Making the connection

When you're ready to set up the connection for Remote Assistance, the following is what you need to do. (I'm writing this from the point of view of the person requesting assistance from a guru. If you're the guru in the interaction, you have to kind of stand on your head and read backward, but, hey, you're the guru and no doubt you knew that already, right?)

1. **Make sure that your guru friend is ready.**

   Call or shoot an email to remind your guru friend to have a PC on, connected to the internet, and running a reasonably recent version of Windows. Also, make sure that your friend has an instant messenger program cranked up, will check email frequently, or will wait for you to send a file or make one available on your network.

2. **Start your machine (the PC that your Remote Assistance friend, the guru, will take over), and make sure it's connected to the internet.**

   Make sure you aren't running any programs that you don't want the guru to see. Yes, that includes the Sudoku with the lousy score.

3. **Click or tap the search icon and type** invite. **On the top, choose Invite Someone to Connect to Your PC and Help You.**

   The Windows Remote Assistance dialog box appears, as shown in Figure 3-13.

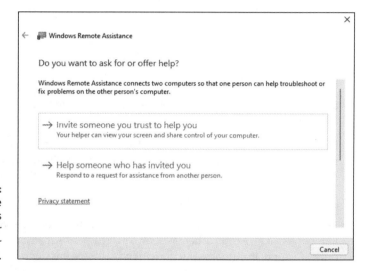

**FIGURE 3-13:**
Windows Remote Assistance wants to know whether you're giving or getting advice.

4. **Click or tap Invite Someone You Trust to Help You.**

   You don't actually have to trust this person but, well, you get the idea. Remote Assistance responds with the dialog box shown in Figure 3-14.

**TECHNICAL STUFF**

Easy Connect is an advanced version of Remote Assistance. It works for some people if they're connecting with another person who's running Windows. Unfortunately, sometimes network routers get in the way. The big gain with Easy Connect is that you set it up once, and then you can reuse the same connection any time you like, without going through the invitation/password routine.

The method I describe in the following steps works whether your router likes it or not. If you want to try Easy Connect, choose that option in Figure 3-14, and see whether your guru can connect. If it works, it's easy.

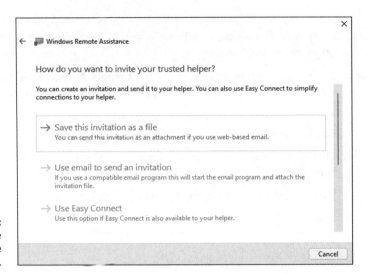

**FIGURE 3-14:**
The best choice
is to save the
invitation as a file.

**5.** **Choose Save This Invitation as a File.**

Even if you're going to email the file, it's easier to save the file first and then attach it to an email message.

Remote Assistance opens the Save As dialog box and prompts you to save the file Invitation.msrcIncident. You can change the name, if you like, but it's easier for your guru friend if you keep the filename extension *msrcIncident*.

**6.** **Save the file in a convenient place.**

Remote Assistance responds with an odd-looking dialog box, the Windows Remote Assistance control bar, as shown in Figure 3-15. It advises you to provide your helper (that's your guru friend) with the invitation file and the automatically generated 12-character password.

Windows 11 waits for your guru friend to contact you. You can continue to work, play Minesweeper, or do whatever it takes to keep you sane until your friend can connect.

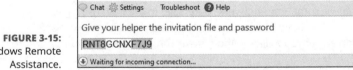

**FIGURE 3-15:**
Windows Remote
Assistance.

**7.** **Send the invitation file and the password to your guru friend via email, in a shared OneDrive folder, or a USB slipped into his hamburger at lunch.**

**8.** **Tell your friend to double-click or double-tap the invitation file to initiate the Remote Assistance session, type the password you've shared, and click or tap OK.**

Windows Remote Assistance then asks whether it's okay to allow your guru friend to connect to your computer (see Figure 3-16).

**FIGURE 3-16:**
Remote
Assistance
requires
your explicit
permission.

**9.** **Click or tap the Yes button.**

Two things happen simultaneously:

● Your computer's Remote Assistance bar shows that your guru is connected, as shown in Figure 3-17.

● Your guru friend's computer sets up a window that displays everything on your computer, as shown in Figure 3-18.

If your guru friend wants to take control of your PC, your friend needs to click or tap the Request Control icon on the Remote Assistance bar. If your guru friend does that, your machine warns you that your guru friend is trying to take control, as shown in Figure 3-19.

**FIGURE 3-17:**
Your computer
gets this Remote
Assistance bar.

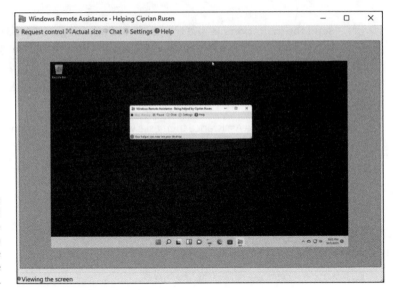

**FIGURE 3-18:**
Your guru friend
sees your entire
desktop in a
special Remote
Assistance
window.

**FIGURE 3-19:**
Allow your
guru friend to
take over.

**10.** **On your machine, click or tap Yes to allow your guru friend to take control of your PC.**

Your guru friend can now control your computer, move the mouse cursor, and type while you watch.

**11.** **Any time you want to sever the connection, click or tap X on the Remote Assistance bar.**

Your guru friend can sever the connection in the same way. In addition, you — the person who requested the session — can cancel the session at any time by pressing Esc.

It's a good idea to chat with your guru friend over the phone during the Remote Assistance session to make it more productive.

TIP

**REMEMBER**

After a Remote Assistance session is underway and you release control to your friend, your friend can do anything to your computer that you can do — anything at all, except change users. (If either logs off, the Remote Assistance connection is canceled.) Both of you have simultaneous control over the mouse pointer. If either or both of you type on the keyboard, the letters appear onscreen. You can stop your friend's control of your computer by pressing Esc.

**TECHNICAL STUFF**

Your friend can rest assured that this is a one-way connection. Your friend can take control of your computer, but you can't do anything on your friend's computer. Your friend can see everything that you can see on your desktop, but you aren't allowed to look at your friend's desktop. Whoever said life was fair?

## Troubleshooting Remote Assistance

Plenty of pitfalls lurk around the edges of Remote Assistance, but it mostly rates as an amazingly useful, powerful tool. The following are among the potential problems:

>> You and your guru friend must be connected to the internet or to the same local network. If you can't connect to the internet — especially if that's the problem you're trying to solve — you're out of luck.

>> Both of you must be running a version of Windows or another operating system that supports Remote Assistance. Sorry, your iPad doesn't qualify, but you can mix and match — you can be running Windows 11, while your friend is on Windows 10. Go ahead and gloat.

>> You must be able to give (or send) your guru friend a file so your friend can use the invitation to connect to your PC.

>> If a firewall sits between either of you and the internet, it may interfere with Remote Assistance. Windows Defender Firewall (the firewall included in Windows 11) doesn't intentionally block Remote Assistance, but other firewalls may. If you can't get through, contact your system administrator or dig into the firewall's documentation and unblock Port 3389 — the communication channel that Remote Assistance uses.

You — the person with the PC that will be taken over — must initiate the Remote Assistance session. Your guru friend can't tap you on the shoulder, electronically, and say something like this (with apologies to Dire Straits): "You an' me, babe, how 'bout it?"

# Getting Better Help Online

Microsoft is finally making it easier to chat with a real, live human being. But you may find better answers (and ones that conform less to the Microsoft Party Line) if you hop on to the Microsoft Answers forum at `https://answers.microsoft.com/`.

Lots of people join in on the forums to help (see the nearby sidebar). Many of the helpers are Microsoft MVPs (Most Valued Professionals) who work without pay, just for the joy of knowing that they're helping people. Microsoft gives the MVPs recognition and thanks, and some occasional benefits such as being able to talk with people on the development teams. In exchange, the MVPs give generally good — and sometimes excellent — support to anyone who asks.

## MICROSOFT ANSWERS FORUM

The Microsoft Answers forum is one of the great resources for Windows 11 customers. There are sections for just about every nook and cranny of every Microsoft product. You post questions, other people post answers, and it's free for everyone.

But it's important that you understand the limitations.

Most of the people on the Answers forum are not Microsoft employees — in fact, it's pretty rare to see Microsoft employees on the forum. (They're identified as Microsoft employees in their tag line.)

Although the typical forum denizen may be well intentioned, they aren't necessarily well informed. You must keep that in mind while wading through the questions and answers.

The Answers forum is a great place to go with immediate problems that may affect other people. It's one of the few ways that you can register a gripe and expect that, if it's a valid gripe, somebody at Microsoft will read it — and maybe respond to it.

In particular, realize that both the moderators and the Microsoft *Most Valued Professionals, or MVPs* (also identified in their tag lines) are volunteers. No, the moderators are not Microsoft employees. No, Microsoft doesn't pay the MVPs either. They help on the forums out of the goodness of their hearts. Hard to believe that in this day and age, but it's true. So be kind!

**REMEMBER**

Realize that support techs aren't frontline programmers or testers. Mostly, they're quite familiar with the most common problems and have access to lots of support systems that can answer myriad questions that aren't so common. Some of the techs may even have copies of this book on their desks.

If you have a really, really tough question and the tech you talk to can't solve it, ask to have your question escalated. Support has three levels of escalation, and in rare cases, some problems are escalated to the fourth level — which is where the product developers live. Kind of like Dante's *Paradiso*. If your problem is replicable — meaning it isn't caused by bad hardware or cosmic rays — and the tech can't solve it, you should politely ask for escalation.

**TIP**

If you or someone you know is at the beginner stage, do both of you a favor and get Andy Rathbone's *Windows 11 For Dummies*. The book will answer all your beginner's questions in terminology that you can understand.

# Chapter **4**

# Storing in Storage Spaces

For people who want to make sure that they never suffer a data loss — in spite of dying hard drives or backup routines that don't run properly — the Storage Spaces feature may, in and of itself, justify buying, installing, and using Windows 11.

Storage Spaces should not be mistaken with Storage Sense. The latter, which is entirely different, is used for cleaning up unnecessary files from Windows 11. You can learn more about it in Book 3, Chapter 7.

Some people prefer to back up to the cloud with OneDrive or Dropbox, but even if you do save backups on the internet, you'll feel a whole lot better knowing that the data you have here on earth is not going to disappear when a hard drive spins its last. On the other hand, if all your data is in the cloud all the time, you don't need to worry about local drives failing, and you can skip this chapter.

In this chapter, I introduce you to the Windows 11 approach to drive virtualization and how it enables Storage Spaces to work. Then, I go through setting up Storage Spaces and the tips and tricks you need to make Storages Spaces work for you. Using Storage Spaces for backup is quick and easy.

# Understanding the Virtualization of Storage

Windows 11's Storage Spaces takes care of disk management behind the scenes, so you don't have to. You'll never know (or care) which hard drives on your computer hold what folders or which files go where. Volumes and folders get extended as needed, and you don't have to lift a finger.

You don't have to worry about your D: drive running out of space because you don't *have* a D: drive. Or an E: drive. Windows 11 just grabs all the hard drive real estate you give it and hands out pieces of the hard drive as needed.

REMEMBER

If you have two or more physical hard drives of sufficient capacity, any data you store in a Storage Spaces pool is automatically mirrored between two or more independent hard drives. If one of the hard drives dies, you can still work with the ones that are alive, and you never miss a beat — not one bit is out of place. Run out and buy a new drive, stick it in the computer, tell Windows 11 that it can accept the new drive into Storage Spaces, wait an hour or two while Windows performs its magic, and all your data is back to normal. It's really that simple.

When your computer starts running out of disk space, Windows tells you. Install another drive — internal, external, USB, eSATA, whatever — and, with your permission, it's absorbed into the pool. More space becomes available, and you don't need to care about any of the details — no new drive letters, no partitions, no massive copying or moving files from one drive to another, no home brew backup hacks. For those accustomed to Windows' whining, the Storage Spaces approach to disk management feels like a breath of fresh air.

When you add a new hard drive to the Storage Spaces pool, everything that was on that new hard drive gets obliterated. You don't have any choice. No data on the drive survives — it's all wiped out. That's the price the drive pays for being absorbed into Storage Spaces.

Here's a high-level overview of how you set up Storage Spaces with data mirroring:

1. Tell Windows 11 that it can use two or more drives as a storage pool.

   Your C: drive — the drive that contains Windows — cannot be part of the pool.

**TIP**

   The best configuration for Storage Spaces: Get a fast solid-state drive for your system files and make that the C: drive. Then get two or more big drives for storing all your data. The big drives can be slow, but you'll hardly notice. You can use a mixture of spinning disks and solid-state disks if you like.

2. After you set up a pool of physical hard drives, you can create one or more spaces.

   In practice, most home and small business users will want only one space. But you can create more if you like.

3. Establish a maximum size for each space, and choose a mirroring technology, if you want the data mirrored.

   The maximum size can be much bigger than the total amount of space available on all your hard drives. That's one of the advantages of virtualization: If you run out of physical hard drive space, instead of turning belly up and croaking, Windows 11 just asks you to feed it another drive.

**TECHNICAL STUFF**

   For a discussion of the available mirroring technologies, see the sidebar "Mirroring technologies in Storage Spaces."

4. If a drive dies, keep going and put in a new drive when you can. If you want to replace a drive with a bigger (or more reliable) one, tell Windows to get rid of (*dismount*) the old drive, wait an hour or so, turn off the PC, yank the drive, stick in a new one, and away you go.

   It's that simple.

## MIRRORING TECHNOLOGIES IN STORAGE SPACES

When it comes to mirroring — Microsoft calls it *resiliency* — you have four choices. You can

- Choose to *not mirror* at all. That way, you lose the automatic real-time backup, but you still get the benefits of pooled storage.

- Designate a space as a *two-way mirrored* space, thus telling Windows 11 that it should automatically keep backup copies of everything in the space on at least two separate hard drives and recover from dead hard drives automatically as well. It's important to realize that your programs don't even know that the data's being mirrored. Storage Spaces takes care of all the details behind the scenes.

- Use *three-way mirroring,* which is only for the most fanatical people with acres of hard drive space to spare.

- Use another form of redundancy called *parity,* which calculates check sums on your data and stores the sums in such a way that the data can be reconstructed from dead disks without having two full copies of the original file sitting around. This approach takes up less room than full mirroring, but there's higher overhead in processing input and output. Microsoft recommends that you use parity mirroring only on big files accessed sequentially — videos, for example — or on files you don't update very often.

**TIP**

If you've ever heard of RAID (Redundant Array of Inexpensive Disks) technology, you may think that Storage Spaces sounds familiar. The concepts are similar in some respects, but Storage Spaces doesn't use RAID. Instead of relying on specialized hardware and fancy controllers — both hallmarks of a RAID installation — all of Storage Spaces is built into Windows 11 itself, and Storage Spaces can use any kind of hard drive — internal, external, IDE, SATA, USB, eSATA, you name it — in any size, mix or match. No need for any special hardware or software.

# Setting Up Storage Spaces

Even though you can set up Storage Spaces with just two hard drives — your C: system drive plus one data drive — you don't get much benefit out of it until you move up to three drives. So, in this section, I assume that you have your C: drive, plus two more hard drives — internal, external, eternal, infernal, whatever — hooked up to your PC. I further assume that those two hard drives have absolutely nothing on them that you want to keep — because they will get blasted. Guaranteed.

Ready to set up a space? Here's how:

**1.** **Hook up your drives, log in to Windows 11 using an administrator account, and then go to File Explorer and verify that Windows 11 has identified three drives.**

In Figure 4-1, I have three drives. The C: drive has my Windows 11 operating system on it; C:'s the boot drive. The other two (E: and F:) have miscellaneous junk that I don't want to keep, and the D: drive is my Blu-Ray disc reader.

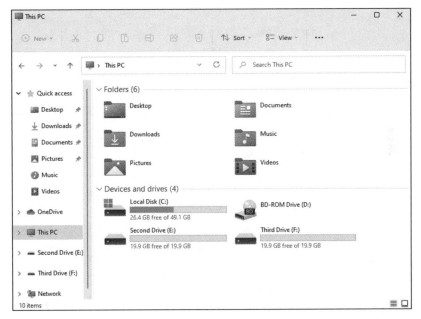

**FIGURE 4-1:**
Start with three drives, two for your storage pool.

**2.** **Bring up the Control Panel. Click or tap System and Security, and then click or tap Storage Spaces.**

Or type **storage spaces** in the Windows 11 Start menu.

If you choose either Storage Spaces or Manage Storage Spaces, you see the Storage Spaces screen, as shown in Figure 4-2.

**3.** **Click or tap the Create a New Pool and Storage Space link and then answer Yes to the UAC prompt that shows up.**

You must create a storage pool first — that is, assign physical hard drives to the storage pool. Windows 11 offers to create a storage pool, as shown in Figure 4-3.

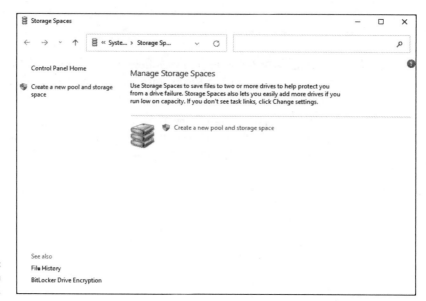

**FIGURE 4-2:**
Create a
storage pool.

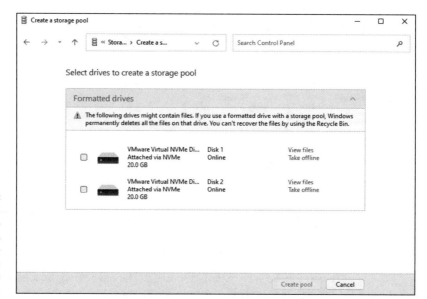

**FIGURE 4-3:**
Windows 11
allows you to
pool any drives
other than those
that contain the
boot and system
partitions.

WARNING

**4.** **Select the check boxes next to the drives that you want to include in the storage pool. Be careful! If you accidentally select a drive that contains useful data, your data is going to disappear. Irretrievably.**

And I do mean *irretrievably*. You can't use Recuva or some other disk-scanning tool to bring back your data. After the drive is absorbed into the storage pool, it's gone.

## 5. Click or tap Create Pool.

Windows 11 whizzes and wheezes and whirs for a while, and displays the Create a Storage Space dialog box, as shown in Figure 4-4.

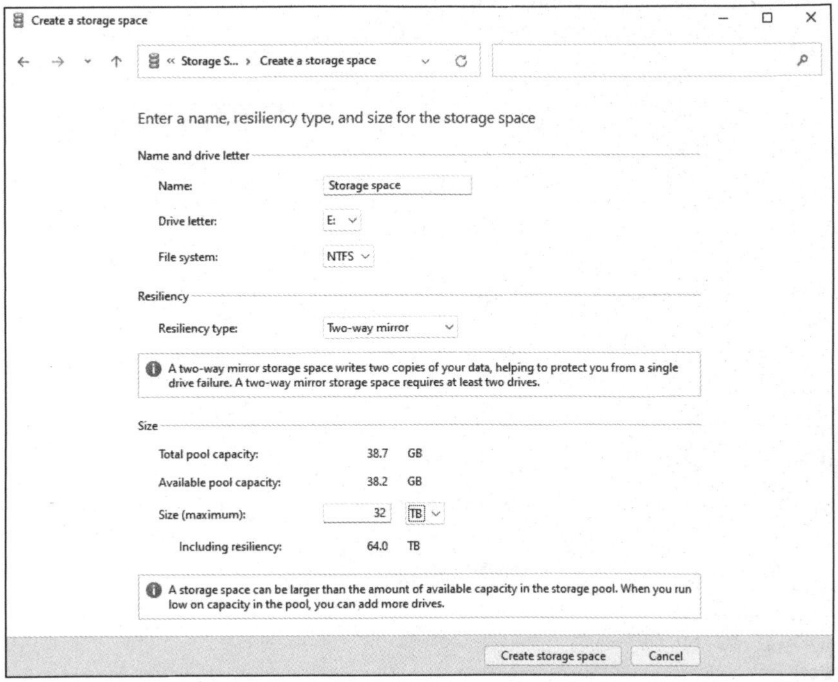

**FIGURE 4-4:**
Windows 11 wants you to give the new storage space a name and drive letter and choose the mirroring and the maximum size.

## 6. Give your storage space a name and a drive letter.

You use the name and the letter in the same way that you now use a drive letter and drive name — even though the storage space spans two or more hard drives. You can format the storage space drive, copy data to or from the drive, and even partition the drive, even though there's no real, physical drive involved.

## 7. Choose a resiliency type.

For a discussion of your four choices — no mirroring, two-way, three-way, and parity — see the sidebar "Mirroring technologies in Storage Spaces" earlier in this chapter.

## 8. Set a logical size for the storage space.

As mentioned, the logical size of the storage space can greatly exceed the available hard drive space. There's no downside to having an exceptionally large logical size, other than a bit of overhead in some internal tables. Shoot for the moon. In this case, I turned less than 1 terabyte of actual, physical storage into a 32TB virtual monstrosity.

**9.** Click or tap **Create Storage Space.**

Windows 11 whirs and sets up a freshly formatted storage space.

**10.** **Go back to File Explorer and verify that you have a new drive, which is, in fact, an enormously humongous storage space.**

You see something like Figure 4-5.

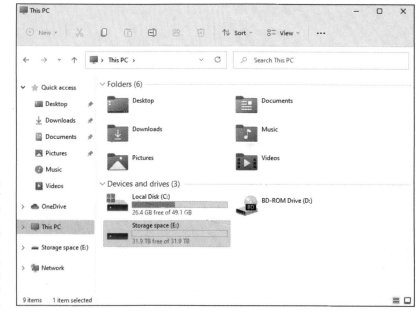

**FIGURE 4-5:** If it weren't for the fact that you just created it, you probably wouldn't be able to tell that the new storage space isn't a real drive.

# Working with Storage Spaces

First, realize that to the outside world, your storage space looks just like any other hard drive. You can use the drive letter the same way you'd use any other drive letter. The folders inside work like any other folders. And if you have a cranky old program that requires a simple drive letter, the storage space won't do anything to spoil the illusion. That said, storage space drives can't be defragmented or run through the Check Disk utility.

Here's the grand tour of the inner workings of your storage space:

1.  **Bring up the Control Panel. Click or tap System and Security, and then Storage Spaces.**

    An alternative is to go to the Windows 11 Start menu and type **storage spaces**. If you choose either Storage Spaces or Manage Storage Spaces, the Storage Spaces screen appears, this time with a storage space.

2.  **At the bottom, click or tap the down arrow next to Physical Drives.**

    The full Storage Spaces status report appears, as shown in Figure 4-6.

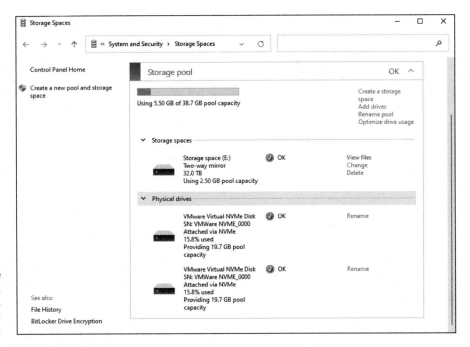

**FIGURE 4-6:** Full details of your storage space and the storage pool it sits in.

The Storage Spaces report tells you how much real, physical hard drive space you're using; what the storage space looks like to your Windows 11 programs; and how your physical hard drives have been carved up to support all that glorious, unfettered space.

It's quite a testament to the designers of Storage Spaces that all this works so well — and invisibly to the rest of Windows. This is the way storage should've been implemented years ago!

# Storage Space Strategies

You can save yourself a headache by following a few simple tricks:

>> Use your fastest hard drive as your C: drive. (If you have a solid-state drive, use it for C:) Don't tie it into a storage space.

>> If a hard drive starts acting up — you see an error report, in any of a dozen different places — remove it from the storage space. Refer to the Take Offline option in Figure 4-3. Replace it at your earliest convenience.

>> Remember, in a three-drive installation, where two drives are in the storage space, the two-way mirror option limits you to the amount of room available on the smaller storage space drive.

>> When you need to add more drives, don't take out the existing drives. The more drives in storage space, the greater your flexibility.

# Chapter **5**

# Working with Printers

The paperless office. What a wonderful concept! No more file cabinets bulging with misfiled flotsam. No more hernias from hauling cartons of copy paper, dumping the sheets 500 at a time into a thankless plastic maw. No more trees dying in agony, relinquishing their last gasps to provide pulp as a substrate for heat-fused carbon toner. No more coffee-stained reports. No more paper cuts.

No more . . . oh, who am I trying to kid? No way.

Industry prognosticators have been telling people for decades that the paperless office is right around the corner. Yeah, sure. Maybe around *your* corner. Around *my* corner, I predict that PC printers will disappear about the same time as the last *Star Trek* sequel. We're talking geologic time here, folks. We're slowly getting rid of printers, but like fax machines, they're not going to vanish with the next version of Windows.

The biggest problem? Finding a printer that doesn't cost two arms and three legs to, uh, print. Toner cartridges cost a fortune. Ink costs two fortunes. That bargain-basement printer you can get for $65 will probably print about twenty pages before it starts begging for a refill. And four or five refills can easily cost as much as the printer.

**TIP**

One of the best developments in the printing world is the network-connected printer — one that attaches to a network router, either through a wired or Wi-Fi connection, bypassing PCs entirely — and now this type of printer is finally affordable. In my experience, printers attached to and used by one PC work best. However, failing a one-to-one correspondence, network-attached printers have far fewer problems than the ones tethered to a specific machine on a network.

And 3D printers? Whoa, Nelly! They're here — and from what I've seen, they hook up just as easily as laser printers. Paying for them and running them is another story, of course.

And because you're here to learn about printers, you should know that Windows 11 has excellent printer support. Getting your printer to work well is easy after you grasp a few basic skills.

In this chapter, I show you how to install a printer in a home network, as well as the basics about using and troubleshooting your printer. Eventually, we all run into problems at some point, no matter how expensive and advanced our printer is.

# Installing a Printer

You have three ways to make a printer available to your computer:

>> Attach the printer directly to the computer.

>> Connect your computer to a network and attach the printer to another computer on the same network.

>> If the printer can attach directly to a network, connect your computer to the same network and attach the printer directly to the network's router or switch, either with a network cable or via a Wi-Fi connection.

Having used all three attachment methods for many years, I can tell you without reservation that, if you have a home network, it's worth getting a Wi-Fi-connected printer.

**REMEMBER**

Connecting a computer directly to a network router or switch isn't difficult if you have the right hardware. Each printer is different, though, so follow the manufacturer's instructions.

## Attaching a local printer

So, you have a new printer and want to use it. Attaching it *locally* — which is to say, plugging it directly into your PC — is the simplest way to install a printer, and it's the only option if you don't have a network.

All modern printers that connect to a PC have a USB connector that plugs into your computer. (Network-attached printers work differently; see the next section.) In theory, you plug the connector into your PC's USB port and turn on the printer, and then Windows 11 recognizes it and installs the appropriate drivers. You're done!

**TIP**

However, it's a good idea to use the CD that came with the printer or go to the manufacturer's website and download the latest drivers for your printer model. Older printers don't have Windows 11 drivers on their CDs, so a visit to the manufacturer's website will be mandatory. To help you with that, refer to Table 5-1.

**WARNING**

While I recommend that you install the manufacturer's software, keep in mind not to blindly accept all the recommended apps. Some are junk. For example, my Canon Pixma G7000 series printer offers the utilities shown in Figure 5-1 alongside the drivers that make it tick. I don't need most of those utilities, although some people do. Select what makes sense for you.

When the printer is installed properly, you can see it in the Printers & Scanners list. To get there, click or tap the Start icon and then the Settings icon. Next, go to Bluetooth & Devices and click or tap Printers & Scanners. You see a list similar to the one in Figure 5-2.

**REMEMBER**

If you don't know where to find the latest drivers for your printer, check out the list of websites in Table 5-1. Note that these links might change as companies revamp or reorganize their sites. Can't find the right site? Google is your friend.

Working with Printers

**TABLE 5-1**

## Driver Sites for Major Printer Manufacturers

| Manufacturer | Find Drivers at This URL |
|---|---|
| Brother | www.brother-usa.com/brother-support |
| Canon | https://global.canon/en/support/ |
| Dell | www.dell.com/support/home/en-us//products |
| Epson | https://epson.com/Support/sl/s |
| HP | https://support.hp.com/us-en/drivers |
| Samsung | www.samsung.com/us/support/downloads/ |

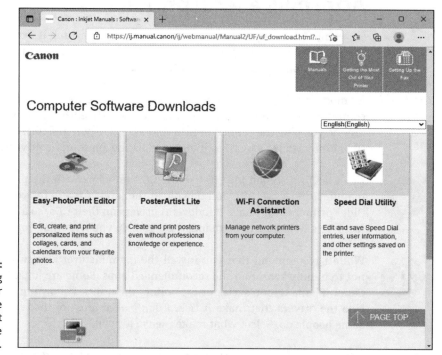

**FIGURE 5-1:**
When installing drivers for your printer, be mindful of what other software you install.

## Installing a network printer

If you have a network, you can attach a printer to (almost) any computer on the network and have it accessible to all users on (almost) all computers in the network. You can also attach different printers to different computers and let network users select the printer they want to use as the need arises. However, the best idea is to buy one Wi-Fi printer, connect it to the wireless network broadcast by your router, and then add it to all the computers that you want to have access to it.

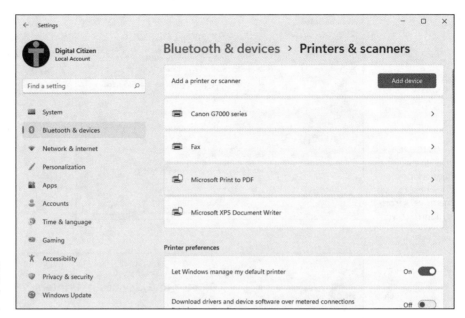

**FIGURE 5-2:**
Your printers and
scanners appear
in this list.

Before you install a network printer, first download the latest drivers from the manufacturer's website and use those to guide you through the setup process. Again, refer to Table 5-1 for the list of websites with drivers for the major printer manufacturers.

The setup wizard for my Canon Pixma G7000 series printer carefully guided me through the setup process based on the connection method I choose, as shown in Figure 5-3.

If you don't like the setup process offered by the printer's manufacturer or you can't find the printer's drivers, you can use the options offered by Windows 11 to install it. Here's how:

1. **Click or tap the Start icon and then Settings. On the left, choose Bluetooth & Devices.**

2. **On the right, click or tap Printers & Scanners.**

   The Printer list appears, as shown previously in Figure 5-2.

3. **At the top, click or tap the Add Device button.**

   Windows 11 looks all through your network to see whether any printers are available and displays any printers that are turned on, as shown in Figure 5-4.

**Working with Printers**

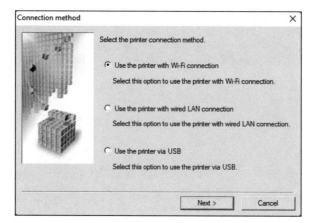

**FIGURE 5-3:**
When installing a network printer, it's best to use the drivers from its manufacturer.

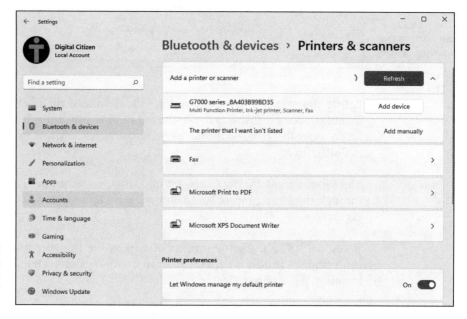

**FIGURE 5-4:**
Windows 11 lists the printers that it finds on your network.

4. **Click or tap Add Device next to the name of the printer you want to install.**

   Windows 11 looks to see whether it has a driver handy for that printer. It whirs and clanks for a while and then tells you that the printer is ready.

5. **To set the newly added printer as your default, scroll down and set to off the Let Windows Manage My Default Printer switch, by clicking or tapping it.**

**6.** **Click or tap the name of your printer.**

Windows 11 displays several links and buttons for configuring your printer, as shown in Figure 5-5.

**7.** **Click or tap the Set as Default button, and then close Settings.**

Your new printer appears in the Printers & Scanners list and is set as the default.

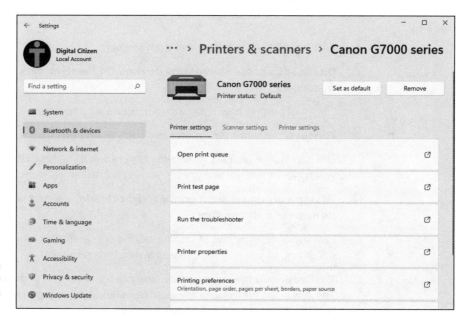

**FIGURE 5-5:**
Setting the new printer as the default.

# Using the Print Queue

You may have noticed that when you print a document from an application, the application reports that printing is finished before the printer finishes printing. If the document is long enough, you can print several more documents from one or more applications while the printer works on the first one. This is possible because Windows 11 saves printed documents in a *print queue* until it can print them.

If more than one printer is installed on your computer or network, each one has its own print queue. The queue is maintained on the host PC — that is, the PC to which the printer is attached.

If you have a network-attached printer, the printer itself maintains a print queue. Windows 11 uses print queues automatically, so you don't even have to know that they exist. If you know the tricks though, you can control them in several useful ways.

## Displaying a print queue

You can display information about any documents that you currently have in a printer's queue by following these steps:

1. **Click or tap the Start icon and then Settings.**

2. **On the left, choose Bluetooth & Devices. On the right, click or tap Printers & Scanners.**

   The list of printers previously shown in Figure 5-2 appears.

3. **Click or tap the printer's name and then Open Print Queue.**

   The print queue appears, as shown in Figure 5-6. If you have documents waiting for more than one printer, you get more than one print queue report.

4. **To stop a document from printing, right-click (or tap and hold down on) its name and choose Cancel.**

   In many cases, Windows 11 must notify the printer that it's canceling the document, so you may have to wait awhile for a response.

   The Owner column tells you which user put the document in the print queue. The jobs in the print queue are listed from oldest at the top to newest at the bottom. The Status column shows which job is printing.

5. **Keep the print queue window open for later use or minimize the print queue window and keep it on the taskbar.**

   Keeping it open can be handy if you're running a long or complex print job.

TIP

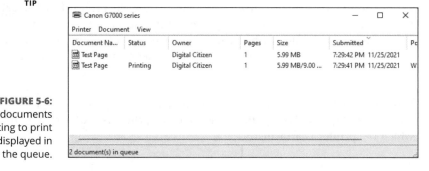

**FIGURE 5-6:**
The documents waiting to print are displayed in the queue.

# Pausing and resuming a print queue

When you *pause* a print queue, Windows 11 stops printing documents from it. If a document is printing when you pause the queue, Windows tries to finish printing the document and then stops. When you *resume* a print queue, Windows starts printing documents from the queue again. Follow these guidelines to pause and resume a print queue:

>> **To pause a print queue,** when you're looking at the print queue window (refer to Figure 5-6), choose Printer and then Pause Printing.

>> **To resume the print queue,** choose the same command again. The check mark in front of the Pause Printing line disappears, and the printing resumes.

**TIP**

Why would you want to pause the print queue? Say you want to print a page for later reference, but you don't want to bother turning on your printer to print just one page. Pause the printer's queue, and then print the page. The next time you turn on the printer and resume the print queue, the remaining pages will be printed.

Sometimes, Windows 11 has a tough time finishing the document — for example, you may be dealing with print buffer overruns (see the "Troubleshooting Printing" section, later in this chapter) — and every time you clear the printer, it may try to reprint the overrun pages. If that happens to you, pause the print queue, and turn off the printer. As soon as the printer comes back online, Windows is smart enough to pick up where it left off.

Also, depending on how your network is set up, you may or may not be able to pause and resume a print queue on a printer attached to another user's computer or to a network.

# Pausing, restarting, and resuming a document

Here are some other reasons you may want to pause a document. Consider the following:

>> Suppose you're printing a web page that documents an online order you just placed, and the printer jams. You've already finished entering the order, and you have no way to display the page again to reprint it. Pause the document, clear the printer, and restart the document.

>> Here's another common situation where pausing comes in handy. You're printing a long document, and the phone rings. You don't want to hear the printer while you talk, so pause the document. When you're finished talking, resume printing the document.

Here's how pausing, restarting, and resuming work:

>> **Pause a document:** When you pause a document, Windows 11 is prevented from printing that document. It skips the document and prints later documents in the queue. If you pause a document while Windows is printing it, Windows halts in the middle of the document and prints nothing on that printer until you take further action.

>> **Restart a document:** When you restart a document, Windows 11 is again allowed to print it. If the document is at the top of the queue, Windows prints it as soon as it finishes the document that it's now printing. If the document was being printed when it was paused, Windows stops printing it and starts again at the beginning.

>> **Resume a document:** Resuming a document is meaningful only if you paused it while Windows was printing it. When you resume a document, Windows resumes printing it where it paused.

REMEMBER

To pause a document, right-click (or tap and hold down on) the document in the print queue and choose Pause. The window displays the document's status as Paused. To resume the paused document, right-click or tap and hold down on that document and choose Resume.

## Canceling a document

When you cancel a document, Windows removes it from the print queue without printing it. You may have heard computer jocks use the term *purged* or *zapped* or something unprintable.

TIP

Here's a common situation where document canceling comes in handy. You start printing a long document, and as soon as the first page comes out, you realize that you forgot to set the heading. What to do? Cancel the document, change the heading, and print the document again.

To cancel a document, select that document. In the print queue window, choose Document, and then Cancel. Or right-click (or tap and hold down on) the document in the print queue window and choose Cancel. You can also select the document and press Delete on your keyboard.

REMEMBER

No Recycle Bin exists for the print queue. When you delete a document from the print queue, it's gone from the printing process. However, the document still remains available as a file on your computer.

Conversely, most printers have built-in memory that stores pages while they're being printed. Network-attached printers can have sizable buffers. You may go to the print queue to look for a document, only to discover that it isn't there. If the document has already been shuffled off to the printer's internal memory, the only way to cancel it is to turn off the printer.

# Troubleshooting Printing

The following list describes some typical problems with printers and the solutions to those sticky spots:

>> **I'm trying to install a printer. I connected it to my computer, and Windows doesn't detect its presence.** Be sure that the printer is turned on and that the cable from the printer to your computer is properly connected at both ends. Check the printer's manual; you may have to follow a procedure (such as push a button) to make the printer ready for use.

>> **I'm trying to install a printer that's connected to another computer on my network, and Windows doesn't detect its presence.** I know that the printer is okay; it's already installed and working as a local printer on that system! If the printer is attached to a Windows 10 PC, the PC may be set to treat the network as a public network — in which case, it doesn't share anything. To rectify the problem, set the network as private, and then right-click (or tap and hold down on) the printer and choose Sharing. (For details, see *Windows 10 All-in-One For Dummies,* published by John Wiley & Sons.)

>> **I can't use a shared printer that I've used successfully in the past.** Windows 11 says that it isn't available when I try to use it, or Windows doesn't even show it as an installed printer anymore. This situation can happen if something interferes with your connection to the network or the connection to the printer's host computer. It can also happen if something interferes with the availability of the printer — for example, if the host computer's user has turned off sharing.

If you can't find a problem or if you find and correct a problem (such as file and printer sharing being turned off), but you still can't use the printer, try restarting Windows on your own system. If that doesn't help, remove the printer from your system and reinstall it.

To remove the printer from your system, follow the instructions in the next section. To reinstall the printer on your system, use the same procedure you used to install it originally. (See the "Installing a network printer" section, earlier in this chapter.)

**Working with Printers**

» **I printed a document, but it never came out of the printer.** If the printer is attached to just one PC, check the printer's print queue on the host PC (the one directly attached to the printer). If the printer is attached to a network, check the print queue on any attached PC. Is the document there? If not, investigate several possible reasons:

- *The printer isn't turned on or is out of paper.* Hey, don't laugh. I've done it. In some cases, Windows 11 can't distinguish a printer that's connected but not turned on from a printer that's ready, and it sends documents to a printer that isn't operating.

- *You accidentally sent the document to some other printer.* Hey, don't laugh — you've heard that one.

- *Someone else unintentionally picked up your document and walked off with it.*

- *The printer is turned on but not ready to print, and the printer (as opposed to the host PC) is holding your entire document in its internal memory until it can start printing.* A printer can hold several hundred — or even several thousand — pages of output internally, depending on the size of its internal memory and the complexity of the pages. Network-attached printers frequently have 16MB or more of dedicated buffer memory, which is enough for a hundred or more pages of lightly formatted text.

If your document is in the print queue but isn't printing, check for these problems:

- *The printer may not be ready to print.* See whether it's plugged in, turned on, and properly connected to your computer or its host computer.

- *Your document may be paused.*

- *The print queue itself may be paused.*

- *The printer may be printing another document that's paused.*

- *The printer may be thinking.* If it's a laser printer or another type of printer that composes an entire page in internal memory *before* it starts to print, it appears to do nothing while it processes photographs or other complex graphics. Processing may take as long as several minutes.

  Look at the printer and study its manual. The printer may have a blinking light or a status display that tells you it's doing something. As you become familiar with the printer, you'll develop a feel for how long various types of jobs should take.

- *The printer is offline, out of paper, jammed, or unready to print for some other reason.*

# Removing a printer

If you need to uninstall a printer from Windows 11 for troubleshooting or just because you don't use it anymore, follow these steps:

1. **Click or tap the Start icon and then Settings.**

2. **On the left, choose Bluetooth & Devices. On the right, click or tap Printers & Scanners.**

   You see the list of printers previously shown in Figure 5-2.

3. **Click or tap the printer's name and then the Remove button (at the top).**

   Windows 11 asks you to confirm that you want to remove the device, as shown in Figure 5-7.

4. **Click or tap Yes.**

   The printer is removed, and you won't see the its name in the list of available printers unless you reinstall it.

**FIGURE 5-7:** Windows asks you to confirm that you want to remove your printer.

# Stopping a print job you've sent by mistake

Mistakenly starting a print job must be the most common, most frustrating problems in printer–dumb.

**REMEMBER**

You print a document and, as it starts to come out the printer, you realize that you're printing a zillion pages you don't want. How do you stop the printer and reset it so that it doesn't try to print the same bad stuff, all over again?

Here's what you do:

1. **Turn off the printer. Pull the paper out of the printer's paper feeder.**

   Be careful with this step to avoid roller damage or paper tears that will cause problems later.

   This step stops the immediate problem, uh, immediately.

2. **On the desktop, in the lower-right corner, look among the icons for one that looks like a printer; double-click or double-tap it.**

   The print queue appears (refer to Figure 5-6).

3. **Right-click (or tap and hold down on) the runaway print job and choose Cancel.**

   If this step deletes the bad print job, good for you.

4. **If the bad print job was not deleted, reboot Windows 11. When Windows comes back, turn the printer back on.**

   Your bad job should be banished forever.

# Chapter 6

# Working with USB and Bluetooth Devices

N obody uses CDs, DVDs, or Blu-Ray discs anymore. The world has been swept away by USB flash drives and USB hard disks instead. And for good reasons: They are cheap, small, and easy to carry around. You can write any data on them, and they work plug-and-play with all operating systems — even with Android, if you have a USB Type C flash drive to connect to your smartphone.

Therefore, it makes sense to have a USB flash drive around. And if you're using one or more, it's a good idea to know how to get around some annoyances, like the AutoPlay dialog you see every time you plug in a USB device. Also, even if Microsoft says otherwise, it's good to know when it's safe to unplug a USB device from your computer, so, I share some tips on that.

Continuing the discussion about devices, Bluetooth devices are popular too, due to everyone using smartphones and tablets. Windows 11 works with Bluetooth devices if your computer has a Bluetooth chip. Most Windows laptops and tablets have Bluetooth, while most desktop PCs don't. If you need Bluetooth and you don't have it inside your PC, just buy a Bluetooth USB adapter. They're cheap and easily found on Amazon and at other places.

But why do you need Bluetooth? You may want to connect a Bluetooth mouse and keyboard and get rid of wires. You may want to connect a Bluetooth speaker to listen to music with better sound than your laptop can provide or a Bluetooth headset for conference calls.

In this chapter, I show you how to do all that, as well as how to disconnect Bluetooth devices from Windows 11.

# Connecting USB Devices

Attaching a USB device to a Windows 11 computer is easy. Simply plug in your device into a free USB port. The operating system detects the device automatically and displays an AutoPlay notification in the bottom-right corner of the screen, as shown in Figure 6-1. This notification tells you that a USB drive was detected and its drive letter, and asks you to choose what happens with removable drives.

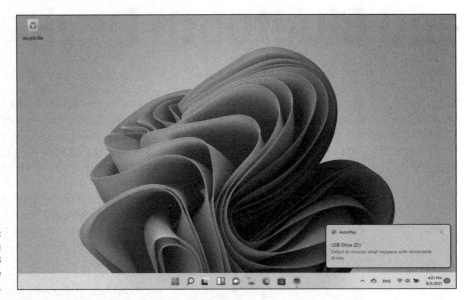

**FIGURE 6-1:**
Each time you plug in a USB device, you see this notification.

You can ignore the notification; it will go to the notification center (see Book 2, Chapter 3 to learn more). Or you can click or tap it and choose what you want Windows to do. The options you see depend on the apps installed in Windows 11 and the device you plugged in. For example, if you don't have Dropbox installed, you won't see the Import Photos and Videos option shown in Figure 6-2.

USB Drive (D:)

Choose what to do with removable drives.

Configure storage settings
Settings

Import photos and videos
Dropbox

Open folder to view files
File Explorer

Take no action

**FIGURE 6-2:**
Options for
handling
removable drives.

TECHNICAL
STUFF

Windows 11 remembers your choice, and the next time you plug in a USB drive, it automatically does what you selected. It doesn't matter whether you plug in the same USB flash drive or another. This action is repeated over and over.

## Configuring AutoPlay for removable devices

If you work with many USB devices, you may not like the AutoPlay dialogs you see each time you plug in something. Or you may have made the wrong choice when asked what to do with removable devices, and you want Windows 11 to stop. Here's how to disable or configure AutoPlay to do what you want:

1. **Click or tap the Start icon and then Settings. Alternatively, press Windows+I on your keyboard.**

   The Settings app is shown on the screen.

2. **In the column on the left, choose Bluetooth & Devices.**

3. **On the right, scroll down to AutoPlay and click or tap it.**

   The AutoPlay settings appear, as shown in Figure 6-3.

4. **If you want to disable the AutoPlay dialogs completely, set the Use AutoPlay for All Media And Devices switch to off by clicking or tapping it.**

   The feature is now disabled, and you will no longer see any prompts when you plug something into your Windows 11 computer.

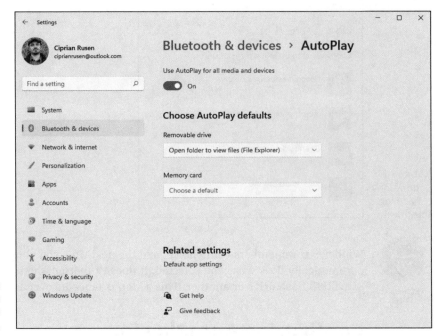

**FIGURE 6-3:**
You can choose
to disable
AutoPlay.

5. **If you want to change what AutoPlay does for removable devices, click or tap the drop-down list for Removable Drive (under Choose AutoPlay Defaults).**

   A list of options appears, as shown in Figure 6-4.

6. **Choose an action from the list.**

   If you don't want AutoPlay to do anything, select Take No Action. If you want it to ask you what you want each time you plug in a USB device, choose Ask Me Every Time.

7. **Close the Settings app.**

   Your settings are applied immediately.

## Removing USB devices

In Windows 10, Microsoft developed a feature called quick removal, which lets you unplug a USB drive anytime you want. This is the default setting for both Windows 10 and Windows 11, and most people will tell you that when you want to disconnect a USB flash drive or hard disk from your PC, you just yank it out of the USB port.

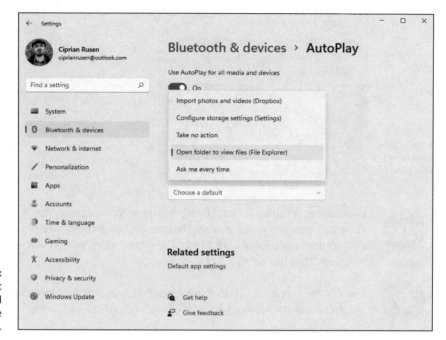

**FIGURE 6-4:**
Choose what AutoPlay should do for removable drives.

However, you may not know whether an app or Windows is actively writing data on it. If this happens and you eject the drive, the data on it might get corrupted. Also, you don't get to save the latest modifications made to it. To avoid such situations, I recommend using the Safely Remove Hardware option, like you used to do back in the days of Windows 7. Here's how it works in Windows 11:

**1.** **With the USB drive still plugged in, click or tap the arrow pointing upwards, in the bottom-right corner of the desktop.**

The icon is named show hidden icons, and after you click it, it shows a list of, well, hidden icons.

**2.** **In the list of hidden icons, click or tap the icon that looks like a USB flash drive.**

You see a list with the USB devices connected to your computer, as shown in Figure 6-5.

**3.** **Click or tap the Eject option for the USB device that you want to unplug.**

After a few seconds, Windows tells you that it's Safe to Remove Hardware, in a notification at the bottom-right corner of the screen.

**4.** **Unplug the USB device from your computer.**

**FIGURE 6-5:**
Choose the USB
device you want
to remove safely.

**WARNING**

If Windows 11 tells you that the device is currently in use, don't unplug it until you close all open apps, and ensure that no data is actively written on it. Once you do that, repeat the process, and eject the device after you receive confirmation from Windows that it's safe to do so.

**TIP**

You can remove a USB flash drive from File Explorer too: go to This PC, right-click (or press and hold down on) the USB drive, and select Eject.

# Connecting Bluetooth Devices

Connecting Bluetooth devices to a Windows 11 laptop or tablet starts with pairing them. Consider it as a mandatory approval process before Bluetooth devices can transmit data to each other. When you connect Bluetooth devices to Windows 11, you follow the same steps, with a few minor differences: Bluetooth keyboards require an additional step than other types of Bluetooth devices such as mice or headsets. Let's see how to connect your Windows 11 computer with a Bluetooth device:

1. **Click or tap the Start icon and then Settings.**

   The Settings app appears on the screen.

2. **In the column on the left, choose Bluetooth & Devices, and make sure that the Bluetooth switch is on.**

   You see all the options and settings for handling Bluetooth and other types of devices, as shown in Figure 6-6.

3. **To start the connection process, click or tap the + Add Device button on the right.**

   The Add a Device window appears, as shown in Figure 6-7, with options for connecting all kinds of wireless devices.

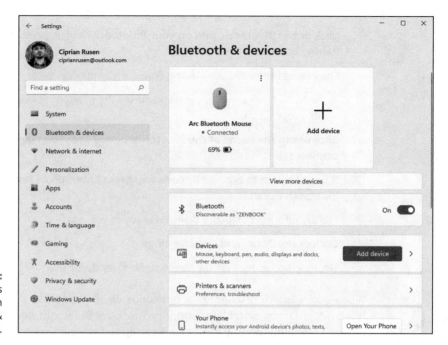

**FIGURE 6-6:**
Adding devices
starts in
Bluetooth &
devices.

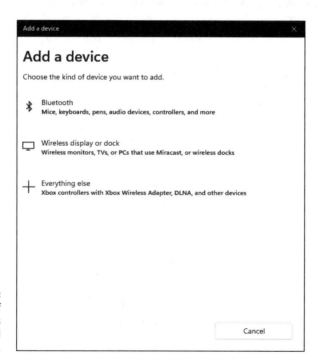

**FIGURE 6-7:**
The types of
wireless devices
that you can add
to Windows 11.

4. **Click or tap Bluetooth, and on your Bluetooth device, press the Pairing button.**

   The Pairing button usually has the Bluetooth symbol on it.

   In the Add a Device window, you should see the Bluetooth device that you want to connect to.

5. **Click or tap the name of the Bluetooth device that you want to connect to.**

6. **If you're asked to type a PIN code and press Enter, do as requested on the Bluetooth device.**

   You are informed that your device is ready to go.

7. **Click or tap Done, and close Settings.**

   The Bluetooth device is now connected and ready for use.

TIP

When you want to disconnect a Bluetooth device but leave it paired with your Windows 11 laptop or tablet, simply turn off the Bluetooth device. Alternatively, to stop using Bluetooth, you can click or tap the network icon or the volume icon on the right end of the taskbar to open Quick Settings, and then click or tap the Bluetooth icon.

# Unpairing Bluetooth Devices

If you no longer want to use a Bluetooth device, it's a good idea to remove it from Windows 11 so that your computer no longer searches for it. The process is quick and painless:

1. **Click or tap the Start icon and then Settings.**

   The Settings app appears.

2. **In the column on the left, choose Bluetooth & Devices.**

3. **On the right, click or tap Devices.**

   You see all the devices connected to Windows 11 (Bluetooth and others), as shown in Figure 6-8.

4. **Find the Bluetooth device that you don't want to use anymore and click or tap the three dots to the right of its name.**

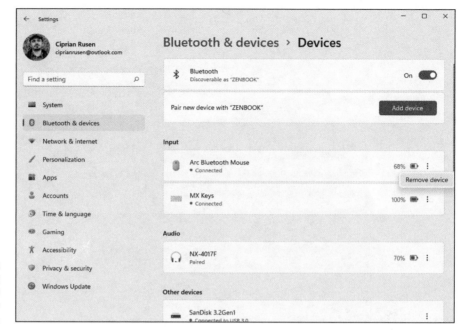

FIGURE 6-8:
Removing
Bluetooth devices
requires a few
clicks or taps.

**5.** **Click or tap Remove Device, and then Yes, to confirm.**

The Bluetooth device is removed from the list, and Windows 11 no longer connects to it.

As you can see, working with Bluetooth devices in Windows 11 is quite easy, and the process for connecting and disconnecting such devices works the same.

# 8 Maintaining Windows

# Contents at a Glance

# Chapter **1**

# Backing Up Data

I f you're accustomed to using earlier versions of Windows to back up or restore data, to ghost (clone) an entire drive, or to set restore points, you're probably in this chapter looking for something that no longer exists. Microsoft is *deprecating* (killing, zapping) all the old backup and restore functions, in favor of new (and easier-to-use) options.

In Windows 11, the main tools promoted by Microsoft for this task are OneDrive (which stores everything in Microsoft's cloud) and File History (which stores everything on a storage drive you own).

In this chapter, I talk mostly about File History and how to set it up so that it makes backups of your data on an external drive or a network drive. The tool works well, is easy to use, and pretty reliable. I also discuss the benefits of storing your data in the cloud, and the privacy concerns you may have. As you'll see for yourself, online backups make your life easier!

# Finding Windows 7's Backup Options in Windows 11

If you're an experienced Windows 7 user, you may be looking for specific features that have been renamed, morphed, or axed in Windows 11. Here's a little cheat sheet to help you figure out the landmarks:

>> **Shadow copies (or previous versions) of files are now called File History.** File History is functionally similar to the Apple Time Machine — just not as good looking, from a user interface perspective.

>> **Image backup (or system image or ghosting) is buried deep.** If you really want to use Windows 11 to create a full disk image, open the Control Panel. Then, under System and Security, click or tap the Backup and Restore (Windows 7) link. On the left, click or tap Create a System Image, and continue from there.

>> **Windows Backup and the Backup and Restore Center are in Windows 11 but are difficult to find.** They were present in Windows 8, got tossed out of Windows 8.1, but now they're back. Again, open the Control Panel, and click or tap the Backup and Restore (Windows 7) link. In the Backup and Restore (Windows 7) window (see Figure 1-1), click or tap Set Up Backup.

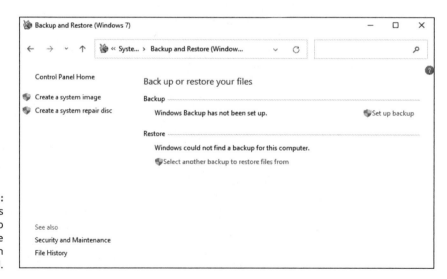

**FIGURE 1-1:** The old Windows 7's Backup options are hidden deep in the Control Panel.

# The Future of Reliable Storage Is in the Cloud

Microsoft has turned into a big-time fan of cloud storage, and it wants you to store your data on its servers. New features in Windows are designed to make it easier for you to put your data in the cloud — preferably Microsoft's cloud, One-Drive. Yes, part of the motivation is to get you to pay for cloud storage or at least lock you into Microsoft's cloud offerings. But a big part of the reason for steering you to cloud storage is that it's better. That, in turn, translates into fewer support headaches.

Yes, you read that right. I'm telling you that cloud storage is better than local storage, for most people in most situations. One of the big reasons why is backup. You don't have to sweat backup when your data is in the cloud, (although I admit that in rare cases, people have lost data saved in one of the cloud storage systems — OneDrive, Google Drive, iCloud, Dropbox, and so on.)

Contrast cloud storage with local storage. If you've been using computers for any length of time at all, chances are good that you've lost some data. If you know ten people who store data on their own PCs, I'd guess that ten of them have lost data. So, scoff at cloud storage if you like. Worry about the privacy problems. (Microsoft says it doesn't look into your files, although it does scan your photos to create albums.) Fret over maintaining an internet connection. But contrast that with the possibility — no, the likelihood — that you'll lose data by managing it yourself. No contest, from my point of view.

I cover OneDrive cloud storage in Book 4, Chapter 5.

# Backing Up and Restoring Files with File History

File History backs up not only your data files but also many versions of those files, making it easy to retrieve the latest version as well as multiple earlier versions.

By default, File History takes snapshots of all the files in user folders (Documents, Pictures, Movies, Videos, and so on) and on your desktop. It can also take snapshots of OneDrive, if you set your user folders to use OneDrive as their default location. The snapshots get taken once an hour and are kept until your backup drive runs out of space or for a time of your choosing, if you personalize File History's settings. I explain how later in this section.

# Setting up File History

To use File History, Windows 11 demands that you have an external hard drive, a second hard drive, or a network connection that leads to a hard drive. In this example, I connect to an external USB drive that is connected to my PC. You can also use a cheap external hard drive, which you can pick up at any computer store, or use a hard drive on another computer on your network.

**REMEMBER**

If you have lots of pictures in your Photos folder or a zillion files in the Documents folder, the first File History backup takes hours and hours. If you have lots of data and this is your first time backing up, make sure you're ready to leave the machine to do its thing for a long time.

To get File History going, attach an external drive to your computer and follow these steps:

**1.** **Click or tap the search icon (magnifying glass) on the taskbar, and enter** file history.

The search results are displayed.

**2.** **Click or tap the File History search result.**

The File History window pops up, displaying your external drive, as shown in Figure 1-2.

**FIGURE 1-2:**
With an external drive connected, it's time to turn on File History.

3. **If multiple drives are connected, click or tap Select Drive, select the drive you want to use for File History and then click or tap OK.**

4. **Click or tap the Turn On button.**

   File History is started, and it tells you that it's copying your files for the first time.

5. **If you want, close the Control Panel.**

   You can perform other tasks while File History works in the background.

## Checking whether File History backed up your data

Instead of relying on the File History program to tell you that the backup occurred, take matters into your own hands, and look for the backup with File Explorer. To find and check your backup files, follow these steps:

1. **Click or tap the File Explorer icon on the taskbar.**

   File Explorer opens.

2. **Navigate to the drive that you just used in the preceding steps for a File History backup.**

   This may be an external or a networked drive; it may even be a second drive on your PC, although I don't recommend that.

3. **Double-click or double-tap your way through the folder hierarchy:**

   - File History
   - Your username
   - Your PC name
   - Data
   - The main drive you backed up (probably C : )
   - Users
   - Your username (again)
   - Desktop (assuming you had any files on your desktop that you backed up), or Pictures, or some other folder of interest

   A File Explorer screen like the one shown in Figure 1-3 appears.

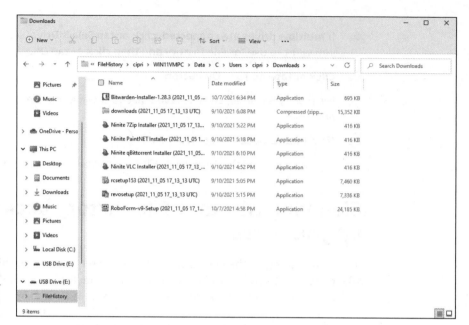

**FIGURE 1-3:**
Your backup data appears way down in a chain of folders.

4. **Check whether the filenames match the files on your desktop, in your Pictures folder, or in any other folder of interest, with dates and times added at the end of their name.**

5. **Do one of the following:**

   - *If the files match, close File Explorer and close the File History dialog box.* Although you can restore data from this location via File Explorer, it's easier to use the File History retrieval tools. (See the next section for details.)

   - *If you don't see filenames that mimic the files on your desktop, go back to Step 1 of the preceding list and make sure File History is set up right!*

**REMEMBER**

File History doesn't run if the backup drive gets disconnected or the network connection to the backup drive drops — but Windows 11 produces File History files anyway. As soon as the drive is reconnected or the network starts behaving, File History dumps all its data to the correct location, automatically.

## Restoring data from File History

File History stores snapshots of your files, taken every hour, unless you change the frequency. If you've been working on a spreadsheet for the past six hours and discovered that you made a big mistake sometime in the last half hour, you can retrieve a copy of the spreadsheet that's less than an hour old. If you've been working on your résumé over the past three months and decide that you really don't like the way your design changed five weeks ago, File History can help you there too.

Here's how to bring back your files from File History:

1. **Click or tap the search icon on the taskbar and enter** file history.

   The search results are shown.

2. **Click or tap the File History search result.**

3. **Click or tap Restore Personal Files.**

   The File History Restore Home page, shown in Figure 1-4, appears.

**FIGURE 1-4:**
You need to find
the file you want
to restore,
starting at
the top.

4. **Navigate to the location of the file you want to restore.**

   In Figure 1-5, I went to the Downloads folder, where the file I want to resuscitate is stored.

TIP

   You can use several familiar File Explorer navigation methods in the File History program, including the up arrow to move up one level, the forward and back arrows, and the search box in the upper-right corner.

5. **Check the time and date in the upper-left corner and do one of the following:**

   - *If you see the time and date of the file you want to bring back, click or tap the file to select it, and then click or tap the arrow-in-a-circle (restore).* You can also drag the file to whatever location you like. You can even preview the file by double-clicking it.

- *If this isn't the right time and date, click or tap the left arrow at the bottom to go back to the previous snapshot. Click or tap the left and right arrows to move to earlier and later versions of the files, respectively.*

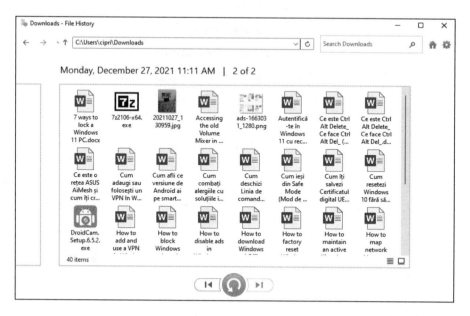

**FIGURE 1-5:**
First, find the
location. Then
find the correct
version.

6.  **If you want to restore all the files displayed in the File History window, click or tap the arrow-in-a-circle at the bottom of the screen, without selecting a specific file first.**

7.  **Choose to Replace the Files in the Destination (which deletes the latest version of each file) or select which files you want to replace, as shown in Figure 1-6.**

If you accidentally replace a good file, be of good cheer. A snapshot of that file was taken less than an hour ago. You just have to find it. Kinda cool how that works, isn't it? And that old copy stays around for a long time — years, if you have enough disk space and your backup drive doesn't die.

## Changing File History settings

File History backs up *every file in every user folder* on your computer. If you have a folder that you want to have backed up, just put it in one of the standard user folders. File History takes care of all the details.

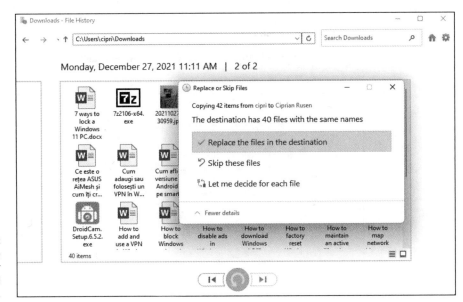

**FIGURE 1-6:**
You can restore an entire folder full of files all at once.

However, if you want to change how often it backs up your data and how long it stores it, you need to access its advanced settings. Here's how:

**1.** **Click or tap the search icon on the taskbar, and type** file history.

You see the search results.

**2.** **Click or tap the File History search result.**

The File History window pops up (refer to Figure 1-2).

**3.** **If you want to exclude some folders in your libraries so they don't get backed up:**

a. *Choose Exclude Folders (on the left).* File History opens a simple dialog box.

b. *Click or tap the Add button and select a folder to put it in the exclude list.* For example, in Figure 1-7, I excluded a folder in the Documents library.

c. *Repeat Step 2b until you have selected all the folders you want to exclude.*

d. *Save your changes and click or tap the back arrow to go back to the File History home page.*

**4.** **To change how frequently backups are made:**

a. *Click or tap the Advanced Settings link (on the left).* The Advanced Settings dialog box appears, as shown in Figure 1-8.

b. *Change the frequency of backups and how long versions should be kept.* See my recommendations for these settings in Table 1-1.

## 5. Click or tap Save Changes.

Your next File History backup follows the new rules.

**FIGURE 1-7:**
Exclude individual
folders from
File History.

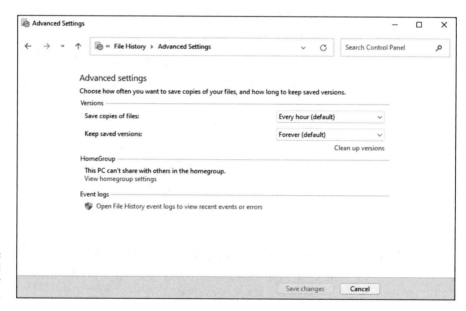

**FIGURE 1-8:**
Take control
of your
backups here.

| TABLE 1-1 | File History Advanced Settings | |
|---|---|---|
| Setting | Recommendation | Why |
| Save Copies of Files | Every 30 Minutes | This is mostly a tradeoff between space (more frequent backups take a tiny bit of extra space) and time — your time. If you have lots of backups, you increase the likelihood of getting back a usable version of a file, but you must wade through many more versions. I find 30 minutes strikes the right balance, but you may want to back up more frequently. |
| Keep Saved Versions | Forever (default) | If you choose Until Space Is Needed, File History won't raise a holy stink if you run out of room on your backup drive. By leaving it at Forever, File History sends notifications when the hard drive gets close to full capacity, so you can run out and buy another backup drive. |

# Storing to and through the Cloud

File History's a great product. I use it religiously. But it isn't the be-all-and-end-all of backup storage. What happens if my office burns down? What if I need to get at a file when I'm away from the office?

The best solution I've found is to have File History do its thing but also keep my most important files — the ones I'm using right now — in the cloud. That's how I wrote this book, with the text files and the screen shots in Dropbox. I also used Dropbox to hand off the files to my editors and receive edited versions back.

The only question with the editorial team nowadays is which cloud storage vendor to use. Believe me, things have really changed.

**TIP**

Backing up to the internet has one additional big plus: Depending on which package you use and how you use it, the data can be accessible to you no matter where you need it — on the road, on your iPad, even on your Android smartphone. You can set up folders to share with friends or co-workers, and in some cases, have them help you work on a file while you're working on it, too.

Many years ago, only one big player — Dropbox — was in the online storage and sharing business. Now there's Dropbox, Microsoft OneDrive, Google Drive, the Apple iCloud — all from huge companies — and SugarSync, Box (formerly Box. net), and others from smaller companies.

What happened? People have discovered just how handy cloud storage can be. And the price of cloud storage has plummeted to nearly nothing.

**REMEMBER**

The cloud storage I'm talking about is designed to allow you to store data on the internet and retrieve it from anywhere, on just about any kind of device — including a smartphone or tablet. It also has varying degrees of interoperability and sharing, so, for example, you can upload a file and have a dozen people look at it simultaneously. Some cloud storage services (notably OneDrive and Google Drive) have associated programs (such as Microsoft Office and Google's Work-space, respectively) that let two or more people edit the same file simultaneously.

## Considering cloud storage privacy concerns

I don't know how many times people have told me that they just don't trust putting their data on some company's website. But although many people are rightfully concerned about privacy issues and the specter of Big Brother, the fact is that the demand for storage in the cloud is growing by leaps and bounds.

The concerns I hear go something like this:

>> **I must have a working internet connection to get data to or from the online storage.** Absolutely true, and there's no way around it. If you use cloud storage for only offsite backup, it's sufficient to be connected whenever you want to back up your data or restore it. Some of the cloud storage services have ways to cache data on your computer when, say, you're going to be on an airplane. But in general, you have to be online.

>> **The data can be taken or copied by law enforcement and local govern-ments.** True. The big cloud storage companies get several court orders a day. The storage company's legal staff takes a look, and if it's a valid order, your data gets sent to the cops, the feds, or some other law enforcement agency.

**REMEMBER**

Moral of the story: If you're going to store data that you don't want to appear in the next issue of a certain British tabloid, it would be smart to encrypt the file before you store it. Word and Excel use remarkably effective encryption techniques, and 7-Zip (see Book 10, Chapter 6) also makes nearly unbreakable ZIPs. Couple that with a strong password, and your data isn't going anywhere soon. Unless, of course, you're required by the court to give up the password, or the NSA sets one of its teraflops password crackers to the job.

>> **Programs at the cloud storage firm can scan my data.** True, once again, for most (but not all) cloud storage firms. With a few notable exceptions — Mega, Spider Oak, and others — cloud storage company programs can see your data. There's been a big push in the past few years to hold cloud storage companies responsible for storing copyrighted material: If you upload a pirate copy of *Men in Black 4,* the people who hold the copyright are going to get upset.

Different cloud storage companies handle the task differently, but with the takedown of Megaupload in January 2012, everybody is concerned about incurring the wrath of the MPAA and RIAA, the companies that defend movie and music copyrights, respectively.

» **Employees at the cloud storage firm can look at my data.** True again. Certain cloud storage company employees *can* see your data — at least in the larger companies. They must be able to see your data to comply with court orders. Does that mean Billy the intern can look at your financial data or your family photos? Well, no. It's more complicated than that. Every cloud storage company has strict, logged, and monitored rules for who can view customer data and why. Am I absolutely sure that every company obeys all its rules? No, not at all. But I don't think my information is interesting enough to draw much attention from Billy, unless Billy is trying to swipe the manuscript of my next book.

» **Somebody can break into the cloud storage site and steal my data.** Well, yes, that's true, but it probably isn't much of a concern. Each of the cloud storage services scrambles its data and uses two-step verification, so it'd be difficult for anyone to break in, steal, and then decrypt the stolen data. Can it happen? Sure. Will I lose sleep over it? Nah. That said, you should enable two-factor authentication when it's offered (so the backup service sends an entry code to your email address, or sends you a message on your phone, requiring the entry code to get into your data). And if you want to be triple-sure, you can encrypt the data before you store it — 7-Zip, among many others, makes it easy to encrypt files when you ZIP them.

## Reaping the benefits of backup and storage in the cloud

So much for the negatives. Time to look at the positives. On the plus side, a good cloud storage setup gives you the following:

» **Offsite backups** that won't get destroyed if your house or business burns down.

» **Access to your data from anywhere,** using just about any imaginable kind of computer, including smartphones and tablets.

» **Controlled sharing** so you can password-protect specific files or folders. Hand the password to a friend, and he can look at the file or folder.

» **Broadcast sharing** from a public folder that anyone can see.

>> **Direct access from application programs that run in the cloud.** Both Google Apps and the many forms of Microsoft Office are good examples. The list includes iWork (the Apple Productivity apps) if you're using Apple's iCloud. Office apps now have direct access to Dropbox data, too.

>> **Free packages, up to a certain size limit,** offered by most of the cloud storage services.

## Choosing an online backup and sharing service

So which cloud storage service is best? Tough question. I use four of them — three for PCs and Android, and iCloud for my Mac, iPad, and iPhone stuff — different services for different purposes.

Dropbox, Microsoft OneDrive, and Google Drive have programs that you run on your PC or Mac to set up folders that are shared. Drag a file into the shared folder, and it appears on all the computers you have connected (with a password) to the shared folder. Go on the web and log in to the site, and your data's available there. Install an app on your iPhone or Android smartphone or tablet, and the data's there as well. Here's a rundown of what each cloud storage service offers:

>> **Dropbox,** shown in Figure 1-9, offers 2GB of free storage, with 2TB for $10 per month. It's easy to use, reliable, and fast. I use it for synchronizing project files — including the files for this book. Visit www.dropbox.com for details.

>> **OneDrive** has 5GB of free storage, with 200GB for $2 per month. The amounts offered change from time to time. Also note that many Microsoft 365 (formerly known as Office 365) subscription levels have 1TB of OneDrive storage free, for as long as you're a subscriber. I talk about OneDrive in Book 4, Chapter 5. Also, visit www.onedrive.com for details.

>> **Google Drive (also known as Google One),** shown in Figure 1-10, has 15GB of free storage, with 100GB for $2 per month and 2TB for $10 per month. Google Drive isn't as slick as the other two, but it works well enough for most people. See Book 10, Chapter 4 and visit www.drive.google.com for details.

>> **Apple iCloud,** shown in Figure 1-11, is intended to be an Apple-centric service. The first 5GB is free, and then it's $0.99 per month for an additional 50GB. It works great with iPads and iPhones and even Macs, with extraordinarily simple backup of photos. In fact, photo and video backup and sharing take place automatically, and you don't have to do a thing. Visit www.icloud.com for details.

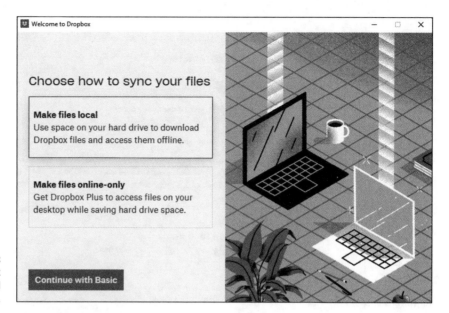

**FIGURE 1-9:**
Dropbox
popularized
cloud storage.

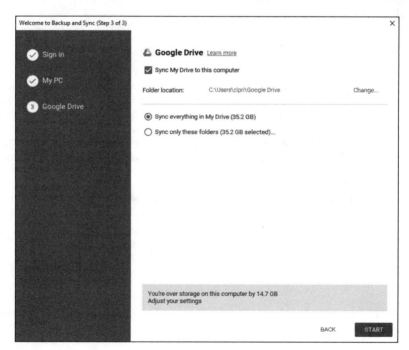

**FIGURE 1-10:**
Google Drive
works very well
with Google apps.

FIGURE 1-11:
iCloud works with
Apple products
but makes it
difficult to share
files among PCs.

The other services have specific strong points:

>> **Amazon Drive** (www.amazon.com/clouddrive) ties in with Amazon
   purchases and the Kindle but not much else. If you pay for Amazon Prime
   ($119/year), you also get unlimited free photo storage.

>> **SugarSync** (www.sugarsync.com) lets you synchronize arbitrary folders on
   your PC. That's a big deal if you don't want to drag your sync folders into
   one location.

>> **Box** (www.box.com) is designed for large companies, providing tools to control
   employees sharing files.

Chapter **2**

# Resetting Windows to a Working State

I f you've worked with Windows for any length of time, you know that from time to time your Windows PC simply goes out to lunch . . . and stays there. The problem could stem from a hardware component that's suddenly malfunctioning, a scrambled Windows registry entry, a driver that's taken on a mind of its own, a new program that's throwing its own revolution, or that dicey tuna sandwich you had for lunch.

Windows is a computer program, and it will have problems. The trick lies in making sure that *you* don't have problems too. This chapter walks you through the important Windows 11 tools you have at hand to solve problems as they (inevitably!) occur. I talk about how to use the different Reset options to make your PC functional again. I also teach you how to bring back the old and trusty System Restore, and have it ready to help, before going down the more drastic Reset route.

# Resuscitating Malfunctioning Windows 11 PCs

When resuscitating a machine when Windows 11 has gone bad, consider the three Rs: remove the latest update (read Book 7, Chapter 2), reset but keep your programs and data, and reset with the data going bye–bye. It's important that you watch carefully when you apply any of these Rs. The implications of your actions are spelled out reasonably well on all the screens that Windows uses, but it's still easy to get confused.

Here are the basics every Windows 11 troubleshooter needs to know:

>> **Reset** has two variants that are as different as night and day:

- **Reset with Keep My Files** keeps some Windows settings (accounts, passwords, the desktop, Microsoft Edge favorites, wireless network settings, drive letter assignments, and BitLocker settings) and all personal data (in the Users folder). It wipes out all programs and then restores the apps available in the Microsoft Store. This option is pretty drastic, but at least it keeps the data stored in the most common locations — Documents folder, the Desktop folder, Downloads, and the like. And as a bonus, the Reset with Keep My Files routine keeps a list of the apps it zapped and puts that list on your desktop, so you can look at it when your machine's back to its chirpy self.

- **Reset with Remove Everything** removes everything on your PC and reinstalls Windows. Your programs, data, and settings all get wiped out — they're irretrievably lost. This option is the most drastic thing you can do with your computer. Most hardware manufacturers have the command jury-rigged to put their crapware back on your PC. If you run Reset with Remove Everything on those systems, you don't get a clean copy of Windows 11; you get the factory settings version. Yes, that means you get the original manufacturer's drivers (see the "Why would you want factory drivers?" sidebar). But it also means you get the manufacturer's crapware.

  If you like, you can tell Reset with Remove Everything to do a *thorough* reformatting of the hard drive, in which case random patterns of data are written to the hard drive to make it almost impossible to retrieve anything you used to store on the disk. But in the end, you get the same crapware that comes with a new computer.

>> **Restore** (or System Restore), which rolls Windows 11 back to an earlier *restore point* (as described later in the chapter), is hard to find — Microsoft doesn't want everyday users to find it. Restore doesn't touch your data or programs; it

simply rolls back the registry to an earlier point in time. If your problems stem from a bad driver or a problematic program change you made recently, Restore may do all you need.

Why does Microsoft make it hard to find System Restore? As far as I know, the logic goes something like this: If you don't use Restore correctly, you can incapacitate your machine; in which case, you'll bother the folks at Microsoft mercilessly and accuse them of all sorts of mean things. Even if you *do* use Restore right, it fixes only a small percentage of all Windows-breaking problems, so if you try Restore and it doesn't work, you'll also bother the folks at Microsoft mercilessly — a classic lose-lose situation for the company. Importantly, there's nothing analogous to System Restore with any competing operating system, tablet, or smartphone. In short, only Windows has a registry, and System Restore works almost exclusively on the registry, so only Windows needs a Restore. There's not much competitive benefit — and lots of downside — to offering Restore to the average Windows consumer.

» **Go Back** tells Windows to remove the last applied cumulative update. Use it when one of Microsoft's mighty forced cumulative updates (see Book 7, Chapter 2) cripples your machine. I've had mixed results with Go Back, but when it works, it's a fast and easy solution to a congenital problem — Microsoft forcing Windows 11 updates down your throat.

REMEMBER

All three resuscitation methods play out in the *Windows Recovery Environment (WRE)*. If you run Reset, you won't even know that WRE is at work behind the scenes, but it's there. Read Book 8, Chapter 3 for more about WRE.

## WHY WOULD YOU WANT FACTORY DRIVERS?

There's an obvious downside to running a Reset with Remove Everything: You get all the junk that manufacturers ship with their new computers. Some of the apps they ship are supposed to make managing your PC better. Others are simply advertising, for which the advertiser pays. You really don't want either.

The one upside to running a Reset with Remove Everything? You get back the original drivers. I can't say that I've ever seen a situation where a clean install of Windows 11 resulted in useless drivers. In the unusual situation where you get suboptimal drivers, one trip through Windows Update should get you up to speed.

But if you're worried that a truly clean install will leave you begging, Reset with Remove Everything is for you.

When there's trouble and Windows 11 can't boot normally, the operating system instead boots into WRE, not into Windows itself. WRE has the special task of giving you advanced tools and options for fixing things that have gone bump in the night.

I talk about WRE — and your advanced boot options — toward the end of this chapter.

# Resetting Your Windows 11 PC

You don't really need to know or care about restore points, and you don't want to dig into Windows 11 to make it work right. Mostly, you just want a one-click (or tap) solution that reams out the old, replaces it with known good stuff, and might or might not destroy your files in the process — at your option. You get the manufacturer's drivers, but you also get the manufacturer's crapware. That's what Microsoft has tried to offer with Reset.

Reset runs in two different ways:

>> The **Keep My Files** option tries to work its magic without disturbing any of your personal data files.

>> The **Remove Everything** option blasts everything away, including your data. It's the scorched-earth approach, to be used when nothing else works.

REMEMBER

Running a Keep My Files reset *keeps* all these:

>> **Some of your Windows 11 settings:** These include user accounts and passwords, wireless network connections and their settings, BitLocker settings and passwords, drive letter assignments, and your Windows 11 installation key.

>> **Files in the Users folder:** That includes files in every user's Documents folder, Desktop folder, Downloads folder, and so on. Reset with Keep My Files keeps File History versions, and it keeps folders stored on drives and in partitions that don't contain Windows (typically, that means it doesn't touch anything outside of the C: drive).

>> **Windows 11 apps from the Microsoft Store:** Their settings are saved too. So, if you're up to the 927th level of Cut the Rope before you run a Reset with Keep My Files, afterward, you're still at the 927th level. Confusingly, if you bought a desktop app in the Microsoft Store, its settings get obliterated. Only your Windows 11 apps come through unscathed.

**WARNING**

Running Reset with the Keep My Files option *destroys* the following:

>> **Many of your Windows 11 settings:** Display settings, firewall customizations, and file type associations are wiped out. Windows 11 must zap most of your settings because they could be causing problems.

>> **Files — including data files — not in the Users folder:** If you have files tucked away in some unusual location on the C: drive, don't expect them to survive Reset. However, partitions other than C: are not touched by Reset.

>> **Desktop apps or programs:** Their settings disappear too, including the keys you need to install them, passwords in such programs as Outlook — everything. You need to reinstall them all.

The Reset routine, helpfully, makes a list of the programs that it identifies on the kill list and puts it on your desktop.

Here's how to run a Reset with the Keep My Files option:

1. **Log in using an account with administrator permissions. Also make sure you understand what will come through and what won't.**

   See the previous bullet lists.

2. **Click or tap the Start icon and then the Settings icon.**

   The System entry should be selected on the left.

3. **On the right, choose Recovery.**

   You see the recovery options shown in Figure 2-1.

4. **Click or tap Reset PC.**

   Windows 11 asks if you want to keep your files or obliterate everything, as shown in Figure 2-2.

5. **Unless you're going to recycle your computer — give it to charity or the kids — first try the less-destructive approach. Click or tap Keep My Files and choose whether you want a Cloud Download or Local Reinstall.**

   The first option takes more time because it downloads the Windows 11 Setup files from Microsoft servers. You then see a summary of your current settings.

6. **Click or tap Next, and you're informed about what the resetting will do to your machine. Click or tap Reset.**

   If you have apps that won't make it through a Reset with Keep My Files option, click or tap the View Apps That Will Be Removed link before starting the Reset. A list appears on your screen, as shown in Figure 2-3.

The entire process involves several restarts and takes about 10 minutes on a reasonably well-seasoned PC. It can take longer, though, particularly on a slow tablet. When Reset is finished, you end up on the Windows 11 sign-in screen.

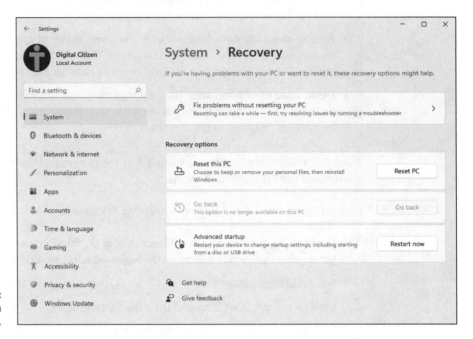

**FIGURE 2-1:**
Run Reset from
the Settings app.

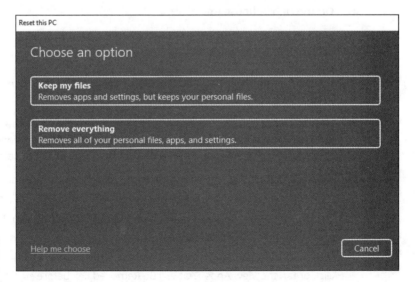

**FIGURE 2-2:**
Choose the kind
of reset you want.

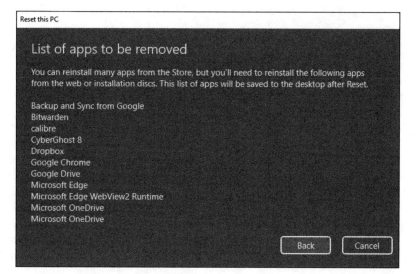

**FIGURE 2-3:**
These apps — yes,
even some apps
from Microsoft —
won't survive
a reset.

7. **Log in to Windows 11, wait for the Welcome dialog to finish, and choose the privacy settings for your device.**

8. **Double-click or double-tap the new Removed Apps file on the desktop.**

   Microsoft Edge appears and shows you a list of all the programs it identified that didn't make it through Reset.

**WARNING**

If Windows 11 can't boot normally, you're tossed into the Windows Recovery Environment. See the last section in this chapter for a description of how to start Reset from the Windows Recovery Environment.

# Resetting Your PC to Factory Settings

The Reset with the Remove Everything option is similar to running Reset with Save My Files except . . .

**WARNING**

Warning! Resetting with Remove Everything on your PC wipes out everything and forces you to start from scratch, all over again. You must even enter new account names and passwords, and reinstall everything, including all your Windows 11 apps. Your Microsoft account settings remain intact, as does any data you've stored in the cloud (for example, in OneDrive or in Dropbox). But the rest gets hurled down the drain.

In addition, when you're done, you'll have a factory-fresh copy of Windows 11. If you're running one of the (many) Windows 11 PCs that ship with crapware pre-installed, all of it will suddenly reappear.

If you're selling your PC, giving it away, or even sending it off to a recycling service, Reset with Remove Everything is a good idea. If you're keeping your PC, only attempt Reset with Remove Everything after you've run Reset with Keep My Files, and you haven't solved your problem(s). Reset with Remove Everything is similar to a clean install. You're nuking everything on your PC, although you get your factory drivers back, along with all the factory-installed crapware.

With that as a preamble, here's how to Reset your PC with Remove Everything:

**1. Log in using an account with administrator permissions. Also make sure you understand what will happen if you go ahead with this procedure.**

See the preceding warning.

**2. Click or tap the Start icon and then the Settings icon.**

The System entry is selected on the left.

**3. On the right, choose Recovery.**

You see the Reset options (refer to Figure 2-1).

**4. Click or tap Reset PC.**

Windows 11 asks if you want to keep your files or obliterate everything (refer to Figure 2-2).

**5. Click or tap Remove Everything, and choose whether you want a Cloud Download of Windows 11 (from Microsoft's servers) or a Local Reinstall.**

The second option is faster. A summary of your current settings is displayed, as shown in Figure 2-4.

**6. Click or tap Next.**

You're informed about what the resetting will do to your machine.

**7. Click or tap Reset.**

The entire process involves several restarts and takes about 15 minutes on most PCs. It can take longer, though, particularly on a slow tablet. When Reset is finished, you end up at the Personalization wizard, which allows you to configure Windows 11 as if it were newly installed.

**8. Set up Windows 11 from scratch.**

Now that's a complete reinstall.

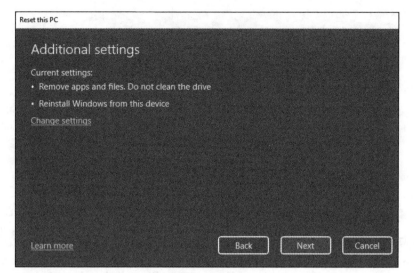

**FIGURE 2-4:**
What Reset your
PC with Remove
Everything does.

# Restoring to an Earlier Point

If you've used Windows 7 or earlier, you may have stumbled upon the System Restore feature. Windows 11 has full support for System Restore and restore points; it just hides all the pieces from you.

With a few exceptions (see the next section on system image), Reset takes you all the way back in time to when you first set up your PC; it adds the Windows 11 apps that ship with the operating system, and it's careful not to step on your data. Aside from a few Windows 11 settings, that's about it. Reset is a sledgehammer, when sometimes the tap of a fingernail may be all that you need.

Smashing with a sledgehammer is easy. Tapping your fingernail requires a great deal more finesse. And that brings me to System Restore in Windows 11.

If you enable System Protection, Windows 11 takes snapshots of its settings, or *restore points,* before you make any major changes to your computer — install a new hardware driver, perhaps, or a new program. You can roll back your system settings to any of the restore points. (See the "System protection and restore points" sidebar.)

A restore point contains registry entries and copies of certain critical programs including, notably, drivers and key system files — a *snapshot* of crucial system settings and programs. When you roll back (or restore) to a restore point, you replace the current settings and programs with the older versions.

## SYSTEM PROTECTION AND RESTORE POINTS

Windows 7 created restore points for your system drive (usually C:) by default. Windows 11 doesn't. Restore points take up space on your hard drive, and Microsoft would rather that you just trust its cloud-based recovery options. But if you want to take your system into your own hands, properly maintained and used restore points can change a gut-wrenching Reset into a simple rollback to an earlier restore point.

**TIP**

When Windows can tell that you're going to try to do something complicated, such as install a new network card, it sets a restore point — as long as you have System Protection turned on. Unfortunately, Windows can't always tell when you're going to do something drastic — perhaps you have a new CD player and the instructions tell you to turn off your PC and install the player before you run the setup program. So, it doesn't hurt one little bit to run System Restore — er, System Protection — from time to time, and set a restore point, all by yourself.

## Enabling System Protection

System Protection is disabled by default in Windows 11, and you must turn it on manually. Here's how:

1. **Click or tap the search icon on the taskbar and type** restore.

   The first result in the search is Create a Restore Point.

2. **Click or tap the Create a Restore Point link.**

   Windows 11 displays the System Properties window open to the System Protection tab, as shown in Figure 2-5.

3. **With the C: drive selected, click or tap the Configure button.**

   The System Protection window appears, shown in Figure 2-6.

4. **Choose Turn On System Protection, select the disk space usage (no need to go higher than 5 percent), and click or tap OK.**

5. **Click or tap OK one more time to enable System Protection.**

   System Protection is now turned on, and it will create restore points automatically.

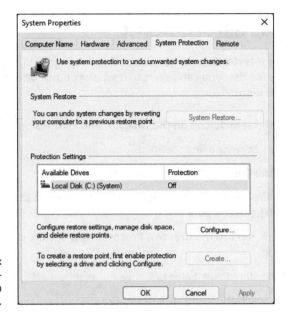

**FIGURE 2-5:**
The hard-to-find System Restore option.

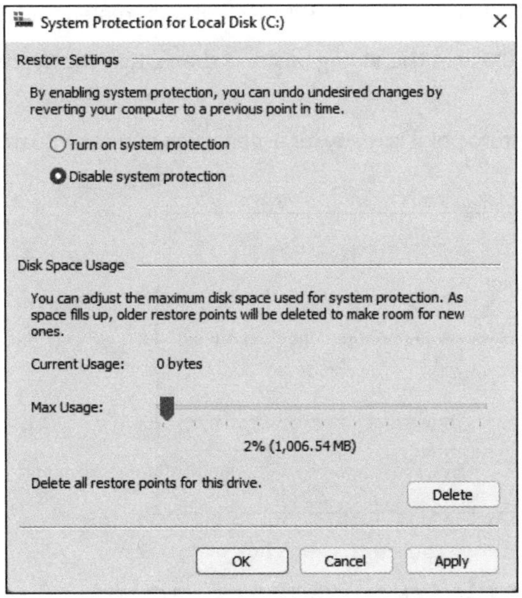

**FIGURE 2-6:**
Enable and configure System Restore here.

# Creating a restore point

You should create a restore point when your Windows 11 PC is running smoothly, without problems, so that you can revert to it when you run into them. Here's how to create a restore point:

**1.** **Click or tap the search icon on the taskbar, and type** restore point.

The first result is Create a Restore Point.

**2.** **Click or tap the Create a Restore Point link.**

Windows 11 displays the System Properties window open to the System Protection tab (refer to Figure 2-5).

**3.** **At the bottom, next to the Create a Restore Point option, click or tap the Create button.**

The Create a Restore Point dialog box appears, as shown in Figure 2-7.

**4.** **Type a good description and click or tap Create.**

Windows 11 says that it's creating a restore point. When it's finished, it displays a dialog box to tell you that the restore point was created successfully.

**5.** **Click or tap Close in the dialog box and then OK in the System Properties window.**

Your new restore point is ready for action when you run into trouble.

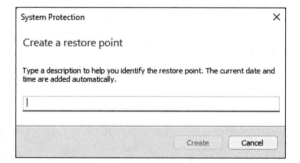

**FIGURE 2-7:**
Give your restore
point a name.

# Rolling back to a restore point

If you don't mind getting your hands a little dirty, the next time you think about running Reset, see whether you can instead roll your PC back to a previous restore point manually and get things working right. Here's how:

1. **Save your work and close all running programs.**

   System Restore doesn't muck with any data files, documents, pictures, or anything like that. It works only on system files, such as drivers, and the registry. Your data is safe. But System Restore can mess up settings, so if you recently installed a new program, for example, you may have to install it again after System Restore is finished.

2. **Click or tap the search icon on the taskbar, and type** restore point.

   The first search result is Create a Restore Point.

3. **Click or tap the Create a Restore Point tile.**

   Windows 11 flips you over to the System Properties window open to the System Protection tab (refer to Figure 2-5). Protection for your C: drive should be on. (If it isn't on, you don't have any restore points.)

4. **In the System Restore area, click or tap the System Restore button.**

   The System Restore wizard appears, as shown in Figure 2-8.

5. **Click or tap Next.**

   A list of recent restore points appears, as shown in Figure 2-9.

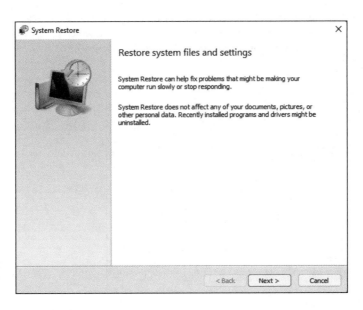

**FIGURE 2-8:** System Restore to the rescue.

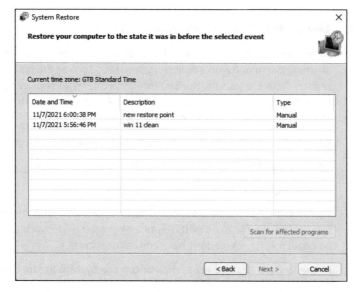

FIGURE 2-9:
The latest restore
point isn't
always the best
restore point.

6. **Before you roll your PC back to a restore point, click or tap to select the restore point you're considering and then click or tap the Scan for Affected Programs button.**

System Restore tells you which programs and drivers have system entries (typically in the registry) that will be altered and which programs will be deleted if you select that specific restore point. See Figure 2-10.

FIGURE 2-10:
Windows can
scan the restore
point to see what
programs will
be affected by
rolling back.

7. **If you don't see any major problems with the restore point — it doesn't wipe out something you need —click or tap Close and then Next.**

   (If you do see a potential problem, go back and choose a different restore point, or consider using Reset, as I describe earlier in this chapter.)

   You're warned that rolling back to a restore point requires a restart of the computer and that you should close all open programs before continuing.

8. **Follow the instructions to save any open files, close all programs, click or tap Finish, and then confirm by clicking or tapping Yes.**

   True to its word, System Restore reverts to the selected restore point and restarts your computer.

TIP

If Reset and System Restore didn't help, your last chances are the Windows Recovery Environment and safe mode. Read the next chapter to learn more.

# Chapter **3**

# Troubleshooting with Safe Mode

A useful troubleshooting tool that can bring your computer back to life is safe mode. Windows 11 has several safe modes, and in this chapter I explain the differences between them. Most people won't need more than two safe modes, thank goodness!

Unlike in the days of the ill-famed Windows 8, you no longer enter safe mode by pressing F8 during the boot process. The procedure is now a lot more complicated. You also have more ways to start safe mode.

Furthermore, Windows provides a Recovery Environment that starts automatically after Windows fails to successfully boot three times in a row. Therefore, if you find yourself in a pinch and unable to use Windows, the Windows Recovery Environment might save you. In this chapter, I show you how to access this environment and give you a brief description of the tools included. You may find them useful!

# Working in Safe Mode

Safe mode is a special way of starting Windows in which the operating system loads only its basic user interface. This mode uses only essential drivers and services, so most of the things that can cause crashes or problems are out of the way. This approach makes it easier to troubleshoot Windows.

In safe mode, you can uninstall misbehaving apps and drivers, change important system settings, or perform maintenance tasks such as checking the drive for errors and repairing it.

You can access three safe modes:

>> **Safe mode:** The standard safe mode that most people need. It doesn't load any networking drivers and services. You can see it in all its glory in Figure 3-1.

>> **Safe mode with networking:** A safe mode that also loads networking drivers and services. This mode is useful when you need to troubleshoot Windows 11 with a working internet connection available.

>> **Safe mode with command prompt:** Automatically loads a command prompt window, for when you need quick access to the command line. You can't do anything in this mode except type commands. However, because the command prompt is available also in the standard safe mode, most people don't need this last safe mode.

## Accessing safe mode

Unfortunately, Windows 11 requires UEFI, and it doesn't work with old BIOSes from older generations of motherboards.

**TECHNICAL STUFF**

BIOS is an acronym for basic input/output system. Think of it as the software that allows communication and facilitates data transfers between the hardware components of a computer and the users or the software installed on it. UEFI stands for Unified Extensible Firmware Interface, and you can look at it as a modern and more powerful BIOS. It has the same role as the traditional BIOS but includes more features such as cryptography and remote diagnostics and computer repair.

Therefore, the old ways of booting into safe mode, such as pressing F8 or Shift+F8 on your keyboard, no longer function. However, there are plenty of other ways to get into Windows 11 safe mode. One of them that works well is the following:

**FIGURE 3-1:**
Safe mode loads only the essentials.

1. **Save your work and close all running programs. Then click or tap the Start icon.**

   The Start menu appears.

2. **Press and hold down the Shift key on your keyboard while you click or tap the Power button and select Restart.**

   Windows 11 reboots. Then it asks you to choose an option, as shown in Figure 3-2.

3. **Click or tap Troubleshoot and then Advanced Options.**

   You see several advanced options, as shown in Figure 3-3.

4. **Select Start-up Settings. If you don't have this option, first click or tap the link See More Recovery Options to get to it.**

   Windows 11 loads a screen called Startup Settings, where it informs you that, after you restart your PC, you can change several Windows options. One option is enabling safe mode.

5. **Click or tap the Restart button.**

   A new Startup Settings screen appears, as shown in Figure 3-4.

**6.** **Press 4 or F4 on your keyboard to start Windows 11 in safe mode or press 5 or F5 to enter safe mode with networking.**

Windows 11 starts in safe mode, and you can log in using an administrator account and start troubleshooting.

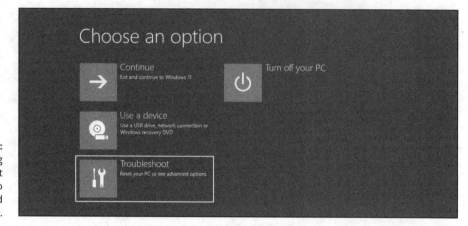

**FIGURE 3-2:**
Choosing
Troubleshoot
leads you to
several advanced
options.

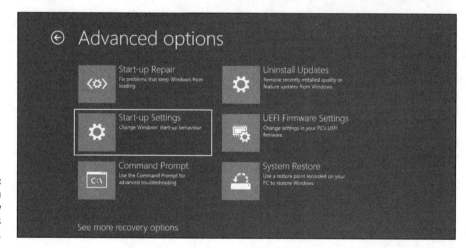

**FIGURE 3-3:**
From here you
can change how
Windows behaves
at startup.

**TIP**

Another way to enter safe mode is to interrupt Windows 11's normal boot process three consecutive times. Press the physical Restart or Power button on your Windows 11 computer or device to stop it during its startup process. Then Windows 11 will load its automatic repair mode. On the Automatic Repair screen, click or tap the Advanced Options button and then follow Steps 3 to 6 in the preceding list.

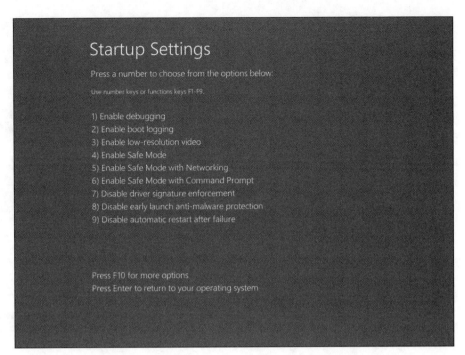

Startup Settings

Press a number to choose from the options below:

Use number keys or functions keys F1-F9.

1) Enable debugging
2) Enable boot logging
3) Enable low-resolution video
4) Enable Safe Mode
5) Enable Safe Mode with Networking
6) Enable Safe Mode with Command Prompt
7) Disable driver signature enforcement
8) Disable early launch anti-malware protection
9) Disable automatic restart after failure

Press F10 for more options
Press Enter to return to your operating system

**FIGURE 3-4:**
Press 4 or 5 to start into safe mode or safe mode with networking.

# Using safe mode for troubleshooting

The most useful of the three safe modes is *safe mode with networking* because it starts by giving you access to the network and the internet. It even loads Microsoft's support site automatically, as shown in Figure 3-5.

Using safe mode is the same as using Windows 11 normally. You can click, tap, right-click, press and hold down, and drag-and-drop as usual. However, many Windows services and features don't work. You can access only the features you need for troubleshooting and repairing your PC: Settings, Control Panel, Command Prompt, PowerShell, and several Windows tools such as Event Viewer, Disk Management, and Disk Cleanup.

**WARNING**

Search doesn't work in safe mode, limiting your capability to find stuff fast. However, File Explorer starts, and you can use it to browse to the files or apps you need for troubleshooting.

**TIP**

Depending on your problem, you may find the troubleshooter you need in the Settings app, by going to System ➪ Troubleshoot. To learn more about troubleshooting Windows, read Book 7, Chapter 3.

Troubleshooting with Safe Mode

**FIGURE 3-5:**
Safe mode with networking.

# Entering the Windows Recovery Environment

The Windows Recovery Environment has become a sophisticated tool. It appears when your machine fails to boot three times in a row. You can even trigger it yourself by pressing — three times in a row — the physical Restart or Power button on your Windows 11 computer or device to stop it during its startup process. You know you're in the Windows Recovery Environment after Windows 11 displays messages that it is Preparing Automatic Repair and then Diagnosing Your PC. You then see a blue Automatic Repair screen like the one in Figure 3-6.

In the Automatic Repair screen, click or tap Advanced Options, and then Troubleshoot. From the Troubleshoot screen, you can run Refresh or Reset directly: They behave as described in the Chapter 2 of this minibook. You can also choose Advanced Options in the Troubleshoot screen, which brings you to several interesting — if little-used — options, as shown in Figure 3-7.

**FIGURE 3-6:**
The Windows
Recovery
Environment
has loaded.

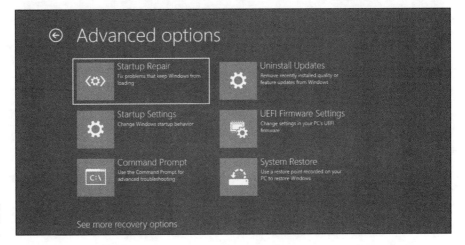

**FIGURE 3-7:**
Advanced
boot options.

Here's what the Advanced Options can do:

>> **System Restore:** Puts your system back to a chosen restore point, as described in Chapter 2 of this minibook. It won't work, though, unless you've turned on system protection/restore points for one or more drives on your computer.

>> **Startup Repair:** Reboots to a specific Windows Recovery Environment program and runs a diagnosis and repair routine that seeks to make your PC bootable again. I've seen this program run spontaneously when I'm having hardware problems. A Start Repair log file is generated at \Windows\ System32\Logfiles\Srt\SrtTrail.txt. If your computer is running Automatic Repair, you can't do anything: Just hold on and see whether it works.

>> **Uninstall Updates:** Allows you to remove the latest quality or feature update for Windows 11. This option is useful when your problems are caused by low-quality updates.

>> **UEFI Firmware Settings:** Displays the UEFI/BIOS for your computer, where you can set how its motherboard, processor, and other components work.

>> **Command Prompt:** Brings up an old-fashioned DOS command prompt, just like you get if you go into safe mode. Only for the geek at heart — you can hurt your device in there.

>> **Startup Settings:** Reboots Windows and lets you go into safe mode, change the video resolution, start debugging mode or boot logging, run in safe mode, disable driver signature checks, disable early launch antimalware scans, and disable automatic restart on system failure. Not for the faint of heart.

# Chapter **4**

# Monitoring Windows

**W**indows 11 ships with an array of tools designed to help you look at your system and warn you if something's wrong. In this chapter, I talk about two of them: Event Viewer and Reliability Monitor. The purpose of Event Viewer is to collect all Windows logs into one place, so that you can find them when you need them, while Reliability Monitor gives you a visual perspective of what's wrong with your Windows 11 computer or device.

Both Event Viewer and Reliability Monitor are designed for support technicians rather than end users. Because the information these tools present is complex and hard to interpret, scammers often use them to trick people into paying for expensive "tech support from Microsoft" that they don't need. However, you may sometimes find these tools useful for troubleshooting Windows. In this chapter, I provide a brief overview of both and share why and how you should use them.

## Viewing Events

Every Windows user needs to know about Event Viewer, if only to protect themselves from scammers and con artists who make big bucks preying on peoples' fears.

As I explain in Book 9, Chapter 1, scammers are calling people in North America, Europe, Australia, and other locations all around the world, trying to talk Windows users into allowing them to take over their systems via Remote Assistance. They typically claim to be from Microsoft or associated with Microsoft. They may get your phone number by looking up names of people posting to help forums.

**WARNING**

Some of them just cold call: Any random phone call to a household in North America or Europe stands a good chance of striking a resonating chord when the topic turns to Windows problems. If you randomly called ten people in your town and said you were calling on behalf of Microsoft to help with a Windows problem, and you sounded as if you knew what you were talking about, I bet at least one or two of your neighbors would take you up on the offer.

The scam hinges around the Windows Event Viewer feature. It's an interesting, useful tool — but only if *you* take the initiative to use it, and don't let some fast talkers use it to scam you out of hundreds of bucks.

## Using Event Viewer

Windows has had an Event Viewer for decades, but few people know about it. At its heart, Event Viewer looks at a small handful of logs that Windows maintains on your PC. The logs are simple text files, written in a special structured format called XML, which enables apps to treat them like database entries. Although you may think of Windows as having one event log file, there are many — administrative event logs, hardware event logs, security logs, system logs, and many other logs.

Every program that starts on your PC posts a notification in an event log, and every well-behaved app posts a notification before it stops. Every system access, security change, operating system twitch, hardware failure, and driver hiccup ends up in an event log. Event Viewer scans those text log files, aggregates them, and puts a pretty interface on a dull, voluminous set of machine-generated data. Think of Event Viewer as a database reporting program, where the underlying database is just a handful of text files.

**REMEMBER**

In theory, the event logs track significant events on your PC. In practice, the term *significant* is in the eyes of the beholder. In the normal course of events, few people ever need to look at any of the event logs from Windows 11. But if your PC starts to turn sour, Event Viewer may give you important insight to the source of the problem. To use Event Viewer, you must log into Windows 11 using an administrator account. Standard user accounts barely see any useful data in Event Viewer.

Here's how to use Event Viewer:

**1.** **Right-click or tap and hold down on the Start icon. Choose Event Viewer.**

Event Viewer appears.

**2.** **On the left, expand the Custom Views section and click or tap Administrative Events.**

It may take a while, but eventually you see a list of notable events, as shown in Figure 4-1.

**3.** **Navigate through the Event Viewer logs while not freaking out.**

Even the best-kept system (well, my production system anyway) boasts reams of scary-looking error messages — hundreds, if not thousands of them. That's normal. See Table 4-1 for a breakdown.

**4.** **When you've finished using Event Viewer, click or tap X in the top-right corner.**

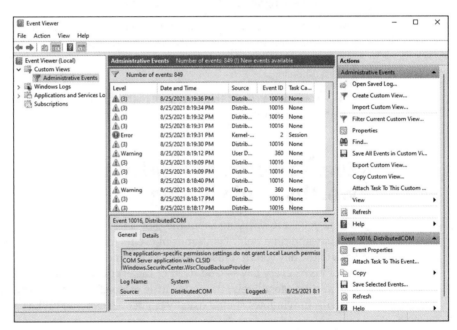

**FIGURE 4-1:**
Events logged by Windows.

The Administrative Events log isn't the only one you can see; it's a distillation of the other event logs, with an emphasis on the kinds of things a mere human might want to view.

**TABLE 4-1**

## Events and What They Mean

| Event | What Caused the Event |
|---|---|
| Error | Significant problem, possibly including loss of data |
| Warning | Not necessarily significant, but might indicate that there's a problem brewing |
| Information | Just a program calling home to say it's okay |

**TECHNICAL
STUFF**

Other logs include the following:

>> **Application events:** Programs report on their problems.

>> **Security events:** They're called *audits* and show the results of a security action. Results can be either successful or failed depending on the event, such as when a user tries to log in.

>> **Setup events:** This type of event primarily refers to domain controllers, which is something you don't need to worry about.

>> **System events:** Most of the errors and warnings you see in the Administrative Events log come from system events. They're reports from Windows system files about problems they've encountered. Almost all are self-healing.

>> **Forwarded events:** These are sent to this computer from other computers in the same network.

## Events worthy — and not worthy — of viewing

Before you start worrying about the thousands of errors on your PC, look closely at the date and time field. Thousands of events may be listed, but those probably date back to the day you first installed the PC. Chances are good that you can see a handful of items every day — and most of the events are just repeats of the same error or warning. Most likely, they have little or no effect on the way you use Windows. An *error* to Windows should usually trigger a yawn and "Who cares?" from you.

For example, looking through my most recent event log, I see a bunch of error ID 10010 generated by a source called DistributedCOM, telling me that the server didn't register with DCOM within the required timeout. Really and truly, no biggie.

If you aren't experiencing problems, don't sweat what's in Event Viewer. Even if you *are* experiencing problems, Event Viewer may or may not be able to help you.

**TIP**

How might Event Viewer help? In the Event ID column, note the ID number and then look it up at www.myeventlog.com. They may be able to point you in the right direction or at least translate the event ID into something resembling plain English. Figure 4-2 shows the results when I went looking for event ID 10010 — the DCOM problem.

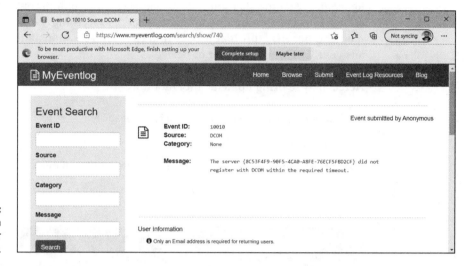

**FIGURE 4-2:**
The result of an event lookup for the error 10010.

If you are trying to track down a specific problem and notice an event that may relate to the problem, use Google or Bing to see whether you can find somebody else who's had the same problem. Event Viewer can also help you nail down network access problems because the Windows programs that control network communication spill a large amount of details into the event logs. Unfortunately, translating the logs into English can be a daunting task, but at least you may be able to tell where the problem occurs — even if you haven't a clue how to solve it.

# Gauging System Reliability

Every Windows routine leaves traces of itself in the Windows event log. Start a program, and the event gets logged. Stop it, and the log gets updated. Install an antivirus solution or a security update for Windows, and the log knows all, sees all. Every security-related event you can imagine goes in the log. Windows services leave their traces, as do errors of many stripes. Things that should've happened but didn't get logged, as well as things that shouldn't have happened but did.

The event log contains items that mere humans can understand. Sometimes. As mentioned, the event log consists of a mash-up of several files maintained by different Windows system programs in different ways. Event Viewer, discussed in the preceding section, looks at the trees. Reliability Monitor tries to put the forest in perspective.

**TIP**

Reliability Monitor slices and dices the event log, pulling out information that relates to your PC's stability. It doesn't catch everything — more about that in a moment. But the stuff that it does find can give you an instant insight into what ails your Windows computer or device.

Here's how to bring up Reliability Monitor:

**1. Click or tap the search icon and type** reliability.

You see a list of search results.

**2. At the top of the list, click or tap View Reliability History.**

Reliability Monitor springs to life, as shown in Figure 4-3.

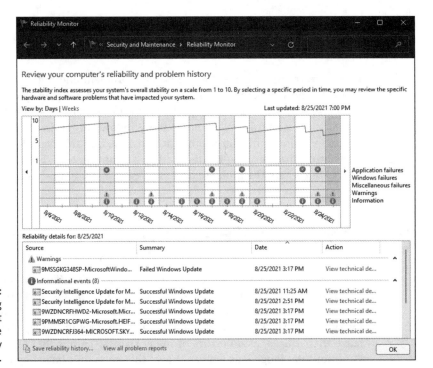

**FIGURE 4-3:** When something goes wrong, it leaves a trace in Reliability Monitor.

3. **Above the reliability graph, in the View By line, flip between Days and Weeks.**

   Reliability Monitor goes back and forth between a detailed daily view and a weekly overview. The box at the bottom shows you the corresponding entries in your event log.

4. **In the Reliability Details section in the bottom half the screen, click or tap the View Technical Details link for one of the entries.**

   Reliability Monitor presents a detailed explanation about the event that it logged.

5. **Click or tap OK to get back to the reliability graph, and then click or tap the View Technical Details link for other entries.**

6. **Click or tap the View All Problem Reports link at the bottom of Reliability Monitor.**

   You get a summary of problem reports, as shown in Figure 4-4.

7. **Close Reliability Monitor by clicking or tapping X in the top-right corner.**

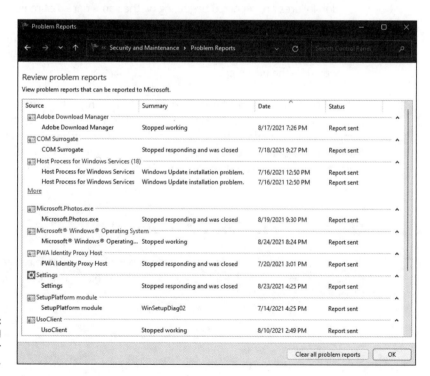

**FIGURE 4-4:**
A more detailed view of your problem reports.

**TECHNICAL STUFF**

Again, please don't freak out. There's a reason why Microsoft makes it hard to get to this report. It figures that if you're sophisticated enough to find it, you can bear to see the cold, hard facts.

The top line in the reliability graph is supposed to give you a rating, from one to ten, of your system's stability. In fact, it doesn't do anything of the sort, but if you see the line drop as shown in Figure 4-3, something undoubtedly has gone amiss.

**REMEMBER**

Your rating more or less reflects the number and severity of problematic event log events in four categories: application, Windows failures, miscellaneous failures, and warnings. The information icons (*i*-in-a-circle) generally represent updates to programs and drivers; if you installed a new printer driver, for example, there should be an information icon on the day it was installed. Microsoft has a detailed list of the types of data being reported in its TechNet documentation at `https://docs.microsoft.com/en-us/previous-versions/windows/it-pro/windows-vista/cc749583(v=ws.10)`. Here's what they say:

> Since you can see all of the activity on a single date in one report, you can make informed decisions about how to troubleshoot. For example, if frequent application failures are reported beginning on the same date that memory failures appear in the Hardware section, you can replace the faulty memory as a first step. If the application failures stop, they may have been a result of problems accessing the memory. If application failures continue, uninstalling and reinstalling those apps would be the next step.

**REMEMBER**

Reliability Monitor isn't meant to provide a comprehensive list of all the bad things that have happened to your PC, and in that respect, it certainly meets its design goals. It isn't much of a stability tracker, either. The one-to-ten rating uses a trailing average of daily scores, where more recent scores have greater weight than old ones, but in my experience, the line doesn't track reality.

## OTHER PERFORMANCE MONITORS

Windows 11 has two other monitors — *perfmon*, Performance Monitor, and *resmon*, Resource Monitor — that have been largely rendered obsolete because of Task Manager. I talk about Task Manager in Chapter 5 of this minibook. If you really want to see perfmon or resmon in action, type the appropriate name in the search box and then click or tap the only app that appears.

But I think you're going to like the new Task Manager much better.

The real value of Reliability Monitor lies in showing you a time sequence of key events — connecting the temporal dots so you might be able to discern a cause and effect. For example, if you suddenly start seeing blue screens repeatedly, check Reliability Monitor to see whether something untoward has happened to your system. Installing a new driver, say, can make your system unstable, and Reliability Monitor can readily show you when it was installed. If you see your rating tumble on the same day that a driver update got installed, something's fishy, and you may be able to readily identify the culprit.

The proverbial bottom line: Reliability Monitor doesn't keep track of everything and some of it is a bit deceptive, but it can provide some worthwhile information when Windows 11 starts misbehaving. Reliability Monitor is well worth adding to your bag of tricks.

IN THIS CHAPTER

» **Unveiling Task Manager**

» **Viewing and ending running apps and processes**

» **Keeping an eye on performance**

» **Viewing details about running processes and services**

» **Managing startup apps**

Chapter **5**

# Managing Running Apps, Processes, and Startup Apps

I t's easy to run apps in Windows 11. All you have to do is install them and then click or tap their shortcuts. However, some apps can cause problems. For example, your Windows 11 PC or device may become sluggish because lots of apps are starting automatically when you log into Windows. Some apps may crash or become unresponsive for no good reason. To help you manage this complexity, Windows 11 includes Task Manager, which makes it easy to see which apps and processes are running and to close those that are no longer responding to your commands. You can use Task Manager also to keep an eye on performance and identify the apps that eat up the most of your processor or network traffic, for example.

In this chapter I show you everything you need to know about using Task Manager. Then you can keep your running apps and startup apps in check, not the other way around.

# Using Task Manager

Task Manager is a versatile app that can handle any of the following jobs:

**REMEMBER**

» **Kill, or stop, an app or a program from running.** It doesn't matter if you're trying to kill a Windows 11 app from the Microsoft Store or an old-fashioned desktop app. Either way, one trip to Task Manager and *zap!*

» **Switch to any program.** This feature is convenient if you find yourself stuck somewhere — in a game, say, that doesn't let go — and you want to jump over to a different application. You can easily go to a Windows 11 app or desktop program.

» **See which processes are slowing down your PC.** *Processes* are all the executable files run by the apps you're using, by Windows itself, by your drivers, and so on. Task Manager shows you a list of all running processes. That list is invaluable if your PC is running like a slug and you can't figure out what is hogging the processor, eating up all your RAM, using the hard drive intensively, and so on.

» **Get real-time graphs of CPU, memory, disk, GPU, or network usage.** These graphs are cool and informative, and may even help you decide whether you need to buy more memory.

» **See which Microsoft Store apps use the most resources over a specified time period.** Did the Camera take up the most time on your PC in the past month? Instagram or maybe Mail and Calendar?

» **Turn off autostarting programs.** This procedure used to be a headache, but now it's surprisingly easy. Almost everyone has automaticallystarting programs that take up boot time and add to system overhead. Task Manager shows you the major programs that start automatically and gives you the option to disable them.

» **Send a message to other users on your PC.** The message shows up on the lock screen when you log off.

» **Display details about processes and services.** Task Manager lists all processes and services and allows you to start them, stop them, restart them, or find out more details about them online, so that you know what's what.

It's quite an impressive feature list, isn't it?

# Starting Task Manager

Before you can use Task Manager, you need to know how to start it and then close it. Follow these steps:

**1.** **Do one of the following:**

- Press Ctrl+Shift+Esc.

- Press Ctrl+Alt+Delete and then click or tap the Task Manager link in the screen that appears.

- Right-click (or press and hold down on) the Windows logo on the taskbar, and choose Task Manager in the menu that opens.

- Click or tap the search icon on the taskbar, type **task**, and at the top of the list of search results, click or tap Task Manager.

The Task Manager appears in its compact view, showing a list of running apps (see Figure 5-1).

**2.** **Click or tap More Details at the bottom.**

The full Task Manager is displayed with the Processes tab open, as shown in Figure 5-2.

**3.** **To get back to the compact view of Task Manager, click or tap Fewer Details.**

**4.** **To close Task Manager, click or tap the X in its top-right corner.**

You're back at the desktop.

# Viewing running apps and processes

The compact view of Task Manager (refer to Figure 5-1) displays only apps you've opened. You don't see all running processes, including those run by Windows 11, your drivers, antivirus, and so on. When you click or tap More Details, the Processes tab is displayed (refer to Figure 5-2). Here, Task Manager groups running programs depending on the type of program:

>> **Apps** are regular, everyday programs. They're the ones you started or the ones that are set to start automatically. (You may think that *apps* mean just desktop apps or touch-friendly Windows 11 apps — but no. These are programs of any stripe — whatever happens to be running.)

>> **Background processes** are run "hidden" from view by your installed apps, drivers, antivirus, and even Windows. Unlike apps, background processes don't have a user interface that you can see and click (or tap).

>> **Windows processes** are similar to background processes, except they are part of Windows itself and are started automatically by the operating system.

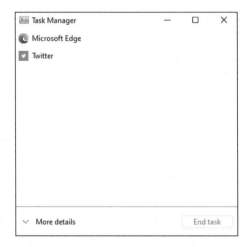

**FIGURE 5-1:**
The compact view of Task Manager.

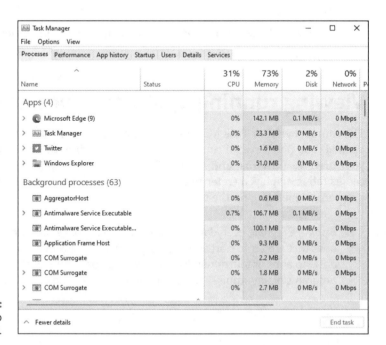

**FIGURE 5-2:**
The Processes tab in Task Manager.

When your Windows 11 PC is sluggish, you can use the Processes tab in Task Manager to identify which apps are eating up your CPU, memory, disk, or network bandwidth. Here's how:

1. **Start Task Manager by pressing Ctrl+Shift+Esc.**

   You see Task Manager's compact view.

2. **Click or tap More Details.**

   The Processes tab opens.

3. **To view which apps and processes are eating up the most of your processor's power, click or tap the CPU column on the right.**

   You see all apps and processes ordered by processor utilization, in decreasing order, as shown in Figure 5-3. To reverse the sort order, click or tap the heading of the current sort column.

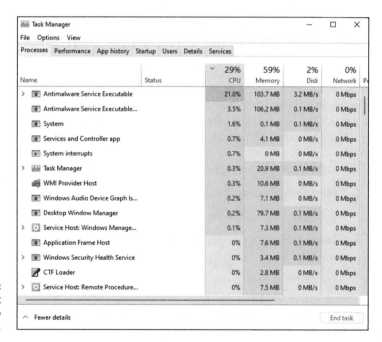

**FIGURE 5-3:**
View all apps that are eating up your CPU.

4. **To view which apps and processes are using the most RAM, click or tap the Memory column.**

   All running apps and processes are ordered by memory use, in decreasing order.

5. **Do the same with the Disk and Network columns, to view apps and processes sorted by their disk and network utilization, respectively.**

6. **To switch back to Task Manager's default view, click or tap the Name column.**

   Task Manager now lists everything in the Processes tab like it did when you started this exercise.

# Dealing with Misbehaving Apps

Are you using an app that is stuck and is no longer answering your commands? Or do you think some running apps are using too much RAM or eating up too much network bandwidth but you don't know which ones? In this section, you see how to deal with both situations.

## Killing apps that don't respond

When an app no longer responds to your commands, it's time to force-close it. You don't need to reboot Windows 11 — just use Task Manager. To see how to force-close an app, let's use Microsoft Edge as a guinea pig. I have nothing against guinea pigs — I think they're cute animals — and I like Microsoft Edge too. It's just that I have to choose an app to help you understand how it all works:

1. **Start Microsoft Edge by clicking or tapping its icon on the taskbar.**

2. **Start Task Manager by pressing Ctrl+Shift+Esc.**

   You see Task Manager's compact view.

3. **Select Microsoft Edge by clicking or tapping it in the Task Manager window.**

   The End Task button in the bottom-right corner changes color and is now usable, as shown in Figure 5-4.

4. **To force-stop Microsoft Edge, click or tap End Task.**

   Microsoft Edge closes immediately, without requesting confirmation.

**WARNING**

When you force-close an app in Windows, any edits you've made in the app are lost. For example, if you were working on an Excel spreadsheet and Excel stopped working, force-closing it means you would lose the latest changes between the moment the spreadsheet was last saved and when you clicked or tapped End Task.

**FIGURE 5-4:**
Task Manager allows you to force-close any running app.

# Keeping an eye on performance

The Performance tab displays live graphs of CPU usage, allocated memory, disk activity, video card GPU activity (if you have one or more separate graphic cards), and the volume of data running into and out of your machine on an Ethernet connection, a Wi-Fi connection, or both. If Bluetooth is turned on, the Performance tab also shows you the activity over your Bluetooth connection.

The number of items you see in the Performance tab varies based on your computer's hardware configuration. For example, if you have an SSD and a classic HDD, you'll see two Disk entries instead of one. If you have multiple network cards, they will all be listed.

Here's how to navigate the Performance tab in Task Manager:

**1.** **Start Task Manager by pressing Ctrl+Shift+Esc.**

You see Task Manager's compact view.

**2.** **Click or tap More Details.**

The Processes tab opens.

**3.** **Click or tap the Performance tab.**

The tab is split into several graphs: CPU, memory, disk, Wi-Fi, and so on.

**4.** **Click or tap CPU.**

The graph and data display in real time how much of your computer's processor is being utilized, as shown in Figure 5-5.

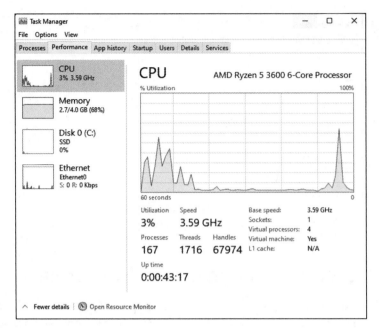

FIGURE 5-5:
Keep tabs on the
key components
of your PC's
performance.

**5.** **In turn, click or tap the other items on the Performance tab (Memory, Disk, and so on).**

Note the graphs and information displayed about the utilization of each hardware resource in your Windows 11 computer or device.

**6.** **To close Task Manager, click or tap the X in its top-right corner.**

You return to the desktop.

TECHNICAL
STUFF

If you want to see more detailed information — including the utilization of each of the cores of a multi-core CPU — click or tap the Open Resource Monitor link at the bottom of the Performance tab. The screen shown in Figure 5-6 appears.

I frequently keep Resource Monitor scrunched down and running on my desktop, so I can see my computer's current state of affairs at a glance.

Resource Monitor is my go-to app when anything starts acting wonky. Which is not all that uncommon in Windows, eh?

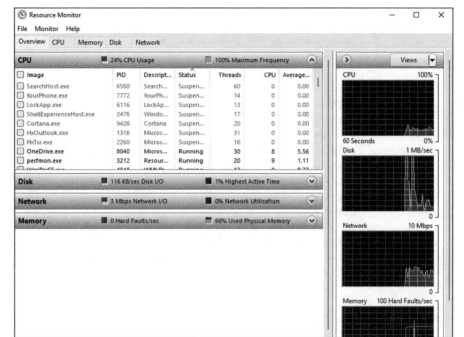

**FIGURE 5-6:**
Resource Monitor tells you at a glance what's going wrong with your machine.

# Getting More Info from Task Manager

So far, I've covered the most common ways in which people use Task Manager. However, what this app can do doesn't stop here. In this section, you discover some other useful features that will help you understand more about the apps you're using as well as manage the apps allowed to start with Windows.

## Viewing App History

The App History tab keeps a cumulative count of all the time you've spent in each of the various Windows 11 apps from the Microsoft Store. Here's how to use it:

1. **Start Task Manager by pressing Ctrl+Shift+Esc.**

2. **If you see the compact view, click or tap More Details.**

   The Processes tab opens.

3. **Click or tap the App History tab.**

   You see a list with all the Windows 11 apps you have, as shown in Figure 5-7.

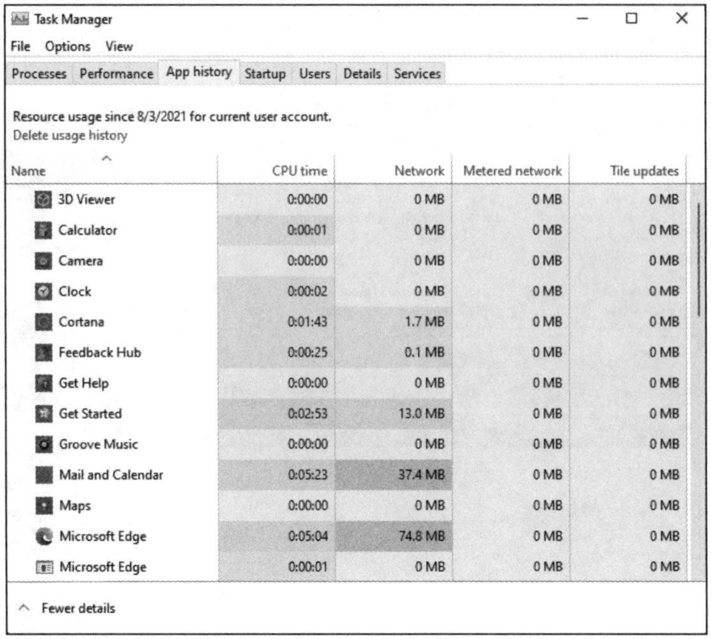

**FIGURE 5-7:**
A comprehensive list of all the time you've spent using each Windows 11 app.

4. **Click or tap the CPU Time column.**

   The list of apps is ordered based on how much they used your computer's processor.

5. **Click or tap the Network column.**

   The apps are ordered by how much data they transferred through your network connection.

6. **To return the App History tab to its default view, click or tap the Name column.**

7. **To close Task Manager, click or tap the X in its top-right corner.**

   You return to the desktop.

## Managing startup programs

Windows 11 automatically runs certain programs every time you start it, and those programs can slow down the boot procedure. This is especially true a couple of months after you start using your PC if you've installed many apps and games. The Startup tab in Task Manager displays all the programs that start automatically each time you log in, and enables you to disable them. For each startup program you see its name, publisher (the company who made it), status (enabled or disabled), and startup impact (high, medium, low, and so on).

If you want to disable an autorunning program, here's what you have to do:

1. **Start Task Manager by pressing Ctrl+Shift+Esc.**

2. **If you see compact view, click or tap More Details.**

   The Processes tab opens.

3. **Click or tap the Startup tab.**

   All apps and programs that run at your Windows 11's startup are listed, as shown in Figure 5-8.

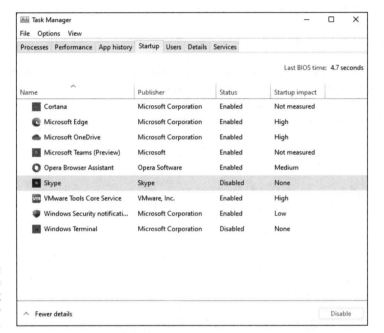

**FIGURE 5-8:**
A subset of those cycle-stealing auto-startup programs.

4. **Click or tap the program that you no longer want to run when Windows 11 starts.**

   The program is selected.

5. **Click or tap the Disable button in the bottom-right corner.**

   The program is now disabled from running at Windows 11 startup.

6. **To close Task Manager, click or tap its X.**

The Task Manager Startup tab shows you the application programs, their helper programs, and sometimes problematic programs that use well-known tricks to run every time Windows starts. Unfortunately, really bad programs frequently find ways to squirrel themselves away so that they don't appear on this list.

**REMEMBER**

Microsoft distributes an Autoruns program that digs into every nook and cranny of Windows and lists absolutely everything running during startup, including the hidden stuff.

Autoruns started as a free product from the small Sysinternals company and owes its existence to Mark Russinovich (now a celebrated novelist) and Bryce Cogswell, two of the most knowledgeable Windows folks on the planet. In July 2006, Microsoft bought Sysinternals and promised that all the free Sysinternals products would remain free. And wonder of wonders, that's exactly what happened.

To get Autoruns working, download it as a ZIP file from `https://docs.microsoft.com/en-us/sysinternals/downloads/autoruns` and extract the ZIP file. Autoruns.exe is the program you want. Double-click or double-tap to run it; no installation is required. See Figure 5-9.

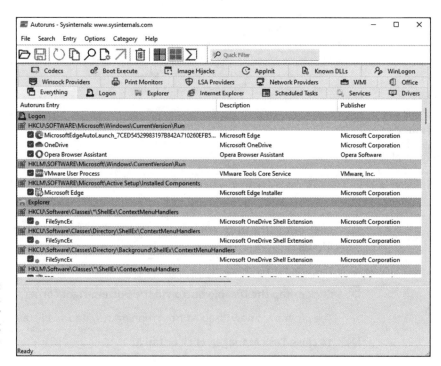

**FIGURE 5-9:**
Autoruns finds more sneaky autorunning programs than Task Manager.

**TIP**

After Autoruns is working on your computer, the following tips can help you start using the program:

>> **Autoruns lists an enormous number of autostarting programs.** Some appear in the most obscure corners of Windows. The Everything list shows all autostarting programs in the order they're run.

>> **Autoruns has many options.** You can get a good overview on its product page at https://docs.microsoft.com/en-us/sysinternals/downloads/autoruns. The option I use most is the capability to hide all autostarting Microsoft programs. Choose Options, and then select Hide Microsoft Entries. The result is a clean list of all the foreign stuff being launched automatically by Windows.

>> **Autoruns can suspend an autostarting program.** To suspend a program, deselect the box to the left of the program's name and reboot Windows. If you zap an autostarting program and your computer doesn't work right, run Autoruns again and select the box. Easy.

**WARNING**

You shouldn't disable an autostarting program just because it looks superfluous or even because you figure it contributes to global warming or slow startups, whichever comes first. As a general rule, if you don't know *exactly* what an autostarting program does, don't touch it.

On the other hand, if you concentrate on autostarting programs that don't come from Microsoft, you may find a few things that you don't want or need — items that deserve to get consigned to the bit bucket.

## Checking out details and services

If you used Task Manager in Windows 7 or earlier, you've seen the version shown in Figure 5-10. The Details tab shows all the running processes, regardless of which user is attached to the process.

The Services tab, similarly, displays all Windows services that have been started, as shown in Figure 5-11. Once in a blue moon, you may find a Windows error message that some service or another (say, the printer service or some sort of networking service) isn't running. This tab is where you can tell whether the service is really running.

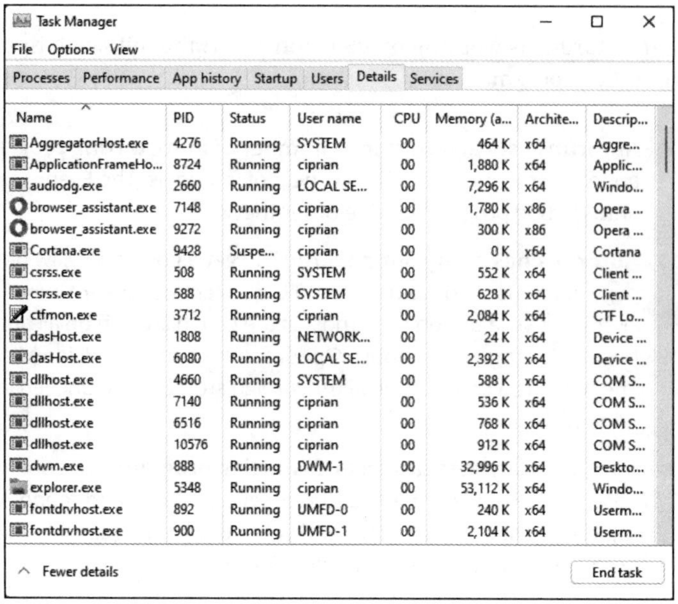

**FIGURE 5-10:**
All details about every process appear here.

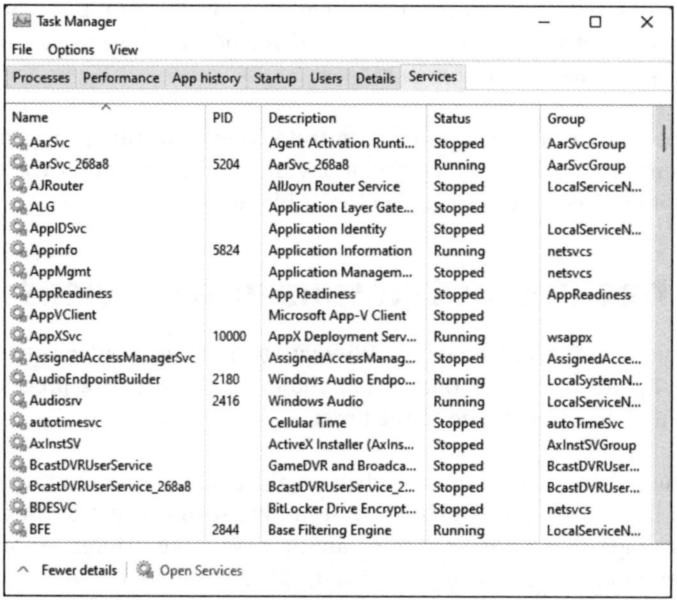

**FIGURE 5-11:**
See details about Windows services.

# Managing Startup Apps from Settings

Another easy way to manage startup apps is from Settings, which has the advantage of working well with tablets and other Windows 11 touchscreen devices. Just tap your finger in a few places, and you're done. Here's how it works:

**1.** **Click or tap the Start icon and then the Settings icon.**

The Settings app is loaded.

**2.** **Go to Apps and then to Startup.**

All apps that can be configured to start when you log into Windows 11 are displayed, as shown in Figure 5-12. For each app (or program), you see its name, the company who made it, its effect on the Windows 11 startup, and whether it's turned on or off.

**3.** **For each app that you want to stop from automatically starting with Windows, click or tap its switch to turn it off.**

The next time you log into Windows 11, your startup settings will be applied.

Managing Running Apps, Processes, and Startup Apps

**FIGURE 5-12:** Managing Windows 11 startup apps from Settings.

# Securing Windows

# Contents at a Glance

# Chapter 1

# Spies, Spams, and Scams Are Out to Get You

Windows XP had more security holes than a prairie-dog field. Windows Vista was built on top of Windows XP, and the holes were hidden better. Windows 7 followed Windows Vista and included innovative security capabilities and represented the first significant break from XP's lethargic approach to security. Windows 8 included marginal security improvements to Windows itself, as well as better safety nets to keep you from shooting yourself in the foot and a fully functional, very capable antivirus program.

Windows 10 introduced a Windows Security app that acts as a control panel for all security tools built into the operating system. And luckily, they were many of them, including a much-improved Microsoft Defender Antivirus. Windows 11 further fine-tunes the security tools from Windows 10, but its biggest contribution to your security is that Microsoft finally got rid of Internet Explorer.

TIP

The single best security recommendation I can give you: Don't run Internet Explorer. Ever. Yes, you don't have it in Windows 11, but maybe there's a Windows 10 PC around. Second-best security recommendation: Disable Flash and Java if you still have them around. Third: Use anything but Adobe Reader to open PDFs. By default, Windows 11 uses Microsoft Edge to open PDFs, and that's a good choice.

**REMEMBER**

Those three simple no's —no Flash, no Java, no Adobe Reader — combined with periodic security updates, some restraint in clicking OK in every dialog box, and paying attention when installing software of any type will protect you from at least 90 percent of all common infections with viruses, ransomware, and other types of malware.

Targeted infections, though, are another story. There's a lot of money to be made — and wealthy governments to please — with very narrowly defined information-gathering techniques. Unless you work for a defense contractor or a Tibetan relief organization or are trying to keep a big company such as Target away from the bad guys, you probably don't have much to worry about. But it doesn't hurt to keep your guard up.

In this chapter, I explain the source of real threats. I bet it'll surprise you to find out that Adobe (Flash, Reader) and Oracle (Java) let more bad guys into Windows systems than Microsoft. I also take you outside the box, to show you the kinds of problems people face with their computer systems and to look at a few key solutions. And I look even farther outside the box, to mass password leaks — think Verizon, Equifax, Uber, Target, Home Depot, MasterCard, Visa, Yahoo!, Facebook, LinkedIn, and the billion-plus compromised accounts (many with deciphered passwords, credit card numbers, and personal info) that are being sold every day like electronic trading cards. Then I concentrate on the problem *du jour* — ransomware, an increasingly distressing threat to every computer.

Most of all, I want you to understand that (1) you shouldn't take a loaded gun, point it at your foot, aim carefully, and pull the trigger, (2) any information online is vulnerable, and (3) if you're smart and can control your clicking finger, you don't need to spend a penny on malware protection. Windows 11 offers you enough protection.

# Understanding the Hazards — and the Hoaxes

Many of the best-known internet-borne scares in the past two decades — WannaCry, NotPetya, Rustock, Waledac, Esthost, Conficker, Mebroot, Netsky, Melissa, ILOVEYOU, and their ilk — work by using the programmability built into specific operating systems and apps or by taking advantage of Windows holes to inject themselves into unprotected machines (see Figure 1-1).

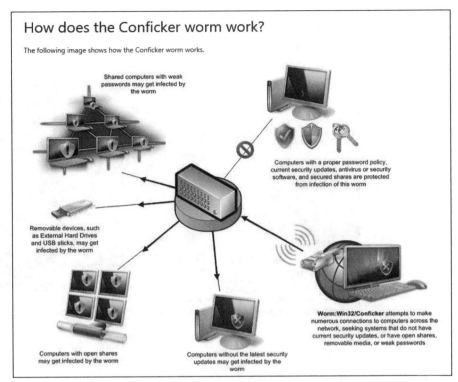

## How does the Conficker worm work?

The following image shows how the Conficker worm works.

Shared computers with weak passwords may get infected by the worm

Computers with a proper password policy, current security updates, antivirus or security software, and secured shares are protected from infection of this worm

Removable devices, such as External Hard Drives and USB sticks, may get infected by the worm

Worm:Win32/Conficker attempts to make numerous connections to computers across the network, seeking systems that do not have current security updates, or have open shares, removable media, or weak passwords

Computers with open shares may get infected by the worm

Computers without the latest security updates may get infected by the worm

**FIGURE 1-1:**
The Conficker worm employed programmability built into Windows and exploited security holes that had been patched months earlier.

*Source: Microsoft*

Fast-forward a dozen years or more, and the concepts have changed. The old threats are still there, but they've taken on a new twist: The scent of money, and sometimes political motivation, has made *cracking* (or breaking in to PCs for nefarious ends) far more sophisticated. What started as a bunch of miscreants playing programmer one-upmanship at your expense has turned into a profitable — sometimes highly profitable — business enterprise.

**WARNING**

Where's the money? At least at this moment — and for the foreseeable future — the greatest profits are made by using botnets and phishing attacks, to scramble data and demand a ransom. That's where you should expect the most sophisticated, most damnably difficult attacks. Unless you're running a nuclear reactor or an antigovernment campaign, of course. You get to choose which government.

## The primary infection vectors

How do computers *really* get infected?

According to Microsoft's Security Intelligence Report 11, the single greatest security gap is the one between your ears. See Figure 1-2. (Pro tip: You can find the latest MS Security Intelligence Report at www.microsoft.com/sir. They're always intriguing.)

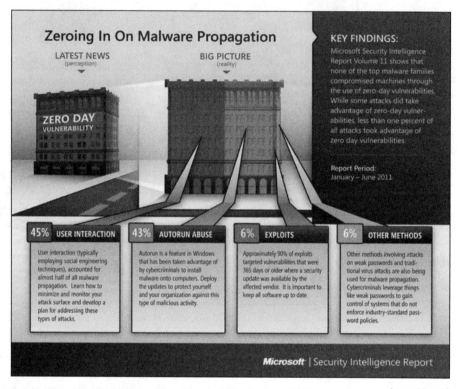

**FIGURE 1-2:**
Most infections happen when people don't think about what they're doing.

*Source: Microsoft*

Many years ago, the biggest PC threat came from newly discovered security holes: The bad guys use the holes before you get your machine patched, and you're toast. They traded them like baseball cards. Those holes still get lots of attention, especially in the press, but they aren't the leading cause of widespread infection. Not even close. A large majority of infections happen when people get tricked into clicking something they shouldn't.

Narrow, targeted infections, though, tend to rely on previously unknown security holes. It's hard for the big boys to protect against that kind of attack. Little folks like you and me don't really stand a chance.

Then there are the EternalBlue-style exploits that borrow sneaky techniques developed by government think tanks. These security holes, discovered by well-funded governmental organizations, find their way from top-secret incubators to $50 black market Script Kiddie bundles.

# Zombies and botnets

Every month, Microsoft posts a new Malicious Software Removal Tool that scans PCs for malware and, in many cases, removes it. In a study, Microsoft reported that 62 percent of all PC systems that were found to have malicious software also had backdoors. That's a sobering figure.

A *backdoor* program breaks through the usual Windows security measures and allows a scumbag to take control of your computer over the internet, effectively turning your machine into a zombie. The most sophisticated backdoors allow creeps to adapt (upgrade, if you will) the malicious software running on a subverted machine. And they do it by remote control.

Backdoors frequently arrive on your PC when you install a program you want, not realizing that the backdoor came along for the ride.

Less commonly, PCs acquire backdoors when they come down with some sort of infection: The Conficker, Mebroot, Mydoom, Sobig, TDL4/Alureon, Rustock, Waledac, and ZeuS worms installed backdoors. Many of the infections occur on PCs that haven't kept Java, Flash, or the Adobe Acrobat Reader up to date. The most common mechanism for infection is a *buffer overflow* (see the nearby "What's a buffer overflow?" sidebar).

An evildoer who controls one machine by way of a backdoor can't claim much street cred. But someone who puts together a *botnet* — a collection of hundreds or thousands of PCs — can take his zombies to the bank:

>> A botnet running a *keylogger* (a program that watches what you type and sporadically sends the data to the botnet's controller) can gather all sorts of valuable information. The single biggest problem facing those who gather and disseminate keylogger information? Bulk — the sheer volume of stolen information. How do you scan millions of characters of logged data and retrieve a bank account number or a password?

>> Unscrupulous businesses hire botnet controllers to disseminate spam, harvest email addresses, and even direct coordinated distributed denial-of-service (DDoS) attacks against rivals' websites. (A *DDoS attack* guides thousands of PCs to send requests to a particular website simultaneously, blocking legitimate use.)

There's a fortune to be made in botnets. The Rustock botnet alone was responsible for somewhere between 10 and 30 *billion* pieces of spam per day. Spammers paid the Rustock handlers, either directly or on commission.

## WHAT'S A BUFFER OVERFLOW?

If you've been following the progress of malware in general, and the beatings delivered to Windows in particular, you've no doubt run across the term *buffer overflow* or *buffer overrun* — a favorite tool in the arsenal of many virus writers. A buffer overflow may sound mysterious, but it is, at its heart, quite simple.

Programmers set aside small areas in their programs to transfer data from one program to another. Those places are buffers. A problem arises when too much data is put in a buffer (or if you look at it from the other direction, when the buffer is too small to hold all the data that's being put in it). You may think that having ten pounds of meat in a five-pound bag would make the program scream murder, but many programs aren't smart enough to look, much less cry uncle and give up.

When too much data exists in the buffer, some of it can spill into the program itself. If the bad players who are stuffing too much data into the buffer are clever, they may be able to convince the program that the extra data isn't data but is instead another part of the program, waiting to be run. The worm sticks lots of data in a small space and ensures that the piece that flops out will perform whatever malicious deed the worm's creator wants. Then, the program finds itself executing data that was stuffed into the buffer — running a program that was written by the worm's creator. That's how a buffer overrun can take control of your computer.

Every worm that uses a buffer-overrun security hole in Windows takes advantage of a programming error inside Windows, but nowadays it's more common for the buffer overflows to happen in Flash, Java, or some other program.

The most successful botnets run as *rootkits,* programs (or collections of programs) that operate deep inside Windows, concealing files and making it extremely difficult to detect their presence.

**TECHNICAL STUFF**

Many people first heard about rootkits in late 2005, when a couple of security researchers discovered that certain CDs from Sony BMG surreptitiously installed rootkits on computers: If you merely played the CD on your computer, the rootkit took hold. Several lawsuits later, Sony finally saw the error of its ways and vowed to stop distributing rootkits with its CDs. Nice guys. The researchers who discovered the problem, Mark Russinovich and Bryce Cogswell, were later hired by Microsoft.

Preinstalled software — crapware, installed by the folks who sell you computers — has opened significant security holes on machines made by Acer, Asus, Dell, HP, and Lenovo (see `https://duo.com/assets/pdf/out-of-box-exploitation_oem-updaters.pdf`). All the more reason to run the Start Fresh routine on any new machine as soon as you get it — or buy a Signature machine from the Microsoft Store.

Microsoft deserves lots of credit for taking down botnets in innovative, lawyer-laden ways. In October 2010, 116 people were arrested worldwide for running fraudulent banking transactions, thanks to Microsoft's tracking abilities. When the folks of Microsoft went after the ZeuS botnet, they convinced a handful of companies whose logos were being used to propagate the botnet to go to court. The assembled group used the RICO laws — the racketeering laws in the United States — to get a takedown order. On March 23, 2012, US Marshals took out two command centers — one in Illinois, the other in Pennsylvania — and effectively shut down ZeuS. Microsoft also led the efforts to take down the Waledac, Rustock, and Kelihos botnets.

## Phishing

WARNING

Do you think that message from Wells Fargo (or eBay, the IRS, PayPal, Citibank, a smaller regional bank, Visa, MasterCard, or whatever) asking to verify your account password (Social Security number, account number, address, telephone number, mother's maiden name, or whatever) looks official? Think again.

### WHAT ABOUT STUXNET?

Few computer topics have sucked in the mainstream press as thoroughly as the Stuxnet worm — the Windows-borne piece of malware that apparently took out several centrifuges in Iran's uranium enrichment facility.

Here's what I know for sure about Stuxnet: It's carried by Windows but doesn't do anything dastardly until it finds that it's connected to a specific kind of Siemens computer that's used for industrial automation. When it finds that it's connected to that specific kind of Siemens computer, it plants a rootkit on the computer that disrupts operation of whatever the computer's controlling. And that specific Siemens computer controlled the centrifuges at Iran's enrichment plant.

The people who wrote Stuxnet are adept at both Windows infection methods and Siemens computer programming. David Sanger, chief Washington correspondent for *The New York Times,* claims convincingly in his book *Confront and Conceal* (published by Crown) that Stuxnet originated as a collaboration between the US National Security Agency and a secret Israeli military unit, and subsequent revelations have confirmed that's almost undoubtedly the case.

Did you get a message from someone on eBay saying that you had better pay for the computer you bought or else he'll report you? Gotcha. Perhaps a notification that you have received an online greeting card from a family member — and when you try to retrieve it, you have to join the greeting card site and enter a credit card number? Gotcha again.

*Phishing* — sending email that attempts to extract personal information from you, usually by using a bogus website — has in many cases reached levels of sophistication that exceed the standards of the financial institutions themselves. Some phishing messages, such as the bogus message in Figure 1-3, warn you about the evils of phishing, in an attempt to persuade you to send your account number and password to a scammer in Kazbukistan (or New York).

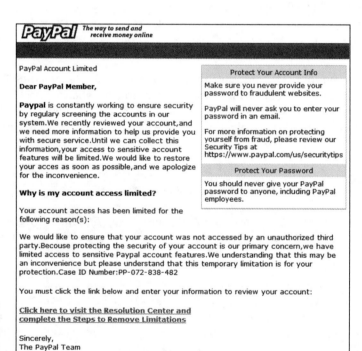

**FIGURE 1-3:**
If you click the link, you open a page that looks much like the PayPal page, and any information you enter is sent to a scammer.

Here's how phishing works:

**1.** A scammer, often using a fake name and a stolen credit card, sets up a website.

Usually it's quite a professional-looking site — in some cases, indistinguishable from the authentic site it tries to clone.

**2.** The website asks for personal information — most commonly, your account number and password or the PIN for your ATM card. See Figure 1-4 for an example.

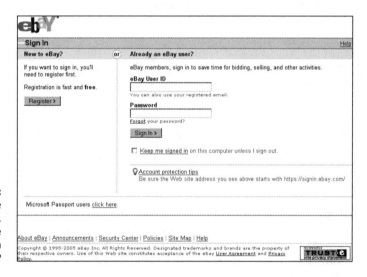

**FIGURE 1-4:**
This is a fake eBay sign-on site. Can you tell the difference from the original?

**3.** The scammer turns spammer and sends hundreds of thousands of bogus messages.

The messages include a clickable link to the fake website and a plausible story about how you must go to the website, log in, and do something to avoid dire consequences. The From address on the messages is spoofed so that the message appears to come from the company in question.

The message usually includes official logos — many even include links to the real website, even though they encourage you to click through to the fake site.

**4.** A small percentage of the recipients of the spam email open it and click through to the fake site.

**5.** If they enter their information, it's sent directly to the scammer.

6. The scammer watches incoming traffic from the fake website, gathers the information typed by gullible people, and uses it quickly — typically, by logging on to the bank's website and attempting a transfer or by burning a fake ATM card and using the PIN.

7. Within a day or two — or sometimes just hours — the website is shut down, and everything disappears into thin air.

Phishing has become hugely popular because of the sheer numbers involved. Say a scammer sends 1 million email messages advising Wells Fargo customers to log in to their accounts. Only a small fraction of all the people who receive the phishing message will be Wells Fargo customers, but if the hit rate is just 1 percent, that's 10,000 customers.

Most of the Wells Fargo customers who receive the message are smart enough to ignore it. But a sizable percentage — maybe 10 percent, maybe just 1 percent — will click through. That's somewhere between 100 and 1,000 suckers, er, customers.

If half the people who click through provide their account details, the scammer gets 50 to 500 account numbers and passwords. If most of those arrive within a day of sending the phishing message, the scammer stands to make a pretty penny indeed — and can disappear with hardly a trace.

I'm not talking about using your credit card online. Online credit card transactions are as safe as they are face to face — more so, actually, because if you use a US-based credit card, you aren't liable for any loss caused by somebody snatching your card information or any other form of fraud. I use my credit cards online all the time. You should, too. (See "Using your credit card safely online," later in this chapter, for more information.)

Here's how to fight against phishing:

>> **Use the latest versions of Microsoft Edge, Firefox, Opera, or Google Chrome.** All browsers contain sophisticated — although not perfect — antiphishing features that warn you before you venture to a dodgy site. See the warning in Figure 1-5.

>> **If you encounter a website that looks like it may be a phishing site, report it.** Use the tools in Microsoft Edge, Firefox, Opera, or Chrome. Use all four if you have a chance! Chrome and Firefox use the same malicious site database. To report a site, go to www.google.com/safebrowsing/report_phish.

**WARNING**

>> **If you receive an email message that contains any links to the web, don't click them.** Nowadays, almost all messages with links to commercial sites are phishing come-ons. Financial institutions, in particular, don't send messages with links any more — and few other companies would dare. If you feel motivated to check out a dire message — for example, if it looks like somebody on eBay is planning to sue you for something you didn't do — open your favorite browser and type the address of the company by hand.

>> **Never include personal information in an email message and send it.** Personal information includes your address, Social Security or government ID number, passport number, phone number, or bank account information. Don't give out any of your personal information unless you manually log in to the company's website. Remember that unless you encrypt your email messages, they travel over the internet in plain-text form. Anybody (or any government) that's "sniffing" the mail can see everything you've written. It's roughly analogous to sending a postcard, with the NSA as the addressee, and Google and Microsoft on the cc list.

>> **If you receive a phishing message that may be new or different, check the linked site by using the PhishTank database at** www.phishtank.com. If you don't see your phishing site listed, submit a copy to PhishTank (which is a service of OpenDNS).

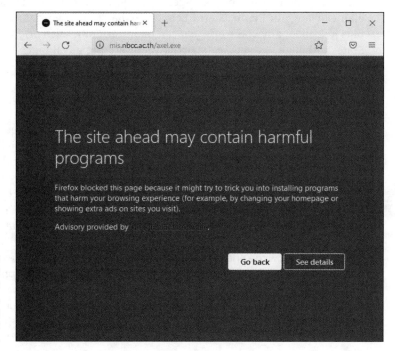

**FIGURE 1-5:**
If enough people report a site as being dangerous, you see a warning like this one from Firefox.

# 419 scams

*Greetings,*

*I am writing this letter to you in good faith and I hope my contact with you will transpire into a mutual relationship now and forever. I am Mrs. Omigod Mugambi, wife of the late General Rufus Mugambi, former Director of Mines for the Dufus Diamond Dust Co Ltd of Central Eastern Lower Leone . . .*

I'm sure you're smart enough to pass over email like that. At least, I hope so. It's an obvious setup for the classic 419 ("four one nine") scam — a scam so common that it has a widely accepted name, which derives from Nigerian Criminal Code Chapter 38, Article 419.

Much more sophisticated versions of the 419 scam are making the rounds today. The basic approach is to convince you to send money to someone, usually via Western Union. If you send the money, you'll never see it again, no matter how hard the sell or dire the threatened consequences.

**REMEMBER**

There's a reason why everybody gets so much 419 scam email. It's a huge business. Some people reckon it's the third to fifth largest revenue-generating business in Nigeria. I have no way of verifying independently whether that's true, but certainly these folks are raking in an enormous amount of money. And, in many cases, they don't work out of Nigeria: 419 scams are a significant source of foreign exchange in Benin, Sierra Leone, Ghana, Togo, Senegal, and Burkina Faso, plus just about anywhere else you can mention. Some even originate in the United States although, as you see shortly, there are big advantages to working out of small countries.

Here's one of the new variations of the old 419. It all starts when you place an ad that appears online. It doesn't really matter what you're selling, as long as it's physically large and valuable. It doesn't matter where you advertise — I've seen reports of this scam being played on Craigslist advertisers and major online sites, tiny nickel ad publishers, local newspapers, and anywhere else ads are placed.

**WARNING**

The scammer sends you an email from a Gmail address. I got one recently that said, "I will like to know if this item is still available for sale?" I wrote back and said, yes, it is, and can be looked at anytime. The scammer wrote back:

"Let me know the price in USD? I am OK with the item it looks like new in the photos I am from Liverpool U.K., i am sorry i will not be able to come for the viewing, i will arrange for the pickup after payment has been made, all documentation will be done by the shipper, so you don't have to worry about that. Thanks"

Three key points: the scammer

>> Is using a Gmail address, which can't be traced with anything short of a court order.

>> Claims to be out of the country, which makes pursuing the person very difficult.

>> Claims that a shipper will pick up the item. The plot thickens.

Also, the grammar falls somewhere between atrocious and unintelligible. Unfortunately, that isn't a sure sign, but it's not bound to inspire confidence.

I wrote back and gave the person a price, but I expressed concern about the shipper. The person then wrote that the shipper would be sent from the UK for pickup and said, "I will be paying the PayPal charges from my account and i will be paying directly into your PayPal account without any delay, and i hope you have a PayPal account."

I gave the scammer a dormant PayPal account, listing my address as that of the local police station. The scammer wrote back quite quickly:

"I have just completed the Payment and i am sure you have received the confirmation from PayPal regarding the Payment. You can check your paypal email for confirmation of payment.a total of 25,982usd was sent, 24,728usd for the item and the extra 1,200usd for my shipper's charges, which you will be sending to the address below via western union."

And then the scammer gave me the name of someone in Devon, UK:

"You should send the money soon so that the Pick Up would be scheduled and you would know when the Pick Up would commence, make sure you're home. I advise you to check both your inbox and junk/spam folder for the payment confirmation message."

I then received a message that claimed to be from Service-Intl.PayPal.Com:

"The Transaction will appear as soon as the western union information is received from you, we have to follow this procedure due to some security reason . . . the Money was sent through the Service Option Secure Payment so that the transaction can be protected with adequate security measures for you to be able to receive your money. The Shipping Company only accept payment through Western Union You have nothing to doubt about, You are safe and secured doing this transaction and your account will be credited immediately the western union receipt of *1,200USD* is received from you."

There's the hook. Of course, the message didn't come from PayPal, much less from www.paypal.com. I strung the scammer along for several days. Ultimately the person threatened me with legal action, invoking PayPal and the FBI as antagonists; see Figure 1-6.

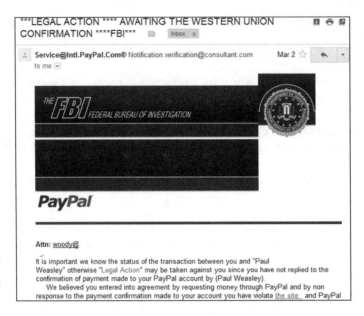

**FIGURE 1-6:**
Oh me, oh my, he's going to send the FBI.

In the end, the scammer and any cohorts were quite sloppy. Most of the time when scammers send email from "PayPal," they use a virtual private network (VPN; see Chapter 4 in this minibook) to make it look like the mail came from the United States. But on three separate occasions, the scammer I was conversing with forgot to turn on the VPN. Using a very simple technique, I traced all three messages back to one specific internet service provider in Lagos, Nigeria.

So I had three scamming messages with identified IP addresses, the name of a large internet service provider in Nigeria, and a compelling case for PayPal (to defend its name) and Western Union (which was being used as a drop) to follow up.

REMEMBER

I sent copies of the messages to Western Union and PayPal. I got back form letters — it's unlikely that a human even read them. I wrote to the ISP, MTN Nigeria. They responded, but the upshot is disheartening:

> "All our 3G network subscribers now sit behind a small number of IP addresses. This is done via a technology called network address translation (NAT). In essence, it means that 1 million subscribers may appear to the outside world as one subscriber because they are all using the same IP address."

So now you know why Nigerians love to conduct their scams over the Nigerian 3G network. No doubt MTN Nigeria could sift through its NAT logs and find out who was connected at precisely the right time, but tracing a specific email back to an individual would be difficult, if not impossible — and it would certainly require a court order.

If you know people who post ads online, you may want to warn them.

## I'm from Microsoft, and I'm here to help

The scam that supposedly involves Microsoft's support people really hurts me because I've made a career out of helping people with Microsoft problems.

**WARNING**

Someone calls and says they've been referred by Microsoft to help with your Windows problem. They are convincing and say that they heard about your problem from a post you made online, or from your internet service provider, or from a computer user group. They even give a website as reference, a very convincing site that has the Microsoft Registered Partner logo.

You explain the problem. Then one of two things happens. Either they request your 25-character Windows activation key or ask for permission to connect to your computer, typically using Remote Assistance (see Book 7, Chapter 3).

If you let them onto your machine, heaven knows what they'll do. If you give them your activation key — or they look up your validation key while controlling your PC — they'll pretend to refer to the "Microsoft registration database" (or something similar) and give you the bad news that your machine is all screwed up and out of warranty, but they can fix it for a mere $189.

**REMEMBER**

As proof positive that your machine's on its last legs, they'll probably show you Event Viewer. As I mention in Book 8, Chapter 4, Event Viewer on a *normal* machine shows all sorts of scary-looking warnings. And that Microsoft Registered Partner stuff? Anybody can become a Microsoft Registered Partner — it takes maybe two minutes, and all you need is a Microsoft account — a Hotmail, Live, or Outlook.com ID. Don't believe it? Go to `https://partner.microsoft.com/` and fill out the forms.

The overwhelming con give-away — the big red flag — in all this: *Microsoft doesn't work that way.* Think about it. Microsoft isn't going to call you to solve your problems, unless you've received a very specific commitment from a specific individual in the organization — a commitment that invariably comes only after repeated phone calls on your part, generally accompanied by elevation to lofty levels of the support organization on multiple continents. Microsoft doesn't respond to random online requests for help by calling a customer. Sorry. Doesn't happen.

**TIP**

If you aren't sure whether you're being conned, ask the person on the other end of the line for your Microsoft Support Case *tracking number* — every tech support interaction has a tracking number or Support ID. Then ask for a phone number and offer to call the person back. Con artists won't leave trails.

If the con is being run from overseas — much more common in these days of nearly free VoIP cold calling — your chances of nailing the perpetrator runs from extremely slim to none. So be overly suspicious of any "Microsoft Expert" who doesn't seem to be calling from your country.

Microsoft knows all about the tech support scams — one of their blog posts claimed that "three million [Microsoft] customers this year alone" had been hit by scummy scammers. In the first legal action of its kind, in late December 2014, Microsoft sued Omnitech Support, a division of Customer Focus Services, "and related entities," claiming unfair and deceptive business practices and trademark infringement.

Microsoft's filing says the scammers "have utilized the Microsoft trademarks and service marks to enhance their credentials and confuse customers about their affiliation with Microsoft. Defendants then use their enhanced credibility to convince consumers that their personal computers are infected with malware in order to sell them unnecessary technical support and security services to clean their computers."

The Customer Focus Services website says it's "A pioneer in India-based offshoring with over a decade of experience in call center outsourcing . . . [with] Multi-location delivery (offshore and onshore) centers in India (Bangalore)." Wonder how long it'll take for them to fold up their company in the US, and continue overseas?

If you've already been conned — given out personal information or a credit card number — start by contacting your bank or the credit card issuing company and follow its procedures for reporting identity theft.

## 0day exploits

What do you do when you discover a brand-new security hole in Windows or Office or another Microsoft product? Why, you sell it, of course.

When a person writes a malicious program that takes advantage of a newly discovered security hole — a hole that even the manufacturer doesn't know about — that malicious program is a *0day exploit.* (Fuddy-duddies call it "zero-day exploit." The hopelessly hip say "zero day" or "sploit.")

0days are valuable. In some cases, very valuable. The Trend Micro antivirus company has a subsidiary — *TippingPoint* — that buys 0day exploits. TippingPoint works with the software manufacturer to come up with a fix for the exploit, but at the same time, it sells corporate customers immediate protection against the exploit. "TippingPoint's goal for the Zero Day Initiative is to provide our customers with the world's best intrusion prevention systems and secure converged networking infrastructure." TippingPoint offers up to $10,000 for a solid security hole.

Rumor has it that several less-than-scrupulous sites arrange for the buying and selling of new security holes. Apparently, the Russian hacker group that discovered a vulnerability in the way Windows handles WMF graphics files sold its new hole for $4,000, not realizing that it could've made much more. In 2012, *Forbes Magazine* estimated the value of 0days as ranging from $5,000 to $250,000. You can check it out at the following URL: `www.forbes.com/sites/andygreenberg/2012/03/23/shopping-for-zero-days-an-price-list-for-hackers-secret-software-exploits`.

Bounties keep getting bigger. Google's Pwnium competition offers up to $2.7 million for hacks against its Chrome OS, and significant bonuses for other cracks. The Zero Day Initiative (from TippingPoint) now offers more than $500,000 in prize money for the best cracks in the Pwn2Own contest — and an additional $400,000 for the separate Mobile Pwn2Own.

According to *Forbes,* some government agencies are in the market. Governments certainly buy 0day exploits from a notorious 0day brokering firm. The problem (some would say "opportunity") is getting worse, not better. Governments are now widely rumored to have thousands — some of them, tens of thousands — of stockpiled 0day exploits at hand.

How do you protect yourself from 0day exploits? In some ways, you can't: By definition, nobody sees a 0day coming, although most antivirus products employ some sort of heuristic detection that tries to clamp down on exploits based solely on the behavior of the offensive program. Mostly, you have to rely on the common-sense protection that I describe in the section "Getting Protected," later in this chapter. You must also stay informed, which I talk about in the next section.

# Staying Informed

When you rely on the evening news to keep yourself informed about the latest threats to your computer's well-being, you quickly discover that the mainstream press frequently doesn't get the details right. Hey, if you were a news writer with a deadline ten minutes away and you had to figure out how the new Bandersnatch 0day exploit shreds through a Windows TCP/IP stack buffer — and you had to explain your discoveries to a TV audience, at a presumed sixth-grade intelligence level — what would you do?

The following sections offer tips on getting the facts.

## Relying on reliable sources

Fortunately, some reliable sources of information exist on the internet. It would behoove you to check them out from time to time, particularly when you hear about a new computer security hole, real or imagined:

**REMEMBER**

>> **The Microsoft Security Response Center (MSRC) blog** presents thoroughly researched analyses of outstanding threats, from a Microsoft perspective (https://msrc-blog.microsoft.com/category/msrc/).

The information you see on the MSRC blog is 100-percent Microsoft Party Line — so there's a tendency to add more than a little "spin control" to the announcements. Nevertheless, Microsoft has the most extensive and best resources to analyze and solve Windows problems, and the MSRC blog frequently has inside information that you can't find anywhere else.

>> **SANS Internet Storm Center (ISC)** pools observations and analyses from thousands of active security researchers. You can generally get the news first — and accurately — from the ISC (https://isc.sans.org/).

**TIP**

Take a moment right now to look up those sites and add them to your Firefox or Chrome bookmarks or Microsoft Edge favorites. Unlike the antimalware software manufacturers' websites, these sites have no particular ax to grind or product to sell. (Well, okay, Microsoft wants to sell you something, but you already bought it, yes?)

From time to time, Microsoft also releases security advisories, which generally warn about newly discovered 0day threats in Microsoft products. You can find those, too, at the MSRC blog.

## Ditching the hoaxes

Tell me whether you've heard any of these:

>> "Amazing Speech by Joe Biden!" "CNN News Alert!" "UPS Delivery Failure," "Hundreds killed in *[insert a disaster of your choice]*," "Budweiser Frogs Screensaver!" "Microsoft Security Patch Attached."

>> A virus hits your computer if you read any message that includes the phrase "Good Times" in the subject line. (That one was a biggie in late 1994.) Ditto for any of the following messages: "It Takes Guts to Say 'Jesus'," "Win a Holiday," "Help a poor dog win a holiday," "Join the Crew," "pool party," "A Moment of Silence," "an Internet flower for you," "a virtual card for you," or "Valentine's Greetings."

>> A deadly virus is on the Microsoft *[or insert your favorite company name here]* home page. Don't go there or else your system will die.

>> If you have a file named *[insert filename here]* on your PC, it contains a virus. Delete it immediately!

They're all hoaxes — not a breath of truth in any of them. Fake news that's really and truly fake.

**WARNING**

Some hoaxes serve as fronts for real viruses: The message itself is a hoax, a red herring, designed to convince you to do something stupid and infect your system. The message asks (or commands!) you to download a file or run a video that acts suspiciously like an .exe file.

I'm not talking about YouTube videos, or Vimeo, or links to any of the other established video sites. Steer clear of attachments that appear to be videos, but in fact turn out to be something else. If you tell Windows to show you filename extensions, you have most of the bases covered.

Other hoaxes are just rumors that circulate among well-intentioned people who haven't a clue. Those hoaxes hurt, too. Sometimes, when real worms hit, so much email traffic is generated from warning people to avoid the worm that the well-intentioned watchdogs do more damage than the worm itself! Strange but true.

**TIP**

Do yourself (and me) a favor: If somebody sends you a message that sounds like the following examples, just delete it, eh?

>> A horrible virus is on the loose that's going to bring down the internet. (Sheesh. I get enough of that garbage on the nightly news.)

>> Send a copy of this message to ten of your best friends, and for every copy that's forwarded, Bill Gates will give *[pick your favorite charity]* $10.

>> Forward a copy of this message to ten of your friends and put your name at the bottom of the list. In *[pick a random amount of time]*, you will receive $10,000 in the mail, or your luck will change for the better. Your eyelids will fall off if you don't forward this message.

>> Microsoft (Intel, McAfee, Norton, Compaq — whatever) says that you need to double-click the attached file, download something, don't download something, go to a specific place, avoid a specific place, and on and on.

If you think you've stumbled on the world's most important virus alert, by way of your uncle's sister-in-law's roommate's hairdresser's soon-to-be-ex-boyfriend (the one who's a computer nerd but kind of smelly?), count to ten twice and keep these four important points in mind:

**REMEMBER**

>> No reputable software company (including Microsoft) distributes patches by email. You should never, ever, open or run an attachment to an email message until you contact the person who sent it to you and confirm that the person intended to send it to you.

>> Chances are very good (I'd say, oh, 99.9999 percent or more) that you're looking at a half-baked hoax that's documented on the web, most likely on the Snopes urban myths site (www.snopes.com).

>> If the virus or worm is real, Brian Krebs has already written about it. Go to www.krebsonsecurity.com.

>> If the internet world is about to collapse, clogged with gazillions of email worms, the worst possible way to notify friends and family is by email. Pick up the phone, walk over to the water cooler, or send a carrier pigeon, and give your intended recipients a reliable web address to check for updates. I bet you they've already heard about it anyway.

Try hard to be part of the solution, not part of the problem, okay? And if friends forward you a virus warning in an email, do everyone a big favor: Shoot them a copy of the preceding bullet points, ask them to tape it to the side of their computers, and beg them to refer to it the next time they get the forwarding urge.

# Is My Computer Infected?

So how do you know whether your computer is infected?

The short answer is this: Many times, you don't. If you think that your PC is infected, chances are very good that it isn't. Why? Because malware these days doesn't usually cause the kinds of problems people normally associate with infections.

Whatever you do, don't fall for the scamware that tells you it removed 39 infections from your computer but you need to pay in order to remove the other 179 (see "Shunning scareware," a little later in this chapter).

# Evaluating telltale signs

Here are a few telltale signs that may — *may* — mean that your PC is infected, or that one of your online accounts has been hacked:

>> **Someone tells you that you sent them an email message with an attachment — and you didn't send it.** In fact, most email malware these days is smart enough to spoof the From address, so any infected message that appears to come from you probably didn't. Still, some dumb old viruses that aren't capable of hiding your email address are still around. And, if you receive an infected attachment from a friend, chances are good that both your email address and your friend's email address are on an infected computer somewhere. Six degrees of separation and all that.

>> **You suddenly see files with two filename extensions scattered around your computer.** Filenames such as kournikova.jpg.vbs (a VBScript file masquerading as a JPG image file) or somedoc.txt.exe (a Windows program that wants to appear to be a text file) should send you running for your antivirus software.

TIP

Always, always, always have Windows show you filename extensions (see Book 3, Chapter 4).

>> **Your antivirus software suddenly stops working.** If the icon for your antivirus product disappears from the notification area (near the clock), something killed it — and chances are very good that the culprit was a virus.

>> **You can't reach websites that are associated with antimalware manufacturers.** For example, Firefox or Edge or Chrome works fine with most websites, but you can't get through to www.microsoft.com, www.symantec.com, or www.bitdefender.com. This problem is a key give-away for several infections.

# Where did that message come from?

In my discussion of 419 scams, I mention that I can trace several scammer messages back to Nigeria. If you've never traced a message before, you'll probably find it intriguing — and frustrating.

You know that return addresses lie. Just like an antagonist in the TV series *House.* You can't trust a return address because "spoofing" one is absolutely trivial. So what can you do?

If you receive a message and want to know where it came from, the first step is to find the header. In the normal course of events, you never see message headers. They look like the gibberish in Figure 1-7.

Delivered-To: woodyleonhard@gmail.com
Received: by 10.220.141.7 with SMTP id k7csp30829vcu;
        Fri, 2 Mar 2012 06:21:05 -0800 (PST)
Return-Path: <johnlaryy1@gmail.com>
Received-SPF: pass (google.com: domain of johnlaryy1@gmail.com designates
10.68.193.138 as permitted sender) client-ip=10.68.193.138;
Authentication-Results: mr.google.com; spf=pass (google.com: domain of
johnlaryy1@gmail.com designates 10.68.193.138 as permitted sender)
smtp.mail=johnlaryy1@gmail.com; dkim=pass header.i=johnlaryy1@gmail.com
Received: from mr.google.com ([10.68.193.138])
        by 10.68.193.138 with SMTP id ho10mr13926198pbc.80.1330698064713 (num_hops
= 1);
        Fri, 02 Mar 2012 06:21:04 -0800 (PST)
DKIM-Signature: v=1; a=rsa-sha256; c=relaxed/relaxed;
        d=gmail.com; s=20120113;
        h=mime-version:sender:date:x-google-sender-auth:message-id:subject
         :from:to:content-type;
        bh=FQrOCNbGPL/umBzdiTsxV9X+TQHfa9z35bSkQZz4rEo=;
        b=GfFPnzZ+QudFuwR7xCsfltOYJ6buvj2xpe0EH/jIJLDv+GdUAYYdNmcPv0QQm8nkH1
         Yy3c5coyOoivEviVrAFwGMP6UwxjEHX4DSBHvwWn6nAp7oEKOSZxS3q5RkjZS94hNVHA
         r4UbU1UPPW9S+CUNEzIDeC2Y24QbVHt+jzDcFLtqC6W8Dvq2UPoUg2HZg4HKIp0YwMtd
         YKepzUcrtlmiL0CWeAEYR6DFoNjYzbhSafZFkN5PQOROpIGJnm/6Dn7ff1hiJ9m3v8Gf
         PRYadRSomuGYJZ6e9wWDr1RfLm7UGFWqeoFztNxXRAJrvtvQ1vgg1aGZ/c6ud1C525iU
         Q7JQ==
MIME-Version: 1.0
Received: by 10.68.193.138 with SMTP id ho10mr13926198pbc.80.1330698064708;
 Fri, 02 Mar 2012 06:21:04 -0800 (PST)
Sender: johnlaryy1@gmail.com
Received: by 10.68.42.67 with HTTP; Fri, 2 Mar 2012 06:21:04 -0800 (PST)
Date: Fri, 2 Mar 2012 15:21:04 +0100
X-Google-Sender-Auth: ceb0jx6AUXsF4JVYhoZOLxC1z1g
Message-ID: <CAL-raB42Ms8Au2M=gHyw9w4d++PvKk3yMx3dTTVr541oqCg4ow@mail.gmail.com>
Subject: =?UTF-8?B?
KioqTEVHQUwgQUNUSU9OICoqKiogQVdBSBSVRJTkcgVEhFIFFdFU1RFU4k4gVU5JT04gQ090Rg==?=
        =?ISO-8859-1?B?SVJNQVRJT04gKioqKKkZCSeKAjyoqKg==?=
From: =?ISO-8859-1?B?U2Vydml1Z1ZUBJbnRsLlBheVBhbC5D5Db22u?=
<Notification.verification@consultant.com>
To: woodyleonhard@gmail.com
Content-Type: multipart/alternative; boundary=047d7b15af4373449104ba4349a1

**FIGURE 1-7:**
The header for
the 419 message
in Figure 1-6.

Here's how to find a message's header:

>> **Outlook** will show you the header, but only if you know the secret handshake.
Open the message in its own window. Then, in the message window, click or
tap File and then Properties. The header is listed in the box marked
Internet Headers.

>> **In Gmail,** click or tap the three dots next to the message sender and choose
Show Original. That shows you the entire message, including the header.

>> **In Hotmail or Outlook.com,** click or tap the three dots next to the message
sender and choose View ⇨ View Message Source.

Other email programs work differently. You may have to jump on to Google to
figure out how to see a message's header.

After you have the header, copy it, and head over to the ipTracker site, www.
iptrackeronline.com/header.php. Paste the message's header into the top box,
and click or tap Submit Header for Analysis. A report like the one in Figure 1-8
appears.

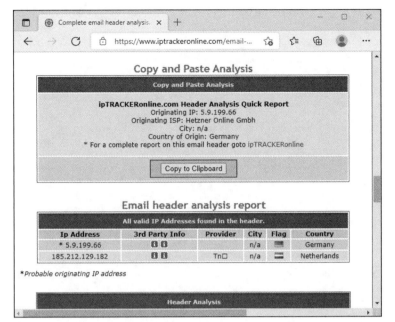

**FIGURE 1-8:**
Checking where
a scam email
came from.

**WARNING**

Realize that the header can be faked, too. Really clever scammers can disguise the origin of a message by faking the header. It's difficult, though, and scammers tend not to be, uh, the brightest bulbs on the tree.

## What to do next

If you think that your computer is infected, follow these steps:

**1.** **Don't panic.**

Chances are very good that you're not infected.

**2.** **DO NOT REBOOT YOUR COMPUTER.**

You may trigger a virus update when you reboot. Stay cool.

**3.** **Click or tap the search icon on the taskbar, type** windows security, **and then choose Windows Security.**

If you aren't using Windows Security, get your antivirus package to run a full scan.

The Windows Security main interface appears (see Figure 1-9). See Chapter 3 in this minibook for details about Microsoft Defender Antivirus.

**FIGURE 1-9:**
Windows
Security, ready
for action.

4. **In the right pane, click or tap Virus & Threat Protection and then Scan Options.**

5. **Choose Full Scan and click or tap Scan Now.**

   A full scan can take a long time. Go have a latte or two.

6. **If Step 5 still doesn't solve the problem, go to the Malwarebytes Removal forum at** `https://forums.malwarebytes.com` **and post your problem on the Windows Malware Removal Help & Support forum.**

   Make sure that you follow the instructions precisely. The good folks at Malwarebytes are all volunteers. You can save them — and yourself — lots of headaches by following their instructions to the letter.

7. **Do not — I repeat — do not send messages to all your friends advising them of the new virus.**

   Messages about a new virus can outnumber infected messages generated by the virus itself — in some cases causing more havoc than the virus itself. Try not to become part of the problem. Besides, you may be wrong.

**REMEMBER**

In recent years, I've come to view the mainstream press accounts of virus and malware outbreaks with increasing skepticism. The antivirus companies are usually slower to post news than the mainstream press, but the information they post tends to be much more reliable. Not infallible, mind you, but better.

# Shunning scareware

A friend of mine brought me their computer the other day and showed me a giant warning about all the viruses residing on it (see Figure 1-10). My friend knew that they needed XP Antivirus but didn't know how to install it. Thank heaven.

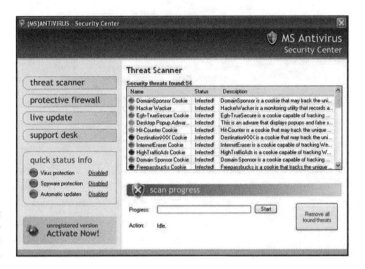

**FIGURE 1-10:**
Rogue antimalware gives you reason to pay.

Another friend brought me a computer that always booted to a Blue Screen of Death that said

```
Error 0x00000050 PAGE_FAULT_IN_NON_PAGED_AREA
```

It took a whole day to unwind all the junkware on that computer, but when I got to the bottom of the dreck, I found Vista Antivirus 2009.

I've received messages from all over the world from people who want to know about this fabulous new program, Antivirus Pro 2017 or WioniAntiVirus Pro (or XP Antivirus or MS Antivirus Security Center or Total Win7 Security or similar wording). Here's what you need to know: It's malware, plain and simple, and if you install it, you're handing over your computer to some sophisticated folks who will install keyloggers, bot software, and the scummiest, dirtiest stuff you've ever seen on any PC.

Here's the crazy part: Most people install this kind of scareware voluntarily. One particular family of rogue antivirus products, named Win32/FakeSecSen, has infected more than a million computers; see Figure 1-11.

**FIGURE 1-11:**
Win32/
FakeSecSen
scares you into
thinking you
must pay to clean
your computer.

The exact method of infection can vary, as will the payloads. Almost always, people install rogue antivirus programs when they think they're installing the latest, greatest virus chaser — and they're hastened to get it working because they just *know* there are 179 more viruses on their computers that have to be cleaned.

If you have it, how do you remove it? For starters, don't even bother with Windows Add or Remove Programs. Any company clever enough to call a piece of scum Antivirus 2021 won't make it easy for you to zap it. I rely on www.malwarebytes. com — but removing some of these critters is very difficult (see Chapter 4 in this minibook).

# Getting Protected

The internet is wild and woolly and wonderful — and, by and large, it's unregu-lated, in a Wild West sort of way. Some would say it cannot be regulated, and I agree. Although some central bodies control basic internet coordination questions — how the computers talk to each other, who doles out domain names such as Dummies.com, and what a web browser should do when it encounters a particular piece of HyperText Markup Language (HTML) — no central authority or Web Fashion Police exists.

Despite its Wild West lineage and complete lack of couth, the internet doesn't need to be a scary place. If you follow a handful of simple, common-sense rules, you'll go a long way toward making your internet travels more like Happy Trails and less like *Grand Theft Auto V.*

## Protecting against malware

"Everybody" knows that viruses are easily found on the internet. "Everybody" knows that bad viruses can drain your bank account, encrypt your hard drive and give you terminal halitosis — just by looking at an email message with *Good Times* in the Subject line. Right.

**TIP**

In fact, botnets and keyloggers can hurt you, but hoaxes and lousy advice abound. Every Windows user should follow these tips:

>> **Don't install weird programs, cute icons, automatic email signers, or products that promise to keep your computer oh-so-wonderfully safe.** Unless the software comes from a reputable manufacturer whom you trust and you know precisely *why* you need it, you don't want it. Don't be fooled by products that claim to clean your Registry or clobber imaginary infections.

  You may think that you absolutely must synchronize the Windows clock (which Windows does amazingly well, no extra program needed), tune up your computer (give me a break), use those cute little smiley icons (they aren't that cute if you look at them closely), install a pop-up blocker (Edge, Firefox, Opera, and Chrome do that well), or install an automatic email signer (your email program already can sign your messages). What you end up with is an unending barrage of hassles and hustles. The Microsoft Store goes a long way in culling the junk, but even there you can find awful programs.

>> **Never, ever, open a file attached to an email message until you contact the person who sent you the file and verify that they did, in fact, send you the file intentionally.** You should also apply a bit of discretion and ask yourself whether the sender is smart enough to avoid sending you an infected file. After you contact the person who sent you the file, don't open the file directly. Save it to your hard drive and run Windows Security on it before you open it.

>> **Follow the instructions in Book 3, Chapter 4 to force Windows 11 to show you the full name of all the files on your computer.** That way, if you see a file named something.cpl or iloveyou.vbs, you stand a fighting chance of understanding that it may be an infectious program waiting for your itchy finger.

>> **Don't trust email.** Every single part of an email message can be faked, easily. The return address can be spoofed. Even the header information, which you don't normally see, can be pure fiction. Links inside email messages may not point where you think they point. Anything you put in a message can be viewed by anybody with even a nodding interest — to use the old analogy, sending unencrypted email is much like sending a postcard.

>> **Check your accounts.** Look at your credit card and bank statements, and if you see a charge you don't understand, question it. Log in to all your financial websites frequently, and if somebody changed your password, scream bloody murder.

## Stop using Java and Flash

As I'm fond of saying, "It's time to run Java out of town." More precisely, I think developers should stop developing programs that require the Java Runtime Environment, or JRE, to run on your computer.

I also salute the death of Flash, and the switch to HTML5, which does a better job in a faster and more secure way. Few sites still use Flash, but they're rapidly disappearing. If you know of a site that requires Flash, send those at the site a nasty message telling them that they're showing enormous disrespect for their customers. And you can quote me.

Luckily, all modern browsers have stopped supporting Flash. So unless you go out of your way to turn on Flash support in Microsoft Edge or Google Chrome (a difficult process), you can't see the contents of a Flash website.

REMEMBER

If you use Firefox, get the free NoScript Firefox extension (www.noscript.net), which automatically blocks Java and all kinds of scripts. You can allow Java to run, on a case-by-case basis, but for general surfing, NoScript and Firefox are the safest ways to go.

Google's browser Chrome has some serious malware-blocking capabilities too, combined with a custom-built Java engine that make surfing the web rather secure. Microsoft Edge is developing some interesting safe-browsing capabilities too.

TECHNICAL
STUFF

When I talk about Java, I'm not talking about JavaScript. Although the two names are similar, they're as different as chalk and cheese. JavaScript is a language that automates actions on web pages. Java (in our case, the JRE) is a set of programs inside your computer that web pages can call. JavaScript is relatively benign (although it has been exploited). Java has led to millions of infections.

# Using your credit card safely online

Many people who use the web refuse to order anything online because they're afraid that their credit card numbers will be stolen, and they'll be liable for enormous bills. Or they think the products will never arrive and they won't get their money back.

If your credit card was issued in the United States and you're ordering from a US company, that's simply not the case. Here's why:

>> **The Fair Credit Billing Act protects you from being charged by a company for an item you don't receive.** It's the same law that governs orders placed over the telephone or by mail. A vendor generally has 30 days to send the merchandise, or it has to give you a formal written chance to cancel your order. For details, go to the Federal Trade Commission (FTC) website (www.consumer.ftc.gov).

>> **Your maximum liability for charges fraudulently made on the card is $50 per card.** The minute you notify the credit card company that somebody else is using your card, you have no further liability. If you have any questions, the Federal Trade Commission can help (www.consumer.ftc.gov/articles/0213-lost-or-stolen-credit-atm-and-debit-cards).

The rules are different if you're not dealing with a US company and using a US credit card. For example, if you buy something in an online auction from an individual, you don't have the same level of protection. Make sure that you understand the rules before you hand out credit card information. Unfortunately, there's no central repository of information about overseas purchase protection for US credit card holders: Each credit card seems to handle cases individually. If you buy things overseas using a US credit card, your relationship with your credit card company generally provides your only protection.

**REMEMBER**

Some online vendors, such as Amazon, absolutely guarantee that your shopping will be safe. The Fair Credit Billing Act protects any charges fraudulently made in excess of $50, but Amazon says that it reimburses any fraudulent charges under $50 that occurred as a result of using its website. Many credit card companies now offer similar assurances.

Regardless, take a few simple precautions to make sure that you aren't giving away your credit card information:

>> **When you place an order online, make sure that you're dealing with a company you know.** In particular, don't click a link in an email message and expect to go to the company's website. Type the company's address into Edge

or Chrome or Firefox, or use a link that you stored in your Edge Favorites or the Chrome or Firefox Bookmarks list.

WARNING

>> **Type your credit card number only when you're sure that you've arrived at the company's site and when the site is using a secure web page.** The easy way to tell whether a web page is secure is to look for a picture of a lock (see Figure 1-12). Secure websites scramble data so that anything you type on the web page is encrypted before it's sent to the vendor's computer. In addition, Firefox tells you a site's registration and pedigree when you click or tap the icon to the left of the web address.

Be aware that crafty web programmers can fake the lock icon and show an https:// (secure) address to try to lull you into thinking that you're on a secure web page. To be safe, confirm the site's address and click or tap the icon to the left of the address at the top to show the full security certificate.

>> **Don't send your credit card number in an ordinary email message.** Email is just too easy to intercept. And for heaven's sake, don't give out any personal information when you're chatting online.

>> **Don't send sensitive information back by way of email.** If you receive an email message requesting credit card information that seems to be from your bank, credit card company, internet service provider, or even sainted Aunt Martha, do not send the information in an email. Insist on using a secure website, and type the company's address into your browser.

FIGURE 1-12:
The lock indicates
a secure site.

TIP

Identity theft continues to be a problem all over the world. Widespread availability of personal information online only adds fuel to the flame. If you think someone may be posing as you — to run up debts in your name, for example — see the US government's main website on the topic at `www.consumer.ftc.gov/features/feature-0014-identity-theft`.

## Defending your privacy

*"You have zero privacy anyway. Get over it."*

That's what Scott McNealy, former CEO of Sun Microsystems, said to a group of reporters on January 25, 1999. Scott, who has been known to make provocative statements for dramatic effect, was exaggerating — but the exaggeration comes awfully close to reality.

I continue to be amazed at Windows users' odd attitudes toward privacy. People who wouldn't dream of giving a stranger their telephone number fill out their mailing address for online service profiles and post tons of sensitive data on Facebook and other social media services. People who are scared to death at the thought of using their credit cards online to place an order with a major retailer (a very safe procedure, by the way) dutifully type their Social Security numbers on web-based forms.

**TIP**

I suggest that you follow these few important privacy points:

>> **Use work systems only for work.** Why use your company email ID for personal messages? Sign up for a free web-based email account, such as Gmail (www.gmail.com), Yahoo! Mail (www.mail.yahoo.com), or Hotmail/Outlook.com (www.hotmail.com and www.outlook.com).

**REMEMBER**

In the United States, with few exceptions, anything you do on a company PC at work can be monitored and examined by your employer. Email, website history files, and even stored documents and settings are all fair game. At work, you have zero privacy.

>> **Don't give it away.** Why use your real name when you sign up for a free email account? Why tell a random survey that your annual income is between $20,000 and $30,000? (Or is it between $150,000 and $200,000?)

All sorts of websites — particularly Microsoft — ask questions about topics that, simply put, are none of their business. Don't put your personal details out where they can be harvested.

>> **Follow the privacy suggestions in this book.** You know that Google keeps track of what you type in the Google search engine, and Microsoft keeps track of what you say to Cortana or type in Bing. You know that both Google and Microsoft scan your email — and that Google, at least, admits to using the contents of emails (on free accounts) in order to direct ads at you. You know that files stored in the cloud can be opened by all sorts of people, in response to court orders, anyway.

>> **Know your rights.** Although cyberspace doesn't provide the same level of personal protection you have come to expect in *meatspace* (real life), you still have rights and recourses. Check out www.privacyrights.org for some thought-provoking notices.

Keep your head low and your powder dry!

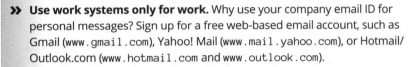

## THE DOUBLECLICK SHTICK

A website plants a cookie on your computer. Only that website can retrieve the cookie. The information is shielded from other websites. ZDNet.com can figure out that I have been reading reviews of digital cameras. Dealtime.com knows that I buy shoes. But a cookie from ZDNet can't be read by DealTime and vice versa. So what's the big deal?

Enter Doubleclick.net, which is a division of Google. For the better part of a decade, both ZDNet.com and Dealtime.com have included ads from a company named Doubleclick. net. Unless ZDNet or DealTime has changed advertisers, you see Doubleclick.net featured prominently in each site's privacy report.

Here's the trick: You surf to a ZDNet web page that contains a Doubleclick.net ad. DoubleClick kicks in and plants a cookie on your PC that says you were looking at a specific page on ZDNet. Two hours (or days or weeks) later, you surf to a DealTime page that also contains a Doubleclick.net ad — a different ad, no doubt — but one distributed by DoubleClick. DoubleClick kicks in again and discovers that you were looking at that specific ZDNet page two hours (or days or weeks) earlier.

Now consider the consequences if a hundred sites that you visit in an average week all have DoubleClick ads. They can be tiny ads — 1 pixel high, so small that you can't see them. All the information about all your surfing to those sites can be accumulated by DoubleClick and used to target you for advertising, recommendations, or whatever. It's scary.

Want to look at who's watching you? Install the Ghostery browser add-in (www. ghostery.com). It shows you exactly which cookies are tracking you on every page you visit.

## Reducing spam

Everybody hates spam, but nobody has any idea how to stop it. Not the government. Not Bill Gates. Not your sainted aunt's podiatrist's second cousin.

You think legislation can reduce the amount of spam? Since the US CAN-SPAM Act became law on January 7, 2003, has the volume of spam you've received increased or decreased? Heck, I've had more spam from politicians lately than from almost any other group. The very people who are supposed to be enforcing the antispam laws seem to be spewing out spam overtime.

By and large, Windows is only tangentially involved in the spam game — it's the messenger, as it were. But every Windows user I know receives email. And every email user I know gets spam. Lots of it.

Spam is an intractable problem, but you can do certain things to minimize your exposure:

>> **Don't encourage 'em.** Don't buy anything that's offered by way of spam (or any other email that you didn't specifically request). Don't click through to the website, and don't reply, asking to be removed from their emailing list. Simply delete the message. If you see something that may be interesting, use Google Chrome or another web browser to look for other companies that sell the same item.

>> **Opt out of mailings only if you know and trust the company that's sending you messages.** If you're on the Costco mailing list and you're not interested in its email anymore, click or tap the Opt Out button at the bottom of the page. But don't opt out with a company you don't trust: It may just be trying to verify your email address.

>> **Never post your email address on a website or in a newsgroup.** Spammers have spiders that devour web pages by the gazillion, crawling around the web, gathering email addresses and other information automatically. If you post something in a newsgroup and want to let people respond, use a name that's hard for spiders to swallow: *contact (at) digital citizen (dot) life,* for example.

>> **Never open an attachment to an email message or view pictures in a message.** Spammers use both methods to verify that they've reached a real, live address. And, you wouldn't open an attachment anyway — unless you know the person who sent it to you, you verified with the person that they intended to send you the attachment, and you trust the sender to be savvy enough to avoid sending infected attachments.

>> **Never trust a website that you arrive at by clicking through a hot link in an email message.** Be cautious about websites you reach from other websites.

>> **Most important of all, if spam really bugs you, stop using your current email program and switch to Gmail or Outlook.com.** Both of them have superb spam filters that are updated every nanosecond. You'll be very pleasantly surprised, I guarantee.

Ultimately, the only long-lasting solution to spam is to change your email address and give out your address to only close friends and business associates. Use a fake phone number or email address or both whenever you can. Even that strategy doesn't solve the problem, but it should reduce the level of spam significantly.

# Dealing with Data Breaches

In recent years we've seen a breathtaking rise in the number of data breaches — where scumbags have broken into company computers and stolen data for millions of customers. Verizon, 14 million. Equifax, 143 million. Home Depot, 56 million. JP Morgan Chase, 76 million. Target, 70 million. eBay, 145 million. Adobe, 36 million. Evernote, 50 million. Activision, 14 million. Sony, 77 million (and almost every key internal document). T.J. Maxx, 94 million. AOL, 92 million, then 20 million more. Kmart, 7-Eleven, JC Penney, Dow Jones, Snapchat, Staples, Facebook, Twitter, and on and on.

## RANSOMWARE

So you're staring at a screen that says all of your files have been scrambled, and you need to pay a Bitcoin or two to get them back. Don't panic. It happens.

First, realize that data you've stored in the cloud (in Dropbox or OneDrive or Google Drive) may be safe — not all ransomware is smart enough to reach out to online services. Second, if the ransomware just locks up your browser or your computer, chances are good you can bypass it easily. (For browser locks, press Ctrl+Shift+Esc; then in Task Manager, on the Processes tab, click pr tap the browser and choose End Task. For screen locks, just unplug your computer.)

But if you have a data-scrambling version — you can't open your Office docs or look at your photos — you should go through all the normal channels to look for a solution. Take a picture of your screen (the police may want it), disconnect your computer from any and all networks, unplug any external drives, and if you can get a web browser going, head to the No More Ransom! Crypto Sheriff site, www.nomoreransom.org/crypto-sheriff.php. Follow the instructions there to see what kind of ransomware you have and whether there's a known antidote.

If there are no effective rescue programs, you have a tough decision to make. Most authorities, including Microsoft, recommend against paying the ransom — it only encourages other cretins to take up a new profession. In addition, a substantial percentage of ransomware hijackers don't send a key even after you've paid them (indeed, some scares are set up so there's no feasible way for the perp to send a key). Wish I had a definitive solution for you, but I don't.

Usually the thieves get away with email addresses and some personal information. If you're one of the unfortunate victims and your password was stolen, you can hope that the password was stored in a very secure way. Sometimes you're lucky. Sometimes you're not.

Researchers recently found a database with 1.2 *billion* stolen IDs.

Lots of people want to know what they can do to keep from being the next statistic. The short answer is, mostly you need to constantly monitor your credit card statements, bank statements, and other financial accounts, to catch problems as quickly as you can. That's a fatalistic analysis of the situation: You can't do much to stop it, so you have to watch to see if the cows have run out of the barn.

That said, there are a few things you should be doing to keep the bad actors guessing as much as possible:

**1.** **Don't use the same password twice.**

Yeah, I know. *Everybody* reuses passwords. I do, too. But I try to reuse passwords on sites that aren't important — and leave the unique passwords for financial sites, personal email, and so on.

**2.** **Use a password-remembering program such as Bitwarden, LastPass, 1Password, Dashlane, RoboForm, or IronKey.**

The only chance you have at remembering passwords *just on your financial sites* is to rely on some computer assistance. There are plenty of pros and cons to the products and methods — do you want to trust the cloud, can you remember to take a USB drive everywhere, where and how securely should the master password be manipulated — but the bottom line is that you need some sort of automated password helper.

I use Bitwarden. Read Book 10, Chapter 6 to see why.

**3.** **Assume that the bad actors have your email address and some additional identifying information.**

They may even have the passwords to your not-sensitive websites. Act accordingly.

4. **If you receive notification that your account has been compromised, don't worry so much about changing the password on the hacked account — look to your other accounts, to see if any of those need changing.**

   After the deed's done, there isn't much you can do — kind of like putting the toothpaste back in the tube. But you can, and should, take a hard look at what might've been taken, and move to mitigate the disclosure.

A lot of companies offer free credit monitoring after they've had a data breach and some banks may offer the service free. Credit monitoring sites scan the credit reporting sites for unusual activity and report to you if they detect any suspicious activity.

# Chapter **2**

# Fighting Viruses and Other Malware

Windows 8 was the first version of Windows to ship with a complete antivirus and antimalware package baked right into the operating system. Windows 10 expanded on those goodies surprisingly well. At launch, Windows 11 didn't have any new Windows Security features. However, I don't view this as a problem because the tools offered by Microsoft are solid and work well. Most people don't need to buy an antivirus, firewall, or anti-everything product. Windows 11 has all you need.

On the other hand, you need to hold up your end of the bargain by not doing questionable things on your computer. I wanted to say "stupid," but some of the tricks of cybercriminals these days can get you even if you *aren't* stupid. Luckily, Chapter 1 in this minibook helps you understand the tactics online creeps use and keep your guard up.

Moving on to Chapter 2, I start with a simple list of do's and don'ts for protecting your computer and your identity. They're important. Even if you don't read the rest of this chapter, make sure you read — and understand and follow — the rules in each list.

Then I talk about how your web browsers protect you through the icons they display while visiting web pages on the internet. Taking them into consideration does help to keep you safer.

# Basic Windows Security Do's and Don'ts

TIP

Here are the ten most important things you need to do, to keep your computer secure:

>> **Check daily to make sure Windows Security is running.** If something's amiss, a red X appears on the Windows Security shield, down in the notification area, near the time. To check its status, double-click or double-tap the shield in the notification area. If Windows Security is running and all's well, green check marks appear, as shown in Figure 2-1.

Windows 11 should tell you if Windows Security stops, either via a notification from the right side or a red X on the flag in the lower-right corner of the desktop. But if you want to be sure, there's no better way than to check it yourself. Only takes a second.

>> **Don't use old versions of web browsers.** One good recommendation is Firefox. It's as secure as Google Chrome or Microsoft Edge, or Opera. Firefox doesn't snoop as much as Chrome, has lots of custom extensions, and performs well — despite what Microsoft may splash on your screen about Edge. However, no matter which browser you choose, make sure it is the latest version, not one released a year ago.

>> **Use anything other than Adobe Reader to look at PDF files.** All the major browsers have their own PDF readers, just because Adobe Reader has caused so many infections. For a stand-alone reader, download and install an alternative to Adobe Reader. However, certain users need to use only Adobe Reader when working with custom PDF forms for the IRS and other government institutions.

>> **Every two months or so, run Microsoft Defender Offline (MDO).** MDO scans for rootkits. You can find it in the scan options offered by Windows Security, in its Virus & Threat Protection section.

>> **Every month or so, run Malwarebytes.** The Malwarebytes program gives you a second opinion, possibly pointing out questionable programs that Windows Security doesn't flag.

**FIGURE 2-1:**
Windows Security is up and running.

>> **Delete chain mail.** I'm sure that you'll be bringing down the wrath of several lesser deities for the rest of your days, but do everyone a favor and don't forward junk. Please. If something you receive in an email sounds really, really cool, it's probably fake — an urban legend or a come-on of some sort. Look it up at www.snopes.com.

>> **Keep up to date with Windows 11 patches and (especially) patches to other programs running on your computer.** Windows should be keeping itself updated, although you can take control of Windows Update if you're reasonably vigilant.

>> **Check your credit cards and bank balances regularly.** I check my charges and balances every couple of days and suggest you do the same. Credit-monitoring services keep a constant eye on your credit report, watching for any unexpected behavior. Most companies that get hacked will offer free credit monitoring to potentially ripped-off customers. Many big banks offer the service free, too.

>> **If you don't need a program anymore, get rid of it.** Use the uninstall feature in Windows 11. If the unwanted program doesn't blast away easily, use Revo Uninstaller, which I describe in Book 10, Chapter 6.

Fighting Viruses and Other Malware

**REMEMBER**

>> **Change your passwords regularly.** Yeah, another one of those things everybody recommends, but nobody does. Except you really should because someone might see you typing your password and use it later without your consent. See the admonitions in Book 2, Chapter 4 about choosing good passwords, but especially look at Bitwarden and RoboForm, which I describe in Chapter 4 of this minibook.

Here are the ten most important things you *shouldn't* do, to keep your computer secure:

>> **Don't trust any PC unless you, personally, have been taking close care of it.** Even then, be skeptical. Treat every PC you may encounter as if it's infected. Don't stick a USB drive into a public computer, for example, unless you're prepared to disinfect the USB drive immediately when you get back to a safe computer. Don't use the business center computer in a hotel or FedEx if you must type anything sensitive. Assume that everything you type in a public PC is being logged and sent to a pimply-face genius who wants to be a millionaire.

>> **Don't install a new program unless you know what it does, and you've checked to make sure you have a legitimate copy.**

**WARNING**

Yes, even if an online scanner told you that you have 139 viruses on your computer, and you need to pay just $49.99 to get rid of them.

If you install apps from the Microsoft Store, you're generally safe — although the Store has its share of crappy programs. But any programs you install from other sources should be vetted ten ways from Tuesday, downloaded from a reputable source (such as www.cnet.com, www.softpedia.com, www.majorgeeks.com, www.snapfiles.com), and *even then* you need to ask yourself whether you really need the program, and have to be careful that the installer doesn't bring in some crappy extras.

Similarly, Firefox and Chrome add-ons are generally safe, as long as you stick to the well-known ones.

>> **Don't use the same password for two or more sites.** Okay, if you reuse your passwords, make sure you don't reuse the passwords on any of your email or financial accounts. Email accounts are different. If you reuse the passwords on any of your email accounts and somebody gets the password, that person may be able to break into everything, steal your money, and besmirch your reputation. See the nearby "Don't reuse your email password" sidebar.

>> **Don't use Wi-Fi in a public place unless you're running exclusively on HTTPS-encrypted sites or through a virtual private network (VPN).**

**REMEMBER**

If you don't know what HTTPS is and have never set up a VPN, that's okay. Just realize that anybody else who can connect to the same Wi-Fi network you're using can see *every single thing* that goes into or comes out of your computer. See Chapter 4 in this minibook.

» **Don't fall for Nigerian 419 scams, "I've been mugged and I need $500 scams," or anything else where you have to send money.** There are lots of scams — and if you see the words *Western Union* or *Postal Money Order,* run for the exit. See Chapter 1 in this minibook.

» **Don't click or tap a link in an email message or document and expect it to take you to a financial site.** Take the time to type the address into your browser. You've heard it a thousand times, but it's true.

» **Don't open an attachment to any email message until you've contacted the person who sent it to you and verified that the person intentionally sent you the file.** Even if the person did send it, you need to use your judgment as to whether the sender is savvy enough to refrain from sending you something infectious. No, UPS didn't send you a non-delivery notice in a ZIP file, Microsoft didn't send you an update to Windows attached to a message, and your winning lottery notification won't come as an attachment.

» **Don't forget to change your passwords.** Yeah, another one of those things everybody recommends, but nobody does. Except you really should.

**WARNING**

» **Don't trust anybody who calls you and offers to fix your computer.** The "I'm from Microsoft and I'm here to help" scam has tricked too many people. Stay skeptical, and don't let anybody else into your computer, unless you know who they are. See Chapter 1 in this minibook.

» **Don't forget that the biggest security gap is between your ears.** Use your head to make decisions on what you open or not, not your clicking or tapping finger.

## DON'T REUSE YOUR EMAIL PASSWORD

Say you have a Gmail account. You run over to an online classified advertising site and sign up for an account there. You're lazy, so you use the same password for both accounts.

A day, month, or year later, you place an ad on the classified advertising site. You have to provide your email address. Hey, no problem.

*(continued)*

Fighting Viruses and Other Malware

(continued)

The next week, somebody breaks into the classified advertising site and steals the information from 10,000 accounts. Unbeknownst to you, the people who created and maintain the classified advertising site stored the passwords and email addresses in a way that can be easily cracked.

The person who broke into the site posts his booty on some underground file-sharing site, and within minutes of the break-in, two dozen people are trying every combination of your Gmail address and password, trying to break into banking sites, brokerage sites, PayPal, whatever.

If they hit on a financial site that requires only an email address in order to retrieve the account information, bingo, they use your Gmail address and ask for a new password. They log in to Gmail with your password and wait for the password reset instructions. Thirty seconds later, they're logged in to the financial site.

If they hit a site that will send you a password reset code and send it to your email address, there you go again.

The site doesn't have to be financial. Just about any site that stores your Social Security number or includes sensitive information like a hospital site might be similarly vulnerable.

Happens every day.

Your best bet: Turn on two-factor authentication (2FA) wherever it's offered. If you have an email account with 2FA, for example, you can insist that access to that account from a new computer must respond to an SMS sent to your smartphone. There are many variations, but two-factor authentication can save your tail.

# Making Sense of Malware

Although most people are more familiar with the term *virus*, viruses are only part of the problem — a problem known as malware. *Malware* is made up of the elements described in this list:

>> **Viruses:** A computer virus is a program that replicates. That's all. Viruses generally replicate by attaching themselves to files — programs, documents, or spreadsheets — or replacing genuine operating system files with bogus ones. They usually make copies of themselves whenever they're run. You probably think that viruses delete files or make programs go belly-up or wreak

havoc in other nefarious ways. Some of them do. Many of them don't. Viruses sound scary, but most of them aren't. Most viruses have such ridiculous bugs in them that they don't get far in the wild.

>> **Trojans:** Trojans (short for Trojan horses) may or may not be able to reproduce, but they always require that the user do something to get them started. The most common Trojans these days appear as programs downloaded from the internet, or email attachments, or programs that helpfully offer to install themselves from the internet: You double-click or double-tap an attachment, expecting to open a picture or a document, and you get bit when a program comes in and clobbers your computer, frequently sending out a gazillion messages, all with infected attachments, without your knowledge or consent.

>> **Worms:** Worms move from one computer to another over a network. The worst ones replicate quickly by shooting copies of themselves over the internet, taking advantage of holes in the operating systems (which all too frequently is Windows).

>> **Rootkits:** These programs operate deep inside the operating system, concealing files and making it extremely difficult to detect their presence, while having access to privileged computer resources.

>> **Ransomware:** Ransomware takes control of your files and folders by encrypting them. Then it tries to force you to pay substantial amounts of money to get them back. And even if you pay, you can't be sure that you can get your data back.

Viruses, trojans, worms, rootkits and ransomware are getting much more sophisticated than they were just a few years ago. Lots of money can be made with advanced malware, especially for those who figure out how to break in without being detected.

Some malware can carry bad *payloads* (programs that wreak destruction on your system), but many of the worst offenders cause the most harm by clogging networks (nearly bringing down the internet itself, at times) and by turning PCs into zombies, frequently called *bots,* which can be operated by remote control. (I talk about bots and botnets in Chapter 1 in this minibook.)

The most successful pieces of malware these days run as *rootkits* — programs that evade detection by stealthily hooking into Windows in tricky ways. Some nominally respectable companies (notably, Sony) have employed rootkit technology to hide programs for their own profit. Rootkits are extremely difficult to detect and even harder to clean. Microsoft Defender Offline, discussed in Chapter 3 of this minibook, is a great choice for clobbering the beasts.

## LIES AND MALWARE STATISTICS

Computer crime has evolved into a money-making operation, with some espionage tacked on for good measure, but when you hear statistics about how many viruses are out and about and how much they cost everyone, take those statistics with a grain of salt, even though they sound alarming, as in this article from *Forbes:* www.forbes. com/sites/chuckbrooks/2021/03/02/alarming-cybersecurity-stats-------- what-you-need-to-know-for-2021/?sh=1f42eb8e58d3

Here's what you need to know about those cost estimates:

- There's no way to tell how much a virus outbreak costs. You should expect that any dollar estimates you see are designed to raise your eyebrows more than providing a realistic metric.

- Although corporate cyberespionage certainly takes place all the time, it's hard to identify — much less quantify. For that matter, how can you quantify the effects of plain-old, everyday industrial espionage?

- Instead of flinging meaningless numbers around, it's more important to consider the amount of hassle people and companies encounter when they must clean up after a group of cybercriminals. One hundred thousand filched credit card credentials may not lead to lots of lost money, but it'll certainly cause no end of mayhem for lots of people.

Although the major antivirus companies release virus-catching files that identify tens of millions of signatures, most infections in any given year come from a handful of viruses. The threat is real, but it's overblown.

All these definitions are becoming more academic and less relevant as the trend shifts to *blended-threat* malware. Blended threats incorporate elements of all traditional kinds of malware — and more. Most of the most successful viruses and malware you read about in the press these days — WannaCry, Petya and NotPetya, Conficker, Rustock, Aleuron, and the like — are, in fact, blended-threat malware. They have come a long way from old-fashioned viruses, and are increasingly being built into $99 Script Kiddie kits.

# Deciphering Browsers' Inscrutable Warnings

One last trick that may help you head off an unfortunate online incident: Each browser has subtle ways of telling you that you may be in trouble. I'm not talking about the giant Warning: Suspected Phishing Site or Reported Web Forgery signs. Those are supposed to hit you upside the head, and they do.

I'm talking about the gentle indications each browser has that tell you whether there's something strange about the site you're looking at. Historically, if you're on a secured page — where encryption is in force between you and the website — you see a padlock on the address bar. That simple padlock indicator has grown up a bit, so you can understand more about your secure (or not-so-secure) connection with a glance.

## Google Chrome

Chrome has three different icons that can appear to the left of a site's URL, as shown in Figure 2-2.

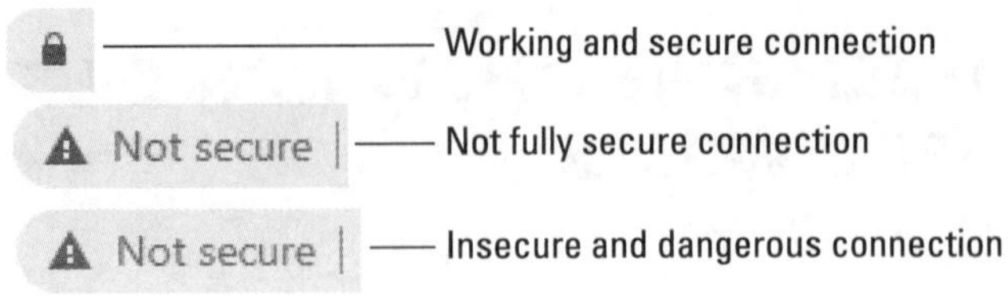

FIGURE 2-2:
The three
different HTTPS
padlocks in
Chrome.

🔒 ——————————— Working and secure connection

⚠ Not secure | —— Not fully secure connection

⚠ Not secure | —— Insecure and dangerous connection

Here's what they mean:

>> **Gray padlock:** The connection is secure and working. As long as you're looking at the correct domain — you didn't mistype the domain name, for example — you're safe.

If the site has an Extended Validation certificate (see the nearby "What is extended validation?" sidebar), you can see more details about the company who owns it.

>> **Gray warning triangle and *Not Secure* label:** Chrome has set up a secure connection, but parts of the page can, conceivably, snoop on what you're typing. That's what the "Not Secure" warning means.

>> **Red warning triangle and *Not Secure* label:** There are problems with the site's certificate or insecure content on the page is known to be high risk. When you hit a red warning triangle, you must ask yourself whether the site's handlers just let the certificate lapse (I've seen that on sites and other sites that shouldn't go bad) or if there's something genuinely wrong with the site.

## WHAT IS EXTENDED VALIDATION?

Companies must pay to get a secure certificate and use it correctly on their sites before the major browsers will display a padlock for them. Unfortunately, in recent years, there have been many problems with faked, stolen, or otherwise dubious certificates. Part of the difficulty lies in the fact that just about anybody can get a website security certificate.

Because of that, starting in April 2008, a second level of certification, an *Extended Validation certificate,* was put into effect. To buy an EV certificate, the organization or individual applying for the certificate has to jump through many hoops to establish its legal identity and physical location, and prove that the people applying for the certificate do, in fact, own the domain name that they're trying to certify. EV certificates aren't infallible, but they're much more trustworthy than regular certificates.

# Mozilla Firefox

Firefox handles things a little differently than Chrome. When you visit a web page, the site identity icon (a padlock), shown in Figure 2-3, appears in the address bar to the left. You can quickly find out if the connection to the website you're viewing is encrypted and, in some cases, who owns the website. This should help you avoid malicious websites that are trying to obtain your personal information.

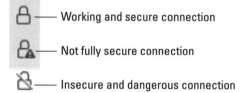

**FIGURE 2-3:** Firefox gives detailed, site security information.

The three states of the padlock indicate the following:

>> **Gray padlock:** The site is secure, with full encryption that prevents eavesdropping. Click or tap the gray padlock to find out if the website is using an EV certificate.

>> **Gray padlock with a warning triangle:** The connection between you and the website is only partially encrypted and doesn't prevent eavesdropping.

>> **Gray padlock with a red slash:** The site uses an insecure protocol or is known to be high risk.

# Microsoft Edge

Edge uses an approach that's similar to Chrome. It too has three icons (see Figure 2-4) that appear to the left of the address bar.

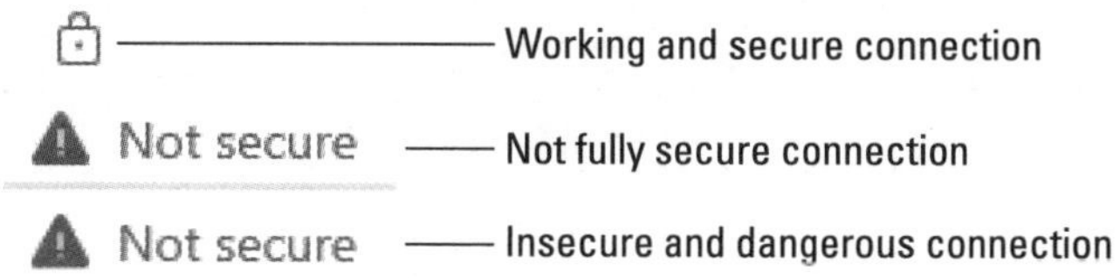

🔒 ———————— Working and secure connection

⚠ Not secure ——— Not fully secure connection

⚠ Not secure ——— Insecure and dangerous connection

**FIGURE 2-4:** Microsoft Edge has a padlock too.

They mean the following:

- **Gray padlock:** A secure connection is in place and working. Click or tap the padlock for more information.

- **Gray warning triangle and *Not Secure* label:** Edge has set up a secure connection, but parts of the page may be able to snoop on what you're doing.

- **Red warning triangle and *Not Secure* label:** There are problems with the site's certificate or insecure content on the page is known to be high risk.

IN THIS CHAPTER

» **Making Windows Security work your way**

» **Blocking ransomware with controlled folder access**

» **Coping with SmartScreen**

» **Working with UEFI and Secure Boot**

» **Controlling User Account Control**

» **Understanding Windows Defender Firewall**

Chapter **3**

# Running Built-In Security Programs

W indows 11, right out of the box, ships with a myriad of security programs, including a handful that you can control and tweak to offer you the best balance between what you need and how they protect you.

This chapter looks at the things you can do with the programs on offer: Windows Security, Controlled Folder Access for blocking ransomware, SmartScreen for blocking dodgy downloads from the internet, UEFI (don't judge it by its name alone), User Account Control, and Windows Defender Firewall.

This chapter is a survey of the tip of the iceberg. Even if you don't change anything, you'll come away with a better understanding of what's available and how the pieces fit together. With a little luck, you'll also have a better idea of what can go wrong, and how you can fix it.

Before we get started, I should warn you that this chapter is more technical than the others, but I make sure to explain all the specialized jargon.

# Working with Windows Security

If you've ever put up with a bloated and expensive security suite exhorting/extorting you for more money, or you've struggled with free antivirus packages that want to install a little toolbar here and a funny monitoring program there — and *then* ask you for money — you're in for a refreshing change from an unexpected source.

Windows Security takes over antivirus and antispyware duties and tosses in bot detection, ransomware protection, and antirootkit features for good measure. For years, in independent tests, Microsoft Windows Security has consistently received high detection and removal scores.

This tool has been rebranded many times: from Microsoft Security Essentials to Windows Defender to Windows Defender Antivirus to Windows Defender Security to Microsoft Defender Antivirus, to Windows Security, and from Windows Defender Offline to Microsoft Defender Offline. To make things even more confusing, Microsoft is not consistent about how it names this product in its Windows 11 notifications. Sometimes you see notifications from Windows Security but other times from Microsoft Defender Antivirus. If you search for Windows Defender in Windows 11, you get shortcuts to Windows Defender Firewall, previously known as the Windows Firewall, and not to the antivirus product that you used to know. No matter what Microsoft calls it, Windows Security is just an improved version of the former Windows Defender and now encompasses more security tools in one easy-to-use app.

Windows Security conducts periodic scans and watches out for malware in real time. It vets email attachments, catches downloads, deletes or quarantines at your command, and in general, does everything you'd expect an antivirus, antimalware, and antirootkit product to do.

Is Windows Security the best antivirus package on the market? No. It depends on how you define *best*, but Microsoft has no intention of coming out on top of the competitive antimalware tests. I think Lowell Heddings said it best, in his "How-To Geek" article (`www.howtogeek.com/225385/what's-the-best-antivirus-for-windows-10-is-windows-defender-good-enough/`) in January 2020:

*"Other antivirus programs may occasionally do a bit better in monthly tests, but they also come with a lot of bloat, like browser extensions that actually make you less safe, registry cleaners that are terrible and unnecessary, loads of unsafe junkware, and even the ability to track your browsing habits so they can make money. Furthermore, the way they hook themselves into your*

*browser and operating system often causes more problems than it solves. Something that protects you against viruses but opens you up to other vectors of attack is not good security.*

*Just look at all the extra garbage Avast tries to install alongside its antivirus.*

*Windows Defender does not do any of these things — it does one thing well, for free, and without getting in your way. Plus, Windows 10 already includes the various other protections introduced in Windows 8, like the SmartScreen filter that should prevent you from downloading and running malware, whatever antivirus you use. Chrome and Firefox, similarly, include Google's Safe Browsing, which blocks many malware downloads."*

I think *Windows 11 All-in-One For Dummies* readers tend to be experienced and involved and would agree wholeheartedly.

**REMEMBER**

The beauty of Windows Security is that it just works. You don't have to do anything — although you should check from time to time to make sure it hasn't been accidentally (or maliciously) turned off. To check whether Windows Security is running, click or tap the search icon (magnifying glass), type **sec**, and in the list of apps choose Windows Security. If you see green check marks (see Figure 3-1), you're doing fine.

**FIGURE 3-1:**
The Windows
Security
home page.

Microsoft maintains an active online support forum for Windows Security at Microsoft Answers, `https://answers.microsoft.com/en-us/windows/forum/windows_11-security`.

When you use Windows Security, you should be aware of these caveats:

>> It's *never* a good idea to run two or more antivirus products simultaneously, and Windows Security is no exception: If you have a second antivirus product running on your machine, Windows Security has been disabled, and you shouldn't try to bring it back. That's because each may detect the other as malware, try to access the same system files at the same time, and simply block your computer from functioning.

>> If you don't like your antivirus product and don't particularly want to keep paying and paying and paying for it, you should remove it. Open Settings (press Windows+I) and then click or tap Apps. On the right choose Apps & Features. Wait for the list to fill out. Then pick the antivirus program you want to remove and choose Uninstall. Reboot your machine, and Windows Security returns.

>> You may see updates listed for Windows Security if you go into Windows Update and look. Just leave them alone. They'll install all by themselves.

>> No matter how you slice it, real-time protection eats into your privacy. How? Say Windows Security (or any other antivirus product) encounters a suspicious-looking file that isn't on its zap list. In order to get the latest information about that suspicious-looking file, Windows Security has to phone back to Microsoft, drop off pieces of the file, and ask whether there's anything new. You can opt out of real-time protection, but if you do, you won't have the latest virus information — and some viruses travel fast.

## Adjusting Windows Security

Unlike many other antivirus products, Windows Security has a blissfully small number of things that you can or should tweak. Here's how to get to the settings:

**1.** **Click or tap the search icon (magnifying glass) on the taskbar and type sec. At the top, click or tap Windows Security.**

The main Windows Security screen appears (refer to Figure 3-1).

**2.** **Click or tap Virus & Threat Protection and then click or tap the Scan Options link.**

You see the options for manually running a quick scan, full scan, custom scan, or Microsoft Defender Offline scan. (See the "Microsoft Defender Offline" sidebar.) If you go back to Virus & Threat Protection, you can also change Windows Security's behavior. If you really want to turn off the main antivirus protections, you can do so here.

**3.** **If you have any reason to fear that your machine's been taken over by a rootkit, select the Microsoft Defender Offline scan, click or tap Scan Now, and confirm your choice.**

You are signed out of Windows 11. Go have a cup of coffee, and by the time you come back, Microsoft Defender Offline will show you a list of any scummy stuff it caught.

## MICROSOFT DEFENDER OFFLINE

Microsoft Defender Offline (MDO) sniffs out and removes *rootkits,* which are malicious programs that run underneath Windows. Rootkits can be devilishly difficult to identify. The "best" ones may not even have symptoms. They sit in the background, swipe your data, and send it out to listening posts.

MDO should occupy a key spot in your bag of tricks. It works like a champ on Windows systems and should be able to catch a wide variety of nasties that evade detection by more traditional methods.

It's important to understand that MDO is not a Windows application, even though Microsoft makes and distributes it. MDO is self-contained. When you choose to run an offline scan, Windows 11 reboots for you, and MDO looks at your system without interference from the installed copy of Windows. MDO runs all by itself and, when it's done, brings Windows back.

To find rootkits, a rootkit detector has to do its job when Windows isn't running. If the detector were running on Windows, it would never be able to see underneath Windows to catch the rootkits. That's why it has to run offline — without Windows.

# Running Windows Security manually

Windows Security works without you doing a thing, but you can tell it to run a scan if something on your computer is giving you the willies. Here's how:

**1.** **Click or tap the search icon on the taskbar and type** sec. **Click or tap Windows Security in the list of search results.**

The main Windows Security screen appears (refer to Figure 3-1).

**2.** **Click or tap Virus & Threat Protection.**

**3.** **Under Virus & Threat Protection Updates, click or tap Protection Updates.**

**4.** **On the resulting Protection Updates pane (see Figure 3-2), click or tap Check for Updates to get the latest antimalware definitions.**

When you tap or click Check for Updates, Windows Security retrieves the latest signature files from Microsoft but doesn't run a scan. If you want to run a scan, you need to go back to the Virus & Threat Protection screen and run it.

**FIGURE 3-2:**
The current status of Windows Security signature file updates.

5. **Click or tap the back arrow in the top-left corner. Then, to perform a manual scan, click or tap Scan Options. Choose one of the following three options (see Figure 3-3):**

- *To perform a quick scan, which looks in locations where viruses and other kinds of malware are likely to hide, select the Quick Scan option and then click or tap Scan Now.*

- *To run a full scan, which runs a bit-by-bit scan of every file and folder on the PC, select the Full Scan option and then click or tap Scan Now.*

- *To run a custom scan, which is like a full scan, but you get to choose which drives and folders get scanned, select the Custom Scan option, and then click or tap Scan Now and select the folder/partition you want scanned.*

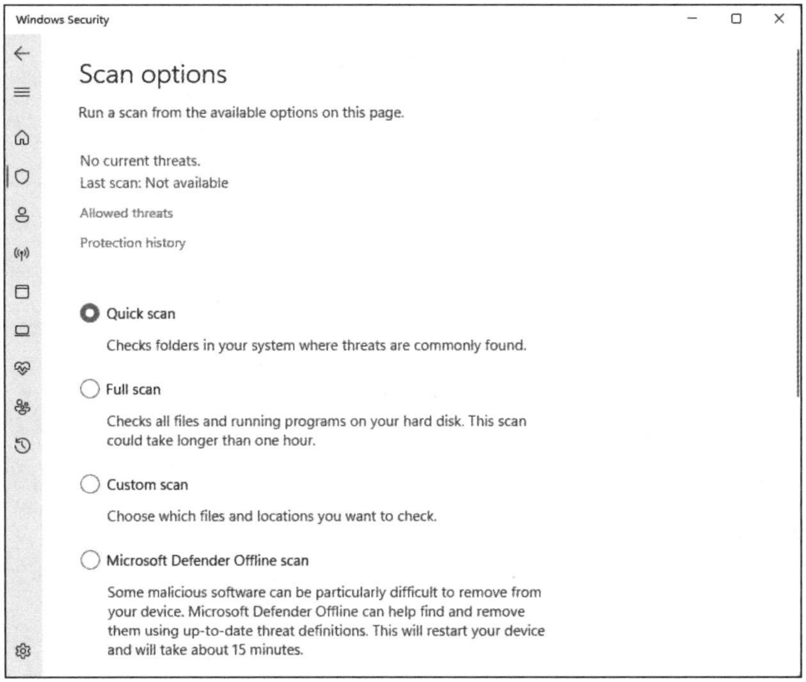

**FIGURE 3-3:**
Scan settings
for Windows
Security.

6. **To see what Windows Security has caught and zapped historically, click or tap the Protection History link in the Virus & Threat Protection pane.**

The screen shown in Figure 3-4 appears. Once upon a time, Windows Security would flag infected files and offer them up for you to decide what to do with the offensive file. It appears as if that behavior has been scaled back radically. As best I can tell, in almost all circumstances, when Windows Security hits a dicey file, it *quarantines* the file — sticks it in a place you won't accidentally find — and just keeps going. You're rarely notified (although a notification may slide out from the right side of the screen), but the file just disappears from where it should've been.

If you just downloaded a file and it disappeared, there's a good chance that it's infected and Windows Security has whisked it away to a well-guarded location, and the only way you'll ever find it is in the Protection History tab of the Windows Security program.

Should you decide to bring the file back, for whatever reason, click or tap the name of the threat, Actions, Allow on Device, and then Yes in the UAC (User Account Control) prompt.

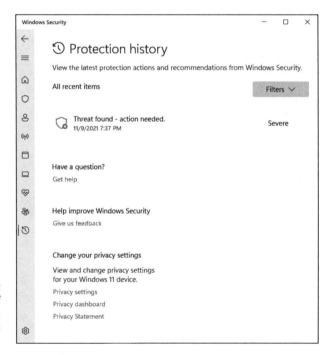

**FIGURE 3-4:**
A full history of the protection actions taken appear here.

# Controlling Folder Access

Ransomware — software that scrambles files and demands a payment before unscrambling — has become quite the rage. It's an easy way for script kiddies to monetize their malware. I talk about ransomware in Book 9, Chapter 1.

Microsoft has come up with a way to preemptively block many kinds of ransom-ware by simply restricting access to folders that contain files the ransomware may want to zap.

**WARNING**

There's just one problem. Restricting, or controlling, folder access is a pain in the neck — it blocks every program unless you specifically give a specific program access. So, for example, you can turn off access to your Documents folder but allow access to Word and Excel. That may work well until you want to run Notepad on a file in the Documents folder.

That's the reason why Microsoft doesn't turn on Controlled Folder Access (CFA) by default. If you really want CFA, you must dig deep and find it. If you do make the effort, stick CFA on all the right folders and whitelist any program that may need to use files in the controlled folders.

To enable CFA, you need to jump through the following hoops:

**1.** **Click or tap the search icon on the taskbar and type** sec. **Click or tap Windows Security in the list of search results.**

**2.** **Click or tap the Virus & Threat Protection icon, scroll way down, and click or tap Manage Ransomware Protection.**

The Controlled Folder Access (CFA) settings screen appears, as shown in Figure 3-5.

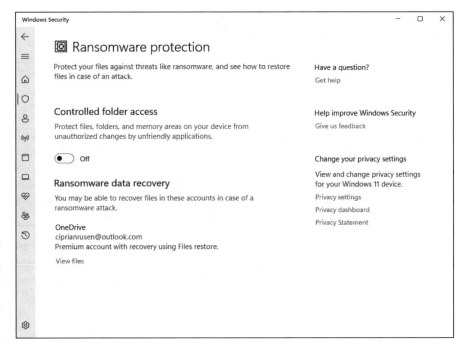

**FIGURE 3-5:**
You have to set up Controlled Folder Access manually — and doing so is problematic on many systems.

3. **Set the Controlled Folder Access switch to on and, then click or tap the Protected Folders link. Click or tap Yes when asked to confirm your choice.**

   You see a list of all folders protected by CFA — Documents, Pictures, Videos, Music, Favorites, and so on. However, ransomware frequently attacks files in other locations too.

4. **If you want to add another folder to the blocked list, click or tap the Add a Protected Folder button and navigate to and select the folder. Repeat as necessary.**

   Note that Windows has an automatically created (but not disclosed!) set of programs that it deems to be friendly.

5. **Click or tap the back arrow in the upper-left corner to return to the window shown in Figure 3-5.**

6. **If you have any programs that need access to those folders, and the apps aren't automatically identified as friendly, click or tap the Allow an App through Controlled Folder Access link, and then click or tap Yes.**

7. **Click or tap the Add an Allowed App button, click or tap Browse All Apps, and then navigate to and select the app. Repeat as necessary.**

   The app is added to the whitelist.

# Judging SmartScreen

Have you ever downloaded a program from the internet, clicked to install it — and then, a second later, thought, "Why did I do that?"

Microsoft came up with an interesting technique called SmartScreen that gives you an extra chance to change your mind, if the software you're trying to install has drawn criticism from other Windows customers. SmartScreen was built into an older version of Internet Explorer, version 7 (it was called Phishing Filter). It's now part of Windows 11 in Microsoft Edge. Google Chrome and Firefox have similar technologies, but the SmartScreen settings apply only to Internet Explorer (in Windows 10 or older) and in Microsoft Edge.

One part of SmartScreen works with Windows Security. In fact, sometimes I've seen an infected file trigger a notification from Windows Security, and later had the same infected file prompt the SmartScreen warning shown in Figure 3-6.

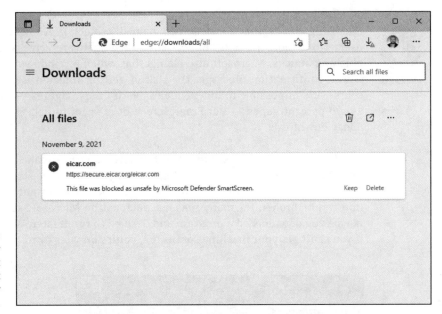

**FIGURE 3-6:**
SmartScreen may
take the credit
for the bust, but
Windows Security
did the work.

If you don't run the program, it gets stuffed into the same location that Windows Security puts its quarantined programs — out of the way where you can't find it, unless you go in through Windows Security's Protection History tab (refer to Figure 3-4).

There's a second part of SmartScreen that works differently, something like this:

1. You download something — anything — from the internet.

   Most browsers and many email programs and other online services (including instant messengers) set a property on the downloaded file that indicates where the file came from.

2. When you try to launch the file, Windows 11 checks the name of the file and the URL of origin to see whether they're on a trusted whitelist.

3. If the file doesn't pass muster, you see a notification like the one in Figure 3-6.

4. The more people who install the program from that site, the more trusted the program becomes.

   Again, Microsoft is collecting information about your system — in this case, about your downloads — but it's for a worthy cause.

Microsoft has an excellent, official description of the precise way the tracking mechanism works at `https://support.microsoft.com/en-us/microsoft-edge/what-is-smartscreen-and-how-can-it-help-protect-me-1c9a874a-6826-be5e-45b1-67fa445a74c8`.

Microsoft claims that SmartScreen helped protect previous Internet Explorer users from more than 1.5 billion attempted malware attacks and 150 million phishing attacks. Microsoft also claims that, when a Windows user is confronted with a confirmation message, the risk of getting infected is 25–70 percent. Of course, it's impossible to independently verify those figures — and the gap from 25–70 percent gapes — but SmartScreen does seem to help in the fight against dodgy downloads.

So what can go wrong? Not much. If SmartScreen can't make a connection to its main database when it hits something fishy, you see a blue screen like the one in Figure 3-7 telling you that SmartScreen can't be reached right now. The connection can be broken for many reasons, such as the Microsoft servers go down or maybe you downloaded a program and decided to run it later. When that happens, if you can't get your machine connected, you're on your own.

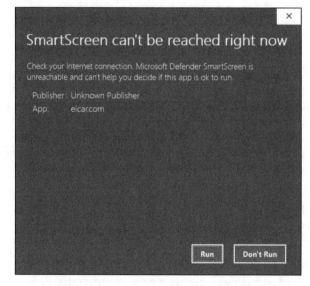

**FIGURE 3-7:**
If SmartScreen can't phone home, it leaves you on your own.

Normally, overriding a SmartScreen warning requires the okay of someone with an administrator account. You can change that, too. Here's how:

**1. Click or tap the search icon and type** smartscreen. **Click or tap the Reputation-Based Protection search result.**

The Windows Security Reputation-Based Protection pane appears (see Figure 3-8).

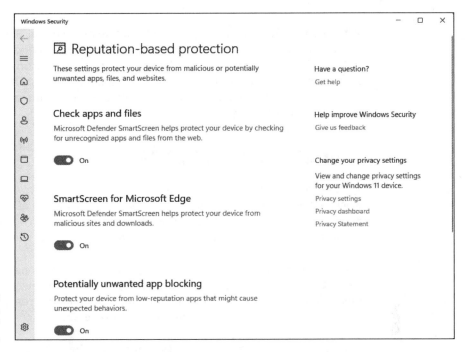

2. **(Optional) To change the default warning behavior for SmartScreen when you run it on downloaded files, click or tap the switch for Check Apps and Files. Click or tap Yes when asked to confirm your choice.**

   You won't receive a warning when something bad is downloaded by Google Chrome, Firefox, or any non-Microsoft browser, but you will be warned if you try to open or run the file.

3. **(Optional) To change the default warning behavior for Edge, adjust the SmartScreen For Microsoft Edge switch.**

4. **(Optional) Turn off SmartScreen for potentially unwanted Apps as well as for Microsoft Store apps by setting the last two switches to off. Click or tap Yes when asked to confirm your choice.**

   Don't forget to close Windows Security when done. Also, its icon in the notification area will be busy with warning messages.

# Booting Securely with UEFI

If you've ever struggled with your PC's BIOS — or been kneecapped by a capable rootkit — you know that BIOS should've been retired more than a decade ago.

Windows 11 pulled the industry kicking and screaming out of the BIOS generation and into a far more capable *Unified Extensible Firmware Interface* (UEFI). Although UEFI machines in the time of Windows 7 were unusual, starting with Windows 8, every new machine with a Runs Windows sticker is required to have UEFI; it's part of the licensing requirement. Windows 11 enforces this requirement by refusing to install on non-UEFI systems.

## A brief history of BIOS

To understand where Windows is headed, it's best to look at where it's been. And where it's been with BIOS inside PCs spans the entire history of the personal computer. That makes PC-resident BIOS more than 40 years old. The first IBM PC had a BIOS, and it didn't look all that different from the inscrutable one you swear at now.

The Basic Input/Output System, or *BIOS*, is a program responsible for getting all your PC's hardware in order and then firing up the operating system (OS) — in this case, Windows — and finally handing control of the computer over to the OS. BIOS runs automatically when the PC is turned on.

Older operating systems, such as DOS, relied on the BIOS to perform input and output functions. More modern operating systems, including Windows, have their own device drivers that make BIOS control obsolete, after the OS is running.

Every BIOS has a user interface, which looks much like the one in Figure 3-9. You press a key while the BIOS is starting and, using different keyboard incantations, take some control over your PC's hardware, select boot devices (in other words, tell BIOS where the operating system is located), overclock the processor, disable or rearrange hard drives, and the like.

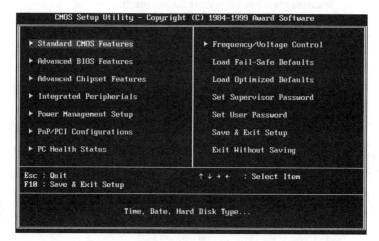

**FIGURE 3-9:**
The AwardBIOS
Setup Utility.

# How UEFI is different from and better than BIOS

BIOS has all sorts of problems, not the least of which is its susceptibility to malware. Rootkits like to hook themselves into the earliest part of the booting process — permitting them to run underneath Windows — and BIOS has a big Kick Me sign on its tail.

**TECHNICAL
STUFF**

UEFI and BIOS can coexist: UEFI can run on top of BIOS, hooking itself into the program locations where the operating system may call BIOS, basically usurping all the BIOS functions after UEFI gets going. UEFI can also run without BIOS, taking care of all the runtime functions. The only thing UEFI can't do is perform the power-on self-test (POST) or run the initial setup. PCs that have UEFI without BIOS need separate programs for POST and setup that run automatically when the PC is started.

Unlike BIOS, which sits inside a chip on your PC's motherboard, UEFI can exist on a disk, just like any other program, or in non-volatile memory on the motherboard or even on a network share.

UEFI is very much like an operating system that runs before your final operating system kicks in. UEFI has access to all the PC's hardware, including the mouse and network connections. It can take advantage of your fancy video card and monitor, as shown in Figure 3-10. It can even access the internet. If you've ever played with BIOS, you know that this is in a whole new dimension.

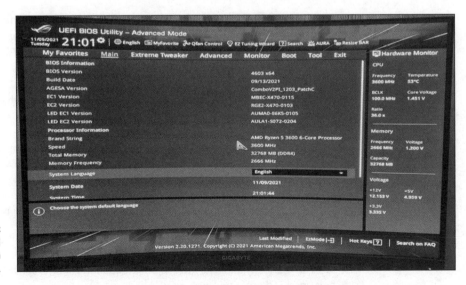

**FIGURE 3-10:**
The UEFI
interface on an
ASUS PC.

Compare Figure 3-9 with Figure 3-10, and you'll have some idea where technology's been and where it's heading.

BIOS — the entire process surrounding BIOS, including POST — takes a long, long time. UEFI, by contrast, can go by quite quickly. The BIOS program itself is easy to reverse-engineer and has no internal security protection. In the malware maelstrom, it's a sitting duck. UEFI can run in any malware-dodging way its inventors contrive.

Dual boot in the old world involves a handoff to a clunky text program; in the new world, it can be much simpler, more visual, and controlled by mouse or touch.

More to the point, UEFI can police operating systems before loading them. That could make rootkit writers' lives considerably more difficult by, for example, refusing to run an OS unless it has a proper digital security signature. Windows Security can work with UEFI to validate OSs before they're loaded. And that's where the controversy begins.

## How Windows 11 uses UEFI

A UEFI *Secure Boot* option validates programs before allowing them to run. If Secure Boot is turned on, operating system loaders have to be signed using a digital certificate. If you want to dual boot between Windows 11 and Linux, the Linux program must have a digital certificate — something Linux programs have never required before.

After UEFI validates the digital key, UEFI calls on Windows Security to verify the certificate for the operating system loader. Windows Security (or another security program) can go out to the internet and check to see whether UEFI is about to run an OS that has had its certificate yanked.

In essence, in a dual-boot system, Windows Security decides whether an operating system gets loaded on your Secure Boot-enabled machine.

That curls the toes of many Linux fans. Why should their operating systems be subject to Microsoft's rules, if you want to dual boot between Windows 11 and Linux?

If you have a PC with UEFI and Secure Boot and you want to boot an operating system that doesn't have a Microsoft-approved digital signature, you have two options:

>> You can turn off Secure Boot.

>> You can manually add a key to the UEFI validation routine, specifically allowing that unsigned operating system to load.

**TECHNICAL
STUFF**

Some PCs won't let you turn off Secure Boot. So, if you want to dual boot Windows 11 and some other operating system on a Windows 11-certified computer, you may have lots of hoops to jump through. Check with your hardware manufacturer.

# Controlling User Account Control

User Account Control *(UAC)* is a pain in the neck, but then again, it's supposed to be that. If you try to install a program that's going to make system-level changes, you may see the obnoxious prompt in Figure 3-11.

**FIGURE 3-11:**
User Account
Control tries to
keep you from
clobbering your
system.

UAC's a drama queen, too. The approval dialog box in Figure 3-11 appears front and center, but at the same time, your entire desktop dims, and you're forced to deal with the UAC prompt.

**REMEMBER**

UAC does all this for a good reason: It's telling you that a program wants to make changes to your system — not piddling things like changing a document or opening a picture, but earth-shaking things like modifying Windows Registry or poking around inside system folders.

If you go into your system folders manually or if you fire up the Editor and start making loose and fancy with registry keys, UAC figures you know what you're doing and leaves you alone. But the minute a program tries to do those kinds of things, Windows warns you that a potentially dangerous program is on the prowl and gives you a chance to kill the program in its tracks.

Windows lets you adjust User Account Control so it isn't quite as dramatic — or you can get rid of it entirely.

To adjust your computer's UAC level, follow these steps:

1. **Click or tap the search icon and type** uac. **At the top of the ensuing list, choose Change User Account Control Settings.**

   The slider shown in Figure 3-12 appears.

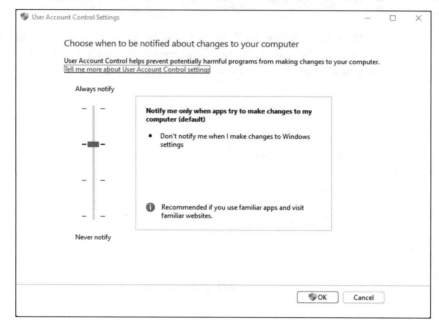

**FIGURE 3-12:**
Windows 11
allows you to
change the
level of UAC
intrusiveness.

2. **Adjust the slider according to Table 3-1, and then click or tap OK.**

   Perhaps surprisingly, as soon as you try to change your UAC level, Windows 11 hits you with a User Account Control prompt. If you're using a standard account, you have to provide an administrator username and password (or PIN) to make the change. If you're using an administrator account, you must confirm the change.

3. **Click or tap Yes.**

   Your changes take effect immediately.

TECHNICAL
STUFF

This description sounds simple, but the details are quite complex. Microsoft's Help system says that if your computer is at Level 2, the default setting in Windows, "You will be notified if a program outside of Windows tries to make changes to a Windows setting." So how does Windows tell when a program is out-side Windows — and thus whether actions taken by the program are worthy of a UAC prompt at Levels 2 or 3?

**TABLE 3-1**

## User Account Control Levels

| Slider | What It Means | Recommendations |
|---|---|---|
| Level 1 (top) | Always brings up the full UAC notification whenever a program tries to install software or make changes to the computer that require an administrator account, or when you try to make changes to Windows settings that require an administrator account. You see these notifications even if you're using an administrator account. The screen blacks out, and you can't do anything until the UAC screen is answered. | This level offers the highest security but also the highest hassle factor. |
| Level 2 | Brings up the UAC notification whenever a program tries to make changes to your computer, but generally doesn't bring up a UAC notification when you make changes directly. | The default — and probably the best choice. |
| Level 3 | This level is the same as Level 2 except that the UAC notification doesn't lock and dim your desktop. | Potentially problematic. Dimming and locking the screen present a high hurdle for malware. |
| Level 4 (bottom) | UAC is disabled — programs can install other programs or make changes to Windows settings, and you can change anything you like, without triggering any UAC prompts. Note that this doesn't override other security settings. For example, if you're using a standard account, you still need to provide an administrator's ID and password before you can install a program that runs for all users. | Automatically turns off all UAC warnings — NOT recommended. |

UAC-level rules are interpreted according to a special Windows security certificate. Programs signed with that certificate are deemed to be part of Windows. Programs that aren't signed with that specific certificate are outside Windows and thus trigger UAC prompts if your computer is at Level 1, 2, or 3.

# Poking at Windows Defender Firewall

A *firewall* is a program that sits between your computer and the internet, protecting you from the big, mean, nasty gorillas riding around on the information superhighway. An *inbound firewall* acts like a traffic cop that allows only good stuff into your computer and keeps all the bad stuff out on the internet, where it belongs. An *outbound firewall* prevents your computer from sending bad stuff to the internet, such as when your computer becomes infected with a virus or has another security problem.

Windows includes a decent inbound firewall. It also includes a snarly, hard-to-configure, rudimentary outbound firewall, which has all the social graces of a junkyard dog. Unless you know the magic incantations, you never even see the outbound firewall — it's completely muzzled unless you dig into the Windows doghouse and teach it some tricks.

**REMEMBER**

Everybody needs an inbound firewall, without a doubt. You already have one, in Windows 11, and you don't need to do anything to it.

Outbound firewalls tend to bother you mercilessly with inscrutable warnings saying that obscure processes are trying to send data. If you simply click through and let the program phone home, you're defeating the purpose of the outbound firewall. On the other hand, if you take the time to track down every single outbound event warning, you may spend half your life dealing with prompts from your firewall.

I think outbound firewalls are mostly a waste of time. Although I'm sure some people have been alerted to Windows infections when their outbound firewall goes bananas, most of the time, the outbound warnings are just noise. Outbound firewalls don't catch the cleverest malware, anyway. However, I have a few friends who insist on running an outbound firewall. If you want one too, I recommend GlassWire, which is available in a free-for-personal-use version at www.glasswire.com

## Understanding Defender Firewall basic features

All versions of Windows 11 ship with a decent and capable, but not foolproof, *stateful* firewall named Windows Defender Firewall (WDF). (See the nearby sidebar, "What's a stateful firewall?")

## HARDWARE FIREWALLS

Most modern routers and wireless access points include significant firewalling capability as part of their firmware. The firewalling capabilities are automatically activated when they share an internet connection among many computers.

Routers and wireless access points add an extra step between your computer and the internet. That extra jump — named network address translation — combined with built-in intelligence on the router's part can provide an extra layer of protection that works independently from, but in conjunction with, the firewall running on your PC.

## WHAT'S A STATEFUL FIREWALL?

At the risk of oversimplifying a bit, a *stateful* firewall is an inbound firewall that remembers. It keeps track of packets of information going out of your computer and where they're headed. When a packet arrives and tries to get in, the inbound firewall matches the originating address of the incoming packet against the log of addresses of the outgoing packets to make sure that any packet allowed through the firewall comes from an expected location.

Stateful packet filtering isn't 100-percent foolproof. And you must have some exceptions so that unexpected packets can come through for reasons discussed elsewhere in this chapter. But a stateful firewall is a fast, reliable way to minimize your exposure to potentially destructive probes from out on the big bad internet.

Windows Defender Firewall inbound protection is on by default. Unless you change something, Windows Defender Firewall is turned on for all connections on your PC. For example, if you have a LAN cable, a wireless networking card, and a 4G USB card on a specific PC, WDF is turned on for them all. The only way Windows Defender Firewall gets turned off is if you deliberately turn it off or if the network administrator on your big corporate network decides to disable it by remote control or install Windows with Windows Defender Firewall turned off.

**WARNING**

In unusual and rare circumstances, malware (viruses, Trojans, whatever) have been known to turn off Windows Defender Firewall. If your firewall kicks out, Windows lets you know loud and clear with balloon notifications near the system clock on the desktop.

You can change WDF settings for inbound protection relatively easily. When you make changes, they apply to all connections on your PC. On the other hand, WDF settings for outbound protection make the rules of cricket look like child's play.

WDF kicks in before the computer is connected to the network. Back in the not-so-good old days, many PCs got infected between the time they were connected and when the firewall came up.

## Speaking your firewall's lingo

At this point, I must go through a bunch of jargon so that you can take control of Windows Defender Firewall. Hold your nose and dive in. The concepts aren't that difficult, although the terminology sounds like a first-year advertising student invented it. Refer to this section if you become bewildered when wading through the WDF dialog boxes.

As you no doubt realize, the amount of data that can be sent from one computer to another over a network can be tiny or huge. Computers talk with each other by breaking the data into *packets* (or small chunks of data with a wrapper that identifies where the data came from and where it's going).

On the internet, packets can be sent in two ways:

>> **User Datagram Protocol (UDP):** UDP is fast and sloppy. The computer sending the packets doesn't keep track of which packets were sent, and the computer receiving the packets doesn't make any attempt to get the sender to resend packets that vanish mysteriously into the bowels of the internet. UDP is the kind of *protocol* (transmission method) that can work with live broadcasts, where short gaps wouldn't be nearly as disruptive as long pauses, while the computers wait to resend a dropped packet.

>> **Transmission Control Protocol (TCP):** TCP is methodical and complete. The sending computer keeps track of which packets it has sent. If the receiving computer doesn't get a packet, it notifies the sending computer, which resends the packet. These days, almost all communication over the internet goes by way of TCP.

TECHNICAL
STUFF

Every computer on a network has an *IP address*, which is a collection of four sets of numbers, each between 0 and 255. For example, 192.168.0.2 is a common IP address for computers connected to a local network; the web server that handles the Dummies.com website is at 104.18.4.55. You can think of the IP address as analogous to a telephone number.

## Peeking into your firewall

When you use a firewall — and you should — you change the way your computer communicates with other computers on the internet. This section explains what Windows Defender Firewall does behind the scenes so that when it gets in the way, you understand how to tweak it. (You find the ins and outs of working around the firewall in the "Making inbound exceptions" section, later in this chapter.)

TECHNICAL
STUFF

When two computers communicate, they need not only each other's IP address but also a specific entry point called a *port* — think of it as a telephone extension — to talk to each other. For example, most websites respond to requests sent to port 80 when using HTTP and port 443 when using HTTPS. There's nothing magical about the number 80 or 443; it's just the port number that people have agreed to use when trying to get to a website's computer. If your web browser wants to look at the Dummies.com website, it sends a packet to 104.18.4.55, port 80 or 443, depending on whether you're using HTTP or HTTPS.

Windows Defender Firewall works by handling all these duties simultaneously:

>> **It keeps track of outgoing packets and allows incoming packets to go through the firewall if they can be matched with an outgoing packet.** In other words, WDF works as a stateful inbound firewall.

>> **If your computer is attached to a private network, Windows Defender Firewall allows packets to come and go on ports 139 and 445, but only if they came from another computer on your local network and only if they're using TCP.** Windows Defender Firewall needs to open those ports for file and printer sharing. It also opens several ports for Windows Media Player if you've chosen to share your media files, for example.

>> **Similarly, if your computer is attached to a private network, Windows Defender Firewall automatically opens ports 137, 138, and 5355 for UDP, but only for packets that originate on your local network.**

>> **If you specifically told Windows Defender Firewall that you want it to allow packets to come in on a specific port and the Block All Incoming Connections check box isn't selected, WDF follows your orders.** You may need to open a port in this way for online gaming, for example.

>> **Windows Defender Firewall allows packets to come into your computer if they're sent to the Remote Assistance program, as long as you created a Remote Assistance request on this PC and told Windows to open your firewall (see Book 7, Chapter 3).** Remote Assistance allows other users to take control of your PC, but it has its own security settings and strong password protection. Still, it's a known security hole that's enabled when you create a request.

>> **You can tell Windows Defender Firewall to accept packets directed at specific programs.** Usually, any company that makes a program designed to listen for incoming internet traffic (Skype is a prime example, as are any instant-messaging apps) adds its program to the list of designated exceptions when the program is installed.

>> **Unless an inbound packet meets one of the preceding criteria, it's simply ignored.** Windows Defender Firewall swallows it without a peep. Conversely, unless you've changed something, any and all outbound traffic goes through unobstructed.

## Making inbound exceptions

Firewalls can be infuriating. You may have a program that has worked for a hundred years on all sorts of computers, but the minute you install it on a Windows

11 machine with Windows Defender Firewall in action, it just stops working, for absolutely no apparent reason.

You can get mad at Microsoft and scream at Windows Defender Firewall, but when you do, realize that at least part of the problem lies in the way the firewall has to work. (See the "Peeking into your firewall" section, earlier in this chapter, for an explanation of what your firewall does behind the scenes.) It has to block packets that are trying to get in, unless you explicitly tell the firewall to allow them to get in.

Perhaps most infuriatingly, WDF blocks those packets by simply swallowing them, not by notifying the computer that sent the packet. Windows Defender Firewall has to remain stealthy because if it sends back a packet that says, "Hey, I got your packet, but I can't let it through," the bad guys get an acknowledgment that your computer exists, they can probably figure out which firewall you're using, and they may be able to combine those two pieces of information to give you a headache. It's far better for Windows Defender Firewall to act like a black hole.

Some programs need to listen to incoming traffic from the internet; they wait until they're contacted and then respond. Usually, you know whether you have this type of program because the installer tells you that you need to tell your firewall to back off.

TIP

If you have a program that doesn't (or can't) poke its own hole through Windows Defender Firewall, you can tell WDF to allow packets destined for that specific program — and only that program — in through the firewall. You may want to do that with a game that needs to accept incoming traffic, for example, or for an Outlook extender program that interacts with smartphones.

To poke a hole in the inbound Windows Defender Firewall for a specific program:

**1.** **Make sure that the program you want to allow through Windows Defender Firewall is installed.**

**2.** **Click or tap the search icon and type** firewall. **Choose Allow an App through Windows Firewall.**

Windows Defender Firewall presents you with a lengthy list of apps that you may want to allow (see Figure 3-13). If a box is selected, Windows Defender Firewall allows unsolicited incoming packets of data directed to that program and that program alone, and the column tells you whether the connection is allowed for private or public connections.

REMEMBER

These settings don't apply to incoming packets of data that are received in response to a request from your computer; they apply only when a packet of data appears on your firewall's doorstep without an invitation.

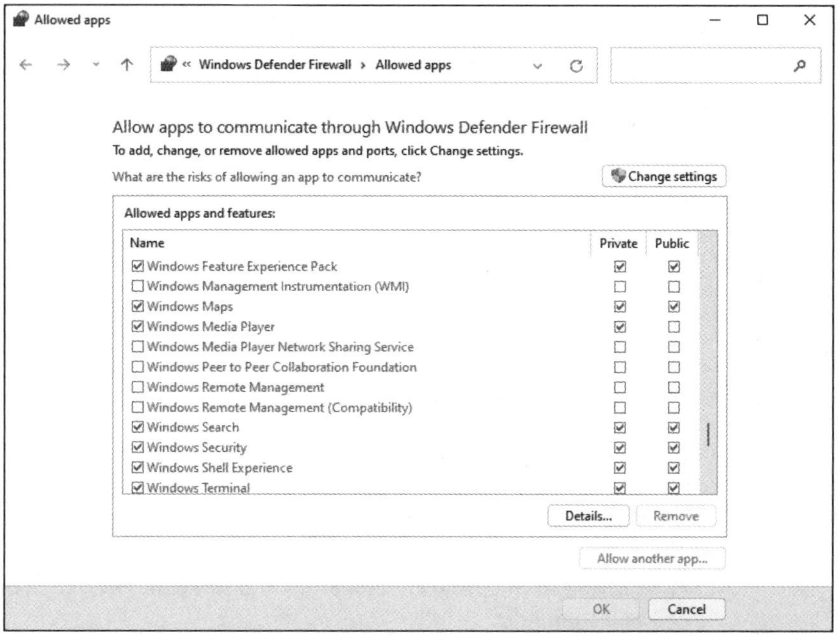

FIGURE 3-13:
Allow installed
programs to
poke through
the firewall.

In Figure 3-13, the Windows Maps app is allowed to receive inbound packets whether you're connected to a private or public network. Windows Media Player, on the other hand, may accept unsolicited inbound data from other computers only if you're connected to a private network: If you're attached to a public network, inbound packets headed for Windows Media Player are swallowed by the Windows Defender Firewall Black Hole (patent pending).

**3.** **Click or tap Change Settings, and do one of the following:**

- *If you can find the program that you want to poke through the firewall listed in the Allow Programs list, select the check boxes that correspond to whether you want to allow the unsolicited incoming data when connected to a home or work network and whether you want to allow the incoming packets when connected to a public network.* It's rare indeed that you'd allow access when connected to a public network but not to a home or work network.

- *If you can't find the program that you want to poke through the firewall, you need to go out and look for it. Click or tap the Allow Another App button at the bottom and then click or tap Browse.*

Windows Defender Firewall goes out to all common program locations and finally presents you with the Whack a Mol . . . er, Add an App list like the one shown in Figure 3-14. It can take a while.

**FIGURE 3-14:**
Allow a program (that you've thoroughly vetted!) to break through the firewall.

4. **Browse to the program's location and select it. Then click or tap Open, and then Add.**

   You return to the Windows Defender Firewall Allowed Apps list (refer to Figure 3-13), and your newly selected program is now available.

5. **Select the check boxes to allow your poked-through program to accept incoming data while you're connected to a private or a public network. Then click or tap OK.**

   Your poked-through program can immediately start handling inbound data.

**TECHNICAL STUFF**

In many cases, poking through Windows Defender Firewall doesn't solve the whole problem. You may have to poke through your modem or router as well — unsolicited packets that arrive at the router may get kicked back according to the router's rules, even if Windows 11 would allow them in. Unfortunately, each router and the method for poking holes in the router's inbound firewall differ. Check the site `https://portforward.com/router.htm` for an enormous amount of information about poking through routers.

# Chapter **4**

# Enhancing Your Security

I n Chapter 3 of this minibook, I talk about built-in Windows security programs available to every Windows 11 owner. In this chapter, I continue with the adventure of securing your PC and start by presenting BitLocker. Unfortunately, this encryption tool is available only for Windows 11 Pro, so Home users are out of luck.

I continue with helping you manage your passwords online. Considering how many accounts we have all over the internet, having a system in place to manage them for us is vital to protecting our security and privacy. Many password managers are available, but I present two services that I like.

Then, I discuss a bit more about handling infections. Your device might get an infection that even Windows Security (and Microsoft Defender Offline) can't handle. Usually it's because you installed a program you didn't research. If you get hit bad, there's one place to turn. *Malwarebytes,* a combination of software and a very competent website, can crack just about any infection.

Lastly, if you want to connect to a website and make sure nobody can snoop on your connection — particularly important if you access financial sites from public Wi-Fi networks, like in a coffee shop or an airport — you should figure out how to use a VPN. Windows 11 can help you set up a VPN connection with ease, and there are some cool VPN services you can try. Some services have a strict no-logs policy, which is useful when a dodgy government or government agency tries to spy on your activities.

# Encrypting Your PC with BitLocker

BitLocker encrypts an entire drive. Unlike Encrypting File System (see the nearby "Encrypting File System [EFS]" sidebar), you have to encrypt full drives (or, more accurately, volumes) or nothing at all. BitLocker runs *underneath* Windows: It starts before Windows starts. The Windows partition on a BitLocker–protected drive is completely encrypted. Even if thieves get their hands on your laptop or hard drive, they can't view anything on it — not even your settings or system files.

BitLocker To Go is similar to BitLocker, except it works on USB drives like flash memory sticks and external hard disks.

BitLocker is part of Windows 11 Pro. It is not part of the Home edition of Windows 11. If you have Windows 11 and want to get BitLocker, you must upgrade to Windows 11 Pro. I talk about the various versions and editions of Windows 11 in Book 1, Chapter 3. Some people feel their information is sufficiently valuable that BitLocker, all by itself, justifies paying the extra bucks for Windows 11 Pro.

Here's how to encrypt your hard drive with BitLocker:

1.  **Click or tap the search icon (magnifying glass) and type** bitlocker. **Click or tap Manage BitLocker.**

    The BitLocker Drive Encryption window appears, as shown in Figure 4-1.

## ENCRYPTING FILE SYSTEM (EFS)

Microsoft *Encrypting File System* (EFS) works with or without BitLocker. EFS is a method for encrypting individual files or groups of files on a hard drive. EFS starts after Windows boots: It runs as a program under Windows, which means it can leave traces of itself and the data that's being encrypted in temporary Windows places that may be sniffed by exploit programs. The Windows directory isn't encrypted by EFS, so bad guys (and girls!) who can get access to the directory can hammer it with brute-force password attacks. Widely available tools can crack EFS if the cracker can reboot the target computer. Thus, for example, EFS can't protect the hard drive on a stolen laptop or notebook. Windows has supported Encrypting File System since the halcyon days of Windows 2000, and it still does in Windows 11.

BitLocker and EFS protect against two different kinds of attacks. Given a choice, you probably want BitLocker.

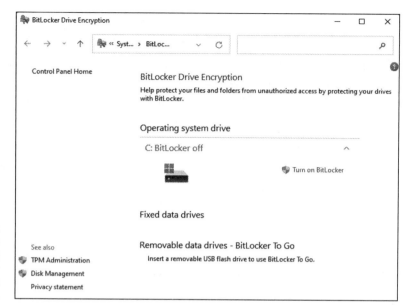

**FIGURE 4-1:**
Manage
everything from
the BitLocker
Drive Encryption
window.

2. **Next to the drive (volume) you want to encrypt, click or tap Turn on BitLocker.**

   The BitLocker Drive Encryption setup wizard appears, and Windows 11 checks whether it meets the requirements for running BitLocker.

**TECHNICAL STUFF**

   If your PC doesn't have a built-in Trusted Platform Module system, you see a message that says *Your administrator must set the 'Allow BitLocker without a compatible TPM' option.* The only easy way to solve that problem is to run the Local Group Policy Editor program, gpedit.msc. If you need advice, check out this tutorial: `www.digitalcitizen.life/how-enable-bitlocker-without-tpm-chip-windows-7-windows-8/`.

   If everything is well, you're asked how you want to unlock your drive at startup. Using a password is the most convenient method.

3. **Choose Enter a Password, type the password you want to use, confirm it, and click or tap Next.**

   The password must be at least eight characters long and must include uppercase and lowercase letters, numbers, symbols, and spaces.

   After encrypting your PC with BitLocker, the recovery key is the only way to access your files when you have problems unlocking your PC. See Figure 4-2. You have options to save the key to your Microsoft account (on Microsoft's servers in the cloud), to save the key to a file on your computer or USB flash drive, or to print the recovery key.

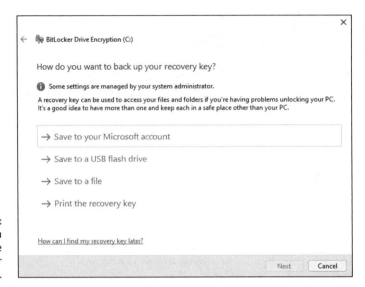

**FIGURE 4-2:**
Choose how you
want to save
the BitLocker
recovery key.

4. **Choose how you want to back up your recovery key, and then click or tap Next.**

5. **When asked to choose between encrypting used disk space only or the entire drive, make your choice and click or tap Next.**

   If you want the encryption to finish faster, choose to encrypt only the used disk space. Encrypting the entire drive may take many hours.

6. **Choose which encryption mode to use, and then click or tap Next.**

   The new encryption mode, which I highly recommend, uses a more secure type of encryption.

7. **Select the option to Run BitLocker System Check and click or tap Continue (instead of Start Encryption).**

   The system check ensures that BitLocker can read the recovery and encryption keys correctly before encrypting the drive, which is a great idea.

8. **When asked to restart your computer, close all your open apps and files, and then click or tap Restart Now.**

   When you log back into Windows 11, BitLocker encrypts your drive automatically, in the background. You can continue using your PC as usual. The BitLocker icon appears in the system tray, on the right side of the taskbar. If you click or tap it, you see the progress of the encryption process.

**TIP**

In case you were wondering, yes, you can use BitLocker on Storage Spaces too. BitLocker encrypts the entire Storage Space.

# Managing Your Passwords

You can find no end of advice on creating strong passwords, using clever tricks, stats, mnemonics, and such. But all too frequently people tend to reuse passwords on what they think are inconsequential sites. It's a big mistake. If somebody hacks into that small-time site and steals your password — an event that's frighteningly common these days — any other place where you've used that same password is immediately vulnerable.

**WARNING**

In the past few years, there have been some spectacular examples of ultra-secure sites getting hacked because the hacker stole a username and password from an inconsequential site and then discovered that the same username and password opened the doors to a trove of top-secret — even politically sensitive — corporate email or customer bank account information. The usernames and passwords were stolen from seasoned security professionals and admins at sensitive sites. You'd think they'd know better.

## Using password managers

I don't know about you, but I have dozens of usernames and passwords that I use fairly regularly. There's just no way I can remember them all. And my monitor isn't big enough to handle all the yellow sticky notes they'd demand.

**TIP**

That's where a password manager comes in. A *password manager* keeps track of all your online passwords. It can generate truly random passwords with the click of a button. Most of all, it remembers the username and password necessary to log in to a specific website.

Every time I go to www.ebay.com, for example, my password manager fills in my username and password. Amazon, too. Facebook. Twitter. My bank. Stock brokerage house. I have to remember the one password for the password manager, but after that, everything else gets filled in automatically. It's a huge timesaver.

A password manager won't log into Windows for you, and it won't remember the passwords on documents or spreadsheets. But it does keep track of every online password and autocompletes the passwords you need with no hassle.

## My recommendations

Many password management services are available, including ones built into web browsers such as Chrome, Edge, Opera, and Firefox. However, I like and trust two more than others.

The big difference between them? One was originally designed to run on a USB drive; the other has always been in the cloud, which is to say, on the internet:

>> **RoboForm** initially could store passwords on your hard drive or on a USB drive. However, this capability has been retired from recent versions and now this service is based in the cloud, works with all major web browsers, and has simple tools for synchronizing passwords.

>> **Bitwarden,** which stores passwords on its website, uses an encryption technique (AES-256) that guarantees your passwords won't get stolen or cracked. One cool aspect is that it's an open-source platform and its source code, features, and infrastructure security are vetted and improved by a global community.

Which one is better? It depends on how you use your computer.

If you always use the same computer, you may want the free plan offered by RoboForm. However, if you use many devices and you want password management on all, a solution like Bitwarden is better. Opinions run all over the place, but I prefer the interface of Bitwarden to that of RoboForm Everywhere. You should feel comfortable using either one.

## Rockin' RoboForm

The RoboForm app (www.roboform.com/) has all the features you need in a password manager. It manages your passwords with excellent recognition of websites, automatically filling in your login details. But it will also generate random passwords for you, if you like, and fill in forms on the web.

### WHAT IS AES-256?

The most effective encryption method commonly used on PCs conforms to the US National Institute of Standards and Technology's Advanced Encryption Standard 256-bit specification.

AES is the first widely available, open encryption technique (yes, you can look at the program) approved by the US National Security Agency for Top Secret information. Of course, that fact has led to speculation (without corroboration) that the NSA has cracked the algorithm, so it can decrypt AES-256 data.

RoboForm stores all its data in AES-256 encrypted format too. If somebody steals your RoboForm database, you needn't worry. Without the master key — which only you have — the entire database is gibberish.

RoboForm has versions for Windows, Mac, Linux, iPhone, iPad, and Android smartphones and tablets. There's a free plan for one computer or device, and paid plans that cover all your devices. There's even a family plan that helps save some money. You can also enjoy a 30-day trial version of RoboForm Everywhere, so that you can make an informed decision before buying. A yearly plan costs $23.88.

RoboForm can read the passwords from any web browser and migrate them over to your RoboForm account, as shown in Figure 4-3.

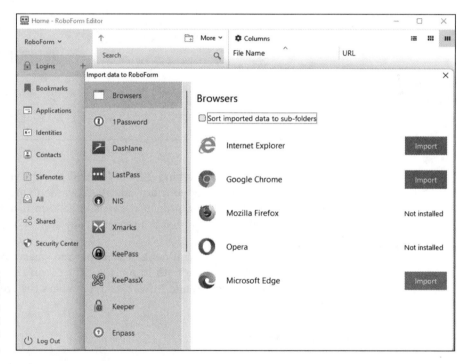

**FIGURE 4-3:** RoboForm is easy to use and can import passwords from all browsers.

# Liking Bitwarden

Bitwarden (https://bitwarden.com/) stores everything in the cloud on its company servers. Like RoboForm, Bitwarden keeps track of your user IDs, passwords, automatic form-filling information (think name, address, phone, credit card number), and other settings, and offers them to you with a click.

Using Bitwarden can't be simpler. Download and install it, and it'll **appear with a blue and white icon in the upper-right corner of your browser (see Figure 4-4).**

**FIGURE 4-4:**
Bitwarden is on the job if you can see its icon in the upper-right corner.

You don't really need to do anything. Bitwarden will prompt you for the master password when you start using your browser. If Bitwarden is turned off, its icon displays a red dot. Click or tap it, provide the master password, and the Bitwarden icon removes the red dot, a sign that it's ready to roll.

When you go to a site that requires a username and password, if Bitwarden recognizes the site, it fills them both in for you. If it doesn't recognize the site, you fill in the blanks and click, and Bitwarden remembers the credentials for the next time you surf this way.

Form filling works similarly.

**TIP**

You can maintain two (or more) separate usernames and passwords for any specific site — for example, if you log in to a banking site with two different accounts. If Bitwarden has more than one set of credentials stored for a specific site, it takes its best guess as to which one you want but then gives you the option of using one of the others. In Figure 4-4, I have three separate credentials for the site — that's why the Bitwarden icon has a 3.

Any time you want to look at the usernames and passwords that Bitwarden has squirreled away, click or tap the Bitwarden icon. You have a chance to look at your *Vault* — which is your password database — or look up recently used passwords and much more. You can even keep encrypted notes to yourself.

**REMEMBER**

The way Bitwarden handles your data is clever: All your passwords are encrypted using AES-256. They're encrypted and decrypted *on your PC*. Only you have the master password. So if the data is pilfered off the Bitwarden servers or somebody is sniffing your online communication, all the interlopers get is a bunch of useless bits.

You can also store secure notes, form-filling information such as your credit card information and address, and other data in Bitwarden.

One last cool bit is that, unlike RoboForm, Bitwarden hasn't phased out its portable USB app. On its download page, you can still find a Portable App for Flash Drives that you can use.

Bitwarden is free for individual use, and it works on all major PC and mobile platforms. If you want some advanced features, such as sharing passwords with others, two-step authentication, or priority support, you need the Premium edition, which costs $10 a year.

# Fighting Back at Tough Scumware

Windows Security works great. But sometimes you need a second opinion. Sometimes you get hit with an infection that's so nasty, absolutely nothing will clean it up.

That's when you want to check out Malwarebytes (www.malwarebytes.org/).

**REMEMBER**

Malwarebytes is a last resort. If your system is running normally, there's no reason to bother with it. And if your system is really messed up, you can probably fix things with a full scan in Windows Security (see Chapter 3 in this minibook) or Microsoft Defender Offline — or even a System Refresh (see Book 8, Chapter 2). If you've tried all that and still can't get your machine to work properly, it's time to haul out the big guns.

Malwarebytes has long been a great choice for going after absolutely intractable infections. Viruses, Trojans, spyware, you name it, Malwarebytes can probably get rid of it.

When you've run Windows Security, Microsoft Defender Offline, and Refresh, but you *still* can't get rid of the beast that's plaguing your system, do the following:

1. **Go to the Malwarebytes support forum at** `https://forums.malwarebytes.com/`, **see whether anyone has the same problem, and if so, log in and talk to that person.**

2. **If that doesn't work, go to the Malwarebytes Anti-Malware Free site at** `www.malwarebytes.com/mwb-download`, **and install the free version of its antimalware package.**

   During the installation phase, Malwarebytes disables parts of Windows Security. Not to worry. You don't want to run two antivirus packages at the same time.

3. **Run Malwarebytes:**

   - *If it doesn't get rid of your problem, post your results on the support forum.* Start at `https://forums.malwarebytes.com/topic/9573-im-infected-what-do-i-do-now/`, and follow the instructions precisely.

   - *If Malwarebytes fixes your problem, maybe pay for its Premium package.* It's only $3.33 /month (when purchasing an annual plan), and you're helping to keep the Malwarebytes effort solvent.

# Securing Your Communication with VPN

If you are serious about protecting your web surfing from prying eyes and have ever used a public, unencrypted Wi-Fi connection, the onus is on you to lock down your connections. If you connect to a wireless access point that uses WPA2 or WPA3 encryption, you're protected. But if you're using a public hotspot with no password required, you're definitely at risk. And the best way I know to protect against surreptitious sniffing — and a dozen other problems — involves a technology known as Virtual Private Networking, or VPN.

## What's a VPN?

You may have heard of VPN but figured it was just too difficult for regular Windows users to hook together. Big companies have VPN, but they also have experts to keep them running. Ends up that we little guys have good choices now, too.

VPN started as a way for big companies to securely connect PCs over the regular phone network. It used to take lots of specialty hardware, but if you worked for a bank and had to get into the bank's main computers from a laptop in another country, VPN was the only choice. Times have changed. Now you can get free or low-cost VPN connections that don't require any special hardware on your end, and they work surprisingly well.

# FIRESHEEP AND SIDEJACKING

In October 2010, ethical hacker Eric Butler released a startling Firefox add-on called Firesheep. If you run Firesheep on your computer, and other people using the same network aren't careful, you can sniff other people logging into websites. Click or tap a link inside Firefox, and you can take over the login credentials for the other person.

Eric Butler describes it this way: "When logging into a website, you usually start by submitting your username and password. The server then checks to see if an account matching this information exists and if so, replies back to you with a cookie, which is used by your browser for all subsequent requests. While most websites protect your username and password by forcing you to log on over a secure (https) connection, some websites immediately drop back into unsecure (http) communication. If the cookie comes back to you over an unsecured connection, anybody snooping on your conversation can make a copy of the cookie and use it to interact with the website in precisely the same way you do — a process known as sidejacking. Firesheep makes it point-and-click easy to monitor Wi-Fi signals, looking for cookies shouted out in the clear. It specifically sidejacks interactions with Amazon, CNET, Dropbox, Facebook, Flickr, Microsoft, Twitter, WordPress, and Yahoo!, among many others."

When you set up a VPN connection with a server, you create a secure tunnel between your PC and the server. The tunnel encrypts all the data flowing between your PC and the server, provides integrity checks so no data gets scrambled, and continuously looks to make sure no other computer has taken over the connection.

VPNs prevent sidejacking because the connection between your PC and the wireless access point runs inside the tunnel: Firesheep or any other sniffer can see the data going by, but can't decipher what it means. VPNs do much more than simply foil Firesheep attacks: They provide complete end-to-end security, so nobody — not even your internet service provider — can snoop on your communication, or look to see if you're using a service such as BitTorrent. If you're traveling in a country subject to governmental eavesdropping, VPN is necessary. However, keep in mind that some countries, such as Russia, China, and Turkey, have banned people from using state-unapproved VPN services.

With a VPN, data goes into the tunnel from your PC, out of the tunnel at the VPN server, then to whatever location you're accessing, back into the VPN server, and out at your PC. A remarkably effective cloaking device hides your data everywhere in between. The people running the VPN server can match you up with your data stream, but nobody else can.

# Setting up a VPN in Windows 11

You can set up your wireless router to work as a VPN server and connect to it from anywhere on the internet so that you remain protected. Or maybe your workplace has set up a VPN server for you to connect to directly from Windows, so it's easier to access the company's apps and internal websites. No matter the situation you're in, all you need is the domain name or the IP address of the VPN server, a username, and a password, and you can connect to that VPN server directly from Windows.

Here's how to add a VPN to Windows 11 and how to connect to it:

1. **Click or tap the Start icon and then the Settings icon (or press Windows+I).**

2. **In the Settings app, choose Network & Internet on the left, and then click or tap VPN on the right.**

   The VPN settings appear, as shown in Figure 4-5.

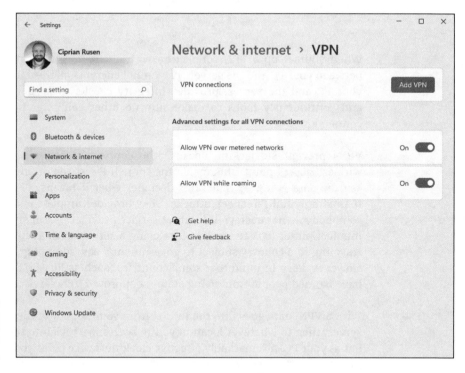

**FIGURE 4-5:**
Windows 11 can manage VPN connections with ease.

3. **Click or tap the Add VPN button.**

   The Add a VPN Connection dialog opens, as shown in Figure 4-6.

4. **Under VPN Provider, choose Windows (Built-In).**

5. **Enter a descriptive name for your VPN connection.**

6. **Type the IP address or the name of the VPN server (something like vpnserver.dummies.com).**

7. **Choose the VPN type and then type the user name and password.**

8. **Don't forget to check the box for "Remember My Sign-In Info" and click or tap Save.**

   The VPN connection is added below the Add VPN button.

9. **Click or tap the Connect button next to the VPN connection.**

   If your internet connection and the VPN server are working, you should be connected in a matter of seconds.

**FIGURE 4-6:**
Add the details of your VPN connection.

# Which paid VPN services should you consider?

If you want a VPN that offers useful features such as no logs of your activities, super-strong encryption, and the option to unlock services you don't normally have access to (like watching Netflix and its entire USA portfolio, using your computer from UK, Italy, or some other country), consider the following paid services:

>> **NordVPN** (`https://nordvpn.com/`): This is one of the fastest and best-rated VPN services on the internet. It offers a strict no-logs policy, and easy-to-use VPN apps for all platforms, including Windows.

>> **CyberGhost** (`www.cyberghostvpn.com`): Another fast service, CyberGhost also blocks ads while you browse the web. One aspect that makes it stand out from other VPN services is that it has the largest server network. See Figure 4-7.

>> **Surfshark** (`https://surfshark.com/`): Alongside its no-logs policy and easy-to-use apps, it also includes an antivirus engine that protects you while connected to its VPN servers.

**TIP**

All these services have free trials, so you can try them out before subscribing. Also, if you don't like the current price, subscribe to their e-mail newsletter. In a few weeks, you're sure to receive an email with a discount offer. The competition is tough between VPN services, so discounts occur frequently.

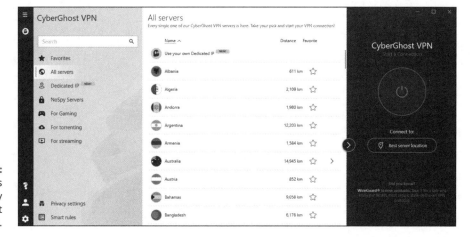

**FIGURE 4-7:**
CyberGhost has an impressively lengthy list of servers.

# Enhancing Windows

# Contents at a Glance

# Chapter **1**

# Linking Android to Windows

We all know the saying: If you can't beat them, join them! Well, that's exactly what Microsoft did: It lost the mobile war and it decided to integrate itself into the mobile ecosystem that beat it: Android. Microsoft partnered with Samsung, the world's biggest manufacturer of Android devices, and made a tight-knit integration with its ecosystem. As a result, owners of Samsung devices get Microsoft's OneDrive, Office, and Your Phone Companion apps preinstalled by default. What's Your Phone Companion, you ask? Well, it's how Microsoft wants you to link your Android devices with your Windows ones.

With Your Phone, you can pair an Android smartphone with a Windows 11 PC, and access your smartphone from your PC, with a mouse and keyboard. If that sounds cool to you, you should read this chapter, because I also present Samsung's take on this integration: Samsung DeX. You can try both apps and approaches and stick to the one you like best.

Lastly, in this brave new world, where many people must work from home, webcams have become both more expensive and hard to find in shops. One smart way to fix this problem is to use your smartphone as a webcam for the PC. In this chapter, you learn about the app you should use, which has a free version that works well.

# Making Windows Talk to Your Android Device

If you're trying to get your Android smartphone or tablet to interact with your Windows 11 PC, you need to know several tricks.

First, take the USB charging cable you're using for your device, and plug it into your computer and your device. Every Android device I know about can connect to a USB port. Chances are good that Windows 11 will recognize the device and install a driver for it. On your smartphone, you may be asked to choose how you want to use the USB connection that was just established, as shown in Figure 1-1. Choose to use it to transfer files.

**FIGURE 1-1:**
On an Android smartphone, choose to use the USB connection for transferring files.

Then Windows 11 should display an AutoPlay notification, as shown in Figure 1-2. Click or tap it, and you see several options for actions you can perform: importing photos and videos, synchronizing digital media, and opening the device to view files.

You can access all the files on the Android device through File Explorer. The Android device shows up in the This PC section of File Explorer. Depending on what kind of device you attached, you'll see one or two folders: The one labeled Internal Storage or Phone is for the phone or tablet itself, and the other, labeled SD Card, is for any additional storage you have on the device. On my Samsung Galaxy S20 smartphone, the pictures I took with my phone are in the folder \Phone\DCIM\Camera, as shown in Figure 1-3. The path should be similar on your smartphone.

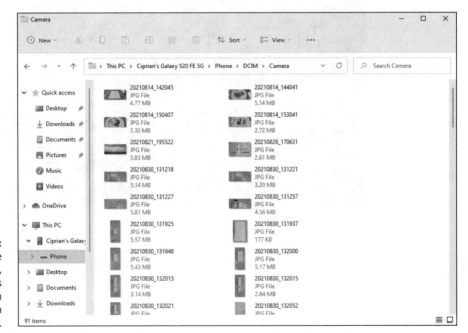

**FIGURE 1-3:**
If the device
installs properly,
you can access
the files on
it through
File Explorer.

From File Explorer, you can cut or copy files, moving them to your PC. You can edit or delete them. And you can print them.

## Trying Samsung DeX

Samsung DeX brings your smartphone or tablet directly onto your PC. You can use it to run all your Android apps, check notifications, and interact with the files on your smartphone. For example, you can easily drag and drop files between devices, or use a mouse and keyboard to get even more done on your phone — from your PC. As shown in Figure 1-4, Samsung DeX is like having a remote connection from your Windows desktop to your Android home screen.

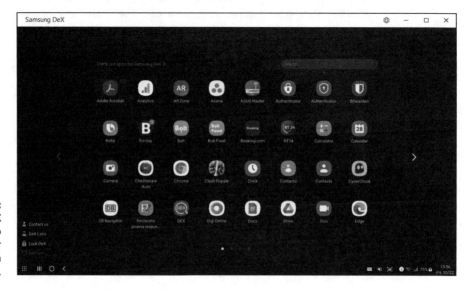

**FIGURE 1-4:**
Samsung DeX makes it easy to interact with your smartphone in Windows 11.

If you own a Samsung flagship smartphone or tablet introduced to the market after 2017, starting with the Galaxy S8, you can use Samsung DeX. When you connect it to your Windows 11 PC, you see a prompt to install DeX, like in Figure 1-5.

**TIP**

Samsung DeX is not just about making your Windows PC interact with your Samsung devices, but also for transforming your smartphone or tablet into a PC, without having a PC around. To learn more, I recommend that you visit this page: www.samsung.com/us/explore/dex/

**FIGURE 1-5:**
Premium
Samsung
smartphones
can use
Samsung DeX.

# Linking an Android Smartphone to a PC

When you install Windows 11, it asks you to link your phone with your PC, using the Your Phone app. When you click or tap Settings and then Bluetooth & Devices, there's a Your Phone entry where you can add your smartphone. The Your Phone app sounds useful, at least in theory: It displays live notifications from your Android device and allows you to respond to messages from your computer, make calls, and access the photos from your mobile device. And with select Samsung phones, you can even launch Android apps from Windows 11. Unfortunately, the Your Phone app is buggy, and it has the nasty habit of losing the connection exactly when you start to like it. But hey, Microsoft will improve it over time.

Until then, here's how to link your Android smartphone with your Windows 11 PC:

1. **Click or tap the Start icon and then the Settings icon.**

2. **In the Settings app, go to Bluetooth & Devices. On the right, click or tap Open Your Phone.**

   The Your Phone app opens, sharing information about what you can do with it, as shown in Figure 1-6.

3. **Click or tap Get Started.**

Your Phone

Microsoft

View your recent photos

**Use your Android phone from your PC**

Get started

To experience the full functionality of the Your Phone app, your mobile phone must be running Android 7.0 or later. Privacy Statement

**FIGURE 1-6:**
Starting the
setup process is
easy. Finishing
it is hard.

4. **On your Android smartphone, open Google Play, install the Your Phone Companion — Link to Windows app, and open it.**

   On new Samsung devices, the app is already installed.

5. **On your Windows 11 PC, select I Have the Your Phone Companion — Link to Windows App Ready, as shown in Figure 1-7.**

6. **In Windows 11, click or tap Pair with QR Code.**

   Wait while Windows 11 generates a QR code for your Microsoft account.

7. **On your Android smartphone, tap Link Your Phone and PC, and then Continue. If asked to give this app permission to use the camera to scan the QR code, allow it to do so.**

8. **Scan the QR code from your PC with your smartphone.**

9. **On your smartphone, tap Continue and then allow Your Phone Companion to receive all the permissions it requests.**

   The phone requests permission to access contacts, manage phone calls, access files, and manage SMS messages. Some phones also ask for permission to run in the background.

10. **Tap Done.**

    Your Windows 11 PC informs you that it's all set.

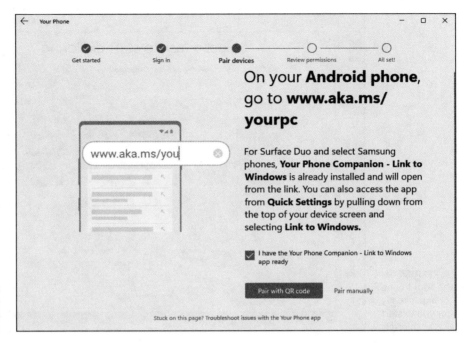

**11.** **On your Windows 11 PC, click or tap Continue and then Get Started. Choose if you want to pin the app to the taskbar.**

The Your Phone app opens on your Windows 11 PC, as shown in Figure 1-8, and you can start using it.

REMEMBER

To use the Your Phone app, you must use the same Microsoft account on your Windows 11 PC and Android smartphone. Also, if you want to take calls from your PC, Bluetooth discovery must be enabled on your smartphone and PC.

WARNING

While you use the different sections in the Your Phone app in Windows 11, you'll notice that it needs even more permissions than the ones you've given it during the initial link. If you want to use it fully, follow the instructions you get from the app and give it all the permissions it needs on your Android smartphone.

## Using the Your Phone app

The user interface of the Your Phone app is easy to understand. On the left you have shortcuts to its features: Notifications, Messages, Photos, Apps, and Calls. Click or tap one, and on the right you'll see the appropriate content, which you can interact with as shown in Figure 1-9.

**FIGURE 1-8:**
The Your Phone app is ready for you to start exploring.

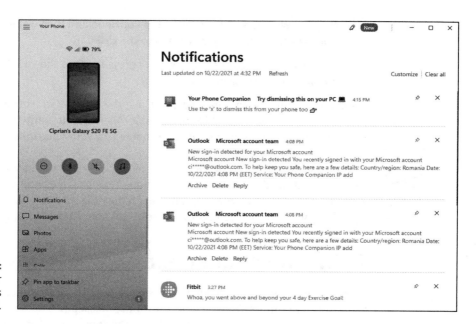

**FIGURE 1-9:**
The Your Phone app is straightforward.

I found the app finicky, although the user interface of this app and its features will evolve. Also, the first time I tried to do anything with it, I was annoyed that it asked me for more permissions. But unless you give them, the Your Phone app is pretty much useless.

REMEMBER

The features you get vary from phone to phone. For example, only owners of Samsung and Surface Duo smartphones can run Android apps with Your Phone. If you have a smartphone from Motorola or some other vendor, you're out of luck: No running Android apps for you. Also, unless you have your smartphone unlocked, you can't run Android apps. I prefer the Samsung DeX experience because it offers a more fine-tuned and well-thought-out experience. Try both, and then decide which one you like most.

## Removing your Android device from the Your Phone app

If you tried the Your Phone app and you decided that you dislike it, here's how to remove your Android smartphone from it:

1. **Click or tap the Start icon and then the Settings icon. In the Settings app, go to Bluetooth & Devices.**

2. **On the right, click or tap Open Your Phone.**

3. **If you see a prompt about adding other Android phones, click or tap Cancel to dismiss it.**

4. **On the left side of Your Phone, click or tap the gear icon (settings) and then choose My Devices.**

   You see the Android devices that you've added to the app, as shown in Figure 1-10.

5. **Click or tap the three dots icon in the top-right corner of the Android device that you want to unlink and then choose Remove.**

6. **Select the I Understand Removing This Device Means I'm Resetting the Your Phone App on This PC option, and then click or tap Yes, Remove.**

7. **Close Your Phone.**

TIP

At this point you can also uninstall the Your Phone Companion app from your Android smartphone.

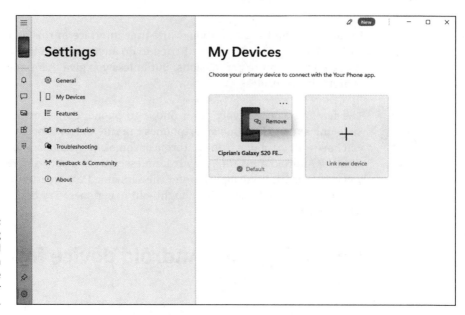

**FIGURE 1-10:**
Removing
an Android
smartphone from
the Your Phone
app is simpler
than adding it.

# Turning a Smartphone into a PC Webcam

The COVID-19 pandemic has made webcams an expensive and difficult-to-find commodity. Help is here, because you can use your smartphone as a webcam for your PC. Simply install a specialized app on your Windows 11 PC and your Android smartphone or tablet. Many solutions are available; the one I like best is DroidCam. Head over to www.dev47apps.com/ and download the app on both your PC and smartphone or tablet.

The DroidCam setup is easy and involves having both your smartphone and your Windows 11 PC in the same network. If you need help setting it up, the folks at Digital Citizen have a detailed tutorial that's updated regularly at www.digitalcitizen.life/turn-android-smartphone-webcam-windows.

DroidCam has both free and paid versions, and I've found that the free version is good enough for most people. See it in action in Figure 1-11.

**FIGURE 1-11:**
DroidCam helps
you use your
smartphone as
a webcam for
your PC.

# Chapter **2**

# Using Your iPhone with Windows

**M**any people own an iPhone or an iPad or both, and love using them regularly. However, they may also have not a Mac but a Windows laptop or PC. If that's the case for you, too, you might be interested in making your Apple and Windows devices work together, and sync pictures and music between your iPhone or iPad and Windows 11.

Unfortunately, the integration offered by Microsoft and Apple is not nearly as good as that with Microsoft and Android. There's no compatibility between the Your Phone app from Windows 11 and the iPhone. Also, if you plug into your Windows PC an iPhone or iPad, you can't simply access its files from File Explorer, as you do with Android devices. You need iTunes or iCloud or both.

In this chapter, I share the basics about installing and using both iTunes and iCloud, so that you can get access from Windows to the files on your iPhone and iPad. I also give you some tips on how to remotely control Windows from your iPhone and iPad.

# Installing iTunes on Windows 11

iTunes was one of the snarliest Windows programs I had ever used: It took over the computer and didn't let go until it was good and ready. It was slow to switch services — double-clicking anything resulted in odd behavior. All in all, it did not look or work like a Windows app. This nightmare ended in 2018 when Apple finally deployed a new iTunes app in the Microsoft Store that works like any other app. The Microsoft Store version of iTunes looks better, is responsive, and is relatively easy to use.

Here's how to get your Windows PC iTuned:

1. **Open the Microsoft Store and search for** iTunes **or go to** `https://apple.co/ms` **in your web browser.**

   Apple redirects your browser to a different page, but that's okay. You end up in the right place, which looks like Figure 2-1.

2. **Click or tap Get or Install.**

   The progress of the installation is shown below the Install button.

**FIGURE 2-1:**
The Microsoft
Store page for
installing iTunes.

**3.** **Click or tap Open, and then agree to the iTunes license terms.**

The iTunes app shows up on the screen, asking whether you agree to share details about your music library with Apple.

**4.** **Click or tap Agree to let iTunes access your Music folders.**

You can quit at this point, or you can continue to use iTunes for the first time, as described in the next section.

**TIP**

If you're not familiar with how the Microsoft Store works, I recommend reading Book 5, Chapter 1 first.

## Setting up iTunes

Before you use iTunes for the first time, you must run through the iTunes Setup Assistant program. Here's how:

**1.** **If you quit immediately after iTunes was installed (see the preceding section) or if iTunes was preinstalled on your PC, click or tap the Start icon, All Apps, and then iTunes.**

If you didn't quit iTunes, you automatically come to this step after iTunes has been successfully installed.

2. **If you see any license terms being shown, read them and click or tap Agree. Then click or tap the Library tab if it's not already selected.**

3. **On the Library tab, click or tap Sign In to The iTunes Store, as shown in Figure 2-2.**

4. **Enter your Apple ID and password, and then click or tap Sign In.**

   If you enabled two-step verification for your Apple ID, you may need to approve the sign-in on your iPhone and enter a temporary code.

5. **Click or tap Go to the iTunes Store, or click or tap the Store tab on the top.**

   You now have access to Apple's Music store, where you can buy anything you want.

**FIGURE 2-2:**
Accessing the iTunes Store with your Apple ID.

# Synchronizing the iPhone with Windows 11

One reason for moving some of your music from your Windows 11 PC to the iPhone is so you can listen to it on the go, without consuming your data plan with music streaming, or when you'll be disconnected from the internet for a few days.

Here's how to get music from Windows 11 to your iPhone. The procedure for moving music and videos from your PC to your iPhone or iPad is similar:

1. **Using the Lightning-to-USB cable, connect your iPhone to your Windows 11 PC.**

2. **On your iPhone, look for the Trust This Computer pop-up, tap Trust, and enter your passcode.**

   Your iPhone now trusts your computer.

3. **Start iTunes by clicking or tapping its shortcut in the Start menu's All Apps list.**

4. **When you're asked whether you want to allow your computer to access information on your iPhone, click or tap Continue.**

   You see the Welcome to Your New iPhone screen, as shown in Figure 2-3.

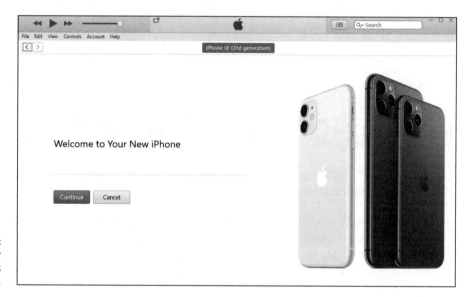

**FIGURE 2-3:**
Adding your
iPhone to iTunes
on Windows.

5. **Click or tap Continue and then Get Started.**

   You see the Summary screen, which shows details and settings about your iPhone, as shown in Figure 2-4.

6. **Use the Settings menu on the left to specify what you want from your iPhone: Music, Movies, TV Shows, Photos, Info, or File Sharing.**

7. **Click or tap Sync.**

Using Your iPhone with Windows

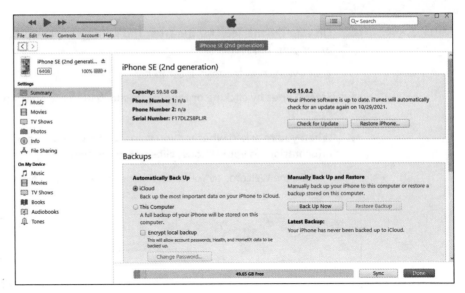

**FIGURE 2-4:**
Options for using
iTunes to sync
stuff between
the PC and
the iPhone.

# Installing iCloud on Windows 11

Your iPhone uses iCloud to back up your photos, mail, contacts, bookmarks and other items. Or at least it should if you let it.

Switching your iPad or iPhone over to using iCloud is simple: In the iPad or iPhone Settings app, tap your Apple ID, and then tap iCloud. Make sure you have the right account set up. (You don't want to hassle with mismatched accounts.) Tap iCloud Backup and turn its switch on. Then wait — my initial backup took two hours.

This can be handy if you need something from your iPhone on your Windows 11 PC and you don't want to use iTunes. You can just install iCloud, and get everything you need from there. Here's how to install and configure iCloud on your Windows 11 PC:

1. **Open the Microsoft Store and search for** icloud **and click or tap Install.**

   The progress of the installation is shown below the Install button.

2. **In the Microsoft Store window, click or tap Open. In the User Account Control prompt that asks for permissions, click or tap Yes.**

   You're asked to sign in with your Apple ID.

3. **Type your Apple ID and password, and then click or tap Sign In.**

   A verification code is sent to your iPhone.

4. **On your iPhone, tap Allow to see the verification code.**

5. **In the iCloud app's prompt on your Windows 11 PC, type the verification from your iPhone.**

6. **If you're asked whether you want to send diagnostic and usage information to Apple, click or tap Don't Send.**

   You see the iCloud user interface, as shown in Figure 2-5.

**FIGURE 2-5:**
Choosing what to sync from iCloud.

7. **Choose what you want to sync between iCloud and Windows 11, and then click or tap Apply.**

   You may want to sync at least your iCloud Drive content and your Photos.

**TIP**

If you chose iCloud Drive in Step 7, you'll see an entry for it in File Explorer. You can then use it to access what's stored in Apple's cloud storage for your account, even if you don't have your iPhone connected to your Windows 11 PC.

# Controlling Windows from an iPhone or iPad

More than a dozen PC remote–control apps are available in the App Store. Some of them work surprisingly well, including the following:

>> **LogMeIn for iOS:** A favorite among reviewers, LogMeIn must run on both the iPhone or iPad and the Windows machine. If you go with LogMeIn Free on the Windows PC, you can't transfer files, print remotely, hear sounds from the PC, or share desktops. To do any of that, you must spend an additional $350 per year (gulp!) for the Windows PC software.

>> **GoToMyPC:** GoToMyPC also draws good reviews but becomes pricey quickly. Figure on spending $33 per month per computer after the initial 30-day free trial.

>> **Splashtop:** A lesser-known product that works well on a Wi-Fi system, Splashtop connects PCs on the same network. Going outside the local network can be more difficult. I use Splashtop to play videos on my iPad that aren't in MP4 format. Its monthly plan is a lot more affordable at $5 per month.

>> **Remote Desktop Mobile:** This app is free and works well if you're using Windows 11 Pro or Enterprise on your PC. An important downside is that your PC must have a public IP address or be in the same network as your iPhone to establish a remote connection.

>> **TeamViewer:** My favorite remote-control program (free for non-commercial use), TeamViewer can run in one of two ways. Install the TeamViewer program on your Windows PC and let it control the interaction, or run the program on your PC manually when you want to access the Windows PC from your iPhone or iPad. Figure 2-6 shows Windows 11 on an iPhone. When you run the program manually, it generates a random user ID and password that you use on the iPhone to initiate the session.

After TeamViewer is connected, you can use the iPhone or iPad keyboard, pinch to expand or reduce the size of the screen, tap with two fingers to emulate a right-click, use the buttons on the top of the screen for Alt and Ctrl and Esc, and much more.

**FIGURE 2-6:**
TeamViewer
lets you control
your PC from an
iPhone or iPad —
and it's free.

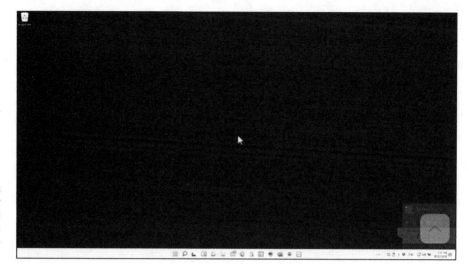

Chapter **3**

# Wrangling E-Book Files

U nfortunately, the increased use of technology means that fewer of us read physical books on a regular basis. It's a sad trend if you ask me, but there's an upside too: We now have access to the world's biggest library online. We can buy and download books online in any language we want. However, because digital books, or e-books, are available in a wide variety of formats, reading them on a variety of devices is difficult.

In this chapter, I discuss the best way to view, read, and manage e-books on your Windows PC: using calibre, an amazing tool everyone should know about. It is free and works great on Windows, Mac, and other platforms. With calibre, you can also convert e-books from one format to another.

While you can read e-books not only on your Windows PC but also on your iPad or your smartphone, the most important platform remains Amazon's Kindle. Therefore I also share how to send e-books from your PC to your Kindle, and how to set up your Amazon account so that your friends can email books directly to your Kindle.

If all this seems interesting to you, it's time to get started.

# Working with E-Book Files

Someday, a single format will exist for all electronic books. In my utopian future, you'll buy a book in one format, and that format will just work, no matter what device you want to use to read it. Unfortunately, the world isn't at that point yet. In fact, it isn't even close. The single biggest headache you're likely to have with electronic books revolves around book formats, and how to get one device to show you books that were made for a competing device.

**REMEMBER**

If you can afford to stick with just one device and bookstore — only buy books from Amazon and read them on the Kindle, for example, or only buy books from Apple Books and read them on the iPad — I congratulate you. Your life will be considerably less complicated. Most people aren't so lucky, especially if they want to purchase books affordably.

Luckily, you can simplify e-book management by buying your books online through your PC's web browser, using a program called *calibre* to convert files into whatever format your reader requires and then syncing your e-books with your e-reader on your PC. You can also read any e-book on your Windows computer, but that may not be so comfortable, right?

## Introducing popular e-book formats

Here are the most popular e-book file formats:

>> **EPUB** comes closest to being a universal format. The iPhone and iPad handle EPUB natively, many third-party Windows EPUB readers are available (more about that after this list), and many Android apps read EPUB. The only major holdout for the EPUB format is the Kindle.

**REMEMBER**

   Given a choice, unless you live in a Kindle-only world, get your books in EPUB format.

>> **MOBI, AZW3, KF8,** and **PRC** formats are the Kindle's bread and butter. Amazon has a format converter called Kindle Previewer that changes EPUB files into MOBI. It works surprisingly well.

>> **PDF** is the original format for publications that have to survive a transition from one kind of computer to another. Although every computer or device can read PDF, most readers just display the original document without trying to reflow pages or add any features, such as note taking. Reading a PDF file in most e-book readers is a frustrating experience.

# Reading e-book files on your PC

Whether or not you have e-books you bought with an e-reader, you can read anything on a Windows 11 PC. Sometimes, though, you must get a little creative and bring in apps that can do the heavy lifting.

If you want to read EPUB files on Windows, your best bet is calibre. PDF files can be read by about any web browser, including the built-in Microsoft Edge.

PDF viewers are also a dime a dozen. The viewer that Microsoft built into Microsoft Edge, shown in Figure 3-1, works reasonably well, with new features added frequently. Google Chrome's PDF viewer works just as well.

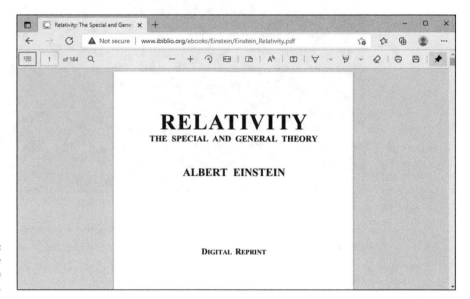

**FIGURE 3-1:**
Microsoft Edge
has a built-in
PDF viewer.

However, if you need to work with protected PDF files that don't look right in Microsoft Edge, it is best that you download Adobe's Acrobat Reader from `https://get.adobe.com/reader/`. For example, PDF files from government agencies have some advanced security features builtin, and they can be handled correctly only with Acrobat Reader.

# Organizing your e-book files with calibre

Before you lose any sleep over different book file formats, keep in mind that one desktop app has been translating among the formats for years. In fact, calibre's more than an e-book converter; it's also a book manager — for free. See Figure 3-2.

**FIGURE 3-2:**
The calibre app translates and organizes.

Calibre keeps track of all your books, translates them into the correct format, if need be, and offers the files up for easy transfer to the reader of your choice.

Here's a quick look at calibre's capabilities:

1. **Open Microsoft Edge, go to** `https://calibre-ebook.com`, **and download and install calibre for Windows.**

   You should download a file named calibre, followed by a version number, such as calibre-5.25.0.

2. **Double-click or double-tap the Calibre — E-Book Management shortcut on the desktop and run calibre for the first time.**

3. **Choose the language for Calibre and the location where your books will be stored. Click or tap Next.**

   The Documents folder works fine as a location, but you can choose another if that's where you store your e-books.

**4.** **When asked, choose your e-book device, as shown in Figure 3-3, and click or tap Next.**

Don't panic — calibre converts any format to any other. This step just makes it easier to choose your most common format.

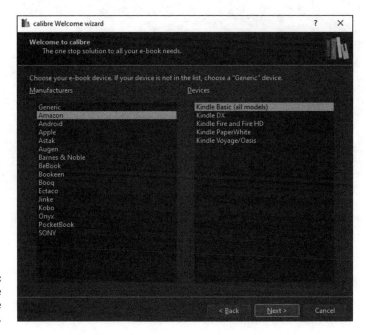

**FIGURE 3-3:**
Choose the device you use most commonly.

**5.** **If you chose Kindle as your e-book device, provide the email of your Amazon account.**

**6.** **Click or tap Next and then Finish.**

Calibre scans your Documents library for books — just about any format you can imagine — and lists each book (refer to Figure 3-2).

TIP

Note that calibre lists books, not files. If you have a book in two different formats — say, a MOBI file and an EPUB file — it appears as only one book on the main screen.

**7.** **To see and edit the details about an individual book:**

a. *Right-click the book and choose Edit Metadata, Edit Metadata Individually.* (Someday, calibre will have a touch option; for now, it's mouse only.) calibre shows you an enormous amount of information about the book, including the available formats, as shown in Figure 3-4.

b. *(Optional) Edit the data and click OK to save your changes.*

c. *Click X to close the dialog box.* You return to the calibre library (refer to Figure 3-2).

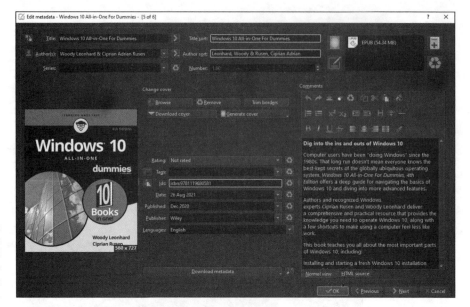

**FIGURE 3-4:**
The calibre app displays and allows you to edit a lot of data about each book.

8. **To convert a book to a different format:**

   a. *Right-click the book and choose Convert Books, Convert Individually.* A Convert dialog box appears, as shown in Figure 3-5.

   b. *In the upper right, choose the Output Format you want to convert the book to; in the lower right, click OK.* The calibre app converts the book to the format you chose and places the new file next to the old ones.

**FIGURE 3-5:**
Choose the new book format in the Output Format box.

This discussion just touches the surface on calibre's capabilities; it's an amazingly versatile program. For a more detailed rundown of what calibre can do, start at `https://manual.calibre-ebook.com/gui.html`.

**REMEMBER**

Keep in mind that calibre translates from one format to another. It doesn't relax digital rights restrictions: If you translate a pirated book from MOBI to PDF, it's still a pirated book.

# Getting e-Books from Your PC to Your Kindle

If you use your PC to manage your books and music, you need a way to get those files onto your e-reader or tablet. This section is here to help. Unfortunately, the methods for each device are specific to that device. So I focus on the Kindle e-reader in this section because it's the most popular e-reader out there.

## Emailing books from your PC to your Kindle

The easiest way to transfer books to your Kindle? Email them via Kindle Personal Documents Service. If you need to transfer a file type listed in Table 3-1, emailing is the best and quickest way.

**TABLE 3-1**

### Documents You Can Email to a Kindle

| File Type (Filename Extension) | What It Is |
|---|---|
| MOBI | Kindle-native MOBI format. |
| TXT | Plain text file (looks surprisingly good on the Kindle). |
| DOC, DOCX | Word document. Kindle doesn't handle complex Word documents very well, but simple ones are fine. |
| RTF | Rich Text Format. |
| HTML | Web page. |
| ZIP, X-ZIP | File archive. Kindle unpacks these files. |
| PDF | Portable Document Format. |
| JPG, GIF, BMP, PNG | Image file. |

Here's how to transfer a file:

1. **Open Microsoft Edge and log in to www.amazon.com with the same account as on your Kindle.**

2. **In the topright, click or tap Account & Lists.**

   You see many options related to your Amazon account.

3. **Scroll down to the Digital Content and Devices section, as shown in Figure 3-6, and click or tap Manage Content and Devices.**

   You see all the digital content you've acquired in recent months.

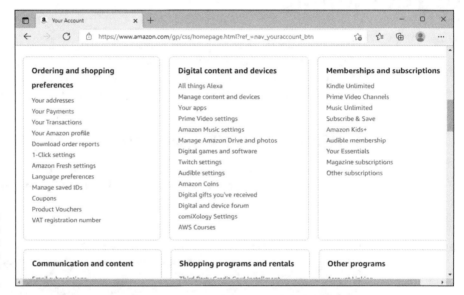

**FIGURE 3-6:**
Scroll to the
Digital Content
And Devices
section of your
Amazon account.

4. **Click or tap Devices.**

   You see all your Amazon devices.

5. **Click or tap Kindle, and then click or tap your Kindle device name.**

   Kindle shows you the registration information, including an email address, such as `ciprianrusen_99@kindle.com`.

6. **Write down the email address.**

7. **On your Windows PC (or any computer, for that matter), send a message to that email address, and attach to the message the file you want to transfer.**

   The file ends up in your Kindle's Documents folder.

**TIP**

Amazon has a Send to Kindle application that lets you right-click or tap and hold down on a file in File Explorer and choose Send to Kindle. This sends the file to your Kindle, using the email address mentioned earlier. You can also print from any desktop application and choose Send to Kindle. You can find the Send to Kindle application at `https://www.amazon.com/gp/sendtokindle`.

# Receiving emailed books from a friend

If you want a friend to send books or documents to your Kindle, you have to give that person permission by adding the friend's email address to your allowed list. Here's how to let others email books and documents directly to your Kindle:

**1.** Open Microsoft Edge and log in to `www.amazon.com` with the same account as on your Kindle.

**2.** In the top right, click or tap Account & Lists.

**3.** Scroll down to the Digital Content and Devices section (refer to Figure 3-6) and click or tap Manage Content and Devices.

You see all the digital content you've acquired in recent months.

**4.** At the top, click or tap the Preferences tab, scroll down to the Personal Document Settings section, and click or tap it to extend it.

The options shown in Figure 3-7 appear.

**5.** Scroll a bit lower and click or tap the Add a New Approved Email Address link.

You see a box that lets you add email addresses.

**6.** Type the address of whom you want to allow to send stuff directly to your Kindle, and click or tap Add Address.

To add multiple addresses, simply repeat Steps 5 and 6. The changes take effect immediately.

You can now enjoy your friends' books, directly on your Kindle.

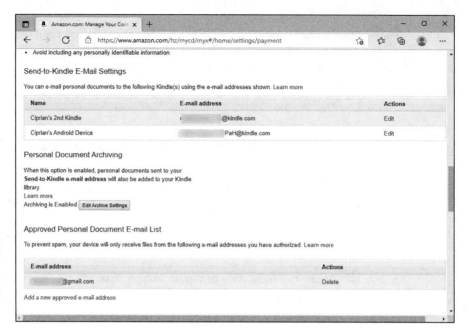

**FIGURE 3-7:**
You can add the email of your friends, so that they send books directly to your Kindle.

# Chapter **4**

# Getting Started with Gmail and Other Google Apps

espite the rivalry between Microsoft and Google, Google's so important to today's computer users that Microsoft builds hooks into Windows 11 that try to get you to add your Gmail account to their Mail app and add your Gmail contacts to the People app. Of course, Google is happy to return the favor, with straightforward ways to put your Outlook.com mail inside Gmail and to import your Outlook.com contacts into Gmail.

There's a reason why Microsoft wants you to put your Google eggs in its basket. Google has good competitors for many Microsoft products, including the following:

» Chrome OS, as explained in the nearby sidebar, obviates the need to run Windows for many people.

>> Outlook.com, the Windows 11 Mail app, the mail part of Microsoft 365, and the Outlook Web App compete with Google Gmail, in different ways.

>> The Windows 11 Calendar app and the various Office Outlook calendars compete with Google Calendar.

>> The Windows 11 People app and Outlook.com contacts compete with Google's Gmail contacts.

Worth noting: Every app in the preceding list, except the mail part of Microsoft 365, is free if you're running Windows 11. Absolutely free. Microsoft and Google give away the apps to draw you in to their ecosystems, with the hope of selling you something in the future.

You can use Gmail to send and receive mail using your own private domain, although you must pay for a Google Workspace account to make it work. So, for example, I can use Gmail to handle all the mail coming into and going out of DigitalCitizen.life without changing my email address and without anyone knowing I'm using Gmail. All the mail going out says it's from `contact@digitalcitizen.life`, and all the mail sent to `contact@digitalcitizen.life` ends up in my Gmail inbox. This feature is in Google Workspace, costs $6 per user per month, and is easy to set up and use.

All this wrangling takes place against a backdrop of increased competition from Apple and new assaults from Facebook. All these companies want to get you hooked to their ways of working.

**REMEMBER**

Don't forget that free services aren't free in the sense of being zero-sum. The companies offering free services gather information about you unabashedly and show you targeted ads, in the hope of generating revenue. Remember this saying: "If you're not paying for it, you're not the customer; you're the product being sold."

In this chapter, I help you familiarize yourself with Google's ecosystem, set up your Gmail account, and use it to send and receive emails. You also find out how to move another email account to your Gmail inbox. Lastly, I show you how to add Google Drive to Windows 11, and use Google apps to create documents, presentations, and other types of files.

# Introducing Google's Ecosystem

Google has many free online products and offerings that warrant your attention. I cover the ones that are most appealing to less technical users who don't need the full power of Windows and what Microsoft has to offer.

Here are the key Google products, other than Chrome OS, that are alternatives to Microsoft offerings:

>> **Gmail:** A free, online mail service, like Microsoft's Outlook.com. Features change constantly, but it's fair to say that if you find a feature you like in Outlook.com, it'll be in Gmail soon — and vice versa. Some people prefer one interface over the other; I'm ambivalent. If you use Google's Chrome web browser, one upside is that you can use Gmail when you aren't connected to the internet to read and compose email.

## CHROME OS — THE WINDOWS KILLER

In a few years, Chromebooks have jumped from scoffed-at toys to genuine Windows rivals. If you are looking for a computer and don't need to do anything directly tied to Windows, getting a Chromebook is a good idea. Compared to Windows laptops, Chromebooks are easier to use, less prone to infection, and all-in-all a whole lot less hassle for troubleshooting problems.

Chromebooks run Chrome OS, which is, to a first approximation, just the Chrome browser you've used before. To a second approximation, Chrome OS can support overlapping resizable windows (each resembling a Chrome window on Windows or macOS), as well as apps built for this operating system and Android apps. Certain apps (such as Gmail, Sheets, Docs) can run even when your Chromebook is offline. Chrome OS also includes a built-in media player and a file manager.

Google has its own "Office Suite," and many people prefer it over Microsoft Office because it is simpler to use, with fewer and more focused features. and everything you do is saved automatically. Also, if you really need Office, you can use Office Web Apps for free at www.office.com. Finally, Microsoft's Office apps for Android run well on Chrome OS too. If you don't want to spend a lot on a laptop and don't need all that Microsoft and Windows have to offer, a Chromebook may be a viable alternative to a Windows laptop.

>> **Google Drive:** A service from Google that gives you up to 15GB of free online storage, more than Microsoft OneDrive's 5GB free allotment, with occasional discounts for various promotions. I talk about the different online storage services in Book 10, Chapter 6. Google Drive's main advantages are its capability to work easily with Google apps and its integration into the affordable Google One subscription plans.

>> **Google Workspace:** Contains online programs for creating and editing word-processing documents (Docs), spreadsheets (Sheets), fill-in-the-blank forms (Forms), presentations (Slides), and drawings. The programs have been gaining new features rapidly and are designed to work collaboratively — two or more people can edit the same document at the same time, with no ill effect and no weird restrictions. And you can get at your docs from your PC, Mac, tablet, or smartphone. Slick, and you don't need to do a thing.

Google Workspace is the official name of the paid version of all those programs and services. The pieces — Gmail, Google Drive, Docs, Sheets, Slides, and more — are free for personal use, but if you use them for business, you need to pay for Google Workspace. In addition to the free-for-personal use features, Google Workspace includes more Google Drive space, more apps, and a collection of administrative tools. Google Workspace subscribers also get additional features in Docs and Sheets. For details, go to https://workspace.google.com/pricing.html, which is shown in Figure 4-1.

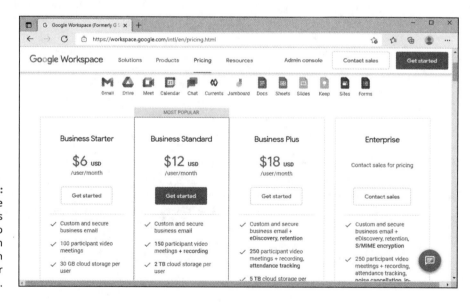

**FIGURE 4-1:** Google Workspace runs from $6 to $18 per person per month, with discounts for yearly payments.

Google Workspace for Education and Google Workspace for Government are identical to Google Workspace but are available only to bona fide educational institutions or government institutions, respectively.

There's another big difference between the free Google apps and Google Workspace. If you don't pay for using the Google apps, Google takes a peek inside your emails and stored files, scanning them to target ads in your direction. If you pay for Google Workspace or have an official free Google Workspace for Education or Google Workspace for Government account, Google does *not* scan your email or your stored data to target ads.

Concerned about privacy? First, *every* online email program (Outlook.com, Yahoo! Mail, and so on) scans your mail for viruses, spam, and scams — some more thoroughly than others. The online storage providers also scan for malware that can clobber their systems. That's part of the ballgame. Scanning, in and of itself, isn't bad. The email provider is protecting both you and itself.

## MICROSOFT 365 IN A NUTSHELL

Microsoft's entry in the office application wars was *Office 365*, now renamed *Microsoft 365*. Over the years, this service has grown from an experiment into a multi-billion-dollar business. Depending on the subscription level — and the amount of money you pay — Microsoft 365 can work for one or six users for home users (and many more for businesses) and provides 1TB of storage on OneDrive for each user, the Microsoft Family Safety mobile app (useful for families with children), minutes on Skype, and the full-blown version of Office for Windows, Office for iPad, and Office for Android.

Ed Bott has a lengthy analysis of the differences between Google Workspace and Microsoft at www.zdnet.com/article/office-365-vs-g-suite-which-productivity-suite-is-best-for-your-business/.

The condensed version goes like this: Google Workspace is browser-centric and it works best in the Google Chrome browser. The apps included are small, easily administered, cover the high points, and don't try to reach into obscure corners. Microsoft 365, on the other hand, offers the best (and most complex) support in the business. I'm continually amazed at how well Microsoft has built out Office, rolling feature upon feature into the mix, yet keeping the entire package remarkably stable, usable, and manageable.

If you need to create complex Office-standard documents, Microsoft 365 has no equal. But if you have less stringent requirements and a willingness to part with 100 percent Office document compatibility, Google Workspace offers a less expensive but reliable alternative.

Second, Google's snooping is expressly for the purpose of directing ads. They aren't sniffing for your bank account numbers, and any organization that wants access to your data has to go through the usual channels — which usually involve a search warrant.

Third, if you use encryption to either protect the body of your email message or to lock up files stored in Google's cloud, Google won't go to the trouble of cracking the encryption. If you want something safe, lock it up yourself.

# Setting Up Gmail

If you don't yet have a Gmail account, get one. Doing so is free and easy. Besides, every new Gmail account gets 15GB of free cloud storage. Here's how to set up an account:

**1.** With your favorite browser, go to www.gmail.com.

**2.** Click or tap the Create an Account button, at the top.

The sign-up form in Figure 4-2 appears.

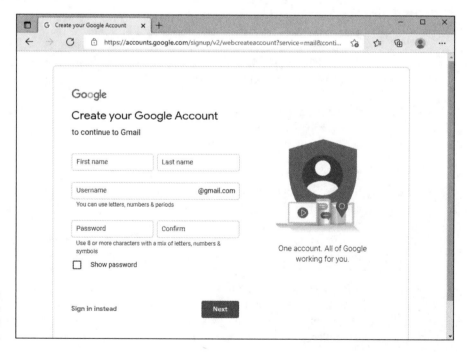

**FIGURE 4-2:**
Signing up for a
Google account
is free.

3. **Fill in the form as creatively as you want, and then click or tap Next.**

4. **On the next form, type the mandatory data requested (gender, birthday, and so on), and then click or tap Next.**

   If you type a real phone number, Google can use it to help you get into your account if you're locked out and or for two-factor authorization. Similarly, your current email address may help you get back into your account if somebody hijacks it.

**REMEMBER**

In some countries, you're required to give a valid mobile number, and Google sends you an SMS to verify that phone number before you can sign in. Currently, the United States, most of the countries in Europe, and India require valid mobile numbers, but the requirement can change from day to day. If you're reticent to give Google your phone number, remember that it could save your tail one day if you get locked out or if you elect to have two-factor authorization added to your account (challenging you with an SMS message every time you log in from a new computer). Google says it "won't use this number for anything else besides account security."

5. **Choose the type of personalization you want (Express or Manual) and click or tap Next.**

   You see information about how your data will be used and how your account is configured.

6. **Confirm that you are okay to go ahead.**

7. **Agree to the privacy and terms, and go through Gmail's personalization wizard.**

   You now have an official Google account and a new Gmail address. Google dangles the default Gmail inbox in front of you, as shown in Figure 4-3, already populated with at least one email message.

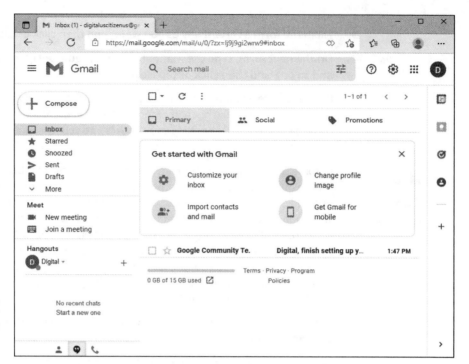

**FIGURE 4-3:**
Your brand-new Gmail account comes with an email message.

# Sending and Reading Emails from Gmail

A clever way to get started is to simply send an email to yourself. Follow these steps for an orientation:

**1.** **In the upper-left corner, click or tap + Compose.**

The mail composition pane appears, as shown in Figure 4-4.

**2.** **In the To field, type your new Gmail address, add a subject, write a message, and try formatting parts of the message using the string of formatting icons at the bottom of the New Message box.**

**3.** **When you tire of talking to yourself, click or tap Send, in the lower-left corner.**

Wait a few seconds. If you get bored, click or tap the round refresh arrow at the top, to force your browser to look again.

**4.** **When the message arrives, click or tap it to open it.**

Gmail is different than other email services. For starters, it groups messages by subject. With one click, you can change to a conversation view that looks like a conversation on a forum.

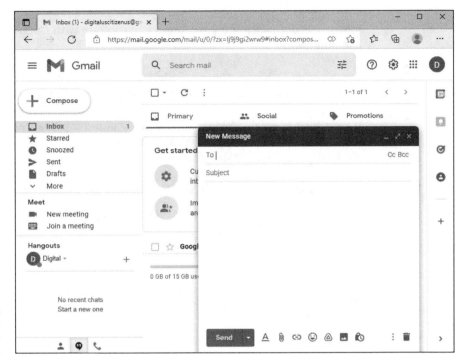

FIGURE 4-4:
Create a new
email message
here.

TIP

After you have a few messages under your belt, hop over to the Gmail learning center at https://support.google.com/mail and figure out the extensive
and impressive options Gmail offers. It probably won't surprise you to know that
Gmail has search down cold — you can find any message in seconds, if you know
the tricks. But you may be surprised to see how Gmail can work offline (when you
aren't connected to the internet), as long as you use the Chrome browser.

# Moving an Existing Account to Gmail

It's easy to keep your current email address but move all your email handling over
to Gmail. People you write to will never know that you switched to Gmail.

For example, you can move your *name@personaldomain.com* from the Outlook app
and your own email servers to Gmail. You can then check for new messages using
the Gmail app on your smartphone, iPad, Chromebook, or any other device. The
Gmail apps for Apple and Android work well too. Moreover, you no longer have

to worry about backing up .pst files or putting up with Outlook's weird ways of handling IMAP.

**REMEMBER**

And searches? Oh my! Where the Outlook app from Microsoft might take about three minutes to search its Sent Files folder, Gmail takes seconds.

If your current email provider supports POP3 (and it probably does), all you need is your email username, password, and POP server address (your mail provider has it). Here are the details for moving all your mail to Gmail:

**1.** Go to www.gmail.com and sign in with your Gmail account.

**2.** Click or tap the gear icon (right side, above your messages) and then click or tap See All Settings.

You see all your Gmail's settings, split into tabs, as shown in Figure 4-5.

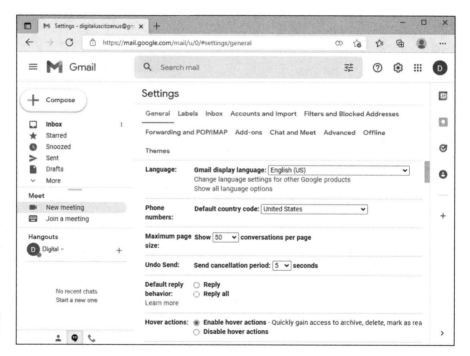

**FIGURE 4-5:**
Here you see all
Gmail settings.

**3.** Click or tap the Accounts tab.

**4.** In the Check Mail from Other Accounts section, click or tap Add a Mail Account.

A dialog box appears.

5. **Do the following:**

   a. *Type the email address you want to add to your Gmail inbox and then click or tap Next.*

   b. *Choose Import Emails from My Other Account (POP3) and click or tap Next.*

   c. *Enter your username and password plus the details for your mail provider's server.*

   In the Add a Mail Account dialog (see Figure 4-6), I typically select the Leave a Copy of Retrieved Message on the Server box; it gives me an emergency out, should something go bump in the night. I also select the Always Use a Secure Connection (SSL) when Retrieving Mail box.

   For Label Incoming Messages, pick the email address from the drop-down list or create a label you want to attach to all the messages you receive in the account you're adding. I don't automatically archive incoming messages.

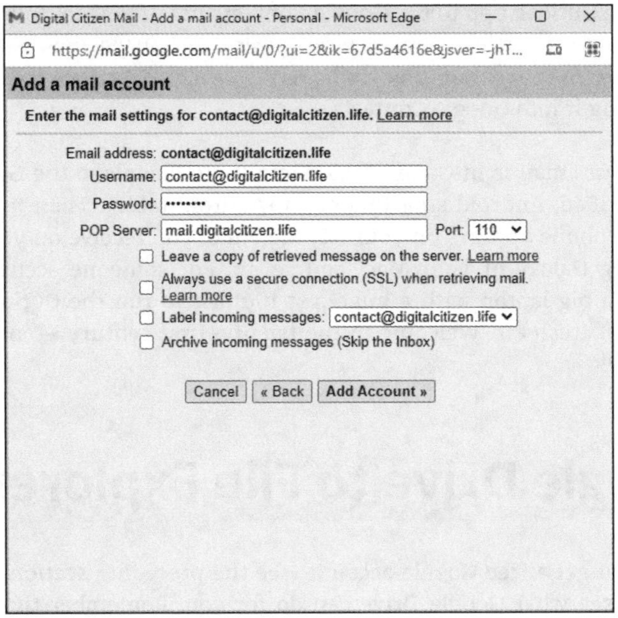

**FIGURE 4-6:**
Adding a POP3 account to Gmail is easy if you know the server's name.

6. **When you're done, click or tap Add Account.**

   Gmail starts sucking up all the mail it can find. While Gmail copies your mail over to its servers, you get a dialog box that asks whether you want to be able to send mail using your original email address.

7. **Select Yes, and then click or tap Next.**

   You'll see another dialog box that confirms the details about your previous username.

**8.** Click or tap Next again.

Gmail asks you to enter the details of the SMTP server that's used for sending emails.

**9.** Add the necessary connection details and then click or tap Add Account.

Gmail asks you to verify the email address you've added.

**10.** Open your email account in the Outlook app, or the client you've used so far to access it, and note the email verification code you've received from Gmail.

**11.** Copy the verification code and paste it into Gmail's verification box. Then, click or tap Verify.

You're done!

**TIP**

Consider carefully whether you want to automatically export all your contacts from the Outlook app to the Google Contacts list. If you do, follow the steps in the How-To Geek article at www.howtogeek.com/201988/how-to-import-export-contacts-between-outlook-and-gmail/, which describes creating a CSV file and importing it into Google Contacts.

After your email is in Gmail, take a minute to download the Gmail apps for your iPhone, iPad, Android smartphone, or Android tablet. Then, the email you send on your phone appears on your PC, the email you receive on your iPad is on your Samsung Galaxy or your Mac, and so on. For someone accustomed to lugging around a big laptop with a huge .pst file just to run the Outlook app, it's like a breath of fresh air. Welcome to the twenty-first century — no Exchange Server required!

# Adding Google Drive to File Explorer

After you get a free Google account (see the preceding section), take a few minutes to see what Google Drive can do for you. Remember that the Google apps for creating documents, spreadsheets, presentations, fill-in-the-blanks forms, and drawings may be referenced in some places as being part of Google Drive or Google Workspace (which is the official name of the paid service but colloquially includes all free-for-personal-use Google stuff) or both. For personal use, everything's free.

Here's how to start with the Google apps:

**1.** With your favorite browser, go to https://drive.google.com/.

2. **If you aren't logged in to Google, provide your Google account and password.**

   The Google Drive page appears, as shown in Figure 4-7.

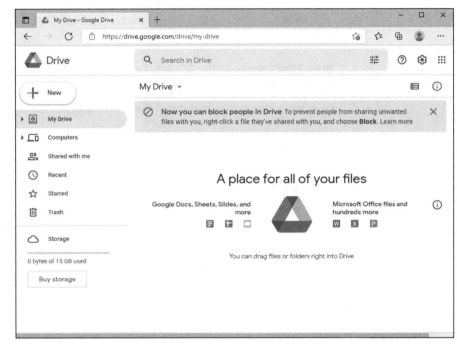

**FIGURE 4-7:**
Google Drive is familiar to anyone who's used a cloud drive.

3. **Download Google Drive by clicking or tapping the gear icon in the upper left and choosing Get Drive for Desktop. Then click or tap the Download Drive for Desktop button.**

4. **Open the GoogleDriveSetup.exe file you just downloaded and install Google Drive by following the instructions shown by the setup wizard.**

   You might need to provide your Google account details again to finalize the setup process.

5. **Open File Explorer and note that you have a new folder called Google Drive in the Quick Access section.**

6. **In the Google Drive folder, open the My Drive subfolder.**

   This is where you can drag and drop files like you normally do on your Windows 11 computer.

# Using Google Apps to View and Edit Files

You can add any files you want to Google Drive after you've added it to File Explorer. Remember that you can copy and paste files to Google Drive, delete them, rename them, and so on. The changes you make on your Windows 11 computer are reflected in the online Google Drive. Here are the basics about how it all works:

1. **Open File Explorer. In the Quick Access section, open the Google Drive folder and then the My Drive folder.**

2. **Copy and paste an assortment of files into the My Drive folder.**

   Try grabbing a simple Word document, a spreadsheet, some graphics files, some PowerPoint slides, and maybe a PDF. Get a handful of them so you can experiment with the Google apps.

3. **Go back to your browser, and navigate to** `https://drive.google.com/`.

   All the files you put in the Google Drive folder appear, as shown in Figure 4-8.

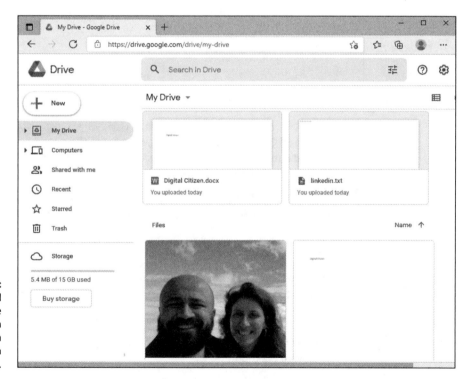

**FIGURE 4-8:**
The files you add to the Google Drive folder on your PC appear in Google Drive on the internet.

4. **Open one of the documents (a Word document, an Excel spreadsheet, or a PowerPoint slide, if you have one) you copied into the Google Drive folder.**

   Google Drive opens the document inside the appropriate app. As you can see in Figure 4-9, Google Drive does a reasonably good job of rendering it — showing it on the screen.

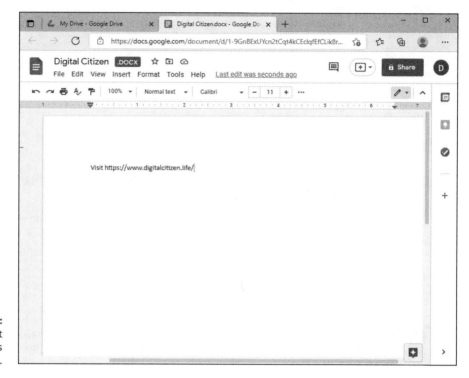

Visit https://www.digitalcitizen.life/

**FIGURE 4-9:**
Simple Microsoft Office documents render well.

**WARNING**

More complex documents, though, can have all sorts of problems, from missing pieces to jumbled text. Although Google Drive does yeoman's work trying to display Office documents, it's far from 100 percent accurate — and it doesn't play well with complex templates and doesn't work at all with macros.

5. **To create a document, open the tab with the Google Drive home page, click or tap the +New button and choose what kind of document you want.**

   You can create a document, presentation, spreadsheet, or drawing (which is stored as a .gdraw file). See Figure 4-10.

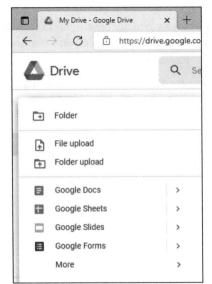

**FIGURE 4-10:**
You'll get more
consistent results
creating new
documents from
Google Drive
rather than
importing and
switching from
the Microsoft
Office format.

**6.** **Edit the file using the tools available in the app you've chosen. Don't forget to give it a name too.**

You can also click or tap Share, and choose a person who can edit the file simultaneously.

**7.** **When you're finished, close the browser tab.**

Your file is saved automatically, and the latest version appears almost immediately in the Google Drive folder in File Explorer.

**TIP**

After you play with Google Drive a bit, take a few minutes to read the manual. You can find the Google Docs help system at `https://support.google.com/`.

# MORE ABOUT GOOGLE WORKSPACE

Google has several apps — word processing, spreadsheet, presentation, drawing, forms, calendar, and so on. The apps are tied together with a Dropbox-like, online file storage and synchronization app called Google Drive.

All those apps and 15GB of online synced storage are available free for anybody, anytime. You can also purchase a Google One plan that increases the storage from 15GB to 100GB, 200GB, or 2TB. For details, go to https://one.google.com/about/plans.

In the next level up from the free basic account, Google Workspace ties together organizations (companies, yes, but charities and clubs and all sorts of other kinds of organizations). This level is particularly useful for organizations that operate with a single domain, such as DigitalCitizen.life or Dummies.com. When your organization (and your domain) hooks up with Google Workspace, you get to use Gmail for handling all your mail and you aren't tied to @gmail.com email addresses.

Why would an individual or small group want Google Workspace? Good question. The most persuasive arguments I know are these:

- It's simple, effective, cheap (or free, if you're with a nonprofit or school), and easy, especially if you know and like Gmail.

- If the Google apps do everything you need, you can save yourself and your organization a ton of money by not buying Microsoft Office. This, to me, is the crucial question: Do you need to spend the money to get all the frills in the Office apps, or do the Google apps give you enough of what you need? Tough question, and one only you can answer after you try it for a while.

- If you set up things properly, you can share documents with everyone in your group, and it doesn't take any extra work. Arranging the collaboration is zero effort.

Edit because otherwise, the amount of effort collaborating is zero.

- Group members can work on the device they prefer. Whether the device is a PC, a Mac, an iPad, a Pixel, or a Chromebook, the Google apps have you covered. And you can switch from machine to machine, location to location, without any concerns about syncing or dropping files.

- Google's reliability is second to none. It isn't up 100 percent of the time, but it's mighty close.

*(continued)*

*(continued)*

Before you go screeching to your terminal to sign up for Google Workspace, understand that setting it up has a couple of gotchas, although the day-to-day use of Google Workspace is as simple as using Gmail. Converting to the free versions of the Google apps isn't too difficult, but moving your group's domain to use Gmail has a few tough spots. You would be wise to make sure that you understand the steps before you commit yourself.

Also ensure that you understand what will and won't happen with your email after you switch. For example, Google Workspace doesn't move your old messages over to Gmail. If you want your old messages to come across, you have to run its migration program. You can find a comprehensive discussion about moving to Gmail at `https://support.google.com/a/users/answer/9259748`.

I assume that you already have a domain name for yourself or your organization. If not, you can register a domain name from one of thousands of web-hosting companies.

If you want to use Google Workspace, go to `https://workspace.google.com/pricing.html` and click or tap the Get Start button for the plan you want. Follow Google's instructions from there.

# Chapter **5**

# Using Outlook.com and Microsoft 365

I n 2012, Microsoft decided that Hotmail — one of the best-recognized brands on the planet — would be retired, replaced by something completely different. Yes, Microsoft tossed out a brand as well-known as Coca-Cola or the terms *taxi* or *Visa* and replaced it with Outlook.com.

If you think that the name Outlook.com was chosen because Microsoft's new flagship online email-service-formerly-known-as-Hotmail looked or acted like Outlook in Microsoft Office or anything else that's ever been called *Outlook*, you'd be wrong. Outlook.com started out as the old Hotmail, with a few internal changes and a new boxy interface. In the years that followed, Microsoft gradually made Outlook.com look and behave more like the other Outlooks — and made the other Outlooks look and behave more like Outlook.com. The match-up is still not perfect, but it's a lot better than it used to be.

In this chapter, I take you through Outlook.com, with a nod and a wink to Hotmail, which is now officially dead. Then I talk a bit about the Office app from Windows 11, and the "new" Microsoft 365 subscriptions, which are the former Office 365 subscriptions with a new name. Why would Microsoft rebrand Office? I don't know but someone close to the company's CEO thought it would be a great idea, and now the Office brand is also being phased out.

## A BRIEF HISTORY OF HOTMAIL

Hotmail broke new ground as the first major, free, web-based email service when Sabeer Bhatia (a native of Bangalore and a graduate of Caltech and Stanford) spent $300,000 to launch it in 1996.

On December 29, 1997, Microsoft bought Hotmail for $450 million, cash, and the service has never been the same. Microsoft struggled with Hotmail for many years, adding new users like flies, but the service suffered from severe performance problems and crashes heard round the world. Ultimately, Hotmail was shuffled under the Microsoft Network (MSN) wing of the corporate umbrella, its free services were clipped, and its user interface was subjected to more facelifts than an aging Hollywood actor, which is saying something.

As MSN lost its luster and as competitors, such as Gmail and Yahoo! Mail, won the majority of the email market, Hotmail's subscription-based income model died almost overnight, and the company's market share fell precipitously. Why pay for 20MB of Hotmail message storage when Google gives away 1GB for free?

Microsoft has gone through a series of well-intentioned but horrendously implemented rebrandings and a few minor upgrades, passing through (get out your scorecard) MSN Hotmail, Windows Hotmail, Windows Live Hotmail, Microsoft Hotmail, and now Outlook. com. Hotmail's final facelift, pre-Outlook.com, came in early 2012. Few people cared, and among the ones who did, the reaction was not universally positive.

Although email as a whole isn't an endangered species, it isn't growing that much anymore. Social networking sites pick up a substantial portion of traditional, one-to-one email traffic, and instant messages, SMSs (texts), and Skype and WhatsApp calls eat away at the numbers.

Lastly, if you don't want to pay for Microsoft 365, read the last part of the chapter, where I give you some tips about using Office on the web for free.

# Using Outlook.com

When working with Outlook.com, any Microsoft account will do. If you already have an @hotmail.com, @live.com, @outlook.com, or an older @msn.com email address, it's already a Microsoft account. If you don't yet have an @hotmail.com or @outlook.com email address, getting one is easy. To create an Outlook.com/ Microsoft account, read Book 2, Chapter 5.

Once you have your account ready, log in to Outlook.com (www.outlook.com) and familiarize yourself with the user interface (refer to Figure 5-1):

>> **Default folders on the left are Inbox, Junk Email, Drafts, Sent Items, Scheduled, Deleted Items, Archive, and Notes.** You click or tap each folder to open it. Make sure you understand what each one is supposed to contain:

- *Inbox* gets all your mail as it comes in. If you don't do anything with it, the message stays in your inbox. The inbox is split into a Focused tab (with emails from people and services you frequently use) and Other (usually with emails from newsletters or people who rarely write to you).

- *Junk Email* holds mail that was sent to you but Outlook.com has identified as being spam. Outlook.com and Gmail have effective junk identifiers, but occasionally a message will get tossed in here that really isn't junk. If that happens, click or tap the box next to the "good" junk message and, at the top, choose Move To ⇨ Inbox.

  You can also drag and drop the message into whatever folder you like.

**TIP**

  If you get a piece of junk mail in your inbox, don't delete it. You can help the Outlook filters and other Outlook users by marking the message as junk. Just select the box next to the message and, at the top, click or tap Junk.

- *Drafts* holds mail you were working on but didn't send.

- *Sent Items* contains copies of everything that's gone out.

- *Scheduled* contains all emails you've scheduled for sending at a later time. Unfortunately, you can do this only from Outlook.com, not from Windows 11's Mail app.

- *Deleted Items* is the place where messages go when you delete them.

- *Archive* is the place where see the messages that you've archived instead of deleting.

- *Notes* is the place where you can create and view notes. They're automatically synced with the Sticky Notes app from Windows 11 and the OneNote app.

  You can create folders. Just click or tap the New Folder link at the bottom of the Folders list.

>> **The Search box on the top is the most important location on the Outlook.com main page.** People go nuts trying to organize their mail. The Search function finds things amazingly quickly. But that's the topic for the next section.

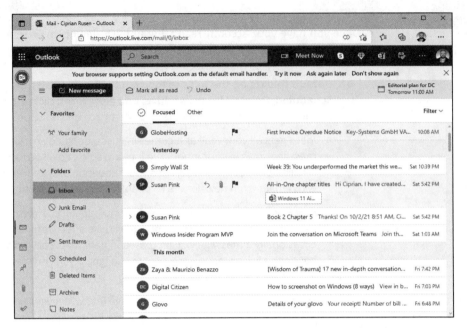

**FIGURE 5-1:**
Your Outlook.
com inbox and all
its options.

TIP

You may find it instructive to see how Outlook.com compares to the Windows 11 Mail app. Although they're dressed up to look similar, they work in different ways. Flip back to Book 4, Chapter 1 and see how the Outlook.com interface differs from the Mail's app interface. In addition to cosmetic differences, there are functional differences:

>> Outlook.com runs in your browser, doesn't store any information on your computer, and works only when you're connected to the internet.

>> The Windows 11 Mail app runs on your computer, stores a small subset of your email on your computer, and will continue to work (albeit on a subset of messages) whether or not you're connected to the internet.

## Sweeping emails in Outlook.com

The sweep feature enables you to move all messages sent from a specific email address into a folder. Select one message from the sender you want to move, choose Sweep, and then choose how you want to sweep:

>> Move All Messages from the Inbox Folder: Takes the action on all mail sent currently in the inbox from this sender.

>> Move All Messages from the Inbox Folder and Any Future Messages: Moves all existing and the future messages from the inbox into the folder you select.

>> **Always Keep the Latest Message and Move the Rest from the Inbox Folder:** Applies to email from only this particular sender. This rule applies to future emails too, not just existing ones.

>> **Always Move Messages Older Than 10 Days from the Inbox Folder** applies to mail from only this particular sender. It does, however, apply to all current and future messages from the sender. Discretion advised.

Here's how to use the Sweep feature in Outlook.com:

1. **Open Microsoft Edge and sign in to Outlook.com.**

2. **In your inbox, select an email from a sender whose messages you want to sweep, and click or tap Sweep on the top.**

   The Sweep Messages dialog box appears, as shown in Figure 5-2.

3. **Select the option you want from the list.**

4. **Click or tap the Move To drop-down list and choose the folder where you want to move the messages from this particular sender. If you want to delete them, select Deleted Items.**

5. **Click or tap OK.**

   All the messages from that sender are moved according to the Sweep rule that you have selected.

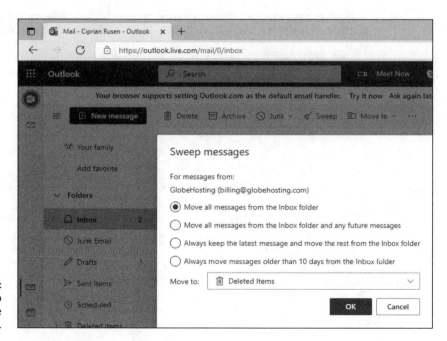

**FIGURE 5-2:** The Sweep options available in Outlook.com.

# Bringing some sanity to your Outlook.com inbox

Here's my number-one tip for Outlook.com users:

**If you have an Archive folder, don't create any new folders.**

That way lies madness. Yes, you can create a folder hierarchy that mimics the filing cabinets in the Pentagon. You can fret for an hour over whether an email about your trip to the beach should go in the Trips folder or the Beaches folder — or both. You can slice and dice and organize 'til you're blue in the face, and all you'll have in the end is a jumbled mess.

Here's my number-two tip for Outlook.com users:

**If you don't have an Archive folder, create one — and use it.**

If you want to save that message about your trip to the beach or that gorgeous Pinterest mail, just click or tap the message and then click or tap the Archive tab at the top of the Outlook.com window. Or drag the message to the Archive folder. See Figure 5-3.

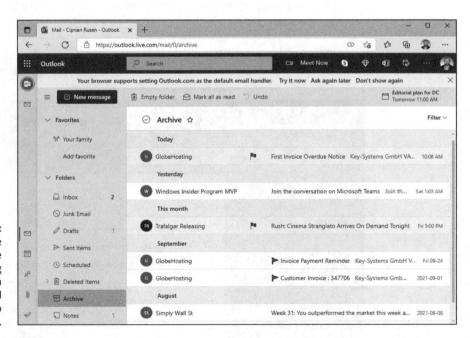

**FIGURE 5-3:**
The Archive folder (note the Archive heading at the top) can hold any mail you don't want to delete.

The first time you click or tap the Archive button at the top of the Outlook.com window, it offers to set up a new Archive folder for you. After that, anything you archive goes into that folder.

Additionally, people get caught up in categories or flags as a way to organize and sort mail. Outlook.com comes with built-in flags and categories too. If you work well that way, hey, knock yourself out. But note that there's only one kind of flag; you can't set up different flag colors as you can in some email programs. My general approach is to blast through email as quickly as I can, responding to what needs responding and deleting or filing the rest immediately. *De gustibus non est disputandum.*

REMEMBER

If you want to find all the messages about trips, use the Search box. If you want to find all the messages about beaches, use the Search box. And if you want to find all the messages about trips *and* beaches . . . wait for it . . . use the Search box!

# Handling Outlook.com Failures

Any computer system in general — and online systems in particular — have failures, Outlook.com included. If Outlook.com starts acting up on you, here are two websites you should consult:

>> **Microsoft's Service Status site** (see Figure 5-4) gives you the latest information about Outlook.com's current health — from Microsoft's point of view. Unfortunately, the site has been criticized for being slow to show updates in real time. In the past few years, Microsoft's network going down has, at times, also taken the status reporting sites down (https://portal.office.com/servicestatus).

>> **Downrightnow,** which isn't aligned with Microsoft, gives you a crowdsourced consensus view of what's happening with Outlook.com/Hotmail. Downrightnow (shown in Figure 5-5) not only actively solicits comments from people who visit the site but also has a Twitter monitoring program that finds some of the tweeted complaints in real time (www.downrightnow.com/hotmail). Yes, the URL is for Hotmail, not Outlook.

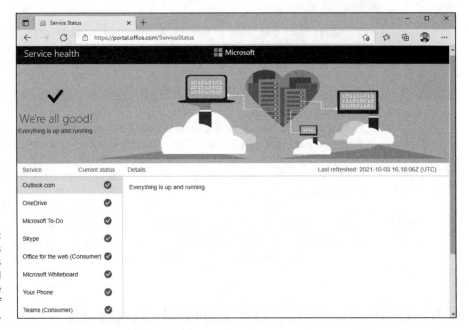

**FIGURE 5-4:**
Microsoft's
Service Status
site gives a broad
overview of the
current status of
Outlook.com.

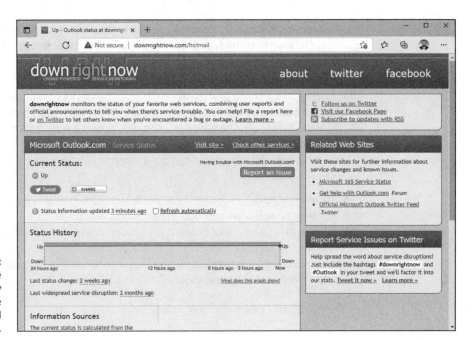

**FIGURE 5-5:**
Compare the
Microsoft party
line with the
crowdsourced
Downrightnow.

# The Office App and Microsoft 365

When you browse the apps preinstalled with Windows 11, you'll stumble upon the Office app. When you start it, you'll see that it's mostly a portal to Microsoft 365 (formerly known as Office 365). The app is useful only if you use a Microsoft account connected to a Microsoft 365 subscription.

To the left of the Office app (see Figure 5-6) are shortcuts to the apps that are part of the Microsoft 365 subscriptions: Word, Excel, PowerPoint, Outlook, OneDrive, Teams, and OneNote. A click or tap on their icons, and the apps start right away. In the middle of the Office app are your recently opened files, and at the top area My Account and Install Office buttons.

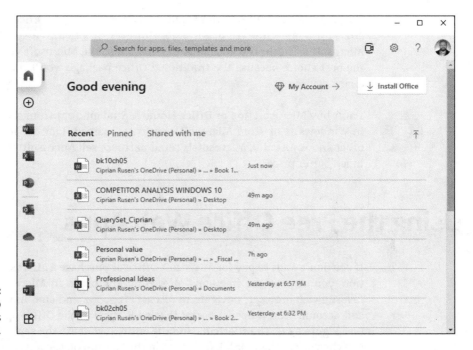

**FIGURE 5-6:**
The Office app promotes Microsoft 365.

**TIP**

On the surface, the Office app may seem useful, but its role is mostly to sell you a Microsoft 365 subscription. If you don't plan on buying one, you're better off uninstalling the Office app to save a bit of storage space.

Now, when it comes to office apps, Microsoft is the king of the hill, and there's no debating that its Office suite is extremely useful and chock-full of features. If you want to use Word, Excel, PowerPoint and all the other apps included, Microsoft 365 subscriptions for home users are available in two types of plans: Personal and Family. Personal is for one person and five devices (Windows, Mac, iPhones, and Android devices), and it costs $69.99 per year. Family is for up to six people and five devices for each and costs $99.99 per year. If you want to compare them, visit this page: `www.microsoft.com/en-us/microsoft-365/buy/compare-all-microsoft-365-products`.

Business subscriptions start with Microsoft 365 Business Basic, which cost $5 per user per month, up to Microsoft 365 Business Premium for $20 per user per month. Their features vary and get more complex as the cost per user increases.

Home users can still buy the traditional Office package, Office Home & Student 2021, for a one-time fee of $149.99. However, it's tied to a specific PC, not to a Microsoft account. If you change devices often, the Microsoft 365 subscription is the best choice because the traditional Office package won't migrate with you to a new device.

TIP

Don't buy Microsoft 365 or Office Home & Student 2021 from the Microsoft Store in Windows 11 or from Microsoft's website. Instead, look for it on Amazon and other shops. Usually, Microsoft's retail partners sell Microsoft 365 and Office at a much better price.

# Using the Free Office Web Apps

If you don't want to pay for Microsoft Office or purchase a Microsoft 365 subscription, you can use the free apps offered by Microsoft. In Microsoft Edge or your favorite web browser, navigate to `www.office.com` and sign in with your Microsoft account. You'll open a portal that's identical to the Office app in Windows 11 (see Figure 5-7). The shortcuts and the entire layout are the same. However, when you click or tap the Word, Excel icons in the column on the left, the free Office web apps open instead of their desktop counterparts.

Office web apps offer slightly fewer features, but they work well and are remarkably similar to the mobile Office apps on Android devices, iPhones, and iPads.

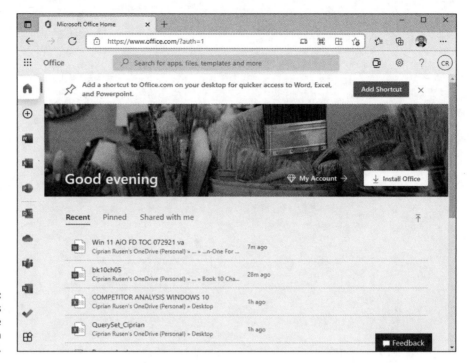

**FIGURE 5-7:**
Office.com is the same as the Office app in Windows 11.

**TIP**

At the top of the office.com web page, check out the notification recommending that you add a shortcut to Office.com to your desktop. Click or tap the Add Shortcut button and select all the places where you want this shortcut. You can have it on the desktop, the taskbar, and the Start menu. When you use the shortcut, it opens the Office.com website, where you can use all Office web apps for free, without paying a penny for Microsoft 365. Try it out, and you may notice that you don't really need the desktop alternatives for Word, Excel, PowerPoint, and so on.

# Chapter **6**

# Discovering the Best Free Windows Add-Ons

Much as I like Windows 11, it has a few glaring holes that can be fixed only by non-Microsoft software. For example, playing video files with the Movies & TV app works well, but it doesn't hold a candle to VLC Media Player. That's why, in this chapter, I step you through two different kinds of software. First come the (few) programs you need to fix holes in Windows. Second is a much larger group of programs that just make Windows work better. Both collections have one thing in common: They're free for personal use.

At the end of this chapter, I turn to one of my favorite topics: Software that you *don't* need and should never pay one cent to acquire. Lots of snake oil salespeople are out there. This chapter tells you why they're just blowing smoke.

## Windows Apps You Absolutely Must Have

Depending on what kind of Windows 11 machine you have, there's a short and sweet list of free software you need.

# VLC Media Player

Although Microsoft made a few minor improvements to its media handling in Windows 11 — adding the capability to play FLAC lossless audio, MKV video, and a handful of less interesting media formats — it remains woefully underpowered in its capability to work with common media files.

**TIP**

Find a DVD or Blu-Ray movie somewhere — if you don't have one, rent one . . . if you can find a place to rent them now — and stick the disc in your PC. A Windows notification appears, and you can click or tap that notification and play the DVD or Blu-Ray. It ought to be like falling off a log.

Unfortunately, some brand-spanking new Windows 11 PCs won't play DVD movies. Why? Microsoft decided that, even though it shipped the DVD-playing capability in previous versions of Windows, putting that capability in Windows 8 and later just cost too much. You can read the details at www.infoworld.com/ article/2616896/microsoft-windows/update--windows-8-won-t-be-able-to-play-dvds.html.

Most PC makers step in and provide DVD and Blu-Ray movie-playing software with their new machines, but they're under no obligation to do so. That's why I suggest you get a DVD movie and use the free VLC Media Player program. In fact, VLC is so good that I use it and recommend it for all media playing — music and movies. VLC includes the small translation programs (called *codecs)* that let you play just about any kind of music or video on your Windows 11 PC.

Unlike other media players, VLC sports simple controls; built-in codecs for almost every file type imaginable; and a large, vocal online support community. VLC plays internet-streaming media with a click, records played media, converts between file types, and even supports individual-frame screen shots. VLC is well-known for tolerating incomplete or damaged media files. It will even start to play downloaded media before the download is finished.

Hop over to VLC (www.videolan.org) and install it (see Figure 6-1). Yeah, it looks spartan, but it works very well indeed.

VLC has played with the idea of shipping a Windows 11 app version of VLC but results as of this writing are disappointing. Unless you're running Windows 11 in S mode — and thus can't run programs on the desktop — I'd give the Microsoft Store version a pass.

**FIGURE 6-1:**
VLC Media Player
plays every song
and video type
imaginable, even
your video DVDs.

## Bitwarden

In Book 9, Chapter 4, I talk about two password managers, Bitwarden and Robo-Form. Both are excellent choices. Most people, in my experience, prefer Bitwarden, but you ought to look at Book 9, Chapter 4 and see if your circumstances are different. I use Bitwarden in all my browsers and on all my computers and devices: Windows, Android, iOS, Chrome OS, Mac, you name it.

Bitwarden (shown in Figure 6-2) keeps track of your user IDs, passwords, and other settings, stores them in the cloud, and offers them to you with a click. Bitwarden does its AES-256 encrypting and decrypting on your PC, using a master password that you must remember. The data that gets stored in the cloud is encrypted, and without the key, the stored passwords can't be broken, unless you know somebody who can crack AES-256 encryption.

Bitwarden works as a browser add-on for Microsoft Edge (see Figure 6-2), Mozilla Firefox, and Google Chrome, so all your passwords are stored in one place, accessible to any PC you happen to be using — if you have the master password.

Bitwarden is free for personal use. The Premium version, which adds two-step login options and other useful features, costs $10 a year.

## Recuva

Deleted files recovery has been a mainstay PC utility since forever. But there's never been an undeleter better than Recuva, which is fast, thorough, and free. See Figure 6-3.

When you throw out the Recycle Bin trash, the files aren't destroyed; rather, the space they occupy is earmarked for new data. Undelete routines scan the flotsam and jetsam and put the pieces back together.

As long as you haven't added new data to a drive, undelete (almost) always works. If you've added some data, there's still a good chance that you can get most of the deleted stuff back.

Recuva can also be used to recover data on a USB drive, an SD card, and many smartphones and digital cameras that can be attached to your PC.

Powerful stuff. For more advanced features, there's a Pro version for about $20.

# The Best of the Rest — All Free

Here are my recommendations for useful software that you may or may not want, depending on your circumstances. Hey, the price is right.

## Ninite

Leading the list of traditional desktop programs is one that helps you install (and update) other programs. Actually, it isn't a program — it's a website. When you start looking at desktop applications, your first stop should be to `https://ninite.com/` (see Figure 6-4). Simply click or tap the applications you want and Ninite will download the latest versions free of crapware, install them, and leave you in the driver's seat.

Need to update your apps? Run Ninite again. Everything's brought up to date, no junkware, no hassle. For the full royal treatment — where Ninite notifies you of changes to programs you've installed —Ninite Updater ($9.99/year) works like a champ.

The beauty of the Ninite approach is that all these apps are a click away — no fuss, no nags, no charge. It's the best way I know to install a bunch of good programs on a new machine in just a few minutes. The downside? It misses a few of my favorite desktop apps.

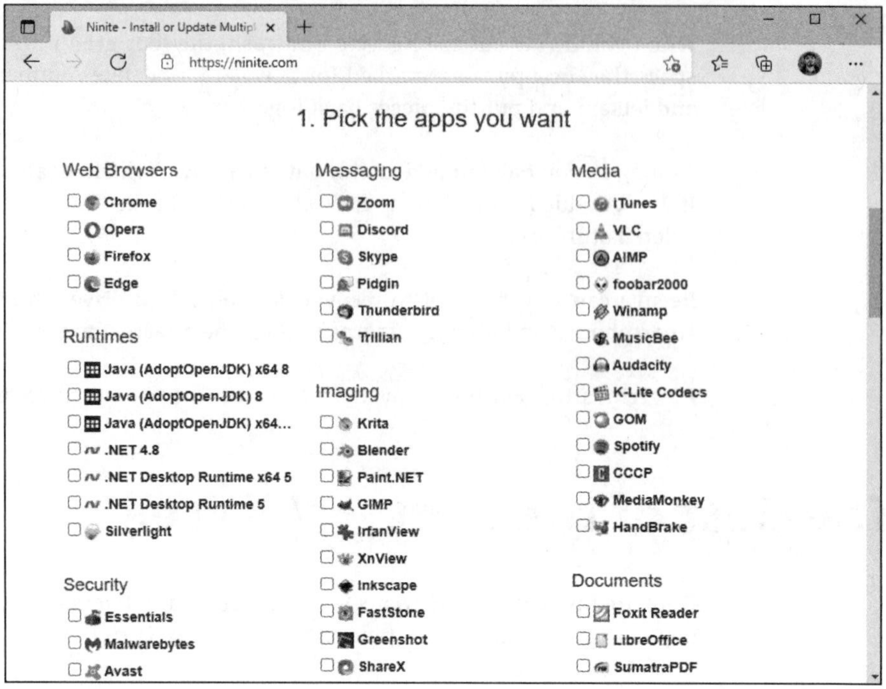

FIGURE 6-4:
Install or update
popular desktop
apps with Ninite.

The figure shows a browser window with the Ninite website (https://ninite.com) displaying "1. Pick the apps you want" with categories:

**Web Browsers**: Chrome, Opera, Firefox, Edge

**Runtimes**: Java (AdoptOpenJDK) x64 8, Java (AdoptOpenJDK) 8, Java (AdoptOpenJDK) x64..., .NET 4.8, .NET Desktop Runtime x64 5, .NET Desktop Runtime 5, Silverlight

**Security**: Essentials, Malwarebytes, Avast

**Messaging**: Zoom, Discord, Skype, Pidgin, Thunderbird, Trillian

**Imaging**: Krita, Blender, Paint.NET, GIMP, IrfanView, XnView, Inkscape, FastStone, Greenshot, ShareX

**Media**: iTunes, VLC, AIMP, foobar2000, Winamp, MusicBee, Audacity, K-Lite Codecs, GOM, Spotify, CCCP, MediaMonkey, HandBrake

**Documents**: Foxit Reader, LibreOffice, SumatraPDF

# Revo Uninstaller

Revo Uninstaller (www.revouninstaller.com/revo_uninstaller_free_download.html) well and truly uninstalls programs, and it does so in an unexpected way.

When you use Revo, it runs the program's uninstaller and watches while the uninstaller works, looking for the location of program files and for registry keys that the uninstaller zaps. It then goes in and removes leftover pieces, based on the locations and keys that the program's uninstaller took out. Revo also consults its own internal database for commonly left-behind bits and roots those out as well.

Revo gives you a great deal of flexibility in deciding just how much you want to clean and what you want to save. For most programs, the recommended Moderate setting strikes a good balance between zapping problematic pieces and deleting things that really shouldn't be deleted.

The paid Pro version monitors your system when you install a program, making removal easier and more complete. Pro will also uninstall remnants of programs that have already been uninstalled.

If you uninstall programs — whether to tidy up your system or to get rid of something that's bothering you — it's worth its weight in gold.

# Paint.NET

In Book 5, Chapter 2, I talk about the Microsoft Paint program, which can help you put together graphics in a pinch. For powerful, easy-to-use photo editing, with layers, plugins, and all sorts of special effects, along with a compact and easily understood interface, I stick with Paint.NET (see Figure 6-5).

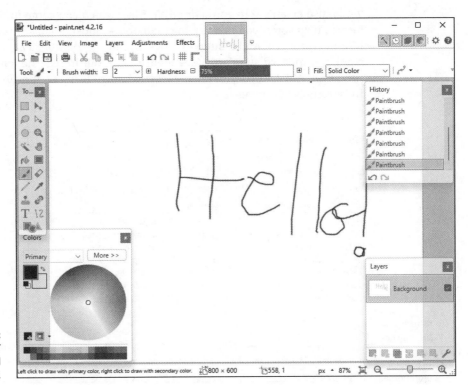

FIGURE 6-5:
Paint.NET
is a powerful
image editor.

The program puts all the editing tools a nonprofessional might reasonably expect into a remarkably intuitive package. Download it at www.getpaint.net and give it a try.

**WARNING**

Pay attention when downloading Paint.NET. Unfortunately, its official site displays many intrusive ads. Make sure to close them all, and don't get tricked into downloading something else. If you want a simpler download process, try this location instead: www.techspot.com/downloads/657-paint-net.html.

With dozens of good — even great — free image editors around, it's hard to choose one above the others. IrfanView, for example, has tremendous viewing, organizing, and resizing capabilities, but it is not as versatile at editing like Paint.NET.

# 7-Zip

Another venerable utility, 7-Zip (www.7-zip.org) still rates as a must-have, even though Windows supports the ZIP format natively. Why? Because some people of the Apple persuasion will send you files in the RAR archive format from time to time, and 7-Zip is the fast, easy, free way to handle them.

7-Zip also creates self-extracting EXE files, which can come in handy (although heaven help you if you ever try to email one — most email scanners won't let an EXE file through). And it supports AES-256 bit encryption. The interface rates as clunky by modern standards (see Figure 6-6), but it gets the job done with ZIP, RAR, CAB, ARJ, TAR, 7z, and many lesser-known formats. It even lets you extract files from ISO CD images.

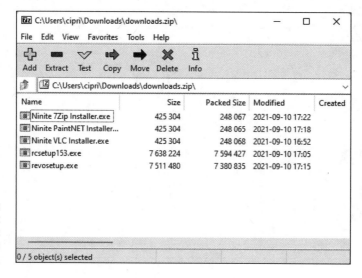

**FIGURE 6-6:**
7-Zip may not have the greatest interface, but it's a workhorse.

Another poster boy for the open-source community, 7-Zip goes in easily, never nags, and wouldn't dream of dropping an unwanted toolbar on your system. Enlightened.

**TIP**

You don't need to register or pay for 7-Zip. Don't fall for a website with a similar name. To get the real, original, one and only free 7-Zip, with a crapware-free installer, go to 7-zip.org. Download it from www.7-zip.org/download.html.

# qBittorrent

If you aren't yet using torrents (a method of distributing files over the internet), now's the time to start. Torrents have taken a bad rap for spreading illegal, pirate software. Although that reputation is entirely deserved, it's also true that many torrents are legitimate. And they are the single most efficient way to distribute files online.

For years I've used and recommended uTorrent, but the current version's installer includes crapware — and in previous versions, it has installed some really obnoxious crapware.

Instead, try qBittorrent, shown in Figure 6-7. It's simple, fast, and easy to use, and it supports magnet links (which simplify downloads), with extensive bandwidth reporting and management. Download it at www.qbittorrent.org.

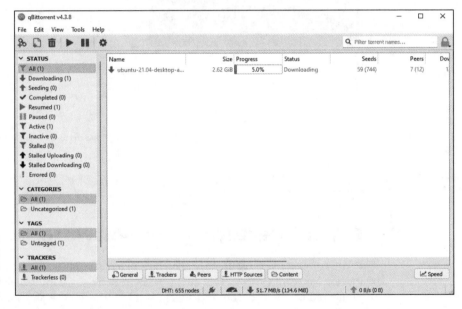

**FIGURE 6-7:** qBittorrent doesn't have uTorrent's baggage.

# Dropbox, Google Drive, OneDrive, or . . .

Even if the thought of putting your data on the internet drives you nuts, sooner or later you're going to want a way to store data away from your main machine, and you're going to want an easy way to share data with other people or other devices (desktops, laptops, tablets, and smartphones).

There's no obvious winner — no cloud storage that's inherently better than any of the others. Just pick one and get it set up. Someday, it'll save your tail. I used Dropbox for the files for this book. I also use OneDrive for most of my personal files, and Google Drive for my blogging work at Digital Citizen.

They all have free introductory options, and some give you an enormous amount of storage for free or for a small fee. Some even provide a large amount of storage if you subscribe to a related service such as the Microsoft 365 subscription. Simply take a look at their plans (see Figure 6-8) and choose the one you consider best.

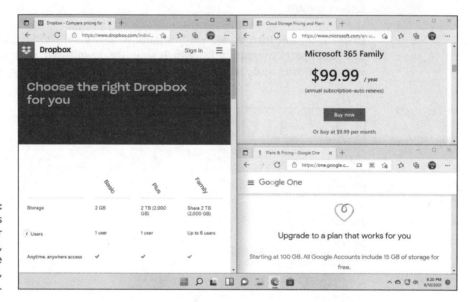

**FIGURE 6-8:**
Check the plans available for Dropbox, OneDrive (Microsoft 365), and Google Drive.

## Other interesting free software

If you connect over public Wi-Fi, such as in a coffee shop, you should use a Virtual Private Network (VPN). I talk about VPNs in Book 9, Chapter 4. Session hijacking, pioneered by the program Firesheep, can let others pose as you, even while your session is in progress. Using secure sockets (SSL) helps, but even those can be subverted in certain circumstances. Your best bet is to stick with VPN.

TIP

Need to rip a DVD? Forget trying to use Windows. Get the open-source, free, and junk-free HandBrake at `https://handbrake.fr`. Works like a champ on any DVD.

Wonder what programs run whenever you start Windows? Look at Microsoft's venerable and free-as-a-breeze Autoruns at `https://technet.microsoft.com/en-us/sysinternals`. Autoruns finds more autostarting programs (add-ins, drivers, codecs, gadgets, shell extensions, whatever) in more obscure places than any other program, anywhere. Autoruns not only lists the autorunning programs but also lets you turn off individual programs. It has many minor features, including the capability to filter out Microsoft-signed programs, a quick way to jump to folders holding autostarting programs, and a command-line version that lets you display file hashes. Autoruns doesn't require installation. It's a program that runs and collects its information, displays it (using a rudimentary user interface), lets you wrangle with your system, and then fades away.

**TIP**

Want to know what hardware you have? It's a common question that's easily answered with a nifty free utility called HWiNFO, available at `www.hwinfo.com`. HWiNFO delves into every nook and cranny. From the summary to detailed Device Manager-style trees of information — entire forests of information — HWiNFO can tell you everything anyone could want to know about your machine. A separate real-time monitoring panel tells you the current status of everything under the sun: temperatures, speeds, usage, clocks, voltages, wattages, hard drive SMART stats, read rates, write rates, GPU load, network throughput, and on and on.

## You may not need to buy Microsoft Office

If your needs are simple and you don't have to edit fancy documents created in Word, Excel, or PowerPoint, you may be able to get by with Google apps (which I discuss in Chapter 4 of this minibook) or LibreOffice. The web-based Office Online apps are also good — and free for personal use. If you're moonlighting with a Mac, the iWork apps might do, too.

**TIP**

Do the math: LibreOffice, free. Google apps, free for personal use. iWork apps, free. Microsoft 365 Family (which includes six licenses) $100/year forever. Office 2021 Home & Student (for personal use only, no Outlook), $150. Home & Business, $220. Office Online, free for personal use.

The big advantage to Microsoft 365: You get not only six licenses of the latest versions of the Office programs — Word, Excel, PowerPoint, Outlook, OneNote, Access, Publisher — for PCs or Macs, but also licenses for five tablets (including Office for iPad, which is a tremendous product), and five licenses for phones (largely forgettable). In addition, you get 1TB of OneDrive online storage per user for up to six users. Unless you have a visceral reaction to renting Office — I can sympathize — Microsoft 365 at $100/year or less comes across as a bargain.

Whenever somebody asks me, "Why do you recommend Office when OpenOffice/LibreOffice does everything for free?" I have to cringe. It's true that Microsoft Office is expensive, and with Microsoft 365 you're locked into the annual fee. It's also true that good, but not great, alternatives exist — including Google Workspace (which I discuss in Chapter 4 of this minibook).

Here are two substantial problems:

>> As much as I would love to recommend a free replacement for Word, Excel, or PowerPoint, the simple fact is that the free alternatives (other than Office Online) aren't 100 percent compatible. In fact, for anything except the simplest formatting and most basic features, they aren't compatible at all. Even Microsoft's free Office Online Apps aren't as full-featured as the real Word, Excel, and PowerPoint. If your needs are modest, by all means, explore the alternatives. But if you have to edit a document that somebody else is going to use and it has any unusual formatting, you may end up with an unusable mess.

>> Many people don't realize it, but OpenOffice.org isn't the same organization it used to be. In fact, there's an ongoing debate about the superiority of the new OpenOffice.org (which now belongs to Apache) and the renegade offshoot LibreOffice (www.libreoffice.org). Basically, some feel that OpenOffice.org moved away from its open-source roots when Oracle owned it, so a new organization, LibreOffice, forked the code (made a copy of the original code and then improved it) and released several new versions that are not associated with OpenOffice.org or Oracle. So you're left with two organizations, slightly different products, and no clear indication of which version (if either) will be around for the long term.

**TIP**

If you can get by with Google Workspace — that's what I use for everything except books — go through the steps in Chapter 4 of this minibook. If you have to use Office, do yourself a favor and first try the free-for-personal-use Office Online, at www.microsoft.com/en-us/microsoft-365/free-office-online-for-the-web.

# Don't Pay for Software You Don't Need!

If you've moved to Windows 11, there's a raft of software — entire *categories* of software — that you simply don't need. Why pay for any of it?

Many people write to ask me for recommendations about antivirus software, utility programs, registry cleaners, or backup programs. The simple fact is, if you've moved up to Windows 11, you don't need lots of this stuff.

In this, the last section of the last chapter of this book, I'm going to lay it on the line — point out what you don't need, in my considered opinion — and try to save you a bunch of money. With any luck, the following handful of tips will save you the price of the book.

# Windows 11 has all the antivirus software you need

Windows Security includes Microsoft Defender Antivirus, formerly known as Windows Defender. It works great and doesn't cost a cent. If you follow the recommendations in this book, you don't need to pay a penny for antivirus, antispyware, anti-anything software, and you don't need a fancy outbound firewall, either. (I talk about Windows Security and Windows Defender Firewall in Book 9, Chapter 3.)

You do need *other* security programs, however. I list those in Book 9, Chapter 4. They're free.

# Windows 11 doesn't need a disk defragger

Because of the way Windows stores data on a hard drive and reclaims the areas left behind when deleting data, your drives can start to look like a patchwork quilt, with data scattered all over the place. *Defragmentation* reorganizes the data, plucking data off the drive and putting files back together again, ostensibly to speed up hard drive access.

It's true that horribly fragmented hard drives — many of them handcrafted by defrag software companies trying to prove their worth — run more slowly than defragged drives. However, in practice, the differences aren't that remarkable, particularly if you defrag your hard drives every month or two or six. (Note that you should never defrag a solid-state drive.) Even moderately bad fragmentation doesn't make a noticeable difference in performance, although running a defrag every now and again helps.

With Windows 11, you don't need to run a defrag. Ever. If you have a solid-state drive, you don't need (or want) a defrag — it wears out your drive and doesn't improve anything. If you have a whirling-platter hard drive, Windows runs a defrag for you, by default, one day every week.

# Windows 11 doesn't need a disk partitioner

I hate disk partitioning, but rather than get into a technical argument (yes, I know that dual-boot systems with a single hard drive need multiple partitions), I will limit myself to extolling the virtues of Windows 11's partition manager.

No, Windows 11's disk partition manager isn't a full-fledged program, but it does everything with partitions that most people need — and it gets the job done without messing up your hard drive. That's more than I can say for some third-party disk partition managers.

To run Windows 11's built-in disk partitioner, type **partition** in the Windows 11 Search box. Click or tap Create and Format Hard Disk Partitions, which should be the first link. That displays the Disk Management program (see Figure 6-9), where it's right-click easy to see, delete, expand, and change your partitions.

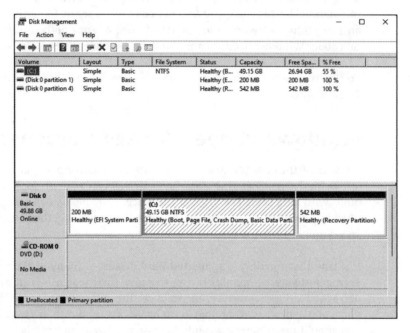

**FIGURE 6-9:** The Disk Management program enables you to manage your partitions with ease.

**WARNING**

If you're not familiar with disk management tools and concepts like partitioning, I think it's best that you don't use Disk Management without a detailed step-by-step tutorial that explains everything you need to know.

If you want to create a partition, right-click or press and hold down on any empty area and choose Create Volume. If you want to make a new partition on a volume that's full, right-click or press and hold down on the volume and choose Shrink Volume.

## Windows 11 doesn't need a registry cleaner

I've never seen a real-world example of a Windows machine that improved in any significant way after running a registry cleaner. As with defraggers, registry cleaners may have served a useful purpose for Windows XP, but I think they're useless nowadays. I've never found a single run of a single registry cleaner that caused anything but grief.

A great quote originated (as best I can tell) on the DSLReports forum in March 2005. A poster who goes by the handle Jabarnut stated, "The Registry is an enormous database, and all this cleaning really doesn't amount to much . . . I've said this before, but I liken it to sweeping out one parking space in a parking lot the size of Montana." And that's the long and short of it.

Jabarnut is correct: The registry is a giant database — a particularly simple one. As with all big databases, sooner or later some of the entries get stale; they refer to programs that have been deleted from the system or to settings for obsolete versions of programs. Sure, you can go in and clean up the pointers that lead nowhere, but why bother? Registry cleaners are notorious for messing up systems by cleaning things that shouldn't be touched.

## Windows 11 doesn't need a backup program

The File History backup option, which I discuss at length in Book 8, Chapter 1, works very well. The only possible exception is if you're paranoid enough to want a full ghost backup of your hard drive. In that case, yes, you have to acquire (possibly buy) a backup program. But why bother? Windows 11's tools work very well indeed.

## Don't turn off services or hack your registry

I just love it when people write to me, all excited because they've found a Windows service that they can turn off with no apparent ill effect. Other people tell me about this neat Windows pre-fetch hack they've found, in which a couple of flipped bits in the registry can significantly speed up their computer. Before the change, Windows boot times were so slow. Now, with the hack, it's like having a new PC all over again!

I call this the Registry Placebo Effect. If you find an article or a book or a YouTube video that shows you how to reach into the bowels of Windows to change something, and the article (or book or video) says that this change makes your machine run faster, well — by golly — when you try it, your machine runs faster! I mean, just try it for yourself: Your machine will run *so* much better.

Yeah. Sure. Once upon a time in the early days of Windows, turning off a few *services* (little Windows background programs that run automatically every time you boot) may have added a minor performance boost to your daily Windows ME routine. Bob may have jumped up faster, or Clippy could have offered his helpful admonitions a fraction of a millisecond more quickly. But these days, turning off Windows services is ineffective. Why? The service you turn off may be needed, oh, once every year. If the service isn't there, your PC may crash or lock up or behave in some strange way. Services are tiny, low-overhead critters. Let them be.

That covers the high points. I hope this chapter alone paid for the book — and the rest is just gravy!

# Index

## Numerics

## A

# X

# About the Author

**Ciprian Adrian Rusen** is a tech blogger and author of several titles about Windows and Office. He has been recognized by Microsoft as a Windows Insider MVP, an honorary title given for his public contribution to and expertise in the Windows ecosystem. This book is one of the many ways in which he helps Windows users worldwide.

Ciprian leads the team at `www.digitalcitizen.life`, a website that provides useful how-to content for Windows, Android, iOS, and macOS. If you want to learn how to tame the computers, smartphones, and gadgets that you use daily, subscribe to his blog.

# Dedications

To Cristina, Codrut, and Diana, who have helped me and supported me through the entire process of writing this book. Each of you is amazing in your own way.

# Author's Acknowledgments

Thanks to Susan Pink, Guy-Hart Davis, Steve Hayes, and the staff at Wiley for helping me bring this massive tome together in record time.

Thanks to ASUS for loaning a cutting-edge ASUS ZenBook Duo, which I used to test things and write portions of this book.

Particular thanks to the editorial team at www.digitalcitizen.life, who keep on top of all the problems — and answers — that make this book and the site tick.

Many thanks to all of you!

## Publisher's Acknowledgments

**Executive Editor:** Steve Hayes

**Project and Copy Editor:** Susan Pink

**Technical Editor:** Guy-Hart Davis

**Production Editor:** Tamilmani Varadharaj

**Proofreader:** Penny Stuart

**Cover Image:** © canadastock/Shutterstock

# PERSONAL ENRICHMENT

**Staying Sharp**
9781119187790
USA $26.00
CAN $31.99
UK £19.99

**Facebook**
Carolyn Abram
9781119179030
USA $21.99
CAN $25.99
UK £16.99

**Guitar**
Mark Phillips
Jon Chappell
9781119293354
USA $24.99
CAN $29.99
UK £17.99

**Investing**
Eric Tyson, MBA
9781119293347
USA $22.99
CAN $27.99
UK £16.99

**Beekeeping**
Howland Blackiston
9781119310068
USA $22.99
CAN $27.99
UK £16.99

**Digital Photography**
Julie Adair King
9781119235606
USA $24.99
CAN $29.99
UK £17.99

**Meditation**
Stephan Bodian
9781119251163
USA $24.99
CAN $29.99
UK £17.99

**Pregnancy**
ALL-IN-ONE
9781119235491
USA $26.99
CAN $31.99
UK £19.99

**Samsung Galaxy S7**
Bill Hughes
9781119279952
USA $24.99
CAN $29.99
UK £17.99

**iPhone**
Edward C. Baig
Bob "Dr. Mac" LeVitus
9781119283133
USA $24.99
CAN $29.99
UK £17.99

**Crocheting**
Karen Manthey
Susan Brittain
9781119287117
USA $24.99
CAN $29.99
UK £16.99

**Nutrition**
Carol Ann Rinzler
9781119130246
USA $22.99
CAN $27.99
UK £16.99

# PROFESSIONAL DEVELOPMENT

**Windows 10**
Andy Rathbone
9781119311041
USA $24.99
CAN $29.99
UK £17.99

**AutoCAD**
Bill Fane
9781119255796
USA $39.99
CAN $47.99
UK £27.99

**Excel 2016**
Greg Harvey, PhD
9781119293439
USA $26.99
CAN $31.99
UK £19.99

**QuickBooks 2017**
9781119281467
USA $26.99
CAN $31.99
UK £19.99

**macOS Sierra**
Bob "Dr. Mac" LeVitus
9781119280651
USA $29.99
CAN $35.99
UK £21.99

**LinkedIn**
Joel Elad, MBAs
9781119251132
USA $24.99
CAN $29.99
UK £17.99

**Windows 10**
ALL-IN-ONE
Woody Leonhard
9781119310563
USA $34.00
CAN $41.99
UK £24.99

**SharePoint 2016**
Rosemarie Withee
Ken Withee
9781119181705
USA $29.99
CAN $35.99
UK £21.99

**Fundamental Analysis**
Matt Krantz
9781119263593
USA $26.99
CAN $31.99
UK £19.99

**Networking**
Doug Lowe
9781119257769
USA $29.99
CAN $35.99
UK £21.99

**Office 2016**
Wallace Wang
9781119293477
USA $26.99
CAN $31.99
UK £19.99

**Office 365**
Rosemarie Withee
Ken Withee
Jennifer Reed
9781119265313
USA $24.99
CAN $29.99
UK £17.99

**Salesforce.com**
Liz Kao
Jon Paz
9781119239314
USA $29.99
CAN $35.99
UK £21.99

**Coding**
Nikhil Abraham
9781119293323
USA $29.99
CAN $35.99
UK £21.99